LIBRARIES IN INDIA'S NATIONAL DEVELOPMENTAL PERSPECTIVE

About the Author

Dr. Mohamed Taher (*b.* 1955-), Librarian trained in India, moved to Canada, trains the trainers in information handling, writer and teacher. He has the distinction of being first among library historians in the world, and second among library professionals in India, to receive the degree of Doctor of Letters (D.Litt.). As a Fulbright Scholar, Dr. Taher was affiliated to Rutgers University, New Jersey, USA, 1990-91. He is an alumni of Mysore University (M.A., M.Lib.Sc), Calicut University (Ph.D.), Osmania University (M.A.), and Agra University (D.Litt.), India. He has been on the board of examiners of B.R. Ambedkar Open University, Hyderabad; Osmania University, Hyderabad; Karnataka University, Dharwad; Pondicherry University, Pondicherry; Ravishankar University, Raipur, and so on.

With 19 books, 50 articles, 30 reviews, and other publications, he has singly and jointly worked on various publications and projects. Serving as information professional since 1978, he is presently an information scientist and consultant in the Middle East. During all these years Dr. Taher has conducted extensive surveys of libraries in USA, UK, India, Middle East, and continues search for user-friendly libraries, a rare commodity in the Third World.

He is also a resource person and associated with various international institutions and academies, including, Information Research Management Association, Hershey, Pa, USA; Indo-American Centre for International Studies, Hyderabad; Aligarh Muslim University, Aligarh; Maulana Azad National Urdu University, Hyderabad; Henry Martin Institute of Islamic Studies, Hyderabad; Institute of Objective Studies, New Delhi; Indian Library Association, New Delhi; Indian Association of Special Libraries and Information Centres, Calcutta; Academy of Library Science and Documentation, Hyderabad; Institute of Library Science, Hyderabad, India; Institute of Banking, Riyadh; King Abdulaziz City for Science and Technology, Riyadh, Saudi Arabia; etc.

Being exposed to Internet and net training programmes, he has developed expertise in web page development, as well as, in the area of indexing of the Internet sites and other electronic publications. He is presently working towards bridging the gaps between the information haves and the have-nots. To fulfil this idea he is developing simple processes, that would ease accessing information—and called as, gateway or directory, one sample is at: www.asrc.freeservers.com. Aimed at 'save the time of the surfer', it presents a short cut to find relevant information for a student, researcher, and scholar in the field of American studies. Such gateways are being planned in other fields.

LIBRARIES IN INDIA'S NATIONAL DEVELOPMENTAL PERSPECTIVE

A Saga of Fifty Years Since Independence

Dr. MOHAMED TAHER
Ph.D., Library Science, Calicut University
D.Litt., History, Agra University

C/o Indo-American Centre for International Studies,
(formerly ASRC) Hyderabad-500 007, India
mt@poboxes.com

CONCEPT PUBLISHING COMPANY, NEW DELHI-110059

ISBN 81-7022-842-5

First Published 2001

Published and Printed by
Ashok Kumar Mittal
Concept Publishing Company
A/15-16, Commercial Block, Mohan Garden
NEW DELHI-110059 (India)

Phones: 5648039, 5649024
Fax: 091-11-5648053
E-mail: publishing@conceptpub.com

DEDICATION

This work is dedicated to the die-hard reference librarians who were trained in the Madras University Library around 1930 and who worked as barefoot librarians, staggered their annual holidays by the statistically ascertained monthly fluctuation in the density of library visitors, offering all the thirteen hours—reference service—all round the year.

It is, also dedicated to my family: Ameena, Amatul Momin, Hafsa Taher, Mohamed Salman.

PREFACE

Books on Indian library development abound with catchy titles, such as, growth of libraries, advances in librarianship, library development in different States, march of libraries, library movement and its advances, libraries at cross roads, and multitudes of phrases. I am aware that in this crowd there are some significant writings on library development by Indians. These are a minority in terms of really contributing to this area, including works by: S.R. Ranganathan, A.K. Ohdedar, Jogesh Mishra, B.S. Kesavan, S.K. Mookerjee, Girija Kumar, and omission of a few is unintentional.

Otherwise a majority of the publications, try to either provide a catalogue of developments or present a superficial story. Catagorizing as catalogues of developmental situation is in fact true, because such books do act as pointers to something significant, but offer no documentary evidences on library development. These publications do provide 'statistics' covering one or two major areas, for instance, growth of books in libraries, number of readers that have grown over a period of time. Shortage of description in such large number of books is striking, particularly about a fundamental criteria of modern librarianship, *i.e.*, user-friendly libraries. What is also missing is data or rationale on 'why there is no growth of a library culture in India' or 'why India lacks a reading culture or book culture'. Obviously, the readers are left in dark about factors and precursors that are the source for such a pathetic situation—and mislead with a standard statement, such as, 'there has been a tremendous growth of libraries in Independent India'.

If the story of deception is so common, then why are such books written, and people all over continue buying? There are different views on this issue. From the book generator's point of view it could be, that publish or perish being the fashion of the day, the marathon has made book generation a necessary evil! From the buyer's point of view, it may be a desire to understand the forces that are contributing to this entire process of a social change. Moreover, the society is beginning to feel that for each rupee they contribute as library cess, and in turn for library development, they have a right to know, how and where it is being utilized!

This brings to the three dimensional focus of my book. First, on the eve of the Golden Jubilee of the independence of India, a survey of library status is important, to recapitulate achievements/failures, in the context of library and information profession's primary goal, *i.e.*, developing 'user-friendly libraries'. Second, people need to know what libraries in independent India are doing in the past fifty years and what they are not doing, from user's point of view, and to demonstrate to them that what they need is, nothing other than 'user-friendly libraries'. Third, there cannot be a stalemate in the libraries, either they are allowed to grow like all living institutions and perform what is happening in the advanced countries in terms of 'user-friendly libraries', or they are made museums, an essential picture for management and government.

Then this book is written with a conviction that everyone wants to know what role are these Indian libraries performing—are these working as 'centres of learning', or 'centres of information and knowledge', or 'community information centres offering survival information', or 'mere reading rooms for newspapers and other light reading materials'? Additionally people want to know, what has gone into the making of modern libraries, and what remains to be done in the process of making libraries live wires of the society. While these are crucial issues, but all the more missing from existing publications. From the point of view of individual's all-round development, they probably are interested in a book on library development, reading about which will make them feel at home—that from the resources in a *user-friendly library* they can assess how to find right type of information, and, thereby pass their life in a more intelligent way. The real picture of whatever little exists in terms of library service and library facilities is apparently not so transparent in the print form, and not marketed well by the libraries. Ironically in this age of information explosion, readable books on library development are short of supply. It is also true that there is no single book, as yet in India, on the state-of-the-art of developments in libraries in general, and user-friendly libraries in particular, analysing in a nutshell whatever has happened in the last fifty years. In this analysis lies the importance of the present work. This is only the beginning of the reviews of half the century developments, and this book is likely to inspire others.

From the community point of view, this book tries to bring into limelight the status of libraries in national developmental perspectives. Of the questions analyzed, a few are listed here: Is library development appropriately incorporated with the national development programmes?

Have there been bridges or hurdles in promoting an integrated development of libraries? Has the library development received due priority in the overall nation building process, or is it otherwise? Is library a priority of primary level or secondary in the national development? What emerges, in this book is an answer in the form of a saga. The enormous data gathered in writing this book, including surveys of literature, libraries, use pattern and behaviour, user's opinion, complaints, suggestions, and observations, all together, will provide a holistic picture, among other things, on the constitutional and democratic vistas of information provision in India. This book is, therefore, useful for authorities in re-tracing their steps, for professionals in reorienting their priorities, and for an enlightened society this will help in creating an awareness and, in turn, prepare them to raise a collective voice for their fundamental right—that is, Right to Information. The latter can constitutionally demand for the establishment and sustenance of usable libraries, which will in turn help for healthy development of our society.

The *summum bonum* of this book in hand has been, in fact, to identify major factors that make a good library or user-friendly library, rather than it being an almanac of all events. Therefore, if friends of libraries, bibliomaniacs, information professionals, etc., find food for thought in these pages on what makes a library usable, I shall presume that the goal of my exercise is fulfilled. I hope that proponents and critics of modern librarianship will use this book as a benchmark to trace user-friendly libraries in India, and if they concur on the absence of usable libraries, they can join with me in pleading with all authorities for "declaring a moratorium on funding 'sick libraries' in India".

This book raises a positive slogan:

> "Management, government, professionals and library users, all *feel* the absence of usable libraries, but now they must also *agree* on the *need* for developing usable libraries for a better tomorrow, and democratically speaking, their *efforts* will change the society, and the millennium 2000 will start with seeds of user-friendly libraries uniformly distributed all over the country".

The book then has two things in specific. First, it has plenty of anecdotes and cases drawn from live situations, represented thematically as, information management, attitudes towards library development, library user profiles, mis-management, lessons of history, legal encounters, etc. These narratives are never mixed with fiction. Second, it has to pass the test of being a book which is glanced and left to pick dust, or, a kind of book which he/she might buy and keep it around—because 'want to look into again someday!' The wish is that it should be the kind of a book that can be read, as well as, referred, on the often—*Amen.*

Dr. MOHAMED TAHER

ACKNOWLEDGEMENTS

I am sure my acknowledgements here have no meaning to all the kindness and consideration that my friends all over have shown me. But as a gesture of appreciation, I still feel it is worth recording. I simply pray, and wish the best to all those who have been so kind and generous in my academic and professional endeavours.

I sincerely thank the prime movers of the idea which has emerged today as a book, namely, Dr. N.K. Ghosh (Department of English, Agra University) and Dr. R.K. Bhatt (IIT Library, New Delhi), incidentally both are the products of Agra University, the University which honoured me with the degree of Doctor of Letters (D.Litt.).

I owe my best regards to the Mysore University, whose faculty in library science made me what I am today, contributing whatever I can to the professional advancement. I also thank and respect other *Gurus* in the profession, some whose names are below, and some whose names are omitted by mistake, but whose contributions in my professional development, nevertheless, has been great.

I salute Prof. Girija Kumar (retired University Librarian, JNU, Delhi) whose review of my earlier book on historic outline of Indian libraries and librarianship and his personal attention to my works, inspired me to work with a narrow speciality, and the result is the book in your hand; Dr. B. Ramesh Babu (former Academic Fellow, ASRC), whose advises are worth and whose attention always rewarding; most importantly three professionals who generously endorsed my work cannot be forgotten here, they are Dr. M.A. Dalvi (retired Librarian, British Library, Pune), also a guiding source for my professional activity, literary efforts and career; Prof. M. Rishwadkar (formerly Professor and Chairman, Department of Library Science, Poona University, Pune) whose critical approaches to research and study have been an added advantage for me; and Dr. S.D. Vyas (University Librarian at Banasthali Vidyapith, Banasthali, Rajasthan)—my former colleague, collaborator and a friend indeed.

A host of historians have helped me intellectually, whose efforts one cannot quantify, and the list has Dr. Edwin David Harrell (Emeritus Professor of History, Auburn University); Dr. B. Richard Burg (former

Director, American Studies Research Centre, Hyderabad); (late) Dr. Robert M. Crunden (Professor of History and Civilization, University of Texas, Austin), whose historiographical approach and whose understanding of my abilities brings me to this stage; Dr. B. Sheikh Ali (former Vice-Chancellor Mangalore and Goa), whose historicism and historical approach guides me always; (late) Dr. Ramesh Jauhari (former board member, ASRC), whose historiographical approach to my work provided much needed inspiration and focus; including Dr. K.K. Sharma, Meerut University; Dr. B.D. Yadav,Rohtak University; Dr. A.K. Mittal, Gorakhpur University; Dr. Bhanu Singh, Agra University; and last but not least, Dr. Donald Gordon Davis, Jr. (Graduate School of Library Studies, University of Texas, Austin), the library historian whose encouragement, co-authorship of my earlier book, and whose historic approaches to Indian library studies is highly cited at the national and international level; I am thankful to the Indian Library Association who heard the pleas of Davis, and other library historians, and agreed to have a Sectional Committee on Library History, on the lines of the IFLA Round Table on Library History, and Davis and I are involved in both these groups.

I had the benefit of interacting, in the process of this study, with some stalwarts in the profession: Prof. A. Neelamegham, Prof. M.A. Gopinath, Prof. S. Seetharama, Prof. Ganesh Bhattacharya [all faculty members, formerly associated with the famous Documentation Research Training Centre (DRTC), Bangalore]; Mr. Abdurrahman Kamaruddin (former Information Advisor, Islamic Development Bank, Jeddah); Prof. S. Parthasarthy (retired Director,INSDOC, Delhi); Prof. P.N. Kaula (retired University Librarian, Banaras Hindu University); Prof. C.P. Vashishth (Deptt. of Library Science, Delhi University); (late) Mr. C.V. Subba Rao (Information Scientists, Delhi); Mr. L.J. Haravu (former Information Manager, ICRISAT, Hyderabad); Dr. H.A. Khan (retired Professor & Head, Department of Library Science, Mysore University); and (late) Prof. N.B. Inamdar (retired University Librarian, Osmania University, Hyderabad).

My indebtedness to professionals all over India, cannot be forgotten for all the help and support they have offered in my work. A large number were kept on active mailing programme to distribute, collect, and re-mail my questionnaires, and these are Dr. Roshan Raina (Librarian, IIM, Lucknow); Dr. Fazle Rab (Sinha Institute of Social Studies, Patna); Mrs. Rukmini Mitra (Librarian, Bose Institute, Calcutta); Mr. Wydande (Librarian, IIT, Bombay); Dr. M.K. Bhandi and Mr. Khaisar Khan

(Mangalore University); Mr. Rakesh Kumar Srivastava, Mrs. Rakesh Srivastava, and Mr. Girish Chander, all active members of Lucknow Library Association, and others who are in different parts of India. I owe also my sincere thanks to Dr. Nishi Pandey (Deptt. of English, Lucknow University); Mrs. D. Rajyalakshmi (Information Officer, NEERI, Nagpur); Mrs. Sonal Singh (Deptt. of Library Science, Vikram University, Ujjain); Mrs. Anuradha (Librarian, GIDS, Lucknow); Mr. Ansari (Asstt. Librarian, Jamia Millia, Delhi); Mr. Mehdi (Librarian, Deptt. of Chemistry, AMU, Aligarh); Mr. Chaube (Asstt. Librarian, IGCFA, Delhi); Mr. G.N. Vyas (Librarian, RCE, Bhopal) for their kind cooperation. Without their kind and generous help I could not have done this large and extensive survey, in such a short time.

My former colleagues (Indo-American Centre for International Studies, Hyderabad), did all their best in cooperating with me, and I am always grateful to each one of them.

I am also indebted to various professional associations, librarians, libraries, archives, museums, who helped me by permitting me to conduct my survey, and record my observations.

Thank you one and all.

Dr. MOHAMED TAHER

CONTENTS

LIST OF TABLES

1

INTRODUCTION

Background

This work is a review of the role of library in national development and *vice-versa, i.e.*, the role of the nation in library development. This review is based on historic precursors in the context of social, political, educational and other vistas in the post-independence India. It uses accepted qualitative and quantitative methods of datas collection, analysis, interpretation and summation.

The work intends to study: General status of history in the nation, position of library in recent history, overall place of nation in the recent library development, the state of library in the national development since India's independence—*i.e.*, a review of the past fifty years' successes, achievements and failures.

A few words about the terms used here is worth before we proceed. Contemporary history or the new history are new fields, and is gaining importance in India too. Contemporary history as a term refers to the history of the twentieth century, or some part of the century. New history as a term is some time in the loose sense is used to connote any novel approach to historical inquiry. Social history refers to historical writing that concentrates on the study of social groups, their relationships, and their roles in economic and cultural structures and processes; often it is characterized by the use of social science theory and quantitative methods.

The concept of history of ideas is gradually becoming a focus for historical studies, more so in the context of intellectual history. Intellectual history, is a new term which in the traditional connotation was used for, philosophical history, art history, and literary history. It is today used for the historical study of ideas in a holistic sense. While it covers the history of articulate thought but it also extends its scope to consciousness in general, for example, assumptions, beliefs/convictions and presuppositions, implicit opinions, feelings, state of mind, and collective mental processes.

Then intellectual history is an extension of the known sub-areas of history, namely social history and causal history—because even in intellectual history one is concerned with the text-context relationship. It is the question of where the text ends and the context begins and the nature of relationship that is the main concern.

Further, 'representativeness' and 'interpretation' are no longer taken as unambiguous possibilities of texts by the intellectual historians. Hence every text, grand or humble, classic or common, is seen to be equally representative, and equally interpretative of its context, the notion of a text that might be treated as especially privileged interpretative model is not an accepted practice by these historians. This is true whether one is explaining (as Comtean's, or Hegelian's or Marxist call it), or reconstructing (as classical philological hermeneutics wish to), or interpreting (as the modern post-Saussurian hermeneutics think about) the past. One can continue to analyze further the text-context relationship without raising the question of language and linguistic intricacies. The present work will deal with intellectually history in this frame of reference of its ability to understand; intellect then refers to power of knowledge or thinking; and from this it means that intellectuals have a better understanding of the world than others and thus their presence or absence can make a difference. We may quote what Arnold Toynbee viewed about growth and decline of civilizations, in essence he said: There are always two factors that make or mar civilizations, one is the existence of a creative minority, and the other is the existence of factors that are neither too favourable nor too unfavourable. A creative minority is what is the intellectuals are referred to in this quote. Intellectuals are in all walks of life, including philosophers; writers of genres like poetry, prose and drama; artists; politicians; bureaucrats; etc.

Intellectualism, or the age of intellectuals, in the modern era has a direct link with enlightenment. Enlightenment was promoted more so by the emergence of the genre, called Encyclopedia. In the history of the book, emergence of this genre, created a great revolution in transfer of ideas. In fact Encyclopedia brought in the fashion of making the knowledge easily accessible to all.

Says, Robert Darnton, in his essay "The Encyclopedic wars of pre-Revolutionary France", The publication of the Encyclopedia has long been recognized as a turning point of the enlightenment. In permitting Diderot's text to appear in print, the state, however, reluctantly and imperfectly, gave the philosophies an opportunity to try their wares in the market place of ideas. . . . No one can pretend to know what message 'took' in the minds of those readers (of the Encyclopedia). Many of them must have bought the Encyclopedia for what it claimed to be: a compendium of all knowledge, rather than philosophic propaganda. As Panckoucke put it, 'The Encyclopedia will always be the first book of any library or cabinet'—but it could have been a book to display on shelves, not to read. In fact Panckoucke reported that some subscribers in Lyons could not read at all. But it is difficult to believe that a high proportion of its owners never got through even its Preliminary Discourse, which is a manifesto of the enlightenment. And far more people must have read the Encyclopedia than owned it, as would be common in an era when books were liberally loaned and when cabinets litteraires were booming. It, therefore, seems legitimate to conclude that the biography of this book—the protection accorded it by French authorities, the struggle to exploit it among book dealers, and its diffusion among clientele of middle-range notables everywhere in the country—that this extraordinary success story reveals an enlightenment that had spread far beyond the elite of court and capital and had penetrated throughout the upper echelons of the Old Regime (in *Studies in Eighteenth-Century Culture*, 1977: pp. 3, 28-29).

In the Indian context there are a few encyclopedias, and these are of both types: general encyclopedias and subject encyclopedias. The trend setters were the Britishers, who introduced this genre in India. In Indian literary sources, some tend to call the *Puranas* as encyclopedias, and interestingly, Ranganathan clarifies this: "But, for those accustomed to the atomising tendency in modern encyclopedias, such a description would be misleading. In our present context, a *Purana* is a conglomerate of several books within books, great and small" (1961: 148).

Again it was the British who popularized the reading habits, by different methods. Priya Joshi, in her doctoral thesis completed at Columbia University in 1995, states, "It is well documented today that the British introduced the Novel in India in the nineteenth century as a means to contain dissent and propagate Englishness in the colony. The dissertation begins by probing the impact of this policy on Indian readers and does so by conducting primary research on the consumption of prose fiction beyond the classroom—where English literature, history, and culture were first introduced to the Indian student—to the informal consumption of this culture from libraries, bookstores, domestic reprints and translations. It documents, for instance, what novels were actually read and discussed in India outside the institutional spaces of colonial schools and universities and establishes the extent to which imperial mandates were eventually subverted toward national ends within the impor d genre of the novel". Then novel is another genre which helps in the writing the history of the growth of 'book' in the overall context of intellectual history.

Jawaharlal Nehru in his *Autobiography*, makes a specific reference to some of the books that influenced him, he states (in the context of his visit to Shantiniketan): "We spent some days there, and I remember C.F. Andrews giving me some book which interested and influenced me greatly. They dealt with the economic aspects of imperialism in Africa. One of these books—Morell's Black Man's Burden—moved me particularly. . . . About this time or a little later, C.F. Andrews wrote a pamphlet advocating independence for India. I think it was called Independence—the immediate Need. This was a brilliant essay based on some of Seeley's writings on India, and it seemed to me not only to make out an unanswerable case for independence but also to mirror the inmost recesses of our hearts. The deep urge that moved us and our half-formed desires seemed to take clear shape in his simple and earnest language.

There was no economic background or socialism in what he had written; it was nationalism pure and simple, the feeling of the humiliation of India and a fierce desire to be rid of it and to put an end to our continuing degradation" (1936: 66).

Books and Intellectual History—Interdisciplinary Approaches

Book and History

Let's begin with what is a book; book has three components: "When we look at the word 'book', the First Law (of Library Science) would employ the well-known rule of *Panchatantra*—Divide and Rule. It would ask us to recognise the composite nature of a book. Indeed it would bring back to our mind that a book is a Trinity. It is a trinity of the: (1) Gross body (the physique, the binding, the paper and the print); (2) Subtle body (the language, the style, and the standard of exposition); and (3) Soul (the thought-content or the subject matter) of the book" (Ranganathan, in Book Selection, Sec DA3).

Here the discussion is on book in history and the history of the book; that is, this history is made up of many elements, which involves the size and composition of the readers of the book, the availability of books, the technical history of book production, the economic history of the book trade, the legal and political issues involving its printing, publishing and distribution, the authors, editors, and the contributors to this idea of a book, and most importantly role of the book in developing a book-based culture, that has emerged in different corners of the world. This holistic analysis of the issues will itself speak of the interdisciplinary approaches in understanding this topic, and a brief discussion on these follows here.

Books have a historic image: As objects of adoration, scholarly standing, as carriers of the sacred word, and as also visible through art and aesthetics—whether in manuscript form or papyrus, or paper copy—in the masterpieces of the bookmaker's art, or in the *Bible's* illuminated or *Quran's* calligraphic artistic achievements. In short, "As an historical and cultural phenomenon, the book can only be fully understood when we recognize that it is more than merely a vehicle for a text" (Feather, 1986: 12).

What is meant by book: It is a series of sources, including the pre-paper reading materials, printed stuff, and other non-printed sources that gradually evolved during industrial revolution, information revolution, media revolution, and the latest computer based revolution. The printed book, brought in its wake the newspaper, journal, report, etc. These led to the emergence of all varieties of secondary and tertiary sources which tried to reduce the problem of scatter and seepage. The book in non-print form, included the documents that were produced in the form of microfilms, audios, videos, slides, and so on, with its latest version in disks, CD-ROM, on-line computer networks, etc.

The intellectual history of modern India cannot be completed without the influence of the book and the libraries which promoted the medium. The growth of libraries was basically due to the availability of the book—Gutenberg revolution made book cheaper, easy to produce as well as handle and the most common means for spreading ideas, information, education and knowledge, in all languages, in all regions, and for all the people.

Any progress in the society requires two types of infrastructure: physical and intellectual. Physical infrastructure that facilitates progress includes roads, bridges, and all communication media. Intellectual infrastructure agencies promote information access and understanding leading to knowledge systems. These include, educational academies leading not only to advances in their research output, but proceed further to develop a network of interaction with new knowledge-intensive companies, products and processes—and the cycle continues for further transformation of the society. West has continuously updated these infrastructures. The intellectual infrastructure is improved in two ways: (a) investment in upgrading universities, and (b) having programmes to stimulate the development and commercialization of new technologies, in the hope of creating high-tech growth clusters. Whether the Indian authorities have adopted these techniques of improvement of the infrastructure is yet to be seen.

What is the level of output of information in document form? There are large number of studies to quantify the growth patterns of literature, all over the world. In India, Ranganathan made one of the first attempts to quantitatively analyze this explosion phenomenon. Incidentally, in terms of quantification studies, bibliometricians (*i.e.*, those of the genre of statistical bibliography), coined the term bibliometrics in 1969; whereas Ranganathan in 1948 took lead even in this naming ceremony, and called, the quantification (of library work, services, and behaviour pertaining to these, or outcome of these which by implication includes citing and citation by library users), as librametrics.

In a chapter 'Emergence of Reference Book' of his book *Reference Service*, Ranganathan, discusses "Accelerated Growth" and states, "During the past century, there has been an accelerated growth in every variety of reference book. Several classes of knowledge of varying degrees of extension have begun to attract every variety of reference book. Here is the result of a rough count of such classes made in 1940" (1961: 261):

TABLE 1.1: Variety of Reference Books

Title	*Numbers*
Atlas	81
Bibliographies	896
Biographies	42
Concordance	80
Dictionaries	428
Encyclopedias	164
Formulae Book	21
Gazetteer	27
Guide Book	52
List	21
Statistical Book	17
Table	153
Yearbook and Directory	148
Total	2,130

The existence of so many reference books (that is secondary sources), is itself an astounding figure, because of the simple fact that if there are thousands of sources to identify primary materials, what is level of growth of primary sources—it has to be in lakhs and billions.

If book has grown in its entirety, its publishing too has been at a pace unheard before in the annals of Indian history. While there are thousands of publishers in India, Oxford University Press (OUP), has been one of the most outstanding. The Indian branch of OUP was set up in 1912. It progressed and has four full-fledged branches in four metros of the country, and many more showrooms. It produces books for schools, academic institutions, etc., to promote the educational curiosity of the society. It reprints and publishes adaptations of books published elsewhere as low cost editions, as well imports and distributes books from Oxford, and the rest of the group. 'Because of its activities people all over the world have come to associate Oxford with books for education and learning' (OUP Indian Branch, General catalogue, 1996).

This catalogue has thousands of titles dealing with books by India for India and on India. A glance at the section on History reveals, sub-sections as historiography, South Asian studies, Indian history—generalia, urban, ancient, medieval, modern, and environmental history. In the context of intellectual history, there are, Romila Thapar's work's dealing with history of ideas, technology transfer in the age of imperialism, social change and political discourse in India, class transformation and political transformation in post-colonial India, writings on South Asian history and society, etc. All these go to make the contributions of the book in the development of intellectualism.

The twentieth century which brought the book culture, inspired directly and indirectly, literacy and education campaigns at a mass level, enabling emergence of distance education programmes—a unique product of the new information age. Again this century, through the same medium, facilitated the progress of industrial revolution, into a seemingly science fiction world. That is, the information based computerized technological revolution has brought hopes of transforming the whole world into a global village.

History of the growth of book in the present form is then a basis of the advances in intellectual history. That is while intellectual historians went ahead and accepted the variety of sources for the purpose of analysis, explication, reading, or interpretation, they also got the advantage of mass media—another form of book to gather information from the non-elite channels. Given the oral tradition that has prevailed all through, this evolution of book culture and its influence on intellectual history is really remarkable.

Books have created history, books have led to war, and books also led to peace. Then books are medium of inspiration, interpretation, and assimilation. Book as a scripture, be it Vedic texts, *Bible, Quran*, has had enormous influence in shaping the life and culture of all civilized people.

Again, there are books which have improved the human communication mechanism, that is, through the language reference books. What is meant by language reference book? These books codify language, examine its past, argue or gently push for reform, offer information to the puzzled of the curious. To a foreigner these reference books, function as, helping them learning a new language. To those who use it as their mother tongue, functions as, resolving usage questions, or explaining difficult word. In short these language reference books develop the idea of a standard language. An intellectual historian uses these to decipher the meaning of words and usage, and thereby promotes the cause of understanding human beings. People spend great effort in learning to speak and to write one's native language well, to discover what is needed, perform important duties, and to learn to interact effectively with others at society's various status levels.

Books have another appeal in the form of stories they contain. Story-telling, or story-reading, is an age old art, and it appeals every one. Whether it is Aesop's *Fables, Hitopadesa, Panchtantra*, or the *Arabian Nights*, all stories that are recorded in books have continued to inspire people all over. With the advent of print and mass media culture these stories easily crossed all geographical and transcendental borders and these stories became universal.

Story-reading, reading text is an interesting topic for the twentieth century historians of language and literature.

Whether a text has something more than what it has always denoted to convey is their concern. These structuralists, deconstructionists and the like are continuously engaged in a discourse and the process of this activity has created a new school of history called historicism and new historicism.

If books contain information, facts, ideas and all this is just to lead to knowledge and knowledge based decisions, let us have a look at utilities of knowledge and the intellectual movement that emerges ultimately due to the use of knowledge.

While there is the use of knowledge, there is also, the mis-use of knowledge. Some call it disinformation, as an alternative term for deception or propaganda. Disinformation as a term emerged in the post World War II period to designate false materials produced with an intention to deceive foreign governments/agencies. Misinformation is a word with broader connotations, encompassing information that is unintentionally as well as knowingly false. This art of deceiving foreign agencies was a popular practice in Indian past as well. Kautilya's *Arthasastra*, contains a reference to this topic. It advises a prince desirous of wining battles, to circulate secret agents among the enemy, spreading rumours of their certain defeat.

Knowledge can emerge based on research, intuition, heresy, etc. The question one may ask is how does research generate useful knowledge? Is their a relation between research and its effect on the society? What is the nature of such knowledge and what is the impact of such knowledge? Does that knowledge get from producers to consumers, who are the consumers, and for what purpose do they use that knowledge? Some of these questions are discussed and analyzed in a collection of essays, and reprinted in '*Knowledge for Policy: Improving Education Through Research*', Edited by Anderson and Biddle, most of these essays were already available in other sources, and the editors felt the need to combine these as the uses of knowledge for policy decisions.

The book gives the dictionary definition of research, both, in its broad and narrow sense. In its broad sense, as: "any investigatory activity, thus it might include (among other things) philosophical inquiry, textual exegesis, or self-exploration via meditation". . . in the narrower sense in which "research is used to denote disciplined empirical investigation or inquiries which gather interpret evidence" (p. 2). So also, the authors have limited the utility of application in social disciplines whose research had had greatest impact on education, namely, social psychology, sociology, anthropology, and occasionally history, political science and economics. A chapter relevant to us in this book is: "If dissemination is the solution, what is the problem?" by Knott and Wildavsky. The issues discussed include, dissemination unlimited, under supply or overload, spreading the wrong word, dissemination by design, and strategies of dissemination. The catch word in all this exercise is "dissemination", which is the *summum bonum* of modern day librarianship!

In our context this brief note brings us to the utility of research in improving the knowledge base, information base and finally to the advancement of science, technology and humanity, in making life simpler, easier, and less costly.

But how does one view what is the knowledge itself? Scholars, scientists, explorers, reporters, government bodies, industrialists, business people, lawyers, engineers, doctors, and others, are all who publish their results of their inquiries, observations, data collections, and contribute whatever they can to the public stock of knowledge. While this is all known, it is also a fact that not every thing that has been found out by people about the mundane is all documented or made public—much remains untold, hidden, unpublished, implicit, and so on. So there is a public knowledge that is known to all, and there is much more that is, though public knowledge, but which is not known to anyone. Then there is the garbage in and garbage out, that is, though there are many publications, and information explosion is the order of the day, yet much that is published is of no value. It is rightly said: "perhaps three quarters of the scientific literature did not deserve to be published at all". Quantitative historians are now stating the same thing that the present age is an age of publish and perish—not publish or perish as some felt earlier. This is the role of the authors, editors and others who contribute their might in production and indirectly also contribute in the process of circulation of the book among the readers.

This leads us to state that what is collected as public knowledge is not knowledge at all! Whereas knowledge lies in between what is existing—in concrete sources and what is in the mind of the sender and receiver of the message, and what exists as knowledge, but, is not published anywhere—which one may call private knowledge. So there are two types of knowledge, one that is published and the other that is never published, but still exists, in the air, in the mind, in the conscience, in gossip, in speeches, in discussions, in observation, interpretation, and so on. Incidentally, the boundary between the private and public is often purely accidental.

It is interesting to quote what Manu (or the man who is associated with the arch in the Indian history = mahanuvu, and who in the *Bible* refers to as Noah, and his arc), says, to express the utility of having access to and a desirability to transfer it to others:

"To carry knowledge to the doors
of those that lack it and to
educate all to perceive the right!
Even to give away the whole earth
cannot equal that form of service"

From the point of having knowledge embodied in manuscripts, books, and other means, it is pertinent to see what is the role of the book in the development of the society. The presence of book, among other influencing factors, has led to a considerably modified, and improved approach of intellectual historians—as visible in the fact that the intellectual history has progressed from representative elite to non-elite social groups; from history of ideas *per se*, to the acceptance of the fact that ideas must be related to social and economic conditions; from mere intellectualism to the inclusion of the mental life of the commoners; and from mere historic perspectives to an interdisciplinary perspective, accepting that ideas must be understood as part of a system in which all elements are logically interconnected. This interdisciplinarity is evident in the framework of fusion of the techniques and aims of history, poetics, aesthetics, quantitative sociology and anthropology. Interestingly, the evolutionary process also retained the original approaches as evidenced by the fathers of the intellectual history—namely, Arthur Lovejoy, Perry Miller, etc.

Book and Intellectualism

There is a direct link between the book—a medium of communication—and the intellectual history. The nineteenth century Bengal witnessed this linkage in its renaissance where the social protest and awakening gathered momentum mainly through the book. So also the spread of literacy and the idea of education for all succeeded to a great extent through the printed book. The nineteenth century saw the establishment of all levels of educational institutions—primary to higher—all over the country and book did play its part in the process.

By intellectual history, it should not confuse any one that the study is limited to literary history. It includes the worlds of its generators, distributors and readers, as well as popular (or mass) history. The focus is, nevertheless, on the role of book in the development of the intellect and hence the main discussion is on the twain—book and the history of the intellectual growth.

One single instance of the relationship of book and intellectual history becomes evident from the point that the present study of the development in Indian libraries and intellectual contribution to the progress of the library movement is based on books and is intended to develop an analysis, and interpret the trends of intellectualism in India today. In doing so the researcher will identify, "read" and highlight, contemporary Indian contributions in all walks of life, as well as research output, scientific, industrial and cultural outlook and analyze the present state-of-the-art.

In short, the intellectual historian studies himself (as a book), studies the growth of ideas and in the process of reading, writing, interpretation, representation, figuration, he completes the cycle. This is not to undermine the fact that the intellectual historian in this process passes through the writings of other discourses, philosophers, linguists, poets, etc., improving simultaneously ideas about others. And any such study of links between book and history must focus on reading, popular culture, bibliographic techniques and apparatus, as well as the society.

Before ending this note, it is appropriate to state that book that was in paper form is today appearing in a computer output. How does a historian and that too an intellectual historian find food for thought? The answer lies in the fact, that the computer age is stepping into the shoes of the intellectuals by bringing in intelligent computers—computers which can store the history, which can read the meaning and text of the word, and can equally well interpret the text—using the hyper text and hyper media technology. To quote the concerns for history, is only worthy thing here,

> ". . . we as historians have to address a series of critical questions about the impact of computers and related technologies on our professional lives. Have computers changed the way we ply aircraft? Have computers opened up new avenues for structuring and probing historical evidences? If so, might these new modes of inquiry alter the way we define specific fields within history and other disciplines? Finally, do long-term developments in computer technologies even offer the possibility of redefining the hierarchies within the historical profession?" (Reiff, 1991: 3).

Libraries and National Development

Developmental Perspectives

Let us first define the terms that are involved: development, information for development, libraries and library development, and then correlate the library as a resource centre alike for both the intellectuals and the masses.

National development as a term here refers to the changing society, human affairs, communication channels, economic progress, etc. History of this change and its relationship to a process of development through the time is the context which is relevant here. The concern is to study the past five decades of independent India which can lead to the discovery of general laws of social development and these in turn may be used to predict future events.

Library, here, refers to information centre, which is actively involved in information collection and promoting use for the development of the individual and the society. Modern libraries are the centres of interaction for all interested in accessing information and interested in participating in the marathon of the present competitive age. Modern libraries in the West have demonstrated their ability to get a place in the society, by involving in the social and economic affairs. The relevant question, then is, has India achieved this. The answer lies in the assessment done in the present work.

There is always a debate on the exact meaning of the term "development". If development refers to progress, then progress is defined as "a pattern of continuous improvement in human society". If development refers to improvement of material conditions, then material development is the advancement "of material prosperity to the exclusion of all interest in religion or even aesthetics".

Then one may ask what are the conditions for progress, if this is one meaning of the term development. Karl Popper in his book, *The Poverty of Historicism*, has discussed this issue. He is of the opinion that progress is demonstrated through certain conditions and social institutions as well as technological support. For him progress is visible in the advances in education, means of continuing education that are improved such as, conferences, scientific congresses, and he adds on "Language is a social institution without which scientific progress is unthinkable, since without it there can be neither science nor a growing and progressive tradition. Writing is a social institution, and so are the organizations of printing and publishing and all other institutional instruments of scientific method. Science, and more especially scientific progress, are the results not of isolated efforts but of the free competition of thought" (1961: 154).

The term development was persistently used to connote economic growth. But the non-economic dimensions of development, that is, political, social, cultural and human are gaining gradual acceptance. Although economists were the first to recognize the importance of human factors in economic development, it was sociologists who brought into focus the social dimensions of the term development—beginning with social determinants and consequences of economic development—

leading to the development of the notion of societal development. Naturally this also showed its impact on the widening of the meaning of the term economic development. Economic development has come to mean long-term changes in GNP and welfare together with complementary changes in social and political structures.

There are critics who differ from the Western definition of the term. According to Gunder "Ever since the European Enlightenment, socio-economic 'development' has been deemed positive and pro-gressive".

"This Western modernist position on socio-economic knowledge, organization, and practice came to dominate the world system with the triumphant march of European powers over the globe. As Western philosophy followed the flag, development came to be universally defined as natural, beneficial and inevitable".

Gunder continues his argument: "With this weltschauung, it is lack of development in any given area that appears to require explanation. At the onset of the cold war, when simplistic racial or climatic explanations of "backwardness" would no longer suffice, various perspectives on development were created that remained nonetheless consistent with this overall orientation. So evolved the "modernization" school.

Lack of development is a consequence of the absence of necessary factors. To discover what those missing factors were, modernization theorists would create an archetypal developmental experience derived from a review of an ideal-type Western industrial state. When a particular country experienced difficulties in achieving socio-economic progress as defined by the West, the explanation would invariably revolve around the lack of the requisite factors . . . (such as) levels of financial investment required for "takeoff" and the necessary transformation in the socio-political sphere consistent with a Western market-oriented democratic society as derived from a reading of English history . . . (also) transformation of values and socio-psychological conceptions must be sufficiently advanced . . . (and) the lack of political institutionalization leads to serious hindrances to the developmental process".

Some wish to call the development as underdevelopment, in the context of developing countries, as against developed countries. That is there is a school of thought, even among the Westerners, which does not accept the Western definition of development. For Gunder the process so far is all to do with the underplaying of forces in the West, against the third world countries. He has a crusade against all this Western game plan and he has all through dealt with this idea of underdevelopment of development.

Andre Gunder Frank is one of those, who insists "that we understand real development not as a stage or state, but as a process encompassing economic, social, and technological changes by which human welfare is improved (we hope, not at the expense of nature) and embellished with its political, cultural, and perhaps spiritual dimensions. . . ."

Then ". . . Actual development", feels this school of which Gunder is the leader, "is instead a cyclical global dynamic by which some regions/people temporarily assume leading "developed" positions while others are underdeveloped as a result". In an interesting analysis of "measuring village commitment to development" Robert F. Krug and associates, present the idea that development project is based on chain reactions. They state: "The intended sequence begins with the immediate project achievements, such as the production of more rice per acre, the introduction of a handicraft industry, or the development of a cadre of highly trained public officials. It continues through a number of intermediate effects, such as higher disposable income or more efficient public administration. It ends with a contribution to the ultimate societal goal of improving the 'quality of life' or overall well-being of the beneficiary group. The flow is from narrow, specific outputs that are closely linked to the nature of the project activities through increasingly broad, remote outcomes that are the common objectives of a large number of entirely different types of development programmes" (in Lasswell, 1976: 104).

The same essay, highlights the realities and presents the limitations of most projects which do not complete the chain, in presenting their rationales or in evaluation of the project, rather, the chain of presumed cause-effect links is given in detail up to the attainment of intermediate outcome; about the remaining links there are sketchy references. Stating the bureaucratic reason for this, the authors feel that because there is considerable overlap in the affairs of the government and the action agencies, they feel this is unavoidable 'most planning occurs within the confines of their respective chapters'. Whereas the technical reasons for this drawback in project proposal and planning, the authors state: "derive from the extreme conceptual and methodological difficulties which encumber analyses that extend to the more ultimate societal goals. There are no entirely acceptable definitions of life-quality, no suitable measures or scales, no known way of accommodating the large individual differences in needs and values in priority judgments. . . . The evaluator cannot confidently attribute an observed change to the effects of one specified intervention when dozens of other factors are also at work and offer equally plausible explanations . . ." (p. 105).

The editors of the same book, *Values and Development: Appraising Asian Experience*, have presented the idea that development is basically, irrespective of the nation, rich, richer, poor, poorer, proceed in the developmental process in the pattern, called as the Lasswellian paradigm of the social processes: participants—seeking to maximize values—utilize institutions—affecting resources. To quote, "In most societies participants maximize at least these eight values: power, wealth, skill, enlightenment, well-being, affection, respect, rectitude. Values in this context are neither 'attitudes' nor 'behaviours' as defined in the conventions of empirical social research. They can be object of systematic analysis and observation, however, when they are conceived in the Lasswell tradition as 'preferred outcomes'. Manifestation of such preferences, and of the efforts to advance them, are important as evidence of both individual and social purpose. They can also serve as useful indicators of the sources and consequences of development. Because of their elusive quality, values usually have been either assumed (in the case of 'growth', for example) or ignored in the name of scientific neutrality in most of the literature on development" (p. viii).

Coming back to the meaning and implications of the term development, according to some social scientists, development is an all round process, including: physical, economic, social, and health aspects. Physical development involves communication, transport, sewage, irrigation, energy, forestry, animal conservation, environment and others; economic development encompasses agriculture, business, industry, etc.; social development covers education, culture, sports, political activities, etc.; and health has nutrition, sanitation, community health, preservation of water and air pollution.

Then to find what development is, the three dimensional picture looks like: one has to identify and examine existing conceptions of social development; review the operational indicators of social development and show their inadequacies; underline the importance of social dimensions of social development. And if one has to see the development of society four key factors may help finding a true answer: (a) material (to do with improvement of levels of living—GNP and mental health); (b) structural (use indicators pertaining to political participation and power distribution); normative (to develop a society which cares for others) and (c) integrative (develop a sense of solidarity, community-measure using the scales of anomie and alienation) (Sharma, in Atal, 1993: 427).

To study what are essential components for development in improving the quality of life, Malgavkar, has listed 13 areas, which are food, health care, clothing, education, housing and supporting constructing needs, transport—air, road, rail, sea—communications, women, population growth, water, energy, ecology, and global interdependence. He has analyzed these areas and discussed the present levels in India's development towards a quality life as well as the context of governance (1996: 315). This is yet another developmental perspective.

For the purpose of our study we take development as that which provides increasing opportunities to all for a better life, based on expansion and improvement of facilities for education, health, nutrition, housing, social welfare, etc. From our context we must also include that developmental process requires access to information and without this access, development that takes place, will be definitely lacking in the required perspective of a holistic approach to the issues one has to deal with. This latter approach presents the developmental issues in an expanded, flexible and humanitarian perspectives.

Information for Development

Coming to information, it is worth considering what is meant by information. How does information become idea, in turn ideas become knowledge and this knowledge provides a basic support in developmental process. How does information, which is actually, raw data/figures become usable and is consumed? How do individuals gather information—what is their information seeking behaviour? One may also like to know how knowledge is represented in documents, how people conduct their information-gathering activities, and how libraries can help to bring knowledge to bear where it is useful? These are some pertinent issues.

Information has two general connotations: one,' that refers to communication of intelligence and knowledge; and two, the technical context it has. The former is widely understood and commonly accepted media concerning all people in all walks of life. The latter, is the handmaiden of the business world—linking storage and retrieval of ideas to produce commodities or to sell the same.

It is the chip which does this wonder, instructing the concerned system—human or machine—what to produce and what to buy. Worth noting is the fact that latter 'information' is vital to the progress of the society. It is the latter type of the information that has demonstrated that societies having access to this type of information are doing better in all respects.

Here it is appropriate to quote Prof. Seetharama on the scope of socio-economic developmental information:

(a) Information that is pivotal to the question of economic and social development, *i.e.*, information that is non-sectoral or cross-sectoral; and
(b) Information that has been generated for other purposes, but which is relevant to the aims and objectives of the development community (including basic economic and social facts and data, and the more aggregated forms of information from individual sectors" (Seetharama, 1996: 2).

In the context of information for development, there must be constant survey and review of the existing knowledge. The public stock of knowledge changes frequently, because there is a constant growth of public and private knowledge. This survey and review is basically documentary research done in the framework of the libraries that collect the concerned resources. This then leads to the stage where there are specialists in each of the branch of universe of knowledge. Specialists are those who gather evaluated information and pass on knowledge to others, whereas non-specialists ask information from the specialists as and when it is required.

Which implies that all knowledge is of two kinds, for instance, (a) we know a subject, or (b) we know where to get the information from. Because of this people generally know who is what: who is a dentist, carpenter, mechanic, etc., and also know which agency may deal with what: market, industry, school, library, book store, etc.

There is a problem in all this knowledge business: No one can simply gather all information; whatever limited information one gathers it is costly to maintain it; there are limits to our ability to understand and use information, even from what little we could have gathered and maintained; what one already knows determines what else is required and where it is to be found; lack of knowledge that is displayed in judgment can be as harmful as lack of useful information; while ignorance is often disadvantageous, it is costly ignorance that is more harmful. By costly ignorance, it means that, in the absence of which we may make worse decisions and continue worse patterns of actions. To avoid this costly ignorance there must be some mechanism, which can separate wants and wishes and demands from what we call as information 'need'. That is, it based upon the exigencies such as, causal, or logical sense of need. We may have to make better decisions, and for this our information need is causal; we may otherwise like to made correct decision and for which we may need logical information. Further, how does one know what amount of information is enough in decision-making, and how does this effect the habit of information gathering? One common answer is, if the amount of information led to positive consequences, then it is because there was enough information; whereas if it led to negative consequences then we are worried about our information supply!

Then one hunts for additional information gathering mechanisms. Information seeking is a complex subject, because it also leads to the way in which people accept or reject changed circumstances, or changed sources of information gathering. Further, changes of position within the environment one works may call for starting a new information gathering process. So also changes in the environment, outside the work place, also calls for adapting to new mechanisms.

All these call for a helpful, user-friendly, library mechanism which can help in identifying the right source, for the right path, and at the right time, in the process of development. Libraries then must be suppliers of information both directly and indirectly to the information 'needs' of the society. That is, some use libraries directly, and some others use the library users to get the information in an indirect manner. Indirect use is also called the spill over benefit which a library enjoys. Indirect use is also in a sense that a non-user may some time come to the library. Nevertheless, the question of the library's role in the effective use of information as a guide to decision and action is the most important question to ask about library roles. Does a library provide information for its member's utility 'most of the time', or 'sometimes', is a more crucial question in finding the role library plays in developmental process of its society. Libraries must serve in reduction of the costly ignorance, by supplementing to the process of formal education, and by complementing to the knowledge base of the specialists—through whose spill over benefit the society is benefited.

Library Development

Library development here is considered as a part of the holistic approach in the development process of the country. Development of libraries is imperative for an overall healthy development of its members. Since libraries are the centres for information, education, and knowledge, it is for the society to have libraries which provide food for thought, food for inspiration and food for survival of human race.

By library development this work refers to the growth, development, and maintenance of libraries in India since independence. It also refers to strategies (for survival, protection, development and participation of libraries) that are adopted by the library profession, the public and the authorities. From the outset this study has considered library as a part of the social set-up and not an independent entity, as a component of the social milieu, and as a proactive role player in the development process of the nation. The study will analyze, interpret and suggest where this part is intact, and where it is not yet integrated into the whole. It is presumed that the society has different components which support its developmental activity and library is one such active participant, and if there are shortcomings in the process of participation the study will attempt to highlight these. For the type of a study this is, it is imperative that we define what is meant by growth. Growth here refers to the growth of individual libraries, call it as case studies, as well as of libraries in general. A case study of few libraries is used here in presenting the growth pattern, which then leads to understand how the library as an institution has emerged to become a development tool, in the larger cause of the national development.

Perspectives on Development: Libraries vs. Nation

Library Development	*National Development*
Developmental perspectives: growth and development of library system	Developmental perspectives: in relation to the nation's informational infrastructure
Society's role: direct and indirect	Professional role: direct and indirect
Planning according to social needs	Planning with information support
Programmes and services to care for present/future	Programmes to integrate incorporate information as an essential
Development must be holistic: users/staff/ stocks all included with a balance	Development must incorporate involvement of libraries as any other essential factor
Training of the professionals to be motivated/skilled	Motivating the management/leaders
Adopt appropriate techniques for marketing	Publicity about developmen information, develop programmes/develop public relations
Organize user education	Organize education and research
Emergence of virtual libraries: plan for the future of the book	Emergence of digital information systems and still dependency on libraries
Right to information	Freedom of expression and right to acquire information

Types of Libraries

A word is necessary about the idea of different types of libraries—a concept which did not explicitly exist in the last centuries. Today we have clearly defined functional role players in the society, which are called as public libraries, academic (school, college, university, etc.) libraries, national libraries, and special (purpose) libraries.

Library which serves the general public—public libraries—is entrusted with educational as well as cultural responsibilities. This library can supplement the school library by providing books required by school students. In the developing countries where no school libraries exist, public libraries have a definite role in promoting the reading habits of the students and the young. Adults use public libraries for formal and professional development and to improve their skills. So also in the context of developing countries where no agency exists to promote functional literacy, libraries have to provide the required types of printed and non-printed materials which may help the adults solve their immediate problems. So also, since all library growth and development is concentrated in urban areas, it is the duty of the public libraries to collect the resources which can cater to the rural society—comprising of illiterates or semi-illiterates and who form the larger group of population in these developing countries. This does not exclude the urban industrial, scientific, and other information needs. In the democratic societies, public libraries are also expected to create sustainable democratic environment, using all possible means and methods that are necessary in the process. Modern public libraries are then expected to promote cultural as well as all-round development of the individual's personality. In the present study, such a multi-purpose society and information need base calls for evaluating the kind of balance a public library has in its collection to cater to the needs of a variety of literates, age groups, and others.

Libraries attached to academic institutions primarily serve to enrich the curricula of their respective institutions. The goal is to enlarge the horizons of the students, teachers, researchers, administrators, etc.; promote interests in reading for education and knowledge, reading for pleasure and reading for improvement of the personality; at basic education level it promotes information and educational interests, and at higher level it promotes publication, extension and research functions of its parent organization; promote informal education—as is today understood by using the terms such as distance education, adult education, and life-long education.

In developing world, academic libraries have another role to play—to supplement and complement the function which is not performed by public libraries—that is providing community information services. In facilitating this, an academic library, provides information for survival, information for development and information for progress, not only to the academic community, but also to the people living in its surrounding—the outside community. And in supplementing the role of other libraries, these libraries effectively contribute for the human resource development programme—a vital prerequisite for the national development. In one sense this is taking the book to whom it has not reached and thereby provide extension service.

National libraries, have emerged to provide information about the nation—for users, within the nation and outside. Since it represents the national literary output, it is expected to preserve the written documents, including all that is produced in the country and such of the documents about the nation produced outside. Adopt legal procedures, if any required, such as copyright act, or, document delivery act—in acquiring all works, published or otherwise, and hence be capable of two distinct activities of a modern national library: first, to develop a mechanism of national bibliographic control (demonstrating transparency about the production pattern and behaviour), and second, to produce a list, periodically, of all the newly added collection.

Special libraries, or special purpose libraries, provide a resource centre for all those in the society, who do not find any place to satisfy their specific tastes, needs and demands for information. A library can be special by its purpose, by its collection focusing on a specific area of study, and by its user needs which are highly focused. These serve specialized users by a variety of services directly intended to satisfy individual needs. Businesses, industries, scientific and technological institutions, cultural centres, and others like hospitals, prisons, places of worship, etc.; are all the different libraries which can come in the definition of the term special libraries.

Role of a Library

Whether an intellectual or commoner that is using books, books as such do not distinguish the users. What distinguishes these two types of users is the purpose for which these use the information/book. Both may use the book for constructive or destructive purposes. That is to say facts, which are mere textual stuff, may mean differently to different users. Facts are one instance to explain this context: 'People learn the "facts" necessary to meet their desired goals in their own cultures, and they find it very upsetting to discover that members of other cultures have different views concerning the "facts"' (Cushner, 1996: 279).

So also, 'a single object can be looked upon with favour or disfavour, and can be valued more at one time than another'. . . the values of any given society dictate, what is a desirable or undesirable state of affairs. At the same time, values "are the resultants of societal demands and psychological needs, they are learned and determined by culture, society, society's institutions, and personal experience" (pp. 318-19).

The question of value in the Indian context may refer to the ethical and moral questions based on its own culture, which may be different for the outsider, and which has to be very carefully dealt. For instance, the value of depicting, publishing, and circulating some material may be against its traditions, which cannot be tested, questioned or argued based on outsider's definition of cultures, values, and factual knowledge. Similarly, the value placed on individual freedom in American context is so high that it is more frequently leading to cross-cultural clashes. Many Americans believe that the concept of freedom includes the right to express oneself openly, and if such expression leads to slight property damage, then the penalty should be light. What is the level of freedom of expression in free India and the values behind the same will be discussed in detail in this work under consideration. What is the right to information in India is another issue which independent India was supposed to spell clearly and enact upon it with due social justice, did India come through this saga, will be also discussed in detail in the concerned chapter.

Why this Survey

1. A survey of literature shows that library history is a very neglected area in India:
   That is, though there are many surveys of overall nature dealing with development of libraries in ancient, medieval and modern India, but hardly any suitable for the type of work undertaken here. That is, there is not much work which can explicitly or implicitly highlight historic nature, style and form, and in short, on the Indian historiographical contexts—given the level and degree of advances that have been made in writing of history and historiography at the national level.
2. The historical literature available today does little to explain the role of books in the developmental process:

By books the study includes, printed and other print and non-print media. There are many questions in this context, the answers to which is difficult to find, and the problem is also multi-dimensional. What is the role of people in building the agencies of transfer of communication? What is the role of the government in promoting such institutions—which on the whole are only for promotion of the institutions of democracy, raise public consciousness about right to access of information and freedom of expression, as well as lead to people's movement. What role the book has played in the past, the present and its role in future? What is the role of the agencies in promoting an understanding of these roles among the public, the authorities and all others who are concerned.

3. The library as a social institution has considerably advanced in post-independence era, but retrospection is overdue of the growth of the nation vis-à-vis growth of the library:
   That is, there is a need to study what forces, factors, precursors have helped the growth? If these are not helping then are these hindering the growth of these two institutions: society and libraries? How far are these libraries effectively serving the society, and how the satisfaction by the society (or user) is being felt? Most importantly, how library development has contributed for the social development and what role libraries have played in this social development? These are the kind of questions that are of immediate concern and warrant urgent attention of all the concerned.
4. There is no convergence among the communication channels that are functioning in the society:
   That is, information handling agencies, such as libraries, media, telecommunications, printers, publishers, book and media promoters, computerized information technologies, etc., are all functioning independently without cooperation, coordination and convergence. A national integrated information system, if developed, may speed the process of national development. What is the role the society can play in integrating the agencies, and what is the role of the library in such a process? Many such questions arouse which require an in-depth analysis and the present study will try to address some of the significant issues.
5. People have no proper awareness about finding means to access information, also about the sources of information which can

support developmental activities—both collectively and individually:
That is, while there is an emerging information society, and while information need for all walks of life is become essential (be it for growth, sustainable development, survival), there is no proper access to information. Providing access to information has become a major goal of the American government under Clinton, which the Indian society is yet to grapple. There are studies which deal with usage rather than with the use behaviour, and with the information seeking behaviour. Awareness of information seeking pattern leads to adoption of appropriate means of providing relevant and significant information. Not enough data exist about the emerging information needs, and in the absence of which it is difficult to project a leading role for future libraries. Then there is a need to assess information use behaviour and seeking behaviour. The present study will identify ways and means of doing so. There is no framework for the integrated approach to writing Indian library history—qualitative and quantitative?

While there have been a few qualitative and fewer historical assessments of the Indian library development, with whatever limitations, there is hardly any study which combines the qualitative and quantitative methods in the study of the Indian library development. Hence in a humble way, this study combines qualitative and quantitative approaches, and, presents a holistic picture of the issues involved.

Presumptions

The following are the assumptions of the present study:

(a) Libraries are underdeveloped in maintaining records of their own development; indicating a lack of attitude in record maintenance and a lack of scope for retrospection:
That is, resultingly, they fail to provide any primary and secondary sources to trace their growth. Evidently, lack of historicity prevails, and the historian is sent from pillar to post for data about the recent or retrospective history. There is no tradition of such record maintenance, nor there is any training programme to create an awareness about such an important activity. In general this highlights the tendency to be too much

involved in matters more current than those relating to the past and future. More specifically it shows the absence of insight and far-sight into matters that require both introspection, and, retrospection.

One reason for this lacuna is the fact that there is hardly any attempt in terms of producing qualitative or quantitative historical evidence which could have convinced the concerned to initiate steps in implementing such practices.

(b) Neither the libraries are involved in planning of the national growth programmes, nor the society has shown any inclination to get involved in planning of library growth:

That is, each ignoring the other—action and reaction are equal and opposite. Wherein libraries are not participating in the national growth, and the society is not participating in the library growth. In fact libraries are the heart of democratic societies—which means that libraries and the collection therein inspires the society towards participatory democracies; and in return libraries become an indispensable part of the society. But such a library and such a participatory democracy is yet to emerge. The question is who is responsible: Is the library profession not fulfilling its obligation of opening up the libraries and promoting the concept of participatory democracy; or is the society not yet prepared to pick up the mantle which was given to it fifty years ago in the form of freedom from foreign hegemony and an opportunity to build its own society using the libraries—centres for free access to knowledge and information?

(c) Society is not made conscious of its democratic rights to information, and, library profession has failed to utilize its democratic right to struggle for image formation in the society:

This is also a two-way failure: the society should have been made aware of the right it has by virtue of being in a democratic setup; and the profession has not utilized the democratic avenues of image formation—by motivation and inspiration—making the public feel that library is the right place to develop a framework and thence an all-round development. In fact today social development starts, continues, and ends up without even the planners entering the corridors of library! Planners and decision-makers get most of their information from sources outside the libraries.

The library profession had an opportunity to play the role of provider of access to information in all walks of life—whereas libraries have created the impression of being a last resort reading room; people are using libraries only if they are bored from, or exhausted, all other centres of social activity. The failure of the profession is this regard is dangerous for its future survival.

(d) This is one of the reasons why authorities do not consider libraries as indispensable institutions, and resultingly a concerted library development lacks:

The authorities are not yet convinced that given the resources libraries can also act as a springboard for the social development. Science libraries have received the priority which other libraries in the country lack; resultingly a lopsided library development and planning in the last fifty years is obvious—the libraries are a dispensable entity today. While the government has prioritized its programming in areas such as literacy, education, and distance education, it has totally ignored a support mechanism—libraries—which could at least help in providing the other essentials, such as, adult education, and, informal education.

How of the Survey

(a) Survey library records, documents, growth patterns, advances in information access and information handling, etc. A few major libraries and their users will provide a sample for analysis and for evaluation of the status. The survey will also enable the assessment of the level of historicity in record maintenance in libraries. Collect both qualitative and quantitative data from all concerned sources.

(b) Analyze prevailing trends in library services vis-a-vis above advances and changing social information needs. This will highlight the work already done, and the areas which can be prioritized for the present and for a future plan of action.

(c) Interpret the changes in information needs and impact of emerging information highway for future of the libraries. That is, an interpretation of user needs and marketing strategies adopted in the libraries, will follow. Also included are an interpretation of the different channels of information that are leading libraries towards extinction, and how the libraries can survive on the information highway.

The study will use the accepted historical method of cliometrics.

Cliometrics relies on counting and reporting of events or behaviours. The study will use the quantitative and the qualitative techniques of analysis and interpretation, to provide a totalistic approach to the problems under consideration.

The methods adopted and the strategy used will try to find out how services were planned initially, improved and modified later to the changing needs, and how far the marketing strategy is helpful in popularizing the library culture in India. The study will analyze the effectiveness of services in libraries in terms of user satisfaction; ability of librarians to be user-friendly and ability to play the role of mediary in information access and retrieval.

2

LIBRARY HISTORY AND HISTORIOGRAPHY IN INDIA

Trends in Indian Historical Writing

Ancient and Medieval

India's past, incidentally, was recorded in a fewer local, and more in foreign sources, all through the ages. Consider the fact that a number of travellers from China, Tibet, Europe, Persia, Arabia, etc., have left enormous details covering different walks of life, and representative of different historic periods. As against these foreign sources, Indians have made comparatively lesser efforts in documenting their own past—and this shortfall is glaring both in terms of quantity and quality! Qualitatively speaking our historic attitude, as well as, a sense of recording history was absent, and whatever existed was less critical, less analytical and least scientific. Quantitatively our past records, which we can boost of, are not only meagre but also not satisfactory, to give a total picture of any walk of life.

There are different opinions of this lack or non-lack of historic roots. But in general there is a possibility that the perceptions of what constitutes history and what constitutes historical sources may not have been clear in this whole debate.

Firstly, Indian kings, saw to it that they established record departments everywhere. Secondly, kings appointed court chronicle writers, or *Sutas*, to record all event and happening around them. Thirdly, there were historical narratives of the court. Fourthly, there were poets, writers, philosophers in all ages who recorded whatever they saw around and also interpreted their age according to the past traditions they had imbibed.

Then it is right to look at the whole issue in another way: While there are lot of sources to write the history afresh, and a lot of resources to dug, they have also discussed causes, consequences, conditions, and processes of events that have occurred in the long ages. Indians did not spend time in this important field of human understanding, called as history. They did provide a source and have left the legacies—oral and documentary—for the future to write what they could not really sit down and write. The *Puranas*, the traditions, the epics, and a lot of other literary sources, all talk of the people, people's creative spirit, people's social, economic, political and cultural institutions.

But doing all this exercise they left it all as pieces and scattered materials—so disjointed, so isolated, so incoherent, and sometimes in so illogical sense that despite seeing all this, a thinking mind would be forced to refuse all this as anything less then fiction and myth, rather than as facts and chips. What they totally lacked, and without any dispute were devoid of, is the art of putting these loose structure of ideas and facts into some mould, they did not draw conclusions, they did not show the relevant connections and did not present in the frame of reference of time and space. Hence, they did not produce one single historian in ancient period of repute who could be cited and quoted. They did produce only philosophers of history, who could sing praises, and develop more literature and reasoning on past ideas and ideals.

On the whole, what are the reasons for this lack of sense of history? One may find some reasons described in detail by leading historians, such as, Sheikh Ali (p. 302):

1. Indians in the past were close to the epic age when the imaginative faculty was so strong that it could soar to any height. What it refers to is that there historical objectivity is a relative term. One can also understand this relativity from what follows. There is a difference between the Western and the Indian subjectivity; when Westerners said something, they said because it was possible, but when Indians said something they went one step further and said something that was impossible. For instance, Megasthenes states, in his book *Indica*, that he heard from the Indians that they had long ears, so long that they could be matched with those of an elephant. . . .
2. The Orientals had a genius of mixing true with false things. What a Westerner would say could be either right or wrong, but what an Indian would say could be both right and wrong. Alberuni says that Indians are the most paradoxical people on earth, for no one could excel them in mixing truth with falsehood. Alberuni cites Aryabhatta on this: Aryabhatta is

perfectly right when he explains the process that is undergoing during lunar eclipse—owing to the alignment of sun, moon, and earth in a particular posture—but the entire remarkable discovery is fully nullified by what Aryabhatta adds to this process, that a heavenly dragon devours the moon and hence the eclipse. Alberuni fails to understand why a scientific theory should thus be killed by a myth.

3. Indians dwell more in the realm of the ideal than the real and hence all aspects of their creative genius whether in art, architecture, sculpture, painting, poetry, or drama, is more concerned with a divine conception than with the depiction of reality in this world. Indian mind is restless if something impossible is not introduced, see how mother earth consumes Sita in the otherwise secular epic, *Ramayana*.

The medieval period however brought some relief to the total absenteeism of history and historiography, and this happened when the Muslims created a true historical consciousness. It all got streamlined, and resulted in a clear idea of what this creation was: from the thirteenth to the fifteenth centuries the Muslim historians regarded Persian historiography as their model to follow in India, and with the advent of Mughals there was far more standardization in the art and skill of writing history. Quantitatively and qualitatively the works that were produced in this period is staggering. Elliot and Dowson spent much of their life time and brought out eight volume of edited works, containing the gist and elaborate bibliographical references.

Modern Period

In the modern period, and more so with the British inspiration, the result of an awakening, in the form of Indian cultural renaissance became more obvious in the spirit of research about the past and its antiquities. This specifically started with the founding of the Asiatic Society of Bengal (*f.* 1784), which influenced both Europeans and Indians, resulting in the progress of the discipline of history and enormous literary contributions.

The promotion in this area came also from the enactment of The Ancient Monuments Preservation Act, which helped in protection of historic structures, and also for getting State control over the excavation historical sites and traffic in antiquities. Archaeological Department also contributed its share in preserving resources for study and research.

Historical research, as a movement, started henceforth and the agencies which provided inspiration included archives, museums, libraries, etc. In addition to these universities and independent research institutions a few more sources have helped the growth of interest in historical studies.

Epigraphical materials and inscriptions, among others, enabled research to an outstanding level, and led to excavations and improvement in the methods of understanding the past. It was due to these advances in historicity that we have today a clearer picture of Mohenjodaro in Sindh, Harappa and Taxila in the Punjab, Pataliputra and Nalanda in Bihar, Paharpur, Mahasthan and Bangad in Bengal, Sanchi in Madhya Pradesh, Sarnath near Varanasi, and Nagarjunakonda in Andhra Pradesh. In addition to these, epigraphic records and the travelogues have enabled us to decipher details about the history and chronology of various dynasties of India.

It is right to say that Indology, study of India as a field of research is only two centuries old; studies in the past—ancient, medieval and modern—are still growing. Researchers continue to debate over the beginning and the end of each of the (ancient, medieval and modern) periods, the differences between India and other countries in social, economic and cultural spheres and whether pre-colonial India was feudal, 'Asiatic' or something otherwise. Because of the efforts of several Indian, British, German, Soviet, French, Japanese, American, and other outstanding scholars of Indology—called as Orientalists, Indologists, South Asian studies specialists—much work has been done in the areas of main stages of history, political processes, agrarian and industrial developments and their mutual relationships, social structures, religious and spiritual intricacies and specialities have been dealt with.

Some of the Indian universities, notably the Universities of Calcutta, Benaras, Madras, Bombay, etc. and institutions, such as, All India Oriental Conference, the Indian History Congress, the Bhandarkar Oriental Research Institute, Bharat Itihasa Samsodhaka Mandala at Poona, the Indian Historical Records Commission, Vangiya Sahitya Parishad, have provided considerable impetus to the detailed study of our past.

Not to undermine our past, one scholar criticizes those who see all greatness in the 'modern' and post-independent India:

> "The stereotype that still lives in the minds of scholars and the general public is that India spent its medieval history absorbed in a mystical trance or lethargy, totally distanced from what is understood as progress or development. This stereotype is somehow made to corroborate with the image of modern, post-independence India,

with its dynamic development and well-known achievements in economy, social reforms, political democracy and culture. Many people think that the country owes its modern dynamism to the brief colonial period that lies between 'traditional' and 'modern India'.

Without under-estimating the Western influence during British colonial rule, let us ask, what soil was it on which the seeds of British influence were sown? Only a short period of time is supposed to divide 'traditional India' from the India of Raja Ram Mohun Roy and other enlightened Indians, from the India of the democratic press and first patriotic-modernist societies. Was a meagre historical space of some decades sufficient to transform the educated elite, that was supposedly 'seeking community with the Universe rather than struggling with mundane problems'? It is an acknowledged fact that India borrowed much from the west, but we should also question why it could borrow, why it could rethink and reconsider many a tradition and dogma. These questions cannot be fully answered if the whole progress of modern India is attributed only to the influence of the British Raj, which also had been established in many countries of Asia and Africa, but with somewhat different results" (Vanina, 1996: 5).

The author continues her argument:

"The cultural legacy of medieval India lives in modern Indian culture as a religious treasure, as a spiritual inspiration, as a foundation for moral and ethical values. There are many reasons for this: the cultural legacy and historical memory of the people is being utilized by different political forces for their specific purposes. . . . But what is more interesting and important, is that many problems, meditated upon by medieval thinkers and sages are vital for modern India also. Some would see this as a proof of the stagnant character of Indian history, but we take a different view. The very fact that many ideas and concerns of medieval sages seem modern now, displays the depth of their insight into the crucial problems of the country" (Vanina: 6).

Contemporary Historical Writings

We may highlight the significant contributions of the Indian historians, who were trained under the Eastern spiritual flame but with a Western orientation, and the list of these includes (Sheik Ali, 1978):

(a) the extremists, such as Rajanarian Bose, Chandranth Basu, Bankim Chandra Chatterji, A.C. Das, K.P. Jayaswal, Bala Gangadhar Tilak, V.D. Savarkar, and others who asserted the superiority of Hindus over Western culture, also called as nationalists;

(b) the rationalist such as, Rajendralal Mitra, R.C. Dutt, R.G. Bhandarkar, Raychaudri, etc., who viewed events more objectively to rectify the errors committed by Westerners in writing Indian history;

(c) the comprising of Maj. D. Basu, A.C. Majumdar, C.Y. Chintamani, Surendranath Banerjee, who exposed the economic exploitation of India by the Britishers, and strengthened the cause of nationalists in their struggle for freedom;

(d) the Marxists, such as, Hiren Mukherjee, R. Palme Dutt, Kosambi, and who influenced others, like, Muhammad Habib, S. Nurul Hassan, Romila Thapar, Bipin Chandra, Harbans Mukhia, Irfan Habib, etc.

(e) the independent historians, who did not wish to be associated any of the above, which included: Jadunath Sarkar, S.N. Sen, Shafat Ahmed Khan, Sardesai, S. Krishnaswamy Iyengar, Srinivasachariar, Venkateshwarlu, B. Sheik Ali, and so on.

Libraries in History: An Overview

Traces in History

Etymologically speaking, 'library' meaning information centre, was not used in ancient India. Let alone, this terminological shortfall, even the other components which form this system—books, users and librarians are nowhere explicit, and if there is a passing reference it requires lot of work to decipher the exact meaning and connotation. For instance, a record section (called as government/administrative record office) is at times confused as a collection of books, or the people officially appointed to write the official records are sometimes mistaken as scribes who copy all texts, including the scholarly and other written matter for academic purposes.

According to Max Muller, "If we take the ordinary modern words for book, paper, ink, writing, etc., not one of them has as yet been discovered in any Sanskrit work of genuine antiquity. Book, in the modern Sanskrit, is Pustam or Pustakam, a word most likely of foreign origin. It (*Pustak*) occurs in such works as the *Hitopadesa*, where we read of a person, 'neither read in books nor taught by a tutor'. The *Hitopadesa* itself is said to be written (*likhyate*) as an extract from the *Panchtantra* and another book. To write is *likh* and *lip*, the former originally used in the sense of scratching, whether on stone or leaves, the latter, in the sense of covering a surface with ink. . . . The words for ink (*masi, kali, mela, gola*) and pen (*kalma*) have all modern appearance; and as Kayastha, the name of the writer-caste, proceeding from a Kshatriya father and a Sudra mother, it does not even occur in Manu". One may add that the usage of the term *kalma* (or *Qalam*) has an Arabic origin, which must have entered the Indian usage sometimes after the tenth century, and used in most of the regional languages to express the tool for writing (chalk, pencil, pen, etc.).

Whatever was meant to be a place of books, is rendered differently in Indian languages. It was these languages who first spelled and pronounced the name for a place of books, and we have in the following a few examples, with variations: Chanakya or Kautilya, the minister of Chandragupta Maurya, (who ruled between 269 and 322 B.C.) is attributed as the author of *Arthasastra*, which mentions an officer, "*adhyaksh*", who is in-charge of manuscripts, and the office is called Nibhanda Pustakasthana. This term '*pustak*' means book. *Arthasastra* certainly existed before seventh century, according to the historian Dr. R.C. Majumdar.

A later scholar of repute, Pandit Danasila, of tenth century, wrote a monograph and its title read as: *Pustaka-pathopaya* (literally meaning, reading a book).

Telugu writers like Tenali Ramakrishna and Allasani Peddana, who lived in sixteenth century, used the terms *Pust-pusthaka bhandagaramulu*.

Pust, is probably taken as the root of the word, meaning piled one above the other and sewn together. The Sanskrit word '*knot*' grantha acquired the sense of book from gathering of loose materials; so also the term *granth kuti* had the same usage, Trikanda uses this term; Interestingly in *Mahabharata* we find the use of the term *Grantha*. The development of a language and its literature speaks a lot of the development of letter and word. Panini, the famous grammarian who lived in fourth century B.C., introduced the alphabet styled Yavanani. The era of Mauryas also saw the composition of the Mahabhasya of Patanjali, an exposition of the grammatical work of Panini. Viniyapitika and Nikyas mention a list of games one of which is called *Aksharika* (lit. lettering).

As important is language, so is the art of writing. There emerged a class of writers or a separate class whose main profession was to write.

These came to be known as Kayastha in the Eastern part of the country; elsewhere they were called Divira or Divirapati. In the Jain parlance, we find *Jnana* (or *Gnana*) Bhandar, and Saraswati Bhandar, lit. storehouse of knowledge; *Jnana* = knowledge, Saraswati = the Goddess of knowledge and learning, *Bhandar* = storehouse.

Similarly, Chalukya king, Deva, had a library, which he called as Bharati-Bhandar. In Bengal the term *Gata Ghar*, came to be used for book house; *gata* for *Grantha* and *ghar* for house. *Granthalaya* is another term commonly used for Indian libraries.

In the chapter on 'Light from Sanskrit'. Ranganathan tries to analyze the term *Grantha*, and states:

> "In Sanskrit, merging is denoted by '*laya*'. And '*alaya*' denotes perfect merging, integration, at-one-ment. It can also mean merging to the limit of the achievement of the purpose sought. *Grantha* denotes expressed thought or work.
>
> The term for library is therefore '*grantha-alaya*', coalesced into the form '*granthalaya*'. Semantically, it means the merging of mind and *grantha* to the limit of the achievement of, the following: Enrichment of memory; Elevation of emotions; Stimulation of intellect; Increase of knowledge; and Release of intuition.
>
> It can also mean the total set-up helping such a merging of mind and *grantha*".

Ranganathan also goes ahead and explains the allied terms, such as *pustakalaya, granthalayi*, etc., as follows:

(a) *Pustakalaya:* "A derived degenerate meaning of '*alaya*' is the point marking off the end of merging—the place of total merging. Moving a little further, it means the abode of the entity to be merged. A place cannot be the abode of mere *granthana* or expressed thought. Because, it is abstract, and place is concrete. To make it abide in a place, the expressed thought should be embodied. The physical embodiment of *grantha* is denoted by '*pustaka*'. It is the Sanskrit equivalent of 'book'. Combining it with '*alaya*' in the sense of place, we get *Pustakalaya.* The term denotes 'library' in its Chaucerian sense of 'place for keeping books'.

(b) *Granthalayi:* '*Granthalayi*' denotes a person helping in the merging of mind and *grantha* to the point of achievement of enrichment of memory, elevation of emotions, stimulation of intellect, increase of knowledge, and release of intuition. To be of efficient help in this, the *granthalayi* has to use many techniques. He should keep continuously sharpening them. These include organization, administration, classification, cataloguing, personal help in the choice of *granthas* pinpointedly, exhaustively, and expeditiously, and service of the *granthas* chosen. Thus, the Sanskrit term '*granthalayi*' is more expressive than the term 'librarian'. 'Library science' has '*Granthalaya-Sastra*' as its equivalent in Sanskrit.

(c) '*Pustakalaya-Pala', or 'Pustaka-pala', or Granthalaya-pala'*: Connote the protector of books, that is those who provide security to the collection—but they are not librarians. Accordingly, '*Anu-laya-seva*', is equivalent for reference service, and '*Anu-laya-sevi*' for reference librarian (1961: 185-186).

He has painstakingly developed a Glossary of Library Terms, stating, "This glossary gives Sanskrit equivalents of library-terms to facilitate the formation of cognate terms in the several Indian languages and the rendering of this book into those languages" (Ranganathan, 1988: 388). In the context of the literary developments and in the context of evolution of the book, the word narrative has an interesting origin.

According to the *Dictionary of the History of Ideas*, the term narrative, is derived from the Sanskrit '*gna*' via the Latin *gnarus* (the known, the knowable)—means a story told by one who knows the fact; and 'story' in the broadest sense, is defined as 'any account, written, oral or in the mind, true or imaginary, of actions in a time sequence'. This goes to indicate the on-going linkage between the cultures of the world, from antiquity to the present. Coming back to the usage of the terms, there are few more instances. In Jaipur the Royal Library, established by Maharaja Sawai Jai Singh II (1699-1743), was called *Pothikhana*; *pothi* (in the dialect) refers to book, and *khana* refers to department. Some used the term *Punti Khana*, for manuscripts department. *Kitab* has an Arabic origin. Muslim rule brought the term to India and used the term '*kitab* (pl. *kutub*) *khana*', lit. book department, and referring to library.

Priolkar called the Indian Incunabula in Marathi as Dolamudrise. He preferred to classify all books printed in India before 1867 as Indian Incunabula.

In the Oriyan literature we find the following terms: *Pathan* (for reading), *Likhan* (for writing), *Patra-likhan* (for letter writing), *Kosa* (for an encyclopedic work), etc.

Dr. S. Radhakrishnan, says "in the old days teachers of India were themselves librarians and they were held in the highest esteem". Such scholars, or, bibliophiles, were according to Newton Mohan Dutt, like 'mobile libraries' and according to Richardson, they were 'memory libraries'.

James Todd, in his *Travels in Western India*, published in 1839, mentioned the rich manuscript collection in the princely states of Bikaner and Jesalmir. As a follow up of this note, Georg Buhler surveyed these collections, and in his report of the trip, recorded finding the oldest extant manuscript in India, dated 1103 A.D. This attempt by Buhler and others was under a larger programme to identify Sanskrit works all over India. This identification of works and the place of availability led to inter-library loans, managed by the convenience of the British Government in India, arranged by the India Office Library, and within a decade 59 works were lent. The countries and numbers of manuscripts borrowed were: Germany (27), Austria (20), Great Britain (9), and Russia (3) (Johnson, 1986: 222).

This was a continuous transfer of Indian works, with the clear approval of the British administration. Incidentally, Indian works had already gone abroad: to U.K., after the Tipu Sultan's Library was transferred (around 1800) to the India Office Library; and to U.S.A., by the end of the eighteenth century—institutionalizing the process with the setting up of the East India Marine Society, in 1799, to house the Indology collection.

While thousands of books have reached the U.S.A. through the Public Law 480, and its subsequent amendment, it is nevertheless true that at present the acquisition is restricted, due to budget constraints, enrollment patterns in American institutions, space problems in the participating libraries in the U.S.A., recent selections being based on subject profile, etc. Beginning with its legislation in 1958 and implementation in 1961, the programme of book acquisition started. These are some of the important findings of two doctoral theses, by M.B. Konnur completed at Poona University (1988) and by Jessie Satyanesan who got her doctorate from SUNY, at Buffalo, in 1992. While Konnur has dealt with the Indo-American influences in the field of librarianship, Jessie deals with the acquisition of Indian print resources by the Library of Congress's cooperative acquisition programme.

While these acquisitions are enormous, and the strategy of skilfully exporting the Indian published works may be criticized by many, the net outcome of this has been single—that is it has opened up a new door for the understanding of India that was and India that is. For this opening of the door one instance is more than enough: the Public Law 480 (more famous as PL480), and India its financial aid, India Wheat Loan programme (along with India Wheat Loan Educational Exchange programme) directly resulted in two different developments, first in the reprinting of several out-of-print Indian titles, which were subsequently made available to the nearly two dozen U.S. participating libraries; and, second in the utility of the Accession List:

India (now Accession List: South Asia), which worked as a substitute of the Indian National Bibliography—being comparatively far more up-to-date, comprehensive and detailed, and which was made accessible all over the world by the Library of Congress. And this economic aid to India, made India strong enough—a power to reckon with. This is the finding of another important doctoral study by Dennis Merill *'Bread and Ballot: The United States and India's Economic Development'*, completed at the University of Connecticut (1986).

As a by-product of this book export, the Western academies and institutions developed extraordinary facilities for the study and research of Indian language, literature, culture, etc., and thus have established centres of learning Sanskrit, Hindi, Urdu, and so on all over the Occident. South Asian studies exchange and interaction programme and conferences of South Asian specialists, linguists, and librarians are a perennial feature in these lands.

A few publications, which reflect this interest in Asian studies, will amplify this topic: V. Raghavan, *Sanskrit and Allied Indological Studies in Europe*. Madras University, 1956; Mohammad Yusufuddin, *Oriental and Islamic Studies in American Universities*. Hyderabad Islamic Society Publications, 1953; J.D. Pearson, *Oriental and Asian Bibliography: An Introduction with Some Reference to Africa*. London, Crosby, 1966; Annual bibliography (supplement) of the *Journal of Asian Studies*; University of Chicago—The College, *Introduction to the Civilization of India: South Asia, An Introductory Bibliography*, comp. by Maureen L.P. Patterson and Ronald B. Inden, 1962; *Third World Resource Directory: A Guide to Organizations and Publications*, ed. by Thomas P. Fenton, and Mary J. Heffron, New York, Orbis Books; etc.

The audience of all these publications are the Western scholars interested in the field of Indology, South Asian Studies, West Asian

Studiès, South East Asian Studies, Asian Studies, and the broader term, reflecting these—Oriental studies, etc.

Use and Abuse of Libraries

What is then the place of library in history? This question is both simple and difficult. Simple in a sense that libraries existed or were burnt in all ages, for whatever reasons. It was difficult because whenever there was a library the only question we can ask, how useful was to its intended audience.

Coming to Indian history, we find there were libraries established by great kings like Akbar. But we are also told by historians that Akbar was illiterate, and he used the services of professional readers to recite the texts. Is it not interesting factor that those who were great patrons of art, letters and libraries were themselves probably not in the category which we today call as literates.

Libraries in history has another meaning. How did the people, thc commoners use the library, or think of its utility?—in an age when there was not much of literacy, and literacy was only for a privileged class. One can infer, from the circumstantial evidence that as temples, courts, and courtyards were exclusively for the chosen few, the libraries, wherever these existed must have also been a showpiece for all outsiders—whether they belonged to the higher class or not, they had no question of access to the collection, howsoever rich, and whatsoever it contained!

In this regard Prof. Kaula rightly states that the existing "libraries as such were not agencies for the dissemination of knowledge for one and all without any restriction whatsoever. . . . These rulers were patrons of learning, no doubt, but knowledge as such was not accessible to any but the chosen few" (1958: 58-59).

Jain traditions have recorded that it was a virtuous practice to reproduce existing texts. Reading whether from memory or by using a manuscript—was stressed as a daily duty of the lay. So also in the Muslim traditions ability to read the scripture is developed from the childhood for all alike—commoners and elites. Such religious compulsions treat development of literacy a must.

We find from historical records that libraries existed in educational institutions and academies, such as, Nalanda, Taxila, among the Buddhist and Brahmin's learning centres; *madrasa* (educational centres) at Gujarat, Delhi, Bidar, etc. among Muslims. What kind of study facilities for students that these libraries extended? From the historical sources of the centres of Buddhists and Brahmins we understand that the student was expected to memorize all the text and the interpretation verbatim. A few instances are found which indicate that reading from a book was not totally out of fashion.

One instance of eminence of famous educational institutions of India, the grandeur it was, is evident from the writings of I-tsing, who states the following about Nalanda and Valabhi:

"Eminent and accomplished men assembled there in crowds, discussed possible and impossible doctrines, and after having been assured of the excellence of their opinions by wise men, became far famed for their wisdom" (Majumdar: 191).

For example, Agraharas, or Vedic schools in post-Gupta period Orissa, had holy scriptures collected, stored and preserved for use by the Sanskrit scholars and for reading the same to the masses who assembled for recreation. Similar collections did exists everywhere, but the question still remains—who had access to it, did the students find ways to refer it, or it was exclusively for the teachers?

Students at *madrasa* had to refer a lot of manuscripts—and books later—to pursue the courses. The difference in behaviour of the two patterns can be seen from an oral culture, which predominated in India, and a book or reading culture which the *madrasa* imported from Arabia.

Stories of book burning and library destruction in ancient and modern world should not surprise that love of one (book) forces the hatred of the other (book), and this is a universal phenomenon.

Book Promotion Programmes

Introduction of reading, publication, press, media and the book in various other forms, have been responsible role players, in the progress of the civilization. Even language and literature, as part of the cultural wheels, have played their own part in this promotional exercise.

The movement to introduce English in India, led to rise of currents which either favoured or opposed the movement. Directly or indirectly, these currents contributed to the development of book. For instance, the establishment of press for the vernacular and English, in a competitive spirit, gave rise to a process of tremendous output of literature.

Christian missionaries—notably William Carey (who founded the Srermapore Mission, Calcutta); government machinery—through the offices of Warren Hastings (who founded Calcutta Madrasa), William Jones (founder of Asiatic Society of Bengal, Calcutta), and Resident

Jonathan Duncan (who founded Sanskrit College, Banaras); and the Indian liberal—prominent among them were David Hare, Raja Ram Mohun Roy, etc., all did their effort in promoting the education and learning process, and thereby promoted books and book culture.

It should not be surprising then to read what British Parliament in its renewal of the Company's Charter in 1813, wanted the East India Company to take measures, for "revival and improvement of literature and the encouragement of the learned natives of India, and for the introduction and promotion of a knowledge of the sciences among the inhabitants of the British territories in India".

School Book Society

The end of the seventeenth century and the beginning of the eighteenth century had many promotional attempts in this regard. The School Book Society at Calcutta, founded in 1817, gave vent to a large scale publishing programme. It aimed at providing school books—basically for religious education, but also had secular content—for a growing number of modern schools. Bombay and Madras presidencies, too established their branches of this Society. It was an Indo-European enterprise, constituting of the missionaries and liberal Indians.

Its Second Annual Report, 1819, gave a call for book donations. It also mentioned that its books are separated under three categories: (1) publications of the parent body; (2) elementary books; and (3) miscellaneous. According to the ambient educationist Mr. Trevelyan, the prevailing spirit of the time is clearly indicated by the fact that "upwards of 31,000 English books were sold by the School Book Society in the course of two years, while the Committee did not dispose of Arabic and Sanskrit volumes enough in three years to pay the expense of keeping them for two months, to say nothing of the printing expenses" (quoted in Majumdar, 1967: 812).

1835 Minutes

The Committee referred to, is the Committee of Public Instruction, which took upon itself the idea of doing 'justice' to both the vernacular and English medium of instruction, as well as publishing books for the students of both types. The proponents of the English in it were called Anglicists, and the proponents of the vernacular were called Orientalists. Whatever, little was spent from the British treasury in India, came to a halt soon. The 1835 Minutes, of the East India Company, under the

Presidentship of Thomas Babington Macaulay, finally declared that 'henceforth the available funds should be spent on English education. The existing oriental institutions like the Sanskrit College and the Madrasa were to continue, but fresh awards to stipends of these institutions and the publication of the classical texts must ease'. This stopping of printing and publication of classical texts effected the growth of the vernacular book production too.

According to many historians it was Macaulay whose attempt, as stated above changed the history of education in India. But some other historians, absolve Macaulay of this tragic drama, and replace the name of Alexander Duff, who 'saw the Indian civilization as a pure obstacle to progress and wanted to undermine it through an educational system based on English language and literature' (quoted in Janardhan Rao). Duff was a missionary, and was a member of the Committee of Public Instruction, and 'he thereby strengthened the hands of the English party' feels Majumdar too. He does not show inclination of adding any more weightage to Duff's role. But whosoever was behind this, in short, wanted the British to adopt a 'filtration theory', as advocated by the Anglicists, thereby government funds and resources could be used only for a westernised education, and not for any other system of education (Majumdar, 1967: 812). As history also has it, it was the same Lord Macaulay who introduced the public library system in India, and thus becomes the father of public libraries in India—opening libraries to the public, in a Western fashion.

Other Efforts

Private attempts at promotion of book also ran parallel. A Bengali Book Shop as early as 1815, was opened by Ganga Kishore Bhattacharya, who was an ex-employee of the Baptist Mission, Serampore. Ganga Kishore, with the help of Pandit Hara Chandra Roy, started the first Bengali Newspaper, *i.e.*, *Bengal Gazette*, 1818.

Distribution of free books was a common practice, either for religious reasons, or otherwise. Copies of *Mahabharata*, in Bengali translation, were distributed free of cost, by the Maharaja of Burdwan, and a famous elite, Kali Prasanna Sinha. "*Gita* is also distributed to Brahmins on all religious occasions to Brahmins even in the present day. . . . Maharaja Monindra Chandra Nundi of Cossimbazar who was a noted Vaishnava philanthropist also distributed Sanskrit *Srimad Bhagavat*, Bengali *Sri Sri Chaitanya Charitrmitra*, etc. to the public free of cost" (Mookerjee, 1969: 247).

Christian missionaries regularly distributed the *Bible* since the appearance of the first printed copy in vernacular languages.

Bengal Haraku, the first daily newspaper, inaugurated an era of reading news on a daily basis. With the growth and development of the educational level, it became next to impossible for all people to buy personal copies of all that was published as magazines and newspapers. Hence emerged the idea of reading rooms.

Book publication increased at a rapid pace. *Samachar Darpan*, another newspaper, in its edition of 14 January, 1826, informs its readers that there were then 14 or 15 presses, which were printing and publishing various kinds of books in the country.

B.S. Kesavan has done a thorough research in the area of how printing has created a cultural awakening, and this is in the context of South Indian scenario, his first volume deals with much more details, it is entitled *History of Printing and Publishing in India: A Story of Cultural Re-awakening*, Volume 1, *South Indian Origins of Printing* (National Book Trust, 1984); Volume 2, bears the title *The Book in India: A Compilation* (National Book Trust, 1992).

The first book has a variety of topics, and the list includes, first printing in Indic characters; The Roman types used in Goa; German tradition in Tamil scholarship; Tamil magazines; printing of literature on Karnataka Music; etc. One can find interesting passages in its pages: "A bibliographic treasure is the memorable Murdoch Catalogue as a source of information on Tamil printing. Except that it ignores the Portuguese phase, it records the many hundreds of titles published in the Tamil country from Tranquebar's early printing to the period up to 1865. One can pick up some of its faults like the omission of the year of publication, etc. But this is offset with the wealth of details given on a number of books which he had carefully examined for comment. His ill-health was responsible for some of the drawbacks of the work. He was so aware of it that he appealed to the English-educated Tamil's to publish a series of works illustrating their native language and literature. "Let them be assured that so long as they despise their mother-tongue, they have merely a thin white-wash of civilization"—an appeal which, one is sorry to say, our people took a long time to accomplish" (p. 68).

Why there was a change of practice from oral tradition to written tradition? Whatever other historians have to say, according to Prof. Kesavan, "the orthodox tradition of the Hindus probably changed after AD 1200 with the collapse of the Hindu Kingdom . . . " (p. 150).

Given these trends, the public reading interest in general, which gradually became general in nature, gave a boost to the promotion of reading culture.

Need for Libraries

By the end of eighteenth century a need to study the Indian history and culture grew, necessitating establishment of the Bombay Branch of Asiatic Society at Bombay (in 1804), and the Royal Asiatic Society Library at Calcutta (in 1784). Sir William Jones was the pioneer who undertook the cause of establishment of this Calcutta Library. It is the kind of scholars like Jones and others who promoted the interest in ancient Indian culture, language and history. In the words of Prof. Abdus Subhan, writing on the same institutional contributions states: "While Calcutta can boast to be the birthplace of the Oriental movement that swept the nation two centuries ago, it is the scholarly achievements and pioneering efforts of a whole generation of British Orientalists that is responsible for initiating the process of our intellectual advancement, leaving behind, in the process, a legacy of literary works in vernacular languages and landmark institutions for oriental studies" (1997: 3).

Further, continues the author, "Hundreds of edited texts and translations of Arabic, Persian and Sanskrit manuscripts have seen the light of day through the Society's famous Bibliotheca Indica Series. The Society, in fact, contributed immensely to the awakening of the native intelligentsia and thereby hastened the growth of vernacular literature" (*ibid.*).

It was the same European influence in general, and British in particular, that contributed further in establishing other modern institutions, namely the Sanskrit College and Calcutta Madrasa. While Warren Hastings, as the historian R.C. Majumdar, states: 'encouraged the revival of Indian learning and to him owe the foundation of Calcutta Madrasa (1781) . . . a Sanskrit College was established at Banaras by the Resident Jonathan Duncan in 1792' (p. 810). In the same zeal was the establishment of Sanskrit College at Calcutta, in 1821. Indian leaders like Raja Ram Mohun Roy, who represented the popular progressives, protested against the setting up of this college, as he was in favour of promoting Western education. Despite the protests the college started functioning and its library came into being in 1824. The American missionaries who were already in India by 1813 started the first college in India, Lucknow Christian College, in 1888. These efforts brought a distinct reading and study culture, and this resulted in a uniformity for later institutions that emerged in India.

Libraries have helped the progress of the country in different ways. While the European and American missionaries established libraries to promote evangelical programmes or dialogue, to spread the word, there are few instances, which include Baptists Theological Seminary (at Bangalore), Carey Library (at Serampore), League of Service Library (at Lahore), etc.; the Muslim rulers, elite, philanthropists, and individuals established mosque libraries—as free reading rooms attached to mosques (an eminent Indian library scientist, D.N. Marshal calls these as forerunners of modern public libraries); bibliophiles, such as, Khuda Bakhsh (at Patna), Salar Jung (at Hyderabad), etc., spent their lifetime fortune and established libraries; similarly Saraswathi Mahal Library (at Tanjore), Asafiya Library (now State Central Library, Hyderabad), Raza Library (at Rampur), were developed by royal patronage.

The educational institutions which started in different places had no systematization until the year 1835. This year saw the Macaulay's minutes aimed at Anglicization of Indian Education and Freedom of Indian Press Enactment. This act emphasized that the great object of the British Government ought to be the promotion of European literature, sciences, etc., among the Indians and that all funds appropriated for the purpose were only for English medium education. Due to this act three types of educational institutions became distinct: Oriental, vernacular, and, English (at some places it was Anglo-Indian mixture).

According to R.C. Majumdar, the chief defect of introduction of English education was 'the disproportionate attention paid to the English education of the middle-class gentry as against the education of the masses through vernacular schools' (p. 813). The Government was aware about these defects, and the report submitted by William Adam (in 1835, 1836 and 1838) had described the miserable condition of the vernacular schools, but it was beneficial for the government to ignore these issues, and it relied on the filtration theory—accepting only those who had English education, and others were systematically ignored. The tragedy that happened due to this was that while middle-class Hindus reaped the benefits, the losers were the Hindu aristocracy and the Muslim community (Majumdar: 813).

Due to such reasons the Indian elite woke up, combined their efforts, and felt a serious need to establish their own institutions and libraries in the nineteenth and early twentieth century. We have instances of this awakening and interest in different parts of the country, including undivided Punjab, Bengal, Bombay Presidency, Madras Province, etc. For instance, Deccan Education Society, Poona (*f.* 1884); Bhandarkar

Oriental Research Institute, Poona (*f.* 1917); Sri Krishna Devaraya Andhra Bhasha Nilayam, Hyderabad (*f.* 1901); Calcutta Library Society (*f.* 1818); Medical Literary Society, Mumbai (*f.* 1789); Madras Literary Society (*f.* 1818); Social Science League, Mumbai (*f.* 1911); etc.

According to historians, including R.C. Majumdar,

> The general awakening of Modern India would not have been possible without significant changes in the educational ideas and institutions of the country. Much in the sphere of education was tried and achieved in India during the nineteenth century, and still more has been accomplished in the present century (Majumdar: 956).

Furthermore,

> Several factors, such as growing contact with the outside world, eager yearning for the revival of the cultural treasures of the past, the desire to reform all aspects of life, and speculations about the problems of common weal and common woe, have profoundly stimulated Indian thought and have caused a comprehensive cultural renaissance, the influence of which is visible on modern Indian Literature as well as Art (Majumdar: 960).

The beginning of this century saw remarkable progress in the study of science, philosophy, politics, religion, and culture. The valuable discoveries of Sir J.C. Bose, Sir P.C. Ray, Sir C.V. Raman, Dr. Meghnad Saha, S.C. Roy, Sir B.N. Seal, Sir S. Radhakrishnan, Dr. Abhanindranth Tagore, Nandalal Bose, Abdur Rahman Chaghtai, Dr. A.K. Coomaraswamy, Dr. Rabindranath Tagore, Dr. Sir Mohammed Iqbal, Ali Brothers, Maulana Abul Kalam Azad, Mr. G.K. Ghokle, Sir Asutosh Mookerjee, are outstanding in the respective fields of study and research.

The establishment of institutions for study and research in other fields also took place in this period, the list includes, Zoological Survey of India, Calcutta (1916), Botanical Survey of India, Calcutta (1911), Geological Survey of India, Indian Science Congress, Indian Institute of Political and Social Science, the Bombay School of Art, etc. The British Administration established five universities in Bombay, Calcutta, Madras, Lahore and Allahabad in between 1857 and 1887.

Around the years 1906-1938, the growth of communal consciousness and provincial patriotism greatly supported the setting up of new universities in places, such as Patna, Lucknow, Aligarh, Banaras, Agra,

Delhi, Nagpur, Waltair, Mysore, Hyderabad, Chidambaram, and Trivandrum. A Women's University in Poona, in 1916, and the Vishwabharati, at Shantiniketan, in 1926, were two distinct establishments. For women it was the first institution of higher learning, and Vishwabharati had a uniqueness in having a cosmopolitan outlook, and a blend of the East and the West, and of Old and the New India. Another way, to find how much were our leaders were interested in libraries, is to read what and wherever they have mentioned about libraries. While the ideas of Tagore are described in another context, in the end of this chapter, we reproduce the part of a speech which was given by Gandhi, while he laid the foundation of Ahmedabad Sanghralaya, and which was reproduced in *Harijan Bandhu*, 1-10-1933:

> "I have some ideas about libraries—about what they should be and what they should do. I will place them before you. First, you may so plan the building of the library that it can be enlarged as the library expands without marring its symmetry. The later additions should not appear as extraneous accretions to the original building. It should provide facilities for arranging occasional lectures and for the students and scholars engaged in research work to come and make use of the books there in an atmosphere of peace. We should aim at making this library the biggest and the best in the world. If we have the will, God will give us the strength to do it. Kakasaheb has suggested that the collection of books with the Vidyapith may be kept here. There is no dearth of art in Gujarat. The famous lattice work in stone in the mosque at Bhadra had no match in the whole world. Similarly, the needle-work of Ahmedabad is perhaps unrivalled. The delicacy of stone-work of the masons of Ahmedabad has surprised me. I have seen them living in dark and dingy hovels. Artists do not wait for encouragement. If we could find another donor ready to offer fifty thousand rupees, for a museum, we could set up on in this very building. We have to work in such a way that the library may grow and develop from day to day. It would be better if we could get one or two men who would devote most of their time to it. Don't choose a money-minded businessman, who would merely keep the books safe and in good condition, for the post of librarian. Choose someone who could be depended upon to appreciate the relative worth of different books and select them. In case no one volunteers his service for it free, you should be ready to offer a good salary and appoint a really qualified man. Harijans should be allowed to use the library without any fee, and if books

are spoiled or damaged or even stolen, the loss should be borne by the library itself. The Harijans are the poorest of the poor and are entitled to special consideration. In fact, you may extend this concession to all the poor people. That will enhance the glory of the institution".

Further, "I also repeat the request made by Bhai Rasiklal, namely, the managing body for the library should be carefully chosen from a body of scholars so as to keep the institution alive and growing. Do not think that this body should be composed only of men of practical wisdom, for scholars understand what a library should be like and how it can be made to shine. Carnegie gave large donations to many libraries. The conditions he attached to his donations were accepted by most scholars, except those of Scotland. They frankly told Carnegie that if he insisted on his conditions they would not accept the donation. How would he know, they asked, what books would be useful to the library? The artists do not sell their art. There are in Gujarati large collections of precious books. But they are in possession of banias. The Jains have fine collections of old books of great historical value, but they are lying useless tied up in silken sheaths. I have wept over the sight of these books which serve no purpose by being in the hands of the banias who know nothing except how to make money. I would go as far as to say that in their hands the Jain religion itself is dying of starvation by being in the strangle-hold of money. It is possible to count *dharma* against money? In fact, money should be only the means of *dharma*. I, therefore, ask you to include able scholars in the managing body of the library. Find out how to do this; and see that you do it".

In December 1928, addressing the All-India Public Library Conference, Rabindra Nath Tagore, said:

"Most libraries are possessed with the passion for accumulation. Three quarters of their books don't come into use; their over-grown proportion even thrusts into a corner the specially selected few that are meant for being actually used. In our popular parlance, the man of large riches is called a great man. When a millionaire comes into a gathering, they view to do him honour—an honour not dependent on what he has to give but merely on what he has. Much in the same way, the bigness of a library is estimated by the number of its volumes, the facilities offered for their use, that should have been its glory, are not deemed necessary for its pride. . . ."

He continued,

> "... The average Librarian, however, rarely takes thought or trouble to bring the largest number of books to the utmost use, because it is always easier to overwhelm the public mind with the mere display of quantitative abundance.... It is not enough that it passively permits visitors: its invitation should be active. For, as the Sanskrit proverb tells us 'Tannashtam Yannadiyate'—that which is not given is wasted".

Then he comes to the details of what libraries are doing in futile: "The usual thing for a library is to say: Here is my catalogue, come and select for yourself. But in the usual catalogue there is no introduction, no invitation, no spirit of welcome. That library alone can be hospitable, which shows an eagerness to invite readers to the feast at its disposal.... That the readers make the library is not the whole truth, the library likewise makes the readers ... I feel that the big library can but function as a store-house and only the small one serves as a refectory to furnish the wherewithal for daily sustenance and enjoyment ... where the Librarian is a true devotee, devoid of ulterior seeking, free from pride in the mere loading of shelves, capable of discriminate rejection ... (Among the periodicals received) ... three-fourths of these, remain unopened, encumbering space and burdening the shelves as they keep on accumulating" (Ohdedar, 1969: 34-37).

The former President of India, Dr. S. Radhakrishnan, in his speech given at the opening ceremony of the Mysore University Library building, on 7 December, 1965, said:

> "True end of education is not the acquisition of information, important though it may be, or acquisition of technical skills, though they are very essential in the modern society, but to have that superior outlook, that outlook which goes beyond information and technical skill; information is not knowledge, nor is knowledge wisdom. You must have the capacity to subsist in the battle and to look at things as they happen without any kind of inward disturbance of perturbation of your being".
>
> "... Everyday, we must read a classic; not a mere text-book, not mere notes given by your teacher, which may serve you for your examination; but turn your attention to some old classics of the East or West, it does not matter which. All of them have the same power to stimulate your minds, soothe your hearts, to enrich your whole

> nature, to make you a new being altogether. That is the purpose of the classics. . . . Our late Prime Minister Jawaharlal Nehru, even during his illness, in spite of his work spent half an hour in studying a classic before going to bed. Everyday he did it, in spite of his illness and preoccupation. Why can't we do it? Why are we not doing it?"

Indirectly these had a considerable influence in a felt need for libraries. Hence, we find that there are instances of individuals and institutions, collectively and singly, promoting the cause of development of libraries in pre-independent India.

Library History: Trends and Prospects

What is history? History is the story of the past, people, societies and cultures. American historian Carl Becker defined history as 'the knowledge of things said and done'. The British historian R.G. Collingwood, defined history as 'science, or an answering of questions; concerned with human actions in the past; pursued by interpretation of evidence for the sake of human self-knowledge'.

A general lack of understanding of the need for writing the past of libraries prevails world over. For instance, a symposium arranged by IFLA's Library History Round Table on Library History Research in the International Context, in 1978, received a response which cannot be called as pinpointed, exhaustive and expeditious. There were papers largely from the European and American continental perspectives. A total absence of Asia and Africa, except for Israel, was glaring and stunning. And also surprising was the low level of historicity even in European countries.

Hence, we find, "Although many papers have been edited lately on the history of the public library in Sweden, it is still an underdeveloped area. The history of public libraries in the cities and towns is still to be written. . . ." (Tortensson, 1990: 23); British past scenario was not either highly productive, because a glance at publications dealing with the category 'study of library history' (appearing between 1971 and 1980) as 5 books, 5 chapters in new books, 1 pamphlet, 6 articles (above 4 pages), and 6 articles (less than 4 pages) (Manley, 1990: 84).

We may quote a few instances from the findings of American library historians, in this regard. Pierce Butler , noting that the librarian seemed curiously immune to the theoretical questions that puzzle most men and that he 'apparently stands alone in the simplicity of his pragmatism: a rationalization of each immediate technical process by itself seems to satisfy his intellectual interest' (1933: 81).

Butler said this in 1933, and 40 years later, Felix Reichman found the situation basically unchanged. Puzzled by this lack of historicity, he opined "On the one hand, we (librarians) have a dark suspicion that historical studies are a waste of time, mere 'dates'. We do like the word 'pioneer'; we share the love of this phrase with American educators, and we are all constantly pioneering in reading services, in technical services, in the application of machines, and so forth. The pioneer, of course, does not have the time nor the interest to look backwards; for him the past is dead and of no consequence, and his main attention is focused on the future" (1964: 37).

Librarians are then pragmatic, they lack time to devote for this digging of the past, and they lack the skills to dig the past, effectively and efficiently. Furthermore, those library histories which exist are not necessarily of any value in assisting another researcher to further the existing historic work. These historical works leave the reader more puzzled and confused about the overall situation.

For instance, Mary Reed, wrote in 1958, in her doctoral thesis on History of the Lakewood Public Library, that, "This record contributes to the understanding of the events described, it seems to me, little more than an ornithologists' anatomical sketch contributes, say to fathoming the flight of a shallow. The essential questions remain. Where is the measure of the tangible and the intangible [effect] of one sentence out of the nine million or so books borrowed by the people of Lakewood from their library during these twenty-five years".

Library's History

What is library history? It is defined as "that branch of history that investigates the actions of people, the activities of agencies, or the effects of social movements within or contributing to the development of librarianship for the sake of professional awareness" (Krzy, 1975: 295).

We may define it as study of the growth of library as a social institution. It is then a study of individual libraries in particular, and of the librarianship in general, which leads to an understanding of the level of contribution the library has in the social development and *vice-versa*, that is level of social contribution in library development. This historical study, therefore, encompasses study of library in holistic sense, taking care of the role played by the public, government and the profession in the growth of the library and also the role played by the elite, masses, and the supporting institutions, such as education, literacy, communications, etc.

What is the use of library history? The answer is simple. To quote, James G. Olle:

> "One value of library history needs little justification. Properly to understand the library world as it is today, one must know how it has reached its present state. . . . There are several valid reasons why we should study library history, but I doubt whether anyone who questions its value will be convinced of its usefulness by argument. The study of library history begins as an act of faith. It is easier to believe that it is worthwhile than it is to prove it" (quoted in Krzy, 1975: 297).

Source Materials

It is pertinent to have a look at the level of historicity that prevails in our libraries to write the history and historiography of Indian libraries?

For this activity one may ask: what are the types of sources and evidences that one can gather to write the history and re-write the same. What are the agencies and institutions that are promoting this academic and educational enterprise? What are the trends in research and study of this field? Who are the main scholars and contributing historians in this century—are they all from the profession of library science or are there other specialists also included? What type of literature is appearing in print, in non-print sources, and in what disciplines are these scattered—history, sociology, geography, anthropology, politics, economics, technology, etc.—What is the present state-of-the-art of library history in India and what is its future?

What is the place of history in the growth of a library as a social institution? The level of time and effort that has been devoted to preserve the records of growth and development of these libraries can be one measure to evaluate this point. Significantly one can find the history of fewer segments of this growth and development, if one is to rely exclusively on the library's own archives and records! For writing this history one has to gather information from as distant sources as possible. One single instance illustrates this point. Indian sources of the past give little evidence of the libraries. And for most of these historical records, narratives, and evidences we have to see the foreign sources—travelogues, biographies, and vast number of other rich databases.

This is then another major hurdle, that is, lack of archival material, restricting the art and craft of library history. Library historians are, to quote Michael Harris, "inextricably tied to, and overwhelmingly dependent upon, the available evidence; the historical record preserved and made available to the scholar" (1974: 3). Sidney Ditzon, rightly says, "Neither, libraries nor library associations, paradoxically, have systematically done for themselves that which they occupationally do for others—organize and maintain their own unprinted thoughts and reports" (1973: 63).

Then library's history is significant in understanding the history of the movement that follows in collecting, storing and making the records of the past accessible to the posterity.

Library Historiography: A Review

What of Historiography

What is historiography? It is the writing of history. The term derives from 'historia' (inquiry) and 'grapheim' (to write). Before venturing to deal with the growth and skills of the library historiography, it is pertinent to note what a historian does if asked to write history, or to re-write the existing state-of-the-art:

1. Historian deals with collections and already existing series of resources; that is a historian does not work with isolated documents, or an obscure pamphlet, rather uses the cause and effect of each chain and link.
2. To deal with a new topic a historian engages in, what can be called, imaginative historical re-creation. In this process he is likely to list persons who are involved; list agencies—government, private, etc.—involved; check sources for local history; identify news and opinion sources which would have reflected the particular topic; and identify libraries, archives, and museums which could easily provide source material.
3. He thinks in terms of mapping out the whole terrain of possible sources, looking through a microscope into each body of relevant documents for scattered sources.
4. No amount of bibliographical control of the existing literature and indexing can satisfy the curiosity and pinpointed search of resources the historian would like to link up. Because, for a historian the potential sources do not constitute a limited class

of materials; the list includes, ranging in between all man-made records: printed sources, ephemera, mimeographed documents, manuscripts, inscriptions, artifacts, etc. The historian will be probably looking for things which an indexer would not have even been alert to record!

5. As against the current research needs, historian relies more on earlier works, rather than latest and recent publications; (this calls for a different approach to arrangement of books—indicating the chronological order of the publication of the concerned book. This change in the existing order is necessary because the normal shelf and catalogue displays are either by subject or by theme, but never by the time—new or old—of the publication. A collection which tries to meet the historians needs for books must adopt some innovative approaches in this regard. By such a modification latest books will emerge first and followed by books of various degrees of obsolescence. So also the books in the catalogue must indicate their dates and preferably arranged according to the chronological order).
6. By mental effort a historian translates himself into the past, not to find curiosities and rarities, but to comprehend the organized world in which the people of the concerned period lived. He is interested in their knowledge as organized knowledge, their ideas as articulated ideas. What helps a historian is easing the tasks is consideration of his specific needs in data collection, analysis, interpretation, etc. The point note worthy is that "he cannot gather his materials in the laboratory or the field, he can only use the records that other men have made or the documents they have accumulated—for their own purposes, not his. He goes to the library not to prepare for his research, but to carry it out" (Bestor: 123).

What of Library Historiography

The question is what is library historiography? Richard Krzy states that it is: (a) the process and a product of the pattern of recording the changes that libraries have undergone in the ages of human history, (b) the way in which the historians isolate the main currents of librarianship to identify the forces that drew them along, and (c) which assist in formulating a theory explaining all the phenomena observed, and stated in short it is "the writing of the history of agencies, people, and movements within or contributing to the development of librarianship" (Krzy, 1975: 294).

According to another historian of libraries, Joanne E. Passet, Library historiography is the writing of the history of people, institutions, and movements that have contributed to the development of the profession (called Librarianship)" (1994: 260).

Library historiography then deals with the art and craft of writing the history of libraries and librarianship along with the forces and precursors that have influenced or that have enabled the historians in documenting the details accurately and meticulously. That is the historical assessment of historians is reviewed to form broader generalizations, to lead to policy-making and to assess the course for future action in this process.

Library historiography, can be classified according to three types, *viz.*, (a) purpose with which it is written; (b) the subject area examined; and (c) the method employed.

One more factor in the study of the library history is worth consideration. According to Krzy "In contrast to historians, librarians, being pragmatic rather than philosophical, have devoted less attention to the nature of their profession's historiography than to the uses of library history . . ." (p. 295).

A statement of priorities was already mentioned by Ranganathan in his Radio talk in April 1956:

> "An account of the libraries in the first four periods (the vedic, the Buddhistic, the Medieval, and the Muslim) must necessarily depend upon the historical research. This has not yet been done. The library profession is too small in India to spare a person to fill up this antiquarian gap. Those trained in the scientific method of tracing history are too preoccupied with dynastic and political history to spare sufficient time for cultural history in general and library history in particular".

This stated in other words, the type of education and training which Ranganathan and others promoted concentrated more on the philosophical and management issues than towards historical and cultural analysis. So interpret's Donald Davis:

> "This developed as a perceived necessity to bring Indian librarianship as quickly as possible into modern, 'scientific' era. A developing and industrializing nation, it seemed, should not devote precious

professional resources to the study of the past. . . . The discouragement that this has brought the profession, itself not unrelated to the lack of a sound historical consciousness, has resulted in an even greater impetus to focus on current problems exclusively. The influence of book and libraries on the cultural development of society is a topic, it would seem, that is best left to senior and retired members of the profession and other scholars . . . because of lack of appreciation of the impact of books and libraries in Indian culture and because of the present state of mind (real library history only began after 1947), there is a reluctance to appear to be documenting failure. Even though librarians may feel that their profession has little history in India worth studying, some reflection frequently causes them to think otherwise. Yet the perception of failure is present, perhaps because the profession at large is preoccupied solely with the public library movement as exemplifying what is of genuine importance to Indian life" (Davis, 1990: 581).

A few distinct features of library historiography are worth mentioning, which are based on the remarks of Krzy's article, as these have an international relevance:

(i) by the end of the nineteenth century and the beginning of the present century librarians became generally so pragmatic in their preoccupation with practical matters of library management that they tended to neglect the writing of library history;
(ii) library historiography has tended to remain oblivious of the main currents of historiography and has most generally taken the form of the narrative chronology;
(iii) when library historiography has been influenced by currents of historiography, the development has been an ancillary one; and
(iv) the scarcity of scholarly library history may be explained by the general lack of training in history among librarians (Krzy, 1975: 324).

Interdisciplinarity

Historiographical studies by very nature are interdisciplinary. This is because historical works make use of the methods and concepts of one or more disciplines other than history. Hence, in this sense the nineteenth century exclusive focus on social sciences ended, and the present century brought the idea of incorporating humanistic and scientific methods and techniques in vogue. To demonstrate the interdisciplinarity of library history, as it also follows the pattern of its parent discipline, we will be collecting sources for the library history from social, cultural, literary and other areas. This is to say that library history draws support from many disciplines, such as, archaeology, epigraphy, paleography, sphragistics, or sigillography, numismatics, philately, genealogy, heraldry, chronology, diplomatic, etc.

The study of library as an institution has now become a serious topic, and is also come to be known as 'Scientific library historiography' since it follows sound research methodology and surveys the library as a social agency.

To quote a library historian,

> "Research in library history is an interdisciplinary area connected, by tradition, usually with historical and philological subjects. But recently, methodological aspects in library history can be discovered that try to show the mutual connections and influences between libraries and their environment. To name only a few topics: the growth of library collections; reading interests and acquisition profiles; and the role of the sponsors in the development of libraries" (Kaegbein, 1990: 1).

Approaches in Indian Library Historiography

A literature survey on this topic reveals two major works, one by O.P. Sharma, and another by Donald Davis. A glance at these is given in the following:

O.P. Sharma

O.P. Sharma's "Literature of the History of the Library Movement", *Herald of Library Science*, 7: 1968, 8-16;

Newton Mohan Dutt's "History of Indian Libraries from Earliest Times to the Present Day", *Modern Libraries*, 2: 1932, 69-76;

Dutt laments on the lack of interest in historiography, or in writing on the subject. "The subject which I have selected for my discourse is the history of ancient and modern Indian libraries, but time will not permit of anything more than a brief survey of the subject. I would commend the topic to any university student for his doctoral dissertation. If we look back to the distant past, we are tempted to think that there were no libraries in ancient India" (p. 69).

Sharma in this literature survey analyzed the state of affairs in the field of Indian library history and identified the characteristics of the literature as follows: redundant coverage of topics; sparsity of chronological details; lack of statistics; rarity of systematic and orderly treatment of a topic; prevalence of a journalistic, rather than a scholarly style; and the paucity of bibliographical references.

M.K. Murthy's "Examination of Primary Sources in Indian Library Historiography", *Library History Review*, 1: 1974, 77-96; this is another important source.

Donald Davis

Donald Davis in his review essay 'status of library history in India' (1989), found that: historiographical writing (in library field) is relatively scarce. He has done an exhaustive survey of library history, the first of its kind in India, reviewing the scenario. One of its aim was the survey of literature to review the existing level of bibliographical control in this sub-branch of Indian librarianship. The questions it deals with require a close study of the literature that already exists. For this end the strategy was, 'a systematic review of English-language printed monographs, collected works and chapters in general works, theses and dissertations, and major journal articles—especially those that treated Indian library historiography as a field" (p. 100).

> The findings indicate "A comprehensive search for printed, secondary treatments of Indian library history reveals about thirty books and several dissertations, about thirty articles and chapters in collected works, and atleast two whole collection of papers that have direct historical significance. . . . (This does not include) publishing and printing history, the history of education, general cultural history, literary history, religious and missions history, and library catalogues, even though these are rich sources for supplementary material relating to library history" (p. 100).

Each of these items must be thoroughly evaluated and a full-fledged project must be initiated to work on this area, with the help of premier historic research institutions in India. Also these works are worth evaluating for their level and degree of historicity these demonstrate. A survey of the citations, as a sample survey for the entire data, may help identifying the citing patterns, citing behaviour, cited sources—original and secondary—that find favour with the historians in the library field, and so on.

The survey of Donald Davis has useful insights:

> "Most of the works deal with general aspects of library history that treat extensive periods of history. The public library movement, largely a twentieth century phenomenon in India, has received the most attention. Others that have attracted scholarly interest include the Muslim influence, the national library and library associations. The conspicuous gaps in the published literature include such topics as academic libraries, library education, private libraries, and the influence of the British on library institutions" (*ibid.*).

The gaps in the existing works, as listed in the last lines helps in improving the nature of the work already completed and in excluding the over worked area. The time gap between the study by Sharma and Davis being twenty years, and Davis found that 'though some improvement has occurred in the intervening years, these characteristics (identified as gaps and problems in historic method by Sharma) are still present" (Davis: 101).

Davis adds on:

> "The literature demonstrates that authors seldom write more than one book; that many works appears either as general surveys used as textbooks or are doctoral dissertations (to a lesser extent, master's theses) done in history departments and later put into monograph form or articles; and that studies of regions and state public library development in limited time periods predominate. Such journal articles as exist tend not to be scholarly nor based on primary source materials. The literature as a whole is confined to Indian journals and publishers".

One single fact which emerges in this literature survey is that all contributions are by library science scholars and librarians. There is not one single write-up from the scholars belonging to different fields and different areas of scholarly activity, such as, general or specialist historians, sociologists, etc.

Other Recent Studies

A review of the literature published since Donald Davis's survey does show some sort of improvement and advances. The recent publications are:

B.D. Panda, *History of Library Development*, New Delhi, Anmol Publications, 1992. Panda has done his work in tracing the history and historical scholarship in librarianship, being an improved version of the author's doctoral dissertation. The book provides a sound base and an elaborate introduction to the existing works and the need for an exhaustive case study of the library development in the State of Orissa. This work provides a pattern for other State library histories, to assess the development individually and collectively and in the process assess the contribution of the respective State in the national library movement.

R. Raman Nair, "Nature and Use of Library History", in *Library Movement and Library Development in India*, Seminar papers, 39th All-India Library Conference, Bangalore, 1994, pp. 1-13.

The author states on the trends in 'analysis of library movement' histories:

> "Some recent library histories done in India applied the scientific methods and attitudes about library history and traced out the waxings and wanings of at least the major principles which have characterized library systems and library legislation in India. Good principles are seen to be good principles on the basis of comparative analysis and factual evidence. Like this bad principles are equally and similarly identified. In a study on Kerala's library movement we find that in Kerala the movement for library development has followed too far a wrong path which is an odd twist given by an organization, a dominant force which led the movement. Everywhere it is a remarkable fact that despite current and former occultations the essential principles of library movement emerge unambiguously and uncontrovertibly from our long history. For a healthy and useful growth, library development should follow directions of proved advantage" (Nair: 7).

Further, the author states in the conclusion:

"Among the historians of libraries and librarianship in India, there has been a tendency to work from the first definition of history, to view events of library development as closed and finite phenomena which may accumulate in the passage of time but which will not change. Public library service in India has been studied usually as a social development with emphasis in India on the factors contributing to the movement for library service rather than on the order in which events occurred or the specific advances were made. The order of events and advances does much to define the nature of movement; but it can be ignored in a study in which assumed order is known.

Similarly, the search for causes of the public library's origins is much simplified if it is assumed that the history of an institution is known and needs only to be explained in the light of some interpretative theory for the causes to become clear. Large number of histories of libraries and librarianship in India may be judged as having failed to meet author's purposes. . . . The history of public library movement in Kerala which we cited as an example illumines a characteristic of history as a way of learning; one which springs from a live concern, deals with life, serves life, for there is apparent in it the national and social movements and the concern to demonstrate it to the public library movement and the function of the people's library movement as a training ground for political leaders" (pp. 11-12).

Mohamed Taher and Donald Gordon Davis, *Librarianship and Library Science in India: An Outline of Historical Perspective*, New Delhi, Concept Publishing Company, 1994.

It is an attempt to cover the development in the field comprehensively. This brief, but complete history, is based on primary and secondary sources available in English, and other languages. Although this work will fill a great gap in the world history of librarianship and library science, it too is only a beginning. As an outline, it serves as a kind of synthesis and bibliographic essay that ties together the long story of libraries in India and points the reader to the existing literature. However, as a contribution to the study of international and comparative librarianship, the work should initiate and facilitate in-depth research in areas which are identified as understudied and in areas which are still unexplored.

R.K. Bhatt, and S.C. Bhatt, "Applications of Historical Method of Research in the Study of Library and Information Science: An Overview", *Annals of Library Science and Documentation*, 41(4), 1994, 155-60.

The author has provided an extensive discussion on the topic and among other things, it lists the sources of data and information which are useful in historical research:

> "Official records, such as laws, deeds, annual reports of organizations, charters, etc.; newspapers and other periodicals; eye-witness accounts of events; archives; manuscripts; letters and personal diaries;

biographies, autobiographies, and memoirs; historical studies; literary writings; oral histories; memorials; catalogues; schedules, agendas, etc.; and archaeological and geological sources (non-documents)" (Bhatt: 156).

Presenting the possibilities of the applications in a theoretical framework, the author concludes:

> ". . . there is a vital scope of the application of historical method in the field. . . . Undoubtedly, in the present day librarianship, there is a continuing need for genuine historical research in librarianship which has remained largely a neglected area. To promote historical research in the field of librarianship, it is advisable for the historical researcher to follow some sort of scientific method of inquiry, including the formulation and testing of a hypothesis and the analysis and interpretation of data. Such processes will not only help him to establish true and healthy results and findings, but will also increase faith among research community in the application of historical research method" (Bhatt: 158).

Davis, Donald and Taher, Mohamed, "Library History and Historical Assessment and Current Trends", *Third World Libraries*, 3 (1993), 40-44 (Revised version of a paper submitted at Library History Round Table, IFLA Conference, New Delhi)

> "The organization structure of research in library history is diffuse, with the best collection of printed materials at the National Library of India. Programmes in library and information science have not given much attention to library history; and even on the doctoral level, most of the dissertations that have appeared have been in other departments or overseas. There are no identifiable groups that bring persons interested in library history together and not many conferences on the subject. The few historically-oriented studies that are produced appear in the general professional journals, or, more likely, in scholarly journals published abroad" (p. 41).

Taher, Mohammed, "Library Historiography: Methodological Issues", a note prepared for the ILA's Central Sectional Committee, 1995 (the author is presently the Convenor of this Committee):

It is another theoretical perspective on the issues of writing library history in India. The note describes the types of library history that have been developed by Western historians in the field; the types of sources—

primary and secondary—that are useful for a library historian, including the more important official and private public records; differences in writing library history of the past and the present; and library historiography relies on the general historiography and borrows equally well from other related disciplines.

In addition to these there are number of case studies of libraries and the list of all such is growing day by day. A survey of two sources in the field reveals the rate of growth: an annual index such as: (1) literature in Library Science, edited by Sewa Singh, and the multi-volume series of *Handbooks of Libraries, Archives and Information Centres*, edited by B.M. Gupta. The latest volume contains a specific collection on history of libraries.

B.M. Gupta, ed. *Library Development in India: Handbook of Libraries, Archives, and Information Centres in India*, Vol. 16, New Delhi, Aditya, 1996.

The book presents a collection of essays by eminent historians of library science in India, who have contributed on general trends concerning library development in India, and in specific, the post-independent scenario. It provides a base for a historian to assess the development, in India, both before and after India independence. Certain case studies, Statewise performance, and development of the National Library, all together go into forming a strong foundation for a future historian of librarianship.

The present work tries to provide a holistic approach in writing the state-of-the-art, and in writing the history of Indian librarianship. It uses the model suggested by a pioneer in American librarianship, which is as follows:

> "The history of librarianship . . . treats of the changes within the library and the impact of those changes upon the services of the library as one agency in the communication process. . . . The kind of historical writing for which we are here arguing would throw a strong light on librarianship today, and provide us with insight at a time when insight is sorely needed. . . . Not until such studies have been made can the profession speak with authority of the meaning of librarianship within its coveal culture" (Shera, 1966: 639).

This writing or re-writing of library history, as Shera envisages, covers the development of each every segment of the field of librarianship, and the present study will attempt to focus on many of these.

3

LIBRARY MOVEMENT: Pre-Independence Era

Social Movements

What is a movement? It can be stated in simple sense as that which involves a group of people moving together *en masse*, in order to achieve a set goal.

Before we go into the details about library movement, let us have a look at what a social movement in fact is, how can it find a similarity in a social institution—such as, library—and in the finale to see what are the dynamics of the relationships of such a library movement to the social system in which it arises.

What characteristics describe a social movement, and how one identifies its subtleties? Below are some of the characteristics:

> A social movement is a "wide variety of collective attempts to bring about a change in social institutions or to create an entirely new social order" (Heberle cited by Gore in Atal: 168).

Most social movements are not chance happenings, rather they are recurrent happenings. The existence of value system provides a support for the continuity of the movement, and a social movement calls for change in the value system as well as change in the social relationships in one or more aspects of social life.

Such changes in relationships, imply changes, in material transactions, emotional interactions, etc.; ideologies governing movements focus on changes in material transactions, rather than other transactions. Further, attempts to mobilize support for changes, results in confrontation, since any existing relationships have proved to be advantageous to some, and disadvantageous to some other members of a society; this leads to division and into groups of potential followers, potential opponents, uninterested members and unaffected onlookers.

Most movements succeed only partially, and sometimes only superficially, because of many reasons: (a) defects in the objectives of the movement, or achievement of fewer objectives; (b) the success may be partial, in a sense that, of the potential beneficiaries, on whose behalf the movement is launched, only a proportion are mobilised as its members; and (c) the success may be partial, in another sense, that the movement may lead to unanticipated consequences which defeat the original objectives.

Movements are likely to succeed if they develop organizational structure with defined authority and clearly set channels of communication. Individuals who lead the movement, if they don't get institutionalized soon leave the whole effort in doldrums. While the first leaders, or founders, carry a sort of *charisma*, it will last long only if the *charisma* is also institutionalized. But the disadvantage with institutionalization is that they soon loose their innovativeness, and due to lack of creative abilities, they merely defend their doctrines and do nothing concrete. The other factor which promotes success is, rather behavioural, and deals with the existence of commitment and involvement among its members, including loyalty to the cause.

Most movements may end up because of varied reasons: (a) their objectives are fulfilled; (b) merged into larger or broad based movements; (c) ceased to be relevant or attractive in a new environment; (d) competition with others having similar aims; (e) crushed by the establishment; and so on.

Library Movement

Library movement refers to the voluntary participation of people to promote the cause of establishment and maintenance of a library. When would people get involved in any activity? They would involve only if they are convinced, motivated and inspired in the right direction. They also would like to see if the involvement would in turn lead to improvement of the quality of life—such as, education, health, etc. That is, it must enable the overall development of the personality of the individual and the development of the society as a whole.

How does one find a relationship of these factors, in the library movements that have flourished in this century, in different countries, and have succeeded or continue to struggle, or have failed—explicitly or implicitly.

Library Movement in Andhra Pradesh

Library movement in Andhra Pradesh is a good sample, for this explanation. The movement of political leaders which started in the State in and around 1914 was immediately for literacy campaign and as an ultimate goal to achieve independence.

The present State of Andhra Pradesh, was formerly under different political divisions; the Nizam's State, Madras Presidency, and others. The movement which emerged in the 1910s was termed as Andhra Library Movement. The background of this movement can be traced in the following:

(a) The growth of literature in the regional language, Telugu, which gained momentum due to the printing technology—the first Telugu book was printed in 1834;

(b) Many libraries were established in the region: a public library at Rajahmundry started by Justice James Thomas in 1839; the opening of the Theosophical Society Library at Guntur in 1850; Sri Mudigonda Sankaradhya set up the Sankarananda Library at Secunderabad in 1872; Saraswathi Nilayam at Vishakhapatnam in 1886 by the efforts of a school teacher, named, Sri Mantena Adinarayana Murthy; founding of the Asafiya Library at Hyderabad in 1886 by a nationalist, Moulvi Abdul Qayyum and Moulvi Syed Hussain Bilgrami, alias Nawab Emadul Mulk; Ram Mohun Library at Vijayawada in 1911; and others at Ongole, Nellore, and so on.

(c) Political stirrings in the region for bringing an *Awareness* through the libraries about need for literacy as well as for joining hands in the national struggle for freedom—some call this as creating awareness and struggle against oppression and the feudal forces (referring to the Nizam's rule), which later stabilized as an integral part of the Andhra Jana Sangham and Andhra Mahasabha who eventually prepared for a revolt against the Nizam;

There are some critics who feel that this fight against the so called feudal forces was only to raise the communal and religion based voice. And so they feel that the Nizam was correct in oppressing the so called anti-feudal, or as we may term them today as anti-secularists. The Nizam was in no sense a bigot and biased, nor favoured Muslims at the cost of Hindus. His was declared as the Secular State, where the government employment was open to all, irrespective of caste, creed, etc., that is, there were Hindus, Muslims, Christians, and the like in his administrative set-up at all levels, including highest and lowest.

(d) The existence of a large number of political and social leaders who could arouse the feelings of cultural affinity and brotherhood, the list of significant names includes: Ayyanki Venkata Ramanayya (1890-1979), Ravichettu Ranga Rao, Paturi Nagabhushanam (1907-), Kommaraju Laxman Rao, Raja Nayani Venkata Ranga Rao, Madapatti Hanumantha Rao (1885-1970), Suravarapu Pratap Reddy, Puvvadu Venkatappayya, Suri Venkata Narsimham (1880-1930), Kasinadhuni Nageswara Rao Pantulu (1862-1938), Kalluri Narasimham Pantulu (1863-1925), Bhupatiraju Tirupati Raju (1867-1951), Gadicherla Harisarvottamrao (1883-1960), Saranu Rama Swamy Choudary (1901-1976), Adusumilli Srinivasrao (1901-1981), Vavilala Gopal Krishnaiah (1906-), Kodati Narayana Rao (1914-), etc.

(e) The movement gathered force with the establishment of its office: Andhradesha Granthalya Sangam (Andhra State Library Association). Mocharla Ramachandra Rao was its first president; Chilkamarthi Laxminarasimham Panthulu and Suri Narasimha Sastry were its vice-presidents; Ayyanki Venkata Ramanayya and Nalam Krishna Rao were its secretaries.

The Association conducted conferences, and meetings at all levels as a regular programme, to promote its cause. They held the first conference, Andhradesha Library Conference in 1914, at Vijayawada.

At this conference Chilakmarthi read out the library manifesto, which he titled as 'Grandhalaya Vedam', stressing the importance of library service. Originally in Telugu, it is transliterated here:

> "O Mother Bless me with knowledge.
> Knowledge
> Like the air we breath
> the water that quenches thirst and
> the Sun's energy that sustain the cycle of life should be available to all universally".

In his speech he said:

> The Sun's light brightens everything;
> So shall knowledge dispel darkness and brighten every life.
> Air gives life to all and is freely accessible;
> So shall knowledge be within the reach of all, breathing life vigour into them clear water quenches the thirst of all;
> So shall knowledge satisfy the curiosity of the curious and the hunger of the hungry for it (Sarada, 1978: 73).

The President while emphasising the urgent need for financial aid from the local government, or municipality, also said: "If the existing provisions of Municipal Act do not facilitate extension of aid to libraries it needs amendment to arrange for such aid".

The slogan, "Grandhalaya Vedam", the Association, and all its activities appear today as small achievement. Though in those days when literacy level was very low, society was tradition bound, let alone women, even men did not have much education, and the imagination, conviction and courage all together led to become a people's movement. To quote from the Report of the Committee on Private Libraries, set up by the Government of Andhra Pradesh:

"In Telangana region of the Nizam's State, as in the then Madras Province, library movement paved the way for and strengthening political, social, and cultural renaissance of the people. In the peculiar conditions obtaining under the Nizam's rule in Hyderabad State, library movement also helped in forging an awareness and unity in the struggle against oppression and the feudal forces. Later it stabilised, as an integral component of the Andhra Jana Sangham and Andhra Mahasabha which eventually prepared the people for the revolt against the Nizam Shahi" (1978: p. 5).

In 1919, to get this support, a delegation of library workers met P.S. Sivaswamy Iyer, the member of the Executive Council, Madras, got an order for release of funds from all local bodies. In 1920, again, D.K.V. Pantulu, moved a resolution in the Madras Legislative Council, directing government to release Rs. 20,000 as aid to libraries. This was approved, though never released. The approval of grant carried the following conditions:

— a library could aspire to benefit by government grants, if registered with the government on payment of Rs. 50;
— such a library should necessarily agree to contribute a matching amount as of the grant money;
— it shall purchase only those books that are approved by the government;
— such a library should subject itself to inspection by officers of the Education Department; and
— such a library should provide admission to all citizens irrespective of caste, creed, and religion.

Incidentally, public objected to the above first four points. They felt that these only favoured the government, and prevented libraries from acquiring books and periodicals needed by people as also it was creating obstacles in the manner of assistance to other libraries.

(f) Published literature in Telugu, including a journal *Granthalaya Sarvasamu*.

(g) Trained the volunteers in ways and means of establishing and maintenance of libraries.

(h) Organized library *yatras* (pilgrimages) to propagate their ideas among the masses. From 1934 to 1937 in West Godavari District, and from 1943 to 1947 in other districts batches of prominent workers went touring extensively for weeks, village after village, in the interior districts of the state. Different activities were performed, which included, poster display, *Bhajan* reciting, lecturing, exhibiting books, and other materials, using gramophones and magic lanterns.

The team would first paste the posters containing *Granthalaya Veda*, and try to contact elders and commoners of the village. Some volunteers would in the meanwhile arrange a book exhibition. Some lectures, book reading (reading *Harikatha* and *Burrakatha*) and puppet show sessions would then follow. *Burrakatha*, an interesting technique of folk narrative, was done in a group of three members—the main story teller, and two supportive characters. The story would revolve around an epic character, drawn from mythology or historical events. Sometimes the contemporary and social events are also converted to heroic dimensions. Consequently, *Burrakatha*, assimilated various literary aspects which were predominant in the society.

The teams carried magic lanterns and audio-visual equipment, such as, gramophone records, and helped in communicating the message of library service. Books were taken to the door steps in bullock carts, cycles, and all other means, including boats. This innovation, of boat library service, was brought in by the help of leaders like Paturi Nagabhushanam of the Sevasram Library, at Pedapalam. The magic lanterns were used to exhibit posters on health, literacy, library propaganda and education.

(i) The Nizam's government also, rather indirectly, participated in the movement, by establishing and funding libraries in the Nizam State: During the reign of the Nizam VII, Mir Osman Ali Khan, there were 63 government funded libraries, 6 reading rooms, 78 mobile (travelling) libraries, and a total of 2,48,428 volumes. As compared to this there were 9 non-governmental libraries, in the Nizam State, with a collection of 9,781 volumes (all figures are of the year 1933).

In the year 1916-17, the expenditure on Public libraries, including Asafiya, was Rs. 42,516 (of which Rs. 6,145 for books), for aided libraries it was Rs. 8,850, number of visitors, 22,756, total volumes 23,663, and book consultation 31,168. Interestingly this rulers patronized education and learning to an extra-ordinary level, and encouraged the opening of colleges, schools and university in the dominion, with a provision for library in each of these institutions. The period saw the development of mobile and travelling libraries, which included books in multiple numbers regularly lent to schools, using the mobile facility. The Osmania University Library, City College Library, Nizam College Library, and a library in each of the degree and professional colleges emerged later. City College Library was set up as a model library in the State, with a librarian (trained on the job), and who made its outlook professional and usable. It was in many ways a leading college library in the State, in providing open access, a catalogue based on Dr. Ranganathan's Classified Catalogue Code, and Browne System for issuing of books.

Further, another sign of support being received by the Nizam for library development, is obvious in the best essay prize, instituted in 1942, in the Hyderabad State. It was to coincide with the Golden Jubilee celebrations and exhibition, on the successful completion of fifty years of the Nizam's rule, and also the other occasion, and that was the meetings of the All-India Oriental Conference, and Indian Historical Congress. The State Asafiya Library, Hyderabad, made this prize announcement, stating three prizes are for the best essay on the topic, entitled 'Deccan Libraries'. The Andhra Pradesh Oriental Manuscript Library, Hyderabad, has nicely preserved these essays considered for the competition.

(j) We can see a few instances of the dedication of the workers and their leaders. The founder of Andhra Vigyana Prakashini Grandha Nilayam at Suryapeta, resigned government service and continued to serve the cause of mass awareness—launched by the elders of the community—which he called as Krishi Pracharini Grandha Mela. This was the library which legally challenged the censorship imposed by the Nizam's government. The Government's objection to Andhra Jana Sangham about holding a conference at Suryapet in 1926, which the organisers got it nullified through the legal intervention. The High Court, established a legal precedent, providing judicial activism as early as this year, by a verdict stating that the Government had no right to prevent the organizers from conducting the conference.

There was another interference from the Government. "The activities of Andhra Desa Library Association led the Government of India to suspect that the Indian National Congress might capture this movement for its own advantage" (Ranganathan, 1968: 41). Hence, the Government created a diversion and got sponsored All-India Library conference at Lahore in 1918, but such diversions were not repeated again.

(k) The dedication of people in creating a spirit of affinity was more so visible in the enthusiasm displayed by them (which library enthusiasts have called as 'library workers') when they organized relief work for victims during the river Krishna floods in 1916; many of the volunteers worked at schools, adult education programmes, and helped organization of clinics and dispensaries, gram panchayats and women and children welfare centres.

(l) From the beginning of this movement the Nizam Government viewed the activities of these leaders with suspicion. The officials were asked to closely watch the programmes of these libraries. The Government passed a ruling to screen the activities of these private institutions. It issued the *Gashti Nishan, no. 53*, to ensure that no institution—including libraries—could be set up without the Government's prior permission.

Again, no *Pathsala* (school) and *Vyayamasala* (physical exercise centre) could be set up without permission.

This state intervention, or call it censorship is common; Governments, state level or national, all followed a similar style of censor. Nehru found similarities all round: "Mysore and Travancore seemed to give some civil liberty and opportunities of political work at the time; in Hyderabad even this was wholly absent; and I felt, in spite of courtesy that surrounded us, stifled and suffocated. Latterly the Mysore and Travancore Governments have withdrawn even the measure of civil liberty and political activity that they had previously permitted".

"In Bangalore, in the Mysore State, I had hoisted at a great gathering a national flag on an enormous ironpole. Not long after my departure this pole was broken up into bits, and the Mysore Government made the display of the flag an offence. This ill-treatment and insult to the flag I had hoisted pained me greatly. . . . There are no newspapers worthy of the name issued there (in Hyderabad), and in order to prevent the germs of corruption from coming from outside, a large number of newspapers published in other parts of India are prevented entry. So strict is this policy of exclusion that even Moderate journals are excluded" (1936: 272-3).

(m) Another conference, was organized in the year 1944, by Sri Chowdavarapu Viswanatham, the Convener of Bharati Grandhalayam, at Gudur in Jangaon Taluq, which was not cleared by the Government. Because he disobeyed the government, he was prosecuted and was sentenced to a week's imprisonment.

Mohan Dutt, in his book *Baroda and Its Libraries*, praised the Andhra Library movement: "The Andhras have developed quite a new type of library, incorporating in its organization amidst other indigenous institutions of Hindu temple and ancient village community and a modern public library".

These historic events, moves, roles, and activities, refer to some kind of activism. The question, however is does it fit into the definition of a social movement, can it be called a mass movement, and if so did it survive the forces of time and tide that passed by, or did it succumb to these hurricanes? The answer lies in the affirmative: that there was an institutionalized attempt, with leadership, motivated workers, and the movement achieved success in the first few decades of its growth. It did get the mass support and hence it was rightly called people's movement. The main focus of the movement was in the development of nationalistic spirit, and in this it did succeed. So far as the growth of library culture and reading culture is concerned, it probably did not gain much success. But once the people felt going smooth, achieving some of the stated objectives—literacy, freedom struggle, awareness about other problems, etc.—the movement started withering.

Apart from nationalism, one more factor, was predominant in the entire process, that is creating an interest for literary works: 'the greatness of the Telugus and the pride of the land'. To achieve this end, one of the technique that worked was the folk narrative, *Burrakatha*. A social anthropologist, Daniel Negers, working for his doctoral research on *Burrakatha*, at the Department of Ethnology, Paris University, deplores the lack of patronage to this, and, is gradually getting replaced by media and television in the land of its origin.

About the purpose that it fulfils, Negers says, that it "is not only a complete and rich art form but also plays a crucial role in integrating various groups in rural areas. . . . Ever since it came into existence during the freedom movement to convey the nationalist and revolutionary messages, *Burrakatha*, had been popular all over the state".

Whether, *Burrakatha*, could promote literacy or not, it was definitely a fun time for the audience. Negers says, "Ever since it came into being, *Burrakatha*, was considered as a means to promote learning, entertainment and propagate a message, although used on different religious and social functions".

There is another school of thought, which feels that the activity that went on in the pre-independent India, was to reduce the barriers of castes, to reduce the cases of child marriage, remove the practice of *Sati*, and so on, and hence these were the focus of the educational and social change, and these were only next to raising the national spirit. There is not much of activism to remove illiteracy or to create a ground for book and information culture. One can see ideas these reflected in the doctoral dissertation of Prof. Y. Vaikuntam, Spread of Education and Social Change in Andhra, 1880-1920 (Osmania University, 1979).

If at all there was some movement in creating library awareness, and in building a platform for literacy eradication, according to another historical research, this was limited to classes, and did not percolate to the masses. The upper classes of the society, including, the Reddy, Valma, Vaishya and Brahmins were all into this activism. The masses did not join the programmes because of lack of consciousness of the value of literacy, lack of governmental support to the activities, and so on. One instance of the daily attendance in a library system, in one district (Karimnagar), which has a population of 30,000 has on an average attendance of 25 to 80 persons, is itself demonstrating that the people were not much interested in reading the books, or newspapers, that were available in these reading rooms (libraries). One can find an interesting discussion on this case history in a chapter 'Library Movement in Karimnagar District' in Narotham K. Reddy's published doctoral thesis, entitled *Freedom Struggle in Erstwhile Nizam State*, with special reference to Karimnagar District (Hyderabad, 1991, pp. 255-82).

There are some more research works, that have studied the social, cultural and political activities, and searched by this researcher, for citations, and, references to what is termed in library literature as library movement: Ch. Veerabhadram, Socio-economic basis of the Agency rebellion in the Madras Province, 1879-1924 (A study of Godavari District), M.Phil thesis, Osmania University, 1982; and B. Bhanumathi, The Development of Local Government in the Nizam Dominion (1869-1941), M.Phil thesis, Osmania University, 1980.

We are still left with the question, as to what can this entire historic event be called: movement, low key activity, etc., and also, what factors contributed to this slowing down of the movement? Was there no farsight in the leadership? Was the process of institutionalization became the main reason? The answers can be many including, the following:

(i) The political participation in the movement was temporary, as the main forces were more busy in the freedom struggle, and that was their main goal. What were the social reformers doing for this. Nehru has an answer in his autobiography. "But the real reason why the Congress and other non-official organizations cannot do much for social reform goes deeper. We suffer from the disease of nationalism, and that absorbs our attention and it will continue to do so till we get political freedom" (p. 383).

It is felt by some that the others who found an opportunity to gain a hold over the reins did exploit the situation and achieved much personal benefit in the name of a social cause. This theory is supported by the argument that these leaders were not professionals—in any sense of the term as we understand today, nor had any idea of what librarianship demands, and so on;

(ii) Lack of regular funding—neither the British Government came forward in this, nor the local enthusiasts could raise the level of funding required to improve the initial level of library development;

(iii) The newly trained graduates in professional ethos had little or no inkling of what it means to work at a mass level, or what can sustain the spirit of library movement which was so enthusiastically brought up by the leaders;

(iv) Institutionalization and technological innovations reduced the common man's proximity and led to man-machine struggle for survival; and

(v) The goal of the leaders was primarily to achieve literacy, rather than create a spirit of library use and library attendance—always neo-literates find the gap between the 3 Rs. which they have learned and kind of material and services the library offers.

We may come out of this Andhra Library Movement, for a while, and see some of the resolutions of the First All-India Librarians Conference, held at Lahore, on 5 January 1918.

The first step to be taken in any measure of reciprocity is compilation of a census of libraries in India and the Government of India be requested to compile and publish such a census, consulting the councils of the Asiatic Society of Bengal and the Bombay Branch of the Royal Asiatic Society, the authorities of the Madras University Library and the Imperial Library and such other authorities as the Government of India may deem it desirable to consult:

(a) That the nature of libraries to be included in the census with reference both to number of volumes and to contents be left to the judgment of the Government, the Conference merely suggesting that purely numerical test is not a test of value.

(b) The census should include collection of manuscript and apply to libraries in Native States as well as British India.

(c) That the information to be collected in the census would include the location of each library, the date of its foundation, its ownership, its income and book budget, amount of admission of accessibility to public, conditions of admission, number of printed books, number of manuscripts of pamphlets and periodicals, nature of the date of catalogue and general contents and staff" (*Hindu*, Lahore, January 5, 1918).

In this conference there is a professional approach to the business of conference, and also a serious concern for library development, collection of data for analysis of the growth patterns, and for whatever other reasons. This much of simple approach is not evident anywhere in the Andhra Desa Library Movement. The names of the participants of this All-India conference, make some sense in this regard, Handerson, Connemara Public Library, Gothskar, Bombay Branch of the Royal Asiatic Society, Newton Mohan Dutt, Curator, Baroda, Nagappa, Mysore University, J.A. Chapman, Imperial Library, and so on.

There is also a possibility that due to the presence of such a library awareness and background of library spirit it was possible that post-independent India could easily enact the library legislation in this State. This hypotheses needs verification. To those who wish to prove this as true, the question remains: Did library legislation (call it regularising the financial support and governmental involvement) lead to the development of library culture. If yes, where is the evidence. If no, why these enactment did not lead to making the library a centre of the society.

To quote Prof. Sarada,

> "These activities formed the hallmark of Andhra Library Movement during the pre-legislation (before 1948) period. After the enactment of Madras Public Libraries Act, 1948 and Andhra Pradesh Public Libraries Act, 1960, the library services tended to acquire professional character. The library service was limited to the four walls of the library. The activities of public libraries were limited to the acquisition and organization of reading materials and providing facilities for reading in the library, and circulation and issues of books to the members of the library. A skeleton of extension activities are being undertaken once in a year during the celebration of National Library Week (November). The involvement of the library in the community information services almost declined during the period after 1948" (1991: pp. 230-1).

One Man Movement

Contrast this entire force and historic drama, with what one man S.R. Ranganathan did to create a chain of movements. His one single book Five Laws of Library Science, was his bible, and based on each law (guiding principle), let us see how he led the movement, to make library a usable place.

First law, states, Books are for use. Finding that the much of the faculty and undergraduate community had no access, and hence much of the books remained unused, he opened the doors of the Madras University Library to these students and to the other teachers, the user attendance went up from 90 to 1636, within one year, 1936.

Second law, states, Every reader his/her book. Ranganathan made it obligatory that every user who comes in the library must be helped, assisted and guided in finding the desired information, so as to see that no reader goes out of the library without getting information. For this he, imported the idea of 'Information desk service, which provided a list of reference on inquiry.

Third law is Every book its reader. That is all books in the library must have users, and none should be left untouched or unused. For this Ranganathan devised the scheme of taking the books to the door steps, through mobile libraries, and sending information to the potential and non-users.

Let us quote one event in the context of taking information to people: Ranganathan once received cash gift, which he used for purchase of a bullock and cart. He got the interior and exterior done, to look like a room, with shelves fitted, and books displayed on the shelf. The cart enters a village, the cart man rings the bell, giving a call to the inhabitants to come and use the mobile unit. The parking done in a prominent place, near a residential area, or near the market, would be for an hour or two. Interested people would come and borrow books for themselves or for others. The cart would then move on, to other place. Due to its slow speed, it hardly covered 10 or 12 miles in a day, and thus reach a few locations (Mookerjee, 1969: 356).

Fourth law enunciated by Ranganathan is Save the time of the reader. Ranganathan, saw to it that was possible in one way by providing instant help to the readers, through the availability of trained staff marked out for 'service to readers'; and in another way by providing access to the users as much as possible, and keeping the library always open and accessible. "The University Library knows no holiday. It works all the 365 days of the year, no matter whether it be a Sunday or a festival day or a sacred day. It works 13 hours each day. It opens at 7 a.m. when people go to the beach for their morning (walk, they) can refresh their intellect as well. The serious full times research workers will be found in the reading rooms all through the day. Again, after the evening walk in the Marina, it is possible for anybody to step into the comfortably in library and do some solid reading till 8 p.m."

In saving the manhours (time of the user) he even went ahead and started the open access system, in 1929, at Madras University library, despite the threat that this new system would increase the book loss.

> "One man spends an hour in a library fumbling in catalogues and lists or wandering confusedly among the books, when all he wants is the date of the second battle of Panipat. Another man goes straight to any of the half a dozen books, that he knows, will tell him; jots it down and in three minutes he is gone. Unhappily the second type of man is so much rare. The daily losses in energy and material, that result from sheer ignorance on the part of otherwise intelligent persons of how to avail themselves of the contents of books, must be colossal and beyond all calculation. Here is the big class of readers who need reference assistance" (Elahi, 1940: 2-3).

The fifth law, Library is a growing organism. Library grows with the user's needs and user's demands. Ranganathan saw to it that every person in the neighbourhood was made a library goer and habitual reader. For this library had no alternative but grow to satisfy the increasing pressures for variety of information needs. He trained the staff to be capable of correlating users with new knowledge that was entering the library; at the same time verifying the utility of old occupants of the library shelves and cabinets.

So was the one man movement which lent a helping hand, on another front, as compared to the Andhra Library Movement.

Library Movement in the West

Coming to the concept of library movement, let us glance at what kind of library movement prevailed in the developed countries, such as U.K., and U.S.A. And based on these trends we can judge whether the above move is worth being called as a library movement, and how far these Western movements influenced the Indian scenario.

The Western countries had many factors which led to a sound basis for the emergence of the library movement as well as for its success. For instance, in Western countries the concept of library for the public use existed in the eighteenth century, the concept of providing access to reading material existed much earlier, the idea of allowing circulation of books (against subscription in most cases, and not free) was there in the nineteenth century. The idea of a professional body to promote the cause of the institutionalization came only in the end of the nineteenth century. Much before this happened, the people were already involved in library development, both in individual capacities and in institutional set-up.

The kind of trends that prevailed in the Western library development are mostly unique than to the soil, culture, political and economic conditions, religious and social atmosphere, and so on. For instance, in the Western culture literacy was not a major problem for the countries to start with. This must then make the point clear: there are cultures, by and large, which are dominated orally—cultures where the knowledge of writing is less in priority; as against this, there are also such cultures which are deeply affected by the use of writing. Due to some peculiar reasons the Western world got influenced by one language—English—since the modern period. This common language—uniformly used for all purposes—in the West made it easy for major part of the Western world to exchange knowledge and ideas across the seas. The uniformity was easily achieved as it was the English people—with their language—who ruled a major part of the globe since the fifteenth century, including America, Africa, Asia and Australia. Before proceeding further it is appropriate to cite the fact that 'user' in a library was not existing in the dictionaries. *New English Dictionary*, published first made an explicit reference in its volume published in 1901, in its definition of library as: "A library is a public institution or establishment charged with the care of a collection of books and the duty of making them accessible to those who require them".

Books, ideas and knowledge all travelled across the boundaries of the globe spreading what was Western and what was desired by the mother of the countries—Great Britain. While the libraries attached to the religious institutions that emerged first, were exclusively for the promotion of medieval religious tradition, it nevertheless led to the libraries which shed the religious bias and took up to secular and non-religious literature's, in the process of building the libraries across regions and States.

How did the West get away from the oral culture, or from the predominance of natural—oral and verbal—communication pattern? The answer is that the invention of printing and the 'bookie' (as it first called, Sir Thomas Elyot's *The Bookie Named the Gouernour*, published in 1534 in London) revolutionized the approach of human traffic of ideas! According to Walter J. Ong, "Writing had reconstituted the originally oral, spoken word in visual space. Print embedded the word in space more definitively. This can be seen in such developments as lists, especially alphabetic indexes, in the use of words (instead of iconographic signs) for labels, in the use of printed drawings of all sorts to convey information, and in the use of abstract typographic space to interact geometrically with printed words in a line of development that runs from Ramism to concrete poetry and to Derrida's logomachy with the (printed, typically, not simply written) text" (1982: 123).

The major effects of the print medium were visible in production of large number of dictionaries—to regularize the correct usage; encyclopedias—to spread at a mass level the universe of knowledge; which also brought in the concept of privacy of an individual as a right—a major symbol of modern society; private ownership of words—intellectual property rights; etc. These are listed here as these have a direct bearing on the library movement in the West—a continuum.

Western library movement had then enthusiasts, or friends of libraries, who would voluntarily contribute all that was possible by them—cash, kind and personal services. This voluntarism added with the philanthrophic foundations that contributed to the libraries, more so in the U.S. is a record achievement of the concerned societies. The single handed support of Carnegie and the Foundation which he left behind is one unique example for all ages in this regard. In this culture libraries are considered, for all practical purposes, as social development agencies, arsenals of democracy, as indispensable social centres, providing information support for all walks of life—satisfying all needs with equal justice and equal opportunity for all—irrespective of individual or groups as whole, for recreation, knowledge, and education.

The role played by Government agencies is also worth mentioning here. Enactment of laws; regularization of the establishment, maintenance and development of libraries; organize the library system, wherever private mobilization was insufficient; providing means for regular funding; subsidizing the trade and tariff for library to access and provide services; and reducing barriers in information transfer between the regions and countries.

Agencies dealing with book trade, printing, literary activities, etc., all did contribute in this process of making library movement a success. Similarly was the role of associate agencies such as adult education, literacy programmes, and others.

The professional spirit also played a major role in this process and in building a usable environment in libraries. The establishment of reference service as a central point in making the public comfortable in the library—use-friendly libraries; development of training programmes to have skilled and trained staff; emergence of literature for the development of the field and its progress; providing opportunities for continuing education of staff; etc.; are other supporting evidences.

The other main promoters of the library movement in the West include: reading habits, intellectual curiosity, information gathering needs, and the like. In addition the culture of learning and seeking knowledge which was developed due to Renaissance and Reformation found its supporter in the industrial revolution, and finally led to what is seen as the most revolutionizing the humanity—information age.

One can see the level of activism that exists in the West, in the involvement of the people in developing libraries and in the involvement of the librarians in development of the society. Of these two dimensions of the involvement, a lot of literature exists on activism in American librarianship, dealing with the social revolution era of 1960s and 1970s. The society had to tackle issues that dealt with civil rights movements, intellectual freedom, war on poverty and community reach, the discriminated ethics and minorities, women's rights movement, etc.

It is appropriate to quote the editors, of a book, entitled *Activism in American Librarianship, 1962-1973*,

> "In the sixties hundreds of American librarians and library school students became involved in championing socially related change in librarianship. They persuaded these ends in libraries, library schools, and their professional associations and in doing so brought the library profession into the social protest movements and in so doing brought the library profession into the social movements of the time. Women's rights, the struggle for social equality, the anti-war movement—these and other movements expressed themselves in library reform efforts of considerable magnitude. As a consequence, the library as an institution experienced the severest internal challenge in the profession's history. The causes were all not new; the extent of the activism generated was" (Bundy, 1987: 1).

The above mentioned book reproduces an advertisement given jointly by the book publishing industry and the American library profession, on the Vietnam War, reads:

> "Mr. President:
>
> We in the book publishing industry and library profession want you to hear our voices raised along with those of many other informed, responsible citizens in the worlds of business, the professions and the arts.
>
> The United States is the most powerful nation on earth. Let us act with responsibility. Let us have 'the wisdom and the courage and the compassion for humanity' to *End The War in Vietnam Now.*
>
> For more than twenty years military assessments of the war in Vietnam have proved tragically wrong. How much longer shall we listen to military 'solutions'? Is not it time, in the American tradition, for a civilized, civilian approach to the problem?
>
> You are a citizen president, a civilian. Your mandate from the people of the United States in the election of 1964 was for peace and for the creation of a Great Society which could not only change the face of our own country but brings a new enlightenment to the world.
>
> We believe that you, as we, want history to record you as giving the world that new enlightenment. The alternatives, as we see them, are that you will be remembered for a Pyrrhic military victory in Vietnam or that you will not be remembered at all because history will have been stopped forever by a world holocaust. Morally and materially, the war in Vietnam is withering away the chances of that new enlightenment in the world.
>
> Let us stop sending the young men of our country across the world to be killed. Let us stop destroying the people and the economy of Vietnam. Let us stop bombing North Vietnam and start negotiating now!" (p. 185).

Interestingly, the first country in Asia to have library legislation was Japan in 1899; Bulgaria had in 1928; Czechoslovakia in 1919; Finland in 1921; Mexico in 1917; Poland in 1946; Russia in 1921; South Africa in 1928; and Sweden in 1930. Library legislation, or getting the Government involved in managing the libraries, and in providing free library service to all, is seen as a best method in all these countries.

For those who state that library legislation is a must for the library development, the supportive evidence comes from many countries of the world who have enacted library laws and this in turn led to the library progress, and one may find these documented in the book, McColvin's Survey of Libraries. But those who feel doubtful about library legislation itself, or feel that there are other ways of promoting library development quote the US example, stating that there is the most advanced country, without any uniform pattern of library legislation (Krishnamurti, 1958: 22).

There are others who feel that library legislation, or desire for providing free library service, in a Third World context, like India, must come from the people. If the people have a desire—and more so a felt desire—only then the Government should come forward to legislate such a library system. "Studies have also revealed that lack of clear cut policy, paucity of funds, low priority are some other factors which have influenced growth of library development" in a negative manner (Aslam, 1996: 8).

Library Movement in Other States of India

In passing we can glance at the trends in which contributed to the progress of the concept of the library movement in Baroda, Bengal, Punjab, and many places all over India had tremors of library movement in various degrees and various ways. While in some places, like Bengal it had a mixed support of the Government (for various reasons), and the elite; in Baroda it was the single and whole hearted support of the ruler; in Kerala it was the people in general who had contributed to the spread of libraries; and hence these trends have interesting patterns for one to look deeper into and find the overall patterns that contributed to the development of libraries. In the following is the description of some prominent places that have demonstrated some singular effect in this process of growth of library and library awareness.

(A) *Bengal*

In the undivided Bengal the introduction of English as a medium of instruction, led to what can be called, as, Bengalee renaissance. This was possible due to the increase in the level of literacy and thereby to an increasing interest in the masses-to use the libraries. Availability of printed books in a variety and style, and these available at a comparatively cheaper prices, access to public libraries against a very small subscription, availability of translated works of patriotism as well as the heroic deeds of the Eastern and Western leaders, and such other means promoted the development of a spirit of libraries, and increased an interest in the promotion of libraries for masses. The development of Government funded libraries, establishment of colleges and schools, and such other facilities also ignited a feeling for the necessity of learning and spreading of knowledge.

In the urban and the rural areas it was a practice to read books to the illiterates; enthusiasm was raised for the adult education by many such programmes. Free night-schools were started all over. At the back of all this was the idea of developing a base for nationalistic feeling and promoting the cause of independence. The British Government soon sensed this 'negative' spirit and raised all efforts to put down this movement of popularising libraries and literacy campaign. To quote from Ohdedar: "The reign of terror let loose on Bengal had no parallel in the country in general. The public and specially the middle class—backbone of the society—had their sympathy in the *swadeshi* movement but were afraid of repression. The night-classes, the gymnasium and the small public libraries had to close down or had their activities" (1969: 28).

This fear of being caught was short lived and due to public pressure many libraries were opened and the national library in Calcutta appeared—despite the Government's negative position and efforts to put down the raising spirit of equality and liberty.

In fact the establishment of the Asiatic Society, led to the beginning of library movement in Bengal. The second step was the opening of the Calcutta Public Library in 1836; and the third step was with the beginning of organised library movement, *i.e.*, formation of All Bengal Library Association in 1925, at Albert Hall, Calcutta. The State provides a lead in establishing a variety of professional bodies, which became the channels, later, for the national library development.

(B) *Baroda*

Baroda had another type of library movement, unique in its existence, and unique in its immediate disappearance. The Maharaja of Baroda, Sir Sayaji Rao Gaekwad III, played a leading role in the development of libraries in the State, the progress is this regard is incomparable with any other State. The Maharaja on his second tour in America selected one expert American librarian, William Alanson Borden. He, was appointed as the first State Library Director, and he served from 1910 to 1913, advising, planning and implementing a statewide library development programme. The entire State was covered by a well-knit programme to connect all library related activities at the State, district and rural levels as a systematic network. It aimed at providing free service, though limited to books in the regional languages. It also had a children's library to cater to the need of the young. The pioneered the cause of library development in a very profound manner, concentrating on training of librarians, publishing of literature, creating an awareness of reading and library habits, professionalizing library practices (by introducing classification, cataloguing and other professional methods), the concept of friends of library club (called Mitra Mandal), and so on.

Borden's efforts are stated in his own words:

> "I determined to introduce into Baroda what we in the United States have recognised as a goal to be ultimately attained, but which we have not yet reached. I mean a system of centrally located book storehouses, each surrounded by a network of small, inter-depending libraries. These small libraries to have the books commonly called for and the storehouses to supplement these small collections. This has been done and the result is now known in India as the Baroda System" . . . If there is any value in this library cooperation throughout a large State let it be remembered that it was first introduced, not in the home of the modern library movement, our own country, but way down in India, 10,000 miles from here. . . ."
>
> And continues in terms of specific details ". . . In addition, I have induced the members of my staff to start the Baroda Library Club, which meets monthly and which already has a reputable membership. They have also started a quarterly magazine, devoted to library matter, called The Library Miscellany. Furthermore, in the way of library extension, we have established a Visual Instruction Branch, for the benefit of the many who cannot read. This branch has four cinematographs and is showing educative films in the villages and towns of the State—free of course" (Borden, 1913: 659).

He is rightly credited with the title of Father of Public Library movement in India; he initiated open access for the first time in India in 1910, started a library journal in 1912, began a library training programme in 1912. The programme went on well, until the life time of its sponsor, the Maharaja. With his death in 1926 came the end of the whole movement. In fact till that day it has reached a glorious height: providing library service to cent per cent service to the urban dwellers, and 65 per cent to the rural community.

One is forced to wonder if at all the public was prepared to accept this generosity of the ruler, which came in as a free public library—anything which comes free is always set aside! There continued some semblance of the movement so heartily initiated by the ruler, and leaders including, Newton Mohan Dutt, T.D. Wakins, Motibhai Amin, Kudalkar, and so on.

(C) *Punjab*

Like the undivided Bengal, undivided Punjab also made a history in its library development. Here again, an American librarian, Asa Don Dickinson, was in the forefront to provide the necessary stimulus and professional guidance. He was appointed as Librarian of the Punjab University, Lahore, in 1915.

Dickinson led the country in the establishment of the first university library system. He became the pioneer, in being the first foreign professional university librarian in India; he started the first Library Training Class in 1915, at Punjab University; he heralded an era of systematic development of university library administration; he set the pace for professional continuing education programme by organizing the first All-India Library Conference, in 1918 under the banner of Punjab Library Association—also founded by him in 1916; he introduced for the first time Dewey Decimal Classification scheme in India; initiated a series of publications and published a useful source for organizing a library, called Panjab Library Primer.

The utility of the primer is stated by the author as:

> "This little book is the fruit of a decade's experience among American libraries, modified by a year's acquaintance with conditions peculiar to India. . . . (It is) an excellent handbook for inexperienced librarians in the public, college and school libraries in India . . . (presuming that) the average Punjab Librarian (who is generally a college matriculate but only rarely a college graduate) by a diligent study of these pages will find himself able to improve very materially the conditions in his library".

The Association and all the other innovations of Dickinson faded soon after a while. However the State of Punjab had the benefit of some leading librarians who contributed their efforts in continuing the spirit of the library movement. The Punjab Public Library provided a lead in offering services to the people, the example of which was followed by a few public libraries in North India. The leading journals, Modern Librarian (organ of the Association, started in 1930) and Indian Librarian (started in 1946) both started here.

Library Use Pattern and Treatment of User

How was the user treated? How much of concern for the user was shown in planning, implementing and interacting with user? What type of attitude did the library staff have in making the library user-friendly? What types of facilities and services were given to the users?

We may find that libraries did lend books. Although it was not usual to lend books, subscription based libraries did lend books, at certain time and with certain rules! For instance, in Goa State Central Library, according to the historical records of 1938, borrowing privilege was extended only to the Government officers and Lyceum teachers, with prior permission from the Government. However, this facility was stopped several times on the pretext that it damaged the books and also deprived the genuine reader from using it in the reading room. Again, this library had, in 1941, a spacious well-ventilated Reading Hall with wooden cupboards along the wall for shelving of books. This library has undergone several changes in its working hours, and as early as 1883, it was kept open till 10 p.m., and sometimes the timings were changed according to seasons (Rodrigues, 1996: 272-3).

In Calcutta, we find the city underwent a number of experiments, in making its place unique in India—as the capital of the East India Company. Due to the European, and more specifically the British influence there emerged, by 1800, a number of libraries which charged different rates, and permitted either only reading, or reading and borrowing, and such other facilities.

It was also due to these Europeans that the habits, such as reading for pleasure, reading for information, reading for pastime, and so also taste for fiction and newspapers, etc., became a fashion first among the Babus and then among the elite in India, as early as the beginning of the eighteenth century. "In Bombay (now Mumbai) and Madras (now Chennai), the Englishmen, who came as District Officers, or Sessions Judges, tried to create small libraries in the localities where they were stationed, primarily with the help of the elite of the town—which were more or less like small club libraries for recreation" (Ohdedar, 1969: 29).

The user had some stated 'rights' in this age. For instance, Delphian Society (founded 1810) in its prospectus listed library rules, rule four stated that, any member has the liberty, at stated times, of visiting the library, and reading and taking extracts from the books and manuscripts (Ohdedar, 1996: 12).

In 1813 Vakeel Reading Room provided reading facility to those who could afford to pay a monthly subscription of Rs. 13, against which one could use the reading room between 7 a.m. and 5 p.m., and again between 6 p.m. and 8 p.m. (Ohdedar, 1996: 14).

Harkaru Circulating Library, another subscription based library (flourished between 1820 and 1832), had three types of subscribers, with respective rates of subscription and privileges: I Class, Rs. 8 (3 to 8 books at a time, also permitted to borrow new novels, pamphlets, latest magazines); II Class, Rs. 6 (2 to 6 books at a time, new novels, plays, pamphlets, and magazines received in a month); and III Class Rs. 4 (1 to 4 books, cannot borrow new novels, plays, pamphlets, and magazines). The Harkaru newspaper subscribers, were entitled to use the Reading Room free of charge, the reading room containing the 'newspapers of the Bengal Presidency and those of Madras, Bombay, Ceylon, Penang, Mauritius, Cape, and so on'.

The subscription libraries apart, there emerged proprietary libraries— a fixed premium paid entitled a person to become a proprietor, as such, had a share in the stock of the library, and this share became the actual property, as it could be transferred or sold, and was expected to increase in value. One such library, Calcutta Library Society (flourished in 1820s), provided 'excellent opportunity of pursuing all the best new works in every department of science at the least possible expense'. The proprietors of the library paid annual amount of Rs. 160 and raised soon to Rs. 200.

User-Friendly Libraries

Ranganathan has given many instances, or case studies, of how he dealt with the users, or how his staff in the library or the reference section provided reference service. He is realistic in narrating the cases, because he does not shy in quoting instances of reference librarians being problem creators, rather than problem solvers.

Case One

"John Bourdillon Bilderbeck was a local celebrity at Madras about the end of the last century. He was a professor and principal in the Presidency College, a government institution".

"One afternoon the office of the Director of Public Instruction wanted details of his career. They were found in the History of Services of gazetted and other officers in the civil department serving in the Madras Presidency corrected up to 1st July 1906 (the year of retirement of Bilderbeck). As the reference librarian began to read out from it, the man at the other end of the wire said:

> 'It is all too much within the next few minutes. The office of the Director of Public Instruction had its own copy of this publication of the Government. But there was no reference librarian in the office. Nor was there any one with ready to look up at that publication. But, it was almost a reflex action for our reference librarian to look it up" (1961: 208-09).

Case Two

"The award of Nobel Prize for literature in 1938 to Mrs. Pearl S. Buck was the occasion for a rush to inquirers. The Who's Who in America gave only four inches of information. Two other books were known to devote some pages for her. . . ." "But these were not available in the library. However, the practice of the reference staff of perusing and mentally noting outstanding facts appearing in periodicals came to our rescue. It was recollected that some information about her had occurred in the Wilson Bulletin. A search of its file disclosed that volume 6 (1931-32) contained six columns of biographical information with a picture and that volume 9 (1934-35) contained two more pictures. From the moment this reference was located, the problem changed over from long-range to ready reference" (pp. 209-10).

Case Three

Ranganathan did tremendous work in promoting the idea of reference service, in pre-independent India. In his book, Reference Service, has cited fifty four queries that were received and attended by himself and his colleagues. He has stated the details of each query, the chain of works consulted, and time taken in responding to these reference requests.

A few of these questions and the sources consulted can be reproduced:

— Addresses of some prominent biochemists of India. (A professor. In person. Handbook of Indian universities, 1938. Year-book of the universities of the Empire, 1939. Official chemical appointments, 1937. 5 times).

— The verses in *Kumarasambhava* describing the wedding of Parvathi. (An artist. In person. Verses 71-91 of Chapter 7. 15 minutes).

— Any material on the art of lettering. [A lady. In person. The article on Calligraphy in the Encyclopedia Britannica, Ed 14. Reference catalogue of current literature, 1938. Wade (Cecil): Modern lettering from A-Z, 1938. 15 minutes].

— A description of the *Ekadasi* festival at Srirangam. (Journalist. In person. . . . The three books in the Library on Hindu festivals were out on loan. Hence, Encyclopedia of religion and ethics. Not of help. Imperial gazetteer of India. Moniker Williams: Brahminism and Hinduism, pp. 448-50. Not available in the library. *Index to Indian Antiquity*, vi, p. 322. 5 minutes).

— Any book or article on beggar problem relating to India in particular. (A local library. No book. Birendranath Ganguly: Street beggars of Calcutta: A Study of the Problem and Its Solution in the *Indian Journal of Economics*, Vol. 8, 1927-28, pp. 373-86. 45 minutes).

— I am told that the words 'Zamorin' and 'Mappilla' are loan words from Persian or Arabic. The original of Zamorin is Tamuir and of Mapilla is Moufla. I shall be much obliged if you will let me know . . . whether there any words in those languages exactly corresponding to them or resembling them . . . (A lecturer. By post. Yule's Hobson-Jobson. 10 minutes).

— A book on Pakistan. (A student. In person. Was told that it can be read only in newspapers and periodicals of the months as the problem was quite new. 1 minute).

— Is Sankara a crypto-Buddhist? (A philosophy student. In person. Student also participated in the search. A series of articles by G.V. Budhekar entitled "Is the Advaita of Sankara Buddhism in disguise?" in the *Quarterly Journal of the Mythic Society*, Vol. 24, 1933-34. One hour).

Case Four

"One morning in 1943, an American lady came and presented to me a confidential letter from the Chief Secretary of the Government of Madras. The letter disclosed that she was the Field Librarian of the South East Asian Theatre of War. She had been given an aeroplane to go out and collect from important libraries in India, the information needed for organising their proposed offensive. In the course of a short discussion with the lady librarian, I noted down in successive slips of paper, the Class Numbers for the publications likely to have the information needed and passed on, one at a time to the Reference Section giving some important hints about the exact kind of information needed. From about an hour thereafter, trolley loads of publications were wheeled into my rooms, with flags at relevant pages. By about 5 p.m. the field librarian told me, 'you seem to have organized your publications as if, for war purposes! I know that you had done this in the natural course of processing work. We in America, do not do our work in such a detailed way'. (The moral of the story is libraries should be prepared as in war instances, for any in-depth search and be ready for immediate offence). (Ranganathan, 1972: Part II, 5).

The colleagues were all whom he trained with so much of vigour and tenacity that they led to the creation of a generation of dedicated and motivated reference librarians in India. These user-friendly attitudes were well received and revolutionized the concept of library, from a store-house to interacting and participating reference centre. This was the result of the rigorous and strenuous training Ranganathan provided to his colleagues.

Case Five

Ranganathan, laid the foundation stone, in this pre-independent era to provide reference service, not only on demand, but also in anticipation. He extended the helping hand to an extent which inspired every user to become horacious reader and effective consumer of information. Being a scholar and librarian, two rare qualities in modern librarianship, he always went a step ahead of all the colleagues in providing the required and relevant information. See for instance, the letter he wrote to a professor of physics, a type of user whom he himself feels is a passive clientele:

University Library, 9 December 1939
My dear friend

I remember your telling me about a year ago about a correspondence, originated by the Surgeon-General during your predecessor's time about the ultra-violet energy content of the solar radiation in our city. You said that the Surgeon-General sought your cooperation in estimating it.

At that time I could only lay my hands on some scrappy materials in the *Journal of Research of the American Bureau of Standards*, the *Journal of the American Institute of Electrical Engineers and the Public Health Bulletin.* I wonder if you are still interested in the subject. If you are, I have come across something which may be of real use to you. This morning the foreign mail brought the October issue of the *Journal of the Franklin Institute.* It contains an article entitled "A four-year record of the ultra-violet energy in daylight", by Mathew Luckiesh and others of the Lighting Research Laboratory of the General Electric Company.

The bibliography at the end of the article mentions the following five titles:. . . .

The first of the above articles gives a detailed description of the necessary apparatus. It may be of great interest to you. There are twelve further references. These too may be of interest to the Secretary-General.

Perhaps you may call at the library for these references.

I have assembled all of them in my room to save your time.

You may call at any time between 9 a.m. and 6 p.m. I am sure it will be very nice if your laboratory can build data for our city.

Yours sincerely
Sd/-
Librarian

Case Six: Imperial Library

How much was the user-friendliness lacking? One has to dig a vast amount to treasures to identify this aspect. But there is one letter published in *The Statesman*, 29 March 1892: "Sir, among the wants I feel in Calcutta is that of good up-to-date reading, which I find I cannot procure except through the medium of a few literary friends. I hear that there is an Imperial Library in Calcutta, which contains some solid works relating to India, and some valuable publications for the student of modern history; and I am told that permission to use this library can be obtained by application in the right quarter. Would any of your readers kindly inform me where this library is situated, and to whom I must apply for admission thereto? A clerical friend tells me that there is an excellent library at St. Paul's Cathedral, which is replete with theological and other works; but I am ignorant of the conditions of membership, and would like information on the point. It is a pity, I think, that the Bentinck Library is such a hodge-podge as to be useless to the systematic reader, and that there is really no good useful library in Calcutta; for there are several like myself who have a taste for serious reading, and cannot stand the trashy publications which seem to be the vogue here" (Ohdedar, 1996: 28).

The situation was not all that bad always. Given one hundred years of struggle for the growth of a library devoted exclusively to the public, the Imperial Library, Calcutta, from 1830s to 1920s, showed some improvement in its aim of providing free access to the universe of knowledge.

The Annual Report of this library, for 1930-31 suggested:

> 'A strong propaganda was required to induce the reading public to avail themselves of the opportunities offered by the Imperial Library in matter of lending books' (Ohdedar, 1996: 70).

Interestingly, the Imperial Library did make clear its intentions of promoting its cause of access to the recorded information. J.A. Chapman, the Imperial Librarian, from 1911 to 1930, stated in an article in *Calcutta Review*, March 1922:

> '. . . (the Imperial Library) is a lending library, and is prepared to send its books to approved persons, anywhere in India and Burma. There are scholars all over India and Burma who do not know this. It is not only to scholars to whom the books may be sent: in practice anyone who applies for the loan of books is approved. . . ."

In another publication Chapman stated:

> "If the Imperial Library, an institution to which, in nine out of ten, if not oftener, the student must come, the benefit of it would be for Calcutta to enjoy, and a restricted Calcutta; for Europeans who read, read at home. I should deplore such a limiting of its usefulness. There are many students scattered throughout India, within whose reach if the Imperial Library were not a lending library, there would not be one. Another fact not to be overlooked is that the life of a modern printed book in India is short. All the world knows how difficult it is to preserve books in India from getting worm-eaten. It

will be a solace to the "future historian of India", who shall find a gap in our shelves, to know that the book was read, while it was still legible" (Ohdedar, 1996: 69-70).

A quantitative analysis of the use pattern in this library of the books requested for reading shows: just before the First World War, religion ranked as most preferred subject (522 books), followed by literature (496 books); just after the war, literature ranked as the highest (5,412 books), and religion had a low ranking (1,403 books). Another glance at the statistics of readers vis-a-vis books read and borrowed, shows that: in 1910, about 39,000 readers visited the library, these used about 10,000 books, and borrowed 958 books; in 1919-20 it was 43,000 readers and 19,000 books, and borrowed 3,000; in 1930-31 it was 45,000 readers and 30,000 books, and borrowed 7,000; and in 1943-44 it was 24,199 readers, 24,536 books and 14,580 borrowed. While the number of readers and books consulted do not lead to any inferences (as the figures are simply fluctuating—very high to low levels), the figures of books borrowed are an indicator of the changing trend in reading away from the library—a facility extended gradually to all and the net outcome seems to indicate that it was a highly appreciated by the users. Reading away from the library meant that, people are changing their reading style!

Case Seven

Another instance of the use of a public reading room, is cited in Letters from Madras (1946), by Julia Thomas—wife of Mr. James Thomas, a judicial officer who started the reading room in 1839. To quote:

> "The reading room is established and much approved. The doors are opened before six in the morning, but there are always waiting outside, ready for the first moment they can get in. Always twenty or thirty at a time are sitting there and about a hundred come in course of the day. The wall is hung divers of your peeny pictures, which are much admired, especially that of the Queen on the horse-back. We have found plenty of suitable books in English, Hindustanee, Tamil and Gentoo (Telugu) and I think it seems to be very petty invention, and likely to give great satisfaction.
>
> "We have received a petition, signed by the Principal people, cheafly Mussalmans, in several villages, begging us to supply them with books of the same kind as those in our reading room mentioning

the names of several that they particularly wish to have and saying that they will thankfully pay for them, if we will procure them. Therefore, we have now a sort of circulating library in the district. We consign a packet of books to the headman in the village, and he passes them to the rest, and when they are all read, we sent out a fresh supply" (quoted in Venkatappaiah, 1996: 139-40).

Case Eight

The service of issuing books grew leaps and bounds in the Madras University Library, from 5,100 in 1914; 15,300 in 1919; 27,629 in 1925 to 1,31,321 in 1930. In fact, it was only after Ranganathan joined the Library, on 4 January, 1924, the situation gained the real momentum. From 30 September 1924 to 21 July 1925, he was at London, studying Library Science and observing library service. Only after his return he planned to organize the entire set-up—classify, re-arrange in classified sequence, introduce open access, practice reference service, and demonstrate the educational and social values of reference service, and as a result of this secure additional staff.

Role of the Government

What are the ways in which we can assess the role of the Government in contributing towards the development of libraries? How many, and for what purpose, did the Government establish or support educational and research institutions. There were a few universities that were set up by the British patronage, some research centres and some public libraries. It is here that the role of the British Government is shown, and the influences which these had in the development or otherwise, that emerges.

There were many positive attempts at promoting a book culture, reading culture, and print culture. There were also many side effects of these attempts, which hampered the process of development in the British India. The attempts to promote th library development were directly in many areas, and indirectly in a few areas.

Its direct role is visible in the development of agricultural education and research, which was done on the basis of the recommendation of the Royal Commission on Agriculture. The first step in this regard was the setting up of Indian Council of Agricultural Research in 1929, and which led to the later development of a chain of libraries attached to the agricultural information system in India (see Gaddagimath, 1995; J.N. Sharma, 1982).

In this context, it is relevant to cite Sharma who has outlined various steps taken like, library surveys (beginning with the setting up of its library in 1930), library study teams, establishment of new agricultural libraries, sponsoring library related seminars, workshops and facilitating cooperation at national and international levels. This example of agricultural development fits the kind of priority India stepped in, based on the kind of agriculture base that it has, and not agriculture or information base as other countries have.

However, much of the library promotion that was done by the British was lopsided, biased, and limited to fewer areas. In many cases, the idea of having a full-fledged library to support the information needs, was not very encouraging. For instance, while the three main universities in India were established in 1857, the libraries attached to these grew very late, Bombay University Library in 1880, Calcutta University Library in 1873, and Madras University Library in 1904. And the appointment of respective university librarian was very late, that is Bombay in 1915, Madras in 1924 and Calcutta in 1937.

What could have been the reasons for this clear disregard for library development. Was it the lack of interest in the education and research activities, or was it a lack of demand for information, or was the system of education which did not give rise to the need for libraries, or what else? The answers are also many to these questions. One answer to these is that the establishing of a university was not really for promoting learning and research—which is its ideal. In fact these universities were only conducting examinations and awarding degrees, rather than fulfilling the aims of institutions of higher learning, as understood world over. The colleges conducted the teaching work, and the universities were only doing the administrative functions.

The main drawbacks of the existing university set-up was clearly highlighted by the Indian Universities Commission, established under the Chairmanship of Sir Thomas Raleigh, in its report submitted in 1902. The report stated:

> "Of the present university libraries there is not much to be said. The library at Madras appears to be entirely neglected. Mumbai has a good collection of oriental and other books; but the library is little used by the graduates and hardly at all by students. Calcutta has a library and money has been granted for the purpose of making it supplementary to other libraries in Calcutta. It is opened to fellows and to persons permitted by the Syndicate to use it for the purpose

of literature search. The Allahabad University has no library. Lahore has not a very large university library".

We may look into the suggestions of the Commission:

"... good reference libraries should be provided in this connection both with universities and colleges in order that students may have an opportunity of forming the habit of independent and intelligent reading".

The Government, may be for whatever reasons, accepted some of the recommendations of the Commission, and we find that in 1904 the British Government enacted the Universities Act. This Act specifically stated the place of the library in a university. While it did have its impact or not, the Government set up another Commission in 1917, called the Calcutta University Commission, among other things to look into the question of 'maintenance of an adequate university library kept up to date as essential to a first class university'.

The findings of the Commission include: library had inadequate books, and hence could not meet the needs of a majority of students and teachers; most disorganized libraries; majority of these libraries neither provided open access, nor, they allowed borrowing of books; the librarian had to pay for the loss of books; of those libraries who, if at all they allowed borrowing, the use of such a privilege was meagre: of the whole 300 or 400 college students, only a few had borrowed—25 books borrowed in a month, on an average; and the library was not an essential part of the teaching programme.

The Commission, after due consideration of all the factors and precursors, recommended:

(a) necessity of a full-fledged librarian for the Calcutta University Library, who must have the salary and status of a professor, and be ex-officio member of the Academic Council—'a man with professional standing with a monthly salary of rupees 600-800';
(b) library collections need to be improved;
(c) students as well as, though sometimes, teachers, be trained in using the library;
(d) make libraries a real centre of intellectual activity;
(e) be it college or university library, it should maintain a good and useful resource, useful both for the students and faculty; and

(f) as seed money the university must be given rupees two lakhs, with annual grant of rupees 50,000.

While this report was probably the most, and the earliest detailed evaluation of the state-of-the-art of the conditions and the remedies it offered, there continued to be a national level deprivation in finding libraries—useful as well as exemplary—to match the counterparts in England or elsewhere.

There were many more committees and commissions, the list of which includes:

(a) Simon Commission, appointed in 1927, and this had an Auxiliary Committee, and this Committee realistically focused on the problems faced by the educational system and states:

'the dispersal of resources for university teaching among a number of colleges had made it difficult to build up university libraries of the type required for advanced work both at the Honours and the research stage . . . (therefore) majority of the university libraries were inadequate and all needed great additions';

(b) Adult Education Committee Report of 1939. It recommended similarly many useful things for the development of libraries, and the role of the library in adult education, but we do not have enough records dealing with the results of these recommendations;

(c) The Ministry of Education, established in 1935, requested the Central Advisory Board of Education, in 1944, to survey conditions of educational system in the country. The report of the Board, submitted by its Chairman, Sergeant, also the report called as Sergeant Report, was strangely silent about the library, and nowhere it made even a passing reference, among its elaborate details of all other educational matters.

Also during this period, was set up the Fyzee Committee, or also known as Library Development Committee, for the assessment of the state of the art and suggesting the course of action. The details of the recommendations of this Committee have been described elsewhere.

Incidentally, there were a number of attempts made to get the school and college libraries opened up for the public at large—given the fact that in a country having mostly villages (30,000 villages), there is only one public library for every 25 villages. The attempts were made by various agencies, including, Pupils Public Library Association in 1934, Fyzee Committee Report, 1940, and so on. Incidentally, the request for the same by Pupils's Association was heard, by the Madras Government, and which issued orders in 1939, to open the school libraries for the public, and the order outlined the technicalities, such as opening hours, responsibility in case of losses, etc. The Fyzee Committee states:

> "These school libraries should be made available to past students . . . general public. . . . The importance of this may not be realised in big towns . . . or . . . smaller towns. . . . (Venkateswara Rao, 1994: 369).

Before we proceed to see the role of the Government in other intellectual pursuits, related to library movement, let us quote Nehru on this fashion of being in Committees and Commissions: "There were also many other committees sitting in London, and there was an undignified scramble behind the scenes for membership of any Committee which meant a free passage and stay in the heart of the Empire" (p. 387). This he was more so referring to the Indians who were envying with each other to be on such missions, and reach London, but on the whole this is true of either side members, that their efforts were after all a futile exercise.

Censorship and Banned Books

Like any other rulers, Britishers also confiscated, proscribed and banned books, for reasons ranging from blasphemyh in religion, to commercial non-viability, and to treason and criticism of the Government. With time and tide, banned books later have got into a rarity status and also sometimes were reprinted many times. Banned in one country, does not mean, banned in another country, and so goes on the story of censorship. The Britishers took to task authors, publishers, printers, etc., for publishing nationalistic literature—books, newspapers, pamphlets, etc. Both the Central and State Gazettes have a variety of titles, and information resources that were listed under this category. The State Governments have not been any way behind the Britishers, in proscribing the unwanted literature.

Specific instances of the censorship are scattered in the literature. One such reference is cited by Ketkar while refering to the Bombay Presidency libraries:

> "Books in these libraries were mostly in English and the administration exercised some control directly or indirectly so that books which may be considered objectionable by Government were excluded from acquisition and the library was not used as a place for political gathering" (1958: 11).

Nehru in 'Autobiography' (1936), in the chapter dealing with prison humours, states:

> "I could not have all the books I wanted, as there were restrictions and a censorship, and the censors were not always very competent for the job. . . . But I must not complain, for I had, on the whole, a good variety of books. Again I seem to have been a favoured person, and many of my colleagues (A Class prisoners) had the greatest difficulty in getting books on current topics. In Bananas Gaol, I was told, even the official White Paper, containing the British Government's constitutional proposals, was not allowed in, as it dealt with political matters. The only books that British officials heartily recommended were religious books or novels. It is wonderful how dear to the heart of the British Government is the subject of religion and how impartially it encourages all brands of it" (p. 350).

He continues, the topic,

> "Writing or the taking of notes of books read are dangerous pastimes in which they must not indulge. This deliberate discouragement of intellectual development is curious and revealing. From the point of view of reclaiming a prisoner and of making him a fit citizen, his mind should be approached and diverted, and he should be made literate and taught some craft. But this point of view has perhaps not struck the prison authorities in India. Certainly it has been conspicuous by its absence in the United Province. Recently attempts has been made to teach reading and writing to the boys and young men in prison, but they were wholly ineffective, and the men in charge of them have no competence. My own experience has been the exact opposite, and I found many of them, who came to me for the purpose, to have a perfect passion for learning to read and write. We used to teach such convicts as came our way, and they worked hard; and sometimes when I woke up in the middle of the night I was surprised to find one or two of them sitting by a dim lantern inside their barrack, learning their lessons for the next day" (pp. 351-52).

From this passage to the future of India, Nehru seems to tell that the role of the Government was to promote intellectual development as well as literacy movement, and in both the fronts the Government was showing little or no concern!

There are innumerable instances of book ban. One such is the banning the *Pather Devi* a novel by Sarat Chandra Chatterjee. The Second All Bengal Library Conference, 1928, in its resolutions resolved to request the provincial Government to withdraw its ban on this Bengali work.

While the Press and Registration Act of 1867, was meant to identify politically correct literature, there has been one attempt to list all banned books, during the British period in India, that is Gerald N. Barrier's Banned Controversial Literature and Political Control in British India, 1907-1947. "Even a cursory look at this list of banned literature reveals how ruthless the British were to retain their hold on India" (Ramaiah, 1994: 99).

> "In India since the early British days the practice of confiscating or proscribing books not for blasphemy in religion, but for treason and criticism of the Government was fairly common . . . the central and state gazettes are replete with such notifications of books being banned" (Mookerjee, 1969: 266).

Obviously, the British, acted as traditional monarchs, and behaving with dictatorial system of Government, they did not allow the freedom of expression for India. This can be illustrated in one or two instances. The first instance, is from the hot bed of India's freedom struggle, Bengal. *Anand Math*, a book by Bankim Chandra Chatterjee, published in 1882, in Bengali, and later translated into English many times. It also contained Vande Mataram, a patriotic song. This song became very popular and its echoes went all over during the freedom struggle.

The other instance is from the Marathi language, the land of Shivaji, and Bhosles. The book is V.D. Savarkar's *The Indian War of Independence*. Even before its printing, news about it spread like wild fire, and all presses that were suspected of printing it in Maharashtra, or any where in India and abroad were all under direct vigil, and despite these currents, the book was printed in English version, from England in 1909. The contents of these two books dealt with nationalism—that brand of nationalism which the British opined will create discontent and hatred against them among the masses and classes. Hence they banned these. A detailed description of the attempts to print and the public appreciation of these books in India is available in the literature (Ramaiah, 1994).

Legislation and Policies

Considering that the development of public libraries is essential for all-round prosperity, health and happiness of all people, and this can be achieved with the active cooperation in providing access to information, the Western countries were the first to adopt a recourse to legal steps. The first legislation in U.S.A. was passed in 1700, by the South Carolina Legislative Assembly, for the regulation and protection of the first library founded in the state; the first Public Libraries Act in U.K. received the Royal approval on 14 August, 1850.

In this context, it is pertinent to mention some of the measures adopted by the Government, which directly or indirectly, helped in promotion of the library movement.

The first library established was that of East India Company in 1715, in Bombay (now Mumbai). What happened to this library and its activities is not known. This was followed by the opening of the Bombay (now called Mumbai) Branch of the Royal Asiatic Society of London in 1804, which became the forerunner of public libraries in the country.

The first Government effort to build strong collection based on the compulsory deposit of books is visible in 1808, when a proposal was issued by the Government of Bombay (now named Mumbai), accordingly, all libraries were to be registered for receiving copies of books published from the 'funds for the encouragement of literature'. This was further strengthened by the Press and Registration of Books Act (XXV of 1867), of 1867.

As per the provision of this Act, copies of all publications, were to be submitted to the Government, for which the government agreed to pay the cost. Later by an amendment of 1890, the Act enabled the Government to acquire copies free of cost; there were further revisions to this Act in 1911, 1914 and the last was in 1922 (as a pre-independence effort) modifying many details. Three copies of each publications were to be deposited at a local Government office—one sent to the British Museum, one to the India Office Library, and one retained in India.

This development of compulsory deposit system was intended for a different reason: The probable hidden aim is spelt as "The literature of a country is no doubt an index of the opinions and conditions of the people and as such an index is essential to good Government that rulers of a country should possess".

And the other intention, though secondary, was "In the interest, too, of history and of the scholars of Europe, it is undoubtedly wise to provide that a complete collection of the publications of the press of this country should be made as well in this country as in England. It cannot, too, but be of benefit to authors and publishers that catalogues of their works, and, to a limited extent, copies of the works themselves, should be accessible to the public at certain well-known places".

The library historian A.K. Ohdedar, states, "In practice, this Act became for India a controlling agency for keeping vigilance over the loyalty of the people, and for England a means for collecting worthwhile printed materials of this country" (1996: 23).

The Imperial Library Act, 1902 (I of 1902), amalgamated many existing collections, in Calcutta such as including Calcutta Public Library; the collections that were housed in the earlier Imperial Library at the civil Secretariat buildings; etc.

The Imperial Library heralded a new era of Government's role in supporting and maintaining of libraries, and in this directly encouraging the development of the concept of free library service—a major departure from subscription based and limited access to 'public libraries'. In the words of A.K. Ohdedar, this change and the clear involvement of the Government "thus marked the beginning of the Government's recognition, in this country, of its obligation to make library service freely available to the public. Thereafter Government assistance towards free public library service came forth in other parts of the country" (1996: 78).

In the due process it could not fulfil its own stated objectives: "to be a library of reference, a working place for students, and a repository of material for the future historians of India, in which, so far as possible, every work written about India at any time can be seen and read".

Then the first problem emerged as the library, from the day one, issued books, acting as the re-incarnation of the defunct Calcutta Public Library; and the second problem emerged as the Imperial Library, had no power to enforce the Copyright Act, and compulsorily collect each and every publication that emerged in the country. Hence, there were protests from the Imperial Librarians, such as John Macfarlane (1903-1906), J.A. Chapman (1911-1930), and K.M. Asadullah (1930-1947). For instance, Chapman, suggested that the Copyright Act was to be made forceful, and that the Indian collections at British Museum and India Office Library be brought back to Imperial Library, and this is 'the only way to atone to India for a great error'. The Government made a lip service response to all these protests, by stating "that storage facilities of material expected to be received and recruitment of staff for processing such material should first be provided before effecting any legislation granting the copyright depository privilege to the Imperial Library".

The other involvement of Government in development of libraries is seen in Baroda, between 1907-1926, which is described elsewhere in this chapter. This was a unique and well-articulated system of library development and had much for being exemplary in the country.

The Congress Ministry in Mumbai, soon after its assumed power, in 1939 appointed a Library Development Committee to investigate the possibilities of and to make recommendations to start a public library movement in Bombay Province. The Chairman of the Committee was A.A.A. Fyzee, who investigated the possibilities of setting up of central and regional libraries. According to the report, the recommendations were to be accomplished in six stages, in establishing the following:

(i) a central library in Bombay and three regional libraries for the three linguistic areas in Province (Ahmedabad, Poona, and Dharwar);
(ii) district libraries;
(iii) taluka libraries; and
(iv) village libraries.

The State Government accepted these, in 1946, and thus began the development of libraries on modern lines. The three regional libraries were made, accordingly, copyright libraries; the Government also took up the suggestion and appointed a Curator of Libraries for library service in the Province, with three assistant curators for the respective regions. All this came in handy for the Maharashtra Public Libraries Act, 1967.

Shortcomings

What role did the British Government play in developing a library movement in the final phase of its rule in India? The answers are to be seen in the number of people who gained education, literacy, and so on, and the number of libraries and library related institutions that grew in the first half of the present century.

To quote Nehru, again,

> "The cultural and other needs of the people, except for a tiny handful, were entirely neglected. The changing conceptions of public

finance which brought free and universal education, improvement of public health, care of poor and feeble-minded, insurance of workers against illness, old age and unemployment, etc., in other countries, were almost entirely beyond the ken of the Government (in India)" (p. 435).

He continues to present the reality of the whole matter, that there must be some limit to what can be expected from aliens.

"I don't think it is very difficult to convert the masses to social reform if the State takes the matter in hand. But alien rulers are always suspect, and they cannot go far in the process of conversion. If the alien element was removed and economic changes were given precedence, an energetic administration could easily introduce far-reaching social reforms" (p. 384).

If these rulers wished to mould India according to their own fashion, they could have easily done so. Because it was the same west which revolutionised itself in the last hundred years! For name sake India too underwent changes: railways, irrigation works, factories, educational academies, offices all have drastically altered the way in which our lives were. But in general what one finds is worse to imagine: poverty, literacy, epidemic, lack of basic sanitary facilities, unemployment, and so on.

It is not all the fault of the rulers, as we too had our input in this situation. Our own kith and kin who got in good books of the rulers behaved as if they were also of the same race: white. The I.C.S. officers became one of these in the categorv of distinct kept classes (Nehru, 1936: 441).

Status of Librarian in the Society

How were the librarians treated by the authorities, and others? An answer to this comes from Ranganathan's case history series in his Reference Service, as follows:

"I was transferred to the Coimbatore College in 1920. I did not find the library of the college adequate. Therefore, I gave the Principal a list of the essential books to be bought. The list came back to me with the laconic remark'Extravagant'. I then had the certitude and the fearlessness of youth; and so I wrote back that I should not be held responsible for the results, unless the books were provided. No doubt, I now realise what a rash act this should have been in a Government College. Through God's grace, the worst did not happen. The Principal sent for me. My trail began.

"Why do you want so many books?"

"For the use of the students".

"Do you really believe that your students are going to use them?"

"Yes, certainly".

"If they really read all these books, each of your students will become Hanumantha Rao or a Ramanujam". "Why not?"

"You are thinking of the students you first met at Mangalore. The students of this place are a poor lot. You can't make much of them".

"Give me a chance, Sir. I do believe that even the boys of this place will shoot up if only we give them their books". "You are too optimistic. Anyhow I shall sanction your wish this year as a special case".

The year came to an end. I was transferred from that college.

I went to the Principal to say 'Good bye'. "When the Director was here a few days ago, he congratulated the college on the excellent results in your group—with the first in the presidency and 17 out of 19 passed! I told the Director that I should not be held responsible for the standard going down again in future years, as you would be no longer with us".

"But the library will still be with you and for the use of the boys. This phenomenal result is traceable largely to the books you were good enough to sanction—and the integration of students' work in the library and classroom work".

K.S. Vaidyanathan, the principal, and myself had a hearty laughter. He stood converted" (1961: 108).

We find from published sources some evidences of how one's services and contribution receive appreciation. How was the society, and the authority considering role played by librarians? One can read a positive note on this issue, by Sir John Sargent, Educational Commissioner, Government of India, in the 'foreword', written for Ranganathan's book, *New Education and School Library*, 1942:

"S.R. Ranganathan needs no introduction to the reading public of India. Few people in this or any other country have devoted more thought or study to library technique than he has done. Even those not accepting all his conclusions nor adopting his methods, will, I am sure, acknowledge the debt under which his industry and erudition have placed them".

"No one loving books and regarding the appreciation of them as one of the main hallmarks of a civilized society, will despise the craft of a librarian. It is an encouraging sign that the status due to this learned profession is beginning at last to receive the recognition, hitherto withheld from it for some mysterious reasons. The extent to which this most desirable change has been done due to Ranganathan's untiring efforts, other people can judge better than I can".

"My gratitude to Ranganathan, and I am sure that of a great many people who like myself cannot claim to be experts in Library Science, arises not so much from his contributions to the techniques of assembling and distributing a large number of books as from the fact that he never allows what I may perhaps almost irrelevantly describe as professional details to obscure his vision of the essential value and function of a library. To him all the complicated business of accessioning, indexing, cataloguing and distributing, however important and even controversial the issues involved in it may be, remains always subordinate to the fundamental aim of getting as many books into as many hands and their contents into as many heads as possible" (p. 16).

The moral is for 'receiving the status' or for that matter receiving acceptability in the society, a librarian has to give respect and only then can expect respect. The state of affairs is that the librarians are recognised wherever and whenever they have done their job well.

Some library historians have raised issues that deal with the status, position and the kind of treatment given to the librarian in the society. Sant Ram Bhatia, is one such, who was the editor of the leading journal *Modern Librarian.*

In an editorial, in 1945 issue of his journal, Sant Ram stated:

"To-day the Indian Librarian is working without the aid of the Government. That is the truth. Ill-paid, half starved, unprotected, ill-equipped, groaning under the impact of the high prices and high expenses he is prey both to the whims of his masters and to his own staggering helplessness. . . . Where does the Indian Librarian stand to-day? What position will the Indian Librarian have in the post-war era? In the changing world will he have security of a free independent man, free from all worries and anxieties in the stress and strain of everyday life? Will he remain the ever-exploited instrument in the hands of a few who claim vested interests in the temples of knowledge? Or will he be allowed to serve the best interests of the society and the nation as a happy man?" (1945, 47-51).

India in pre-independence era remained underdeveloped. It had the direct access to the Western advances in science and technology; it had such benevolent rulers who could have transformed the entire region and brought it on the map of most advanced nations of the twentieth century. Incidentally the British rulers can take the credit of having first opened India's window to the West and brought her a glimpse of Western industrialism and science. But it is also true that the main feature of their rule was their concentration on everything that helped them strengthen their economic and political hold on India. Everything they did or promoted was merely to achieve these larger goals. If Indians became united, and began fighting for freedom, this happened only as a side-product. In this same line of thinking, there are historians who wonder whether India got independence as a gift from the Britishers. May be this line of thinking is supported by the fact that Indians did not fight a war of independence as the Americans or others had to fight!

Role of the Professional Institutions

What is a professional body? A professional body has, as per the report of the Library Advisory Committee, five functions: fosters the growth of a brotherhood among librarians; has a code or an ethics of conduct *vis-à-vis* their communities; organizes training and continuing education programmes; promotes the service conditions; and provides a base for all library extension and integration in the country. These functions are fulfilled in different ways, such as, through publication of literature, holding meetings for the professional get-together, conducting study-circles, exhibitions, and so on.

Based on these five functions, the associations that were established in the first quarter of the present century in India, hardly, had these any idea what all this meant. By 1930 there emerged a sense of professionalism, that was unheard before. For instance, initiated programmes for training of librarians; tried to inculcate the idea of library service, reference service, and the like; they started publishing literature; and led the base for professional activities that resembled the Western World.

Pre-Independent India started professionally with some idea of professional literature, professional training, professional attitude, and so on.

Andhra Desa Library Association

It is historical fact that this body was the first to be set up in the country. There are, however, some limitations of judging whatever in it was 'professional' or otherwise. For instance, this Association was constituted by those social and political leaders of Andhra who were not professionally trained; not professionally oriented towards librarianship (whatever definition was commonly used in that age); not aware of the meaning and implication of using the terms libraries, librarianship, and the like; not into the library movement—as were the later leaders; raising a spirit of nationalism and awakening the people for liberation from existing political set up; and so on. The people who were trained by this Association, were/are all the local participants, and were prepared to be good social workers and not librarians.

Madras Library Association

In fact, apart from the courses that were offered at Imperial Library, Baroda, and Punjab, a truly professional course was started at Madras (now named as Chennai). It was the establishment of Madras Library Association, in 1928, that enabled Ranganathan to regularize the training programme and all other activities. This association started a certificate course in 1929. It was a pioneer, in having a creative leader, Ranganathan, who initiated the idea of reference service, reader's advisory service on the lines of British library world. It was also the first professional in the country to start a movement which became a fashion later, and is now famous as 'library user education', which Ranganathan called 'initiation of the freshmen' in a college library.

Bengal Library Association

The first regional, truly professional, association that emerged after the first quarter of the present century was the Bengal Library Association, founded in 1925 (Mookerjee, 1969: 33). Its Second All Bengal Library Conference was addressed by Rabindranath Tagore, and the address is also reproduced elsewhere. This Association had many firsts to its credit. It did much work in spreading the idea of public library and free service for all. It had both the infrastructures—intellectual and physical—to work for the promotion of library movement. Intellectual support came from both the English and the native elite; and the physical support came from the rich, and the common alike, as well as from the social, political and professional leaders in the region.

Its activities received both approval and tacit support of the local, provincial and national leaders, including Ranganathan, Lala Babu Ram of Punjab, the Minister of Local Self-Government Mr. B.P. Roy, Minister of Education in the Provincial Government Khwaja Nizamuddin, N.M. Dutt who was the Curator of Libraries at Baroda, and so on. It is probably the lone Association in the country which first got the financial help from the Government, and such was its socializing activity that it was acceptable by all, and useful for all (Mookerjee, 1969: 39-40). Its activities include, publishing literature in Bengali, a monthly organ *The Granthagar*, in irregular paper *the Pathagar*, and most importantly is its Library Training Course. It was this Association who, again for the first time, used media—Radio—to spread library awareness, and promote library movement in the region. It could deliver 25 radio lectures on libraries and library movement.

The other leading bodies that emerged in the second quarter include the following:

Punjab Library Association

Punjab Library Association (founded in 1916, and repeatedly revived in 1929, 1969, 1989); founded by Asa Don Dickinson, it flourished with the founder, performed very well, conducted much of professional meetings, including the first All-India Library Conference, held in but got "defunct enthusiasm"; revived by Rattan Chand Manchanda, Librarian, Hailey College, Lahore, and among others by Lala Sant Ram Bhatia in 1929. Manchanda in fact founded a group of librarians—Librarian's Club—who together led to the revival and made the association active, by immediately hosting the Seventh All-India Library Conference in December 1929. This Association published two professional journals: *Modern Librarian* and *Indian Librarian*.

Indian Library Association

Indian Library Association (founded in 1933), was originally set-up as a federation of associations in the country, because those who were responsible in its establishment included representative of libraries and library authorities from all over the country. Because of this it had a national outlook, and had its first President, Dr. M.O. Thomas, Librarian of Annamalai University, and the Imperial Librarian Khan Bahadur K.M. Asadullah, its Secretary. The Association's objectives were to promote the library movement in the country; promote training of professionals; promote research in library science; strive to promote the status and service conditions of the librarians; and cooperate with international library organizations.

According to the research done by the above mentioned journal, *Indian Librarian* (September 1966), Asadullah was the product of the first Library Training Class started by Punjab University, Lahore in 1915 under Dickinson. Asadullah underwent the Examination of the Diploma of Library Association, London, and was the first Indian to have received this Diploma, and was nominated as a Fellow of the Association. It was only a little later, in 1924, that Ranganathan was deputed for training to England, and he was probably the second graduate from British library school. Asadullah, was probably the first and the only Librarian, to be honoured with the title 'Khan Bahadur' by the British on the King Emperor's birthday in 1935. Asadullah was envied by all, and appreciated by his professional colleagues, young and elder, alike, including the pioneers, like, Dr. G.T. Kale, Rattan Chand Manchanda, and others.

What is more pertinent in these roles played by the librarians and the impact it left in the society, is that libraries gained some acceptance in the society. Had it not been for these professional efforts of continuously striving for the promotion of the library service, whatever little that was done by the Government even that would not have been done. For instance, the need to promote public libraries—with the Western notion of free for all and open to all—promote fairly good academic libraries with some semblence of the Western counterparts, in providing open access, in providing clean and usable study and research facilities, etc.

It is also true that the Indian professionals took a longer time than the Western counterparts in making their presence felt in the public and in the Government circles. Different people have left different impressions in this process of professional contribution to the development of the library profession in India. If it was the British and American librarians who founded the modern librarianship in British India—Dickinson, Bordon, A.C. Burnell, W.H. Stacy, J.A. Chapman, *et al.* It was the Indian leaders who later took the lamp and started the marathon, and include, a long list of names, such as, Lal Babu Ram, Sant Ram Bhatia, Dr. Wali Mohammed, Dr. G.T. Kale, Iyyanki Venkata Ramanayya, Hari Sarvothama Rao, N.R. Ray, Dr. Rahatullah Khan, Abdul Majid, K. Selliah, Mohammed Safi, Yusuffuddin Ahmed, S. Mohammed Kaseem Ali Rasulpuri, Fazel Elahi, and *et al.*

It was also the role of these professionals which led to the setting up of some measures for improvement of the working conditions of libraries, including the Fyzee Committee. Its recommendations were taken care and even implemented before the dawn of independence, and the Maharashtra Public Libraries Act took note of the suggestions of this Committee.

There were professionals who attempted during this period to get the Library bills passed in the State legislature. The movement for such attempts, begins with, Madras Library Model Bill, 1930. This bill was thoroughly discussed in the Library Service Section of the First All-Asia Educational Conference at Bananas, in 1930. Newton Mohan Dutt was its President, and Ranganathan its Secretary. Interestingly, in its resolution 11, the Section made an appeal to establish library associations in various States, and requested All-India Library Association to coordinate the activities of library work in all the States.

Before presenting this bill for enactment its discussion went on for over a year, with various local bodies, district boards, municipalities, taluks, panchayats, etc. And this discussion on the bill led to preparing a group of professionals who stood up to champion the same cause all over the country, and the group had, among others, Kumar Munindra Deb Rai Mohasaya of Bengal Library Association, P.N. Kaula (the present President, ILA), S.K. Bole, Vavilala Gopala Krishnaiah, M. Donde, R.L. Mittal, Velga Venkatappaiah, *et al.*

The bill was submitted to the State Legislative Council in 1933, and tabled by a Legislator, Basheer Ahmed Sayeed, and got it approved for further consideration. In 1934 a select committee was appointed and its findings were left unattended, to be taken up again in 1937, 1946, and finally approved in 1948. All the while the details of the bill were improved upon.

Due to these pressures, moves and struggle, many improvements took place. The Connemara Public Library started offering increased library service and began the open access system. There was some development in the professional image and the courses offered by the Associations, were later taken up by respective State and local universities, and the trend set in of training library graduates, on the Western model.

Summing Up

We may end this discussion with a note from Dr. S.R. Ranganathan, who paid a tribute to the success and achievements of Andhra Pradesh in fostering a spirit of library movement in the form of people's movement:

> "The distinctive contribution of Andhra Pradesh to the dawn of library consciousness in India is the demonstration of what private efforts can do in spreading library service inspite of indifference on the part of the Government. Andhra Pradesh may be described as a land of Library Associations, State Associations, District Associations, Taluk Associations, Local Associations, and even associations in different part of the one and the same city. These associations have been holding annual conferences. These conferences have been whipping up popular enthusiasm . . . (quoted from the Diamond Jubilee Souvenir of the Sri Krishna Devaraya Andhra Bhasha Nilayam in 1962, from his article on 'March of Library Science in India')".

4

LIBRARY MOVEMENT: From 1947 to 1996

OVERVIEW

Prologue

A free India had intellectuals, like Dr. S. Radhakrishnan, Maulana Azad, and others, who provided inspiration and guidance to the developmental process of education, in general, and libraries, in particular. As a preface to the survey of the developments of the period, it is appropriate to quote their remarks about the library as a social institution:

So said, Dr. S. Radhakrishnan, as the Chairman of the University Education Commission, (1948-49), in his report:

> "Teaching is a cooperative enterprise. Teachers must have the necessary tools for teaching purposes in the shape of libraries and laboratories and also the right type of students. The library is the heart of all the university's work; directly so, as regards its research work, and indirectly as regards its educational work, which derives its life from research work. Scientific research needs a library as well as its laboratories,while for humanistic research the library is both library and laboratory in one. Training in higher branches of learning and research is mainly a question of learning how to use tools, and if the library tools are not there, how can the student learn to use them. President Truman's Commission on Higher Education says, 'The library is second only to the instructional staff in its importance for high quality instruction and research'. Both for humanistic and scientific studies, a first-class library is essential in a university".

This lends support to the idea that the academic librarians are as much involved in teaching as are the teachers. The Commission further clarifies, this matter, about the faculty status for the librarians:

> "We have already indicated that lectures and tutorials must be supplemented by work in the library. The teacher gives the students some guidances as regards supplementary reading. But the reference assistant, if he is properly qualified, will be in touch with the teachers and guide the students to the proper volume and proper usage in each volume which would be helpful to him. These reference assistants can be of help not only to the students but also to the teachers in their special subjects of study" (1949: 110).

Maulana Azad, as first Union Education Minister, addressed the participants of the UNESCO Seminar on the Development of Public Libraries in Asia, on October 6, 1955, and observed:

> "A District Library service will . . . require support and guidance from a Central Library in every state. These Central Libraries must also be linked up with four National Libraries in Calcutta, Bombay and Madras, with the National Central Library in Delhi as the coping stone of the edifice. It is obvious that such a National Central Library must be built not only to coordinate the library activities within India but also cooperate with UNESCO in organizing adequate library service for this region of the world".
>
> "Global Social forces that promoted the idea of Free Book Service for All, included, development in social thought, development in political thought, development of industrialization, spread of universal education, and creation and production of books in abundance. . . . But none of these had taken shape in India till the beginning of the twentieth century. . . ." (which has in post-World War II era, and more specifically in India led to a universal idea of books for all, books for every time, books for everyone, books for use, and books a must for democracy, equality, fraternity, and for spread of social justice). Ranganathan: *Free Book Service for All* (1968: 26, 40).
>
> "If we look at the budgets that the libraries have planned for the last few years, you will see a tremendous growth: even then we don't always make up for all the requirements we have" Dr. S.C. Sahasrabudhe, Director IIT, Bombay, addressing the IASLIC Seminar, December 1994.

A study of the progress of libraries and library movement in the post-independence era is done in the following in terms of the role played by the Government, profession, the public and the test of five laws to see if these laws still find a place in the country.

Role of Government

So long as it was an alien Government, Ranganathan had the following response:

> "As a matter of fact, Dr. Ranganathan, said one of his friends from a British library remarked on how in India they were building from the top downwards, and that nothing had been done for the masses. It was true, he said, and it was due to the presence of an alien Government unable to understand and sympathize with the needs of the masses" (*Hindu*, 5 April 1953).

How better is our own elected government's performance is discussed below: But before proceeding further let us see the trends in the country, and this will help clearly visualize the pattern and role the Government is expected to play.

The role of the Government, Central and State, in this context deals with the type of support these authorities provide to the development of libraries; policy, if any, on the development of libraries; promotion of library and book culture which the Government undertakes; place of library in the national agenda for planning and implementation of national development; and so on.

Role of Central Government

The Government of India took certain steps in improving the state of affairs. The list is however not very long.

Constitution of India

The Constitution of India laid down the fundamental right of the citizens of India in its preamble, to include Equality of opportunity, and Liberty (Freedom) of thought and expression.

While this is stated in the context of right of expression of ideas and thought—in speech and in print—it does not include, by any extension of the words, and by any implication the right to information, that is, right to have access to information. It is a right to get education, health, sanitation, but it is not a right to get free information, nor information freely. The Government has held back this basic right that the individuals must possess when they are living in a democratic and free society!!! The Constitution has broad outlines and lists essential items that affect the normal life of a citizen. While searching for the presence of the terms libraries, information, knowledge dissemination, and so on, and these are not in the Constitution.

Ranganathan, as early as 1951, made a thorough survey of the Indian Constitution to search something timely and fundamental for a growing nation. He searched therein for explicit or implicit provision for the social institution for the perpetual self-education of all the citizens, which the library has become today.

In his paper on 'Library Organization and the Constitution of India', presented at the Symposium 1, Public Library Provision, Ninth All-India Conference, Indore, 1951, he systematically analyzed the whole constitution—395 articles, augmented by seven schedules, in 251 pages. The same analysis is also in a paper 'Integrated Public Library System: Five Tiers', presented by Ranganathan in a seminar on Public Library System, held in Bangalore in 1972. Indicating that the situation between 1949 and 1972 remains same in the context of status of the library in the Constitution of India. Furthermore, even after fifty years of independence, in 1996, India has not made any improvement on this front in its Constitution.

Ranganathan rightly laments, in 1972, "The public libraries serving the people of a Constituent State have not been declared by Parliament to be institutions of national importance".

Discussing the Fundamental Rights Ranganathan states, "As Article 32 makes the fundamental rights justiceable and as the provision of educational agencies has to depend on the material and human resources available for the purpose, it cannot be complained that part 3 of the Constitution of India had not mentioned education and library service as fundamental rights" (p. 12).

Under the discussion of Directive Principles, in part 4, he is of the opinion that the Article 37 expects the States to implement the meaning of the article, which includes establishment of libraries.

The Article 37 in part 4 carries the directive principles of State policy, "The provisions contained in this Part shall not be enforceable by any court, but the principles therein laid down are nevertheless fundamental in the governance of the country and it shall be the duty of the State to apply these principles in making laws".

In Articles 41 and 45, again in part 4, is a direct reference to education, which can include by implication, perpetual self-education of every citizen, that is leading to setting up of informal centres of life-long education, through libraries. "For adulthood, the only known possible universal agency of education is a comprehensive country-wide Library system" (Ranganathan: 13).

Article 41, states, "The State shall, within the limits of its economic capacity and development, make effective provision for securing the right . . . to education. . . ."

Article 45, states, "The State shall endeavour to provide, within a period of ten years from the commencement of this Constitution, for free and compulsory education for all children until they complete the age of fourteen years".

Ranganathan, read between the lines, and sensed the possibility of Governments not fully implementing the Article 41. "The only deterring factor anticipated by Article 41 of the Constitution of India is 'the limits of economic capacity and development'. It is here that the library profession has to plead with the statesmen of the country that the very increase of the economic capacity and the very development depend upon better informed and better educated citizenship. A vicious circle thus gets formed. We do not see any way of this circle being cut except by straightaway providing for the progressive establishing of a comprehensive library system as an agency for universal perpetual self-education" (p. 15).

Under the Seventh Schedule, Clause 12 reads, "Libraries, museums and other similar institutions controlled or financed by the State, ancient and historical monuments and records other than those declared by Parliament by law to be of national importance".

Further, Clause 62, names National Library, among others, as in the purview of the Government of India. And Clauses 62 to 66 of this Union List deals specifically with educational functions, to be directly dealt by the Union Government. Further, the State List in its Clause 11 directly deals with other matters of education at the State level.

Ranganathan, remarks, on the Clause 12 "But here it is clubbed with Museums, Archives and Archaeological Remains. This is evidently a mechanical copy from the Government of India Act of 1935, which in its turn was perhaps inspired by some British convention of the Victorian Age.

According to this early nineteenth century convention, which has been allowed to smuggle itself into the Constitution of India, the primary and social function of libraries was conversation of books and manuscripts and not the positive and purposeful promotion of their use by one and all of the citizens for their mental and spiritual betterment and thereby for their physical, political, economic and social well-being also" (p. 12).

Commenting on the possibility of approaching the Union Government for a National Library Act, he refers to the above cited Clauses 62-66, as more direct and useful in this regard. "Perhaps, in as much as libraries form in modern times an essential part of 'institutions for higher education or research and scientific and technical institutions', Clause 66, which exclusively entrusts to the Government of India the 'co-ordination and determination of standards in such institutions', may be construed to cover also business libraries and libraries of higher academic bodies. It is thus in Clauses 62 and 66 of the Union List that we find authority for the Union Library Bill which the Indian Library Association has recommended for enactment by the Indian Parliament" (p. 11).

Concludingly, he advises the profession to strive for (a) the establishment of nation-wide library system, (b) search the Constitution, to locate in it the spots where the library function of the State lies latent, and (c) work for its explicit embodiment in special library legislation (p. 11). He appeals on behalf of the Indian Library Association to the Union and each of the States to "take up immediately enactment of library laws and the implementing of the same. The Constitution of India allows it, directs it, and expects it" (p. 15).

Additionally, the Constitution has some more implied references to the areas which can influence the library development, and include intellectual property rights (IPR) and 42nd and 72nd Amendment of the Constitution.

Intellectual Property Rights: Strangely, even Ranganathan, did not get an idea that information is a property which Article 19 directly mentions under the Fundamental Rights, 'Right to Freedom', as including right "to acquire, hold and dispose of property". Today, after fifty years it is essential to read and interpret this clause to also incorporate the intellectual property rights. The United States is taking a lead in asking India to accept this legality in transfer and exchange of the intellectual property at the international level.

Article 45, refers to the efforts which can raise the 'standard of living of its people', referring directly to health, but indirectly definitely to providing access to information which can improve the standard of living and quality of life. This is the more recent understanding which is creating a consciousness in the society to not only run behind progressiveness, but also to maintain a good and healthy way of life. In this process the need to establish community information centres is the duty of the society as well as the Government.

The resolution of the Government of India to establish a Planning Commission, cited from the Directive Principles, two articles, namely, Articles 38 and 39. The aims of planning, as defined in this resolution, included among others, "to promote a rapid rise in the standard of living of the people by efficient exploitation of the resources of the country, increasing production, and offering opportunities to all for employment in the service of the community". Because of the establishment of the Planning Commission, it became possible for libraries to receive a clear place in the implementation of national policies, in the Five Year Plans, which are still in practice and supporting the library development in more than one way.

By implication, the Articles 38 and 39, also refer to the promotion of information centres, community information centres, and the like, which can be pro-active role players in the improvement of standard of living, promoters in exploitation of resources and in a way directly increasing production, and providing an information support base for all round progress of the nation and national development.

Clause 31, Seventh Schedule, lists communication channels under the Union List, and reads as "Posts, telegraphs, telephones, wireless, broadcasting and other like forms of communication". This effects the information technology and libraries too, directly in getting access to national and international telecommunication networks, Internet connectivity, and so on.

A library management must also keep track of the rights and duties given in the Constitution, for the welfare of the profession and the professionals. These are general references, applicable to all citizens, but one can use these in any context.

Article 19(1)(g) Guarantees the freedom to practice any profession, or to carry out any occupation, trade or business. The State's power to restrict the enjoyment of these freedoms is limited to the making of any law imposing reasonable restrictions in the interests of the general public in so far as it relates to: (a) The prescribing the professional or technical qualifications necessary for practicing any profession or carrying on any occupation, trade or business.

Articles 36 to 51 deal with the Directive Principles of State Policy. One of the principles is very important for service law. The State shall direct its policy towards securing . . . (d) equal pay for equal work for both men and women (Article 39). By implication, this article applies to all categories of staff, and also to the overtime payment, consolidated salary, and so on.

42nd and 72nd Amendment of the Constitution

According to the 42nd Amendment of the Indian Constitution, effective 3 January 1977, libraries form part of the Concurrent List. Thereby the Central Government has no role to play in respect of libraries, and the whole burden lies with the States. Whereas with the 72nd Amendment in Bill 158, 1991, came the issue of establishment of Panchayats, as well as their role and status. As per Article 243-G (Eleventh Schedule-20), the Gram Panchayat has to establish and maintain a public library for the villagers. The expenditure for this has to be met from the panchayat resources.

Role of the Ministries

Pilot Project of the Human Resource Development Ministry

Based on the suggestions of various committees, including the recommendations of Committee on National Policy on Library and Information System (also called the Chattopadhyaya Committee), the Ministry decided to set up a scheme of pilot project for rural libraries. According to a press release of last week of August 1994, the Ministry stated:

> The Government plans to set up village libraries to make up for the dearth of reading material for the literates. A sum of rupees one crore has been earmarked for about 500 libraries which will be started this year on a pilot basis. The cost of each library, to be located in selected middle and high schools, is expected to be around Rs. 20,000.

Union Ministry of Rural Development

The ministry has chalked out a plan to establish one lakh community information centres under the panchayats, during the Eighth Five Year Plan. The Ministry has taken the help of the Department of Social Welfare, National Literacy Mission and others to implement the programme.

Case Studies

Role of the Government in improvement of libraries is pertinent. We may hence look at some cases.

Case One (Legal Battles—Employment Issue)

As per the provisions of the Poona University Act, 1974, Clause 77(B) sanction of the Government of Maharashtra is required for any activity of which involves creation of post, recruitment of post or of upgradation of posts or sanction of any allowance which involves payment of money. Due to increase in the workload in the library, proposals were submitted to appoint additional staff in the library. We could not get the sanction from the Government of Maharashtra for this proposal. The Poona University, therefore, appointed persons on temporary basis on consolidated salary per month from the university funds, considering the increased work load in the Jayakar Library and to extend the services for longer hours to users. These staff members were continued in the service of the Poona University by giving breaks of one to ten days. As the Poona University did not receive any sanction from the Government of Maharashtra for over ten years, for additional posts, some of the staff members filed a writ petition in the Bombay High Court in 1988 requesting the Court to direct the University to appoint them on permanent basis in the scale attached to posts. They stated that "the authority deprived of salary and service conditions equal to that of permanent library employees. This act is violative of the petitioners fundamental rights under Articles 14 and 16 of the Constitution of India and also violative of Article 39(d) of the Directive principles.

They also quoted the following cases in which the judiciary had decided to give equal pay for equal work. They also quoted Article 7 of the International Covenant of Economic, Social and Cultural Rights, 1966, which exhorts all state/parties to ensure fair and equal wages for equal work. The Court decided that injustice has been done to the temporary employees. The University of Poona requires additional staff. It is unfair to give less wages to temporary employees and more wages to permanent employees and directed the University of Poona to absorb these employees and pay them wages equal to that of permanent employees.

Some Cases Cited

Daily rated workers of P&T Department *vs.* Union of India AIR 1987

SC, p. 2342; Delhi Municipal Karamchari Ekta Unions *vs.* P.L. Singh and Others, AIR 1988, SC p. 519; U.P. Income Tax Department Contingent Paid Staff Welfare Association *vs.* Union of India and Others, AIR SC p. 517 (Mahajan, 1993: 139-40).

Case Two (User-Library in Legal Battle)

External students right to use the library: In the Poona University in the faculty of law we run a course for LL.M. There are regular as well as external students enrolled for this course. In the year, 1984 we observed that more than 120 candidates have enrolled for LL.M. (external) courses in addition to more than forty regular students. The external students approached the library for extending the library facilities. I realized that we have hardly three copies of textbooks prescribed for LL.M. courses which are reserved for reading in reading hall, three copies were available for home lending and one copy was available for teachers. If all the candidates are permitted to enroll as members of the library, it was not possible for the librarian to give library services to all the candidates. Therefore, the librarian after permitting about thirty external candidates, stopped giving admission to external students.

One of the student being aggrieved filed a writ petition in the High Court of Judicature of Bombay (Appellate side) at Bombay (No. 1538 of 1884). The petitioner said that all LL.M. students have fundamental right of education (citing a Delhi High Court judgment) . . . (and) that by denial of the University even to permit the library hall to be used by external LL.M. students is denial of the fundamental right of education and the consequential denial of the enshrined fundamental rights of the petitioner guaranteed under Article 19 and Article 21 of the Constitution.

The petitioner also said that both the students (regular and external) paid the library fees. Allowing all the regular students to use the library and not allowing all the external students to use the library amounts to discrimination among the equal and violates Article 14. The petitioner also claimed that allowing external students of other faculties to use the library facilities and not allowing the students of law faculty violates Article 14.

Their Lordship heard the arguments in favour of both the parties and finally directed both the parties to arrive at an agreement. The university authorities agreed to admit all the external students to the reading hall of the Jayakar Library from 8.00 a.m. to 11.00 a.m., and after 6.00 p.m. only. Textbooks will be issued on the basis of first come first serve principle.

It was realized that an amendment in the library rules is necessary and the library rules were amended accordingly. The library rules should specifically mention that eligibility to be admitted to the library does not mean that all the students will be admitted to the library and further that admission to the library does not mean availability of the books to all the students.

Secondly, last date for admission to the library for all the external students was to be fixed. Total number of seats available in the reading hall for external students was also to be fixed and incorporated in the library rules. After enunciating this procedure, admissions were to be given to external students, may be on first come first serve basis. After allowing this procedure, the library may admit only a limited number of students. This will not amount to discrimination and consequently violate the provisions of Article 14 . . ." (Mahajan, 1993: 141-42).

Case Three (Practical Experiences)

"At one time, the Madras University Library, did not allow many author later than Browning and Dickens to be represented on its shelves" (Ranganathan, 1958: 22). This is more pertinent in the context when the book selection takes care of only the past, and ignore the recent and contemporary topics. "Today, we face great difficulty in going the right way (in collecting the essential books). We do not have books on sciences, in our languages. Few arts and crafts have books in our languages. Library movement has therefore to be backed, for some years, by a special organization for book-production" (p. 22). This agency was soon established, it was called National Book Trust, which is expected to provide a large quantity and quality of literature to be collected in the library.

Case Four

The Government of Bombay has recently ordered that it is sufficient if books are bundled by headmasters of central schools and the bundles are pushed from village to village by inspectors of schools. According to them, there is no need for the library profession except perhaps for listing them. Again recently the Government of India gave nearly a lakh of rupees to each of many universities and earmarked them for books. But neither the Government nor the universities provided staff to select, purchase, classify, and catalogue the books. With the result the staff was turned on this "behind the screen-work" (p. 23).

Case Five

(The Bombay Government) expects the basic library finance of a locality to be raised by voluntary contribution or subscriptions. It expects local bodies to give an equal amount. It then agrees to give an equal amount from State funds". While the local bodies failed to restore their annual expected contribution, the Government also reduced its contribution. A stalemate resulted, and the local committees were blamed for this! (p. 25).

Case Six

Fascination for number tends to militate against the efficiency of library service. Even 30 years ago, the Government of Uttar Pradesh reported having more than a thousand libraries in the State. Travancore too has been reporting similarly. Recently, Bihar and Bengal spoke of similar numbers. What do they mean by a library? Mostly, an independent tiny book collection with an annual library budget of about Rs. 100. Such a library can only swell statistics and lure us into false satisfaction. Its viability will be deplorable. Its book-resource will be negligible. It is a wrong way of developing the library service of the nation (p. 26).

Case Seven

The first library system in India was built by the Gaikwad Sayajee Rao of Baroda. That was half a century ago. It progressed splendidly during his life-time. But it began to fade after his death. This has been due to the wrong way of basing a state library system on administrative measures. These are subject to all the stresses and strains in political changes, party politics and whims and fancies of the person in power (p. 28).

Case Eight (Implications of Copyright Act)
(Tape Recording of Gramophone Records)

Bal Gandharva was an eminent musician and Marathi theatre artist. His birth centenary was celebrated, in 1987 all over the Maharashtra on 15 May 1987. A news appeared in one of the Marathi daily that the Jayakar Library possesses a rare collection of gramophone records of Bal Gandharva and suggestions are made to copy those records for preservation. Immediately, the Librarian received a registered notice from the copyright holders of these gramophone records stating that 'it is illegal for anyone to copy such copying as provided by the law'. It further stated that the Copyright (Amendment) Act, 1984 has been more stringent and infringement of this Act has been made into a cognizable offence. Minimum punishment is a fine of Rs. 50,000 and imprisonment of six months for the offenders. The letter further requested the Librarian to confirm that he will not indulge in or permit anyone to indulge in taping the records.

The Copyright Act as amended in 1984 permits copying only one copy for academic purpose. Mass copying or copying for commercial purpose is prohibited. Realizing these implications the Librarian confirmed that he will abide by the provisions of the Copyright Act.

The Copyright holders further informed that this company has released a two-cassette pack of Bal Gandharva's old songs which is freely available in the market (Mahajan, 1993: 147-48).

Case studies, of a variety exist in the literature. N. Dutta has compiled many decisions in respect of academic library staff, in relation to UGC guidelines, in his book *Academic Status for University and College Librarians in India.*

The role of the Government is then seen in the acceptance of the library as a social institution. The Government has been pursued by the society to include library in the agenda of the national development, and list it in the Five Year Plans of the Central Planning Commission, in the UGC's guidelines and implementation programmes, in the establishment of a network of public libraries—Delhi Public Library System, etc. While these are a few attempts at promoting the cause of library development, and there is a need for far more involvement and concerted effort on behalf of the authorities, it is upto the society to demand more or be satisfied with bare minimum. Is the society hearing?

Case Nine (Copyright, Intellectual Copyright)

The Mumbai police on May 1, 1997 gave a clean chit to actress Pooja Bhat embroiled in a controversy over her alleged 'nude' photograph in the May (previous year's) issue of Stardust.

> "The police assured her that she was not guilty but a victim of a dirty mischief. To quote the police sources, as reported in *Deccan Chronicle*, May 2, 1997, "We questioned her and also the magazine's editor Omer Qureshi and came to the conclusion that the photo

printed by the magazine was not Pooja's but a computer generated image". The magazine had also claimed that the photograph, showing an unbelievably slim Pooja, was downloaded from the Internet. The concerned file was now missing, it had said. But other facts which could help question the ethics of the magazine in publishing a 'fake' photograph of a well-known actress for generating publicity are also coming to light. 'This particular photograph was on the Internet for over last two years', said Dale Bhagwagar, editor of the *Den Entertainment* magazine on the Internet. "The file called *Pooja gift* from which the photo was downloaded, was actually created at 3.23 p.m. on March 6, 1995, Mr. Bhagwagar said".

If the Intellectual copyright is a matter of international concern, India appears on the map of this controversy, because much that is produced in media and other sources is alleged to be taken from Western sources, without any permission and acknowledgement. Libraries and custodians of knowledge and information also get into these scams. The government is yet to resolve these issues and present a transparent situation to the world at large. The above report, explicitly states, that the file from which the photograph was copied is lost, leaving no trace of the source from where the image was extracted, also creating a doubt in the minds of the public that there is a possibility of much bungling in these troubled waters.

The matter of misusing the information resource, is one danger, faced by us, the other matter of inability to access and thereby create a schism between haves and have-nots is another distinct gift of the modern world, which bothers some, but is not yet the concern of the law makers.

Lessons of History

Ranganathan, states:

> "In 1950, I wrote in a mood of despair, 'When will the statesman in India realize the importance of this? When will our Economy Committee develop a proper sense of value? When will they distinguish between what gives quick but ephemeral political returns to the few money-grubs or power-grubs and what is beneficial in the long run to the people at large? When will they, for example give up tying down libraries to archaeological museums and dropping them together into the depts. of the future, leaving the next

generations to pick them up and develop them if it so wishes. Little do they realize that the world has now reached a stage when a nation, which pushes library provision aside, in order to save its cost for other purposes, is like one whom the common man describes as penny-wise and pound-foolish'. But today I am in a happy position. The elder statesmen in the Planning Commission have become aware of the necessity for country-wide public service. They have provided liberal sums of money. Nearly two crores of rupees for the development of public library service during the first five year period should be said to be almost generous. They are also keen to place public library service on a statutory basis in each of the constituent states".

Soon he found that all that glitters is not gold. "This sum is not, in the first instance, being properly transformed into actual book-service. The reasons for this are many. The ministers, who have to carry out the intention of the Planning Commission, had had no chance to have enjoyed, seen, or even heard of a good library service in their earlier years, which fell in the British period. They are, therefore, unable to judge the proposals put up before them by the bureaucracy. In most cases, a tradition has developed that the implementation of library service belongs to the Department of Education. The officers in this Department are equally without any library experience. On the other hand, this century-old Department has developed a great rigidity in outlook. It begins and ends with the enforcement of the account rules, financial rules, and other Victorian rules of procedure. This is also a third casual cause of trouble. Many of the handful of persons, occupying vantage positions in the library professions, are unprogressive. Some are too idle to act up to standards. Some are clever enough to cover up their idleness by specious social contacts and wise talks; and there is no mixture more ruinous to society than the mixture of cleverness, idleness, and garrulousness. Some are swept away by passing considerations of 'getting on' with personal coverage at the cost of what can be of lasting benefit to the library personality of the country and 'getting honour and getting honest', in that provincial way. Therefore, there is now much leakage in the utilization of the money voted for the library service" (1988: 246-7).

While these state of affairs were stated by Ranganathan in 1958, the question is has the role of the Government improved or worsened, in the last forty years. The question can be understood by looking into the steps taken by the Government, such as passing library related acts at the State and Central levels; setting up Commissions and Committees to (outlast) consider the requirements of time and tide; adopting a plan for national library system for each type of library—national, academic, special, etc.—to facilitate growth of an integrated system of libraries; adopting a national policy for library and information science; establishing an accrediting body to regulate and streamline the education of librarians; facilitating the growth of free public libraries and development of library as an essential (if not indispensable) social institution; place of library in national planning and implementation, and so on. Some of these can be discussed here.

Committees and Commissions

Chattopadhyaya Committee Report

The Department of Culture of the Central Government, set up a Committee in 1985, under the Chairmanship of D.P. Chattopadhyaya, to advise the Government of the formulation of a national policy. The Committee submitted its report, in 1986, to the Union Ministry of Human Resource Development.

The Committee revived the slogan, originally stated in the recommendation of the Secondary Education Commission (1952-53) 'no library no school'.

Regarding the provision of equal access to the all, the Committee in its report, also recommends that "Primary schools where such facilities cannot be provided should share the resources of the community library. In areas where the community library does not exist, the primary school be so developed as to serve as the base of the village library" (quoted in Venkateswara Rao, 1994: 371).

While this does not refer to schools managed by the private agencies and missionaries, the school library concept in government schools is literally non-existent.

The fact of the matter is bad, in the matter of having a library in the school. According to the Report on the Higher Secondary School Buildings in India published by the National Building Organization, New Delhi, "37.3 per cent of schools do not have even a room for the library and in other schools where it is provided, it is used more as a store room than as library" (quoted in Kaula, 1991). This is true despite some standing instructions and guidelines that exists, such as, Delhi Schools Education Act, 1973, and Delhi School Education Rules, 1973, which contain an Article No. 42, entitled 'School Libraries—Instruction for the Maintenance and Use of School Libraries'.

The Planning Commission's Working Group also heard the plea from the library associations, including Indian Library Association, and it emphasized the need for such a policy in their report, entitled, Modernization of Library Services and Information for the Seventh Five Year Plan (1985-90). On the basis of these pressures, the Government set up another committee called Empowered Committee to consider the recommendations on the National Policy, in all aspects and draw plan to action for implementation.

This body submitted its report to the Human Resource Development (HRD) Ministry, on 11 April 1988. The reports have to be presented in the Parliament, which is long overdue.

The Empowered Committee recommended "Charging of nominal membership fee ranging from Rs. 10 to be fixed keeping in view the economic conditions of the target group of users" of public libraries.

A clearly stated policy for library development in India has been missing all through. The profession has sent many messages to the Government, at least in the last few decades to consider the need and implement a policy, which has fallen on deaf ears. The US Government under Clinton and Al-Gore have at last risen up to this and have initiated a National Information Infrastructure (NII) Act, which aims to create free access to information from all corners of the globe, by all and for all. The American Library Association has been making all efforts to get itself totally involved in this implementation programme of the NII.

Apart from this, there are certain issues which are jointly dealt with by the Central and State Governments. One instance, of this is in the managing of the educational institutions, more precisely, the institutions of higher learning in the country, and the area of interests of the University Grants Commission.

While there are certain roles the Central Government can play, there are certain roles, State alone has to play, and hence what follows is the different roles played by these respectively.

Sinha Committee Report

The Government of India, on the recommendations of different bodies, including the ILA, appointed an Advisory Committee, in 1957 to look into various issues, the list had among others: "to inquire into the present reading needs of the people, how they are met, and what part of the existing library set-up plays in meeting the needs".

The Report was submitted in 1958-91, and it found that there are 32,000 large and small libraries in the country, with over 71,00,000 books, as of March 1954, and a total circulation of about 3,77,00,000. It recommended an integrated library system, with national library at the apex, and all others in the same hierarchy. This specifically dealt with public library system in the country, and became a work of reference for all other library committees and discussions. Based on its suggestions the Government took only one action, and that was the appointment of another committee to draft a Model Public Library Bill. It also took note of a lack of regular library service to the public, and recommended that school and college libraries must be opened up for the public, in smaller towns and villages, where public have no access to libraries.

Mudaliar Committee Report

To improve the status of libraries in the academic library system, a number of committees and commissions were set up and each made valuable suggestions. The Mudaliar Commission on Secondary Education was critical about the lack of libraries in schools, emphasizing on the significance of developing a reading habits among the young. It restated a historic practice, and recommended that in small places it is economical to have the school library function, both as, a school library and a public library, for the community in the neighbourhood.

Radhakrishnan Commission Report

This University Education Commission, 1948-49, which deals with the Indian higher education, was chaired by Dr. S. Radhakrishnan. Its report was an eye-opener on the state-of-the-art of libraries, staff, collections, etc. in universities, stating "libraries are hopelessly inadequate to serve the curricular needs of a modern university. They were ill-housed, ill-stocked, and ill-staffed and were totally lacking in standard literary and scientific journals. Service was in the hands of personnel that had hardly any notion of the objectives of university education. The annual appropriation for book purchase seldom exceeded the ten thousand mark". The report heralded an era of consciousness among the academics about the sad state of affairs of the libraries attached to higher learning.

With regards the providing of access to public by school libraries, the Kothari Commission, endorsed the recommendations of the Sinha Committee Report, and added that "School libraries should be integrated with the system of public libraries. We have laid stress on schools being made centres of adult education and extension services". The Report also said, that "It is, therefore, necessary to develop and assist school libraries to perform this new education. Even the remotest schools should be serviced by a neighbouring public library" (quoted in Venkateswara Rao, 1994: 371).

Ranganathan Committee Report

The UGC Library Committee, 1965, chaired by Dr. S.R. Ranganathan, gave a report from both the academic and professional viewpoints to the Government, on the standards of libraries, buildings, pay scales, and education of librarians. The Committee not only surveyed the state of affairs, but also discussed the findings of the Committee with the professionals, before finalizing the report. The report that was submitted dealt with collection development, finance, services, and staff status in the academic environment. The Report made a considerable impact on the college and university libraries in India, by and large improved many issues relating to budget and staff status, and henceforth made it possible for university libraries in each state to receive a grant on par with other university programmes—from central and state grants.

Kothari Commission Report

Nevertheless, a series of Committees and Commissions continued, in the past tradition, and yet another was set up in 1964-66, Dr. D.S. Kothari, as its Chairman, to review the developmental needs of universities. The report was critical on the point that most universities had not implemented the recommendations of Radhakrishnan Commission on spending a clear cut portion of the budget on acquisition of books and periodicals. It recognized the bad shape of the libraries, wherever these existed, and hence took serious note of the urgent need to uplift university libraries. Among its recommendations most prominent were, an academic institution, must first have a library plan, before seeking recognition; improvement of services and working conditions of libraries; etc. It went a step further and strongly felt that since libraries can play a better role in adult education, it recommended that public libraries must be integrated with school libraries for successfully implementing adult education programmes. It also spelt out the need to plan each university library in order to match the growth of users, growth of user needs, growth of research needs, and growth of new subjects.

The report states: "No university or college or department should be set up without taking into account its library needs in terms of staff, books, journals, space, etc. Nothing could be more damaging to a growing department than to neglect its library or give it a low priority. On the contrary, the library should be important centre of attraction on the college or university campus".

It has given extensive details and states how planning is essential for a good library: "A collection of books, even a collection of good books, does not constitute a 'library'. Given enthusiastic teachers who teach with books, and librarians who can cooperate with them in converting the library into an intellectual workshop, even comparatively small collection of sensitively chosen books may work wonders in the life of students. Without such a staff, the most luxurious building or extensive book collection, may have no effect at all. The object of library planning is not to build a collection of books unrelated to class-work, laboratory research and conference room. The object is rather to relate book selection, organization of the books, conditions of access and all library activities to the daily needs and activities of the community, both professors and students".

The report emphatically states the importance of libraries in the informal learning of the students, and goes to imply that the librarians are also teachers in this process, supporting the cause of pleading for a faculty status for librarians:

> "Modern education expects a teacher to initiate the students in the new vistas of the universe of knowledge. The students are to explore further and give final shape to what has been presented already. The search begins with the close of the first phase of learning that is, the class room lecturing. It is in the library that the second, the more vital, phase of learning takes place" (286-87).

UGC Review Committee Report (1981)

The Committee in its report has highlighted the state of the universities in India. In terms of funds and use the Table 4.1 gives a clear picture.

The proportion of funds spent and the number of users that frequent the libraries (rather number of seats in the library) are a good measure for the assessment of library growth pattern. In fact the Review Committee report has taken note of this for assessing the performance of the libraries.

This writer happened to visit one of these South Indian universities, on a Sunday, and found:

> The library was closed completely. Someone happened to pass by and said the library has a reading room. On visiting the so called reading room, it was found that it had a crowd of almost 200 students—busy reading, writing, and discussing. A glance at the register maintained at the desk revealed that few were from post-graduate departments, but most were undergraduates. If this is the interest of the readers, why was the library closed completely. Why did the library managers decide to dump this whole interested group in an isolated room, with a separate entrance from the backside?

TABLE 4.1: Funds and Facilities in Selected Universities

University	*Funds (Rs. in lakhs) (Special assistance)*		*Students*	*Seating capacity*	*% of students having seats in library*
	Allocated	*Used*			
Poona	24.30	24.30	2,773	300	11
Sardar Patel	15.00	15.00	1,220	700	57
Jadavpur	22.00	22.00	1,197	400	33
Calicut	36.55	36.55	791	325	41
Sri Venkateswara	24.45	24.27	1,798	432	24
Madras	42.05	31.83	2,508	290	12
Gauhati	49.80	31.09	1,844	210	11
Calcutta	65.40	63.02	13,057	702	5
Ranchi	16.45	16.45	1,590	40	3
Punjab	53.68	51.98	4,801	500	10
Gorakhpur	21.90	15.18	7,362	100	2
Delhi	28.40	24.66	9,738	400	4

Source: O.P. Gupta, *Development of University Libraries*, 1992.

A glance at the Table 4.1 also shows that the funding has quite a few imbalances, in terms of the size of readership the funds allocated, and space allocated in the library. Coming back to the reports and suggestions of the Committees. Whether all that is suggested in these reports is taken note by authorities, or not, it is obvious that there is an on going process of reminding that the libraries are in a bad shape, and this bad shape reflects on bad learning atmosphere for the users.

Interestingly, in seminars, and publications, this is regularly focused. One can see how vociferously the writer, P.N. Gour, supports the idea of an integration of the adult education—which the Government broadened the programme and called it social education, to not only improve literacy, but also to improve living standards and quality of life—and public library services in India. He squarely blames the Government, bureaucracy, and the library profession for the sad state of affairs (Gour, 1980: 9).

Committee for the National Central Library

For the purpose of planning a national level library development plan, the professional plea found an opportunity in the Central Government constituting a Committee on National Central Library. Ranganathan was a member of this Committee, and according to its recommendations, a draft Union Library Act was prepared and received approval of the Committee on 7 April 1948. It provided for the National Central Library to be at Delhi. The report was submitted to the Government, but received no action. Based on these recommendations and the bills which he prepared, Ranganathan published a book 'Library Development Plan for India: A Thirty Years Programme with Draft Library Bills for the Union Government and the Constituent States, published in 1950.

National Library Act

The Imperial Library was re-named as National Library by an Act of Parliament, in 1948 (change of name act). A Review Committee, under the Chairmanship of V.S. Jha, made many suggestions and recommendations for the improvement of the National Library. In 1976, the Government of India passed the National Library Act, giving the Library the status of an autonomous institution to be managed by a Board and an Executive Council. The Library was to be headed by a Director and the Librarian was placed before the Director.

The Central Government, accordingly, is directly responsible in maintenance of the National Library. Before we proceed, and describe other developments, let us see how this re-naming was discussed in the Parliament:

The Education Minister, Maulana Abul Kalam Azad, moved consideration of the bill to change the name of the Imperial Library. The bill sought to substitute the word "National" for "Imperial" in the name of the Library.

Maulana Azad said that under the changed circumstances it was proper for Indian institutions to have Indian names. . . . As soon as the new constitution is accepted, a committee of experts would be formed for the purpose. For the present it was enough to change the name into National Library.

Mr. H.V. Kamath suggested that the Library instead of being called the National Library should have been named as the Hindu Pustakalaya.

Babu Ramnarain Singh said that he was glad that the Government had made the move, though late by a year. It was a pity that the Education Minister had not succeeded in finding a suitable word for the name of the Library in any of the Indian languages.

Mr. Mahavir Thyagi said that for all practical purposes the change in the name of the Library made no difference. The change was proposed for sentimental reasons and there was no need for the house to have been moved for a thing like that. There was much greater need for bringing about a change in the spirit in which the affairs of the State were being conducted.

Maulana Azad, replying to the debate said that the change was proposed because it was felt that after August 15 there was no place in India for words like 'Imperial'. There were numerous offices and institutions whose English names had to be changed and the task was not easy as the House probably thought. In changing names, it was necessary to follow a well thought out and uniform policy. The Education Minister proposed setting of a board or committee for the purpose after the new constitution was passed.

> The purpose in this particular case, Maulana Azad said, would not have been served by using the word 'Rashtriya' in place of 'national' because it did not convey the same sense. Maulana Azad requested the House to agree to the change till the proposed board had made its recommendations. The Bill was passed (*Hindu*, September 2, 1948).

This apart, the other developments in the National Library are as follows:

The National Library of India Act, 1976, clarified its status. In addition the Government of India has made many amendments to the Registration of Books Act, 1867; it was henceforth called Delivery of Books & Newspaper Act, 1954 and amended in 1956, came to be called as Indian Copyright Act, incorporating the fourth national depository library—Delhi Public Library; again amended in 1994.

The National Library, was expected to be the nation's sole repository, with a primary function of reference and leadership. But owing to conditions beyond the control of its own founding fathers, and beyond the control of the authorities who sat in Delhi, away from the British Capital, and still away from the Viceroy's lodge which houses the National Library, the main role of this has been to act as a local public library!!!

Libraries of National Importance Act

The Central Government took it upon itself the issue of maintenance of some leading libraries. The Parliament passed and approved bills pertaining to libraries such as Khuda Bakhsh Oriental Public Library Act, 1969; Rampur Raza Library Act, 1975; The Asiatic Society Act, 1984; declaring these as 'institutions of national importance'. The President of India gave his consent on these bills, and thus these became important libraries, and were henceforth centrally administered.

Raja Ram Mohun Roy Library Foundation (RRLF)

The Central Government played a key role in the establishment of this Foundation, to commemorate the birth centenary of Raja Ram Mohun Roy, the leading social reformer of nineteenth century India. The Foundation was established in 1972, at Calcutta. It aimed at promotion and support of library movement in the country. Since its inception it has been playing a lead role in the growth as well as the development of public libraries in India by funding for acquisition programmes, and, for library buildings. As per the policy of providing funds, it provides grants matching with the respective State Government grants. Between 1972 and 1986 it has received total grant of Rs. 607.64 lakhs (with 382.19 from Centre and 225.45 lakhs from the States, respectively). A word about its areas of concentration is worth here. The Foundation concentrates on promotion of literacy; supply of regional language books—almost 80 per cent for regional languages and 20 per cent for English and other languages; rural libraries; preservation of rare and out-of-print books; and establishment of Bal Kendras in the country.

The Foundation, as stated in its Newsletter, of December 1995, received contributions from and rendered assistance to States/Union territories during the first three quarters of 1995-96 as shown in Table 4.2.

The pattern of funding is obviously fluctuating in all respects, except in providing a matching share for the funds. This also indicates that libraries cannot function with definite plans if the funds they receive is not regular and not even increasing regularly. India still has to pass another age for getting a carefully planned system of funding for library development. According to Thakur and Gopinath, who have assessed the role of the Union and Federal Government in library movement in India, "A critical review of the functioning of the Foundation will reveal that it spends much less than a paise per capita for public library service. The Foundation, which is dominated by Government officials, is functioning like a crippled body for want of funds and proper imagination" (1994: 154).

TABLE 4.2: Contributions and Assistance Received, Rendered by Raja Ram Mohun Roy Library Foundation

State/U.T.	*Balance as on 31.3.95*	*Contributions Received*	*Matching Share*	*Fund Available*	*Assistance Given*
Andhra Pradesh	1.1	5.0	5.0	60.8	5.3
Arunachal Pradesh	1.1			1.1	
Assam	1.2	5.0	5.0	11.2	0.3
Bihar	10.6			10.6	
Gujarat	3.3	10.0	10.0	23.3	20.6
Goa	1.0			1.0	1.1
Haryana	8.7	4.0	4.0	16.7	7.0
Himachal Pradesh	10.0	14.0	14.0	38.0	0.7
Karnataka	9.2	10.0	10.0	10.7	6.3
Kerala	2.4			2.4	
Madhya Pradesh	6.9	10.0	10.0	26.9	2.7
Maharashtra	15.3			15.3	10.3
Manipur	1.3	3.0	3.0	7.3	0.8
Meghalaya	–0.4	0.7	0.7	0.9	0.5
Mizoram		–0.1	4.0	4.0	7.8
Nagaland	0.3	0.3	0.3		
Orissa	–0.9	10.0	10.0	19.0	17.0
Punjab	5.7			5.7	0.4
Rajasthan	8.9			8.9	4.0
Sikkim	0.8			0.8	
Tamil Nadu	12.8	15.0	15.0	42.8	0.8
Tripura		2.1		2.1	0.9
Uttar Pradesh	21.6			21.6	19.5
West Bengal	–2.0	10.0	10.0	17.8	5.6
Andaman & Nicobar Islands		0.3		0.3	
Chandigarh	11.9	6.0	6.0	23.9	4.6
Lakshadweep	2.1			2.1	0.9
Pondicherry	0.6	0.2	0.2	0.5	

Literacy Patterns

A glance at literacy rates in the past five decades, shows the growth patterns.

TABLE 4.3: Literacy Rates: 1951-1991

Decade	*Per cent*	*Male*	*Female*
1951	18.33	27.16	8.86
1961	28.31	40.40	15.34
1971	34.45	45.95	21.97
1981	43.67	56.50	29.85
1991	52.21	64.13	39.29

The national average is just around 52 per cent, far less than a small neighbour, such as, Sri Lanka. And the female literacy further less in many ways. The progress made, in general, is just 30 per cent in all the fifty years of the independent India. Similarly the rise of male and female literacy is increased just 30 per cent. This speaks volumes about the least progress made in educating and bringing in literacy in the country—a country which is proud to be the largest democracy in the world!!!

Delhi Public Library

This is one of the leading and a model public library system developed in India. It was the initiative of many professionals in India and abroad that led to working and establishment of this unique experiment, and an exemplary model for the third world countries. Its prestigious position as fourth national depository library and a public library network which it has successfully developed places Delhi in forefront among the library-cities of India.

Schemes and Implementation

The Government of India in its New Education Policy, issued in 1985, has a passing reference to the list of 'Essential Facilities at the Primary Stage' which includes 'Reference Books—Dictionaries, encyclopedias; children's books (at least 200), magazines, journals, and newspapers for teachers and children' under the category 'Books for Reading'. Whether this is implemented or not, and whether the Government has made a proportionate budgetary allocation for growth and maintenance—including staff, furniture, equipment, books, etc.—of such a collection is yet to be ascertained.

Planning Commission

The Central Government set up the Planning Commission and planned for Five Year Plans to plan and implement its policies. Library development has been incorporated in this process. Accordingly, the Central Government provides financial assistance to the States for setting up libraries—State, district, mobile, and so on.

Why does the component called 'library' appear in some hidden corner of the planning document? For instance, in the document of Fourth Five Year Plan, libraries are listed in the section education, and sub-section of social education!

One, probable answer, is that library is not an indispensable item—such as, health, education, water, social welfare, social security, etc. It is also possible that library—or information is available even outside libraries, in survey results, opinion polls, in oral and other demonstrative techniques, that is, by using audio-visual, media, and so on. Another probability is total planning is the first phase, planning education, health, and other essential services is the second phase, and planning components of these services—information provision for successful implementation—is the third phase; meaning that library has a tertiary place in the social and economic developmental activities of the nation! To support this, one may add on that library planning is not the end in itself, it must support the main programmes for speedy completion, greater efficiency, and in most economical ways.

National Information System for Science and Technology (NISSAT)

To meet the national information needs in science and technology on the lines of UNISIST, NATIS, etc., and on the plans submitted by various experts, including Dr. Peter Lazer, to the National Committee on Science and Technology (NCST), under the Ministry of Science and Technology, and the Department of Scientific and Industrial Research (DSIR), under the Five Year Plan, the Government decided to implement the recommendations of NCST. This led to establishing of NISSAT, in 1977, an integrated multi-tire national information system for the area of science and technology. The aim was to facilitate all plans relating to the scientific and industrial developments, and in this process NISSAT became a facilitator and promoter, rather than a system.

INFLIBNET

Information and Library Network (INFLIBNET) is a platform connecting academic and research libraries, and was set up in 1988, by UGC. It is a project aimed to provide linkage between libraries which can inter-connect the academic community and library resources all over India.

Its implementation is slowed, due to financial crunch and the delay in the Eighth Plan.

Adult Education Programmes

There is an on-going debate to find the relationship between literacy and librarianship. Carl M. White, the expert librarian, whose report of Delhi University Library, written in 1960s, is still referred, has developed the debate further, in his essay "The Intertwined Destiny of Literate Society and Librarianship", in his edited book entitled: *Bases of Modern Librarianship* (Oxford, Pergamon Press, 1964). From the point of our discussion it has to state that if no literacy there is no need of libraries, and if neo-literate are to continue with their reading interest, it is not private collections, that can satisfy the mass reading and information needs, but it is libraries, and none else!

Prof. H.A. Khan in an essay on rural libraries and literacy, analyses the views of the two schools which are against or favour the idea of linking literacy programmes with libraries, and then states ". . . it is better to have a liberal view of the libraries in our society and allow them to promote literacy and adult education activities along with other kindred agencies or even on their own" (1991: 137).

Quoting from the literature extensively, Prof. Khan identifies ways in which libraries can still come forward and help the agencies concerned with adult education to revitalize their activities, as well as, assists the neo-literate directly in sustaining the level of literacy they have achieved.

The Government of India has laid much emphasis on eradicating illiteracy from the society. According to the census reports the trends in eradication has been working slowly but steadily.

TABLE 4.4: Percentage of Literacy

Year	*Persons*	*Male*	*Female*
1951	18.33	27.16	8.86
1961	28.31	40.40	15.34
1971	34.45	45.95	21.97
1981	43.56	56.37	29.75
1991	52.11	63.86	39.42

While the National Adult Education Programme was inaugurated by the Ministry of Education in 1978, the programme itself has not taken off in a full speed. As early as 1961, Sinha Committee had recommended that "Libraries must interact with the other social education and other adult education programmes". But nothing came out of this.

The Planning Commission is also aware of the crucial problem of adult literacy, the levels achieved and alternatives to be adopted. These are clearly stated in its Draft Outline of "Fourth Five Year Plan". In this it has mentioned that libraries can be approached in getting help in this regard. "Recognizing the importance of follow-up measures to make literacy effective, provision is being made for libraries in the rural areas and for large-scale book production suited for neo-literate in different languages. Stress will be laid on the mobilization of public co-operation in covering the first stage of literacy on the lines of Gram Shikshan Mohim tried out in Maharashtra. Attention will also be paid to the training of literacy workers and library personnel, opening adult schools and night classes especially for low income groups in industrial and establishment of workers' education colleges" (p. 322).

Whereas, the Ekbote Committee report, reviewing the Andhra Pradesh Public Libraries Act, has clearly stated the ways and means in which libraries can play a role in eradicating illiteracy (Chapter V, pp. 55-58). Its main focus is on recommending that libraries must use as many audio-visual materials and spread the programme of eradication. It has highlighted the areas in which libraries can be directly involved, in which areas libraries help the illiterates to help themselves, and so on. The recommendations of Ekbote Committee Report are not yet implemented.

Fund Allocated by Central Government for Library Service

A glance at the allocation for one year, 1988-89, shows the pattern of funding and the priority which the national level library system receives.

TABLE 4.5: Allocation for the Year 1988-89

(in lakhs or hundred thousand)

Library	*Plan*		*Non-Plan*		*Total*	
	Rs.	*%*	*Rs.*	*%*	*Rs.*	*%*
National Library, Calcutta	102	28	194	62	296	44
Delhi Public Library	55	15	69	22	24	18
Central Reference Library	12	3	18	6	30	4
RRLF, Calcutta			140	38	12	4
Khuda Bakhsh Or Public Library			25	7	12	4
Indian Council of World Affairs			6	1	2	1
Saraswati Mahal Library, Thanjavur			15	4		
Raza Library, Rampur			11	3		
Total	367		309.84		676.84	

The Table 4.5 displays the level of allocation under the different heads of budget of the Central Government. As much as 28 per cent is allocated in the plan period for the National Library, and the libraries of national importance received different level of priorities, considering their importance and their activities. For instance, the funding for Khuda Bakhsh has to be more than Raza Library, as the latter is more actively involved in programmes and publications; so also the importance of the Raja Ram Mohun Roy Library Foundation, which is a scheme to improve the public library system in the country, with a special focus on rural and literacy programmes, and it getting 38 per cent is not a surprise.

TABLE 4.6: Total Expenditure

(in lakhs or hundred thousand)

Public libraries	*Expenditure*	*Per Capita*
State Govt.	3,171.7	Re. 0.46
Central Govt.	676.8	Re. 0.16

A break up of the expenditure of each State, given below shows the priority each State considers in the matters relating to library development. The list is in descending order by per capita expenditure:

TABLE 4.7: Expenditure on Public Libraries in States (1986-87)

State	*Expenditure (in lakhs)*	*Population (in lakhs)*	*Per Capita (in Rs.)*	*Literacy % 1980s*
(1)	(2)	(3)	(4)	(5)
Pondicherry	15.0	6.04	2.48	45.71
Arunachal Pradesh	15.0	6.31	2.37	11.32
Meghalaya	30.0	13.35	2.24	33.22
Chandigarh	10.0	4.51	2.21	61.56
Mizoram	10.0	4.93	2.02	54.91
Goa	20.0	10.07	1.98	57.25
Nagaland	15.0	7.74	1.94	42.57
West Bengal	928.2	545.8	1.70	40.88
Sikkim	5.0	3.16	1.58	34.05
Tripura	30.0	20.0	1.46	42.12
Lakshadweep	0.5	0.4	1.24	44.65
Andaman & Nicobar Islands	2.0	1.8	1.06	42.14
Manipur	15.0	14.2	1.05	41.91
Tamil Nadu	451.5	484.0	0.93	45.78
Diu	0.2	0.3	0.82	—
Delhi	50.0	62.2	0.80	61.06

(Contd.)

TABLE 4.7 (*Contd.*)

(1)	(2)	(3)	(4)	(5)
Andhra Pradesh	357.1	535.4	0.66	29.50
Karnataka	232.1	371.4	0.63	38.41
Himachal Pradesh	25.0	42.8	0.58	42.48
Daman	0.2	0.4	0.51	—
Dadra & Nagar Haveli	0.5	1.0	0.48	16.78
Kerala	113.0	254.5	0.44	69.17
Rajasthan	120.0	342.6	0.35	25.00
Gujarat	117.0	340.8	0.35	43.75
Assam	60.0	198.9	0.30	—
Jammu & Kashmir	17.3	59.8	0.29	27.00
Haryana	35.00	129.2	0.27	35.84
Madhya Pradesh	120.0	521.7	0.23	27.82
Orissa	60.0	263.7	0.22	34.10
Maharashtra	123.7	627.8	0.20	47.37
Punjab	30.0	167.8	0.18	40.71
Uttar Pradesh	137.5	1,108.6	0.12	27.38
Bihar	25.8	699.1	0.03	26.21

In a comparative perspective, Table 4.7, displays the Statewise level of expenditure and reflects on the priorities that the libraries receive in each State. One does not need a long interpretation of these figures, to show how the most thickly populated State, such as Uttar Pradesh, has only Re. 0.12 per capita expenditure, whereas a small territory, like, Diu, has per capita expenditure as high as Re. 0.82. If this is the fate of the Statewise expenditure in the country, which is totally disproportionate to its size and needs, then the resulting outcome, the development of libraries, 'live wires of the society' would be equally out of control.

Considering the fact, that rate of literacy has no relationship with the size of the State, nor with the per capita expenditure on the respective state library system, it amazes any one, to find out how is the planning done and on what basis? The analysis of the possible answers are not attempted here!

Role of State Governments

In the Constitution of India, the provision of public library service and library development was made a State subject, bringing it under the State List. Hence it is here that the true implications of the library development are expected to appear in the post-independence era.

A glance at the State maps, in the context of statewise library legislation, we find the scenario as follows:

Library Legislation, or Library Acts exist in Tamil Nadu (1948), Andhra Pradesh (1960), Karnataka (1965), Maharashtra (1967), West Bengal (1979), Manipur (1988), Kerala (1989), Haryana (1989), Mizoram (1993), and Goa (1994).

Without going into much of the details of the library legislation in each State, it is pertinent to have a bird's eye view on one aspect which forms the core area. For instance 'library cess', a main resource for raising revenue for the public libraries in India, is included in few existing acts (example, Tamil Nadu, Andhra Pradesh) and not included in some others (Maharashtra, West Bengal, Manipur). Even in the States which have cess there are variants, between three paise on land tax (as in Karnataka) to eight paise on property tax or house tax (as in Andhra Pradesh). These are the indicators of the fact that all library legislative attempts in the country are not uniform, and all legislative attempts do not lead to uniformity even in one single area: raising regular funds to develop the library system. It is a fact that there is no unanimity in including the public funds in development of public libraries in India. In fact, some feel, library legislation is necessary only to get a regular funding source from the public exchequer. Consider the fact that the Fyzee Committee, appointed by the Bombay State in 1939, did not recommend compulsory legislation, but recommended permissive legislation to authorize Municipality or Local Board to levy a special tax if they so desired to raise money for libraries. Another fact, which the opponents of cess, cite is that the amount collected as cess is not being used for the purpose it is collected, for instance, in Andhra Pradesh.

While Fyzee Committee's report for the Bombay Province helped the passing of the first library act, Kolhapur Public Libraries Act, 1945, it also led to the legislation called Maharashtra Public Libraries Act, there were other trend setters in the country. For instance, the Ekbote Committee in the State of Andhra Pradesh, was appointed in 1976, 'to review the working of the Andhra Pradesh Public Libraries Act, 1960 and to suggest amendments to the Act. Its Report submitted in 1977, made several recommendations in the light of the past experiences with this and other such Acts. The Government accepted the recommendations, but it did not implement these. The report contained valuable recommendations, such as the following:

> "It is interesting to know that Central Institute of Indian Languages has prepared a film entitled 'Learn Devanagri' using the two principles of patterned perception and constructive observation. It

has plans to make some films of other scripts. They should be requested if they have not already prepared, to prepare a film through which Telugu script can be taught to illiterates. Series of programmes and series of programmed script learning books and film strips can be used for this purpose. These and many other audio-visuals could be used with profit for accelerated learning of reading and writing" (p. 56).

Considering the fact that RRLF aims to promote audio-visual collections also, then "It becomes immediately plain that the underlying aim is to help rural area more than the urban because percentage of illiterates is enormous in the rural areas. If that is so, then maximum advantage could be taken of this scheme for the purchase of appropriate audio-visual materials which will help eradicate illiteracy as well as for the purchase of books and other reading material for neo-literate" (p. 57).

In these two short recommendations, the Committee has indicated its economy as well as intellectual input by suggesting ways to utilize the available resources in a way other than the present and thus maximize the utility of graphic records, among the literates, neo-literates, and the illiterates. Yet there was no reaction from the authorities, who put the report to cold storage, as per the traditions of the imperial masters.

Despite this inactivity, another committee headed by Vavilala Gopalkrishnayya, was to suggest measures, for the improvement of private and aided libraries. The report submitted in 1978, carried norms and procedures for various issues involved in the process, such as identification of the eligible libraries—to be called 'public' and which could receive the grant-in-aid—inspection of the site for the suitability of the location, levels of officers who can be appointed as Inspectors, and so on.

There is another similar Committee, in Tamil Nadu, which was constituted to look into certain details of the Tamil Nadu Public Libraries Act, 1948. This Committee had V.N. Subharayan as its Chairman. It recommended appointment of full time District Library Officer to manage the library system at the district level, which was not spelled in the Act. These recommendations were accepted in principle. To identify the implications, these recommendations were then evaluated by an official level committee, under the Chairmanship of S. Srinivasan, and it further recommended some more details for the successful implementation of the above suggestions.

Annual Expenditure for District Libraries—At a Glance

To see what is the ground reality it is pertinent to look into the details of the expenditure for 1975-76, as stated in the Ekbote Report. The expenditure includes books supplied by RRLF, and ratio of staff to population.

TABLE 4.8: Population, Expenditure, Staff Ratio

District Library System	*Total*		*Full Time*	
	Population (In lakhs) Rs.	*Expenditure on Books*	*Per Person (in Paise)*	*Staff Ratio to Population*
Adilabad	12.88	38,992	0.03	1:34,000
Anantapur	21.15	92,022	0.04	1:28,600
Chittoor	22.86	61,536	0.03	1:34,600
Cuddapah	15.77	72,258	0.05	1:18,000
East Godavari	30.87	1,32,278	0.04	1:17,800
Guntur	28.45	1,33,042	0.05	1:16,700
Hyderabad City	61.07	2,60,671	0.16	1:9,400
Hyderabad District	11.85	62,987	0.05	1:20,300
Karimnagar	19.64	41,584	0.02	1:40,700
Khammam	13.70	52,337	0.04	1:38,000
Krishna	24.94	1,92,586	0.08	1:10,900
Kurnool	18.82	62,721	0.03	1:28,300
Mahabubnagar	19.32	38,158	0.02	1:49,500
Medak	14.68	33,262	0.02	1:35,600
Nalgonda	18.20	37,503	0.02	1:20,500
Nellore	16.10	63,076	0.04	1:24,700
Nizamabad	13.13	82,921	0.06	1:20,500
Prakasam	19.20	87,917	0.05	1:34,200
Srikakulam	25.90	38,038	0.01	1:52,800
Vishakhapatnam	28.05	41,916	0.01	1:22,000
Warangal	18.71	45,613	0.02	1:45,400
West Godavari	23.74	1,01,802	0.04	1:24,900
Total 22 District	435.03	17,74,220	0.04	1:20,500

Note: Expenditure incurred by aided libraries and the staff employed in them are not taken into account for want of authentic information" (Report, p. 127)

The above figures are indicative of the expenditure patterns in a State which has a very old history of library movement in the country. The most glaring feature is the staff ratio. One man libraries is the rule here, rather than an exception. Again, one person in the library, is left to perform all the tasks, including technical, public and professional. How far one person can fulfil all these and how far these are a accepted as per the standards laid down in the Public Libraries Act. If the main aim of modern libraries is putting knowledge to work, then the question is can one person be accountable for this aim, or it is the duty of the planners to appoint more staff, and only then such libraries can be expected to put knowledge to work!

TABLE 4.9: Statement showing Progress from 1960-76

Year	*Number of Libraries*	*Books (in lakhs)*	*Readers (in lakhs)*	*Borrowers*	*Cess (in lakhs)*	*Total Funds (cess, contributions & grants— in lakhs)*
1960-61	1,725	9.4	88.35	N.A.	7.37	13.29
1963-64	2,090	14.7	N.A.	N.A.	15.08	24.14
1967-68	2,809	25.0	N.A.	99,900	15.10	31.68
1971-72	3,050	40.0	186.53	1,34,300	25.99	56.39
1975-76	3,464	51.6	243.74	2,56,900	41.64	124.88

N.A. = Data not available.
Source: Ekbote Committee Report, pp. 133-34.

The Table 4.9 displays the progress made in opening new libraries the increase in collection, number of visitors, number of registered borrowers, the Cess (public contribution receivable through the taxes), and the total income amount. What is obvious is that there is some progress made in collecting funds and resources, and also it is obvious that on the whole there is slow, but steady progress made in keeping pace with the increasing user size. But what is requiring further probe and indepth surveys is the fact that these figures relating to one State don't tell us about how much these resources are really meeting the needs of the public—the masses for whom the bell tolls. This primarily constituting illiterates, and only a minority is literates, raises a question as to how far libraries, oriented towards literate, meets the information needs of the neo-literate, as well as the information needs of the non-literate. Ignoring the majority of the illiterates in accessing the information is no where justifiable by any measure of truth, if the aim is to provide information for all!

In short, as per the trend set by the professionals and the Government, all States have the responsibility to establish State supported free library service for the public. But this responsibility is not yet fully dawned on the authorities, that have so far ignored legislation in their States. That is, apart from the ten States, all other States are not yet awakened to issues relating to, free information-access, facility in their States.

To quote Prof. M. Satyanarayana,

> "The policy framework of the State Government towards the public libraries appears that the public library is a book-lending institution. It also provides facilities for reading newspapers, magazines, and books. It serves a small proportion of the community. It is non-responsive to the pressing problems of the community" (1997: 129).

Contact Libraries

What role the Government of independent India played in permitting or by not permitting the establishment of foreign information centres is an important question. British India had already set a model for this area of activity, by permitting all that was 'suitable' to their plans and policies.

While foreigners who entered India exploited the resources of the country in all possible ways, there were certain compelling reasons for these foreign powers to establish their own libraries in India. This need began in the form of establishing information centres first for themselves—whites. Next was the need of libraries for the English knowing, or converted Christians, all basically natives; and then the need to establish evangelical programmes that could enable reading Bible to the intended audience; with the establishment of English as medium of instruction for all it became imperative that the Government had to find books and other reading materials, and hence emerged libraries, such as, subscription libraries, proprietary libraries, elite libraries, and finally free libraries for all.

Examples of British sponsored libraries meant to promote Oriental studies are seen in Asiatic Society libraries in Calcutta and Bombay; American, British and other missionaries all over India established colleges and libraries to develop their programmes and examples of these are seen in the League of Service Library at Lahore, Baptist Theological Seminary, Bangalore, Henry Martin Institute of Islamic Studies, Hyderabad, and Lucknow Christian College (Founded by the American Methodists).

In short, these came to be called as contact libraries. In 1943 the establishment of the first American information centre, at Calcutta, followed by other American information centres all over India, inaugurated a new era of American influences in India. These contact libraries imported the practical aspects of American advances in library and information science. Additionally, the availability of American library experts, and an opportunity to visit America opened up many more vistas. Most of these were pre-independence establishments.

The policy for both American, British and other foreign libraries in Independent India was to first allow the idea of free flow of information in major towns, including the four metros, and Hyderabad, Bangalore, Lucknow, Patna, Trivandrum, etc. In the wake of the Indo-Pak war and Indo-China war, the American presence in India was suspected, and this led in 1969 to the closure of all American information centres in the country, except the four metros which had an Embassy or a Consulate.

The American Congress passed an Act in 1951, known as Public Law 480, according to which U.S.A. gave loan to buy much needed wheat from the U.S. Under the Wheat Loan Programme, India agreed to (a) buy American books periodicals and scientific equipment for promotion of India's development in respective areas, (b) enable acquisition of Indian books for America, and (c) the exchange of scholars, including librarians.

Quantitatively speaking, the Wheat Loan Programme enabled 91 institutions to acquire the essential books, though only from America. The 91 recipient institutions, comprised, 36 universities, 52 research institutions, and 3 university extension libraries; the grants varied between around $500 to $77,000; this enabled, some of the sick institutions to gather a breath of life, with this fresh contingent of supplies.

These foreign libraries, established as information centres for the dissemination of respective cultures, soon became a special type of public libraries in India, in the absence of the Indian public library system. Indian users became addicts of these advanced and well-maintained information centres, that the closure of these was shocking for some, unimaginable for few others, and was taken as an unkindest cut by others. The single difference between the British Council and American Libraries, is the latter are attached to the Embassy, while the former are independent of this diplomatic support. There is however a catch, British Libraries in the metros are called British Council (are under the British High Commission), and in other cities these (under the Government of India's Indian Council of Cultural Relations) are called British Libraries.

The most common users are students, who desired but lacked an ability to find such indigenous resources centres. The elite and the lay alike are the frequenters. American Library was envious at Calcutta, as it had, until 1991, a separate Centre in the Calcutta University Campus, to cater to the exclusive needs of faculty and students. These libraries in general had books in English and could provide most recent and advance knowledge, an idea which was again envious to the vast number of Indian libraries, who were totally incomparable even in the collection they housed.

The PL480 fund enabled the development of a unique resource centre, American Studies Research Centre, at Hyderabad. This became the centre for the research and academic programmes initially in the humanities and later also in the social sciences. This Centre is unique in terms of (a) its collection: Americana; (b) its functioning as most upto-date among all the humanities and social science information centres in the country; and (c) its exemplary leadership in being the first completely automated library with an integrated system in India in 1993.

The presence of foreign librarians, either as visitors, or as experts, or on an assignment, provided ample opportunity for Indian librarians to import foreign ideas and library techniques. Independent India witnessed much of the advancement in Indian librarianship basically due to two factors, first, facility to travel abroad, and, second, availability of foreign consultants and experts. According to the research done by Konnur, there were 45 Indian library professionals who visited US during the period 1948-1988. The present writer himself benefited from this facility, under the umbrella of Fulbright programme. What experiences one carries to and fro and what is the effect of these experiences is difficult to quantify. But on the whole it is a live experience and those who wish to develop their own professional standing must visit and experience the meaning and spirit of the advances in the librarianship abroad. The experience of travel abroad, and sight seeing trips for fun and window shopping apart, the main opportunity which one gets is an exposure and experience of a variety and range unimaginable.

This is not merely to sell the idea of the charisma which the west provides to an Easterner; rather it is the reality that impressed and created a spirit of true professional even to the father of modern library in India, *i.e.*, S.R. Ranganathan. To quote from his foreign experiences is itself a full research work, and he was everywhere observing and taking serious note of the type of the grandeur that was and the aesthetic outlook it offered in anything and everything he passed by. In all his trips to the Western world he did get inspiration, and came home more motivated; probably he never returned frustrated in any case.

That the Indian profession is thankful for all this, and it is necessary to quote a word of appreciation from Prof. Kesavan, "Prof. Bonn, whose tenure of visiting professorship in the Delhi University is a mighty piece of good fortune for the department of Library Science, has contributed a very shrewd and understanding analysis of the State of library education in India" (1968).

Prof. George S. Bonn, hailing from University of Hawaii, was at Delhi in 1968, under the Rockefeller Foundation Grant. Bonn's report of his observations and suggestions on libraries in Delhi and the Library Science Department, was published in the Annals of Library Science.

Role of Library Profession

Independent India, had no problems in re-establishing its institutions. Library education was already set up at various levels, including university, college, and at other levels. For instance, independent India, already had certificate, diploma and degree level library science courses; what was missing was the doctorate or research degree programme. It was also necessary to streamline continuing education programmes.

At the service level much was to be achieved, given the superficial level of achievements that had been made in British period. It was a period of test for the profession to establish itself as a prime-mover of a social cause in establishing free and open public libraries, at State, district, city and local levels. This task demanded all the energies of the profession, in order to motivate the Government, public, and all other concerned in the process of making a library—a library as a nerve centre of the society. The problems in this course of action was thus multi-faceted.

At the symposium arranged by the Delhi Library Association in 1957, on 'Library Movement in India', Ranganathan said:

> "Today, library movement aims at the establishment of an integrated national library system with many cultural, political, economic and educational functions. It is not satisfied with the establishment of either a few huge libraries or of myriad's of small libraries, quite independent of one another and with only a few cultural functions. Even the UNESCO has given a wrong direction in regard to function by locating its Library in its cultural wing. Certain historical factors appear to lead the authorities and even the statesmen in India to take a wrong view of the whole matter. The factors that have diversified library functions and called for a new view took shape only during the last few centuries when our community had been in a State of unawareness due to cultural exhaustion. These factors are: 1. Cheap

and rapid methods of reproduction of copies of books; 2. Great increase in population pressure; 3. Increasing inadequacy of natural and near-natural commodities and means for services to meet the needs of the total population; 4. Invention of new methods of technology, and tapping of new sources of power; 5. Formation of new pattern in the aggregation and the distribution of population; 6. Advent of democracy as a political principle and as a social norm" (pp. 19-20).

Ranganathan was highlighting the issues and problems which were faced by the profession in the 1950s, and which were to be taken care and set right, without any further loss of time. These deal, respectively, with printing and duplicating technology; increasing user needs; shortage of resources; advances in information handling techniques; dynamics of population; and democratic pressures to provide free access to information.

What is the role of the profession, if it must meet the pressures of the modern democratic society? The profession is expected to fulfil the democratic norm; of helping everyone in the society to read—'democracy in fact insists on the right of everybody to be helped to read'. So continues Ranganathan, ". . . the use of books by every citizen down to the last in the intellectual scale is necessary for the well-being of the nation as a whole. In the economic sphere, it is necessary as a step in productive drive. In the political sphere, it is necessary to make the masses take an interest in the work of the State. In the social sphere, it can help in mutual understanding and easing of tension" (pp. 21-22).

Dr. Ranganathan's message to aspirants to library profession, at the Department of Library Science, University of Rajasthan, Jaipur, reminded the library professionals that "the Library Profession is a noble profession. It can do no harm to anybody. . . . If the young aspirants to the library profession, now put above want on a par with other professions, devote themselves to their work with undivided attention, and throw themselves heart and soul to give the library service to every reader at every time . . . they will have the satisfaction of having left not only library service and library science, but also our country at a much more advanced stage than what they found when entered the library profession" (LIBRA, 1965-66: 8). This is, in short, the reason of the existence of the profession in the modern age to promote development of all, in every walk of life.

A survey of the literature of library science, with regards to bibliographic control done by the professionals, in addition to the efforts of allied agencies, one finds some studies and surveys that are conducted to come to terms with explosion of information and the attempts to provide control mechanisms and in the ultimate analysis assists in access to the exploding information. Sarin and Sharma (1972), have made an exhaustive attempts, though of the limited period under study to find the approaches that are being taken all over the country in this context. Vyas (1989) in his doctoral dissertation surveyed the area of social science scenario and Kanakachary did a similar survey of the field of humanities in his doctoral research. Some more surveys are mentioned elsewhere in this chapter.

Case Studies—Profession's Performance

Let us see some instances of what is happening in the country, in terms of the above issues, which in fact are encompassing the major aspects.

Case One

"Under the pressure of the blind imitation of everything of the West, that took possession of us in the days of decadence, there is a tendency among the indolent and the predatory in the profession to adopt mangled forms of outmoded techniques of the West. The classification of the West gives no help in the classification of Indian thought and classics. So it is in cataloguing. And yet, there is a cursed allergy in regard to any good technique developed in India" Ranganathan (p. 24).

Case Two

"Some years ago, the University of Madras was asked to arrange a course of lectures on School Library Work. It was stressed that a teacher of English was the most appropriate person to give the course. At the time of my selection to Librarian's post, my having specialized in mathematics threatened to stand in my way. At about the same time, a former colleague of mine who was teaching languages—Latin and Greek—was easily preferred for the Librarian's post of a science library" (p. 22).

Case Three

A recent Annual Report of a State Central Library describes its Reference Service in the following words:

"Some years back an American Library issued the following invitation to its readers: 'Telephone-in for what you want, get the formula you have forgotten, the quotation you can only half remember, the word you want defined or correctly pronounced or ask for material for your club paper, after dinner or political speech'.

"We extend a hearty welcome to all such inquiries and assist them in their searches without extending a formal invitation as such, as it is one of our regular features of service" (Ranganathan, 1972: Part II, 3).

Case Four (Kannada Mss)

A newspaper representative who was in England happened to visit John Ryland's Library. This is one of the libraries in England well known for its collection of manuscripts, in various languages, written on many types of surfaces—clay, bamboo, papyrus, palm-leaf, cloth and paper. As he was being shown round by the Keeper of the Manuscripts, he noticed three small cupboard boxes labelled 'Canarese Mss'. Since this was the visitor's mother tongue, his curiosity was roused and he asked to see these manuscripts. One was on the Mahabharatha epic called Vani Vilasa and the second on Nala Charita and the third he did not examine. These manuscripts belonged to the collection known as Bibliotheca Lindeseana which the library had acquired from the Earl of Crawford in 1901. On returning to India, he mentioned the existence of these manuscripts to his friend, a Professor of Kannada in Bangalore, and also wrote to us to obtain microfilm copies of these to enable the Professor to do some research on these manuscripts. Although our part in it lay only in negotiating through our London office with John Ryland's library and obtaining the microfilm copies, this involved a certain amount of correspondence and organization. But we were eventually able to do it. These manuscripts were on palm-leaf strips, nearly 2′ in length and the process of reproducing was limited to 12″ × 10″. It was therefore necessary to photograph each strip in two overlapping sections, each photograph comprising 4 strips of palm-leaf. But this was successfully done and after the necessary undertaking was given by the scholar that he would not publish any part of it without the permission from John Ryland's and that he would only use it for the purpose of his research, we were able to obtain the information, thus completing a quadrangular cycle of information—Manchester-Delhi-Madras-Bangalore" (Suseela Kumar: 1974, 235-36).

Case Five (Moplah Rebellion)

"A research scholar on Indian history had chosen the 'Moplah Rebellion' for his subject. He wanted books, articles and documents on the subject".

"He had consulted the available records in the Tamil Nadu Archives and was laboriously going through the microfilm copies of the issues of *The Hindu* from 1920 onwards. He also wanted to know whether we could provide further information".

"A list of manuscript material and articles in periodicals was compiled by our Home Library (British Library) in London. . . . Home Library was also able to enlist the help of the India Office Library and their librarian provided a further list of relevant books and files in the India Office dealing with the Rebellion. . . . The research scholar was also informed of the cost of obtaining positive microfilm copies of the files and Xerox copies of the periodical articles. The books could be borrowed from the India Office Library through the National Library, Calcutta" (Suseela Kumar: 273-74).

Case Six

Job satisfaction for the profession is an issue which creates interest in some sociological experts. The question is what motivates some to be zealous and some others to be otherwise? A study by Pulla Reddy, was done to ascertain answers to some of this kind of questions. He surveyed 104 professionals in Delhi's academic libraries. According to the findings, 2.9 per cent are highly satisfied; 27.9 per cent are satisfied; 41.3 are not worried about this issue; 25 per cent are dissatisfied; and 2.9 per cent are highly dissatisfied. The study has done extensive inquiries on these matters and its findings include:

- there is no difference in satisfaction among the respondents in terms of college or university work areas;
- so also satisfaction has not much to do with the pay;
- promotional matters do depend on the level of institution;
- matters relating to supervision do effect satisfaction;
- there is significant difference in these levels, when it comes to satisfaction with the readers;
- job satisfaction has much to do with age;
- sex of the professional does not differ in this matter.

The role of the profession, does get affected by the level of satisfaction or dissatisfaction, but this is only one small factor in the whole process, and the profession has to contribute its head and heart if the goal is to maximize the use of the graphic records.

Case Seven

Is the profession concerned on what the public, or the user needs are. See for instance what a user feels and desires the library to be, and this statement might be a useful guide to measure the professional performance:

> "I am generally put off by the expression Library Movement. The very word 'movement' endows the whole business with an abstract, unreal air. It produces in one's mind a picture of humanity, jammed together, moving in a mass towards a goal—a very impressive picture no doubt, but having nothing to do with the business of reading. Or am I mistaken in thinking that the champions of the Library Movement are interested in the business of reading? Library Science seems all concerned with furniture, locks, keys, registers, vouchers, and statistics, everything except reading. The most noticeable deficiency in any library to-day seems to be a lack of propaganda for books themselves. It would be useful to inscribe on every library-wall the motto: 'Books are meant to be read and not merely to be classified and preserved'. In every library elaborate rules are being framed for borrowing and returning of books. There is a university library that I visit, where there are so many regulations for book-borrowing that few ever find the time to go in and borrow a volume. You have to spend half an hour before you get through the formalities of picking up a book from the shelf, and another half an hour before you can get through the various entries and signatures and go out of the library. Compared to this the ceremony of getting through a custom's inspection looks like child's play. In every library there are so many involved technicalities for this transaction that I sometimes wonder if they would not do better to keep dummy books with gilt titles in sealed almirahs, so that they may only be seen and counted and never taken out, which seems to be the best way of keeping a library secure, above reproach from auditors, and with unimpeachable stock registers".

The observation continues, "The great handicap for the libraries now is that Governments have begun to take an interest in them, and eminent men utilize them as themes for grandiose speeches. As a result of it most library efforts get entangled in red-tape, and become a matter of cess, authority, statistics, and funds" (R.K. Narayan, *Hindu*, 5 April 1953).

This observation should give the profession a moment to think that its rules of the trade are good, so long as these are not hurdles in use and user convenience. But book keeping as a trade in matters of library-user-friendly relationship is to be always carefully handled. Is the profession willing to ponder in becoming a user-friendly place, atleast now?

Case Eight (Handle-with-Care)

In Bihar . . . "we chanced to come across a newly established college. Many colleges happen to be sign-board colleges in many parts of the country. But this was little more than a sign board college. It had a few rooms and I asked to see the library. There was a steel almirah, the locks and doors were rusted (probably never been opened), and a number of bags, gunny bags. When I asked what did they contain, I was told that they contained books which UGC somehow gave to them or somebody else gave them. They did not care to open them. Essentially, neither anybody is interested in looking at the books nor is anybody interested in distributing those books. I said 'can I have the keys to the cupboards, so that I can look what the books are'? 'No, Sir, how can be the keys with us, the librarian hasn't come, he keeps the keys', I was told. 'Why', I asked. "Librarian can't possibly give the keys to others supposing the books are stolen', was the reply! I am sure the locks won't open if you try with keys" (Yashpal, 1995: 10)

Training Programmes and Other Activities

How far is the profession into the job? How does it fair in its dealings within professional circles, outside the professional circles? What are its other activities that go to promote the cause of professionalism in the country? What types of training and continuing education programmes are offered?

During the post-independence era, the professional activities expanded by leaps and bounds. An observation made by Ranganathan on the enormous number of Associations in Andhra Pradesh has been cited, which speaks, on one hand, on the level of interests among the professionals to promote the cause of progress, and on another hand, on the State of affairs, not to say anything about the justification for so many types of associations at so many levels.

Indian professional publications, in journals, books, published pre-seminar papers, etc., are grown in an explosive manner. But the coverage of these in foreign library indexes is meagre.

The reasons stated, by Prof. Neelameghan, in 1971, are still valid in 1996, with no progress:

(a) The language barrier: enormous amount of literature dealing with library science appears in regional languages;
(b) The standard of articles in periodicals vary considerably: from just a descriptive account of a library through presentation of collection of data, to learned articles propounding new ideas;
(c) The slant in exposition of problems to suit the local conditions; and
(d) Time-lag in the publications (Neelameghan, 1971: 46).

Nevertheless, there are recently a few indigenous attempts to compile bibliographies on the vast literature of library science that are produced in India. The list of such bibliographies, include: B.M. Gupta's *Handbook of Libraries, Archives and Information Centres in India*, Vol. 11 and 12 (1992); Sewa Singh's *Indian Library Literature* (annual bibliographic survey, beginning with the year 1971); Indian Library Science Abstracts; there are also attempts at indexing research completed in India, and this list includes Vijay Pathak and L.S. Ramaiah's *Bibliography of Research in Library and Information Science* (1981), P.S.G. Kumar's *Research in Library and Information Science in India* (1987), etc.

Bibliographic control at the level of regions, is also attempted and has given a good support to the problem of scatter of literature. One district attempt at this, is by A.M. Abdul Huq and Mohammed M. Aman, *Librarianship and the Third World: An Annotated Bibliography of Selected Literature on Developing Nations, 1960-1975*, New York, Garland, 1977. The journal *Third World Libraries*, has been another source of identifying Indian literature to the international audience. Such an attempt at disseminating material on Indian librarianship, has recently commenced, in the journal, *Libraries and Culture* (formerly called *Journal of Library History*).

Lessons of History: One

Indian Library Association, has completed its seventy four years of its existence, has found a voice, in its President, P.S.G. Kumar, to spell out what it has learnt in its past performance and what it can do to live long—duely contributing to the cause of progress.

The lessons, in his words, are:

— A professional body should be headed by a professional;
— The president should have a control over the affairs of the Association;
— There should be a close cooperation and understanding between the president and the general secretary;
— Frequent shifting of the office is not at all good for any association;
— The office of ILA should remain in Delhi forever. If necessary a small office be set up for president or secretary when they stay outside Delhi;
— A person elected as president should also be permitted to hold the office for two terms;
— The membership of the Council be cancelled for all those elected persons who fail to attend two consecutive meetings of the ILA Council without giving reason;
— Charge some fee for each nomination;
— Make ILA Bulletin more informative than enlightening;
— Enlarge the publication programme;
— Publications are to be brought out timely;
— All sub-committees appointed by ILA should be subservient to ILA;
— Create professionalism among individuals;
— Sound and detailed policy formulated with regard to financial management of the Association;
— The action taken on a resolution of a body should be reported to the concerned body to the extent possible in writing before the next meeting; and
— A library need to be created immediately and we should enrich the same so that it will serve as a good reference library.

While these are the lessons it has learnt, the morals and the meanings that are to be read in between the lines speak a lot about the state of affairs, and indicating the patterns of growth and the trends it has set. It does not catalogue the achievements nor identify the goals, objectives, etc., but these are dealt in detail in the Indian Professional Works (Kumar, 1994: 95-99).

Lessons of History: Two

The following is conversation that Ranganathan (SRR) did with a Reference Librarian (Ref. Lib), in the context of the lack of intense reference assistance in the libraries. In the words of Ranganathan: "About a year ago, the Reference Librarian of a big library in India called on me. As most librarians do to-day, he began with thanking me for having succeeded in securing the reader's scale of salary for a Reference Librarian". The dialogue begins:

"*SRR:* Your face shows that you are not fully satisfied. Am I right?

Ref Lib: Yes Sir. Money alone does not give satisfaction. I want also work satisfaction.

SRR: According to me, there is nothing in library work giving greater work satisfaction than Reference Service.

Ref Lib: My work as Reference Librarian is to sit in an enclosure, surrounded by the calendars of several universities. As students ask for information about any university, I find it out in the appropriate calendar and give it. But in our University Library, 99 per cent of the questions are only about examination fees, examination time table and occasionally some point on some syllabus. To do this from morning to evening and from day-to-day is boring—indeed maddening.

SRR: My recommendation of Reader's scale of salary and the corresponding professional qualification in the case of Reference Librarian were certainly not for this kind of Reference Service. This is merely Ready Reference Service. A semi-professional can do this work equally well.

Ref Lib: Sir, it is a pity that our Library Authorities have not understood this. (Ranganathan, 1972: Part II, 2-3).

Lessons of History: Three

The Andhra library movement which started and gained momentum in the pre-independence era, had no energies left after the freedom was gained. Freedom at midnight baffled some, and for some it created a sense of relief from all the struggles that were necessary. The library movement lost its flavour and spirit due to many reasons. We may quote a few here:

"Politicians who provided leadership in the establishment of public libraries for awakening the masses in the pre-independence period lost interest in the library movement after the independence of the country;

"Public library legislation gave wrong signals to the organizations and individuals who were interested in library movement that the Government will do all that is needed for library development and their efforts are no more needed;

"The qualified and salaried librarians started keeping the library workers at a distance" (Kumar, 1996: 16).

A Note of Recognition of Associations

Following is the note from the report of the review of the working of the Andhra Pradesh Public Libraries Act, on the need to revive a long standing association:

"The Andhra Pradesh Library Association has a tradition and past history of pioneering service to the people. It may have fallen on lean days in recent years. That should cause us to think of improving its functioning and not break it. More and more enlightened people should join it, make it a more broad based, representative organization and raise to higher levels of effective functioning. The representation accorded to it in this Act should therefore be bent towards improving the organization by removing defects presently noticed, restructuring where necessary and bringing in changes in leadership and formulation at different levels. It is time that the organization makes attempts to retain the reputation that it is a moribund organization, which survives only on paper.

Professionalism

How many professionals in India register themselves as members of professional bodies? How many encourage their own institutions to be on the list of associations to promote the profession? A glance at the list of members of Indian Library Association, in the Table 4.10 reflects the situation.

Before discussing the trends that appear from these figures, it is appropriate to glance at the same data in a Statewise list. The Table 4.11 displays the ILA Statewise membership pattern.

TABLE 4.10: ILA Membership Pattern

Year	*Donor*	*Patron*	*Honorary*	*Life*	*Ordinary*		*Total*	
					Institutional	*Associations*		
90-91	1	1	1	1,274	453	2,270	38	4,038
91-92	1	1	1	1,368	463	2,381	38	4,253
92-93	1	1	1	1,398	306	657	17	2,381
93-94	1	1	1	1,639	343	893	32	2,910
94-95	1	1	1	1,668	343	1,160	32	3,206
95-96	1	1	1	1,838	345	1,245	33	3,464
Nov. '96	1	1	1	1,935	349	1,391	33	3,711

Source: 63rd Annual Report, ILA, 1995-96, p. 20.

TABLE 4.11: Statewise Membership Pattern, as on November 1996

State/UT	*Life*	*Ordinary*	*Institutional*	*Associations*	*Total*
(1)	(2)	(3)	(4)	(5)	(6)
Andhra Pradesh	164	210	25	1	400
Arunachal Pradesh	1	1	—	—	2
Assam	40	21	6	1	68
Bihar	25	17	7	3	52
Goa	14	25	5	1	45
Gujarat	52	40	23	3	118
Haryana	48	79	4	1	132
Himachal Pradesh	18	—	3	1	22
Jammu & Kashmir	7	7	1	—	15
Karnataka	112	111	10	1	234
Kerala	28	12	10	3	53
Madhya Pradesh	68	53	18	1	140
Meghalaya	1	1	2	—	4
Maharashtra	221	279	41	1	542
Manipur	5	—	2	1	8
Mizoram	—	—	1	1	2
Nagaland	5	5	—	—	10
Orissa	56	27	6	—	89
Punjab	49	20	3	1	73
Rajasthan	63	45	12	2	122
Sikkim	—	—	—	—	—
Tamil Nadu	51	76	11	3	141
Tripura	1	—	2	—	3
Uttar Pradesh	123	70	35	1	229
West Bengal	109	36	28	3	176
Andaman & Nicobar Islands	—	—	2	—	2
Chandigarh	51	13	2	—	66
Dadra & Nagar Haveli	—	—	—	—	—
Daman & Diu	—	—	—	—	—

(*Contd.*)

TABLE 4.11 (*Contd.*)

(1)	(2)	(3)	(4)	(5)	(6)
Delhi	570	221	89	1	881
Lakshadweep	—	—	—	—	—
Pondicherry	3	6	1	—	10
Overseas	36	6	1	2	46
Others	14	10	—	—	24
Total	1,935	1,391	350	32	3,708

Source: 63rd Annual Report, ILA, 1995-96, p. 21.

All discussions are around the four types of membership, viz., life (52.1%), ordinary (37.5%), institutional (9.4%) and associations (0.8%). Given the 60 years that have lapsed after the founding of the Association, it is time for analysis to assess the reasons for the low membership figures, in a country which has thousands of libraries, hundreds of library schools, and lakhs of librarians! A democratic country, such as USA, has thousands of members (over 50,000) in the ALA, and so is the situation with LA in the UK. India has not been able to get even the minimum courtesy even from the professional colleagues for a leading and established body, such as ILA! The questions that arise for this state of affair are many, and few can be listed:

(1) Is there a fault with ILA that it does not attract enough following—which other Associations, such as, IASLIC, SIS; ABGILA; BLA; MELA; MALA; etc., are able to do;

(2) Are there a surplus number of such professional bodies in the country, which divert the attention and money that could have otherwise reached ILA;

(3) Is the training that the library schools give does not inspire the products to join fraternities and associations;

(4) Is the library, where the professionals are employed, short of funds to subscribe to the professional body, such as ILA;

(5) Is the subscription fee of the Association so high that all cadres of professionals and all libraries cannot comfortably pay the annual dues;

(6) Is the Association falling short in its propaganda and marketing to reach the libraries and librarians throughout the length and breadth of the country;

(7) Is there a sense of insecurity among the professionals that forces them to feel the need of an organ or a body to whom they could go for rescue;

(8) Is there enough of publications or publishing ability in the Association that it becomes essential for the professionals to subscribe to its output, or rush for getting enlisted as contributors;

(9) Do the professionals have a sense of competitiveness and a need to improve themselves amongst the colleagues and amongst other parallel agencies of information handling to withstand the waves of challenge and competition;

(10) Does the profession have a true meaning in itself to bring in the spirit of comradeship, the spirit of fraternity, the spirit of being one, the spirit which all established professions today cherish;

(11) Is the library occupation a truly fullfledged profession or semi-profession, or marginal profession, given the theory that it falls short of the characteristics of established professions, such as, medicine, engineering and law. Answers to these are not attempted here, and it is left for someone to take up the matter for an indepth analysis at the national level.

We may also quote in this respect, the observations made by a senior professional of what the professional bodies have not been able to achieve. It is Mr. B.L. Bhardwaj, former President of the All India Conference, and former President of the ILA, lamenting on the eve of the fiftieth year of the All India Library Conference:

"Unlike other professional organizations like the Indian Science Congress Association, the Indian Medical (Conference) Association, the Institute of Engineers, the Institute of Chartered and Cost Accountants, etc., it (All-India Library Conference) has little say in the planning and formulation of policies and programmes for library education and training, laying of standards for the provision of library and information services to various sections of our community".

He continues,

"This lack of recognition on the part of powers that appears to be due to two reasons. Firstly, our library conferences have gradually developed after independence, as gathering of practicing librarians to the exclusion of other important sections of the community whose active cooperation, help and support is absolutely essential for the promotion and propagation of library movement. Lack of interaction between the librarians and the educationists, administrators, social workers and policy-makers including the members of the Government, the Parliament and the State assemblies has created a gulf between us, the librarians, and these important partners in the promotion of library movement. The downgrading of the status of the Academic Librarians some years back, was *inter alia*, a result of this lack of interaction and the widening gulf. Again, no mention of libraries in the National Adult Education Programme, a couple of years ago is another instance and such instances can be multiplied".

"Secondly, librarians as a community, have, of late, chosen to live and function in a state of 'splendid isolation' from the community. Very few of them involve themselves in various educational, literary and cultural movements. For instance, how many of them have taken part in programmes like, family and child welfare, adult education, welfare of the backward and weaker sections of the community or for that matter, in the organization of new libraries, reading rooms, book fairs, art exhibitions and cultural programmes. We have thus segregated ourselves from the community at large and have consequently not been able to enlist their sympathy and support for libraries, librarianship and librarians" (1982: XLVIII).

Training Programmes

The Sinha Committee Report, 1959, recommended that library associations must undertake the responsibility of providing basic level training programmes, continuing education programmes, and states:

> "Where a library association is functioning effectively it should be entrusted with the responsibility of training semi-professional personnel by giving them training in elementary library work and awarding certificates of efficiency in 'Elementary Library Work' to successful candidates. The State Government should however lay down standards with regards to contents of the syllabi, duration of courses and selection of teachers and ensure by conducting the examinations that the standards laid down are maintained. Where no library association exists or where it is functioning ineffectively, the State Government through the State Librarian should take up the entire responsibility of training this type of personnel (para 20. . . Sinha Report).

Most of the professional associations in the country are conducting programmes and despite some overlap and duplication of efforts, there is however considerable progress made in this front. On the other hand, the State Governments have not taken up the matter of streamlining the matter of uniformity, standardization of course contents, and so on.

It was in this post-independence era that training became intense and elaborate. With a few university departments teaching library science, before 1948, soon many took up the task of training and education for library work. In this process Ranganathan got the approval and sanction to run a special training centre, for advanced training in reference services, which he called as documentation. For this in his own words,

> "in 1962, with the concurrence of the Prime Minister, the Indian Statistical Institute (ISI) established its Documentation Research Training Centre (DRTC) in Bangalore. Its finance came virtually from the Union Government via the ISI. The then Director General of the Council of Scientific and Industrial Research came to know about it; and he directed the INSDOC to send to DRTC the candidates for training in Documentation" (1972 Part II: 8).

National Library Policy

The Indian librarians under the umbrella of its leading professional body, Indian Library Association (ILA), have made attempts to initiate the process of getting the policy legally cleared and implemented, but nothing much improves, as late as the 50th year of freedom from foreign yoke. ILA submitted its draft policy statement to the Government of India in 1986, so also Raja Ram Mohun Roy Library Foundation prepared a document on the 'National Policy on Library and Information System—A Projection'.

The Association had its annual meetings of various topics to orient the professionals in the lines of raising debate and discussions, and the recent conferences at Chennai, in 1991, dealt exclusively on the topic of 'National Information Policies and Programmes'; in 1994 the seminar discussed 'Library Movement and Library Development in India'; in 1996, it dealt with 'Role of Library in National Development'; and so on. In fact, as early as 1958, Ranganathan himself had taken much interest in participating in a similar seminar. This was organized by the Delhi Library Association, in 1957, and it was entitled 'Library Movement in India'; yet another was at Jaipur, in 1985, under the topic 'National Policy for Library and Information Services'.

These resolutions of conferences and draft policy statements submitted to the Government apart, there has been no response on this national policy from the Government.

Role of the Public

While it is the duty of the profession to train the people in civic responsibility, it is sometimes found that there has been a total failure in this fulfilment of the duty and even in the fulfilment of the responsibility. We have many instances and this is not mere imagination of the pessimists, that the role of the public in treating the library as a social institution as well as a public property has not been upto the mark.

How does the society perceive the role of librarian? One answer could be that a librarian is a person whose help is sought in finding an information source, in finding a document not traced by the user (because of the feeling among the users that the library is a mysterious place, and the catalogue is a super-mystery!!! But rarely a librarian will be approached to solve a problem, to speak about the research methodology, or on how to go about writing a project—despite the faculty status so strongly demanded by the librarian's tribe universally.

> Some critics in the library profession feel that this is what they sowed and now they reap. "Many librarian's themselves accepted this subordinate 'handmaiden's' role and some had even entered the profession in order not to be burdened with professional challenges. It was a notorious fact that library schools were full of 'retreads', who came to librarianship after they had failed in other, more demanding, professions; and, that library school curricula as well as selection procedures provided havens for genteel bookish types who didn't want to cope with demanding clients or theoretical concepts or organization infighting" (Bundy, 1987: 63).

An academic, Prof. M.K. Naik, makes the following remark on the decline of the reading interest in the public:

> "An unholy alliance of many factors has ensured the decline and fall of the well-read man in our own age. First, we live in a civilization which mistakenly believes that mere locomotion is progress . . . we just want to read as fast as we can, mistaking this to be well-read. . . . It is said that a girl took a course like this (i.e., on rapid reading and) was able to read Tolstoy's *War and Peace*—all the

thousand pages and more—in ten minutes flat. Modern science has not only substituted the ideal of the well-read man by that of the 'fast-read' man; it has also practically eliminated the very necessity to be well-read, by providing us with a number of gadgets with the help of which we can spend our leisure hours—without much mental efforts".

"Another development which is responsible for driving a nail into the coffin of the well-read man is the abnormal rise in the price of books during recent years".

Summing up his essay, Prof. Naik, hastens to add "Nevertheless, all said and done, though the well-read man has doubtless suffered a decline, he is not dead and will perhaps never die (1990: 6).

Case Studies

Case One

"The absence of a properly developed civic responsibility make some readers so unscrupulous as to multilate the costly reference books. Here is an extreme example of this anti-social propensity. Some years ago, the article on 'ethics' in the Encyclopedia Britannica of a big Madras library was lost! Surely the book-vandal responsible for this would not have gained any special advantage in having committed that atrocity. It is only his failure to recognize that there were also others to benefit by that article that should have been responsible for his act. The (civic) sense that 'the greatest good for the greatest number' had not developed in him" (Ranganathan, 1988: 266).

Case Two

"I have come across an interesting case of disfigurement. Every line of some new medical books was found underlined in the Madras University Library. This was a problem for us. A new medical book had arrived. It was put on the recent additions shelf. Everybody was on the alert about it. Its inside was examined quite frequently. Its pages were quite clean at 12 noon. At about 1.30 a reader replaced it on the shelf. The book was promptly examined. The lines in about 20 pages were found underlined. The colour of the ink was just the one used by that reader in signing the gate register. He was a rich doctor with wide practice in the city. He was one respected by all.

I showed him this new book. He was not conscious of having underlined in it. But he recognized the colour of his ink. Then, the old underlined books were all shown to him. He felt his mistake. He said that it was probably his unconscious habits. He further offered not to come to the library any longer" (p. 266).

Case Three

"The new building of the Madras University Library was opened in September 1937. There was an unusual rush. I posted myself at the entrance gate to persuade the people to observe the queue. It was then something unknown to people. A knighted gentleman passed alongside the long line in the que and reached the entrance wicked-gate. When I requested him to take his place in the queue, he asked for the meaning of the word (i.e., queue) and later for its spelling. But a more serious situation arose later. An elderly gentleman was exasperated beyond control, when requested to fall into the line and wait his turn to enter. However mildly and however distantly he was requested to do so, he got exasperated and bowled out, 'We are not school children to stand in a line. I am not going to enter this library so long as we are asked to stand in a line like labourers and sepoys" (p. 272).

Case Four

"A parliamentary secretary ascertained by the phone if the library had books on prohibition. He arrived a few minutes later. He had been a professor becoming parliamentary secretary. He was shown books".

He said, "These discuss for and against prohibition. I don't want them. Show me some books on the social aspect of the problem. Where are they kept?"

"Here! In this section 'social pathology—drink devil". There are just a few books here on the prevention of drink devil".

***

"Even these are not to my point. Have you anything on prohibition law?"

"Yes, here are two books".

***

"These too are no good".

"What is it exactly that you want?" "Have you any book on the administration and enforcement of prohibition policy?"

***

"No, no! These are no good. They only deal with smuggling, bootlegging, and so on".

"Perhaps we may be able to find out something helpful if you can say what particular problem you have in mind".

"I want information about exemption from prohibition law. In the acts, you simply come across the phrase 'unless' exempted".

"I expect that the details about exemptions will be found in the rules framed under the acts. They will be mostly executive orders and may not find a place in other books".

"The *poojarees* insists that wine is necessary for temple worship. You know that it is the thin edge of the wedge. I want to know how similar problem have been met in other countries".

"Ordinary books are not likely to go into such details. Perhaps the annual reports on the working of the prohibition act or reported cases may give some information" (Ranganathan, 1961: 221-222).

The colleagues whom he trained were inspired with so much of vigour and tenacity that they led to the creation of a generation of dedicated and motivated reference librarians in India. These user-friendly attitudes were well received and revolutionized the concept of library, from a storehouse to interacting and participating reference centre. This was the result of the rigorous and strenuous training Ranganathan provided to his colleagues.

Case Five

The Hindu College, Delhi which publishes its college magazine carries a write up by a user of the Library:

> "The locks are gone! One gasps in wonder and amazement. 'No! it can't be!', and similar platitudes spring to one's mind as one gazes in disbelief at the unlocked cupboards of textbooks which line the wall of the Reading Room. A swift renaissance has been triggered within the precincts of the Hindu College Library. To seek knowledge one does not have to fill in Demand Slips: one has just to open the (unlocked) cupboard to carry away armfuls of the books. The 1,500 odd textbooks can be issued out on three separate tickets meant exclusively for them (giving us an option to borrow up to six books at a time). Reference books, too, are easily accessible now. A

fortnightly list of the 'new arrivals' (books, that is) is prepared and they are attractively displayed. Among other improvements is the complete overhauling of the Reserve Section, which now has over 2,000 separately catalogued textbooks (besides the 1,500 loanable ones)".

"Behind these refreshing changes are our Librarian's (who took over about a year ago) sincere efforts to improve everything in his control that needs improving. He runs the largest College Library in Delhi—44,000 volumes varying from Thornton's five-volume. A History of British India (original 1841 edition) to the latest novel by Norman Mailer. All this is on the plus side but what about the other aspect?"

"The Library supposedly receives 150 periodicals but, on repeatedly carrying out random surveys I have unfortunately found many important magazines missing or outdated. Notable among these were expensive weeklies like *The Economist and Eastern Economist, Life, Imprint, Reader's Digest, Popular Science, New Times*, etc., appear sporadically but fortunately *Time and New Statesman* are available regularly".

"It has been confirmed after investigations that no one in the Library is responsible for the regular disappearance of the magazines. There are pressures the Librarian cannot oppose and in this context it is relevant to point out that each student contributes 30 rupees annually (which adds up to 45,000 rupees, i.e., 75% of the Library's budget) and the U.G.C. provides the remaining amount".

"The students are justified in expecting these facilities to be oriented to their benefit. All the latest issues of the magazines should be available to them within the Reading Room and should not be permanently sent to certain other parts of the college campus".

"In conclusion, it must be pointed out to the authorities that one of the root causes of the present indiscipline among students is (besides the bad example set by the elders) the non-availability of productive channels to utilize their excess time and energy. The average Hinduite drifts to the cafe to pass his time in idle gossip till the next class. Perhaps (and it sounds rather trivial) a more up-to-date and complete array of magazines would lure him to the Library" (Chandler, 1971: 75-76).

Chandler, who is reproducing this comment, cannot resist making his own observation, and to quote him is but natural, "The author of this article exposed one reason why students do not get the library facilities they need: the professors and lecturers have, understandably, first choice. This is one explanation why Eastern and Western students flock to public libraries where they normally have parity of treatment with other readers. Unfortunately public libraries in India are underdeveloped and are not able to assist greatly. An exception is the Delhi Public Library" (pp. 76-77).

Case Six

What people do, if they find that a library is being closed or shifted to another area? The users of Mysore University Library, in 1965, protested on the idea of shifting of the University Library to the new campus.

Since many learned and elite used the old library, there was a strong protest against this decision. The authorities agreed to retain, at least 10,000 volumes which were selected to meet the needs of those citizens, with adequate staff to manage the resources.

Case Seven

At a seminar held by the National Book Trust at Bangalore, in 1976, one of the participants—a famous novelist complained that he could not get easy access to any library in the city in order to gather material for one of his novels.

The point is, the university and research libraries, must open their doors, to the reading public. Two factors necessitate this demand: one, the lack of good public libraries in the country; and second, given the shortage of resources, no public library can satisfy all the needs of all users—leading to the idea of resource sharing as well as the idea of university and research libraries must be accessible to all who wish to be informal learners. By implication, one may find that there is another reason for the opening up of doors of different libraries: all academic and research libraries expect their users to find their individual information elsewhere; a scientist has to go to public library or create an ideal community information centre for all information necessary for the daily survival!

Case Eight

Dear X

I am in need of 'Post-structuralism and the Question of History', ed. by Derek Attridge. Can I request you to kindly return the book on

the DUE DATE 28-3-1997? I need it only for a few days—so if your need is greater you will have it back in the first week of April!
Thanks a lot.
Y

This note was placed on a Carrell, and the librarian found this unusual·note. It is unusual because of two reasons: ordinarily members when they see books on other carrels either take it away from the carrel without any notice, and misplace it; or such highly demanded books on literary criticism are being stolen. This note speaks of the genuine interest in accessing the book, through a genuine method of accessing, the required book. With the increase in research and study in literary theory and the shortage of such books in other libraries, the library which possess the largest number of such books has recently got into serious trouble—mutilation and stealing books is the most frequent resort by such users.

Case Nine: Friends of Camels

"Some time ago I was visiting Jaipur and there is very nice organization called 'Balrashmi' for children. In the villages around I found a camel cart on which were fixed a number of almirahs full of books. As the camel travels from one village to the other carrying these books, a librarian collects the books which have already been read and issues new books. Any time the camel arrives in the village all children run to it . . . *baiwala aa gaya! baiwala aa gaya!* As they know, they are friends of the camel, they feed the camel, they bring their old books; they take new ones and the camel goes on. A very nice example of an essential service!" (Yashpal, 1995: 9).

Case Ten: A Word from an Academic

In the 'introduction', to Fazal Elahi's "Reference Assistance to Indian Readers: A Text Book for Librarians", Prof. Radhakamal Mukherjee (Head of the Department of Sociology and Economics, Lucknow University), writes:

"In the Indian libraries reference aid is seldom given. The lack of this service prevents us from getting the best out of our library resources, meagre as these are. In the absence of reference work as a function of Indian libraries, I feel that this excellent handbook, which summarizes reference material usually available in India, will be of great aid to both library workers and general readers".

Case Eleven: A Writer's Impression

R.K. Narayan has the following, interesting observation on how the people have different priorities, even if they are contributing to the so called library movement:

> "Recently when I visited a certain important town I saw a new library building coming up at a feverish speed. The name-boards of the architect, contractor, electrician, and sanitary engineers, stood up on all sides of the compound in letters of gold. The ground was swept, lawns were laid and watered desperately, and all workmen were finishing up their tasks by gas light. I felt pleased: the thought that someone was hurrying on at a desperate speed to provide cultural amenities to the townsmen was a very pleasant and sustaining thought. I felt that you couldn't see that zest in any other part of the world. I felt that the friendship of those who were responsible for this was worth cultivating, I sought them out and expressed my feelings. They were naturally pleased with the compliment and were willing to give me all the facts connected with it. I learnt that the building was costing them two lakhs of rupees. They gave me the names of all technicians who were at work there, and concluded, "According to the terms of the contract the building must be handed over to us by the tenth of this month".
>
> "Why such a firm date?"
>
> "Otherwise it will be of no use for us, Sir . . . will be passing this way on the Tenth and he has agreed to perform the opening ceremony. If the building is not in our hands on that date it will be practically useless for us afterwards". I could not accept the statement. "Why do you say that it will be useless? You may always stock the books and start using the building any moment, irrespective of whether an eminent man is passing this way or not?"
>
> Oh, books! he said, "We are not bothered about that now. We are thinking of only the opening ceremony". I could not help asking, "When are you going to bother about it, anyway?" "Oh, can't say. It will depend upon the funds available at the end of all this".
>
> "If and when you decide to admit books into the library what will be your procedure for acquiring them?"

"We will probably call for tenders for the supply of books. We want to encourage the local booksellers and distribute the patronage evenly".

I couldn't help asking "How are you going to select the volumes?"

"We shall leave it to the booksellers. We shall first measure the total shelf space, get an approximate idea of the number of volumes required to fill them, and call for quotations for the supply of this quantity. Anyway we are not going to worry about this detail now. Our first requirement is building and furniture. After that we must find funds for sending up someone for library training, for which we are already receiving numerous applications".

"And so I gathered the following facts and figures about the library:

Building Rs. 2,00,000; Lighting Rs. 15,000; Plumbing etc. Rs. 12,000; Garden lay-out and Supervisors charges Rs. 5,000; Counter, shelves, and furniture Rs. 30,000; Opening ceremony, printing of invitations, welcome address, president's speech, and secretary's report Rs. 2,000; pandal and tea Rs. 4,000 and Books No budget yet".

"I shall leave it without further comment" (*Hindu*, 5 April 1953). These are the priorities in the country, building, inauguration, pomp and glory in the exterior and interior, books no funds, staff no need, users—who are these, why do they need books?

Misuse of the Libraries

People, as well as, communities have abused libraries. It was a matter of shame for people to hide the idea that they are stealing books from libraries. But with the changing times, it is a fashion to display and proudly claim that they are stealing books from libraries, and justify it too.

The book *The Anatomy of Bibliomania* by Holbrook Jackson, has many types of book lovers, loving book for itself, as fashion—positive attitude, and as a sadist thinking that others should not have access to it—negative attitude. Book stealing also has many reasons. Some steal to do mischief, some enjoy misplacement, some have vengeance and do it with logic of their own, and some go mad in this process of creating a record in such acts.

We may quote certain instances that are recorded in Indian libraries of book stealing, book damaging, book destroying, and so on.

Case One

In a library at 9 a.m., someone is found throwing a book *Princeton Encyclopedia of Poetry and Poetics* from a window. The staff notice this. They catch the library user. The user apologizes, on being confronted by the chief of the library staff. Suspecting that he has been into this for a long, he is told that his house will be searched by the staff members. The user reluctantly agrees. The staff accompany him and he takes them to a house where not a single book is traced. The user returns and is told by the officer incharge that because of his mis-behaviour and misconduct, his membership is terminated and he cannot use the library anymore.

Case Two

A user comes to the library and returns three books. These are not checked out. Still he has taken them home and is approaching the librarian with these three books. He informs the librarian that he is guilty of having taken away these books without following procedure. The librarian enquiries with him, as to why he did so.

The user says that he did it for whatever reason, but also goes on to add: 'I have many more books at my home, and I can show you all those'.

'Is it!', shockingly the librarian responds. By his speech and behaviour, the user looks abnormal. He stammers, and repeats his own words, with such a frequency that it is irritating to hear the same guilt feelings. Later the talk turned into angry conversation, on being questioned about the method adopted in this stealing process. He refused to divulge the trick and said there are ways and means of stealing and he did not wish to disclose the same.

He says again in affirmative, that he does have more books and is willing to show it to any one who wishes to come to his house and have a look. The user willingly gives his address, and phone number too.

The librarian deputes two staff to visit his house, and before they embark on this trip, confirms from the given contact number: 'we have been told there are some books of ours at your place, can we come and have a look at these?'

The respondent on phone says, 'yes, why not, please come'. And admits, 'My son has a problem, and he is not keeping god health, and for this reason he did this nasty job of taking away your books. I am willing to help you in tracing your books, but assure me that you will not harm my son, or harm his reading interests. My son is in need of moral and all kind of support, and hence I request you to be kind towards him".

The librarian assures all positive approach in this whole episode.

The two staff members then reach the house of the user. There is a feeling of unknown type: how will the user treat us—badly, generously, madly, crazily? How will he react to showing the books? What could be the course of action—after being shown around the house?

The loud thinking process ended, when a servant took us in, in a minute the user saw us, and was dead serious, yet he said, 'have your seat!' a great relief indeed. 'See I have no problem in showing you these books!

But retorts again, 'why do you want to see these', I have not done anything wrong. I have these books from so many libraries, and none has suspected me on this, why are you people madly chasing me?'

The servant serves tea, and gives a relief from the haunting eyes of the member—talking to himself, throwing the cigarette, and acting very funny.

The staff have no answer, since the user is annoying to the limits, staring on the face of the staff, as if they were criminals, and he a decent civilian—interrogating them!

He gradually gets up and moves around his house, as if he is too busy and we are wasting his time. He disappeared twice and it looked as if he was searching for more books inside the house. Nothing like that happened. The staff carried no warrant to search, and did not even carry a notice to seek legal entry into his house—they were as if breaking his house and stealing all the precious pearls lying there. He points towards the shelf adjacent to the wall, where hundreds of books are shelved, saying:

'These are all mine, you have no right to search my house?'

'I have paid for xeroxing these!' and there are on the shelves a few more hundreds neatly xeroxed, bound and wrapped up—to hide whatever would have been otherwise evident!

The two keep mum, because of the confrontation with this bibliomaniac was not normal and never quite predictable. Finally, he showed up all the books around, and the two picked up whatever seemed to be the property of their library.

Why was it difficult and a sort of searching in the lot to identify the corpses? It was an uphill task, to gather sand from the mouth of the ants literally.

All books had been so badly mutilated, so neatly cleared off their identification marks, that no expert on the earth could identify these, and then declare as the property of some library. Title pages were cut off. The secret page missing, or the place where one could find the library's seal cleared off with the help of ink-remover, or cut off neatly. Book pockets torn off, and due dates slips did not exist at all. A Sherlock homes case indeed.

With a great reluctance, after continuous persuasion to return these identified books as the property of the concerned library, the user finally agreed to do so. He allowed over a dozen books, seemingly the rightful property, to be taken back. He, however, unhappily, identified the books, and saw to it, that, he was giving away only 'genuine' books, and not any books from his personal or other collections!

He later reached the library, met the librarian, and gave a letter, stating that his was an unpardonable crime, and was out and out guilty for the act of his. He would not divulge on two things: why did he do so, and how did he do so, till the last.

The officer-in-charge looked into the case history, and put up the case for terminating the member from the library. Whether termination of membership is the only course of action, or not, the debate may go on.

Case Three

A person enjoys stealing books from a Contact library. Wilfully admits the act, and justifies it by saying, that is one form of anti-colonial vengeance. See for this Upamnayu Chatterjee's protagonist in his celebrated first novel (English August), Ogu.

Case Four

At 7.15 p.m. a retired scientist (RS) approaches the Reference Librarian (RL) for books on optics. The user is shown books in reference section on the subject. The user returns unsatisfied. RS enquires:

> "Do you have a book or volume or symposium—like thing purely on optics?" He is shown Proceedings of the symposium on modern optics, New York, 1967. Which he finds of no help. "Sir, would you kindly tell me what exactly you are searching for?", enquires RL.
>
> RS writes down the article, on being asked to do, the name of the article: 'Karbowiak, Optics-coherence' and says "This is the article which I remember to have read in this library sometime back.

The author, I am certain, is Karbowiak, but the title of the article may be something like 'optical coherence or coherence optics', etc. I am not sure whether Karbowiak edited the book or he is one of the authors of the book".

RL: "Sir, is it likely that you have read this article from some book you borrowed from our library or some book from the lending collection because, if that is so, we need not search in these Reference Books which are not lent out".

The RS wishes to see the books in the lending collection, from where he returns without the required information.

The RL's guess than leads to searching Recent Additions List. Next they search the indexes and abstracts, but with no success. The RS asks for the journals received on microwaves. One journal which is not available in the library, but is listed in Ulrich is searched for price and other information. RS requests the RL to procure it from any local library.

The journal is procured, in a week's time. That journal had an article, whose citation referred to the required item. The article contained the citation and gave the reference details. It turned out that the citation referred to the Advances in Microwaves, v. 1. This was available in the library and the user was given the same immediately.

(The requirement was not spelled correctly, instead of optical wave guides, the RS asked for optics-coherence. The library didn't have an analytical catalogue either to trace chapters. The book was received and displayed in May 1967, and the RS was insisting that he had seen it recently in 1969; hence the delay) (G.S. Raghavendra Rao, 1986: 543-45).

Case Five: A Typical Day of a Villager

"Dasrath, a small farmer from a typical Indian village, gets up early in the morning most part of the year and almost off to work in his small farm. He takes ore or more hands of labour with him in the agricultural season. He works hand in hand with them. Only he gives them the directions. Ploughing, transplanting, irrigating and right up to threshing is part of his work depending on the season. His work days have no fixed hours. After putting in a few hours in the morning, he takes a break for lunch. He stops by a few close fellow farmers on the way and makes casual inquiries and mostly that is where he updates his local information.

There is always something to do for Dasrath. Straighten the fence, weeding or mending something. He would be back in the fields by later after-noon supervising the labour and giving instructions. A visit to the tea stall or the village bus stand for casual talks with the acquaintances. And almost that is how his days go".

"Dasrath is not formally educated, but as a fairly successful farmer he operates with a fair amount of certainty. He has learnt how to go about fertilizing the field, how much of urea, for instance, is required to make the best of the profits, what brand of seeds to use, and all such things. He talks to other villagers, enquires in the cooperative society and other shops that is where he gets his information. He knows the extension workers. He has been one of the willing adopters of their suggestions. But he has always cross checked with other farmers before going for any change. He makes his finer judgements about people he talks to and is not always readily taken in by all kinds of suggestions. Yes, he wants to fare better".

"What can a library give him? Information about improved agricultural practices? Modern implements for small farmers like him, minimum agricultural prices, rights and duties under PR? Yes, certainly. But he would not be in to read any of them even if he knows how to go about it. For him actually seeing/doing is believing. Yes, he listens to the radio and these days also watches his own TV. That is where his dreams and aspirations come from".

"Naidu, on the other hand, is a successful big farmer. He has a leisurely life and has most of the luxuries a village can name of—tractor, fridge, cable TV, and a house. Many people work for him. He just supervises and takes care of marketing. He has better links with all local and district level agricultural agencies. He knows about the government schemes and the improved agricultural methods. He has the where-withal to risk and experiment. His circle of acquaintances include other farmers in the district and of course friends and relatives. He is a big operator in the local power structure. Most of his day goes in interacting with them. Yes, he knows about a lot of stray things through casual talks, small time leisure readings and watching TV. Would he read a book on new agricultural methods if housed in a big library? Typically he would not" (Satish, 1997: 79-80).

Information, Dissemination and Disinformation

From institutional point of view many public institutions play roles directly and indirectly. The National Institute of Advanced Studies

(NIAS), Bangalore, in its report, presents a list of sponsored programmes and mentions the following:

(a) 'A 4-week Workshop on "Documentation of Performing Arts" organized by the National Centre for the Performing Arts, Mumbai, was held from September 15 to October 12, 1992'. The activity, called documentation, relates to the method of facilitating information access through all possible means. In this Workshop the business is concerned with the documentation of the field of performing arts, i.e., theatre, fine arts, music, drama, etc.

(b) Another programme relates to the context of technology and nuclear disarmament. If technology interests war related efforts, technology related information storage and retrieval also gets into the scene, and this is more relevant in terms of intellectual property rights; the programme details are: 'A high level non-official Indo-US joint meeting on "Technology Transfer and Non-proliferation" was held from January 17 to 21, 1994. The Indian team was headed by Raja Ramanna and the United States team by Mr. Robert S. McNamara'.

(c) Yet another activity relates to women in relation to literacy. If literate mothers can be more responsible and India, more than any body else needs these, then its value in our geo-cultural context is very high, and the details are as follows: 'UNESCO-NIAS National Action Research Conference on "Women and Literacy" on the request from the UNESCO, Institute of Education, Hamburg, was organized by NIAS from December 13 to 15, 1994'.

(d) Information is a raw material, its handling and integration with knowledge has also interested the people in this Institute. The purpose of such an orientation course, is to address the issues relating to knowledge explosion, and the speed which it occurs and thereby it is creating specialization and making it difficult to view the world as one whole. 'This we believe can lead to unbalanced decision. The danger is even greater in a country like India, sitting as we are on the threshold of a great leap forward with economic liberalization and gobalization having been accepted as our national policies". The major themes the conference includes are "The communication revolution: Technological, Social and Psychological Implications for India".

The title of the course is 'an integrated approach to knowledge and information' conducted from 8 January to 3 February, 1996, at NIAS. In terms of the details, if one wishes to see how it integrates the twain: knowledge and information, one has very little detail in its invitation mailed for the potential applicants, or in the report, except that the integration is in terms of understanding the integration in the sense of its base and components and how it can be suitably reconciled as a whole, with the able assistance of the faculty at the Institute, representing disciplines as widely different as Social Anthropology, Science and Technology, Psychology, Environmental Sciences, etc.

Other Comments on the Role of the Public

Carl White, the American library expert, made a critical comment on lack of user reaction, despite the sick condition of Delhi University Library, and stated:

> 'Had the library by some misfortune been suddenly dropped into the Jamuna River during the early years, the loss would have been regrettable but I search in vain for any convincing evidence of daily demands upon it by teachers and teaching assignments which would have caused the academic programmes, as then conducted to suffer from the disaster".

Another professional laments the lack of an interest in the people to demand free library service in the country:

> "Inspite of a quarter of a century of library movement, not more than two States have thought it necessary to have library legislation. Political pressure would have been brought to bear on the legislatures if there was a conscious demand by the vociferous segment of the electorates. But that segment, i.e., the literate industrial proletariat is dormant. With the development of large scale industries in the Five Year Plans, the rise of an army of semi-skilled and literate industrial workers could be foreseen and their demand for intellectual pastime will have to be provided for. It may, therefore, reasonably be hoped that the assurance of the Minister of Education for a net-work of libraries through the country in 1961 will be implemented and a new era of intellectual activity will be ushered in the country" (C.S. Krishnamurthi, 1958: 41).

Prof. Girja Kumar, states the kind of misuse is thus stated:

> "In the Jawaharlal Nehru University Library, with the graph of utilization of the library going up steeply, the instances of the mutilation of books went up alarmingly, thus leading to questioning of the very basis of open access system in an academic library. . . . The idea of an exhibition of mutilated books (189 volumes over a period of nine months, January-September 1979) struck a sympathetic chord" (Kumar, 1986: 322).

The public have made no serious attempts to demonstrate the need for any good libraries, and this may have been due to the existence of different reasons, such as, low literacy, lack of competitive spirit in educational and professional activities, unproductive educational system, lack of serious reading habits, etc.

Philanthropists and Voluntarism

Ford Foundation, Rockefeller, and the like philanthropic agencies, and private or public funding agencies such as USAID, IMF, World Bank, UNIDO, UNO, UNICEF, etc., have set a model in funding for secular and modern libraries and educational academies. These have no parallel in India, let alone the unique contribution made by the Carnegie Foundation in the USA. There were also libraries, such as in Germany, who refused to accept the gift of Carnegie, because the grant explicitly stated, what to buy and for whom, under the Grant for acquisitions. The Germans said in their rejection note that they know better what to buy for their users and do not need an outsider to dictate in this matter. In this sense, one can accept or reject the offer of fund-givers, if the terms and conditions are not suitable or politically incorrect.

In India, we would find hardly any institution rejecting a foreign grant, on any ground whatsoever, rather innumerable grants have poured in the country from the Western world, in the post-independent India. Even UNESCO and other international bodies have contributed enormously in the process of developing the library system in India.

There are a few instances of this category of fund givers in India, including the Tata's, the Birla's, the patronage by former rulers, private trusts, and so on. One attempt, worth citing here, is the establishment of The Sri Venkateswara University, Tirupati, which is run by the Temple funds, to promote study and research on a secular basis.

Religious and other funding agencies, have been enormous, who have established educational institutions all over the country, and this is not limited to any caste or community. The Parsi's, Muslim's, Jain's, Jagat Guru's, Ramakrishna's, and the like, have enormous number of educational institutions that promote the objectives of the parent body.

Birla Institute of Technology, Thapar Institute of Engineering and Technology, Tata Institute of Social Research, Tata Institute of Fundamental Research, Bhaba Atomic Research Centre, Indian Institute of Science (founded by J.N. Tata in 1909 under the Charitable Endowments Act of 1890) are all now Central Government managed institutions, and the name they carry is for the reason that they were only initially financed, and, in some cases, continue to be partially financed.

A case in point is the on-going experiment of the idea of Friends of the Library, at the American Studies Research Centre, Hyderabad. This is the idea of developing fund raising activity, in these days of economic instability and financial crunch. There are pros and cons of this and still experimenting on a new venture is not a bad idea. Strangely, funding a library, or a social cause, even if called secular cause, is still a difficult preposition in India.

One can raise fund for music, dance, and similarly for games like cricket in India today, but one cannot venture on the idea of raising a few lakhs or crores for the purpose of promoting educational and research libraries!!!

A search in Indian library literature revealed that there is some thought being given to developing the idea of Friends of the Library. Prof. Krishan Kumar, makes a clear need of the idea of the friends in the development of libraries (Kumar, 1993: 10).

Further, "Friends of the library associations' are an effective method of utilizing PR (public relations) to enlist support—both financial and material—for the university library. Generally, these are voluntary bodies which invite contributions/subscription from users—past, present and potential, and non-users too for library development. . . . For example, the Library Friends of the University of Illinois at Urbana-Champaign with a total membership of over 3,000 contributed $93,103 to the University Library during 1990-91. Their total contribution since 1972, the year of its founding, is over $1,500,000. 'Library friends' is a designated annual fund membership group with the goal to promote private support and to develop public awareness of the library's vast resources" (Jagga Rao and Prafulla Chandra, 1993: 193-94).

Five Laws and Library Movement

As Ranganathan has suggested the Five Laws watch around every library to see how much are the libraries loyal to them! We may use the same five laws to see if the library developments in post-independent India are befitting the expectations of the five laws, or they are otherwise!!!

The first law, books are for use, relates to the point that in a modernized library system, the idea of having books must be exclusively for use of information which these contain. The second law, every reader his/her book, connotes the idea that each user in the society, must find right information at the right time. The third law, every book its reader, means that each book in the library must have a user, if a book is not used, it must go out and get a user, and if it fails to get a user it must be removed from the otherwise useful collection! The fourth law, save the time of the user, calls for providing the right information to the right reader with a minimum loss of time and other resources. The fifth law, library is a growing organism, dispels the idea that a library like dead body is not in need of life saving sources. Library, in fact is a living and progressing body of the society meant only for use; its readers must find what they need and its collection must not be an idle workshop; its time saving devices must attract more and more to develop the personality—materially and spiritually—and in turn demonstrate that its life giving approach to the society, has to be handled with care, a care that is given to all growing organisms. Also that the location, equipment, furniture, stack-room location and arrangement, extension activity, working hours, reference and referral service, and so on provide a basis for overall test of the situation that prevails all over today.

These tests would demonstrate how far libraries have been modernized and how far these have become user-friendly in the holistic sense of the term? Depending on the prevailing situation, the laws protest, condemn, rejoice, bless and praise, but they do not surrender or submit to the evil designs of the monsters.

Location

To test the loyalty of the library to this facet one has to ask questions, such as, is the library located at a convenient place in the society? Is the library accessible to all-irrespective of mobility or immobility or users? Is the location in such a place where women, children and aged can reach freely without hassles of crossing busy lanes, walking in dark lanes, and so on? Is the location of the reception and reference convenient for those who are shy or otherwise to find out by themselves a help desk? Are the stack room and other sections shown on a map at the entrance, to save time of a new comer to the library? Are there proper guides and bays which help in navigating in the library, and in finding the required section or persons?

Facilities, Equipment, and Furniture

What facilities and amenities make the library usable, and user-friendly? What are the minimum necessary items—which make the library appear as a peaceful and calm place for reading and concentrating? What facilities are required to acquire, store, preserve and retrieve information without any loss of time? What facilities are necessary to prevent the books from hazards—health, human, biological, physical, natural, etc.? What type of light, ventilation, and natural surroundings make reading a fun, reading a pleasure, and reading an educational endeavour? What type of chairs, tables and other furniture are required for the young, old, children, handicapped, etc.? What equipment is essential and what can be of less important in storage and retrieval of information in this age of information revolution and technological revolution? Is the building functional and well designed to save the time of the reader and to cater to the present and immediate future needs of the users?

Reference Service

What is the type of help a library must give irrespective of the type of user, type of collection, type of environment in which it is existing? Service mindedness or the attitude to serve the users calls for basic motivations and orientation—do these exist and do these exist at a level which Ranganathan specifies in the laws of library science?

Initiation of the Fresh Men (User Education)

If there are library staff to help the users, in making them acquainted with the library and acquainted with the search strategies, are these librarians doing the work with a missionary zeal, or doing it for the sake of it? Are the user education skills picked up on the job or it is included in the training and education they receive in the library schools? If picked up on the job, are there continuing education programmes to bring in this some level of maturity and perfection, and not left at a layman's level to handle the daily rounds of user education?

Extension Service

Do libraries outreach and extend the information resource to all those who cannot or normally do not reach the library? Do libraries go out in search of new users? Do libraries go out and inform the actual users about topical materials that interest them? Do libraries aim at initiating the reading habits among the neo-literates? Are there ways and means to sustain the acquired level of literacy among the neo-literates?

These and many more questions are to be answered if the five laws are to be confirmed and if Ranganathan must not roll in the grave!!!

Growth of Cooperation: Libraries and Other Agencies

The discussion of cooperation and interaction here includes information handling agencies, and information promotion agencies, such as archives, publishers, book traders, system's specialists, media and communication specialists, etc.

The history of book is incomplete without the history of the authorship, reading and publishing, all treated as a whole. This is the main intention of this section, which tries to see the development of book from a holistic perspective.

Information is a primary resource for individual and also for institutional development. Hence information is handled with care by all those who take the responsibility of providing access to information. Information handling agencies are many, it includes both formal systems, such as, libraries, and informal systems, such as, media.

It is strange that while all information handling agencies are for acquiring, processing, storing and providing information to the society, none of these have been able to integrate and converge in the interest of providing an efficient and effective service to the society.

How do people get information. People do not wait for anyone agency to bring information. In the age of survival of the fittest, every one manages to get information from wherever one can. For instance, "When ADT-27, a paddy variety, was introduced in Tamil Nadu's Thanjavur District, All-India Radio (AIR) put out a story. Farmers who heard it and adopted this variety informed their neighbours and recommended 'Radio Paddy' meaning ADT-27, to others" (Murthy, 1996: 47). That is, there is a variety of role for each information agency in the society, and each role is equally important. Further, this idea works very well in today's media culture, when the people are addicted to the screens (earlier to radio), and all important information can be easily conveyed.

Another instance can also be relevant, "When child labour eradication personnel interviewed the parents and mentioned that there are several

State and Centrally sponsored programmes to assist them to cross the economic barrier, many of them said that they were not aware of such programmes or facilities" (Murthy, 1996: 47). This refers to the lacunas in the society to transmit really relevant and significant information to the right people at the right time. Socio-economic development of individuals as well as of the country is largely dependent on the availability of information, among other factors, and this is an obvious finding of many studies conducted in the post-World War II era.

The value of information is then as stated by the learned author "It is now an accepted fact the practical and useful agricultural information is an essential as any other input like fertilizers, irrigation and improved seeds for farmers to increase their farm yields. Such information that flows out of agricultural research institutions under the Indian Council of Agricultural Research, New Delhi, if properly taken to farmers by the communication media, will increase the yield per hectare as it happened in the case of dwarf varieties of seeds, or result in any other economic advantage to the farmer" (Murthy, 1996: 48).

How does the Government provide access to information which it generates, in terms of policies, plans, technical matters, etc. This is visible in the output of large amount of information generated by the different ministries. For example the Ministry of Agriculture's Directorate of Extension, has the Farm Information Unit, provides this access through its network of agencies. It publishes four monthly magazines, leaflets, pamphlets, bulletins, posters, etc. Its monthly journal, Intensive Agriculture intends to provide information for the extension workers and progressive farmers. Home Science, another monthly, aims to cater to the issues relating to domestic life of the ruralites. Whatever is generated is circulated to a large audience, including supply of blocks and photographs to newspapers in regional languages, free of cost, for a wider audience. Additionally, it produces, in collaboration with the Ministry of Information and Broadcasting, films. These films, about 40 reels, contain educational, motivational and research topics, among others, these carry the message of improved agriculture to the rural community (Murthy, 1996: 51).

Multiple Media

Such collaborative trends are many, and these are a healthy sign of integration and convergence of the information handling agencies. A mixed media approach alone can attend to the type of illiterate masses which India has.

"We have a national literacy rate of about 52 per cent. The situation of rural areas is much worse than national average. It implies that we have a big chunk of our rural population who are illiterate and cannot take full advantage of the print media. One of the major problems of rural development in India is lack of effective communication strategy with appropriate mix-media, to educate the masses as well as transfer and transmit the development messages. On the one hand we have access to the most modern communication technology and on the other hand we do not have conducive conditions in rural areas to make effective use of this modern communication technology. The lack of infrastructure, lack of electric supply, non-availability of audio-visual equipments are some of the constraints posed by rural areas vis-a-vis new technology. It is, therefore, advisable to look for a media-mix which can effectively be used both to educate people as well to make them aware about various development programmes initiated from time to time for their betterment" (Aslam, 1996: 10).

What is referred to media-mix can be a combination of one or more of the variety of print, non-print, audio-visual, satellite, sources and channels.

There is a greater need to bring all information handling agencies together as a coherent and integrated unit. For this one of the important steps required is to coordinate all the governmental activity that goes in a very clear decentralized manner all through. For instance, a variety of Central and State ministries have programmes and all the developmental programmes have no linkages, and if at all there is a link or connection, it is very superficial. The work relating to rural development is spread over in more than ten ministries, include Ministry of Rural Areas and Employment, Ministry of Welfare, Ministry of Labour, Ministry of Education, Ministry of Industry, Ministry of Civil Supplies, Ministry of Welfare, Ministry of Health, etc. So also the matter of information agencies is with a number of ministries, such as Ministry of Information and Broadcasting, Ministry of Education, Ministry of Culture (which looks after the National Library, among others), etc.

Efforts at Creating a Book Culture

The Central and State Governments in the independent India have made some efforts to spread book culture. These are visible in a number of activities. The list though long, has the following establishments:

National Book Development Council (1967), New Delhi;
National Book Trust (1957), New Delhi;
National Council of Science and Technology Communication (1982), New Delhi;
National Information System in Science and Technology (1977), New Delhi;
National Medical Library (1966), New Delhi;
Indian National Scientific Documentation Centre (1952), New Delhi;
Indian Council of Social Science Research (1969),
National Social Science Documentation Centre (1970), New Delhi;
UNESCO's Book Coupon programme through the Indian National Commission;
National Book Fair, New Delhi (annual feature) (first such exhibition in 1966 at Bombay);
Federation of Indian Library Associations (1966) formed at Chandigarh; etc.

Among others, the list includes:

- Instituting the Office of National Research Professor (1965) and Ranganathan's appointment;
- Constituting of a National Advisory Board (1966) under the Union Ministry of Education to advise on matters relating to library development;
- Establishing Institutes of National Importance Act (1969) (as per this provision, the Parliament approved Khuda Bakhsh Library at Patna in 1969, Raza Library at Rampur in 1974);
- Central Government's acceptance of the Wheat Loan Programme, effective 1954, helped directly and indirectly in promotion of library development in India;
- Establishment of Central Reference Library at National Library, Calcutta (shifted back from Delhi in 1959), this division helps in compilation of Indian National Bibliography;
- The establishment of publication division of each ministry, including that of Union Ministry of Information and Broadcasting;
- Raja Ram Mohun Roy Library Foundation's (f. 1972) Book Assistance Programme, Assistance towards building up adequate stock of books and reading and visual materials, Assistance towards development of rural book deposit centres and mobile

library services, Assistance to Centrally sponsored libraries (such as Jawahar Bal Bhavans, Aurobindo Bal Kendras);
— Award of annual prize, instituted by the Government, for excellence in printing and designing of publications;
— Reduction of mailing charges to half of the acutal for printed matter by the Department of Posts;
— Declaring a separate ministry for libraries (1971), the first Minister of the State for the Libraries was A. Madan Mohan;
— Establishing of the Office of Book Promotion, Ministry of Education & Social Welfare, New Delhi;
— Establishing of a library on wheels (a long distance train) the Jayanti Express carried a library (1973);
— Planning and implementation of education through media, distance education programmes of EMRC and AVRC, in addition to the satellite television network (1975);
— Setting up of the National Cooperative Union of India (1981), to build a network of libraries in India;
— Inaugurating of open university or informal education programmes at State and national level to promote continuing and life-long education among the people, who lack basic educational qualifications;
— National Informatics Centre's (f. 1973) networking project to provide computerized access to information useful for the common man in the country, and its District Information System (DISNIC);
— The UGC's Information and Library Network (INFLIBNET) (f. 1988); and so on.

In addition to these the Government has programmes for development of language, literature and culture, such as Sahitya Academy; Urdu Promotion Bureau; Indian Council of Cultural Relations; etc. Urdu Academy, Telugu Academy, Hindi Prachar Sabha, and many universities and research centres which came up to promote the study of language and literature, such as, Telugu University, Sanskrit University, Central Institute of English and Foreign Languages (a deemed university), and so on.

Similarly the State Governments have their own publishing and distributing agencies, and such other agencies which handle information for the public and information for the government.

Independent bodies, such as universities are also playing their role in building this relationship. UGC's seminar 'From Publisher to Reader:

Work-Flow in University and College Libraries' held during March 4-7, 1959, in which librarians from several academic institutions participated, the proceedings were appended with the UGC Library Committee (1957) report. Haryana Agricultural University, instituted an exemplary University Book Depot (1975) to streamline and support book acquisition programme, which has successfully established the concept in India.

Private efforts to build an image of an integrated information industry in the country, is by and large, lacking. Except the guild of writers, or the Federation of Book Sellers and Publishers in India (f. 1952) in Delhi, Writers Workshop, in Calcutta, and the like agencies, there are many other institutions. The need to have ISBN and ISSN numbers for all publications in the country brought some control in identification of these agencies. The organization of local, regional and national book fairs all over the country, and its systematization resulted in a chain of agencies which coordinate such programmes, and have a better linkage. A single handbook of publishers and libraries has done much to bring the twain together. Similarly the UGC's Good Office Committee, a constituent body comprising book dealers, publishers, and librarians, among others, has built a platform for good relationship. A commercial product, such as, *Indian Books in Print*, has been a leading contribution of the publishing industry in bibliographical control, and acts as a supplement to the National Bibliography, Library of Congress's Accession List—South Asia, etc. The role of National Book Trust in printing, publishing and organizing national level book fairs is remarkable.

So also the establishment of forums of language and literature, led to increased interest in such matters, and such bodies include Dramatic Circle of Hyderabad, Hyderabad Literary Forum, and so on.

Authors and writers, who were exploited by publishing houses, came together to form writers guilds, and writers workshops. The Authors Guild of India is one such which coordinates the literary generation, publishing and distributing activities. Its Delhi Chapter (f. 1981), is probably most productive, as it is in the limelight due to its various contributions. The Guild aims at promoting and protecting the professional and literary interests of its members—membership includes diplomats, judiciary, executives, civil and military personnel, etc. Its activities include, participating in the World Book Fair, organizing a defence orientation course to bring together civil and military personnel, etc. Its published directory of members (1982) carries a Model Contract with terms and conditions of agreement to be entered between the Guild and the Federation of Indian Publishers, in case an author intends to publish a work. Also appended is a Publisher's collaboration scheme, encouraging publication and translation of popular books in Hindi by Indian writers. Some more trends in possible areas of cooperation and sponsorship with publishers are discussed by Prof. Girja Kumar, former librarian, JNU, Delhi.

Writers have various ways of citing others, that quoting or referring others. Some cite others to acknowledge the source they have used. Some cite anything and everything they wish to give as supportive evidence, like citing a newspaper report, or citing a letter from the newspaper, or cite from a popular magazine. This citation behaviour is really a topic which has created a lot of interest in the present century, called as citation and bibliometric studies. One instance, of citing a magazine in a newspaper's letter to the editor is evident from the following:

> While questioning the validity of the theory that the Mecca Masjid was built by Qutub Shahi dynasty, the letter to the editor, by M.A. Azeem, in *Siyasat*, Weekly edition, 30 March 1997, cites a historic research source by Syed Hashmi Fareedabadi, and another source cited is from a popular Urdu magazine, *Pakeeza Anchal*, March 1997. The readership of this magazine is the lay, and accepted research methodology doesn't accept a quotation from popular magazine, mostly because of their general nature, and lack of research that goes into the articles contained therein. The said citation from the magazine, carries no name of the writer or any further details—indicating that the writer of the letter intends to increase the number of sources which have been consulted, irrespective of their nature and research value.

Book awards, film awards, writers awards, best article award, best librarian award, best teacher award, best student award, all are indicators of the interest that is being generated in the increase of use of books. Best authors of children's literature in different State languages, is another booster.

Book Reviews

Book reviews that appear in newspapers, and in periodicals exclusively dealing with book reviews, such as, *Indian Book Chronicle, Indian Book Review, Publishing India, Concept News*, etc., are all working in the book promotion programme. However, there is need for more agencies, such as Girja Kumar (1993: 69) suggests, that there must be a "publication like choice, containing well-considered recommendations of latest books in all major languages of India. . . . An Indian version of Times Literary Supplement is also long overdue".

He opines that Urdu readership did not appreciate low price editions and, despite the attempts of one or two agencies to produce low cost but quality books, there has been in general a lack of tendency to publish at low price. He cites Maktaba Jamia, Delhi, as a case, which received some support from different States, with not much of success. He proposes an Everyman's Urdu Library project to cover hundred best books in Urdu, entrusted to an agency, such as, National Urdu Council (alias Bureau for Promotion of Urdu—*Anjuman Tarraqqi Urdu*), and thereby promote the cause of further developing Urdu readership. Such a collection of best books can be selected by a board to be set up, and suggests prominent writers, who can be on the board, such as, Sardar Jaffery, Shamsur Rahman Farooqui, Gopi Chand Narang, Waris Alvi, etc. Such a selected set, he strongly feels, will interest commoner, academies, and libraries in the field.

He is also of the opinion that, due to a number of reasons, Urdu readers have low interest in buying books, whereas, a Malayalam or Bengali reader will buy serious books, and so also it is better among, Tamil, Marathi, and Punjabi reader. Whatever little interest that is in poetry, is now sometimes reaching them through media, and audio-tapes. Moreover, media is keeping people occupied with entertainment, and gives less time for serious reading. Hence the book production is getting effected.

Many Indian publishers and book dealers, added their efforts to popularize the book. In the Urdu publishing field, with an attempt to promote the book, one publisher, Mashura Book Depot, Delhi, took the lead and printed many books at mere one rupee per book, on the lines of Penguin Pocket Books. *Lughat al-Mashura* (Urdu dictionary), published in 1961. Thousands of titles were published in this cheap edition series. This pocket dictionary carries a note on the back side of the title page: 'Every third month ten new Mashura titles are released, if you are interested in receiving new-title information write to us'. The dictionary carries 14,000 words, spread in 192 pages, and is a handy tool even today, for a student and a lay person. This series carried titles written by reputed authors of Urdu language and literature.

Similar, pocket editions, in Telugu literature, was initiated in Andhra Pradesh, under the inspiration of Hind Pocket Books. The home library scheme introduced by M. Seshachalam was a remarkable achievement in cultivating a literary taste. Books were priced at Rs. 2 each. So also, the efforts by the Yuvabharathi Society ıember scheme led to the popularization of reading habits.

Book week celebration, between November 14 and 20, all over India, as a collaborative effort between libraries, publishers, book sellers, and distributors, has been a source of inspiration for many.

November 14, the birthday of Jawaharlal Nehru, is associated with this week long festival to stimulate interest in books and reading for children and the youth. Exhibits, book displays, seminars and debates are though not very common, but still find a place in many library and related institutions. The Hyderabad Book Fair, which is organized to coincide with this book week celebration, holds a joint seminar to bring together librarians, book sellers, publishers, and all concerned, on a single platform to initiate a sense of fraternity, and this has been a good experiment in mutual understanding.

Late, Dr. R.L. Mittal, has listed a host of issues that confront the two—'Indian Book Trade and Libraries', in his *Magnum Opus, Library Administration: Theory and Practice* (1984).

What part libraries have to play in order to promote book culture. The Library of Congress has a Centre for the Book to promote all book reading and book writing activities that it deems appropriate. The annual international conference on The Book in Islamic World, organized by Library of Congress is yet another step in this regard.

The Library of Congress also has the Centre for the Book (*f.* 1977), to 'organize, focus, and dramatize our nation's interest and attention on the book, to marshal the nation's support—spiritual, physical, and fiscal—for the book'. Among its many successful programmes, the Centre for the Book established "Read more about it", a joint endeavour of the Library of Congress and CBS Television that has recruited more than 70 stars of major prime-time CBS specials to present 30-second messages promoting books and reading on their shows.

The Centre was also responsible for "Books Make a Difference", another promotion effort that built on interviews with more than 300 famous and not-so-famous Americans about the books that played a role in shaping their lives".

The British Council Library in New Delhi, as a part of its book promotion programme, organized a special display on Creative Writing during November 1990; and Dim Silvera's *The India Book*, 1991, lists 15 British books from the displayed ones, dealing with themes like,

Reports (entitled: The Basics of Writing Reports Etcetera, by Nick Moore and Martin Hesp; How to Write a Successful Report by Simon Mort; etc.). For the audio-visual medium (entitled: *Film Script Writing: A Practical Manual* by Dwight V. Swain; *The Way to Write for Television* by Eric Paice; etc.). For the Print Media (*The Craft of Writing Articles* by Gordon Wells; How to Make Money Out of Writing by Graham Stevenson; etc.). Similarly, the annual publication Community of the Book, published in US, did remarkable job of listing all relevant and useful information, that concerned a bibliomania, to know which agency is promoting what, in the realm of book as an agency for social and cultural development of the society.

Dim Silvera's above cited handbook also lists other best books, and the list has Dr. Udai Parekh's Ten New Books on Leadership; Dr. T.V. Rao's 12 Books for the HRD Enthusiasts; Ajit Gulabchand's Favourite Drucker Books; N.K. Singh's 12 Books on Work Culture and Institutional Development; T.V.R. Shenoy's *Essential Reading for Journalists*; and so on. A glance at these titles, should not mislead any, as these are all essentially foreign books, though suiting the Indian needs. India's book production and consumption is still far behind the interests of the citizen's and hence foreign publications are still sold off, in many book stalls, as and when they are displayed, be that at Walden, in Hyderabad, Book Worm in Delhi, or Gangarams in Bangalore.

Library promoting book culture, seems too general, as a topic for this discussion. But it is essential at a time when book promotional activities are being taken up by every one except libraries. A few scattered examples here and there, and once in a way, like, the display of books on the eve of National Library Week, are scant in our country. In this regard, an attempt was recently made, at The American Studies Research Centre, Hyderabad, to display the Fifty Best Black Books, as selected by the African-American journal EBONY. The display was planned to coincide with the National Book Trust's, call for libraries to initiate steps to promote book and reading habits, in November 1996, as a part of the National Library Week Celebrations.

A word about the National Book Trust (NBT), is relevant to describe its role in book and reading promotion programme. NBT is an autonomous agency, working under the Department of Education, Ministry of Human Resource Development. NBT publishes low priced books on a variety of subjects including general books, useful for all, as well as, specialized areas like, physical environment, folklore, etc. Its major area of interest is publishing translations of creative writing in various Indian languages. It has published over 5,400 titles in 13 languages. Its subsidy schemes for book publishing has attracted many publishers, and enabled 780 titles to be printed and published.

The Trust organizes book fairs, seminars, and thereby facilitate interaction among readers, writers, elite, publishers, booksellers, etc. So far it has organized ten book fairs in New Delhi.

Archives vis-a-vis Libraries

Coming to the archives and their connections with libraries in India, we find that there has been much progress in building a cooperative effort among these. Traditional libraries in India are still performing what is expected of archives, collecting information for storage, so there is not much of a difference between the roles of the two. Whereas the modern libraries have moved away from the traditional roles, and embarked on the role of disseminators, as the *summum bonum* of their existence. In this modern role, the modern libraries and archives are expected to interact for jointly operating in fulfilling the information needs of the society, and this is a challenge which is undertaken by both parties.

Archive as term refers to an institution which preserves and serves the needs of non-current reading material, and the focus is more on preservation with a touch-me not attitude. In this sense, libraries have most of its information for current reference, and lesser for non-current material. In addition, libraries have all information only for use, and never for preservation. The functions are then supplementing and complementing, and not very opposite. There must be a library in every society—with archival function—but there may be a society without archives, because libraries by practice have always maintained archival collections. While the art and craft of preservation of archives has advanced, and libraries have gone ahead in the process of dissemination, it is not surprising to see these two agencies today are standing poles apart.

Today's health care centre, or, hospital, maintains an archive, as well as library. The former serves the purpose of storing medical records, and the latter provides print and online access to information required in the efficient administration of the health care system. This double storage and retrieval system is getting merged with the automation process, where all records are mechanically retrieved, as is the access of information across nations, using network systems, such as, Internet. All super-speciality hospitals in India, have entered, into this marathon, to be effective and efficient in the present age.

Media and Libraries

With the advent of talking machines, libraries have been forced to enter a new era. If they don't enter they will be left behind in the race, and none willing to use the outdated book store. Hence the need and importance to go ahead with changing times, While modern gadgets that emerged, took recourse to communication, direct and instant, led libraries also to adapt this non-print media, thereby doubling its role and area of activity.

What libraries always did was to provide access to printed communication, and in this role its image is fixed, as far as the media people are concerned. There emerged a cliff, wider than a geological type, between these two agencies. The department of communications and journalism, world over, function independently with no linkage whatsoever with library science departments. This may now look strange at the outset. But those with power in these spheres feel justified in doing so.

Incidentally, libraries and media centres, share common functions: collect, process, store and disseminate information. The differences are only in micro-level. While media centres mostly modify information suiting the respective audience, libraries in general, pass on the information, without much of re-packing. In this sense, it may sound as if, the media people create information, whereas libraries are only doling out information. This is a far-fetched view, which is not representing the facts and roles, as stated above. To create information is as good as creating history—the question which one may ask is 'do media workers create a story, or simply they spend all their time in beautifying the story, with sugar and spice'? The obvious answer from any would be, they are simply doing make-up!

With new media entering into the libraries, there are nevertheless new issues and questions, which reflect on the image a library has to build. For instance, if libraries are taking up new media, such as, videos, telecommunications, floppies, etc., for input, storage, transmission and output, the questions that need tackling are: what is the impact on the working conditions; what will the future of libraries—virtual extinction of libraries, or tough competition with other information agencies for survival, or what else?

Modern libraries show little user interface, in tackling these universal issues. Libraries are forced to re-consider their role, and restructure the user interface and go according to the changing user needs. The forces leading to this restructuring, are of two dimensions: (a) increased automation of inhouse operations, enabling provision of online public access catalogues; and (b) increased computer literacy among the portion of the population using library services most heavily. The technology that has been applied in the libraries, still lacks user-friendliness, rather expects and demands that the user adapt to the machine. It is then for the libraries to change according to the times and be yet another true agency of communication, or stay behind the times, and be prepared to see a day when users would find alternative means of information, with far Šmore ease and comfort.

One more question which bothers libraries, is that of free or fee based services. Radio, music, film, and television channels are sometimes free, but many channels demand fees, and such need to be subscribed. Even the Internet does not have all access free, there are sites which must be subscribed to. If information is a product, value added—information has value to the extent we give attention to it—then it is imperative that there must be fee for the additional value that it gets, in the process of providing information based products; in the process of providing access to costly information; again, in the process of paying for the royalty, to the author, the library will be at a loss if it does not collect the same amount from the user of that particular information. These call for significant care and consideration, of issues, much as pricing strategy, marketing techniques, and value analysis. These are relevant since, unlike the media which concentrates in creation of information, in libraries most information services involve repackaging.

In short, the issues are multiple, and the steps to be applied in this process of integrating the information handling agencies are far more complicated. If there must be real integration, then the aim must be creating a social awareness for cooperation and convergence of all such agencies. Libraries must continue to coordinate and cooperate with similar agencies in providing maximum access to the information they guard. "... both books and electronic documents are going to stay side by side and each has a definite role to play in information communication" (Kumar and Tejomurthy, 1990: 178).

The Government of India has its own channels to promote books abroad. Different offices of the Government are assigned the tasks, for instance, propagation of Hindi abroad is under the Ministry of External Affairs. The propagation includes, sending Hindi teaching materials, and other paraphernalia. This is distributed to all interested governmental and non-governmental bodies and also individuals engaged in the propagation of the language. The Ministry also donates Hindi teaching aids and kits to universities and institutions which are concerned.

Furthermore, there are, as per the figures given in India Reference Annual, 1992, there are 22 visiting professors deputed by the Indian Council of Cultural Affairs, to universities and institutions in as many foreign countries, who are assigned to teach Indology, Indian languages and allied subjects. Two chairs of Indian studies were created in 1991, for the first time in America, in the University of California, Berkeley. This establishment was to coincide with the 150th anniversary of the Indo-US educational exchanges. One of these chairs, is supported by the expatriate Indians, and the other is set up with the financial assistance of Sarah Kaliath Endowment.

The private attempts to market Indian books include the publishing and distributing industry that spread its network outside India. The leading book promoters are a number of book dealers, and allied institutions having interest in promoting India abroad. There are a few India related agencies, established by Indians residing in Canada, US, UK, etc. who sponsor television programmes, sponsor book publishing programmes related to India and its culture.

Agencies Promoting the Growth of Libraries

On the eve of the fiftieth year of freedom, India has reached a stage of thousands of agencies—which are responsible in increasing the number of libraries. The intensity of their contribution is shown below:

Universities	200
Colleges	7,000
R&D Institutions (Sc. & Tech. Sector)	
Central Govt.	522
Others/private (approx.)	1,500

While the scatter of universities and colleges is not so surprising, the scattered number of Central as well as other/private sector R&D institutions, is glaring from the Table 4.12.

The status of public libraries at a glance is also pertinent here: All the States and the union territories, except Sikkim and Lakshadweep, have state central libraries. Out of the total 5,75,937 villages in the country, only 41,828 (or 7%) have libraries. Apart from this, a Statewise picture of libraries is also most unimpressive. There are no accurate record of the total, however, there are estimates given by (1) Dr. S.K. Pandey Sharma, and (2) RRLF, which is presented in the Table 4.13 (quoted in Ramaiah, 1997: 121).

TABLE 4.12: Scattered Number of Central as well as Other/Private Sector R&D Institutions

	Central	*Others/Private*
State		
Delhi	87	101
West Bengal	43	103
Tamil Nadu	18	122
Maharashtra	46	398
Other Cities having Central R&D Institutions		
Bangalore	39	
Hyderabad	30	
Pune	14	
Dehradun	12	
Lucknow	11	
Ranchi	8	
Chandigarh	7	
Ahmedabad	6	
Bhubaneswar	6	
Kochi	6	
Thiruvanthapuram	6	

TABLE 4.13: Number of Libraries in the States/Union Territories

States/U.T.	*According to Dr. S.K. Pandey Sharma*	*%*	*According to RRLF*	*%*
(1)	(2)	(3)	(4)	(5)
States				
Andhra Pradesh	3,952	9.8	1,528	6.9
Arunachal Pradesh	—	—	73	0.3
Assam	1,128	2.8	252	1.1
Bihar	4,503	11.2	1,705	7.7
Goa	—	—	118	0.5
Gujarat	6,556	16.3	2,155	9.8
Haryana	49	0.2	66	0.2
Himachal Pradesh	55	0.2	117	0.5
Jammu & Kashmir	20	0.1	24	0.1
Karnataka	2,655	6.6	2,137	9.7
Kerala	4,169	10.4	2,096	9.5
Madhya Pradesh	6,281	15.6	2,086	9.4
Maharashtra	2,678	6.7	2,070	9.3

(Contd.)

TABLE 4.13 (*Contd.*)

(1)	(2)	(3)	(4)	(5)
Manipur	—	—	106	0.4
Meghalaya	—	—	7	0.1
Mizoram	—	—	107	0.4
Nagaland	24	0.1	139	0.6
Orissa	626	1.6	1,690	7.7
Punjab	163	0.4	25	0.1
Rajasthan	39	0.2	119	0.5
Sikkim	6	0.1	6	0.1
Tamil Nadu	3,017	7.5	1,540	7.0
Tripura	31	0.1	44	0.1
Uttar Pradesh	1,585	4.0	710	3.2
West Bengal	2,061	5.1	2,803	12.7
Union Territories				
Andaman & Nicobar Islands	—	—	40	0.1
Chandigarh	—	—	7	0.1
Dadra & Nagar Haveli	—	—	4	0.1
Delhi	—	—	4	0.1
Daman & Diu	165	0.4	—	—
Lakshadweep, Minicoy and Amindivi Islands	—	—	11	0.1
Pondicherry	—	—	57	0.2
Total	40,107		21,906	

Book Production

To clearly understand the book production, one way is to search the records of books received under the Delivery of Books Act. The figures relate to books, belonging to respective language, which are given in Table 4.14.

In Table 4.14, of all, English books are in the first place, this can be viewed as follows:

- — the publishing trends in the English language are higher than all other languages of the country;
- — that Hindi is receiving only the second place;
- — that English is the accepted medium of communication;
- — that English publications are almost one-third of the country's total book publications among those received at the National Library, under the Delivery of Books Act.
- — that the Copyright rules are being strictly adhered by those in the English language publishing industry, leading to delivery of more books in one single language.

TABLE 4.14: Number of Books Received under the Delivery of Books Act of Different Languages

Language	*1965-66*			*1986-87*			*1990-91*		
	Quantity	*%*	*Rank*	*Quantity*	*%*	*Rank*	*Quantity*	*%*	*Rank*
Assamese	64	0.3	15	207	12.1	3	232	1.2	12
Bengali	1,422	6.7	4	1,622	9.5	4	1,609	8.7	3
English	10,347	48.8	1	5,318	31.3	1	7,368	40.1	1
Gujarati	922	4.3	7	565	3.3	8	1,140	6.2	4
Hindi	2,376	11.2	2	2,745	16.1	2	1,882	10.2	2
Kannada	241	1.1	11	885	5.2	7	1,138	6.2	4
Kashmiri	10	0.1	16	33	0.1	16	12	0.1	16
Malayalam	573	2.7	8	883	5.2	7	860	4.6	7
Marathi	1,612	7.6	3	1,172	6.9	6	1,119	6.1	5
Oriya	120	0.5	14	393	2.3	11	383	2.0	10
Punjabi	167	0.7	13	408	2.4	10	405	2.1	9
Sanskrit	207	0.9	12	251	1.4	13	77	0.4	13
Sindhi	70	0.4	14	57	0.3	14	—	—	—
Tamil	947	4.4	6	1,434	8.4	5	958	5.2	6
Telugu	518	2.4	9	556	3.2	9	686	3.7	8
Urdu	372	1.7	10	376	2.2	12	377	1.9	11
Others	1,285	6.0	5	52	0.3	15	34	0.2	15
Total	21,185			16,970			18,337		

Source: National Library, Calcutta.

TABLE 4.15: Statewise Book Production and Contribution 1965-66

State	*Quantity*	*%*	*Rank*
(1)	(2)	(3)	(4)
Andaman & Nicobar Islands	3	0.1	20
Andhra Pradesh	1,351	6.3	5
Assam	120	0.5	16
Bihar	417	1.9	13
Delhi	5,900	27.8	1
Goa, Daman and Diu	1	0.1	20
Gujarat	699	3.2	8
Himachal Pradesh	320	1.5	14
Jammu and Kashmir	58	0.2	19
Karnataka	431	2.0	12
Kerala	700	3.3	7
Madhya Pradesh	529	2.5	10
Maharashtra	3,035	14.3	3
Manipur	65	0.3	17
Nagaland	4	0.1	20
Orissa	446	2.1	11

(Contd.)

TABLE 4.15 (*Contd.*)

(1)	(2)	(3)	(4)
Pondicherry	—	—	—
Punjab	670	3.1	9
Rajasthan	204	0.9	15
Tamil Nadu	1,936	9.1	4
Tripura	52	0.2	18
Uttar Pradesh	1,118	5.2	6
West Bengal	3,126	14.7	2
Total	21,185		

According to this ranking, English language books are the top most in the country, and Delhi is the leading State which supplies nearly 30 per cent of the national book produce. If Delhi, is the capital of India, it also enjoys the claim of being the largest facilities, requires for book writing, production, distribution, etc. It is easy to get an import license for a book producer in Delhi, than one in any other city in India. So also, Delhi has a network of resources for these purposes, which other cities in India lack, even the industrial city like Calcutta, and a business city like Mumbai, cannot compete in this regard with Delhi.

TABLE 4.16: Annual Book Production in India

Year	*Books Produced*
1971-72	17,557
1972-73	17,020
1973-74	17,600
1974-75	16,192
1975-76	21,957
1976-77	21,992
1977-78	19,659
1978-79	18,584
1979-80	16,466
1980-81	17,168
1981-82	16,798
1982-83	16,650
1983-84	14,202
1984-85	15,091
1985-86	15,720
1986-87	16,970

Source: National Library, Calcutta.

The Table 4.16 depicts the state of art of the book production as reflected in the delivery of books at the National Library under the provisions of the Delivery of Books Act. It shows that while the world has progressed leaps and bounds and the age of publish or perish has led to information explosion, the Indian authors/editors/publishers/ distributors are not in any way producing more than what they produced since ages!

This is a sample of all the types of agencies which exists forming a system. Apart from these there are thousands of institutions that have grown and the list includes the non-R&D social science and humanities libraries, media production centres, software dealing and generating agencies, and so on. Like population explosion, there is also information, knowledge, print and library explosion and have also become a problem to be tackled. Strangely the Planning Commission, or any other concerned agency doesn't think that explosion here is as serious as population explosion.

> "The world today is passing through a phase of information explosion and informatics as an entirely new branch of activity having a direct bearing on social, political and economic affairs has come into operation. . . . Besides the print media, electronics media have come to occupy a very important position in our life. . . . The print media which is exclusively privately owned is also making an insensate drive to modernization by changing over to computerization and photo processes from hot metal and cold metal technologies" (Raghavachari, 1996).

In the words of the poet Iqbal, *Agar abbhi na jage to nam be na hoga tumahara afsano mein* (if you do not wake up even now, your name will not be even in historic fiction). Though this was in another context, yet the relevance to our purpose is obvious. In the context of shrinking budgets, reduction in staff, and increasing costs of maintaining independent institutions, each and every agency handling information, must strive for an integrated approach to the problems, rather than sailing independently in the troubled waters.

Growth of Institutions Promoting Library History

The study of history is a fascinating subject. The interest in historical study and research is demonstrated in a number of institutions. This is hence considered as potential for the cause of promotion of library history interests.

While there are many agencies in India which are meant for the promotion of historical studies *per se*, there is hardly any specific agency interested in promoting library history. So it is upto library historians and their counterparts to find suitable avenues in building contacts and forging alliances to develop and sustain library history interests in the Indian society.

The institutions which are promoting study and research in history are listed below to give an idea of potential resource centres:

1. The Heras Institute of Indian History and Culture, Mumbai;
2. Indian Council of Historical Research, New Delhi;
3. American Institute of Indian Studies, New Delhi;
4. Asiatic Society, Calcutta;
5. Bhandarkar Oriental Research Institute, Pune;
6. Bharat Itihasa Samshodaka Mandal, Pune;
7. Xavier Centre of Historical Research, Goa; and
8. Nehru Memorial and Museum Library, New Delhi.

The following books give a descriptive information of their activities: R.K. Bhatt, *History and Development of Libraries in India* (Mittal, 1995); B.M. Gupta, (ed.), *Handbook of Libraries, Archives and Information Centres in India*, Vols. 1-16, (Delhi).

Conclusion

Before this discussion ends it is appropriate to restate that a library movement must have some basic functions, and must strive to prove these in practice, in its day-to-day life and activity.

In the light of what was stated in the previous chapter, much of the present developments, and the progress of the library movement falls into the category of what is called as movement. In fact, the base of the movement was already set in the pre-independent India, and with freedom, India could enact some of the desired ideals of the term library movement. If the present fifty years of the independence have demonstrated the ability to come out of the traditional system and adopt to the changing needs and changing circumstances, and most of the libraries today have become somewhat usable, it is one of the primary signs of a movement—from inactivity to activity, and from activity to activism. The progress of the library movement is very slow, almost snails pace, but a few decades later one could see more clearly that India of today is far better in terms of its library developments.

While the libraries in the urban areas are prospering in an unprecedent fashion, the rural libraries—whatsoever this may mean to the large number of ruralites—has not been very much. Even the development of academic and research scenario, is all based on, the urban needs and frustratingly lacks rural information and community information perspectives. All the talk about information at the door step of the villager is a day dream, at the end of the fifty years of independence! To quote Prof. T.N. Rajan,

> "The zeal and enthusiasm shown for the public library movement in the pre-independence days, have been conspicuously absent in the post-independence period. Very little has been achieved in this area, despite the fact that some states have enacted library legislation. The massive adult education programme that has been launched in the last two years, has been indifferent to involve the libraries in this programme" (Rajan, 1980: 19-20).

5

LIBRARIES AND NATIONAL DEVELOPMENT: From 1947 to 1996

Dr. S.R. Ranganathan thus quotes Valmiki to describe what should be the correct attitude of the reference librarian (wherein Sita spoke to Rama) 'I don't instruct; I only remind you out of my love and regards for you'.

We may quote Dr. Susheela Kumar here,

> "One of the main aims and objectives of national development is to become self-supporting. Vast information networks not only within a country but between countries should enable each nation to have access to the ideas and thinking of other nations without having to import physically the originators or interpreters of ideas except for brief periods.
>
> Libraries should therefore be conscious of their role in information linkage. They should be alert to the changing needs of the country and its development plans and ensure that exhaustive and expeditious information service is provided to the users of libraries, and strong networks of information are built up".
>
> Further, "Educational, scientific or cultural development depends on the speed with which information about new developments is made available. Unless such information is available there is likely to be duplication in research or delay in process" (Susheela Kumar, 1974: 155-56).

Prof. H.A. Khan presents another view point ". . . public library and society in India have developed independently of one another to the detriment of both" (Prof. H.A. Khan, 1990: 166).

Agenda for the Library Development

What should be an agenda for a discussion for role of library in national development. An agenda that is appropriate is to cite the remarks made by key speakers in a conference on 'Role of Libraries in National Development', in Trivandrum in 1978, an abridged extract from *Hindu*, 27 May, 1979, is adapted here.

B.S. Kesavan

"Follow the pattern of Kerala: people have literacy; and there is an intellectual alertness among the people making information accessible at inexpensive rates and doing away with the middlemen who are bound to:

- exploit the situation and would make tremendous profit;
- exploit the audio-visual convenience to its maximum;
- make the Government accept the basic principle that the responsibility for libraries is as much a responsibility as water to drink and air to breathe;
- let us not suffer from the illusion that library legislation, in our present state of poverty and chaotic situation, is going to yield the necessary funds to run this remarkably. Let the Library Act include the clause that the funds to run public library system include funds from the Central Government as well.

In the West libraries are flourishing, for the reason that there is a plentitude of things that are written, because there has been a sort of a cornucopia of knowledge pouring out. You find that not only at the higher level, not only at the research level, but even at the ordinary levels . . . wanting to know things, how to do things, how to listen to things, how to look at things; you find that there is a tremendous amount of output to-day. We are lacking in that basic thing. . . . For this the blame is not on educationists, governments, none; there is a certain economic fix in which we are at the moment which makes it very difficult for us to achieve this tempo of publication and distribution of material to the people; if your library system does not cater to the vast mass of people who are to be educated and who are to be thought, you are not doing that job properly; the basic need of the people at the grassroot level is the one that should be the primary pre-occupation of the library field if we are to fulfil the national policy of trying to get the mass of the people aware of what is going in their immediate environment, let alone the international environment.

Library culture already exists in Bengal and Kerala. It is in their blood-stream. If you can possibly catch hold of a book, you see them read in the bus, in the gardens, anywhere. They are remarkable people in their intellectual activity. In other States this is missing. Even the books produced in other States don't have nothing graceful about them. One of the basic things necessary . . . is the production of material attractively in the Indian languages.

In India we have moved more than an inch forward towards sophisticated responses to sophisticated conditions of enquiry and research, we haven't moved even a millimetre as far as the base is concerned—the public library system, for example, the school library system".

K.A. Isaac

"— Library service in Kerala has been so organized as to reach the rural population;

— the rural libraries must be able to draw on the resources of the bigger population, in the form of an integrated library system;

— the ultimate purpose of library legislation should be to bring about a library system and also raise the financial resources to support such a system;

— the ratio of per capita income in India to that in the US is 1:89 and as between India and UK is 1:27. When we come to library expenditure, the ratio as between India and the US is 1:416 and India to UK is 1:200. This is a reflection of the importance given to libraries. It is more a matter of proper allocation of the available resources;

— there are norms of library expenditure: Radhakrishnan Commission in 1949 recommended Rs. 40 per student, a library expenditure at the rate of Rs. 40 per student; and the Kothari Commission recommended Rs. 25 per student and Rs. 300 per teacher; and

— the Ranganathan Committee recommended Rs. 15 per registered student—and Rs. 200 per teacher. The Kothari Commission had also the alternative expenditure of $6^1/_4$ to 10 per cent of the total university budget, depending upon the stage of development of the library;

It is very important that library science courses are designed to make them more relevant to the present day requirements than they are".

Girja Kumar

"— there is library development; but the development is not balanced. For example, adult education is on the top priority of the Government, but it nowhere directly talks of libraries as partners in the process of adult education;

— there must be a consensus on objectives of library development in the country, and only then the contradictions of developing imbalances can be removed;

— there are a number of imbalances that have developed over the last 30 years and it is high time these were redressed in the context of the national perspective;

— there must be proper cost accounting of the system to know whether the investments made are yielding any results or not;

— there must be a direction for development; this direction or guidelines must be spelled in terms of national library policy; the objective stated in the simple sense, is as mentioned in the National Commission on Libraries and Information Science in the United States. It says, to eventually provide every individual in the country with an equal opportunity of access to that part of the total information resource which will satisfy the individual educational, working, cultural and leisure needs and interest, regardless of individual's location, social or physical condition or level of intellectual achievement;

— to achieve this we must develop library culture—improve reading habits—thorough different means, including trying to link the publishing and distribution of books, to enable production and use of books, and thereby develop library culture;

— so long as you don't develop your public library system, you can't develop a healthy library system in the country".

T.K.S. Iyengar

"— You must have standards then you can evolve national policy;

— what are the goals we have for library development;

— what are our libraries doing for the majority of our population—the illiterates? Exploit the audio-visuals for this situation;

— library legislation is the choice if we want to have a equitable development; not top to bottom, like excellent university libraries, excellent research libraries, but inadequate school and public libraries—libraries are not implementing whatever that is evolved;

— the important part of innovation is information, without information there is no innovation and without innovation there is no production;

— There has been a degree of thoughtlessness and irresponsibility in the dispensation of the UGC grants.

— The agenda is hereby set and this gives us a base for the assessment of the library development in the country. What follows here will be in the light of these issues and perspectives".

Using the above agenda as a broad framework we can discuss the topic of national development.

Place of Libraries in the Five Year Plans, 1951-1995

There are attempts at improving the common man's quality of life at all levels. With the First Five Year Plan, the Block Development System under the Community Development Project, has extension work in its scope, and in its stated objective, is the opening of small library units within each block. But in practice, the trend has been to "motivate the people in the villages through other agencies and more important role that libraries could play have been overlooked" (Mookerjee, 1969: 369).

In the First Five Year Plan (1951-56) the Government proposed the setting up of National Central Library at New Delhi. This was to be backed by nine State Central Libraries to be set up in State capitals.

Under each plan period, the development of libraries did receive a mention in passing, under the cover of UGC funds, some or other discussions on the topic of library. During this plan period, did emerge the Delhi Public Library. And inaugurating the Public Library Seminar, Maulana Azad said, which was quoted at the beginning of a previous chapter, that each State must have a network of libraries, with district libraries, networked, and supported by a lower and higher level of libraries, as in a systems approach.

A Copyright Act was passed during the plan period, which was called Delivery of Books Act, 1954.

An intensive programme was drawn up for the public library planning, along with a hierarchical structure—national, State, district, city, village, community centres, mobile libraries, and so on.

In this period, the amount sanctioned by UGC, to purchase books and periodicals, for universities was Rs. 31.13 lakhs.

The Second Five Year Plan (1956-61) went one step further. It suggested the setting up of a countrywide network of libraries in all the 320 districts of the country. In this plan period there was an amendment to the Delivery of Books Act, to include, newspapers. It prescribed that every Indian publisher will gift one copy of a publication to each of the three designated libraries in Bombay (now Mumbai), Madras (now Chennai) and Calcutta. Yet another scheme was added to the Plan: amalgamation of public library service in rural areas with adult education programmes.

This Second Plan aimed at slightly widening the scope of the library development in the country. The Government decided to provide in the budget Rs. 140 lakhs—a Central grant to be matched by the State—alongwith a separate allocation of Rs. 10 lakhs for setting up a national organization for education of librarians.

UGC sanctioned, Rs. 115.79 lakhs for the university system enabling these to acquire books and periodicals, during this plan period.

Under the Third Five Year Plan (1961-66) four designated public libraries in the four metros were re-named as National Libraries, already situated in Delhi, Calcutta, Bombay and Madras. During the period UGC grant was Rs. 183.82 lakhs for university acquisitions.

Under the Fourth Five Year Plan (1969-74) was constituted a Working Group, under the Chairmanship of V.K.R.V. Rao It was aimed at drawing a plan for library development. But apart from this there is no other mention of the developing library system in the Plan. However, the UGC grant did find a place, and it included the sum of Rs. 640.20 lakhs.

Henceforth Working Groups were required to submit their plans and proposals for the developmental programmes, and libraries made very little use of such opportunities! This was revealed in the report of a Working Group. For instance, "it revealed that Government of Orissa paid the lowest grant-in-aid of Rs. 15 to a club library" (Panda, 1992: 264). The findings of this Working Group also state that the total provision for public library in the country varied from State to State, an average of Rs. 8.5 lakhs was spent in the year 1963-64. Of this 80 per cent was spent on Government public libraries, and only 20 per cent was given as grant-in-aid to private and rural libraries. Furthermore, the State spent only 3 paise per capita on public libraries, in the year 1963-64. Compare this with the spending on education, which is 6.4 paise per capita, which is proportionally 1:213 of the educational expenditure.

By this year the scenario of public libraries, stated quantitatively was, 75 per cent of states in the country had State Libraries, 63 per cent districts had district libraries, 27 per cent blocks had block development libraries, and 5 per cent villages had village libraries.

The Working Group hence formulated an overall policy fixing up priorities and programmes for the developmental activities, and recommended a grant of Rs. 30.99 crores during this plan period, which is as follows:

TABLE 5.1: Proposed Grants for Library Development

(*Rs. in lakhs*)

Libraries	*Grant*
State Central Libraries	310
District Libraries	100
Block Libraries	1,375
Branch and Subscription Libraries	100
Model Public Libraries	60
Union Territories/Other States	160
Training Librarians	40
Library Associations	10
Other Govt. Departmental Libraries	44
Total	3,099

According to the survey conducted by Panda, "against a sum of Rs. 22.80 crores, suggested by the Central Planning Group, the State Governments provided only Rs. 7.42 crores for the purpose. Against the low provision, Rs. 3 crores was available for public libraries during the year 1969-70. So the scheme (as envisaged by the Working Group) did not receive any attention and no significant progress could be made" (Panda, 1993: 266).

It was during the Fourth Plan that RRLF was instituted for development of public libraries, more so in the rural areas.

Under the Fifth Plan Period (1974-78) some more activities, were mentioned, though these were almost like providing lip service to the notion of library development programmes! The university acquisitions received in this period a sanction of Rs. 951.74 lakhs from UGC.

In the context of the UGC grants, and the development of different disciplines as a result of these grants, it is pertinent to note that there was a greater bias towards the development of science information sources in the universities. The Table 5.2 displays the patterns that prevail, even to this day due to the bias that science carries, and the social science and humanities are at a stage of deprivation.

In terms of preference, then, the order in descending will be science, social science and humanities. Hence, India has very well equipped science information centres, less equipped are social science and least equipped are humanities resources. This does reflect in the national image—India has a remarkable standing in its scientific achievements, but no special place in the other two areas!

TABLE 5.2: UGC Grants to University Libraries

(*Rs. in thousands*)

Year	*Science*		*Social Science*		*Humanities*	
	Journal	*Book*	*Journal*	*Book*	*Journal*	*Book*
1976-77	845	125	428	150	390	67
1977-78	735	171	322	155	300	31
1978-79	918	208	479	270	407	60
1979-80	711	116	393	143	264	27
1980-81	680	70	395	91	285	19

Source: Girja Kumar, 1986: 34; cited from Annual Reports of UGC.

Case Studies of Libraries and Development

An attempt is made, here to discuss the trends in different areas of interest, and view the present situation in understanding the level of development that Indian libraries have achieved. More than anything else, the concern here is, to assess the role of library is providing the information that matches with the developmental needs of the people.

Library Growth Studies: A Survey

For the purpose of gaining a personal insight into the issues that are involved the present writer made a national survey of libraries, travelling all through the metros and other areas. The questionnaire method was associated with interviews and observations. The analysis of the survey is given below:

Ninety-six academic and research libraries in India were surveyed. The questionnaire was served mostly by personal visit and in a few cases it was mailed to save the time of the respondents. The institutions that were surveyed, among others include the following:

A.N.S. Institute of Social Studies, Patna;
American Studies Research Centre, Hyderabad;
Andhra University, Vishakhapatnam;
B.S.N.V. Degree College, Lucknow;
Bangalore University, Bangalore;

Calcutta University, Calcutta;
Central Institute of English and Foreign Languages, Hyderabad;
Centre for Studies in Social Research (ICSSR), Calcutta;
Chemistry Department Library, A.M.U., Aligarh;
Hindu College, Delhi;
Hyderabad University, Hyderabad;
I.I.M., Lucknow;
IIT, Delhi;
IIT, Mumbai;
I.T.R.C., Lucknow;
Indian Institute of Sugarcane Research, Lucknow;
Indira Gandhi Centre for Fine Arts, Delhi;
Institute of Public Enterprise, Hyderabad;
J.N.U., Delhi;
Kashmir University, Srinagar;
Lajpat Rai Pustakalaya Evam Vachnalaya, Lucknow;
Lucknow University, Lucknow;
M.J. College of Engineering, Hyderabad;
Madras University, Chennai;
Mangalore University, Mangalore;
Medical College, Calcutta;
Medical College, Vellore;
Mysore University, Mysore;
N.E.E.R.I, Nagpur;
National Institute of Rehabilitation Training & Research, Cuttack;
National Institute of Virology, Pune;
Osmania University, Hyderabad;
Poona University, Pune;
Regional College of Education, Bhopal;
S.G.P.G.I.M.S., Lucknow;
St. John's Medical College, Bangalore;
State Law Officer's Library, High Court, Lucknow;
Tanjavur Medical College, Thanjavur;
University of Health Sciences, Vijayawada.

The purpose of this enquiry is to see how far Indian academic and research libraries are developed, and interpret the results in measuring this development vis-a-vis the national development. The assessment may reveal as to how far is library development in line with national development. Hope the responses will help in understanding what a library does (service/products) and how to improve the working conditions and library environments. One hundred and five libraries, responded to the questionnaire, and the results are given below. While most responded to all the questions, a few have not done so, and hence there is an obvious difference in total figures in each analysis.

Personnel

Q. How many professionals work in library?

	Respondents	*Percentage*
1—10	95	82.6
10—20	10	8.6
20—30	5	4.3
More	5	4.3
Total	115	

From the above it is evident that most of the libraries that have responded have ten or less professionals, indicating that the majority is from the middle level libraries, which are not very small, nor as big as large university libraries. There are five libraries which have more than thirty professionals, and this represents the large libraries, that have been also serveyed.

Q. How many other staff are in library?

	Respondents	*Percentage*
1—10	55	91.6
10—20	—	—
20—30	—	—
More	5	8.3
Total	60	

Again, 55 respondents have less than ten non-professionals, working in the library. As in the case of professionals, even among non-professionals there are five libraries who have more than thirty other categories of staff.

Q. Is there a job description for the staff?

	Respondents	*Percentage*
Yes	50	66.6
No	25	33.3
Total	75	

Library management, and human resource development, are the twain, which are gaining their foothold in the libraries. Hence, the first step in planning the human resource, is to have staff organisation, and a clear job description. Almost 67 per cent of the libraries have description of their staff. It is one thing to state what is expected of a person, and it is another thing to define what is expected of a specific job. This distinction, apart, it is not clear if the stated job description, is based on any standard, or any pattern, or it is one line statement of each type of job in the library. On the whole, most have some conception of describing the job, which was non-entity in the past.

Q. Is there a performance evaluation for staff?

	Respondents	*Percentage*
Yes	45	42.8
No	60	57.1
Total	105	

Performance evaluation, refers, to evaluation of specific and over all performance of the staff. In this context, having a proper performance evaluation procedure, by either a confidential report (CR) system, or an open system of evaluation, is another step in strategic planning of the human resource. Majority of the responding libraries have indicated a lacuna, in evaluating staff output. Many institutions in India, including those surveyed here (43%), fulfil an annual ritual of filling the CR formality. But most do not have such a procedure of performance evaluation.

Q. Do the staff have continuing education?

	Respondents	*Percentage*
Yes	80	80.0
No	20	20.0
Total	100	

Q. If yes, is it

	Respondents	*Percentage*
Internal	25	25.0
External	75	75.0
Total	100	

Next question here relates to the on the job training facility, which will improve, both knowledge and skills. If performance has to improve, the staff need much support from the management, including opportunities for inservice training. Interestingly, most libraries have such a facility. It is by and large a set practice in public institutions, where staff are offered the leave travel and official absence absent for attending such programmes outside the place of work! This need to travel is supported by the results of the survey, as shown below, that most have such programmes outside their work place. Only 25 per cent libraries have internally organised programmes for the purpose. It is not clear, whether these continuing education programmes are workshops, or seminars, or courses. Seminars, today have less for education, and more for entertainment. Whereas, if there are programmes which run for a week or more, like ten libraries have indicated below, then it has some concrete effect on the recipients of such a programme.

Q. Duration:

	Respondents	*Percentage*
One Week	5	6.6
More	5	6.6
Not Fixed	65	86.6
Total	75	

Q. Nature:

	Respondents	*Percentage*
Planned	15	18.7
Adhoc	65	81.2
Total	80	

Q. Faculty:

	Respondents	*Percentage*
Librarians	60	66.6
Outsiders	30	33.3
Total	90	

Q. Are there any promotional chances?

	Respondents	*Percentage*
Merit	5	5.5
Seniority	30	33.3
Open	55	61.1
Total	90	

Another issue which the human resource management calls for is clear channels for communication among the staff. Most libraries do have some sort of open forum, for the purpose. But 30 per cent respondents state they have no such avenues, as seen below, to promote human relationship, or to promote mutual understanding within the library system. As many as 40 per cent have monthly meetings, and 47 per cent meet once in a way. Communication channels, must be opened in all directions, horizontal, vertical, and across. But the survey results, shown below, reveal that 60 per cent of the libraries have not understood the need of keeping communication channels constantly opened!

Q. Do the staff have internal meetings and discussions:

	Respondents	*Percentage*
Yes	70	70
No	30	30
Total	100	

Q. If yes, how often:

	Respondents	*Percentage*
Weekly	—	—
Monthly	30	40.0
Rarely	35	46.6
None	10	13.3
Total	75	

Q. How often new staff are appointed:

	Respondents	*Percentage*
Yearly	—	—
Rarely	15	13.6
Only if Position Vacant	95	86.3
Total	110	

Evaluating one's own staff, is difficult. And the librarians here have spelled, something very interesting. 48 per cent respondents feel that the staff are motivated, 39.1 per cent feel that they are committed, and 3 per cent reveal that there is dedication. These responses explicitly state that there is a total lack of what is really called as professionalism. As many as 60 per cent state that staff have no commitment, 53 per cent feel that their staff have no motivation, and 97 per cent observe that there is no dedication!!!

Q. Are the staff generally:

	Respondents	*Percentage*
Committed	45	39.1
Motivated	55	47.8
Dedicated	15	3.0
Total	115	

A professional, again, has much to display, its characteristics independent of pressures from lobbyists, and unions, but the picture as shown in the following responses, is not fitting and upto the required goals. Only 33 per cent observe that new ideas must come from subordinates, and 17 per cent do not with this idea. 11 per cent state that it is not practical. In the reality, participative management calls for interactive process, and in such a work place, there is not much of difference on who is suggesting, it is only important to know what is being said. These are the lessons which are still worth pondering by the library managers in India. In the Indian set-up, most of the subordinate staff get bogged down in technical routines, and have no time to contribute for research or creative thinking. In the absence of these conditions, it is right that 38 per cent respondents have a feeling that getting the ideas from subordinates is partially correct. And so are those who think that such a proposition is not practical in the Indian situation.

Q. Desire for a change/new ideas must come from below:

	Respondents	*Percentage*
Agree	30	33.3
Do not agree	15	16.6
Partially correct	35	38.8
Not practical	10	11.1
Total	90	

In the next question, the matter refers to prioritising the responsibilities which librarians have on them. The question is 'How do librarians keep themselves busy on the job'. As a routine they are busy with administration, and 85 respondents agree to this. Given a chance to rank their priorities, 35 feel that they rank 'finding user needs' as primary task. Whereas in practice they are doing this only after they are free from administrative and bureaucratic jobs. As many as 15 place 'finding user needs' at second place, and they are in fact true to their practical situations.

Q. As a librarian rank three major areas in which you spend at least 20 per cent of your time as part of the routine: (Rank your priorities)

	Respondents
(a) Finding user needs	60
(b) Processing	35
(c) Acquisition	35
(d) Administration	85
(e) Developing new products	20
(f) Staff interaction	30
(g) With management	20

First Rank	*Second Rank*	*Third Rank*
(a) 35	(a) 15	(d) 20
(d) 10	(b) 15	(f) 10
	(c) 10	(g) 10

Acquisition of Reading Materials

Moving from staff to collection *per se*, is important, it is the trinity which makes a library—user, staff, collection—staff can make or mar an institution and the type of collection can increase or decrease the user interest. Hence, the questions now relate to growth and development of the collection.

On collection development policy, 75 per cent responded positively. Whereas 25 per cent put it negatively. It is not clear from this as to what do they mean by collection development policy. Because in the next question, if it is written, only 33 per cent were positive. Which means that there is a vague idea of what is to be developed, and this is a practice—to acquire all that relates to parent institution's needs, and to adopt to changing needs.

This apart, policy has many more implication, which includes, decisions on quality and quantity of material to be acquired, user feedback for quality control, proportionate budget allocations, which fluctuates each year according to the immediate and long term plans of the institutional needs and goals, and so on. Policy also includes set guidelines to be followed in the entire process of collection development for all types of reading material—not mere books and periodicals—including, adding, withdrawing periodically, and maintaining a balanced collection. Hence, most libraries must attempt to write their collection development programme and policy, to make it transparent to one all.

Q. Is there a policy for collection development:

	Respondents	*Percentage*
Yes	75	75.0
No	25	25.0
Total	100	

Q. If yes, is it written:

	Respondents	*Percentage*
Yes	25	33.3
No	50	66.6
Total	75	

Q. Who decides finally:

	Respondents	*Percentage*
Library professionals	35	38.8
Others	55	61.1
Total	90	

Budget is a crucial subject for any growing organism. It is, therefore, pertinent to know who are the decision-makers in finalizing the annual budget. As seen from above, only 39 per cent librarians have a final say in the budget finalization, and it mostly others who have their say in this process!!!

Q. How is the demarcation done:

	Respondents	*Percentage*
Subjectwise	35	41.7
Randomly	5	5.8
Budgetwise	10	11.1
On demand	20	23.5
None	15	17.6
Total	85	

What are the ways in which is budget demarcated? Most have no uniform pattern to say that their budget is in one pattern. There are as many options as many institutions.

Q. What is yearly budget:

	Respondents	*Percentage*
Below 10 lakh	50	55.5
Above 10 lakh	10	11.1
Above 20 lakh	25	27.7
Unstated	5	5.5
Total	90	

As stated earlier, most of the respondents are among the middle level institutions, and hence we find they have an annual budget less than Rs. 10 lakhs. But there is another contradiction, in this generalisation, because there are as many as 28 per cent institutions which have their annual budget higher than 20 lakhs, per year.

Q. How much is the yearly increase:

	Respondents	*Percentage*
10%	5	5.5
15%	25	27.7
Limited	25	27.7
No limit	35	38.8
Total	90	

So also, is the annual increase among these institutions. More than 33 per cent have an annual increase between 10 and 15 per cent in the budget. An increase in 15 per cent, however, only takes care of the inflation, leaving the other factors, in the annual planning untouched. Many factors influence the annual budgets, which includes, rising prices, increasing and diversifying needs, increase in exchange rates for imported materials, etc. And the following questions, explicitly, identify the patterns in which budgeting is being done in Indian libraries of today (the answers are self-explanatory).

Q. Is it (*i.e.*, Lib. Budget) proportional to other departments:

	Respondents	*Percentage*
Yes	20	22.2
No	70	77.7
Total	90	

Q. Is it taking care of inflation:

	Respondents	*Percentage*
Yes	55	57.8
No	40	42.1
Total	95	

Q. It is taking care of changing needs:

	Respondents	*Percentage*
Yes	60	63.1
No	35	38.8
Total	95	

Q. Is there a planning to increase collection:

	Respondents	*Percentage*
Yes	60	75.0
No	20	25.0
Total	80	

Q. If yes, how much was last year's annual increase:

		Respondents	*Percentage*
Books	1—5%	30	37.6
	5—10%	15	18.6
	10—15%	35	43.8
Journals	1—5%	35	58.3
	5—10%	10	16.7
	10—15%	15	25
Reports	1—5%	5	50.0
	5—10%	5	50.0
	10—15%	—	

A/v	1—5%	5	16.7
	5—10%	15	50.0
	10—15%	10	33.3
CD-ROM	1—5%	10	40.0
	5—10%	10	40.0
	10—15%	5	20.0

Q. How long the user must wait for a suggested title:

	Respondents	*Percentage*
Six months	60	92.3
Around two years	5	7.6
More than two years	—	—
Total	65	

Given the fact that some libraries today accept user suggestions and order books accordingly, the question is how long a user must wait for fulfilment of the need? It is around six months that most provide the books demanded, and few other libraries need much more time to procure the material.

Q. What is the total collection (total volumes):

	Libraries
Less than 10,000	15
More than 10,000	20
More than 20,000	20
More than 40,000	10
More than 60,000	10
More than 80,000	10
More than 1,00,000	5
More than 2,00,000	5

From the above it is evident that there are large number of libraries, that are surveyed, which have less than one lakh collections. This supports a finding of the study that middle level libraries are sufficiently sized in terms of collections, staff, and budget. What they are in terms of services and how far effective in providing end-user satisfaction will be discussed in the next pages.

Storage

Q. What major equipment is added since last four years:

	Respondents	*Percentage*
Xerox machine	55	33.3
Computer PCs	55	33.3
Terminals	10	6.0
Fax machine	20	12.0
Microfilm equipment	25	15.1
Total	125	

The questions here relate to what type of machines the responding libraries have recently added, and if they have, how many libraries are common in each type of storage and retrieval medium. The above figures show that while xerox machines and PCs/computers are becoming common, still libraries do not have enough of other common gadgets enabling the libraries to be able to enter the competitive world of twenty-first century.

Q. Is the planning adequate to place equipment/furniture:

	Respondents	*Percentage*
Yes	40	44.4
No	50	55.6
Total	90	

Q. If yes, is it enough for computers/audio-visuals:

	Respondents	*Percentage*
Yes	25	62.5
No	15	37.5
Total	40	

Q. Does its maintenance call for training staff:

	Respondents	*Percentage*
Yes	60	80.0
No	15	20.0
Total	75	

While some of the above questions are self-explanatory, the above does call for a word of clarification. Maintenance of computers, and equipments, is a technical job and the librarians must have minimum skills to know its design and structure. Though technicians must be trained to handle these regularly, the librarians must not be handicapped if these are not immediately available!!!

Q. If yes, are the computers managed by a library staff:

	Respondents	*Percentage*
Yes	50	90.0
No	5	10.0
Total	55	

Contradicting the general belief that libraries have full time systems managers, the above response is revealing and it shows that 90 per cent of the institutions have library staff who manage the computers.

Q. How frequently machines break down:

	Respondents	*Percentage*
Usually	10	18.1
Rarely	45	81.9
Total	55	

Q. Is the budget sufficient for adding new equipment:

	Respondents	*Percentage*
Yes	20	25.0
No	60	75.0
Total	80	

Q. If yes, does the maintenance take away large chunk:

	Respondents	*Percentage*
Yes	5	25.0
No	15	75.0
Total	20	

Q. How often users complain about missing items from shelf:

	Respondents	*Percentage*
Few users	10	10.0
Most users	90	90.0
Total	100	

Storage, includes, shelf, and managing this space is as important as is the acquisition and processing of library materials. And this is the prime place also for evaluation of the library's effectiveness: users in 90 per cent of the libraries complain of this problem. By implication it means most libraries presume that if they have catalogued a book it is bound to be in its right place automatically.

The experiences of libraries which practice shelf-reading are different. Cataloguing a book and shelving it does not presume its right placement in the library. A regular practice of browsing and shelf-rectification is a must if books must be at the right place all the time, not only at the time when the user expects!!! That is why the next question focuses specifically on this matter. And a large number state they have shelf reading done by the staff. If the facts are so, what are the other reasons for missing items, misplaced books, and hidden books. The probable reasons are left for the readers' imagination.

Q. Do you have shelf rectification/shelf reading by staff:

	Respondents	*Percentage*
Yes	70	73.6
No	25	26.4
Total	95	

To quickly store the newly acquired items in the library, the staff must have a speed in processing, which matches with the standards laid down for the purpose. A large number of respondents in the question mentioned below, have stated, that they can process only 5 to 10 books a day, which is below the standard recommended by Ranganathan!

Q. How many books are processed per day:

	Respondents	*Percentage*
5—10	45	47.3
10—20	30	31.5
20—40	15	15.7
More	5	5.4
Total	95	

Q. Technical processing is:

	Respondents	*Percentage*
Manual	75	78.9
Automated	20	21.1
Total	95	

Despite the fact that large number of libraries are manually doing the technical processing, it is heartening that a few have reversed the traditions and come up with mechanical mode of processing the materials. A survey of another type would reveal how many are using their own packages for this purpose, and how many are depending on the scarce market.

Service

Relating to the institutional performance is the question of services offered by libraries. The following questions deal with issues relating to offering services (or helpful assistance) to users in libraries.

Q. Does the library have the following services:

	Respondents	*Percentage*
Circulation	100	29.5
Photocopy	60	17.6
Translation	5	1.5

Inter library loan	70	20.6
On-line	30	8.8
Abstracts	10	2.9
Indexes	15	4.4
CAS	15	4.4
SDI	35	10.3
Total	340	

The most common service is circulation, followed by borrowing books from other libraries, photocopy, and others. Interestingly more libraries today have photocopying facility, as compared to few years ago. Indicating that the technology of document delivery has gained inroads and libraries have accepted the modern dictum that sharing resources is the primary function, rather than preservation and 'touch me not' attitude. But if only 60 per cent of libraries of the survey have xerox facility, then the question is how are the other libraries providing this primary responsibility?

Q. Is there any survey done on the need of library products:

	Respondents	*Percentage*
Yes	40	42.1
No	55	57.9
Total	95	

To perform effectively libraries must have an understanding and so also feedback, to know the pulse of the users. The question here is whether there are such methods to find out the need of library services, or products, such as, those stated above: CAS, SDI, indexes, etc. While only 42 per cent libraries have done this exercise, nevertheless this is an encouraging sign to find out how useful is one service and if the users really need it.

Q. What type of services are expected free:

	Respondents	*Percentage*
Circulation	25	29.4
Xerox	10	11.7
Indexes	15	17.6
Abstracts	10	11.7
On-line	10	11.7
CD-ROM searching	15	17.6
Total	85	

Relating to the idea of having a survey of user needs, is the expectations of the users, regarding matters such as payment for the services, type of services that can be priced, and so on. Expecting 'free' is a universal phenomenon, and so was the question to find out the what is expected free. Most respondents feel they should get circulation services free, more want free products too.

Q. What was acceptable price for library products:

	Respondents	*Percentage*
Subsidized	55	91.6
Actual	5	8.3
Total	60	

On the issue of what is the acceptable price, since there cannot be anything called free, most wanted subsidized rates. It is heartening that library users are sensible to the financial crunch, a regular problem for libraries to make both ends meet.

Q. If no survey done, any other means for feedback on services (Circulation/xeroxing/on-line/CD-ROM searching):

	Respondents	*Percentage*
Yes	20	50.0
No	20	50.0
Total	40	

Q. Are the services having full use:

	Respondents	*Percentage*
Yes	55	68.7
No	25	31.2
Total	80	

Q. Are the services actual need based:

	Respondents	*Percentage*
Yes	75	88.2
No	10	11.7
Total	85	

Q. If yes, how are the needs ascertained:

	Respondents	*Percentage*
Observation	55	45.8
Past behaviour	15	12.5
Circulation pattern	35	29.1
Shelf use behaviour	10	8.3
Other methods	5	4.1
Total	120	

Q. Are there any user satisfaction records:

	Respondents	*Percentage*
Yes	25	33.6
No	50	66.3
Total	75	

Q. If yes, how are these used as feedback to improve the work (please comment):

(a) The complaint/suggestion is considered once in a quarter and necessary measures are taken to implement;

(b) Selecting journals of their interest/importance.

Q. What do users think about the library:

	Respondents	*Percentage*
Very good	40	38.0
All right	20	19.0
Requires improvement	35	33.3
Below average	10	9.5
Total	105	

Q. If required improvement what measures are planned:

	Respondents	*Percentage*
Improve products	10	18.1
Improve staff performance	25	45.4
Make surveys/need funds	20	36.2
Total	55	

Q. Any study done to assess cost-benefit of services:

	Respondents	*Percentage*
Yes	5	5.9
No	80	94.1
Total	85	

Q. What is the daily number of visitors:

	Respondents	*Percentage*
5—50	60	60.0
50—100	20	20.0
100	20	20.0
200	—	—
More	—	—
Total	100	

Q. What is the daily number of issues:

	Respondents	*Percentage*
5—50	35	38.8
50—100	40	21.0
100	20	42.1

200	—	—
More	—	—
Total	95	

Q. Is xeroxing service:

	Respondents	*Percentage*
Free	15	18.75
Priced	65	81.25
Total	80	

Q. Is on-line computer searching:

	Respondents	*Percentage*
Free	5	12.5
Priced (Tick any)	35	87.5
Total	40	

Q. Is CD-ROM searching:

	Respondents	*Percentage*
Free	15	37.5
Priced (Tick any)	25	62.5
Total	40	

Q. Number of daily CD-ROM users:

	Respondents	*Percentage*
5-25	35	77.7
25-50	—	—
More	10	22.2
No record	—	—
Total	45	

Q. Number of daily reference queries:

	Respondents	*Percentage*
5—25	60	85.7
25—50	5	7.1
50—75	5	7.1
More	—	—
No limit	—	—
Total	70	

Technology and Changing User Needs

Q. What are the technological implications on the library (Rank these):

	Respondents
(a) Manpower	50
(b) Collection	55

(c) Storage	50
(d) Acquisition	50
(e) Processing	55

First Rank	*Second Rank*	*Third Rank*
(a) 20	(e) 20	(a) 20
(e) 15	(d) 15	(b) 15
(b) 10	(c) 15	(c) 10
(c) 10	(b) 10	(e) 10

Q. Is there any priority in implementation of technology:

	Respondents	*Percentage*
Yes	180	92.3
No	15	7.6
Total	195	

Q. Is yes, what is to be done first:

	Respondents	*Percentage*
Cataloguing	35	33.3
On-line searching	25	23.8
CD-ROM searching	25	23.8
Acquisition	15	14.3
Serials	5	4.8
Total	105	

Q. What are the implications of changing needs of the users (Rank these):

	Respondents	*Percentage*
(a) Acquisition	35	18.9
(b) Funds	35	18.9
(c) Manpower	30	16.2
(d) Collection	30	16.2
(e) Processing	30	16.2
(f) Storage	25	13.6
Total	185	

User Education

(Questions here concern what are the ways adopted to make the users develop self-help, as an essential attitude for managing the library)

Q. Any courses of educating users are introduced:

	Respondents	*Percentage*
Yes	25	23.8
No	80	77.1
Total	105	

Q. If yes (Tick the following name of the programme):

	Respondents	*Percentage*
User education	15	25.0
Bibliographic instruction	5	8.3
No name (informal)	40	66.6
Total	60	

Q. Teaching methods:

	Respondents	*Percentage*
Lectures	20	33.0
Tours	20	33.0
Audio-visuals	15	25.0
Practicals	5	8.3
Total	60	

Q. If no user education programme exists (give reasons):
Q. Lack of resources:

	Respondents	*Percentage*
Yes	20	66.6
No	10	33.3
Total	30	

Q. Lack of interest in the staff:

	Respondents	*Percentage*
Yes	25	62.5
No	15	37.5
Total	40	

Q. Users are acquainted and prefer timely assistance:

	Respondents	*Percentage*
Yes	45	75.0
No	15	25.0
Total	60	

Future

Questions are on the strategies being adopted to face an era of changing technology, changing user needs, literature explosion, inflation and shrinking budgets, with other information providers competing in the society. It is also on how to survive the present while preparing for the future. Depending on how the planning is done for the present, the path for the future can be easily ascertained.

Q. What are future plans to keep pace with changing needs (Check the following): *(Considering technological advances/user needs/financial cuts)*

Q. By making staff changes:

	Respondents	*Percentage*
Yes	35	46.6
No	40	53.3
Total	75	

Q. By asking for more resources from the management:

	Respondents	*Percentage*
Yes	80	88.9
No	10	11.1
Total	90	

Q. By other methods of strategic planning:

	Respondents	*Percentage*
Yes	65	76.4
No	20	23.6
Total	85	

The three options suggested have received responses that are ranked as: asking more resources, using strategic planning methods, and staff changes. This indicates that the librarians have an idea that by improving the level of resources that they have, they can improve their performance in future. Contradicting this thinking is the idea that the level of staff that are available in the libraries is far more than required. Few of the surveyed libraries are really short of staff, but most have surplus staff. By implication, there is a lack of application of standards, to know (a) size of staff necessary for the existing level of services, (b) number of users and proportionate staff, (c) proportion of annual increase of collection and types of services requiring different levels of staff, etc.

One thing which is rarely tried in Indian libraries is internal staff transfers, and changes in routines. Such practices have less of disadvantages and more of advantages, but conservative leaders do not wish to take chances with such experiments. What is to be tried in libraries is regular shifting, and regular changing routines, to remove (a) the tiresome and boring daily routine, and (b) the mechanical behaviour that gradually emerges among the staff.

Q. What are the implications of the future on the following: The responses to this are as follows, representing the priorities of the libraries [(a)* for instance, is collection development]:

(a)*	(b)	(c)	(d)	(e)	(f)	(g)	(h)	(i)	(j)	(k)	(l)	(m)	(n)
60	80	70	75	80	60	60	85	75	70	75	70	75	70

Ranking these the future action plan is as follows:

I.	(85) (h)
II.	(80) (b), (e)
III.	(75) (d), (i), (k), (m)
IV.	(70) (c), (j), (l), (n)
V.	(60) (a), (f), (g)

A break up of these factors is shown below, depicting where each factor stands, in terms of preferences of librarians:

Q. (a)* Collection development:

	Respondents	*Percentage*
Alter interests	40	66.6
Withdraw	10	16.6
Adhoc	10	16.6
Total	60	

Q. (b) Processing: changes in record entry format:

	Respondents	*Percentage*
Yes	55	68.7
No	25	31.2
Total	80	

Q. (c) Changes in output format:

	Respondents	*Percentage*
Yes	45	64.2
No	25	35.8
Total	70	

Q. (d) Plans to download cataloguing records:

	Respondents	*Percentage*
Yes	60	80.0
No	15	20.0
Total	75	

Q. (e) Storage increase in capacity:

	Respondents	*Percentage*
Yes	70	87.5
No	10	12.5
Total	80	

Q. (f) Change medium/methods:

	Respondents	*Percentage*
Yes	40	66.6
No	20	33.3
Total	60	

Q. (g) Change systems of storage:

	Respondents	*Percentage*
Yes	45	75.0
No	15	25.0
Total	60	

Q. (h) Services: increase new services:

	Respondents	*Percentage*
Yes	80	94.1
No	5	5.9
Total	85	

Q. (i) Price the products:

	Respondents	*Percentage*
Yes	50	66.6
No	25	33.3
Total	75	

Q. (j) Produce/increase library products in phases:

	Respondents	*Percentage*
Yes	65	92.8
No	5	7.2
Total	70	

Q. (k) Marketing: survey the needs:

	Respondents	*Percentage*
Yes	70	92.8
No	5	7.2
Total	75	

Q. (l) Feasibility studies of products/services:

	Respondents	*Percentage*
Yes	65	92.8
No	5	7.2
Total	70	

Q. (m) Get regular feedback:

	Respondents	*Percentage*
Yes	60	80.0
No	15	20.0
Total	75	

Q. (n) Evaluate the products regularly:

	Respondents	*Percentage*
Yes	60	83.7
No	10	16.2
Total	70	

If the above ranked items are listed in descending order of importance, the picture will be as follows: services, processing, storage, and so on. Strategies for future are important, and the trends are as shown above.

Before discussing further the ranking pattern, it is worth to have a look at the different factors, from the point of view of what the responses for each are. For instance, on the question how to tackle the issue of collection development, the respondents have given three types of answers. First, most state they would alter interests, in relation to, preferences, and priorities; second, a few think they will withdraw the material and plan the collection development accordingly; third, a few also think they can make adhoc decisions, based on contingencies and necessities. The main issue, however, is that collection development calls for much more than simple factors stated above. Its calls for a holistic approach to the idea of development a balanced collection, based on a clear policy of what to acquire, and what not to, and so on. As stated in another context, most of these libraries do not have a written policy. Given the complexities involved in this process, these matters are left for another survey.

In terms of what the above figures demonstrate, it is obvious that the highest priority is for increasing new services. This is what 85 out of the 105 responding librarians wish to prioritize for the future. While 80 respondents indicated desire to concentrate on processing, the question focused changes in date entry format. 69 per cent were positive in this regard, whereas the others gave negative reply. Which means there is no need to change the record entry format, in case of automating library collection, according to 31 per cent responding librarians.

A question which arises, by default, is whether record entry format, makes any difference in the planning and implementation of automation? So also, arises the question, as to how many libraries in India, have already experimented alternative formats for data entry—a guess is all have to undergo this experimentation, because each library has a different environment. Answers to such questions are left for a future researcher. For instance, most libraries did enter the data earlier without any regard to standards—CCF/MARC, etc.—considering that each library must have its own database. With the advancement in technology of networking it became essential for all libraries to have a common data exchange format. It has dawned to many now that even a common format may not be essential for networking, as the conversion engines are getting stronger and capable of transfer of records with alternative schemes.

Q. As a librarian what knowledge/skills/training you think are critical for your future (state only critical issues like automation, continuing education, networks, staff motivation, fund raising, etc.)

(a) Needs hands-on training of computers and networking, and some type of training for staff;
(b) Computer education and continuing education or latest technologies, alternate fund raising are necessary;
(c) Skills of communication to be improved. Opportunities should be provided to start continuing education programmes and promotional avenues;
(d) Due to increasing costs of books and journals, library automation is the need of time. Hence, the training of computer skills and other equipment is must to face the new changes taking place in the field of librarianship;
(e) 'State-of-art' information technology products, services and applications;
(f) Improve staff motivation.

Most important concern is all about the computerized skill. Except one mention of improving the communication skill, and another mentioning motivational aspects, there is a total dearth of what makes us better role players in the society, a society which needs information even for survival, not only for progress and development. Libraries are struck with the terror of shrinking funds and increasing pressures for personalized services, but none stated anything about fund raising strategies that need to be evolved in a typical type of institution which has always offered 'free' opportunities for free access to information! Moreover, none has even taken pains to respond how to tackle the burning problem (even related to resource sharing), that is the issue of 'networking', which has so badly failed in this part of the world.

Professional Issues

Q. Can you divide library work into administrative and specialists tasks (two/more divisions):

	Respondents	*Percentage*
Yes	60	70.5
No	25	29.5
Total	85	

If all activities in the library can be divided into technical and public service areas, why not divide the administrative and non-administrative areas also. Such was the premise in asking this question. Most library managers get into bureaucratic issues and have no time for other matters. See for instance, in another context, these respondents have indicated that fewer have time for interaction with management, whereas more are busy with administrative affairs. The contention here is if the senior library managers in India are relieved for specialists tasks and matters non-administrative we are bound to have more time devoted for scholarly persist by librarians. According to studies conducted in America, librarianship is lacking the scholarly approach just because it gets bog down with trivial issues rather than involving in creativity. That is it has no time to devote for research and theory of how the profession is performing and what are, to list one of the main agendas, the ways of improving its image in the society.

One must not confuse this proposal, with what Ranganathan had to say in another context: "The combination of academic and administrative responsibilities, and the practice in the universities all over the world indicate that the status and the salary of the library staff should be the same as that of the teaching and research staff". Here Ranganathan is discussing the question of faculty status, and has no where hinted about splitting the responsibility. Coming back to the questionnaire again, let us proceed with the discussion.

Q. If yes, two/more librarians will have equal status, and the headship will rotate (as per UGC faculty pattern):

	Respondents	*Percentage*
Agree	30	46.1
Do not agree	20	30.7
Not possible	10	15.3
No comment	5	5.1
Total	65	

Q. Can library get involved in national development?

	Respondents	*Percentage*
Yes	80	100.0
No	—	—
Total	80	

On the most neglected question, which is the sole purpose of doing this entire research, nearly. 25 per cent of the respondents have no comment. It is strange that they have no idea of what the simple sentence is all about!

Q. If yes, can the Government involve library in the planning and implementation?

	Respondents	*Percentage*
Yes	50	71.5
No	20	28.5
Total	70	

One respondent comments:

(a) Till this date no communication/request from Government is received.

This comment highlights the tradition of waiting for something from above. If it is the government who has to initiate the process of involving libraries in planning, then there is a different route for libraries. In the case of Ranganathan, it was he who first developed library work to such an extent that it became obvious and necessary for the Government to involve him in the planning. The question one may ask is are there any more such Ranganathans who do so much of rigorous exercise in terms of contribution of the library to the national development, the answer will be there are no such task masters any more!!!

Q. On being asked as to how to gain that level of recognition in the society, so that you are called to be in the planning, and 'How you think library can get that level of priority', the respondents have their viewpoints as given below:

To substantiate the earlier question, the above question is seeking responses on how to go about splitting the managers responsibility. Those who were positive in stating that the Library managers can split their duties, administrative and non-administratively, have more details to offer for further analysis. Nearly 46 per cent librarians feel that it is a practical idea. But one-third do not agree on this matter.

This disagreement is supported by the comment of a respondent, who says, 'that the administrative work can be got done by two assistant librarians of two/more divisions, under the control of one librarian'. What is not clear to this respondent is that such a decentralization has been in practice for long, where duties are assigned to different librarians. The issue rather stated differently means, let the librarians who head the responsibilities be allowed to rotate their hardship, may be with librarians of equal pay, or equal qualifications, such as teaching community under the umbrella of the UGC has been performing since a decade.

It is for the working librarians to try out all the possible ways and find means to improve their performance and elevate their own profession—given the fact that librarianship is not even regarded as profession in the eyes of the world, and (any comment on how to achieve this, who should come forward: the society, Government, professional, etc.: do you see any way of becoming on par with health, education, literacy, science technology, etc. Can the library also find a place of such top priority).

(a) Administrative and financial authority should be given to the librarian;
(b) The profession and Government should see that the maximum use of libraries/public libraries is made by the people, so that literacy, health, development in S&T can be attained/used to the maximum extent;
(c) By providing services which are essential for its users;
(d) Library must provide value based services; anticipation of the need is a must;
(e) Users and professionals can come together to get the priority for libraries definitely on lines with health, education;
(f) Devoted professionals should come forward;
(g) Certainly, without developing the information sources it is, not possible to detect the problem and to solve it, and library is the storehouse of information;
(h) By showing the existence and importance, it is only possible when everyone in the profession will be dedicated in his/her work;
(i) By declaring "right to information" a distinct fundamental right in our constitution;
(j) By creating a public library system in the State in such a manner that public library services may be available to the citizens from grassroot level to the State level.

Most have highlighted that the library is still to become a useful resource, which means the profession is still looking beyond its own shoulders for help, without understanding of its own role in this process. Further, the profession has not set any clear lacuna which can be considered as the primary factor in not getting a place as important as health, education, etc. None has indicated that the library can never gain the status of essentials (basic human needs). This missing message must be sounded to those librarians, who work sincerely, and hope that the society will one day treat it as important as food, clothing or shelter!!! Information reaches one and all, and necessity is the mother of invention, and people always find alternative means of information, if libraries have not been accessible, or if libraries are not at their disposal. None waits for the library to open and then declare an invention, or declare that a bomb is to be made. People have a variety of information sources and libraries are just a drop in the ocean.

Q. Will this involvement improve social image of library?

	Respondents	*Percentage*
Yes	80	100.0
No	—	—
Total	80	

Q. Any views on building a usable library to the society you serve (please comment):

(a) By providing CD-ROM and latest books and journals;
(b) To build up usable library financial, and administrative assistance is required. Resource sharing should be encouraged;
(c) By acquiring a few more journals, books and newspapers, it can be more usable library to the society;
(d) Librarians, clinical practitioners and medical, and social workers have to come together and joint efforts are to be made;
(e) The libraries and their services have to be more user-friendly to the members of the society;
(f) Professionals must pay attention towards their user by means of behaviour, resources, etc. (only by this) library becomes usable for society;
(g) A balanced collection with the system of expeditious dissemination;
(h) Public library services should be made available to every citizen irrespective of caste, creed, race, sex, in the manner that none should be left out of the provision whether he/she resides in the cities, town or village;
(i) Collection development should be based on local needs of the people of that area where the library is situated. Then only a library can be usable;
(j) By promoting development information on crucial issues like, education, health, etc.;
(k) By user training and publicity about information.

Library Growth Studies: Other Surveys

Case Study One

Public Libraries

The Karnataka Public Libraries Act, 1965, came into force with the establishment of the Department of Public Libraries (DPL) in 1966. Prof. Khan (1983) did a survey of the working of the Act in the State, after 16 years of its enactment. The survey covered 12 District Central Libraries (DCL) and 6 City Central Libraries (CCL). The findings are:

(a) *Collection:* The overall average availability of Kannada titles in DCLs is between 35 to 50 per cent. The relative holdings of

Kannada titles in urban libraries is 59 per cent and in rural libraries 45 per cent. "Hence, public libraries in the State have to make a vigorous drive to acquire publications in Kannada language covering various subjects". The conclusion is based on the fact "that Kannada is not the only official language of the State, but it is (nevertheless) the medium of communication among the majority of the people in Karnataka".

In respect of subject literature it is found that libraries have a strong collection of books in literature (fiction and criticism) where availability is above 70 per cent. But the libraries have a very poor collection of books in other subject areas. Religious literature and reference collection in Kannada is poorly represented. Non-book materials like maps, charts, atlases in Kannada language are conspicuously absent. "This calls for an early remedial action on the part of the DPL".

(b) *Staff Resources:* One reason why DPL has not attracted talented professionals is its poor pay structure. A problem in relation to staff is the lack of variety which in turn is correlated to lack of variety in library services. For instance, library services to children now-a-days demand specialized training on the part of the qualified staff. There are no specialists in the DPL to render such services.

"This takes us to the consideration of the nature of training provided for a professional working in public libraries. None of the university schools in India which provide professional staff for different types of libraries impart instructions and training in Public librarianship. Some library schools have optional courses but these are inadequate and do not provide a wholesome training especially suiting the Indian environment. As the present author has argued elsewhere, there is a need to have an Institute of Public Librarianship to provide facilities for study and research in this area. Preferably this could be done on all-India basis".

(c) *Financial Resources:* Since 1980-81 surcharge on tax on entry of goods (octroi), etc. has been deleted (by the Government). "It would be better if the State Government gives to the Local Library Authorities adequate compensation for the loss of revenue due to the abolition of the Octroi duty. This measure is long overdue".

As per the annual report of the DPL, 1981-82, the details are:

Type of Libraries	*Income*	*Expenditure*
	(In rupees)	
CCL	43,83,249	49,90,771
DCL	53,18,282	40,95,973
Total	97,01,531	90,86,744

Note: The income includes library cess amount collected by CCL and DCL; and also the State Government's grant. There is a saving of rupees seven lakhs, as seen in the above table.

"On the whole the policy of the Karnataka Act of levying library cess . . . (3% of the land revenue) collected as its contribution to the District Library Authority has proved to be quite beneficial".

(d) *Material Resources:* Functional library building is absent, except in CCL's at Belgaum and Mangalore. All the libraries (CCLs and DCLs) are located in places which are accessible to local community. Except CCLs Belgaum, Dharwar and Mysore, and DCLs Bellary and Bijapur, all others provide easy access to the pedestrians including the senior citizens and the children. Reading tables/chairs are non-functional and uncomfortable in all libraries. Most libraries have shelf system that hampers the ease of use and involves wastage of space.

(e) *User Satisfaction:* Each district has certain unique socio-economic and at times cultural features which can easily be differentiated from others. (Considering this) stereo-typed collections and services of our public libraries are quite ineffective in meeting the differential needs. Except Bangalore District, all other districts have predominantly rural population living in small towns, villages and hamlets. This necessitates strengthening of the present rural libraries and their services and creating new ones almost on war footing. As population is sparse, commissioning of different types of model library services in these areas could be explored. Since literacy level in rural areas is very low, oral and audio-visual communications are a must. Most of the borderline districts have populations whose mother tongue is other than Kannada, and for these suitable literature must be made available. The Bangalore city on account of its demographic and socio-cultural features (basically multi-cultural and cosmopolitan) needs to be provided with library services to meet its individual needs. The pattern of library organization has to be on different footing. Each district has a variety of cottage industries. Informative and educative materials in printed and audio-visual form correlating the specific cottage industries in each district have to be provided. There is a need to create 'Rural Information Centre' to provide general information on issues like health and hygiene, sanitation, family planning, child care, nutrition, trade and commerce, and so on.

Case Study Two

Prof. Khan (1983), cites Nagappa's survey and presents the following trends in public library user need satisfaction:

1. The public libraries have failed to attract the children below 14 years;
2. The public libraries have not been able to attract the literate/ educated women. The ratio between male and female respondents is 87:13;
3. The main segment of users (54%) is (comprises) of students, and employees in offices, firms, etc.;
4. The educational level of the majority of the respondents is below undergraduate level;
5. The largest number of readers are interested in reading novels (66%), story books (52%), biographies (41%), and religious works (35%). Indicating that there is not much of interest in scientific works*;
6. Most respondents (61%) felt that the number and variety of titles in the areas of their choices are insufficient;
7. Nearly 70 per cent find that the arrangement of and accessibility to books is helpful and easy;
8. Staff are helpful to the readers. They are cordial and friendly;
9. Library catalogues are inadequate**.

---

* In following survey the present author has found more details.

** Library catalogues are not always adequate, given the 'presumed' cataloguing entry formats, mysterious skills required to search and specialised skills needed to venture into this system of accessing the library collection. For complexities and perplexities of the catalogue and its critics, one may read the present writer's paper "How User-Friendly Are We" in the All-India Library Seminar proceedings, 1995, Vijayawada, and published by ILA.

Case Study Three

User-friendly libraries for whom? A case in view:

A visit to the City Central Library at Jayanagar (Bangalore), City Central Library, Mysore, and State Central Library, Bangalore, was made to observe the reading pattern of the users.

Most users, in the descending order of priority, are busy with:

(a) Newspaper/magazine
(b) Textbook
(c) Reference
(d) Stacks/catalogue

Case Study Four

Near the city of Mangalore, is located the famous Jain Temple, Dharmastala. Outside the temple, is the shopping centre, and amidst this is the Library, opposite the Guest House. The Library is called *Vachnalaya* (or Reading Room). The *Dharmastala Vachnalaya,* is located in the verandah and a room houses the museum, another room houses the old magazines.

On display there are newspapers, four English dailies and four Kannada dailies. 16 general magazines/comic books lie on the librarian's desk, with no users. The time is between 5 and 6 p.m., and the day is Tuesday, a working day. There are five readers, of different age groups, and sex (one female), one is a labourer too, among the readers, busy reading Kannada daily, line by line, and so engrossed he is in the newspapers, that he does not notice an eyewitness around.

There is no seating for readers of news, as newspaper stands cannot accommodate such facility. There are, however, benches kept aside. The museum is small, housing antiques and excavated items, kept open for visitors. The room has none inside to view the rarities. The readers are probably from neighbourhood, and may be already acquainted with this display, or they may be more interested in gathering news—the crux of the present life.

Such verandah based newspaper rooms are popular in many towns and cities, and those who pass the place are free to stop by and read the news, without any charge or membership. The single factor that emerges on the whole is that news-hungry public does not need books, let alone serious books, scientific books, which Prof. Nagappa laments in his above cited survey result. Where is then all that is called as library movement and what is then the cry about library legislation and its demand for?

Use Behaviour and User Studies

Use and user studies are growing and have received much attention in India. While most of such studies deal with use patterns, some have dealt with use behaviour, user information seeking attitudes, etc. If we are to understand the user the better way suggested by management experts is to have a personal rapport with the users. For this purpose it is necessary to interact with the users, and one way to do so is through the process called user education. Prof. Girja Kumar and Prof. Krishan Kumar have done an exhaustive survey of the trends in user education, in their book, *Philosophy of User Education* (1983). They have also dealt with use and user studies in this work.

Use Behaviour and User Studies: A National Survey

As in the case of institutional growth, the present writer made an exhaustive survey of people in different walks of life in Indian society, across different cities. The results of the survey are analysed below.

A total of 400 people were surveyed. The respondents live and work in different metros and are from teaching, research, various professions, and other fields. The purpose of this enquiry is to know what user's feel about libraries, and what kind of satisfaction the library provides. These responses may help understanding role of library in society and enable planning a strategy for better libraries.

Background of the Users

To begin with, the study tried to identify the background about the users of a library in India. As stated earlier, the survey tried to find samples from different academic and research institutions in the country.

Q. Present qualification?

	Respondents	*Percentage*
Master's	215	50.58
M.Phil	35	8.23
Ph.D.	170	40.00
D.Litt.	5	1.17
Total	425	

While holding a doctorate degree became common in the 1980s and 1990s, but the equal number of respondents having master's degree shows that the fashion did not appeal many, and still there is a generation with master's only. Further the low number of respondents with M.Phil degree hints at a low level of attraction for this degree, as it leaves the beholder with no status or name worth it, which the doctorate degree confers on a person! Coming to the next issue in the survey, it deals with academic status. There are more respondents from the researchers category and hence it is not correct here to say that academics have stopped pursuing their advance studies, as is visible from the responses given below:

Q. Present academic status:

	Respondents	*Percentage*
Teacher	100	23.25
Researcher	200	46.51
Student	85	19.76
Others	45	10.50
Total	430	

While this survey concentrated on academic and research libraries, it did try to identify other library users, and hence there is a 10 per cent response from such people too. This minority is not from non-academic fields, rather these are also in allied and pseudo-academic environments. This becomes obvious from the following question, dealing with the field of affiliation.

In terms of their subject interests, the survey tried to gather a broad idea of the fields which the respondents belonged, and the results are as given below. The main indicator is that the respondents in descending order are from the area of social sciences, followed by humanities and sciences.

Q. Subject of your interest, state any three, in order of preference:

	Respondents	*Percentage*
Humanities	140	29.47
Social sciences	260	54.73
Science	75	15.78
Total	475	

Another question, which tries to find their 'academic' temperament, relates to the question of their past attendance in libraries. The idea is to see the connections of library mindedness among the academicians in India.

Q. What libraries have you used in past:

	Respondents	*Percentage*
Private collection	120	9.75
Public library	200	16.26
School library	140	11.38
College library	265	21.54
University library	295	23.98
Research library	160	13.00
Other collections	50	4.00
Total	1230	

Less then one-fifth are the users of public library, and less than one-sixth have used school libraries. These two are the major interests in foreign countries, whereas in India if public libraries are not yet common, school libraries are still least common.

Related to the idea of using a library, is that, more and more academics travel abroad, for different reasons. The idea of asking about foreign visits was to find out two related issues. First, if they have visited abroad, have they been to libraries in those countries; secondly, how easy it is, or how difficult it is to use those libraries? Incidentally, 80 (or one-fifth of the total respondents) did go abroad, and did use the libraries there. Of these, a great majority did ask for help in the libraries.

Q. Have you used libraries abroad (Name the countries*):

	Respondents	*Percentage*
Yes	80	94.11
No	5	5.89
Total	85	

[* France, England, Japan, UK, USA, Saudi Arabia, Kenya, Pakistan, Singapore, Canada.]

Interestingly, a great majority did ask for help! This is striking because, most Indians, when they are in India did not have the opportunity to ask for help. As the present study shows, India lacks a reference desk in most libraries. Whereas, all libraries in the West have a desk where one can, unhesitatingly, approach for help. And given this helping scenario, for the next question, most users felt, that they had no difficulty in finding what they were looking for!!! A lesson for the librarians and the management in India, to have a ready-made enquiry or information desk in all libraries. In fact Ranganathan imported this idea of information desk, as early as 1925, but today it is a rare species.

Q. Have you sought the help of librarians there:

	Respondents	*Percentage*
Yes	55	78.57
No	15	21.43
Total	70	

Q. Have you faced any difficulties in finding information:

	Respondents	*Percentage*
Yes	10	13.33
No	65	86.66
Total	75	

The next issue that was important was to find out what type of awareness and use these had to the academics and the learned, in India, have about the various types of information sources available in the country. The question relates to, other than library, what are the other sources that are of your interests?

Q. What other source of information you find useful (rank):

	Respondents	*Percentage*
(a) News from friends	105	13.2
(b) Newspaper	240	30.2
(c) Doordarshan	165	20.7
(d) Cable TV	75	9.4
(e) Radio	90	11.3
(f) Electronic mail	30	3.7
(g) Internet	35	3.9
(h) Others	50	6.2
Total	790	

First Rank	*Second Rank*	*Third Rank*
(b) 95	(c) 45	(c) 20
(a) 25	(e) 25	(h) 15
(h) 25	(d) 15	(d) 15
(c) 15	(b) 15	(e) 10
(d) 15	(h) 10	(a) 10

In terms of interests, newspaper is the most preferred source of information. If one-third of the people find newspaper as the most important source, and rank it as the top-most source, it implies that Indian literates are addicts of news! The second most important source is again, media based, that is doordarshan. It again indicates that reading books, and other pastimes are becoming of least interest.

Ninety-five people feel that (b) newspaper is of primary interest, whereas 15 have ranked it at second place, and a fewer have ranked it as of least importance. Again 25 respondents feel that (a) news from friends is primary source, whereas fewer have ranked it at third place. Compared to these only 15 have ranked (c) doordarshan as primary, and 45 rank it as secondary and fewer have placed it as least important.

Another question that related to the awareness of the public is about the existence of the computerized network that the Government has established in the country, and the access points for this are at various Government and academic centres all over India.

While a majority were aware of this, many have access to it in the university library. In fact NICNET is a resource of all variety of useful information for the public, and its publicity is highly desirable, given the fact, that 41 per cent respondents have no idea of such an important official source.

Q. Do you know that the Government of India has a national network (called NICNET), to provide the rural and urban public, some essential information for survival:

	Respondents	*Percentage*
Yes	245	58.33
No	175	41.66
Total	420	

Q. If yes, where do you use this:

	Respondents	*Percentage*
University library	55	35.48
Public library	35	22.58
Research library	40	25.80
Others	25	16.12
Total	155	

Information revolution and information superhighway are no more catch terms for the Western world, rather these are very much in the Indian menu even and hence as high as 74 per cent of respondents have shown their awareness about such means to access information. So also, is the next question, which inquires about the level of awareness of the people about the various Government and private funding agencies for research and related works. Most of the respondents are aware of such agencies.

Q. Are you aware that there are private and public access points electronic mail/ letter/information any where in the world:

	Respondents	*Percentage*
Yes	295	73.75
No	105	26.25
Total	400	

Q. Are you aware that there are many institutions and foundations who can help in funding your research/travel, etc.:

	Respondents	*Percentage*
Yes	335	80.72
No	80	19.27
Total	415	

Of the large number of positive respondents, as many as 60 per cent have used Indian funding for their projects. Less than one-third have availed foreign funding. This trend of using Indian funds for academic activities, seems to be of recent origin. Till the 1960s and even in 1970s, most of the projects were funded by Western institutions—to name a few Fulbright Fellowship, British Council Awards, World Bank, IMF, US Aid, etc.

Q. If yes, have you availed such a facility from:

	Respondents	*Percentage*
Indian institution	110	59.4
American	35	18.9
British	30	16.2
Others	10	5.4
Total	185	

About the Library You Use Most

Please name it:
IIM Library, Lucknow
British Library, Lucknow
USIS, Chennai
GIDS (Lucknow)
Gujarat University, Ahmedabad
ASRC, Hyderabad
CIEFL, Hyderabad
University of Hyderabad
L.P. Vidyaptih, Patna University
JNU, Delhi
Delhi University
Lal Bahadur Shastri Vidyapith, Delhi

IGNCA Library, Delhi
NEERI, Nagpur
District Central Library, Madurai
State Central Library, Chennai
Agricultural College, Nagpur
National Library, Calcutta
College Library, Midnapur (W.B.)
Regional Institute of Education, Bhopal
Andhra University, Vishakhapatnam
Deccan College, Pune
AMU Library, Aligarh
Medical College, Aligarh
Chemistry Department Library, AMU, Aligarh
Kashmir University
SK Agricultural University
AN Sinha Institute of Social Studies, Patna
Punjab University, Chandigarh
Patna University, Patna
Mangalore University
Bangalore University
Tagore Library
Lajpat Rai Pustakalaya Evam Vachnalaya
British Library, Bhopal
Information Centre, Suchna Kendra, Government of Madhya Pradesh, Bhopal

Q. Do you visit your library:

	Respondents	*Percentage*
Frequently	385	92.7
Rarely	30	7.3
Total	415	

Q. Your evaluation of library collection:

	Respondents	*Percentage*
Adequate	155	42.46
Inadequate	65	17.80
Fairly well	145	39.72
Total	365	

Since most of these questions and answers are self-explanatory, there are no remarks given. But the question below is worth looking at. It pertains to the usefulness of the library collection. If the collection is inadequate, is it in terms of books, to which 23 per cent feel positive.

But more than this, 38 per cent feel the inadequacy is in terms of lack of periodicals of their choice! Since the last century a number of periodicals in all possible specialisations emerged, and in the ultimate analysis, it came to the libraries to own, or at least provide access to majority of these, at whatever cost. The other inadequacies relate to services (9%), staff (6%), and no proper catalogue (9%).

If the library is inadequate in services, or in staff, no library can be expected to be inadequate in its catalogue—the key to a library!!!

Q. If inadequate, in what ways:

	Respondents	*Percentage*
Books	40	22.85
Journals	65	37.14
Reports	30	17.14
Services	15	8.57
Staff	10	5.57
No proper catalogue	15	8.57
Total	175	

Q. If the library has a catalogue, is it:

	Respondents	*Percentage*
Computerised	130	30.5
Card catalogue	295	69.5
Total	425	

Q. Are you familiar with catalogue:

	Respondents	*Percentage*
Yes	410	97.6
No	10	2.3
Total	420	

In the above question, it is about if one is familiar with the catalogue. While 2.3 per cent are not familiar at all, in the next question, interestingly, 4.7 per cent feel that though there is a catalogue, it is not easy to use. Even those who are familiar with the catalogue, as many as, 38 per cent, as shown below, use it only sometimes. Is it a fact that a catalogue is a mystery to some, or is that they feel bored using an index, or what are the other reasons for this lacuna? The answers could be many, and are left to the imaginations of those who are concerned!!!

Q. If yes, do you think it is:

	Respondents	*Percentage*
Easy	400	95.2
Difficult to use	20	4.7
Total	420	

Q. If easy, how often you consult the same:

	Respondents	*Percentage*
Regularly	240	62.3
Sometimes	145	37.6
Total	385	

Q. If difficult: Do you normally ignore the catalogue:

	Respondents	*Percentage*
Yes	60	35.2
No	110	64.7
Total	170	

The possible reasons, why people do not use a catalogue, include the point that they have to ask the library staff (which as many as 60% do), or as many as 40 per cent feel that the arrangement of the catalogue is difficult to use. Additionally, nearly 17 per cent opine that the catalogue is difficult to use, because it has an unimaginable arrangement!!!

Q. If no:

	Respondents	*Percentage*
Ask library staff	105	60.0
Go directly to the shelf	65	37.1
Struggle with catalogue	5	2.9
Total	175	

Q. If difficult to use, it is because of:

	Respondents	*Percentage*
Its arrangement	25	41.6
Its inconvenient location	25	41.6
Unimaginable order	10	16.6
Total	60	

In the next question, on subject approach to the catalogue, as many as 15 per cent feel that the subject approach is not helpful. And that the arrangement of the shelf is also not understandable, to an equal number of users. Considering this as a minority, is easy, and the management will be happy to sideline any minority voice, but is it not on the part of the profession that it cares for the maximum user satisfaction!!!

Q. Is your searching of the catalogue by subject helpful:

	Respondents	*Percentage*
Yes	340	85.0
No	60	15.0
Total	400	

Q. Arrangement (or classification) of books on the shelf is understandable:

	Respondents	*Percentage*
Yes	380	95.0
No	20	5.0
Total	400	

Q. If yes, is it helpful:

	Respondents	*Percentage*
Yes	355	94.6
No	20	3.3
Total	375	

Users of a library need help at different times. It is the duty of the library to have user-friendly staff! While most users ask for help, 8 per cent do things on their own. And to those who approach for help, 6 per cent feels that the staff are not available!

Q. If no, do you ask for help:

	Respondents	*Percentage*
Yes	170	91.9
No	15	8.1
Total	185	

Q. If yes, are the staff available:

	Respondents	*Percentage*
Yes	160	94.1
No	10	5.9
Total	170	

Q. If you do not find the required materials, do you still try:

	Respondents	*Percentage*
Yes	370	90.2
No	40	9.7
Total	410	

Q. If yes, through whom:

	Respondents	*Percentage*
Friends	70	17.7
Library staff	160	40.5
Colleagues	55	13.9
Other libraries	110	27.8
Total	395	

Even if the users of a library politely say, 'yes there are staff available', the question is how helping, how sincere and how concerned are the staff for the need fulfilment of their own clientele? Only 65 per cent feel, library staff is helping, 19 per cent feel that there is sincerity, and as few as 15 per cent feel that the staff show a concern. Again, there is a minority of 1.2 per cent who feels that none of these qualities are available in the staff.

Q. Do you find the library staff:

	Respondents	*Percentage*
Helping	320	64.6
Sincere	95	19.1
Concerned	75	15.1
None	5	1.2
Total	495	

Q. Do you have friendly relations with library staff:

	Respondents	*Percentage*
Yes	385	96.2
No	15	3.7
Total	400	

Q. If yes, how friendly they are:

	Respondents	*Percentage*
Very much	200	53.3
Not so much	70	18.6
For finding information	105	28.0
Total	375	

How friendly are the librarians? They are friendly only in terms of business, that is what is the feeling of almost one-third of the users. Almost 19 per cent have no friendship with the librarians. This however, also speaks of the mode and introvertness of the users.

Mere presence of the staff is not a criteria for fulfilment of the user's need satisfaction. There must be staff who are professionals, and who must be capable in all ways, to provide a helping hand to the users. In the absence of such factors, the users look down at the librarians. See the questionary below and it simply means, that as many as 60 per cent users feel that the staff lack in their skills, and that 40 per cent lack even professional training! Only 9 per cent state there is motivation in the staff in helping the users, in turn this is a very sad state of affairs.

Q. Are they:

	Respondents	*Percentage*
Professionally trained	210	60.8
Up to date in their skills	105	30.4
Motivated	30	8.8
Total	345	

There are all types of 'professionals', and the survey results, as shown below, reveal that there are many careless, negligent and misbehaving librarians, and all are not careful, sincere, and considerate!!!

Q. Or are they:

	Respondents	*Percentage*
Careless	25	35.7
Negligent	25	35.7
Misbehaving	20	28.6
Total	70	

Services

Q. Do you know that the library has many indexes and bibliographies on your subject matter in articles/books/dissertations:

	Respondents	*Percentage*
Yes	325	82.2
No	70	17.7
Total	395	

Q. If yes, how often do you use (tick any):

	Respondents	*Percentage*
Regularly	115	32.8
Occasionally	215	61.4
Never	20	5.7
Total	350	

Q. Can you name two or three indexes:

	Respondents	*Percentage*
Yes	100	25.0
No	300	75.0
Total	400	

Q. If you do not use indexes, how do you find articles/essays/chapters:

	Respondents	*Percentage*
Through friends	45	21.9
Through citations	125	60.9
Others	35	17.1
Total	205	

Q. How often do you scan through periodicals:

	Respondents	*Percentage*
Regularly	195	49.3
Occasionally	190	48.1
Never	10	2.5
Total	395	

Q. Do you know that the library can borrow materials from other libraries for you:

	Respondents	*Percentage*
Yes	305	73.4
No	110	26.5
Total	415	

Q. If yes, how often do you use this privilege:

	Respondents	*Percentage*
Regularly	15	6.3
Occasionally	165	67.3
Never	65	26.3
Total	245	

Q. Do you pay charges for any service in the library:

	Respondents	*Percentage*
Yes	150	37.5
No	250	62.5
Total	400	

Q. How happy are you with the charges:

	Respondents	*Percentage*
Very much	25	17.2
Not much	45	31.0
O.K.	75	51.7
Total	145	

A debate which is unending is about the charges—which are incurred in procuring reading material—that are passed on the user of the library. The discussion is here about these charges which the libraries, given the shortage of funds, are forced to ask the users to pay for. In this survey, only 38 per cent pay for the services. And those who pay, most think that the charges are not pinching. Only 18 per cent feel the charges are very much.

Q. Do you use your library for other than research:

	Respondents	*Percentage*
Yes	360	90.0
No	40	10.0
Total	400	

Q. If yes, is it for:

	Respondents	*Percentage*
Recreation	40	7.6
Information	225	42.8
Knowledge	250	47.6
Meeting friends	10	1.9
Total	525	

User Education

Education of the user, about the intricacies and difficulties involved in finding right information at the right time, requires that there must be some method of making the user comfortable in the library.

Q. Do you think the library must train the users:

	Respondents	*Percentage*
Yes	380	95.0
No	20	5.0
Total	400	

Q. If yes, to what level:

	Respondents	*Percentage*
Use catalogue	45	11.2
Use all areas	215	53.7
Use indexes	45	11.2
New technologies	95	23.8
Total	400	

Q. Have you ever undergone this training:

	Respondents	*Percentage*
Yes	85	21.2
No	315	78.7
Total	400	

Q. How do you feel its impact:

	Respondents	*Percentage*
Useful	75	93.7
Not necessary	5	6.3
Total	80	

Q. If you are positive, does this training help you understand the staff and resources:

	Respondents	*Percentage*
Yes	70	70
No comment	30	30
Total	100	

Q. Do you think the library must be user-friendly:

	Respondents	*Percentage*
Yes	395	98.7
No	5	1.2
Total	400	

Q. If yes, is it lacking in:

	Respondents	*Percentage*
Services	60	16.2
Products	35	9.4
Staff	40	10.8
Resources	155	41.9
Performance	80	21.6
Total	370	

Q. Is the library always useful in development of your career:

	Respondents	*Percentage*
Yes	350	90.9
No	35	9.1
Total	385	

Q. If no, what you think are the sources of information for keeping yourself abreast:

	Respondents	*Percentage*
Personal library	15	33.3
Friends	5	11.1
Teachers	15	33.3
Others—Libraries	5	11.1
—Experts	5	11.1
Total	45	

Q. Do you think library is a societal need, as important as education, health, sanitation, market, social welfare:

	Respondents	*Percentage*
Yes	390	97.5
No	10	2.5
Total	400	

Q. Do you think that libraries are unable to attract users for serious reading:

	Respondents	*Percentage*
Yes	205	51.9
No	190	48.1
Total	395	

As many as 52 per cent feel that libraries are not able to attract users for reasons other than light reading, or, for entertainment and news sources. There could be reasons for this lacuna in providing facilities for serious reading. One reason which appears is that the society has not stated its demand in terms of what information, other than newspapers, and light reading materials, it expects the libraries to provide. Or from another point of view, as stated elsewhere, if most of the libraries are crowded in newspaper and magazine section, and hardly a few are in busy in reading books and using the reference resources, this pressure of demand has to be reflected in the collection development pattern too.

Hence the question which was asked next related to asking the responding members of the society, as to how otherwise the library can improve its facilities, collection, area of interest, and so on.

Q. What remedial measures you suggest to improve the library performance for social change: (such as ways of improvement in searching literature; providing quick access to literature; providing more help in order to save time; increase user training methods; mail recent acquisition list; etc.)? The responses are important feedback for the study, and these help in testing, a hypothesis of the present study. To restate the hypothesis, it is 'Neither the libraries are involved in planning of the national growth programmes, nor the society has shown any inclination to get involved in planning of library growth'.

A. By Responding Members:

(a) The habit of visiting libraries should be inducted in the people right from the childhood. It can start from small stories in the younger age which can slowly progress with age into more informative and serious reading habits. Libraries are the source of information for every individual for a healthy and inquisitive mind which can lead to healthy society in general;

(b) The functioning hours of the libraries should be so that they meet the needs of not only students, teachers, researchers, but also the Government and non-government officials who can use the library only after the general working hours, or on holidays. Staff should be more cordial and friendly to its users;

(c) Journals are in small scale and not in sequence means not regular. So librarians take keen interest in this. CD-ROM facility is not available;

(d) Number of libraries should be increased, computerized searching system of book and periodicals should be adopted, library employees should be trained;

(e) By improvement in searching literature;
(f) Prepare/update user profile, their needs and arrange materials as per their need (computerization is a must to customize) and then send list of new additions, resumes and maintaining folders on needed areas, etc.;
(g) Mass awareness of library services are needed. People must be informed about what is a library and what it can offer them even at village/mohalla level. Then only we can expect some social change in Indian society;
(h) Catalogue of books acquired by libraries should be published yearly. New arrival should be dispatched;
(i) Recent publication should be available in the library on all subjects;
(j) Provide more help and save time, increase user training methods;
(k) Number of books should be increased, staff should be trained, computerized system should be adopted, budget for library should be increased;
(l) Pragmatic collection, adequate branches in rural and virgin areas as well;
(m) Introduce the computer facility in library by showing each book in a particular rack and position;
(n) Make searching more simpler and quick access to the required literature;
(o) People should be made aware of the books available in the libraries. The staff should be increased so as to guide and help people in searching the concerned books/periodicals;
(p) Libraries should stock material consistent with the local needs such as that of students in a college, etc. To make people more aware, cable TV ads might be used to inform people of the sources provided. Most of all the staff needs to be friendly and helpful to encourage readers;
(q) Computerization of libraries on various parameters, *viz.*, acc. no., users, subjects, authors, etc. in order to reduce/minimize searching time;
(r) Make the library as user friendly as possible. The process of selection of books should be easy and easily comprehendable;
(s) By helping people in finding out access to intensive topic through more recent acquisition and user training methods;
(t) Matters relating to social change must be collected at one place as per requirement of different sections of readers. The collection should also take care of recent trends in society and tastes and preferences of its users;
(u) Libraries should be in search of the public and should not be for restricted use. Easy access to children is a must;
(v) For literature search electronic media or at least LAN is needed. Adequate fund should be provided;
(w) The card catalogue method should be discarded and computerized system should be introduced. Latest editions of books should be made available;
(x) Publicizing the facilities of the library. Displaying the contents of library;
(y) Good photocopying facility at normal charges. Ensuring that pages, books are not stolen by users. Ensuring that material is kept at assigned place strictly. Ensuring that the material is as per users' requirements;
(z) A regular staff member to guide a new visitor so as to familiarize him/her with various areas of library—like reference, journals, catalogue, etc. Telephone service to provide quick and important information;
(y) All the areas of human life should be covered by the material available in the library;
(x) To provide computer facility (user-friendly) for searching the relevant material. Access to other libraries (in the country/abroad) of some material

is asked for. Proper xeroxing facility (24 hours access). Big reading hall with proper light and within arrangement;

(w) More need based acquisitions. Well classified and communicated to the user;

(v) Developing library to up-to-date technology is very essential. It should be a real treasure for knowledge hunting people;

(u) More easily accessible libraries throughout country;

(t) Apart from a good collection of reading materials . . . libraries (administrative heads/staff) need to be sincere in their effort to increase membership and for that matter the reading conditions must be improved;

(s) Buy the journal (national and international publication). People have to be attracted to the library for improving knowledge;

(r) The library staff must make use of electronic media to inculcate reading habits among users. In this connection they may inform about the facilities existing, like, electronic mail, computerized networks, etc.;

(q) Personal relationship is the key to use the library successfully;

(p) There should be separate compartments for different subjects. Library user should be given training on how to use a catalogue, indices, etc., for a specific period;

(o) As far as the university libraries are concerned: we need to train the staff, the readers. Make use of latest technologies. Encourage readers in making best of library facilities;

(n) Advanced literacy, awareness programmes, library user's consortium, discussion groups/reading classes. Why, even by giving occasional courses on the library: reading the library/reading in the library;

(m) Increase user training methods;

(l) Library administration should be transparent. Those who are not satisfying the eligibility of membership, some other provision should be made for those (who wish) to know;

(k) Search via electronic means—networks. Training, access to national and international networks;

(j) Reviews on new books. In subjectwise list of new books for reference;

(i) More conducive atmosphere in libraries, efficient services, scientific cataloguing including computer services, up-to-date good collection of books and periodicals;

(h) Users must be trained for using new methods of consulting library;

(g) Libraries should be well equipped to provide quick access to literature and every year new titles should be acquired;

(f) Providing good materials on general knowledge. Providing new literature and statistics;

(e) In a good library, there should be everything, *i.e.*, catalogue, books, journals, and other information, keep in order. Library staff should behave well and very cooperative. They should be well trained. In a good library there should be new books;

(d) Store more books for leisure reading. This will attract people initially and then they would be exposed to the vast knowledge to be unearthed here. Mail recent acquisition, provide quick access;

(c) Increase in working hours specially in summer. Selective journals and magazines should be available;

(b) A commission at national level be set up to give rank to journal, magazines, to encourage the mass what to read which to read;

(a) rapprochement between library staff, authorities, and users of the library;

(b) The library must have adequate collection of books/journals, reports on all subjects. Adequate infrastructure, computerized system of cataloguing and well-connected with other libraries and research centres;

(c) Increase user training methods. Publicize facilities available;

(d) Proper cataloguing, proper placement of titles as per classification and indexing at appropriate places, computerising library materials, proper training of library staff and their involvement in the library job;

(e) On-line searches. More CD-ROM material particularly periodicals;

(f) To increase our knowledge, to educate the society, etc.

(g) Basic facilities should be there in each and every library, like proper seating arrangements, ventilation, fans, light, etc. All kinds of reading materials should be available to the readers;

(h) In line with the changing technology, the library personnel must be properly trained to handle new technologies;

(i) New arrival information. Books should be purchased/recommended by researchers. Photocopy of rare books.

These prove the idea that library development is still an on-going process and there is much for the improvement. Most of the suggestions deal with library environment and there is by and large lack of marketing in libraries. Obviously, the first part of the hypotheses is proved to be correct that there has been no attempt to involve library in national development. The second part of the hypotheses has also been validated in the fact that the society will offer its ideas and opinions, but will not involve in the library development, as no respondent has spelled out the possibilities of this involvement!

Q. Do you think library is an indispensable institution for your information needs:

	Respondents	*Percentage*
Yes	385	96.2
No	15	3.7
Total	400	

Q. If yes, how will you help its survival (*e.g.*, if the library is declared as closed what will you do):

	Respondents	*Percentage*
React	175	47.2
Protest	170	45.9
Remain neutral	20	5.4
Others	5	3.5
Total	370	

Q. How will you protest:

	Respondents	*Percentage*
Take up the matter	120	64.8
Raise funds	40	21.6
Go to other library	25	13.5
Total	185	

Q. How will you react:

	Respondents	*Percentage*
Take up the matter	120	61.5
Raise funds	25	12.8
Go to other library	50	25.6
Total	195	

This survey has a large amount of food for thought, for those who wish to have a square meal, on the agenda for library development and a strategy for the development of libraries in India. They can see that user-friendliness is, by and large, a missing item in the total set-up. Further, there is a total lack of awareness of library culture, that a culture is not merely of people who appreciate their past and praise it all over! It is more so in spreading the world through the advanced techniques of recorded communication—no more pure oral systems! And that library as a vehicle of communication, can do wonders, even in this age of information superhighway!!!

Use Behaviour and User Studies: Other Surveys

Case One

Rural Information Centre: This was established in 1964, and caters to the needs centre of the districts of Chittoor, Cuddappah, Kurnool and Ananthapur. Its collection is 60,000 books, 125 subscribed periodicals. It has about 3,200 registered borrowers who use this facility. The study covered 50 residential houses in the neighbourhood, and therein needs:

A study was conducted in Chikmagalur District, with a sample of 495 people, in January 1995. The users were ranked in terms of areas of information needs and the total resources available in the district library system, the details are as follows:

	Area of Needs (Percentage)	*Matching Resources (Percentage)*
Education	50.5	6.94
Health	49.5	1.04

Agriculture	63.2	0.83
Horticulture	39.4	0.64
Legal Issues	41.0	0.42
Banking facility	33.9	0.41
Consumerism	36.9	0.08
Employment	35.5	0.07
Rural development	43.8	0.03
Credit facility	39.6	0.01

The District Library System comprises of 1 District Central Library, 10 Taluk/Branch Libraries, 39 Gram Panchayat Libraries, and 7 Book Delivery Stations. The top ten areas of information needs as listed above, are a part of the 32 areas identified in the study. The inference drawn are:

(1) There is total inadequacy of information resources in these libraries;
(2) The ranking of education at a higher proportion is not to mislead anyone, it includes a large number of copies of textbooks for schools and colleges;
(3) Agriculture and health information needs are the higher ranking areas, and the resources are very meagre; and there is a need to augment the resources almost thousand fold (100%) (Khan, 1997: 221).

Case Two

Regional Library, Tirupati: With 210 residents; the findings are 78 per cent are educated; only 10 per cent are registered borrowers of the library (to borrow books one has to deposit the required amount); 24 per cent habitually visit the library; 13.5 per cent expressed their inability to deposit such amount; 29.7 per cent are not aware of the existence of the library (a tale about the lack of marketing strategy); 62.1 per cent are not in favour of the present working hours (presently three hours each in two shifts); 61.5 per cent desired educational, rather than recreational material; 18 per cent complained about non-availability of required books, and 16 per cent said that there recommended titles were not even acquired; for 40.5 per cent the library books are received through friends; nearly 25 per cent are not very happy about the personal attention given towards the users (Chandran and Ramesh Babu, 1997: 280). There should not be a surprise on these findings. The Ekbote

Committee report had taken care of most of these problems, when they did extensive study of the issues and problems encountered by the library, library users and all concerned. What ails the system is the overall attitude that does not protest for lack of resources, that doesn't fulfil until there is a protest, and that is not going to happen in the near future.

Case Three

Rath and Mohanta, surveyed the public libraries, users and professionals in Calcutta, to analyze the practical problems faced in providing free library service. 30 librarians and 60 users were surveyed—with interviews and questionnaires. The survey covered 2 Government town libraries; 15 Government primary unit libraries; and 12 private libraries. Except, for one, all charged membership fees. Hence, the importance of the pros and cons of the fee based or free service libraries. 70 per cent of librarians think the users must be charged for services to prevent misuse of books. 80 per cent librarians opined that libraries should charge fees for providing lending facilities.

The users' view is also in favour of charging fees. 85 per cent said libraries should charge fees on the various services to meet the expenditure at least to some extent. Like the librarians, 60 per cent favour fees for the reason that it brings a sense of responsibility among the users—'fees will enhance the sense of responsibility of the users so that they will be instigated to exploit fully the resources of the library, besides, it will also infuse a sort of obligation on the part of the library staff to serve in a better way'. 40 per cent feel that people will not realize the value of proper library service, if it is provided free of cost. 85 per cent say public libraries should charge for reprographic services. 60 per cent support the idea of charging for lending services. 40 per cent favoured fees for reference service (Rath & Mohanta, 1994: 184-91).

Case Four

Social Sciences: A. Girja Kumar has reported few studies conducted in India, in his own library, Jawaharlal Nehru University. In one such study of the sociological literature citations of Indian writers, the findings are:

"The study about sociology literature is based on citations of foreign periodicals to be found in 697 articles published by Indian academics in six prestigious Indian sociological publications periodicals ranging from the year 1970 to 1979. Only 332 citations are to be found, thus indicating a low count of less than half a citation per academic piece of writing. . . . It is equally disturbing to note that only 28 foreign sociology periodicals were ever quoted in the whole range of 697 periodical articles published by Indian sociologists over the period of a decade. It is to be contrasted with the fact that 189 foreign periodicals in sociology (and anthropology) are received in the capital city of India alone. Not more than 15 per cent of foreign literature is subjected to effective utilization". Indicating the trends in the use of periodicals by Indian scholars. It also shows that a sample survey of one field and in one period can be repeated to find the similarities and dissimilarities in the results, and apply these to planning of development of libraries.

Case Five

In another study of economic literature, Prof. Kumar found interesting pattern of non-use, dealing with the citations in 80 doctoral works submitted to the Delhi School of Economics, and limited to 152 periodicals in economics received at this library, which were also listed in *SSCI* and *Journal of Economic Literature*, "half of the periodicals received in the Delhi School of Economics received not a single citation in our sample of 80 doctoral dissertations . . . 202 periodicals were found missing from the Indian subscription list confirming the suspicion that the subscription lists have not been updated for practically all purposes during the last three years" (Kumar, 1986: 460-61). This shows that there are periodicals that are not used and there are at the same time periodicals that are important but are not available in the libraries. If half of the citations cited are not from the main resource, from where the doctoral work, is presumably, done than the planners have to re-consider the collection development policies.

Case Six

Satish surveyed the attitude towards information among the social scientists. The study also examines personal and organizational attributes influencing the magnitude of attitude. The data was collected from three universities, and eight social science research and training institutions in the twin cities of Hyderabad-Secunderabad. The findings point out the importance of attitudinal measurement in the user research. Though it is assumed in the information use studies that the scholars in general tend to be ready (*i.e.*, invariably possessing a favourable attitudinal disposition) to make use of the information sources and attempt to keep abreast as well up-to-date, the fact is, it does not seem to be so in all the cases. In the context of this study the favourability of ATI of the response population is not very much pronounced, though it tends to be in the positive direction.

The data indicate that in most of the cases strength of ATI and information source use relations tend to improve when personal and psychological attributes are also considered in the analysis. That is, higher job satisfaction, dedication, level of aspiration, and motivation to work and also higher educational attainment and professional experience have been revealed to strengthen the attitude-behaviour relations (Satish, 1994).

Case Seven

D. Maheswarappa, B.S. and others studied the foreign language barrier among Indian statisticians. The 68 respondents were all academics, most had masters and a few had research degrees; nearly 78 per cent male, over 70 per cent were between the age group of 25 and 45; of these 43 per cent knew French, 38 per cent knew German, 37 per cent knew Russian, 32 per cent knew Japanese and 32 per cent knew Chinese. Infact, hardly 8 per cent had qualified in basic course in French, and 2 per cent in German. The question arises then in this case, how do these academics get access to foreign language materials?

The answer lies in the results of study: 48 per cent look for an English summary, 42 per cent do not care about this material in European languages. While India has taken considerable steps in translation services, 26 per cent of these statisticians are aware of this service provided by INSDOC and 24 per cent are aware of the ISI Library's service in this regard. Again, 32 per cent have commissioned translations, but 63 per cent treat this translation technically accurate as just acceptable, and not very good; whereas nearly 50 per cent feel its readability is good. The study thus remarks "The knowledge, qualification and the reading ability of statisticians in India is very poor. Many of them are scanning current issues of scientific periodicals (83%) abstracting and indexing journals (62%) and other methods. There is a probability and possibility of missing important research reported in the foreign languages" (1993: 234).

Case Eight

In another significant study of the citation behaviour of the Social

Scientists, Girja Kumar, has cited three studies, conducted to find out the pattern of use of information by social scientists in India. The study is of the citations. The results are as follows:

TABLE 5.3: Pattern of Use of Information by Social Scientists in India

Type of Documents	*1**	*2***	*3†*
Books	46.9	48.4	45.8
Periodicals	30.0	34.6	34.7
Other sources	23.0	16.9	19.3
Reports	13.0	n.d.	10.8
Newspapers	5.4	n.d.	2.6
Unpublished sources	4.6	n.d.	5.9

Sources of study:
*1. Girja Kumar and Jayaswal, P.K., in Library Herald (1982).
**2. Singh. S.N., Pune University, (1984).
†3. Parekh, Harsh and Sheth, Tara, *ibid.*

These three citation studies are indicative of the type of documents the users in the field of social sciences prefer. To quote Prof. Girja Kumar "Practically half of the citations are confined to book literature. While annual budget varying from 50 to 75 per cent is devoted to ordering periodicals, the citations to periodical literature are one-third of the total, thus indicating extremely low percentage of utilization of periodical literature by Indian researchers. This is true of most of the developing countries, indicating once again that there was little relationship between information need, information use and collection development. It is extremely disturbing in the context of viewing information as a resource in developmental process of less developed countries" (Girja Kumar, 1986: 461-62).

Case Nine

Humanities: A recent survey of the Indian user behaviour in Humanities, is done by M. Kanakachary, as part of the doctoral research. The survey covers ten institutions, from different parts of the country (see Table 5.4).

The Tables 5.4 and 5.5 have sufficient data to display the prevailing trends among the users of humanities information. For instance, the Table 5.4 represents the types of audience, whom the institutions serve and who are also the primary respondents of this survey. The Table 5.4 also shows, the author's bias towards the institution (CIEFL) where he

TABLE 5.4: Institutional Distribution of Respondents

Library	*Teachers*	*Researchers*	*Students*	*Others*	*Total*
Adyar	6	13	8	28	55
ASRC	25	26	—	1	52
ASB	4	10	4	15	33
BSP	9	13	10	10	42
BORI	7	6	3	25	41
CIEFL	90	34	5	4	133
CIIL	19	18	2	13	52
ICHR	8	14	8	5	35
LKA	2	5	2	13	22
SA	13	14	6	12	45
Total	183	153	48	126	510

Note: Adyar—Adyar Library, Chennai;
ASRC—American Studies Research Centre, Hyderabad:
ASB—Asiatic Society of Bengal, Calcutta;
BSP—Bangiya Sahitya Parisad, Calcutta;
BORI—Bhandarkar Oriental Research Institute, Pune;
CIEFL—Central Institute of English and Foreign Language, Hyderabad;
CIIL—Central Institute of Indian Languages, Mysore;
ICHR—Indian Council of Historical Research, Delhi;
LKA—Lalit Kala Akademi, Delhi;
SA—Sahitya Akademi, Delhi.

TABLE 5.5: Use of Library Services

Users	*Borrowing*	*Consultation*	*ILL*	*Reservations*	*Xerox*	*Reference*	*Referral*	*Total*
Teacher	168	148	54	87	140	112	70	183
Resident	136	106	30	64	105	83	55	153
Student	38	23	3	7	20	13	9	48
Others	104	81	23	29	56	44	34	126
Total	446	358	110	187	321	252	168	510

is serving. The Table 5.5 displays the fact that borrowing is the most important service, which the users prefer, and is at the top of the list as most highly preferred service. The other service, in decreasing order are consultation, photocopy (xerox), reference/referral, reservations and inter-library loan (ILL). One must not be struck at the high rate of borrowing which the users do in humanities: in fact humanities, as citation studies have universally shown, rely more on books, and which most libraries permit borrowing for outside library use. This is also reflecting on the trend that Indians have not got into the use of research library (or using the books within the library premises, with no borrowing privilege at all).

Growth of Ideas of Right to Information and Censorship

"There is also the further limitation that information can be put to wrong uses. History has on record instances when scientific discoveries have been misused for destroying civilizations—as in the case of Nazi Racialism or Hiroshima and the nuclear bomb. Librarians cannot forecast or prevent the use to which information is put but their duty lies, except in unusual circumstances, such as war-time conditions, in ensuring that information reaches the person who requires it with the least delay" (Susheela Kumar, 1974: 182).

Rights, as introduced in a democratic environment, have a meaning which has been used and misused for political and other convenience. If politicians, and the monarchs, banned books, there were other social agencies, too, who were doing this. Take for instance, every country has the religious, or non-secular elements who wish to ban a certain book for reasons better known to them. An instance of Satanic Verses or Lady Chatterley's lover, brings to mind a host of other such issues which this society has witnessed.

Right to information, presumes, that there is a right to all basic human needs, and so also the need to know. People have the right to know under what situations they can cooperate with the Government, and till what limits, and so on. So also information must be available to the people as and when it effects them, both directly and indirectly. For instance, they have a right to know which road widening or dam projects will displace them, and if displaced, what are the plans for their rehabilitation? This type of information is not mere information for the sake of it. It relates to survival and/or developmental needs of the common man, and hence right to information is a life supporting need.

There was definitely some attempt to initiate the freedom of information in a way by opening libraries for the public. To quote Prof. Girja Kumar "Let it not be forgotten it (that is the idea of a free public library) owed its existence to Sir Charles Metcalf, the man who abolished the Act No. XI of 1835 and thus paved the way for the freedom of information in British India" (1996).

Several leading democracies have provided this right long back. Sweden has a freedom of information law for more than 200 years. The Freedom of Information Act was passed in US in 1966. Australia had it in 1982, and Canada in 1983.

But the Indian citizen waits for a life time for this simple facility. In the context Article 19(a) of the Constitution has been interpreted by the judiciary to demonstrate that Right of Freedom of Speech also includes the citizen's right to know what the State is doing and why it is doing so in all matters of public interest, except in cases of national security (See Rajasthan High Court's ruling in the case of L.K. Koolwal *vs.* The State AIR 1988 Rajas 2; cited in Dim Silvera's *The India Book*, 1991, pp. 230-31 as a section under "Advocate Srikant Bhat's 12 landmark judgements of the last two decades").

The Press Council of India has prepared a draft Right to Information Bill, 1996. It does not confer any new right on the citizen, rather, it will only provide a procedure for the enforcement of an existing fundamental right [Article 19(A)], which the legislature has no right to curtail; still less is the right with the executive. The draft reads as follows:

"(i) Every citizen shall have a right to information from the public body;

(ii) It shall be the duty of the public body to maintain all records duly catalogued and indexed;

(iii) The public body shall be under a duty to make available to the person requesting information, the information sought for including such information and it is under an obligation to obtain and furnish and shall not withhold any information or limit its availability to the public except the information specified in Section 4;

(iv) All individuals whether citizens or not shall have right to such information as affects their life and liberty. If relevant information accelerates national development, right to information then must be constitutionally guaranteed. This is a fact, because the only difference between the developed and developing world is in terms of haves and havenots of information, respectively".

According to the National Policy on Library and Information System, drafted by RRLF, "Every citizen must have the right to obtain the information he needs irrespective of his physical, social and economic condition". By implication the libraries have to give free access to information, and the barriers created or present in accessing information for the development of the commoners must be removed.

Bengal Library Association states "Right to free public library service to read and to acquire information should be guaranteed as one of the fundamental rights of the citizen". This has a bearing on the public exchequer, that the libraries which are run by public funds must receive their due grants at the appropriate time, and the Government has the right to implement the idea that free public library service is available at all levels, throughout the country.

In a historic announcement, the Rajasthan Government declared in 1995, that citizens had the right to information to receive details of expenditure on work done in their villages, and all documents could be photocopied as evidence. However, the bureaucracy obstructed the process. Resultingly, the agitation against this called by the Mazdoor Kisan Shakti Sangathan evoked massive popular support.

In this wake of series of debates that were going on, the U.P. Library Association organized a seminar on the 'Right to Information, Democracy and Role of Public Libraries' in 1992.

The seminar made the following recommendations:

(i) Right to information should be included as an explicit fundamental right in the Constitution of India, by amending the Constitution.

(ii) Freedom of Information Act, similar to the Freedom of Information Act, 1966 of U.S.A., should be enacted forthwith as a specific corollary to Article 19 of the Constitution. While passing such Act the Official Secrets Act, 1923, the Custom Act, the P&T Act, etc. should also be amended accordingly.

(iii) National and State level reference and archival centres should be established where all official publications, both of the Central and State Governments should be collected and made available to the public;

(iv) A 'Public Records Act' on the lines of U.K. (1958), should also be enacted, according to which, Government records are de-classified after a period, and then made available to the public.

Dasgupta (1996) in an interesting article highlights the barriers one finds in the flow of official information. To quote from the paper: "The objective of this presentation, is to focus on the barriers to the free flow of information imposed by the Government through its policy of secrecy as well as by the operation of an all pervasive Official Secrets Act of 1923. In this context, it also argues the imperative necessity to grant citizens the right to information which is implicit in Article 19(1)(a) of our Constitution and also acknowledged in Article of both the Universal

Declaration of Human Rights (December 1948) and the International Covenant on Civil and Political Rights (December 1966). . . ."

He concludes the paper with critical remarks:

> "With the disclosure, with monotonous regularity, of corruptions and scams in recent time, the need of the hour is greater transparency in governance. If records were open to public inspection, numerous multicrore scams could have been averted. Although the thrust of this presentation has been on the imperative need for making official information on development available for grass-roots level population, the academic community would equally derive the benefit of a Freedom of Information Act. They would be in a position to demand legally date needed for their research work. For example, although, the Eighth Five Year Plan has almost reached the terminal date, the mid-term plan appraisal is yet to be published. . . . Unfortunately, the academic community has not played any significant role in the battle against indiscriminate censor, banning of books, and secrecy. The professed role of library and information professionals is to collect, analyse, store and disseminate information. They should therefore be in forefront in the battle for freedom of information".

A futurist has gone one step ahead and proposed what is called as a Bill of Rights for the Information Age which recognises the third world (Roode, J.D., and Plooy, N.F. du; 1995). There are many more information sources on this topic in the bibliography.

User's Survey

The modern societies have provided many facilities, including democratic ideas of life and culture. In this context, what is the level of awareness about this right, as essential in our times, and as a pre-requisite for our socio-economic development, are the issues that concern here.

The present study hypothesises that 'society is not made conscious of its democratic rights to information, and library profession has failed to utilize its democratic right to struggle for image formation in the society'. One aspect of this deals with the social perception and the other deals with library profession's responsibilities. Ironically, both these perceptions are negative, despite, the fact that the society has explicit ideas of democratic rights to speak, express, etc., but is unaware of another equally important segment of life! In a survey conducted on this issue among users of different libraries the respondents have reacted on these, and the results are given below:

Q. Do you agree that right to information means no censorship:

	Respondents	*Percentage*
Yes	40	47.0
No	45	53.0
Total	85	

(a) I don't want to get involve in this relative question right now;
(b) As long as it does not provoke the young mind;

Q. If yes, do you recommend freedom of access for subjects, like:

	Respondents	*Percentage*
Irreligious	15	27.2
Obscene	5	9.1
Pornographic	5	9.1
Unhealthy books	10	18.2
Politically sensitive information	20	36.4
Total	55	

Q. Did you know that you have a democratic right to demand library services or facilities in the library:

	Respondents	*Percentage*
Yes	290	73.4
No	105	26.6
Total	395	

As many as 26 per cent in this democratic society, have not given a serious thought on the need to 'right to information' that it must be their stated and secured right, as is the right to freedom, right to speech, and so on.

Most of the respondents have given a positive reply, implying that the society is aware of their rights. It also implies that, though such a provision is not stated anywhere in the Constitution nor in the Government policies, and yet people have presumed that they enjoy such a right by the virtue of being in a democratic society!!! If 26 per cent are not aware, then it is possibly an indicator of a lack of idea as to what it means, or, as to which context they can use it: for instance, in accessing the Government information, or information which is public but not made publicly accessible, or defence information, and so on.

Q. If yes, how to communicate this right to people:

	Respondents	*Percentage*
Publicity	175	68.6
Propaganda	25	9.8
Movement by masses	55	21.6
Total	255	

Survey of Librarians

See how librarians, though also from the same society, as are the users of the library, perceive the issues relating to censorship, freedom of information access, and related matters.

Q. Did you ever think that users have a democratic right to demand library services or facilities in the library?

	Respondents	*Percentage*
Yes	80	94.1
No	5	5.9
Total	85	

Q. If yes, what are the ways of communicating this right to people:

	Respondents	*Percentage*
Publicity	45	42.8
Propaganda	15	14.2
Mass movement	45	42.8
Total	105	

Q. Does right to information means no censorship:

	Respondents	*Percentage*
Yes	195	49.3
No	200	50.6
Total	395	

Q. If yes, do you recommend freedom of access to information on reading materials on subjects such as:

		Respondents	*Percentage*
Anti religion		12	
Obscene		3	
Pornographic		6	
'Unhealthy' books		5	
Politically sensitive information		21	
Other (any comments)		7	
Yes	185		94.8
No	10		5.1
Total	195		

This is another dimension to find out what is meant by freedom of access to information, or democratic right to information! The hypotheses is that 'society is not made conscious of their democratic rights to information, and library profession has failed to utilize its democratic right to struggle for image formation in the society'. By implication it means that the society must know what it wants in the library, and what it thinks should not be in the library. The majority (95%) of the respondents suggest that freedom of access to information is a right, and we cannot make decisions on what is good or what is bad for the society!!!

(a) No, I do not recommend freedom of access to such information which is not necessary for the development of a healthy mind and a nice citizen. This applies only to the knowledge in the field necessary for a betterment of a healthy individual and society and their well-being.
(b) Any type of literature should not be restricted. Restriction should be any of the age group;
(c) Books are meant to broaden an individual's outlook rather than narrowing it by writing things which are anti-religion, obscene, etc.;
(d) Some censorship is useful;
(e) Rare books;
(f) All materials;
(g) All this may be recommended if it is having constructive objective logically;
(h) To adults only;
(i) Not clear what is desired under freedom;
(j) It depends upon the individual, the situations and circumstances he faces in childhood, at present, etc. So it should be open to everybody keeping an eye;
(k) These items to be 'classified' and 'certifies' in the interests of research. Identify genuine researchers. Make these available to only those whose research is genuine and professionally motivated and beneficent;
(l) Certainly not. Freedom does not mean license—a library is meant for spread of knowledge and love and care for humanity—unhealthy conditions, disharmony have no place in a library;
(m) Of course there should be no censorship on those sources of information which does not violate the sentiments of people nor create obscenity in the society;

(n) All the required material must be available without any hindrance specially for research;
(o) So that they can be evaluated critically so as to set the things right. Critical study is a broad subject;
(p) If the books relating to the subject mentioned here is available any reader can read that if he wants;
(q) Since the library users are supposed to have a fair amount of good sense to judge themselves in matters of everything related to their lives, freedom of access to reading of all categories of materials is desirable.

In a country like India, with nearly half the population being illiterate, and majority in villages, it is appropriate to quote Mookerjee's views on how to really get the libraries involved in the society:

> "In creating the social climate and the attitudes which will produce a new village outlook and motivate village people to want to improve the way they live and their traditional practices and methods of making a living—the contribution of the social role of the library is considerable. The contribution towards this social change is the business of all people both official and non-official who are concerned with the Community Development and National Extension Programmes. It is to be noted that there are no short-cuts to this social change of changing village attitudes. Changing attitudes as has been stated previously is a process of creating new social values and new wants which become important to individuals, families and villages. It has been compared to the step by step process of harvesting of crop which must await the different stages of preparing the soil, selecting the seed, planting the seed, applying fertilizer, weeding and tilling the growing crop. . . . Our public libraries if properly planned and organized should be able to play an important role in this sphere of activity. Though the Community Development Project as such has not given any priority to the working of public libraries for achieving the goal, but it has incorporated the idea of starting small library units within each Block to facilitate exchange of ideas and circulation of reading materials amongst the neo-literates and those already literate. The current trend has been to motivate the people in the villages through other agencies and the more important role that libraries could play have been overlooked" (1969: 368-69).

Conclusion

Thus the main points of the role of the nation in the library development, and vice-versa, as discussed above, reveals that the public library system in the country has been more recreation centered, rather than education centered; no efforts exist to understand the information seeking behaviour of these libraries; there has been least interaction between the public libraries and the community whom they serve. Public libraries and the Indian society have developed independently of one another, and the one is taking minimum assistance from the other (Khan, 1990: 168).

These statements are very true, and there can be no dispute about the whole matter. The added stand that the Constitution of India has placed in the case of library development is not one which can facilitate the unified and holistic approach to the entire subject of setting up a library system in the country—The Constitution has placed library development as a subject which is the concern of the State, and not of the Centre. This Federalism has though advantages of allowing free hand in state matters and in implementation of schemes, has nevertheless dampened the process of a systematic library development programme for the entire country.

6

GROWTH OF LIBRARY MOVEMENT
Statewise Analysis

The reorganization of States in 1956, according to the linguistic pattern, has its direct relevance in collection, development and planning for libraries. For instance, the State of Andhra Pradesh was formed in 1953. Telugu [users of other languages, such as, Urdu (7.7%), Kannada (0.9%)], the language of 84.5 per cent people is State language, but there are Hindi (2.5%), Marathi (0.8%), Oriya (0.4%), etc. So also states in the Hindi belt, the North India, have similar cases. While the Constitution of India, in its Eighth Schedule, has national languages, there are many more languages, where unity is in its diversity. Each State has its own pattern of library development and history, and hence it is imperative to survey their achievements in the post-independence era.

The place of libraries and their contribution to national development is the focus of the chapter. The analysis in the following pages will try to assess with the available data and facts, to ascertain the fulfilment of their respective roles in national development; to highlight the role libraries are playing in terms of their value in the society; to see the place of libraries as development tools; and suggest possible solutions faced by the libraries in India.

The status of public libraries at a glance is also pertinent here: All the States and the Union territories, except Sikkim and Lakshadweep, have state central libraries. Out of the total 5,75,937 villages in the country, only 41,828 (or 7%) have libraries. Apart from this, a detailed picture of libraries is also most unimpressive, which is described in respective States.

There are no accurate record of the total, however, there are estimates given by (1) Dr. S.K. Pandey Sharma and, (2) RRLF, which is presented in Table 6.1 (quoted in Ramaiah, 1997: 121).

TABLE 6.1: Statewise List of Library in Villages

State/U.T.	*Pandey*	*%*	*RRLF*	*%*
Andhra Pradesh	3,952	9.8	1,528	6.9
Arunachal Pradesh	—	—	73	0.3
Assam	1,128	2.8	252	1.1
Bihar	4,503	11.2	1,705	7.7
Goa (incl. Diu & Daman)	165	0.4	118	0.5
Gujarat	6,556	16.3	2,155	9.8
Haryana	49	0.2	66	0.2
Himachal Pradesh	55	0.2	117	0.5
Jammu and Kashmir	20	0.1	24	0.1
Karnataka	2,655	6.6	2,137	9.7
Kerala	4,169	10.4	2,096	9.5
Madhya Pradesh	6,281	15.6	2,086	9.4
Maharashtra	2,678	6.7	2,070	9.3
Manipur	—	—	106	0.4
Meghalaya	—	—	7	0.1
Mizoram	—	—	107	0.4
Nagaland	24	0.1	139	0.6
Orissa	626	1.6	1690	7.7
Punjab	163	0.4	25	0.1
Rajasthan	39	0.2	119	0.5
Sikkim	6	0.1	6	0.1
Tamil Nadu	3,017	7.5	1,540	7.0
Tripura	31	0.1	44	0.1
Uttar Pradesh	1,585	4.0	710	3.2
West Bengal	2,061	5.1	2,803	12.7
Union Territories				
Andaman & Nicobar	—	—	40	0.1
Chandigarh	—	—	7	0.1
Dadra & Nagar Haveli	—	—	4	0.1
Delhi	—	—	4	0.1
Lakshadweep (Minicoy & Amindivi Islands)	—	—	11	0.1
Pondicherry	—	—	57	0.2
Total	40,107		21,906	

Library Expenditure at a Glance

A break up of the expenditure of each State, given below shows the priority each state considers in the matters relating to library development. The list is in descending order by per capita expenditure.

TABLE 6.2: Total Expenditure

(*Rs. in lakhs*)

Public Libraries	*Expenditure*	*Per Capita*
State Govt.	3,171.7	Re. 0.46
Central Govt.	676.8	Re. 0.16

TABLE 6.3: Expenditure on Public Libraries in the States (1986-87)

State/U.T.	*Expenditure (in lakhs)*	*Population (in lakhs)*	*Per Capita (in Rs.)*	*Literacy % 1980s*
Pondicherry	15.0	6.04	2.48	45.71
Arunachal Pradesh	15.0	6.31	2.37	11.32
Meghalaya	30.0	13.35	2.24	33.22
Chandigarh	10.0	4.51	2.21	61.56
Mizoram	10.0	4.93	2.02	54.91
Goa	20.0	10.07	1.98	57.25
Nagaland	15.0	7.74	1.94	42.57
West Bengal	928.2	545.8	1.70	40.88
Sikkim	5.0	3.16	1.58	34.05
Tripura	30.0	20.0	1.46	42.12
Lakshadweep	0.5	0.4	1.24	44.65
Andaman & Nicobar Islands	2.0	1.8	1.06	42.14
Manipur	15.0	14.2	1.05	41.91
Tamil Nadu	451.5	484.0	0.93	45.78
Diu	0.2	0.3	0.82	—
Delhi	50.0	62.2	0.80	61.06
Andhra Pradesh	357.1	535.4	0.66	29.50
Karnataka	232.1	371.4	0.63	38.41
Himachal Pradesh	25.0	42.8	0.58	42.48
Daman	0.2	0.4	0.51	—
Dadra & Nagar Haveli	0.5	1.0	0.48	16.78
Kerala	113.0	254.5	0.44	69.17
Rajasthan	120.0	342.6	0.35	25.00
Gujarat	117.0	340.8	0.35	43.75
Assam	60.0	198.9	0.30	—
Jammu & Kashmir	17.3	59.8	0.29	27.00
Haryana	35.0	129.2	0.27	35.84
Madhya Pradesh	120.0	521.7	0.23	27.82
Orissa	60.0	263.7	0.22	34.10
Maharashtra	123.7	627.8	0.20	47.37
Punjab	30.0	167.8	0.18	40.71
Uttar Pradesh	137.5	1,108.6	0.12	27.38
Bihar	25.8	699.1	0.03	26.21

In a comparative perspective, Table 6.3, display the statewise level of expenditure and reflects on the priorities that the libraries receive in each State.

Book Production

To clearly understand the book production, one approach is to search the records of books received under the Delivery of Books Act. The figures are for the year 1965-66, and 1986-87, relating to books received from respective language and States, which are as follows: The Development of Libraries, 'Live Wires of the Society' would be and on what basis? The analysis of the possible answers are not attempted here!

One does not need a long interpretation of these figures, to show how the most thickly populated State, such as Uttar Pradesh, has only Re. 0.12 per capita expenditure, whereas a small territory, like Diu, has per capita expenditure as high as Re. 0.82. If this is the fate of the statewise expenditure in the country, which is totally disproportionate to its size and needs, then the resulting outcome, the development of libraries, 'Live Wires of the Society' would be equally out of control.

Considering the fact, that rate of literacy has no relationship with the size of the State, nor with the per capita expenditure on the respective

TABLE 6.4: Language-wise Book Received under the Delivery of Books Act in 1965-66 and 1986-87

Language	*1965-66*	*%*	*Rank*	*1986-87*	*%*	*Rank*
Assamese	64	0.3	15	207	1.2	11
Bengali	1,422	6.7	4	1,622	9.5	3
English	10,347	48.8	1	5,318	31.3	1
Gujarati	922	4.3	7	565	0.3	15
Hindi	2,376	11.2	2	2,745	16.1	2
Kannada	241	1.1	11	885	5.2	6
Kashmiri	10	0.1	16	33	0.1	14
Malayalam	573	2.7	8	883	5.2	6
Marathi	1,612	7.6	3	1,172	6.9	5
Oriya	120	0.5	14	393	2.3	8
Punjabi	167	0.7	13	408	2.4	7
Sanskrit	207	0.9	12	251	1.4	10
Tamil	947	4.4	6	1,434	8.4	4
Telugu	518	2.4	9	556	0.3	13
Urdu	372	1.7	10	376	2.2	9
Others	1,285	6.0	5	112	0.6	12
Total	21,185			16,970		

State library system, it amazes any one, to find out how is the planning done and on what basis? The analysis of the possible answers are not attempted here!

TABLE 6.5: State-wise Book Received under the Delivery of Books Act in 1965-66 and 1986-87

State	*1965-66*	*%*	*Rank*	*1986-87*	*%*	*Rank*
Andaman & Nicobar Islands	3	0.1	20	7	0.1	21
Andhra Pradesh	1,351	6.3	5	595	3.5	9
Arunachal Pradesh	—	—	—	5	0.1	21
Assam	120	0.5	16	281	1.6	12
Bihar	417	1.9	13	248	1.4	13
Chandigarh	—	—	—	84	0.4	18
Delhi	5,900	27.8	1	4,028	23.7	1
Goa-Daman-Diu	1	0.1	20	40	0.2	20
Gujarat	699	3.2	8	600	3.6	8
Haryana	n.d.	—	—	104	0.6	17
Himachal Pradesh	320	1.5	14	146	0.8	16
Jammu and Kashmir	58	0.2	19	52	0.3	19
Karnataka	431	2.0	12	1,046	6.1	7
Kerala	700	3.3	7	1,090	6.4	6
Lakshadweep	n.d.	—	—	n.d.	—	—
Madhya Pradesh	529	2.5	10	231	1.3	14
Maharashtra	3,035	14.3	3	1,893	11.1	3
Manipur	65	0.3	17	1	0.1	21
Meghalaya	n.d.	—	—	21	0.1	21
Mizoram	n.d.	—	—	4	0.1	21
Nagaland	4	0.1	20	7	0.1	21
Orissa	446	2.1	11	438	2.5	10
Pondicherry	n.d.	—	—	80	0.4	18
Punjab	670	3.1	9	366	2.1	11
Rajasthan	204	0.9	15	181	1.0	15
Sikkim	n.d.	—	—	n.d.	—	—
Tamil Nadu	1,936	9.1	4	1,775	10.4	4
Tripura	52	0.2	18	48	0.2	20
Uttar Pradesh	1,118	5.2	6	1,223	7.2	5
West Bengal	3,126	14.7	2	2,222	13.0	2
Total	21,185			16,970		

According to this ranking, English language books are the top most in the country, and Delhi is the leading State which supplies nearly 30 per cent of the national book produce. If Delhi, is the capital of India, it also enjoys the claim of being the largest facilities, requires for book writing, production, distribution, etc. It is easy to get an import license for a book producer in Delhi, than one in any other city in India. So also, Delhi has a network of resources for these purposes, which other cities in India lack, even the industrial city like Calcutta, and a business city like Mumbai, cannot compete in this regard with Delhi.

A State Sample

A single sample of at state level book production is given here to have a feel of the production pattern. The case in view is Andhra Pradesh, and the figures are from The Office of the Registrar of Publication, Directorate of Public Libraries, A.P. As per the Delivery of Books Act, every printer/publisher must send 3 copies of a book, and 2 copies of a periodical or newspaper, to the Registrar of Publications. The regionwise books and periodicals received are given below, pertaining to the year 1993-94:

TABLE 6.6: Books Received under Delivery of Books Act from Andhra Region in 1993-94

Andhra Region	*Books*	*Periodicals*
Ananthapur	4	398
Chittoor	7	585
Cuddapah	4	78
East Godavari	44	1,204
Guntur	115	185
Krishna	765	3,524
Kurnool	2	22
Nellore	25	153
Prakasam	9	91
Srikakulam	3	48
Vishakhapatnam	5	1,994
Vizianagaram	—	650
West Godavari	24	1389
Total	1,007	10,321

TABLE 6.7: Books Received under Delivery of Books Act from Telangana Region in 1993-94

Telangana Region	*Books*	*Periodicals**
(1)	(2)	(3)
Adilabad	—	24
Hyderabad	545	7,801
Karimnagar	9	331

(*Contd.*)

TABLE 6.7 (*Contd.*)

(1)	(2)	(3)
Khammam	7	—
Mahaboobnagar	—	19
Medak	4	—
Nalgonda	5	12
Nizamabad	—	494
Ranga Reddy	1	48
Warangal	12	425
Total	583	9,154

* Refers to issues of periodicals, the actual titles received is 294 for the year 1993-94.

In terms of ranking these districts, it reveals the descending order as, Krishna, Hyderabad, Guntur, and East Godavari. The same Office provides a languagewise breakup of publications that have been received from 1984 to 1994, as given in the Table 6.8.

TABLE 6.8: Language-wise Publications Received at this from 1984 to 1994

Language	*Books*		*Periodicals*	
	1984	*%*	*1994*	*%*
Telugu	11,995	89.4	2,402	74.9
Hindi	209	1.6	49	1.5
Urdu	329	2.5	146	4.6
Sanskrit	36	0.3	9	0.3
Tamil	4	0.03	21	0.7
Kannada	8	0.06	29	0.9
Marathi	1	0.01	—	—
English & European	819	6.1	365	11.4
Bilingual & Polyglot	14	0.1	188	5.9
Total	13,415		3,209	

While this is the input for the national record of book production, this is also a telling tale of the other side of the story. The Office of the Registrar has no hold on those who don't submit copies of their publications, and so also there are many other problems, of lack of staff, lack of publication collection centres, etc., which effect the collection and implementation of the Copyright Act (Jagga Rao and Prafulla Chandra, 1997: 270).

This is a sample of all the types of agencies which exists forming a system. Apart from these there are thousands of institutions that have grown and the list includes the non-R&D social science and humanities libraries, media production centres, software dealing and generating agencies, and so on. Like population explosion, there is also information, knowledge, print and library explosion and have also become a problem to be tackled. Strangely the Planning Commission, or any other concerned agency doesn't think that explosion here is as serious as population explosions. "The world today is passing through a phase of information explosion and informatics as an entirely new branch of activity having a direct bearing on social, political and economic affairs has come into operation. . . . Besides the print media, electronics media have come to occupy a very important position in our life. . . . The print media which is exclusively privately owned is also making an insensate drive to modernization by changing over to computerization and photo processes from hot metal and cold metal technologies" (Raghavachari, 1996).

It is also pertinent to compare states with library acts and so also compare States without library acts, to see how the enactment makes difference in performing their role in the society.

TABLE 6.9: States having Library Acts, as in 1972

Particulars	*Tamil Nadu*	*Andhra Pradesh*	*Mysore*	*Maharashtra*
(1)	(2)	(3)	(4)	(5)
Library Service Unit				
Central Library:				
State	1	1	1	nil
City	nil	1	4	1
District	13	21	7	8
Divisional Lib.	nil	nil	nil	3
Regional Lib.	nil	4	nil	nil
Branch Lib.	1,438	517	49	166 (Taluk Libs.)
Aided Lib.	173	1,832	298	390
Librachine	16	1	1	8
Delivery station	2,223	502	35	602
Finance (Rs. in lakhs)				
Income	91.44	38.49	47.50	52.83
Lib. Cess	31.61	20.22	22.00	nil
State Govt. Grant	20.23	18.27	16.50	12.71
Plan Grant	27.01	nil	nil	nil
Other Sources	12.52	nil	0.90	40.11
Expenditure	87.02	97.71	45.47	37.97

(*Contd.*)

TABLE 6.9 (*Contd.*)

(1)	(2)	(3)	(4)	(5)
Reading material	7.58	nil	4.78	nil
Salary	48.38	nil	5.30	nil
Others	31.05	nil	·35.38	nil
Book Stock (in lakhs)	44.31	30.30	nil	26.35
Readers (in lakhs):				
Registered members	4.73	1.00	0.19	0.39
Visitors	310.20	150.04	8.69	19.98
Books Used Consulted (in lakhs)	154.25	49.37	14.79	1.18
Borrowed (in lakhs)	71.24	48.38	3.39	60.53
Per Capita Loan	15	nil	18	73

nil = data not available.

TABLE 6.10: State not having Library Acts, as in 1972

Particulars	*Assam*	*Bihar*	*Kerala*	*Madhya Pradesh*	*Punjab*	*Uttar Pradesh*
Library Service Unit						
Central Library:						
State	1	1	1	nil	nil	1
City	nil	nil	nil	nil	7	nil
District	12	7	9	24	nil	12
Divisional Lib.	10	27 (sub-div. libs.)	nil	nil	nil	nil
Regional Lib.	nil	nil	nil	5	nil	nil
Branch Lib.	nil	nil	nil	1	nil	nil
Aided Lib.	nil	2,330	2,370	250	12	129
Librachine	4	17	9	14	nil	1
Delivery station	170	17	580	700	nil	nil
Finance (Rs. in lakhs)						
Income	6.00	9.57	47.82	nil	nil	nil
Lib. Cess	nil	nil	nil	nil	nil	nil
State Govt. Grant	nil	6.57	7.74	nil	nil	nil
Plan Grant	6.00	2.50	nil	nil	nil	nil
Other Sources	6.00	0.50	40.08	nil	nil	nil
Expenditure	6.00	8.17	44.42	nil	nil	9.26
Reading material	1.20	3.80	nil	1.25	nil	nil
Salary	3.60	3.52	0.68	nil	nil	nil
Others	1.20	nil	nil	nil	nil	nil
Readers (in lakhs):						
Registered members	0.83	nil	6.05	0.10	nil	0.08
Visitors	2.45	nil	nil	0.02	nil	0.69
Books Used Consulted (in lakhs)	0.87	nil	nil	1.21	nil	nil
Borrowed (in lakhs)	7.48	nil	146.84	0.19	nil	nil
Per Capita Loan	9	nil	24	nil	nil	nil

nil = data not available.

The above comparison gives ample data for understanding the scenario. The comparison is more obvious in terms of finance and readership. For instance the highest income of one State among without-act, is almost equal to the lowest income of with-act States. Whereas there is no such glaring figures of registered members among the two categories. But per capita loan is better among the States with library acts. One may, however, State that a comparison of States, irrespective of their other demographic factors, is incorrect. One may also say that library data in isolation being compared as above, would give inaccurate results, and hence any generalizations in this context are not attempted here.

STATE: ANDHRA PRADESH

This is the land of rice and chillies, Tirupati and Nagarjunakonda, Charminar and Salar Jung, bagara baigan and double ka mitha (both are special dishes in Mughlai tradition).

The State was formed in 1953 and expanded to include parts of Raichur, Gulbarga, Bidar and Nanded Districts, in 1956; based on boundaries that formed (a) a major part of the Nizam's territory, called as Hyderabad State; (b) part of Vijayanagara dynasty; and (c) a part of the land ruled by Bahmani dynasty. The language of the majority is Telugu, which is also the official State language; Urdu is its second State language, and is official language for the regions in the part of the State, called as Telangana. The political activism in the State is always ripe, as is in Bengal, Kerala, etc. This activism earlier was for nationalism and later for claiming equality for the regional rights; the problem lies in the political division of the State into three regions: Telangana, Rayalseema and Andhra. The present activism since the last two decades is for gaining power in the State; Telugu Desam, Congress, BJP, MIM, etc. The level of literacy in the State has been less than 50 per cent; 3.3 per cent in 1951, 12 per cent in 1961, 21 per cent in 1971, 29.5 per cent in 1981, and 45 per cent in 1991.

Its area is 2,75,068 sq. kms. The population density is 241 persons per sq. kms. The sex ratio of the State is 972 females per 1000 males. The literacy rate of males is 56.2 per cent and females is 33.7 per cent. The main language groups as per 1981 Census are: Telugu (84.5%) (it is State language); Urdu (7.7%), Kannada (0.9%), Hindi (2.5%), Marathi (0.8%), Oriya (0.4%), etc. The religious groups according to the 1981 Census are: Hindus (88.7%); Muslims (8.4%); Christians (2.6%); Jains (0.03%); Sikhs (0.03%); Buddhists (0.02%); and others.

Public Libraries

The growth of the concept of free public libraries began in the earlier part of this century, with the existence of Asafiya Library (later re-named as State Central Library, under the provision of the Public Libraries Act), Sri Krishna Devaraya Andhra Bhasha Nilayam, etc.

But a true sense of public library development is a post-independence phenomena. The passing of the Hyderabad Public Libraries Act, 1955, inaugurated the era of Government support for a systematic and integrated library development in the entire State. In 1989, the Andhra Pradesh Public Libraries Act, 1960, was amended to constitute the Andhra Pradesh Grandhalaya Parishad. The Parishad is the State level autonomous body, with statutory powers to formulate policies.

There are regional libraries, aimed to provide linkage, in a future date, between the State Library and the City/District libraries. The State Institute of Library Education and Training (*f.* 1986) offers regular training for new and in-service librarians.

TABLE 6.11: Public Library System in the State

	1960s	*1980s*	*1990s*
Government Libraries:			
State Central Library	1	1	1*
Regional Libraries	6	6	6
Mobile Library	1	11	
District Library System:			
District Libraries	20	22	22
City Central Library	1	1	1
Branch Libraries	425	790	1,426
Book Deposit Centres	506	**	546
Village Libraries	1,876$	199	344
Mobile Libraries	2	98	
Other Libraries:			
Aided Libraries	2,315	1,884	
Unaided Libraries	3,200$	**	

Note: * Includes merging figures of other libraries.
** Figures not available.
$ Data from Status Report on Public libraries in A.P., 1994 (Dept. of Public Libraries, Hyderabad).

The public library system is centralized, with the Directorate of Public Libraries at the apex, followed by regional libraries, city central library, district libraries, etc. The funding of the public library system is from two sources, the salary expenditure is met by the State Government, and all other expenditures including acquisition of reading materials, as well as maintenance is by the District Library Authority [Zilla Grandhalaya Samstha (ZGS)], through the library cess and a few other sources.

The number of different types of libraries at the end of 1980s was above 4,000—8 government libraries; 179 district libraries (ZGS libraries); and 2,331 aided libraries. The Government libraries are fully financed by the State, the District Libraries receive a matching grant, as per the provision of the Act. While the staff working in libraries attached to local bodies were given status on par with the Government library staff, the services are not yet streamlined in these provincial libraries.

The Raja Ram Mohun Roy Library Foundation funds the infrastructure and collection development needs to a certain extent. It has a centralized acquisition and processing system. The acquisition is based on the suggestions of the State Library Committee.

The book selection procedure is prescribed under an Order No. G.O.Ms. No. 1580, dated 14 August 1970. The State level Book Selection Committee selects books for the Regional Libraries, State Central Library, and for books to be purchased under the RRLF funds. The District Library Authority (ZGS) as a Selection Committee for all the libraries under its control.

Library Expenditure

The figures, in Table 6.12, are representative of what is the priority in the State for expenditure related to libraries. The State has grown in its socio-economic status and its industrial output is well advanced. And despite these developments the per capita of the State in the last decade stands at 16th place among all the States in the country.

TABLE 6.12: Expenditure on Public Libraries in the State (1986-87)

Expenditure (in lakhs)	*Population (in lakhs)*	*Per Capita (in Rs.)*	*Literacy % 1980s*
357.1	535.4	0.66	29.50

Book Collection

The library book collection as of 31 March 1994, in the Government libraries and in the Zilla Grandhalaya Samsthas (ZGS or District Library Authority) is as given the Table 6.13.

TABLE 6.13: Total Collection, 31 March 1994

	Books	*Periodicals*
Govt. Libraries	8,26,003	369
ZGS	91,08,013	33,924

Library Use: A sample survey of the libraries, indicates the following:

TABLE 6.14: Govt. Libraries: Use Pattern

	1964-65	*1965-66*	*1993-94*
Consultations	1,25,000	1,27,000	8,45,076
Registered members	1,06,000	1,08,000	2,23,984
Books borrowed	1,04,000	1,05,000	2,46,891

A glance at some of these is pertinent to get an overview of the details of the working libraries:

State Central Library, Hyderabad

It was established in 1885, as Asafiya Library. The intention of the founders was to build a leading lending library. As per the provisions of the Public Library Act, 1955, amended in 1960, it was renamed as the State Central Library. The functions of this library are not stated in the Act, and hence some have suggested necessary improvements (Raju, 1991: 19; Taher, 1997, 19-25).

Collection: The collection has grown in the following pattern, in terms of books acquired and added to the collection.

TABLE 6.15: Books Added in the State Central Library, Hyderabad

Year	*Quantity*
1951	62,332
1967	1,75,000
1977	1,93,599
1978	2,01,019
1979	2,11,188
1980	2,35,017
1981	2,47,896
1982	3,00,656
1983	3,06,030
1984	3,20,978
1985	3,33,092
1986	3,41,297
1987	3,51,400
1988	3,63,473
1989	3,72,239

TABLE 6.16: Periodical Subscriptions in State Central Library, Hyderabad

Language	*Year*					
	1984	*1985*	*1986*	*1987*	*1988*	*1989*
English	503	352	233	263	263	194
Telugu	41	28	29	32	32	28
Hindi	37	29	18	24	24	20
Urdu	44	33	15	25	25	16
Marathi	6	5	4	5	5	4
Kannada	9	8	7	4	4	5
Total	640	465	306	353	353	267

Service: While the State Central Library, according to the Public Library Act, must be a reference library, but in practice it is a local public library, with no major role to play in fulfilling its place as an apex library in the State.

TABLE 6.17: Collection Evaluation

Year	*Annual Addition*	*Visitors*	*Library Rate %*	*Registered Borrowers*	*Books Borrowed*	*Book Rate %*
1977	8,582	1,94,442	22.6	6,484	40,194	6.1
1978	7,420	2,42,002	32.6	7,201	47,868	6.6
1979	10,169	2,34,502	23.0	7,968	68,107	8.5
1980	23,829	2,75,495	11.5	8,008	60,254	7.5
1981	12,879	2,40,000	18.6	8,836	54,963	6.2
1982	52,760	2,65,576	5.0	9,678	63,543	6.5
1983	5,374	2,67,502	49.7	10,679	68,543	6.4
1984	14,948	2,85,681	19.1	11,478	53,707	4.6
1985	12,114	2,34,087	19.3	12,380	57,597	4.6
1986	10,103	2,19,821	21.7	13,346	65,860	4.9
1987	8,205	2,08,874	25.4	14,300	41,243	2.8
1988	12,073	2,20,381	18.2	15,313	64,765	4.2
1989	8,766	1,87,476	21.3	16,178	52,149	3.2

Given the above numbers, indicating the pattern of growth, it is evident that there is a fluctuating rate of visitors, a constant increase in the number of registered borrowers and borrowing of books. What is not increasing proportionately is the additions of the library (*i.e.*, collections). Further, it is a reflection on the state-of-the-art: that it is neither expected to be a lending library, nor it is to act as a local library, allowing visitors to be in and out all the time!

This is apt to present the inferences as follows:

- — The State Central Library is presently not acting as a central repository for all the publications of the State;
- — Does not have nor publishes a list of all the State's literary output;
- — Not in a position to centralize its technical services;
- — Unable to plan or take part in the development of library system in the State;
- — Does not even have sufficient resources, staff, skills, and the orientation to properly store the publications it had collected all through; and
- — Unable to produce even its own annual report, which reflects on the lack of ability to state its activities, and difficulties.

One can see the literature that is published on the suggestions to improve the working of the State libraries, in general, and this library in particular (Taher, 1996: 250-57).

District Library: *District Central Library,Medak District*

Situated at Sangareddy, the district headquarters, it was founded in 1958, and presently has in 1996, 2,516 members.

Collection: 29,176 books, subscribes to 57 magazines, and 19 newspapers, in Telugu the principal language, and in English, Urdu and Hindi.

Service: Lending; reference service on demand; book exhibitions; film shows; essay writing and debate competitions; celebration of library week, annually.

Mandal Library, Medak District

This is situated in Narasapur Mandal, 20 miles away from Sangareddy, and established in 1967. It has 818 members, including child members.

Collection: 6,813 books, subscribes to 14 magazines, and 4 newspapers.

Service: It organizes book exhibition, film shows, essay writing competition, during the annual Library Week celebrations.

Village Library

Baddipadaga Village, Medak District: This is the only library maintained by the District Library Authority of Medak District. It is located in

Nanganur Mandal near Siddipet. It subscribes to only two newspapers, and does not have enough reading material.

District Library: East Godavari District

It is located at the district headquarters, Kakinada. Established in 1954, it has 8,640 members.

Collection: It has totally 60,000 books, which includes the collections at its branch libraries.

Service: Book circulation; reference service on demand; organizes book exhibitions, debates, lectures, competitions; mobile library service; maintains a separate collection for children.

Mandal Library

Pamarru Mandal Library, East Godavari District: It is nearly 32 miles away from Kakinada. The library has no regular staff, not even regular non-professionals, and hence works irregularly—in fact it is managed by an attendant, who travels from a nearby village to attend to his duties. The inhabitants, reportedly, go to the neighbouring village, called Amujuru, 3 miles away, to use the library facilities.

Village Library

Amujuru Village Library, East Godavari District: This library (*f.* 1974). Attracts its users from neighbouring areas, including the Pamarru villagers.

Collection: It has a total collection of 8,318 books, subscribes to 27 magazines, and 6 newspapers.

Services: Lending books; reference service on demand and sometimes in anticipation; organizes essay writing and other cultural competitions; celebrates library week by mobilizing funds from the public; display advertisements, important news; etc.

Overview

The efforts of the leaders to bring in legislation and get a regular support for public library development, was successful with the enactment of the Public Libraries Act, 1955. But what has been the outcome of this legislative effort. The picture on the whole shows that in a large number of areas the Act had very little impact in promoting literacy, libraries and reading culture.

Library experts are almost unanimous in stating that "even in the States (including Andhra Pradesh) that have library legislation the growth of libraries was inadequate and improper" (Kumar, 1996: 16).

Further, even in cases where village or panchayat libraries are essential for a country which has largest number of villages, the situation is still bleak. "There were 315 libraries in villages which had a population of 5,000 or more; 320 libraries and 591 book deposit centres in villages which had a population between 1,000 to 5,000. There were 1,540 gram panchayat libraries as per 1981 census. About 8,862 villages had been left out without a library or book deposit centre. It amounts to 9 out of 10 villages had had no library facility" (Kumar, 1996: 16).

> "All the 16,408 villages with a population of less than 1,000 do not have library service. This is the position in Andhra Pradesh which has a glorious library movement and an early record of library legislation" (Sarada, 1996: 29).

Dr. Venkatappaiah, a leading public library specialist, feels:

> "Somehow even forty years after library legislation, it has not been possible to cover even 20 per cent of the Gram Panchayats with the Public Libraries or rendering some type of library service. On the other hand, it is rather a pity that the library cess is collected from even illiterates and neo-literates in the villages and most of it is being spent for literates living in towns and cities. Not even a single pie of library cess was spent for illiterates during the last four decades or more. This is a social injustice. This is to be considered by administrators and planners and rectify this great social injustice. This is an issue of a great gamut of the society" (Venkatappaiah, 1996: 37).

In general the public libraries are catering to the literates, and even to the literates these are providing only material which can be useful for "recreational and light reading needs. . . . The illiterate section of the society are neglected by the Public Libraries. Audio-visual aids of communication are not available in the libraries. Libraries hardly provide information relating to socio-economic change and the problems faced by the people in live situation. Therefore, the effectiveness of Public Libraries in the society is negligible" (Sarada, 1996: 30).

The situation has come to stay because all those who matter, the public leaders, the elite, the bureaucrats, the policy-makers, and the last, the library professionals all are equally responsible in this sad state of affairs. While the public leaders have not cared to appreciate the role a library plays in the socio-economic development, the professionals have cultivated a passive image by ignoring potential users, and by not actively participating in the library development programme (Sarada, 1996: 30).

There are a number of specialists who have contributed extensively on the library movement in the State. The place of Venkatappaiah is, one of the leader in this regard. The festschrift released to celebrate his long time contributions, is: Vasishth, C.P., *et al.* (ed.), *New Horizons in Library and Information Science.* Dr. Velaga Venkatappaiah Festschrift, Chennai, T.R. Publications, 1994, p. 602.

A glance at some of his contributions indicates how varied are the contributions of this great person. He has 1,122 total publications to his credit, as tabulated in the Table 6.18.

TABLE 6.18: Publications of Dr. Velaga Venkatappaiah

Theme	*Books*	*Edited Works*	*Bibliographies Compiled*	*Articles*	*Reviews*
Library Science:					
Telugu	33	27	13	350	145
English	12	10	4	150	73
Adult education:					
Telugu	15	80	—	60	2
English	—	—	—	6	1
Children's Litt.:					
Telugu	8	13	—	30	14
English	—	3	—	10	30
Telugu Litt.	5	—	—	14	—
Total	75	135	17	616	279

Case Studies

Example of Book Reading Interests

A continuation of the past trends to promote reading and literacy, is seen in the post-independent Andhra Pradesh, in the growth of different programmes, though localized in their nature. One such attempt is seen in the programme called as "Home Library Plan" (HLP), of an agency, Andhra Pradesh Book Distributors (ABPD), which continues its programme to this day. It is a subscriber based book purchase programme, successfully managed by a few commercial dealers. The agency issued a journal called *Book World* (*Pustaka Prapanchamu*), and its editor as well as the programme coordinator was Mr. M.N. Rao.

A word of how the system worked is pertinent here. The members who wished to develop this home based library, had to be subscribers of this scheme. It was a direct-mail order scheme to any of the subscribers, and sometimes the offer would carry a reward, 'order two get two more free'.

Readership Survey

A survey of book reading habits of its audience was conducted as early as 1960, by Artur Isenberg, Senior Ford Foundation Consultant to the Southern Languages Book Trust, Chennai. The inserted questionnaire, in the Book World, August 1960, read:

> "Dear Home Library Plan Subscribers!
>
> We would really like to know a lot more about you. This is not just idle curiosity: we honestly believe that the more we do know about you, the better the service we can render you. That is why we are earnestly inviting you to give us your confidence and to answer the Questionnaire fully, and frankly. It will only take you a few minutes and cost just a few naye paise in postage.
>
> We sincerely appreciate our co-operation in this matter. What's more, we shall tell you about the outcome of this questionnaire inquiry in *Book World*, in due course. Naturally, we shall not disclose any individual replies: that would be indiscrete. But we shall tabulate your responses and give you a complete overall statistical portrait of yourselves.
>
> It's really quite simple: just write the figures called for in the questions neatly within the boxes provided; and place a check-mark into the appropriate smaller boxes, as indicated in the Questionnaire. If you want to be extra nice to us, please let us have your complete questionnaire before 31 August 1960. To all those of you who will fill out this questionnaire and send it to us, we say: 'Thank you over so much!'
>
> Faithfully Yours
> M.N. Rao
> Editor, *Book World*

The survey was based on questionnaires sent to all the subscribers of *Book World.* Only 470 (17%) responded, and the results are given below:

On question No. 9, "How many books did you actually own before subscribing to the Home Library Plan (HLP)?" the answer are:

TABLE 6.19: Possession of Library Prior to HLP

Had a Library Earlier	*Male* %	*Female* %
Yes	44.9	45.9
No	50.2	54.1

Given the lack of clarity in the question asked, the responses included all types of answers: Some reported owning as few as twenty books—presuming that twenty books are sufficient to call the collection as Home Library. This is supported by another set of responses which stated that they have sixty books, but they did not consider those to constitute a library. The figures above stated also indicate that a higher number of female respondents did own a collection prior to receiving the subscription based book acquisition programme.

Another question 13(a), related to "Are there any libraries in your town or village?" to which the response state:

TABLE 6.20: Libraries Located Near the Residence

Libraries	*Male*	*Female*
Yes	72.5	84.7
No	29.3	15.3

On, being asked 13(b), "If yes, do you make use of such libraries?", the respondents feel:

TABLE 6.21: Usage of Libraries where Present

Usage	*Male*	*Female*
Yes	70.8	68.4
No	29.2	31.6

Respondents to question 13(c), "Local library available within 10 miles of respondent's home", response is as follows:

TABLE 6.22: Library Available within 10 Miles of Residence

Libraries	*Male*	*Female*
Yes	50.9	75.0
No	49.1	25.0

The results show that there are libraries and this leads to the fact that Andhra Pradesh is far better served by libraries near the residences than by book shops only 47.7 per cent reported that book shops are in neighbourhood, whereas 75 per cent report the presence of libraries near their residence. It is unfortunate, however, that 22 per cent reported have neither a bookshop nor library in the residential area, and furthermore, 13 per cent have neither facility within 30 miles of their homes. Respondents to question 13(c), have shown that more than two-thirds do make use of such local libraries, without any significant difference between male and female patterns. In the absence of more information about the type of local libraries, stock, access hours, borrowing conditions, etc.; it is not possible to "say whether the percentage of local library users could not be increased still further". There is a strong evidence, from these responses, of the fact that female respondents typically reside either in urban centres or in villages near such centres. "Taken by themselves, the responses to question 13(c) constitute a strong argument in favour of the future expansion of the public library system".

Another significant issue, relating to multi-lingual situation which is the case of India, the question No. 15, asked was "In what other language(s) (*i.e.*, in addition to Telugu) would you like to read books?" The responses are:

TABLE 6.23: Language Preference

Language	*Male*	*Female*
English	83.4	74.0
Hindi	39.9	40.6
Urdu	2.9	0.0
Others (Kannada, Tamil, Malayalam, etc.)	4.9	11.1

Interestingly, the percentages shown in Table 6.23 do not add up to 100 per cent because several respondents desired for more than one language. In fact, nearly one-third of the respondents desired to read books in English and in Hindi. Of the respondents if 83 per cent are interested in reading English books, it shows that the respondents of this question, are probably urban based. This idea is supported by the fact that the activity was managed from Secunderabad, and the natural outcome is then the same. But the survey respondents, as shown in the results elsewhere, are only 14.8 per cent from city, 22.5 per cent from town, and as many as 62 per cent are from villages. There could be any other reasons for this English bias among the respondents, which the report, under review did not interpret. Such is the trend in promoting the reading habits among the people.

Purpose of Visiting Library

To understand the level of use of public libraries, a survey of a District Library is available. The respondents have indicated their purpose of visiting the library at the time of the interview, conducted by Satyanarayana (1996):

TABLE 6.24: Purpose of Visiting the Library

Lending:	
Return	120
Renew	39
Borrow	78
Reading:	
Textbooks	12
Magazines	30
Newspapers	29

This is the state-of-the art of the use behaviour of a public library located at Vishakhapatnam District. The figures indicate: that the home use of library books by the users is predominant; reading newspapers and magazines—all light reading material—is the main interest of the users; textbook and course material is used by a small group of users; users are interested in keeping the books for longer duration—by availing the renewal facility—indicating that renewal as a practice is common among users; newspapers and magazines are on a high demand—requiring the library to spend more on subscribing the latest in major languages of the area; etc.

The major indicator of this use behaviour is that public libraries are expected to educate, inform, and entertain, but the users are more in the area of spending their time in consuming news—doled out through international news agencies, for whatever reasons, and for whatever cost. And that the expected purpose of the public library is not being fulfilled, either because of lack of resources in these libraries, or because of lack of user demands, or due to any other reason.

British Library Use

One may like to compare this use pattern with another survey done at British Library, Hyderabad, by this writer. The visit on a week day, at noon, shows in the Table 6.25.

TABLE 6.25: The Visit on a Week Day at British Library, Hyderabad

Sections	*Users*
Newspapers	12
Magazines	5
Book stack	15
Reading	25
Borrowing	3
Renewals & Returns	3
Catalogue	4
Student Advise	4
Membership	3
Waiting to be Filed	3
Xerox	2
Reference Desk	2

The Table 6.25, basically indicate that a library has much more than news and magazine type of resources—it is used because it has all types of reading materials and also because it encourages developing an interest in books and a desire to find the world of information by oneself. Though there are guided tours, and reference librarians, available to provide help, the users by and large navigate by themselves in all corners of this small but compact system of libraries.

This is amply demonstrated in the different sections which are fully crowded on all working days, and Hyderabad branch of the British Library is not distinct in attracting the users. All British, and for that matter all American libraries, located in different cities present the same crowd and rush for information.

The British Library is a subscription based information resource, and has thousands of members—individual and institutional. It performs all that is expected of a user-friendly public library. It does achieve this objective, despite the fact that unlike the Indian public libraries it is not free, nor all its services are free. It charges for membership, book reservation, photocopy, searching online catalogues and CD-Rom databases, interlibrary facility from branches within the country and outside the country, etc. The public by paying for these, has shown acceptance as well willingness to this idea of getting information against price, and accepted the fact that information as a commodity has to be purchased. The acceptance and popularity of the British libraries in Indian society, has indicated two facts:

(a) that good libraries—having minimum resources but are usable and are convenient for all types of members of the society—are on demand all the time.
(b) that the Government has accepted that British libraries are useful for the country, and are doing a better service than other existing libraries in the country. India has successfully coordinated its role in promoting the growth of British libraries by joining hands in this process—One should not be surprised that since 1970s the Indian Council for Cultural Relations (ICCR) has undertaken the responsibility of jointly managing the British libraries situated in nine cities. The British High Commission in India, however, is allowed to manage directly the libraries in four metros attached to the High Commission or the Embassy.

Similar to these subscription based foreign libraries, India has yet another private type of subscription libraries. These are privately owned, un-registered circulating libraries in residential communities. Though the British were the pioneers of this in India, when the first such a library was started in Calcutta, in 1787, the Indians have gladly picked up this as a business enterprise. In the small town of Tirupati, Chandraiah (1993), made a study of ten such circulating libraries, and has interesting findings. These circulating libraries were managed by untrained and unemployed graduates; the average stock of these ranges between 120 to 800 volumes (including books, magazines, etc.); the middle class was the maximum user of this service; the customers suggested two reasons for not visiting the public libraries: the public library was not accessible (64%), and books of one's choice were not available (20%). In short the country is in dire need of good public libraries, which can provide free access to all, be open to all, and contribute in the overall development of the personality of its members. Where are such libraries, not even in the

State which is supposed to have 'people's movement' in promoting the cause of library development in this same century!!!

Efforts at Enactment

1953 Hyderabad Public Libraries Bill—drafted by Dr. S.R. Ranganathan (SRR). This bill suggested an independent status for the library development in the newly reformed State. The State had a many regions which were managed under the Madras Public Libraries Act. Hence, a fresh enactment was necessary to the newly constituted geographical areas.

1955 Hyderabad State Public Libraries Act. Based on the draft bill, and the efforts of Justice Gopalrao Ekbote and K.M. Ujlamkar, the Act was passed, which was primarily concerned with the Telangana region of the State of the Andhra Pradesh.

1957 Andhra Pradesh Public Libraries Bill—drafted by SRR. The further re-organization of the States, in 1956, necessitated expanding the legal jurisdiction of the Act, and hence the newly formed State of Andhra Pradesh draft bill became necessary. It also had modifications necessary to change the jurisdiction of the Madras Public Libraries Act, that effected the regions in Andhra Pradesh.

1959 Andhra Pradesh Public Libraries Bill. This was yet another attempt to get the bill passed in the legislature, but it failed.

1960 Andhra Pradesh State Public Libraries Act. This Act re-named the Hyderabad Public Libraries Act, re-defined the regions in the jurisdiction, added many new clauses to the existing legislation, and thus became a model for other States to follow. One of its good features is the getting rid of the benumbing hand of the non-librarian secretary of the Local Library authorities.

1969 Andhra Pradesh Public Libraries Amendment Bill. This was another move to amend the provisions of the Act, but did not get a legislative clearance. With a view to strengthen the cause of library development, and on the persistent demands from public, the Government appointed a fourteen member committee in February 1976, under the Chairmanship of Justice Ekbote. It was called Review Committee, on the Working of the Andhra Pradesh Public Libraries Act. The Committee submitted its report in 1977.

Not much was implemented, but soon another Committee was constituted under the Chairmanship of Vavilala Gopala Krishnaiah, which submitted its report in 1978. This Committee made certain distinct recommendations of the Private Libraries, on their status and improvements required. While the Government has accepted these recommendations, the implementation has not been satisfactory.

1979 Andhra Pradesh Public Libraries (Comprehensive) Bill drafted by Dr. Venkatappaiah.

The other attempts at suggesting improvements to the Act, are:

1986 Andhra Pradesh Public Libraries Amendment Bill
1989 Andhra Pradesh Public Libraries Amendment Bill to amend the name: Andhra Pradesh Granthalaya Parishad
1990 Andhra Pradesh Public Libraries Amendment Bill

Academic Libraries

There are several school, college and university libraries in the State, and mapping there growth and development is not in the scope of this chapter.

The leading universities of the State are Osmania University Hyderabad; Andhra University, Waltair; Sri Venkateswara University, Tirupati; are prominent in terms of historic value and well-established systems. There are some more universities that have emerged in the last few decades, such as Hyderabad Central University, Hyderabad; Jawaharlal Nehru Technological University, Hyderabad; Central Institute of English and Foreign Languages, Hyderabad; Kakatiya University, Warangal; Telugu University, Hyderabad; Agricultural University, Hyderabad; Health University, Vijayawada; Sri Krishnadevaraya University, Ananthapur; Ambedkar Open University, etc.

TABLE 6.26: Collection in the Universities, 1994

	Books	*Serials*
A.P. Agricultural University	2,56,000	1,600
Andhra University	n.d.	n.d.
CIEFL	1,11,000	450
Dr. B.R. Ambedkar Open University	30,000	127
Jawaharlal Nehru Tech. University	34,000	56
Osmania University	5,02,000	388
Sri Krishnadevaraya University	77,287	270
Sri Venkateswara University	2,85,009	300
Telugu University	74,000	156
Sri Padmavati Mahila Viswavidyalaya	25,932	267
Sri Satya Sai Inst. Higher Learning	90,000	—

In addition to these there are the following institutions offering education at the universities and other allied agencies:

	Degree Colleges
353	Colleges of Education
11	Colleges of Engg. & Tech.
28	Colleges of Agriculture
5	Medical Colleges
9	Music Colleges

The above table shows the mushrooming of academic institutions, which started with the process of privatization of education. The advantage with privatization is visible in opening new colleges, but the disadvantage is seen in lack of standards, as many private colleges don't have proper and sufficient libraries, and whatever little budget is officially sanctioned, is not spent in full, leaving the place as useless as any other isolated corner.

Special Libraries

If we can classify the special libraries, as those devoted to research and development, and those attached to traditional centres of specialized study, we have two extreme positions. The first, that is, the libraries attached to R&D centres (scientific and industrial research centres) are the most modernized and are as advanced in their set-up and infrastructure as are the counterparts in developed countries. The other type of libraries, are in a very bad shape, and are not different from the special archives and museums—all maintaining the traditional purpose of 'storing' the material for posterity.

A sample of both of these types is presented in the following to indicate the status of each of these:

Centre of Cellular and Molecular Biology, Hyderabad (CCMB): It is the super-speciality centre. It is, systematically, hooked up with international databases and is a very advanced research and development centre in the world. Its importance and value can be judged by the fact that the scientists who work here are internationally established and highly cited in the concerned field. The Centre in collaboration with the Indian Institute of Chemical Biology, situated on the same campus is equally advanced and is the leading centre for various scientific and technological research, and these days it is in limelight also because of its speciality in DNA research—in ascertaining the parental genes.

The library of these two institutions together has 80,000 books, and subscribes to 550 scientific journals. The library attached to the Centre is well developed and provides all help in document access and document delivery to satisfy the information needs of scientists. It is online with computerized databases, such as, Dialogue, MEDLARS, NICNET, etc. It has CD-Rom and other databases to provide fulltext and bibliographic services. Its document delivery service includes photocopy, inter-library loan service, and procurement of material from anywhere in Andhra Pradesh Oriental Manuscripts Library & Research Institute, Hyderabad.

The other example of special library, from non-R&D type, is this Manuscripts Library and Research Institute. The activities of this library are preserving and providing access to the researchers who visit the library. The total manuscript collection it has is 23,161, with over 82 per cent in paper form, and 18 per cent in palm leaf; these palm leaf are 27 per cent Telegu, 68 per cent Sanskrit, and others Tamil and Kannada; its 16,926 collection, which is a major portion, pertains to 37 per cent Arabic, 52 per cent Persian, and 11 per cent Urdu language material all in paper form. Its services are limited to providing reading room, research grants to scholars (Rs. 400 per month to full-time researcher, and Rs. 200 for part-time), microfilming of these rare documents, and occasionally providing photocopy service. It publishes a research journal, and the Director of the Institute is recognized as a research guide by the neighbouring universities. These are all its special feature, and special activities. Its working conditions are now getting improved with its new premises in the Osmania University Campus.

It lacks all amenities which are required for its survival and prosperity. It has machines and equipments which don't work; it has no professional manpower which can perform the skills and tasks accepted for improving the work environment and special services a 'research' institute is expected to perform; and a modern manuscript library is expected to dwell into. Its grants are wavering, its 'scholarship' is namesake and shamefully less than a tip which Indian restaurant bearers will receive; its claim of 'providing access to the concerned scholars' is totally restricted by any standard—one or two theft cases did occur in the premises of this place, and the material was finally retrieved. Theft and losses are bound to occur, even in the biggest research library, Library of Congress—which does not however restrict any access to anyone, living anywhere. The photocopy of the manuscripts, in the Oriental Library, is not an easy task for a research scholar.

Much bureaucracy is to be crossed for obtaining permission, even to see a particular document. Access to the documents it has, then is not its motto, nor it can be given the kind of enquiries we have to face if something goes wrong prompts a response from sources in the Institute.

Library Profession

Library Associations

Andhra Pradesh has the benefit of having an active people's support, either in its freedom struggle, or its literacy campaign since the first decade of this century. The profession has reaped the advantages of this activism. Today the professional activity in the State, at least, in terms of fraternity and activism, in whatever smaller way, is one of significance and repute in the country. Its activism, though, not as high as, Bengal, Kerala, Punjab, Tamil Nadu and so on, is yet worth noticing, because of various reasons. The Andhra Pradesh Library Association (*f.* 1914), is still active, and it hosted the All-India Library Conference, in 1995.

The other professional bodies in the State, worth their names, are Academy of Library Science and Documentation (ALSD), Andhra Pradesh Public Library Association, and so on. These bodies are in one way or the other, contributing to the growth of the profession. These conduct training and continuing education programmes for the benefit of the profession. For instance, ALSD has been involved in development programmes for the benefit of its members, all over the twin-cities of Hyderabad and Secunderabad. The Andhra Pradesh Public Library Association has its network and conducts similar programmes for its members.

Library Education

Education for library work, has been on the agenda of the State, and it got its first opening in 1935 at Andhra University, as a summer course, and a diploma course was started in 1937; followed in 1959, by Osmania University, starting a post-graduate diploma in library science, Sri Venkateswara in 1974, and Sri Krishnadevaraya in 1985. Open University started its distance education in 1985 which was then followed by Kakatiya University, in 1989. Today all the universities in the State offer Bachelor, Master's and Doctoral/M.Phil. programmes.

Institute of Library Science

A catalogue of all other institutions offering education for library science is out of place, but to mention one or two in detail, is appropriate. A premier professional association, Hyderabad Library Association (*f.* 1951), as per its stated objective, started a certificate course of three months duration, and laid the foundation of what came to be later called as Institute of Library Science. The moving spirit behind all these was K.M. Ujlambkar, Librarian, Nizam College, Hyderabad, later Director of Public Libraries, Maharashtra.

Ranganathan, wrote to the founder, appreciating the services in a letter in 1953—which speaks of quality and efficiency: "I am very proud of the excellent work you have done. I was greatly impressed by the result of your leadership so potently visible during my visit to Hyderabad in October. It is not easy to induce so much of devotion and loyalty in other people unless leadership of a high order is intrinsic in a person". Further, he adds, "The performance of the candidates in the examination has more than surprised me of course in an agreeable direction. I am not exaggerating when I say that during the 3 months you have made your students understand Classification more efficiently than what is being done by the teachers in Delhi. This proved to me that your leadership is not of demagogic or corruptive type but of constructive and elevating type".

Concludingly, remarks "Convey to your students my great admiration . . . admiration which began when I met them in person and which culminated when I saw their performance in the answer books" (quoted by Inamdar, 1991).

History repeats itself, is not very wrong in the case of this Institute. It gave up a diploma course (the present incarnation of Bachelor Degree), to allow Osmania University to start it in 1960s. For which an old faculty laments "This event in its history, tough tragic, intrinsically, did not, however, take away from it the prestige and standing it had by dint of its performance earned (Riswadkar, 1991). But again in 1990s, the Institute, started the degree course, while Osmania continued to offer the same, and made a history when Osmania recognized the course and agreed to conduct examinations and offer degrees for the course conducted by the Institute.

Voluntarism was at the base of all that went on in the development of this Institute. A series of voluntary faculty and office bearers of the board of management contributed their might in making it an asset (Riswadkar).

While there are few more institutes offering this short term training programme, uniformly conducted, all over the State for five months, and its examinations are conducted by the Commissioner of Examinations, Govt. of Andhra Pradesh. Incidentally, the Institute is the first to receive its recognition from the State Government.

Continuing Education

Among facilities for continuing education programmes are the agencies that take lead, and the list includes, Academy of Library Science and Documentation, Hyderabad; ICSSR's Southern Regional Centre, Hyderabad; UGC's Refresher Courses offered at Academic Staff College at the Osmania University; Department of Public Libraries, departments of library science in the State, a series of seminars and workshops conducted at the British Library, Hyderabad; and the American Studies Research Centre, Hyderabad.

National Institute for Small Industry Extension Training (NISIET), however, leads in a regular training programme for continuing education of librarians, more so for information storage and retrieval systems. Its unique place in the map of Third World libraries is obvious from the fact that it conducts intensive training programmes at national and international level, and has been recognized everywhere for these since a long time.

Library Networks

There is considerable debate on resource sharing and networking in the State's library systems—ranging from public library network as envisaged in the legislation, to university library network, to special libraries consortium, and to metropolitan library networks. All is in the thin air, and all that is going on is not really in practice, with a few exceptions. A survey of the libraries in Hyderabad was conducted, as a part of the HYLIBNET network planning exercise. The survey covered 40 academic, research and other special libraries in Hyderabad, and response came from 22 institutions.

Interesting findings are, fourteen libraries reported having another library with similar or common interests within a distance of 10 kms.; 7 within a distance between 10 and 50 kms. Seven reported that the duplication in their collection and those of the nearest library was high, so also in serials subscribed, 10 libraries felt that there was high duplication.

Only 4 libraries had inter-library loan, at a higher rate, whereas 11 had it at low level, 7 had it very low and 2 never had this exchange. In terms of acquiring photocopy of articles, 45 per cent mostly used other libraries in India, 5 preferred the services of INSDOC, 10 sometimes used other Indian libraries. Interaction between libraries was not the main agenda, among the respondents. Even specialized libraries, such as, the engineering and technology libraries, or management and human resource development centres having common interests, had no interaction (Haravu, 1995: 40).

Among public libraries, the District Library Authority (ZGS) has a network of centralized processing and decentralized retrieval pattern. For instance, the City Central Library, Hyderabad-Secunderabad, which works as a District Library for the Hyderabad District, has a radius of 30 kms., with 87 branch libraries, 3 mobile libraries, and 3 women's branch libraries. 10 branches have separate children's sections, and 6 have separate textbook sections. A glance at any of the branch or the main City Central Library, at any time gives an impression that the main attraction for the visitors are the magazine and newspaper sections.

Hence, the concentration of 30 daily newspapers, in 7 languages, and the Chief Librarian is rightly observing this 'It is a test for the eyes for any one to see that the Reading Rooms of these libraries are packed to their capacity by the readers' (Reddy, 1991). By implication, whatever in lakhs and crores is spent to develop other areas is neither for a test nor for anyone to view the sad state of affairs.

The mobile libraries, cover 190 points, in the two cities, operated between 7 a.m. and 7 p.m., these have 8,000 registered borrowers—that is each mobile van has on average 2,666 members, and each van reaches 63 points, by rotation. At each point the van halts for one hour, making it possible to reach each point once a week. A glance at the collection housed in the van, gives an idea of the varied collection, ranging from fiction to prose and poetry, which is expected to be 'useful' for its primary audience: house-wife. The procedure to enroll is simple, an attestation, by a gazetted officer, and a security deposit against the number of books one intends to borrow, the upper limit is four per head.

The library system has a collection, and a user population, as follows:

Visitors per year	40,00,000
Books consulted	12,00,000
Registered borrowers	50,000
Total collection	8,00,000
Annual additions	50,000
Periodicals subscribed	150

It is hooked up to the NICNET for online access, and the dial up services provided a linkage to the national database on all walks of life. Prof. Soma Raju has suggested a network of university library system in the State, which is as follows: it can be a three part system, with specialization in each branch of universe of knowledge,

Andhra University Library	—	Science and Technology
Osmania University Library	—	Social Sciences
Sri Venkateswara University Library	—	Humanities.

There are obvious problems in this proposal. The main problem is of resource sharing—Indian libraries are yet to get the culture of resource sharing. Prof. Soma Raju suggested this in 1986, and to this date there is not even a hope of such a system approach in analysis nor any consideration by any authority in this direction. The much talked about network system, at the Hyderabad City Level (HYLIBNET) has not become fully effective, and a system at the State level at this rate may not appear at all.

Summary

The library development in the State on the whole is not upto the mark as was envisaged by the proponents of library development and the leaders of library movement in the State. They feel depressed at the state-of-the-art and have made many recommendations to the authorities. The problem then lies in the three dimensional view: users, the authorities, and the profession. Who has how much of role and what can remedy the problems faced by the libraries is for any one to guess, less said the better. The public library development committees and commissions, such as, Ekbote Committee, Vavilala Committee, have made their suggestions and the problems are discussed at length.

UNION TERRITORY: ANDAMAN & NICOBAR

This Union Territory comprises of 306 islands, with only 38 Islands inhabited. As per the Census of 1991, it has a population of eight lakhs, and a literacy of 73.58 per cent (which is improved from 53 per cent in 1981). The main issues for this State, in relation to establishing libraries, are the scattered islands, distance from the main land, lack of communication system between these islands and the main land, difficulty in collection of library materials, etc.

Its area is 8,249 sq.kms. The population density is 34 persons per sq.km. The sex ratio of the State is 820 females per 1000 males. The literacy rate of males is 79.6 per cent and females is 66.2 per cent. The main language groups are as per 1981 Census: Bengali (23.4%); Hindi (17.2%); Tamil (14.0%); Nicobarese (11.3%); Malayalam (9.88%); Telugu (9.3%); etc. The religious groups as per the records of the 1981 Census are: Hindus (64.5%); Christians (25.5%); Muslims (8.5%); etc.

Public Libraries

Its library history dates back to the Cellular Jail Library (*f.* 1911). A few inmates took interest in the establishment of this, and the names include, some of the prominent political prisoners, like Vinayak Savarkar, Barin Ghosh, Bhai Permanand, Prithwi Singh Azad, Shri Bangeswar Ray, etc. These people got inspired from the library movement and political activists in Mumbai, Calcutta, and Delhi. It lent books, and prepared brief abstracts of the collection in order to build interest. It had a study circle and reading room facility. Seminars were held that dealt with Marxists influence on India, nationalism, planning and development, and so on. This library served well till 1939, and apart from this there was no other major attempt in library development.

The post-independent scenario shows that the first attempt in library development started in 1959, with the establishment of Hindi Library at Port Blair, the capital city of the Island. This establishment was done with much publicity, and for its inauguration the founders invited Shrimati Violet Alva. This Hindi Library, was opened with the purpose of promoting language teaching and learning centres, under the National Language Teaching Scheme. Within one year another Hindi Library emerged this was located at Car Nicobar. The Hindi Library was first declared as District Library, and later, in 1974, it was designated as the State Library. It is located at Port Blair.

TABLE 6.27: Collection of Books at a Glance 1977-78

Library	*No. of Libraries*	*Book Stock*
State Library	1	35,000
Zonal Library	3	6,000
Community Centres	12	2,400
School Libraries	22	65,000
Public Subscription Libraries	4	5,000
College Libraries	1	10,000
Special Libraries	5	n.d.

Library Expenditure

TABLE 6.28: Expenditure on Public Libraries in States (1986-87)

Expenditure	*Population (in lakhs)*	*Per Capita (in Rs.)*	*Literacy %*
2.0	1.8	1.06	42.14

These figures, Table 6.28, are representative of what is the priority in the State for expenditure related to libraries. The State has grown in its socio-economic status and its industrial output is well advanced. And despite these developments the per capita of the State in the last decade stands at 12th place among all the States in the country.

Administration

The public library system in this State is managed by the Department of Education. Administratively, the two districts Andaman and Nicobar, are divided into ten zones, and the library system consists of ten zonal public libraries, and all under the advisory management of the State Library. The acquisition process is centralized, under the State Library, acquiring for all the ten public libraries, as well as, for the school libraries. The annual budget in 1988, was around Rs. 80,000, for acquisition, and for other expenditures it was Rs. 2.7 lakhs. The financial support given by RRLF, for the year 1988, enabled acquiring 208 books, worth Rs. 19,173.00 (each book on an average costing Rs. 92). Whereas in the year 1986 RRLF funds enabled acquiring 422 books worth Rs. 44,428 (each costing Rs. 105), and in 1987 for acquiring 431 books worth Rs. 41,465 (each Rs. 96).

A comparison of average prices, as shown above, with another comparison of books published abroad, reveals that the average book price will be around \$30 (*i.e.*, Rs. 36 × \$30) or Rs. 1,080. At this rate, Indian libraries can buy 1,000 Indian books in Rs. 1,00,000, or only 100 foreign books. One implication of this is foreign books are out of reach for Indian public library users, and hence they have to live with cheap Indian prints (if at all available, such as ELBS editions, or Indo-American reprint programme), or cheap Indian books, with no control over quality of the contents, quality of material, and quality of the binding either.

Coming back to the status of the acquisitions at the State Library. The annual acquisition is around 1,000 books, along with annual subscription to 14 daily newspapers, and 25 magazines. These acquisition figures are indicative of the trends in the State. In 80,000 whatever little it purchases, the other expenditures would take away much of the fund. The entire staff in the State Library comprises of one Senior Librarian, three junior librarians, eight skilled and semi-skilled assistants (non-professionals) and one clerk (typist).

Since most of the public libraries in the State are located in the school buildings, the centralized acquisition is seemingly suitable. But the other drawback in this centralization process is that there is not a single representative from the different Zones in the state book selection committee, nor there are local book selection committees. Even the State Library Planning Committee comprises of bureaucrats from the State level, and no representation is given from public or from the local zones.

State Library

The State Library has 53,000 books, the zonal libraries have totally 14,000 books. The budget of the zonal libraries, varies annually, between Rs. 3,000 to 5,000, which is again very meagre. This helps in adding around 200 to 500 volumes a year.

The services of State Library are lending (limited to its registered borrowers); reading room (open to all); reference service (open to all); and reprography. It has a children's section too. By implication the State Library is playing the role of a city library, and not the role of a State library (see Taher: 1996). The zonal libraries are also doing the same functions, lending and providing reading room facility, and this supports the thesis that all State libraries, and the national library in India, are not fulfilling their roles which they are expected to, rather these are just doing well.

Again, district level libraries are yet to be established. If there were district libraries, they relieve much of the pressure which the State library otherwise receives. There are, in addition, 11 other public libraries and 8 information centres working under the Deputy Commissioner, of the Andaman District, to serve the rural areas for the District. Additionally, voluntary organizations, run public reading rooms, and as a part of assistance programme, the RRLF supports two such reading rooms in the State.

Academic Libraries

Being a newly formed State, Andaman & Nicobar, started the educational programmes with affiliation from neighbouring States.

Library Profession

Professionalism, as a means to demonstrate the spirit-de-corps, is visible in the State too. The Andaman & Nicobar Library Association (*f.* 1977), has been in the front to promote library development, and for library legislation in the State. Due to its contact efforts, the State Government agreed to constitute "Andaman and Nicobar Library Planning Committee", in 1978. Recommendations have been taken up for implementation, and the first phase, and second phase, saw the opening of libraries in additional places in both the districts.

The Association has been regularly sponsoring book exhibitions, seminars, and such other activities. Interestingly, its activities are being communicated by the media and press, and hence reaching wider audience. This acceptability, of library related matters as worthy for public consumption, is itself a great achievement. For instance, a seminar, organized by the Association, on "One village-one library" was well covered in the local press and duly reported by All India Radio, in its news bulletin. It is ironical, that this being one exception, even national media does not consider library related programmes, as worth taking the time, which is allotted for more important political VIP and VVIPs.

Library Education

Professional education and training needs received attention, in different ways. The Association made a simple beginning in 1978, and offered a certificate course in library science. The Directorate of Education started a six-week course, but due to lack of recognition, it was soon abandoned. The Directorate offered an orientation course for librarians in 1980.

The Association made its first attempt in 1987, to start a regular course of Bachelor's degree in library science. Located in the Teachers Training Institute, Port Blair, its affiliation is from Central University, Pondicherry.

STATE: ARUNACHAL PRADESH

This is the land of the mythic age, but its existence in records is traced 16th century when the Ahom kings began to rule the region. After independence it was a part of the North Eastern Frontier Agency, and in 1972 it became a Union Territory, and gained the status of statehood in 1987. This is a land of Brahmkund and Tawang, war dances and Buddhist Chams.

Its area is 83,743 sq. kms. The population density is 10 persons per sq. km. The sex ratio of the State is 861 females per 1000 males. The literacy rate of males is 51.1 per cent and females is 29.3 per cent, with an average of 41.22 per cent as per the Census of 1991. The major language groups are according to the 1981 Census report are as follows: Nissi/Dafla (22.1%); Adi (18.9%); Gorkha/Nepali (7.2%); Bengali (7.1%); Monpa (5.2%); Wancho (5.0%); Nocte (4.3%); Assamese (4.2%); Hindi (3.7%); Mishmi (3.7%); Tangsa (2.6%); Tibetan (0.9%). According to the 1981 Census, the main religious groups are: Hindus (30.0%); Buddhists (13.7%); Christians (4.3%); Muslims (0.8%); Sikhs (0.2%).

Public Libraries

Library Expenditure

TABLE 6.29: Expenditure on Public Libraries in States (1986-87)

Expenditure (in lakhs)	*Population (in lakhs)*	*Per Capita (in Rs.)*	*Literacy % 1980s*
15.0	6.31	2.37	11.32

These figures, Table 6.29, are representative of what is the priority in the State for expenditure related to libraries. The State has grown in its socio-economic status and its industrial output is well advanced. And despite these developments the per capita of the State in the last decade stands at 2nd place among all the States in the country.

STATE: ASSAM

Situated in the northeast of India, its literacy has grown from 3 per cent in 1951, 27.4 per cent in 1961 and to 43.2 per cent 1991. The first language of the State is Assamese, its earliest book in this language, was Prahlad Charita, by Hema Saraswathi.

The State is considered as underdeveloped in libraries, despite its long literary history, and its famous prose work of Buranji, of 13th century.

Much of the history of the State, is shared with the neighbouring States, and the library development seemed slow, on the whole, due to this frequent political dislocation. The State was split to form independent States: Nagaland (1963); Meghalaya (1970); Mizoram (1971); and

Arunachal Pradesh (1972). Its area is 78,438 sq. kms. The population density is 284 persons per sq. km. The sex ratio of the State is 925 females per 1000 males. The literacy rate of males is 62.3 per cent and females is 43.7 per cent.

Public Libraries

The State Central Library, acts as a informal network for the library system in the State. The State Library came into existence in 1956, with the re-naming of the Assam Government Public Library. The latter (*f.* 1903) was first established at Shillong, and later moved to Gauhati (or Guwahati). The collection in the State Central Library, after Meghalaya was given away its share, stands at 35,459 volumes, which is housed in the District Library Building.

In the Five Year Plans, earlier there was no fund for library building, though the planners called it as "Improvement of Library Service" scheme. The later amendments however, took care of this lacuna, and the State had permanent buildings for different public libraries.

The public library system in the State, is yet to get a library legislation, and all the activities are going on without any such regulatory mechanism. The Government has set up libraries at all levels of the administrative system: at present there are 17 district libraries, 11 sub-divisional libraries. In 1983, the State Library Service was upgraded as a separate section under the Department of Education, enabling far more freedom and for increased efficiency. By 1988, 181 rural libraries were functioning in respective panchayats, and the plan is to have such libraries for all the Gaon Panchayats in the State.

There is a centralised scheme of acquisition, of all books, at the State Library, and the Directorate has constituted a Purchase Board to oversee the pertinent issues, for all the different types of libraries, State to rural levels. To support voluntarism in the State, books from the extra stock are given as gift to libraries managed by voluntary bodies in rural areas.

Library Finance

The RRLF funds do support library development in the State, and provide matching grants. For instance, in the year 1988-89, the State government sanctioned a matching grant of Rs. 1,25,000.

Library Expenditure

TABLE 6.30: Expenditure on Public Libraries in States (1986-87)

Expenditure (in lakhs)	*Population (in lakhs)*	*Per Capita (in Rs.)*	*Literacy % 1980s*
60.0	198.9	0.30	—

These figures, Table 6.30, are representative of what is the priority in the State for expenditure related to libraries. The State has grown in its socio-economic status and its industrial output is well advanced. And despite these developments the per capita of the State in the last decade stands at 23rd place among all the States in the country.

Efforts for Enactment

There is no legislation, and this is the state of affairs despite the attempts by Ranganathan, as early as 1964. A draft public library bill was also prepared then. There have been a variety of other attempts in this regard, without much success as of this day.

1964 Public Libraries Bill for Assam—prepared by SRR: The Assam Library Association collaborated with SRR in preparing a draft bill, and submitted it to the authorities for consideration, but no result emerged.

1972 Assam Public Libraries Bill—prepared by Dr. R.L. Mittal

1986 Assam Public Libraries Bill.

Academic Libraries

The State has three universities, *viz.*, Gauhati University (*f.* 1947), Dibrugarh University (*f.* 1965), and Assam Agricultural University (AAUL) (*f.* 1969). The Gauhati University Library is called K.K. Handique Library (KKHL); Dibrugarh University Library is called Sahityarathi Lakshminath Bezbarua Library (SLBL). The growth of these three university libraries is interesting and presents a comparative perspective for an indepth analysis. A survey by Barman (1994), reveals the following patterns that prevail in the development of these libraries. In terms of growth of collection a comparison of these three libraries shows the priorities that each has.

Barman, feels "Still the annual addition of KKHL is much below the expectation. It may be mentioned here that Jaykar Library of Pune University (*f.* 1949) has an average annual addition of 10,763 during the

TABLE 6.31: Collection Growth

Library	*Years*			*Average Annual Growth, 1972-92*
	1972	*1982*	*1992*	
KKHL	1,23,735	1,90,076	2,36,938	5,662
SLBL	47,000	1,10,366	1,39,899	4,645
AAUL	1,510	61,916	89,205	3,896

same period. Even, Jadavpur University, established in 1955, had annual addition of 10,212 for the year 1982-83" (p. 289). Comparing another growth of current periodicals, the survey, gives the figures of the three university libraries. The Table 6.32 shows the growth of one aspect of periodical collection, that is, current subscriptions to magazines, and periodicals, both foreign and Indian.

TABLE 6.32: Subscription to Periodicals

Library	*Years*			
	1970	*1983*	*1988*	*1991*
KKHL	830	621	849	362
SLBL	400	613	722	547
AAUL	NA	150	NA	441

While the Table 6.32 depicts a lack of uniformity in the subscription of periodicals, it also shows that proportionately there is not much of difference between a library meant for a professional course such as Agriculture, in AAUL, and general education that is provided in the universities attached to KKHL and SLBL. This disproportional pattern is more glaring from two more perspectives: first, KKHL has 33 teaching departments, but its subscription is not on the increase (rather it has decreased heavily); second, in the same years, 1982-83, Pune had subscribed to 1,674 periodicals, and Jadavpur had 1,208 titles. These show how far the budget allocation is influencing the growth or stagnation of the collection of the university libraries.

The growth of the library is also to be seen in terms of users and the size of the staff. The Table 6.33 shows the increase of users, including under-graduates, post-graduates, researchers, and faculty.

These figures, Table 6.33, show interesting points for consideration and understanding the trends. For instance, the AAUL has higher number of staff, against the other two university libraries. Again, AAUL is

TABLE 6.33: Growth of Users and Staff

Library	*Years*			*Average Annual Growth (1980-92)*
	1980	*1983*	*1992*	
KKHL				
Users	2,513	3,423	3,681	97
Staff	42	52	68	26
SLBL				
Users	763	1,000	1,480	60
Staff	24	32	37	13
AAUL				
Users	729	914	1,427	58
Staff	44	63	72	28

comparatively, specialized and focused, and as per the trend in scientific and industrial research libraries in India, these are well staffed, and hence are capable of providing more direct services to the users, as against the other universities. The proportion of users and readers in AAUL is comparable with SLBL, but not with KKHL. SLBL, though general in nature has kept its growth at a low pace, and is steadily growing. On the whole the average growth rate in terms of users and staff is better in AAUL, not so good in SLBL, but it is very poor in KKHL.

TABLE 6.34: Growth in Expenditure (Both Plan and Non-plan)

(Rupees in lakhs)

Library	*1982/83*		*1986/87*		*1991/92*	
	Library	*University*	*Library*	*University*	*Library*	*University*
KKHL	6.05	223.61 (2.43%)	13.86	469.65	24.72	1,050.71 (2.35%)
SLBL	8.36	160.45 (5.2%)	11.68	219.68 (5.3%)	16.07	718.63 (2.2%)
AAUL	16.06	116.67 (13.7%)	N.A.	N.A.	61.88	2,406.66 (2.5%)

Note: Figures in brackets indicate percentage of total expenditure of whole university, spent on library.

Interestingly, higher is the percentage of AAUL, a specialized university library, and lesser is that of larger universities. This is correlating the above stated bias which the science libraries in the country enjoy. While the proportionate expenditure in all university libraries has not been uniformly increasing, there is also no correlation between the past and present in any of the libraries. This is more so obvious in the case of AAUL which earlier had 13.7 per cent and later it has declined to 2.5 per cent—a real calamity faced by all libraries, irrespective of their being science or non-science libraries.

This expenditure pattern is reflected in all the functions of the university libraries. So also the services get better or worse depending upon the availability of such resources. The Table 6.35 displays the types of services offered and growth or decline in services.

TABLE 6.35: Public Services

Service	*1980*			*1992*		
	KKHL	*SLBL*	*AAUL*	*KKHL*	*SLBL*	*AAUL*
Circulation	y	y	y	y	y	y
Reference	y	y	y	y	y	y
Reading Room	y	y	y	y	y	y
Bibliography	y	y	y	n	y	y
Reprography	y	y	y	n	n	n
Translation	n	n	n	n	y	y
Documentation	n	n	n	n	y	y
CAS/SDI	n	n	n	n	n	y
Microforms	y	y	n	n	y	y
Online search	n	n	n	—proposed—		
User's education	n	n	n	n	y	y
Inter-Library Loan	y	n	y	y	y	y
Weekly work-hour	60	72	72	49	54	72

The Table 6.35 shows that some services are common to all, some are only in one or two universities, and some are non-existent. The non-existent services include working for longer hours, extended hours, and so on—the maximum that these work is for 72 hours a week, or on an average 10 hours a day. The Table 6.35 also shows how a decade has brought improvement or otherwise in some areas of services. For instance, bibliography and documentation were common in 1980s and less common in 1990s. As against this user education is prevalent only in one library—considering the fact that university librarians claim and get the faculty status, and this single teaching instance is absent in other university libraries. Similarly, reprographic service was available earlier all the three libraries, but later it has been stopped, due to whatever reasons. The main complaint has been bad machines and unmanageable working conditions. The survey by Barman, in its findings, states "reference service in KKHL which was full and up-to-date in 1980 became partial in 1992. This is due to outdated and obsolete reference tools. Most of the reference tools procured during 1970's have lost their usefulness. Librarian of KKHL admitted this drawback but expressed helplessness due to financial crunch" (p. 294). Considering this fact as a general statement, it is worth mentioning that majority of the university libraries in the country, have such outdated and obsolete tools. Even if they have tools, these are damaged, and mostly have sections missing.

College Libraries

There are 145 colleges under deficit system, 37 colleges under the adhoc system, and 3 Government colleges. In addition to these there are professional colleges which include 3 Engineering Colleges, 3 Medical Colleges, one each Ayurvedic College, Regional Dental College, Regional Nursing College, College of Pharmacy, and College of Veterinary Sciences. A glance at the status of college libraries is pertinent here, to indicate the prevailing conditions.

TABLE 6.36: Collection in College Libraries

	Colleges	*Percentage*	*Books and Periodicals*
	35	20.0	Below 5,000
	40	22.8	5,001 to 20,000
	85	48.5	20,001 to 30,000
	15	8.5	Above 30,001
Total	175		

The figures given in Table 6.36 are indicative of higher proportion of libraries having less than 30,000 collection. A college library which has to cater to the specific teaching, learning, and research needs must be up-to-date, exhaustive and more than all be useful. Another way to test the utility by the size of the population is seen in the Table 6.37.

These figures, Table 6.37, reveal the fact that there is a proportionate growth in size with the growth in the size of the enrolment of new and potential users in the college. But it nowhere speaks of actual users, and their actual demands. Nor it speaks of actual staff strength that is essential, for the respective college—professional or general, as the case may be. There is some semblance of libraries in a few schools, and some are trying to provide professional approach at school libraries, but the scenario on the whole is not very encouraging.

TABLE 6.37: Existence Proportion of Users/Staff/Collection

Student Enrollment	*Library Collection*	*Staff*
Upto 500	Upto 5,000	1 Librarian 1 Bearer
501 to 1,000	5,001 to 20,000	1 Librarian 1 Library Assistant 1 Bearer
1001 to 2,000	20,001 to 30,000	1 Librarian 1 Library Assistant 2 Bearers
Above 2,001	Above 30,001	1 Librarian 1 Assistant Librarian 1 Library Assistant 2 Bearers

Special Libraries

The scene of special libraries, with their advanced status in scientific and industrial environments is very good, as is in other parts of the country. These are visible in institutions such as, Regional Research Laboratory, Jorhat (*f.* 1960); Tea Research Centre, Toklai; NEIBM; Coal Survey Laboratory, Jorhat (*f.* 1957); etc.

Library Profession

Assam Library Association (*f.* 1939), has a long history, and has contributed extensively to the development of professionalism in the State as well as in the entire region. But it had its period of inactivity, which led to mushrooming of other bodies. The Assam College Librarians Association (*f.* 1976), All Assam Rural Libraries Association (*f.* 1987), The Government Assam Library Services Association (*f.* 1969), Gauhati Library Association, etc., are some important bodies in the State. Granthalok, the library journal in Assamese, appeared in 1970s but its publication was suspended later.

Library Education

The attempts to create a base for training and education for librarians in the State, is still in the developmental process. The library science department at the Gauhati University was the only place for the entire north-east India, for a long time, to offer training in librarianship. The Gauhati University started a bachelor's course in 1966. It was the first and still retains its place as only one to offer the Bachelor's degree in library science. It started as an evening course, and the department was headed by the University Librarian. Soon a department of library science was set up, which was re-named, in 1985, as Department of Library and Information Science, along with a new syllabus.

In 1979, the department started Master's degree in library science. The year 1983 saw the bifurcation of the department from the University Library, and the Reader in the department took over as head of the department. While this bifurcation has brought autonomy, status, and much more, it has been cut off from the distinction of having a laboratory (the students learn and experiment the theory in the library). Added to this distancing the library, the idea of internship is also absent in the profession. Ultimately the products that emerge all over the country, are the ones who are devoid of working knowledge and away from the realities.

Inservice training for the librarians is at Gauhati University, as an irregular programme. In the absence of a strong professional body, the department has the complete responsibility to offer professional avenues for the continuing education of the working librarians.

The State Central Library, does offer an adhoc six weeks training for the professionals in the State. But this adhocism is the main hurdle and the profession suffers from lack of regular sources for inservice training and continuing education facilities.

Library Networks

The setting up of North-Eastern Council, in 1970s, and its concern for the development of library information networking in the region is a strong point, given the geo-political situation of these north-eastern States. It has set-up an "Advisory Committee on Improvement of Library and Information Service in the North East Region", to plan, fund and implement all library related matters in the region. It assigned several projects to different institutions. To the Department of Library and Information Science, Gauhati University, it assigned the project, namely "Bibliographic and Documentation Study on the Socio-cultural and Socio-economic Life of the People of the North-Eastern Region".

Not much has been achieved other than this in the sphere of cooperation and coordination in the region, and hence networking is still incomplete.

STATE: BIHAR

There are different theories as to why this State is called as Bihar. One theory is that Vihar, or learning centres, that flourished in the past, led the State to get a literary name, as representative of the glory that was Nalanda University, a place once situated near the present State capital Patna. The proponents of this theory, are probably Muslims, who saw many Buddhist monasteries, or viharas, in this region. Bihar is still important for its Buddhist and Jain origins. Bihar has a record in being an educational State: its Minister of Education, Dr. Syed Mahmood, a champion of literacy, set up thousands of literacy centres, while he was in the office, in 1935. It has a long tradition of *madrasas, qanqahs, pathshalas*, and modern academies of education and learning. It was here that the Khuda Bakhsh Oriental Public Library got its origins, as a one man's life long contribution to the development of learning, and which is recognised as institution of national importance, by an Act of Indian Parliament, in 1969.

This is the land of Buddha and Mahavira, coal and Tata steel, extreme poverty amidst wealth of minerals (the State owns nearly 40 per cent of India's mineral output). Its area 1,73,877 sq. kms. The population density is 497 persons per sq. km. The sex ratio of the State is 912 females per 1000 males. The literacy rate of males is 52.6 per cent and females is 23.1 per cent. The main language groups as per 1981 Census are: Hindi (79.8%); Urdu (9.9%); Santali (3.0%); Bengali (3%); Mundari (0.9%); and others. The religious groups as per the 1981 Census are: Hindus (82.9%); Muslims (14.1%); Christians (1%); Sikhs (0.1%); Jains (0.04%); etc. Its literacy ratio is the lowest: 10 per cent in 1951; 18 per cent in 1961; 20 per cent in 1971; 26.2 per cent in 1981 and 38.5 per cent in 1991.

Public Libraries

Its library history is traced in three different phases, first, in the foundation of the library movement, 1882-1889; second in the flourishing of the library movement, 1901-1960; and third in the progressive awakening of the library movement, 1961-1990 (Esperanza, 1996: 147).

But the learned author has not defined what constitutes the main currents, to understand these phases, or what could be reasons of the backwardness of the State, in terms of (a) low literacy rate, (b) under-development of libraries, and (c) State's inability to lead even its own library development in an exemplary manner given its phased "development". Describing the growth of libraries is different, and explaining the causal relationship that enables the development is another thing.

There was a literacy movement too in the State, as early as 1935. The details of the movement are: "The ministry formed in Bihar after the India Act of 1935 tried to reorganise the whole method and function of education. The most notable achievement was the mass literacy movement initiated by the Hon'ble Dr. Syed Mahmood, Minister of Education, for eradicating adult illiteracy and spreading enlightenment among the masses. It was organised with the help of about 14,000 volunteers drawn from student community, inspecting staff of Education Department and other social workers. More than 12,000 literacy centres were started with an average attendance of one and half lakhs per term of six weeks. This movement also spread into the jails and almost every prisoner was turned literate" (Singh, 1991: 194).

One can contend that the literacy movement that was so forcefully administered should have resulted at least in a steep increase in the rate of literacy. But nothing of the kind was visible, in the State, in 1947. Rather the growth pattern of literacy in the State, as shown above, is unfortunately one the lowest literacy States.

The public library system in the State consists of the State library, divisional and district libraries, subdivisional libraries, block libraries, village libraries, mobile and children's libraries.

TABLE 6.38: Public Libraries in the State (Amount received from RRLF)

Year	*Amount in lakhs*	*State Library*	*District Library*	*Sub. div. +Spl.*	*Block Library*	*Village Library*	*Total*
1978-79	4.29	1	31+7	25	110	200	374
1979-80	4.08	1	31+7	25	210	310	584
1980-81	6.04	1	31+7	25	113	310	487
1981-82	4.34	1	31+7	25	175	310	549
1982-83	6.60	1	31+7	25	175	310	549
1983-84	4.78	1	31+7	25	100	394	559
Total	30.17						

The Table 6.38 reveals the fact that the matching grant given to the public libraries in Bihar, is fluctuating as is the fluctuation in the number of village and block libraries. This fluctuation is understandable if the number of district and sub-divisional libraries also fluctuates, but this is not the case.

Library Expenditure

TABLE 6.39: Expenditure on Public Libraries in States (1986-87)

Expenditure (in lakhs)	*Population (in lakhs)*	*Per Capita (in Rs.)*	*Literacy % 1980s*
25.8	699.1	0.03	26.21

These figures, Table 6.39, are representative of what is the priority in the State for expenditure related to libraries. The State has grown in its socio-economic status and its industrial output is well advanced. And despite these developments the per capita of the State in the last decade stands at 31st place among all the States in the country.

TABLE 6.40: Expenditure of Libraries (All types of libraries included)

(Rs. in lakhs)

Year	*Non-Plan*	*Plan*
1980-81	5.16	—
1981-82	6.66	—
1982-83	—	5.11
1983-84	6.64	—
1984-85	5.75	—
1985-86	—	2.69

There does not seem to be any reason for the reduction of the expenditure year after year. And it is interesting to note that in some years the reduction is so much that it is almost half the size of the previous year, in 1985-86! Is it that the expenses are reduced, or the user needs are shrinking or that the capacity to serve the users is going down, or what? The answers to such questions are not available to this writer.

Efforts for Enactment

1973 Bihar Public Libraries Bill—prepared by Bihar Library Association

1981 Bihar Public Libraries Bill—prepared by R.S.P. Singh

Academic Libraries

This State has 9 universities, and the Table 6.41 shows the number of colleges and affiliated institutions under each university.

TABLE 6.41: Universities and Colleges

University	*Constituent Colleges*	*Affiliated Colleges*	*Attached Institutes***	*Total*
Patna University (*f.* 1917) Patna	14	—	—	14
Bihar University (*f.* 1952) Muzaffarpur	24	44	1	69
Bhagalpur University (*f.* 1960) Bhagalpur	35	7	—	42
Ranchi University (*f.* 1960) Ranchi	42	29	1	72
Kameshwara University (*f.* 1961) Darbhanga	40	—	—	40
Magadh University (*f.* 1962) Bodhgaya	70	—	3	73
Rajendra Agricultural University* (*f.* 1970) Samastipur	7	—	—	7
L.N. Mithila University (*f.* 1972) Darbhanga	60	10	—	70
Birsa Agricultural University* (*f.* 1981) Ranchi	3	—	—	3
Total	295	90	5	390

Note: * Agricultural universities, and the agricultural colleges that are in the States.
** Affiliated institutes are academies and research bodies, that are not independent administratively, and hence are attached to the respective universities. Each university has a tradition of giving recognition and affiliation to private, and semi-private institutions to promote multi-disciplinary programmes, such as areas studies, religious studies, social studies, etc.

One case of a college is described below with some detail to understand the prevailing trends. Under the Rajendra Agricultural University, is the Veterinary College. We may have a look at its growth pattern.

TABLE 6.42: Growth of Veterinary College Library

Year	*Collection*	*Subscribed*		*Staff*	*Budget*	*Users*	*Borrowers*
		Indian	*Foreign*		*(in lakhs)**		
1983-84	17,378	87	53	2	5.1	n.d.	n.d.
1984-85	17,411	87	53	2	5.8	n.d.	n.d.
1985-86	17,636	89	51	2	6.1	n.d.	n.d.
1986-87	18,121	91	49	2	6.5	7,331	784
1987-88	18,166	91	49	2	6.3	8,461	1,174

Note: * Number of readers who have visited the library.
n.d. = No data available.

The figures given in Table 6.42 do not show any major improvements in the five year history. It does show that the budget is unable to provide for any serious improvement in any way. It does not even help improve collection development proportionate to the increasing users and user needs. The budget does not support for having one or two more staff, and so on. The limitations abound, and the development also naturally gets effected.

Special Libraries

If one were to define special purpose libraries, one would definitely include the Khuda Bakhsh Oriental Public Library, Patna, as a specialised library, but open to public. It is not in a way a general collection, nor a resource useful for all. Nevertheless, it has thrown opened its Orientalia collection, the result of one-man's life long dedication to collect rare and valuable books from all over in Persian, Arabic, Urdu, etc. Founded in 1888, in 1969 it was recognized as a Library of National Importance, by an Act of Parliament. It has a total collection of 30,000 books and over 10,000 Mss. It has in its resources original manuscripts with golden illustrations, and this includes some of the rarities that moved out of the Imperial Mughal Library, after 1857.

Library Profession

Bihar Library Association, now called, Bihar Raja Pustakalaya Sangh, was founded in 1936. It is a leading professional body and publishes, Pustakalaya, as its official organ. A concluding note from a seasoned librarian, is appropriate to be cited here: "Living in the last decade of the 20th century today, one experiences the progress, the dynamism and the re-awakening. But together with this there is a struggle that the modern library movement in the State is facing and the libraries are working hard for their survival.

The deficiency of funds has led to many libraries in the State to languish. Although there are many courses to produce well qualified librarians, many of the libraries in the State do not have trained staff to work in them. The result is that the libraries are ill-managed and ill-organised giving the minimum routine services to its readers" (Esperanza, 1996: 148).

UNION TERRITORY: CHANDIGARH

Punjab as the State stood till 1966, was split into three different States,

Haryana, Punjab, and Chandigarh. In 1966, Chandigarh emerged as a Union Territory, and has a constant growth of literacy, 61.6 per cent in 1971, 64.7 per cent in 1981, 78.7 per cent in 1991—it takes the credit of being the city of most literates. For various reasons, political, geographic, etc., this State is still the centre of activities of Haryana, Punjab, and other neighbouring States, this becomes obvious in terms of the location of a number of libraries, with their original intent and name, such as Punjab Civil Secretariat Library, Chandigarh; Haryana Civil Secretariat Library, Chandigarh, and so on.

Its area is 114 sq. kms. The population density is 5,620 persons per sq. km. The sex ratio of the State is 793 females per 1000 males. The literacy rate of males is 82.6 per cent and females is 73.6 per cent. The main language groups are as per 1981 Census: Hindi (53.8%); Punjabi (40.2%); etc. The religious groups as per the 1981 Census are: Hindus (75.2%); Sikhs (21.1%); Muslims (2.0%); Christians (0.9%); Jains (0.4%); Buddhists (0.1%); and others.

Public Libraries

Like many other States, Chandigarh, has no library legislation, and hence lacks any efforts at concerted library development. But like, many others, it has a tradition of maintaining a State library, and has the famous T.S. Central State Library. It has its own distinguishing features, including its location in a prime place, its children's section, and its Mobile Library Service.

The Central State Library (CSL) has a total staff of 82, with six branch libraries. The statistics, relating to the year, 1992-93, at a glance are given in Table 6.43.

TABLE 6.43: Central State Library Statistics Relating to 1992-93

Membership		
General Public	8,171	(cumulative membership for all 35 years 44,000)
Student/children	1,925	
Government employees	2,915	
Total	13,011	
Collection		
Book collection	1,80,000	
Annual addition of books	5,000	
Journals	175	
Newspapers	9	

Table 6.43 statistical figures are compiled on the verge of computerization of the State library. It is hoped that once the automation is complete the library will be hooked up to the NICNET and other online databases. The NICNET has already installed its terminal. And probably this State Library is the first in the public library system in the country to have this hook up. The working of this network, when initiated will perhaps indicate what it is status is in the country, the most effective or one among the least useful NICNET access points.

Other public libraries of importance, are Dwarka Dass Public Library, Gandhi Smarak Nidhi Library, etc.

Library Finances

The budgets allocation of the State library system is given in Table 6.44.

TABLE 6.44: Budget Allocation

(Rs. in lakhs)

Year	*Salaries*	*Office Expenses*	*Materials & Supplies*	*Vehicles*	*Matching RRLF Fund*	*Total*
1987-88	11.94	1.25	2.35	0.07	0.50	16.11
1988-89	14.55	1.39	3.85	0.11	1.50	21.40
1989-90	17.90	1.39	3.58	0.26	2.00	25.13
1990-91	23.50	1.48	9.01	0.23	2.75	36.97
1991-92	n.d.	n.d.	n.d.	n.d.	n.d.	37.30

Source: Ramola, 1993.

This allocation includes plan and non-plan expenditure of the respective financial years. The allocation for vehicles, includes the mobile library expenditure. The matching RRLF fund is to have a provision to met the RRLF agreement and support such projects that are under the scheme suggested by RRLF. Material and supplies includes books and reading materials, and it should not surprise any one that this allocated amount is less than the amount marked for salaries. Salaries everywhere require a major funding and take away more than 60 or 70 per cent of the funds.

Library Expenditure

TABLE 6.45: Expenditure on Public Libraries in States (1986-87)

Expenditure (in lakhs)	*Population (in lakhs)*	*Per Capita (in Rs.)*	*Literacy % 1980s*
10.0	4.51	2.21	61.56

The figures given in Table 6.45 representative of what is the priority in the State for expenditure related to libraries. The State has grown in its socio-economic status and its industrial output is well advanced. And despite these developments the per capita of the State in the last decade stands at 1th place among all the States in the country.

Academic Libraries

Punjab University Library (*f.* 1947) is the only university library in this State. It has 10 degree colleges, each having professionally trained librarians in these, and some have even six senior librarians in each. Since 1970s some of the private schools have good libraries, but of others the picture is no good. As against this, the Government schools, as many as 26, have libraries with full time trained librarians.

Special Libraries

These libraries are as advanced and as traditional as is the case of special libraries in other States. There are some very well advanced special libraries, and the list includes, Post-graduate Institute of Medical Education and Research Library (*f.* 1962), Central Scientific Instrument Organization Library (*f.* 1959), Institute of Engineers Library (*f.* 1964), etc.

Library Profession

Much of the professional activity started before the emergence of Chandigarh as an independent State, under the banner of the Punjab State. Hence, the professional activity, that went on before 1966, is all described and discussed under Punjab Library Association.

Library Association

There are a number of professional bodies, such as, Punjab Library Association, Punjab University Library Staff Association (*f.* 1977), Chandigarh Librarian's Association, North Indian Librarian's Association (*f.* 1974), etc. The most prominent of these, Punjab Library Association, will be discussed under the State of Punjab.

The North Indian Librarian's Association was established as a body, under the presidentship of Nasib Chand and the secretaryship of Mrs. S.A. Bhagi.

Library Education

The Library Science Department (*f.* 1960) with one year post-graduate diploma in library science. At present it has bachelor's, master's and doctoral programme. The Government Polytechnic for Women, offers a two year's diploma in library science, on par with other similar institute, in the country, such as in Bangalore.

Library Networks

As part of the national network the State is under the process of getting hooked up to the INFLIBNET, and the other national networks, such as, ernet, is already hooked up and working well.

UNION TERRITORY: DADRA AND NAGAR HAVELI

Its area is 491 sq. kms. the population density is 282 persons per sq. km. The sex ratio of the State is 953 females per 1000 males. The literacy rate of males is 52.0 per cent and females is 26.0 per cent. The main language groups are as per 1981 Census: Gujarati, Marathi and Hindi. The religious groups according to 1981 Census reports are: Hindus (95.5%); Christians (1.9%); Muslims (1.8%); etc.

Public Libraries

Library Expenditure

TABLE 6.46: Expenditure on Public Libraries in the State (1986-87)

Expenditure (in lakhs)	*Population (in lakhs)*	*Per Capita (in Rs.)*	*Literacy % 1980s*
0.5	1.0	0.48	16.78

The figures in Table 6.46 are representative of what is the priority in the State for expenditure related to libraries. The State has grown in its socio-economic status and its industrial output is well advanced. And despite these developments the per capita of the State in the last decade stands at 19th place among all the States in the country.

STATE: DELHI

This is the land of seven cities, and capital of major governments, including the Mughals and British, representing these two in todays, Old and New Delhi, respectively. The City-State, Delhi, has a literacy growth pattern of 37 per cent in 1951; 52.7 per cent in 1961; 56.6 per cent in 1971; 61.06 per cent in 1981 and 76.09 per cent in 1991.

Its area is 1,483 sq. kms. The population density is 6,319 persons per sq. km. The sex ratio of the State is 830 females per 1000 males. The literacy rate of males is 82.6 per cent and females is 68.0 per cent. The main language groups are as per 1981 Census: Hindi (75.7%); Punjabi (13.0%); Urdu (5.8%); Bengali (1.0%) Tamil (0.8%); Sindhi (0.6%); Malayalam (0.5%). The religious groups according to the 1981 Census are: Hindus (83.6%); Muslims (7.7%); Sikhs (6.3%); Jains (1.2%); Christians (0.9%); Buddhists (0.1%); and so on.

Public Libraries

The public library system in the State, is one way exemplary with its Delhi Public Library programme. This programme was initiated as a model public library, through an agreement, signed between the Government of India and UNESCO, in 1950. Based on the success of the library system, to act as a role model, the Delhi Public Library, was designated in 1981, by the Government of India, as fourth recipient depository library under the Delivery of Books Act. Since this public library has a prominent place in the library history of India, it is worth to describe and discuss it at some length.

Delhi Public Library

With the assistance of UNESCO, the Central Government, established Delhi Public Library in 1951. It is the first public library founded on the lines of modern concept of librarianship—as a pilot library project. The Delhi Public Library aims at 'establishing his/her reading skill so that literacy does not remain his/her goal by only a means to reach better ends'. In addition it aims at providing 'information on the problems of public library service for other parts of India and for Asia generally. Its collection in terms of languages it represents, is depicted in Table 6.47, to illustrate the kind of audience it serves.

This means the majority of the users are from the local population, and those who represent the northern States, called, Hindi belt. Whereas Delhi has in the descending order of importance, speakers of Hindi, Punjabi, Urdu, Bengali, Tamil, Sindhi, etc. The question one would then ask, where does English language readership emerge from, which is almost one-third of the readership? The answer lies in the multilingual nature of the country and so also the nature of the State: Delhi—where any literate could be well-versed in atleast two or three languages!

TABLE 6.47: Language-wise Analysis of the Collection

Language	*Percentage*
Hindi	57.9
English	29.7
Urdu	9.0
Punjabi	3.0
Sindhi	0.2
Bengali	0.2

A glance at its membership and use pattern will give an idea of the functioning, of the Delhi Public Library [the statistics are for 1991/92 (Bhatt, 1995: 185)].

TABLE 6.48: Membership and Use Pattern of Delhi Public Library (1991-92)

	Regd. Users			*Book Issues*		
	Adult	*Child*	*Total*	*Adult*	*Child*	*Total*
Central Library Books	16,301 (83%)	2,755 (17%)	19,056	3,33,362 (85%)	48,768 (15%)	3,82,130
Audio/Visuals	—	40,994	40,994	—	40,994	40,994
Zonal Library (South)	4,250 (51%)	2,187 (49%)	6,437	67,383 (96%)	64,962 (4%)	1,32,345
Four Branch Library	8,819 (58%)	5,110 (42%)	13,929	2,05,176 (61%)	58,966 (29%)	2,64,142
Extension Service:						
Mobile Vans Service	7,834	—	7,834	87,712	—	87,712
Deposit Stations	4,566	—	4,566	1,09,354	—	1,09,354
Braille Books	511	—	511	10,406	—	10,406
Jail Inmates	—	—	—	5,668	—	5,668
Hospital Inpatients	—	—	—	5,070	—	5,070

The figures given in Table 6.48 are self-explanatory, but these are also of a good measure to see use level and active users of one service, that is borrowing. One fact that emerges from this is the ratio of membership of adult to child is not uniform in all the divisions. A higher proportion of adult borrowers are in the branch and zonal libraries, indicating that the child in these areas is either not that much interested, or that child here has less desire to borrow as compared to the other division. While figures for some categories are not available, it is pertinent to note that hospital and jail libraries are becoming a fertile zone for the spread of the word, if the library profession cares for the same.

It is appropriate to quote a comment of a senior librarian, about what Delhi Public Library is and will be in future, "It is easy to be wise after the event, but it was a mistake to establish a pilot public library without ensuring that the local library authority would accept full responsibility for its development". Further, "It was an even greater mistake to establish it in makeshift premises which has been barracks during the period of British rule. The neglect of the library as compared with the treatment of the National Library in Calcutta, which is housed in the former Viceroy's residence, is striking. And yet it seemed to me that the future of India would be determined by the poor in the vicinity of the Delhi Public Library rather than the scholars using the National Library" (pp. 77-78).

Public Library Expenditure in the State

TABLE 6.49: Expenditure on Public Libraries in States (1986-87)

Expenditure (in lakhs)	*Population (in lakhs)*	*Per Capita (in Rs.)*	*Literacy % 1980s*
50.0	62.2	0.80	61.06

The figures given in Table 6.49 are representative of what is the priority in the State for expenditure related to libraries. The State has grown in its socio-economic status and its industrial output is well advanced. And despite these developments the per capita of the State in the last decade stands at 15th place among all the States in the country.

Efforts for Enactment

1955 Delhi Public Libraries Bill—prepared by Prof. P.N. Kaula. This bill received no takers, and hence the Act did not get passed in the Assembly.

1964 Library Bill—prepared by Kaula and Ranganathan. This draft library bill aimed at suggesting a library development plan for Delhi State, was accepted by the Government, but not implemented.

Academic Libraries

The University of Delhi (*f.* 1922), originally aimed at providing a residential system of higher education, has today emerged in a different way. In 1964, Carl White reported 35 colleges, and by 1991 it has 72 colleges, of which 13 are located on the campus, one situated in Bhutan and the rest are scattered in the City-State. A survey of these libraries, limited to 59 sample libraries, by Anand (1988), shows the size of the collection, as given in Table 6.50.

TABLE 6.50: Collection in College Libraries

Collection (in thousands)	*Libraries*
1—10	8
11—20	10
21—30	9
31—40	10
41—50	6
51—60	5
61—70	8
71—80	2
Above 100	1

According to the same survey, the lowest collection is 2,158 books in Guru Gobind Singh College Library (*f.* 1984), and the highest 1,51,508 is in School of Correspondence and Continuing Education Library (*f.* 1962), with an average of 39,688 books in these libraries. A similar survey of periodical collection, as shown in the Table 6.51, indicates the trends in collection development.

TABLE 6.51: Periodicals Subscribed

Periodicals	*Colleges*
Less than 100	36
Less than 200	14
Less than 300	2
More than 300	1
Data not available	7

The highest number of periodicals subscribed is 350, in Maulana Azad Medical College Library (*f.* 1958), and the least is 5 in Dayal Singh Evening College Library (*f.* 1959). These indicates that there is no compatibility in collection, that is, size of book collection and size of periodical collection, are not in any way indicative of proportionate collection development policy. This is substantiated also from, the same survey, wherein Maulana Azad Medical College library has only 21,000 books. Dayal Singh Evening College Library has 25,000 books; so also School of Correspondence and Continuing Education has only 126 periodicals, and data of periodicals subscribed, for Guru Dayal Singh College is not available. This reveals the size of collection in the libraries of Delhi.

A glance at the financial situation of the college libraries is also pertinent, to reveal the level of funding these receive, if they are to satisfy the maximum number of users and if they are to be efficient in their performance! In yet another survey by Motilal and Jyothimayi (1988), the financial position of 33 college libraries in Delhi were identified. The survey data was classified into the type of colleges responding, as 26 general colleges, 1 arts, 2 commerce, and 4 professional. This spilt up is beneficial for the purpose of viewing if there is any difference between these, and if so, how much is the difference.

TABLE 6.52: Average Book Budget of the Library

(In thousand rupees)

Type	*1986-87*	*1987-88*	*1988-89*
General			
Day	108	118	141
Evening	62	56	64
Arts	60	60	60
Commerce	78	77	90
Professional	220	220	280

This pattern is obvious sample probably for the entire country. In one way, it is a state-of-art of funding in the higher education too. If the arts college, are receiving less than the commerce and the latter less than the general (which incidentally includes the sciences in their curriculum—calling for large budgets) and all these less than the professional colleges, showing that the priority is in the decreasing order of professional, general, commerce and arts. It is serious lapse on the part of the management that they are ignoring the equally important two: arts versus professional; if professional (which includes management engineering, and medicine) studies are important the study of humanities (or arts) is equally important in the building of the personality of an individual! India of Gandhi is heading towards the race of materialism, without a spiritual support—on this Gandhi would be spinning in his grave!

Yet another estimation, in the Table 6.53, is available to present the level of priorities in these colleges.

TABLE 6.53: Range of Book Budget

(In thousand rupees)

Annual Budget	*1986-87*	*1987-88*	*1988-89*
Upto 60	8	6	4
Upto 100	8	8	10
Upto 120	8	7	6
Above 120	6	7	8
Information not available	3	5	5

Indicating that the average budget is just around one hundred thousand rupees for most of the colleges. Considering the prices of Indian published sources. Obvious hardly a few books—mostly multiple copies—are acquired, ignoring all costly Indian reference material, as well as the more essential foreign sources, also such libraries will be missing all the multiple media facilities that go to make education a real achievement.

Another issue is how do these colleges estimate their finances, and by which method do they arrive at an understanding of the financial needs? The answer is seen in the Table 6.54.

TABLE 6.54: Financial Estimation Method

Method	*College Libraries*
(a) By per capita	
Teachers	4
Students	24
Staff members	—
(b) On a proportion	1
(c) By detail analysis	—
(d) Considering courses	2
(e) On the basis of (a)	2
(f) On the basis of (d) & (e)	2
(g) As per the requirement	2

Obviously, the most important method is relying on the number of student enrollment—to put up with the requirement of the accredition bodies, rather than with the live realities. The deception however, lies in the fact that by adding the number of multiple copies for the proportionate increase of the students each year, the management justifies that its library building activity is in accordance with the increase in the number of the students—yes, in terms of quantity, but in terms of quality it cannot justify that the type of books purchased is also proportionate to the increasing user needs! Infact, only 8 out of 33 colleges, respondents have taken care of the needs, but this minority does not matter much in terms of the output that emerges from the majority of the colleges.

Even the rate per student, at which UGC's recurring grant is calculated, is itself a specimen of the state-of-the art; a meagre amount of rupees ten per student. An Indian student in 1980s (in the study period), would spend an average rupees ten per day, atleast, on essentials in the process of education—giving a contrast of the planners and the users' performance. The irony is that this rupees ten, is the norm, which is not binding on any one to seriously follow!

School Libraries

A survey by Sunil Kumar of the state of affairs in school libraries in Delhi is an interesting piece of information. The study covered 100 Government Schools in Delhi. The findings of the study are as follows:

- More than half of these had more than 10,000 documents, indicating that the collection was not very poor in majority of the libraries;
- 57 per cent used Dewey Decimal Classification and 28 per cent used Colon classification scheme, indicating that there was a conscious need for a systematic classification scheme in schools;
- more than half had a catalogue; implying that there is yet another half of the schools who were yet to have professionals who could streamline the access to resources;
- two-third of the schools have open access libraries, that is to say there is one-third who still believes that closed access to the future citizens is the best!
- user education is not very common, implying that the users are still dependent on the staff for finding information;
- about ten per cent of the libraries have Browne system of charging, and majority of the libraries have the ledger system to record the circulation of books;
- all the schools have one librarian, one-man show is the order of the day;
- single room is all that the schools have for a library;
- seating capacity varies between 20 to 50;
- annual budget varies from Rs. 3,000 to 10,000, depending upon the number of enrolled students;

— collection development is limited to the titles approved by the Directorate of Education, Delhi Administration, indicating that the selection and choice is not the prerogative of the librarian, nor of the specific school needs!

Such is the state-of-the-art of school libraries, which the survey represents, and the story of the country is not, any way better, if not, very much different.

Special Libraries

Delhi has a representative sample of all types of special libraries, including governmental, non-governmental, and those relating to voluntary and private agencies. The listing of these is impossible and analysis of these is not attempted here. If one begins to list, the list has to encompass all those in the disciplines of science, social science and humanities, all those attached to academic institutions and those which are attached to different governmental and non-governmental agencies, etc.

Library Profession

Library Association

The Delhi Library Association (*f.* 1953) is the leading professional body of the City-State. It publishes Library Herald, its official organ. The members of the body are very active. The Indian Library Association (*f.* 1933), at Calcutta, was shifted twice to Delhi in 1946 and 1964, and is now permanently situated in Delhi. It has its official organs, ILA Bulletin and ILA Newsletter. Its activities includes, among others, uplifting the status of the profession and professionals.

Library Education

Delhi has a lead in having maximum education and training institutions for the professional entry and advancement. The leading two agencies are the Department of Library Science, Delhi University, and the training programme offered by INSDOC, IGNOU, located in Delhi, is making an attempt at national level to spread informal education in the field of library science, and has been doing well both at Bachelor's and Master's level.

A significant chapter in Indian academic library, started by Dickinson, in Punjab, of providing advise and consultancy, was continued at Delhi University, by Carl White. While Dr. Ranganathan and Prof. S. Das Gupta, had led the basic foundation of Delhi University, much of the improvements were suggested by Carl White—American Consultant—in his Report (1965). Written in 184 pages, it came to be highly cited and became famous as White Report. It opened yet a new era of university librarianship in India, as it was a first attempt to exhaustively review the problems and suggest the future course of action. This report "has a unique place in the history of university librarianship in India", and it "did attract the attention of librarians in India and abroad" (Konnur, 1990: 22).

Library Networks

Networking: Delnet (Delhi Library Network) is one among the few metros having a city-based local network. Its main function today is limited to sending and receiving e-mail for inter-library requests.

UNION TERRITORY: GOA (Includes Daman and Diu)

It is a State which has a cultural blend of the Orient and the Occident, beaches and churches, fish, feni and football. It gained independence in 1961 from the Portuguese, and joined the Indian Union thence.

Its area is 3,702 sq. kms. The population density is 316 persons per sq. km. The sex ratio of the State is 969 females per 1000 males. The literacy rate of males is 85.4 per cent and females is 68.2 per cent. The main language groups as per 1981 Census are: Konkani (59.5%); Marathi (26.3%); Kannada (3.3%); Urdu (2.7%); Hindi (2.0%). The religious groups according to 1981 Census are: Hindus (65.8%); Christians (29.2%); Muslims (2.7%); and other communities. The literacy rate of this State have grown in the following pattern: 30.07 per cent in 1961; 44.7 per cent in 1971; 55.86 per cent in 1981; and 76.96 per cent in 1991.

Public Libraries

The State Government in 1978 constituted a State Level Expert Committee to suggest ways and means to improve library facilities existing in this territory, with Prof. K.S. Deshpande as its Chairman. The report of the Committee was submitted in 1980. Due to the efforts of successor body, called State Library Advisor Board, under the Chairmanship of Lt. Governor, K.T. Satarwala, the Government published the report in 1984. The report contains 50 recommendations, and provides details of the public library system. It suggests a five tier structure as follows: State Central Library, at the apex, District Libraries, Taluk Libraries, Village Libraries, Mobile Libraries.

It also recommends complete liberalization within a decade through library legislation from the day of the recommendations. Exactly after ten years of the publication of the recommendations, the State Government passed the Library Act. In principle it indicates that the Government is willing to move forward with the idea of library development in the State. The truth is not however so realistic, and the state of the affairs is yet to improve.

There are five Taluka Libraries under the direct control of the State Central Library. In addition to this, there is yet another group of 9 Government libraries, which are controlled by the Directorate of Art and Culture. There are 99 Government public libraries and 21 aided libraries in the State. Additionally, there are 18 privately managed libraries, but to receive aid from the Government. This is not the end of the list of libraries, there are also Municipalities, which have libraries and reading rooms, managed as Municipal libraries.

Library Finances: Income

The Government public libraries are fully financed by the Government. The Table 6.55 presents the allocation for the year 1992-93.

TABLE 6.55: Allocations for Public Libraries

	Plan	*Non-plan*	*Total*
Government Libraries	10,50,000	25,45,000	35,95,000
Taluka Libraries-I	20,000		
Taluka Libraries-II	16,000		
Taluka Libraries-III	10,000		
Village Libraries	3,000		
Other income:			
Membership fees Donations Programmes	n.d		

Grants for Private Libraries

The State gives grants to libraries managed by private libraries. The annual aid these receive from the State is given in Table 6.56.

TABLE 6.56: State Grants to Private Libraries

(In rupees)

Category	*Funds*
I	10,000
II	8,000
III	5,000
Village libraries	1,000

Library Expenditure

The figures, Table 6.57, are representative of what is the priority in the State for expenditure related to libraries. The State has grown in its socio-economic status and its industrial output is well advanced. And despite these developments the per capita of the State in the last decade stands at 6th place among all the States in the country.

TABLE 6.57: Expenditure on Public Libraries in States (1986-87)

State	*Expenditure (in lakhs)*	*Population (in lakhs)*	*Per Capita (in Rs.)*	*Literacy % 1980s*
Goa	20.0	10.07	1.98	57.25
Diu	0.2	0.3	0.82	—
Daman	0.2	0.4	0.51	—

Collection Development

The collection of these public libraries is varied by languages, because of the fact that Goa has a variety of people living in its boundaries. The State Central Libraries has preserved many rare and valuable resources.

State Central Library	1,38,000 volumes
Taluka libraries collection ranges between	3,000 to 10,000 volumes
Village libraries do not have more than	5,000 volumes.

Efforts for Enactment

1983 Goa Public Libraries Bill—prepared by State Library Advisory Board.

1990 Goa Public Libraries Bill—prepared by K.M. Ujlambkar. The passing of the Goa State Public Libraries Act, 1994, by the State Legislature, heralds a new era in the library development.

Academic Libraries

While Goa University is of recent date, its area studies programmes are well advanced and are working well. The Latin American Studies Centre is a prominent department with a well developed Departmental Library.

Special Libraries

Institutes and specialized research centres are developing at a fast pace, and one of these is the Institute of Oceanography, which has a well developed resource centre.

Library Profession

Library Association

In 1983 emerged the Gomantak Granthalaya Sangh, a professional body under the able guidance of B.D. Satoskar. The body has been active in developing a sense of professionalism, and it offers, with this spirit, a certificate course of two months duration.

STATE: GUJARAT

This land of the Gujarat (a sub tribe of Huns), came into existence in 1960, when Bombay State was linguistically divided, Marathi speakers getting Maharashtra, and Gujarati speakers getting Gujarat.

Its area is 1,96,024 sq. kms. The population density is 210 persons per sq. km. The sex ratio of the State is 936 females per 1000 males. The literacy rate of males is 72.5 per cent and females is 48.5 per cent. The main language groups are as per 1981 Census: Gujarati (90.3%); Sindhi (2.1%); Hindi (2.1%); Urdu (1.7%); Marathi (1.1%). The religious groups as per the 1981 Census are: Hindus (89.5%); Muslims (8.5%); Jains (1.3%); Christians (0.4%); and others. Its literacy growth has been 30.0 per cent in 1961; 35.8 per cent in 1971; 43.75 per cent in 1981; and 60.91 per cent in 1991.

Public Libraries

Public libraries in the State had their origin with the movement initiated by the Maharaja, and the expert advise of Borden. The post-independent India, left Gujarat, till this date, without library legislation.

The figures, Table 6.58, of the number of public libraries in the

State is as follows, and includes directly governed and indirectly governed libraries.

TABLE 6.58. Number of Public Libraries Governed Directly and Indirectly

Library	*Government Libraries*	*Grant-in-aid Libraries*
State Central Library	1	1
District Libraries	17	—
City Central Libraries	21	—
Women's Libraries	2	67
Integrated Libraries	2	—
City Branch Libraries	28	—
Town Category-I	125	—
Town Category-II	205	—
Taluk Libraries	36	—
Village Libraries	—	6,351
Children's Libraries	—	49
Special Libraries	—	6
Other Libraries	4	335
Total	62	7,128

TABLE 6.59: Categorization by the Managing Body

Government	*Municipality*	*Education Society*	*Independent Trust*
0.5	1.1	0.3	98%

The break up of these figures by geographic regions showns the following pattern (Table 6.60).

TABLE 6.60: Geographic Regions

Division	*District*	*Total Libraries*
(1)	(2)	(3)
Ahmedabad	Ahmedabad	170
	Kheda	962
	S. Kantha	194
	Total	1,326
Vadodra	Vadodra	1,246
	Bharuch	297
	Panchmahal	1,005
	Total	2,548
Surat	Surat	476
	Valsad	326
	The Dangs	1
	Total	803

(*Contd.*)

TABLE 6.60 (*Contd.*)

(1)	(2)	(3)
Rajkot	Surendranagar	66
	Rajkot	71
	Jamnagar	99
	Total	236
Bhavnagar	Bhavnagar	550
	Junagarh	27
	Amreli	113
	Total	690
Mahesena	Mahesana	1,032
	Gandhinagar	53
	Banaskantha	538
	Total	1,623
Kutchh		24
	Total	24
Total		7,250

Source: Shukla & Soni; see also Upadhyaya & Mehta.

TABLE 6.61: Public Library per Person in the State

District	*Area sq.km.*	*Population (In lakhs)*	*Literacy*	*No. of Libraries*	*Area/lib. per Library*	*Library Persons per (in '000s)*
Ahmedabad	8.7	47.8	30.21	170	51.2	17,771
Amreli	6.7	12.5	6.3	113	59.3	5,601
Banaskantha	12.7	21.5	6.9	538	23.6	1,287
Bharuch	9.0	15.4	8.0	297	30.4	2,722
Bhavnagar	11.1	22.8	11.0	550	20.2	2,016
Gandhinagar	0.6	3.9	2.9	53	12.2	5,544
Jamnagar	14.1	15.4	7.7	99	142.6	7,827
Junagarh	10.6	23.9	12.4	27	392.8	46,017
Kutchh	45.6	12.4	5.4	24	1,902.1	22.733
Kheda	7.1	34.3	19.4	962	7.4	2,027
Mahesana	9.0	29.2	16.1	1,032	8.7	1,566
Panchmahal	8.8	29.4	10.6	1,005	8.8	1,061
Rajkot	11.2	25.0	14.5	71	157.0	20,454
Sabarkantha	7.3	17.5	8.8	194	38.0	4,551
Surat	7.6	33.9	16.8	476	16.0	3,545
Surendranagar	10.4	12.0	5.4	66	158.9	8,320
The Dangs	1.7	1.4	0.5	1	1,764.0	53,651
Vadodra	7.7	30.7	16.8	1,246	6.2	1,359
Valsad	5.2	21.7	12.0	326	16.0	3,689
Total	196.0	212.6	7,250		2,933	

Source: Shukla & Soni.

The Table 6.61 shows how much less important is a library per person (there is only one library on an average at every 27.0 sq. km.) and one library for every 2,933 literates in a State. This is only the average, otherwise there are thousands of people in some areas with bare reading room or 'library' as it is come to be known as!

By ranking the areas which have dense population one can see the library rate, for example, Kutchh has the largest area and but it receives very less support for library development, and there are lesser number of people benefiting the library facilities in this district. As seen in the earlier table, this district has the lowest number of libraries, that is, 24.

Library Expenditure

A glance of the development in the public library system in the State is pertinent to get a view of the holistic picture. The Table 6.62 gives the expenditure versus the per capita status.

TABLE 6.62: Expenditure on Public Libraries in States (1986-87)

Expenditure (in lakhs)	*Population (in lakhs)*	*Per Capita (in Rs.)*	*Literacy % 1980s*
117.0	340.8	0.35	43.75

These figures are representative of what is the priority in the State for expenditure related to libraries. The State has grown in its socio-economic status and its industrial output is well advanced. And despite these developments the per capita of the State in the last decade stands at 22nd place among all the States in the country. A break up of the expenditure in a few types of libraries can be illustrated to explain how the funding works.

The Table 6.63 indicates an important comparison of the input the library system provides and the use that the output receives. For instance, it is interesting to note that the average daily attendance at the 110 branches of the Town Library-I, is 230 a day. If a town library is consulted by 230 population, then the rate of literacy must be very high, and the rate of users who are interested in making use of the library will be still very high. What is not attempted here is a feasibility study to assess the role these users play in the society, if they are all the regular visitors of the public library system.

TABLE 6.63: Statistics at a Glance

Type of Library	*Number*	*Total Volumes*	*Annual (in lakhs)*		*Average Daily*	
			Grant	*Expenditure (in Rs.)*	*Book Issues*	*Visitors*
Central Library	1	1,74,000	0.90	1,30	0.60	600
City Library	19	3,73,000	0.86	2.45	4.90	7,600
City Branch Library	18	1,66,000	0.29	1.44	2.64	4,200
Town Library-I	110	6,56,000	1.39	4.40	7.64	23,000
Town Library-II	120	4,65,000	0.90	2.72	2.91	17,000
Mahila Library	45	93,000	0.20	0.63	1.18	1,600
Bal Library (Children's)	35	76,000	0.04	0.17	0.55	2,400
Village Library	4,000	n.d.	2.49	n.d.	n.d.	n.d.
Other Library	5	3,000	n.d.	0.01	0.02	50
Total	4,353	20,06,000	7.07	13.12	20.45	0.56

Source: Rawal.

The State has set rules for giving grants to the libraries. For instance, the Table 6.64 shows what is the criteria for funding has been from time to time, in the State.

TABLE 6.64: Public Library Grants in Gujarat

(In rupees)

Library	*1964*	*1974*	*1989*
City Library Population 50,000+	8,000	16,000	40,000
City Branch Library 50,000+	2,000	4,000	15,000
Town Category I 25,000 to 50,000	2,000	4,000	12,000
Town Categories II 7,000 to 25,000	15,000	3,000	8,000
Other Libraries	n.d.	n.d.	42,000
Total	27,000	27,000	1,17,000

Source: Shukla & Soni.

Growth of Public Library System at a Glance

The development of public libraries in the State is shown in the Table 6.65 and has been somewhat progressive.

TABLE 6.65: Overall Public Library Development

(All figures in lakhs)

Year	*Libraries*	*Books*	*Issues*	*Users*	*Total Expenditure*
1960	3,476	16.85	14.35	0.44	6.75
1970	4,465	19.05	20.83	0.54	12.79
1980	6,133	26.92	28.57	0.65	53.08
1986	6,845	55.91	49.94	11.57	117.00
1990	7,250	62.48	55.42	18.55	210.07

The Table 6.65 suggests that the growth pattern of expenditure for the library as a whole has been generous, but collection growth could not be commensurate with the growth in number of users of the public library. For instance, if the users have increased ten times between 1980 and 1986, and yet another ten times between 1986 and 1990, the number of books added to the collection has not been proportionate with this increase. Even the so called 'generous' expenditure of the public library system, is not progressing with the ratio of the users. The expenditures have only doubled in each five years, and not been multiples. So also is the slow growth of the libraries, where the total number of these has doubled only after thirty years, 1960 to 1990.

TABLE 6.66: Government Expenditure on Different Libraries

(Rupees in lakhs)

Type of Library	*Expenditure in Total*	*On Reading Material*	*On Salaries etc.*
Government Library	75.2	20.0	55.1
	(33.8)	(26.6)	(72.3)
City Library	14.2	10.0	8.9
	(6.4)	(52.8)	(47.1)
City Branch Library	8.2	4.0	6.9
	(3.6)	(36.7)	(63.2)
Town (I)	13.6	9.1	8.9
	(6.1)	(57.4)	(49.5)
Town (II)	22.38	7.1	22.7
	(10.0)	(23.8)	(76.1)
Women Library	2.6	1.6	1.8
	(1.0)	(46.6)	(53.3)
Children Library	0.9	0.6	0.6
	(0.4)	(49.0)	(50.9)
Village Library	85.1	38.0	47.0
	(38.2)	(44.7)	(55.2)

Source: Majumdar and Shukla.
Note: Figures in parentheses are shown percentage.

The Table 6.66 depicts the pattern of expenditure on public libraries in the State: in terms of the expenditure on different types of libraries, and in terms of the expenditures incurred under different recurring expenses. On the whole 35 per cent of the expenditure is incurred on reading materials, whereas, the major part of the budget is spent on the salaries, rent of the library buildings, and miscellaneous expenses.

Efforts for Enactment

1965 Gujarat Public Libraries Bill—prepared by Library Development Committee, Gujarat Government. The Committee appointed a sub-committee, to draft a library bill for the State. According to Gopinath (1972), "Probably one of the predisposing causes for slowness in library legislation in Gujarat is the same as in Maharashtra—the Fyzee Committee" (p. 25).

1969 Gujarat Public Libraries Bill—tabled in the Assembly by Manohar Sinhji P. Jadeja, MLA.

1973 Gujarat Public Libraries Bill—prepared by Maneklal Gandhi.

1978 Gujarat Public Libraries Bill—prepared by Manohar Sinhji Jadeja.

1981 Gujarat Public Library Bill—by Lakkani.

1990 Gujarat Library Bill—H.J. Upadhyaya.

Academic Libraries

This is a land of the learned, and there is no dearth of learned bodies and academies. The Gujrath Vidyapeeth has a distinction of being the first automated academic library in the country. This is with due acceptance of its limited nature of computerization. But the efforts that have gone in this regard, in a situation where no catalogue exists in most academic libraries, a computerized catalogue was a gift from the blue!

Special Libraries

It is land of industries, with Surat being the foremost, followed by Ahmedabad, and so on. Its special libraries in the areas of textiles are prominent.

Library Profession

The leadership in the State has been better in this State as a whole, guiding and inspiring people in ways that are professional and service oriented. Borden laid the foundation for this process, which was taken up successively and he was followed by many stalwarts. It was in this undivided State that Fyzee was inspired and motivated as a jurist, to promote legislation in the then Bombay Province.

Library education in this State is being offered at seven universities at degree level. Whereas twelve agencies, which includes governmental and non-governmental institutions, offer certificate course of six months duration. Of all the universities in the State, M.S. University at Baroda, offers the programme in English medium, and others do so in Gujarati.

Library Networks

It was in the present State of Gujarat, that the Maharaja of Baroda, initiated a network of public library system in the State, and set a model in the beginning of this century.

In the context of networking, it is in Gujarat, that the INFLIBNET programme is based and it is here that it has its resource base and all its activities. INFLIBNET is a proposed network of academic and research libraries, and which aims at providing a platform for all such libraries in India to the world at large!

ADINET (Ahmedabad Library Network) is one fast growing example of local library network, though not in a major metropolitan context, as is Bombay. Bombay has its own BONET, While ADINET intends to serve 90 plus libraries in the city of Ahmedabad, BONET has much larger audience.

STATE: HARYANA

This is the State which has in it the land of *Mahabharat* and Panipat, tractors and Maruti cars—and further advances. This State emerged in 1966, as a result of separation of Punjabi speakers from Hindi speaking people, who got a separate statehood called Haryana. The Hindi word *hari*, for green and *ayana* for home, denoting its fertile and surplus food production status in the country. This is also the land of *Mahabharat* and Panipat, as well as of tractors and Maruti cars.

Its literacy growth rate is 19.9 per cent in 1961; 26.9 per cent in 1971; 35.84 per cent in 1981; and 55.33 per cent in 1991. How does the State grow agriculturally as a very productive State, if its literacy is just 55 per cent? The answer may be that literacy, as the term also connotes, practical know how which the farmers have, and they do not rely much on the bookish knowledge. Their sources of information gathering are probably, informal, and also the strongest, and this shows that the progress is still possible!

Its area is 44,212 sq. kms. The population density is 369 persons per sq. km. The sex ratio of the State is 874 females per 1000 males. The literacy rate of males is 67.8 per cent; and females is 40.9 per cent. The main language groups are as per 1981 Census: Hindi (88.4%); Punjabi (9.1%); Urdu (1.7%). The religious groups as per the 1981 Census are: Hindus (89.3%); Sikhs (6.2%); Muslims (4%); Jains (0.2%); and others.

Public Libraries

The State has no organized library system for the public libraries. The public library administrator in the State is, as against most States, a part-time office in the Directorate of Public Instruction. The growth of the public libraries at a glance, is shown in the Table 6.67. This compares all the 12 district libraries in the State.

TABLE 6.67: Growth of District Libraries

District	*1*	*2*	*3*	*4*	*5*	*6*
Ambala	1957	3,678	45,008	200	0.60	44.21
Mohindergarh	1962	1,459	31,578	100	0.40	38.04
Hissar	1967	1,238	27,795	60	0.25	29.73
Jind	1970	1,932	22,510	111	0.80	25.99
Bhiwani	1971	n.d.	n.d.	n.d.	n.d.	32.64
Gurgaon	1971	1,761	20,785	200	0.60	34.66
Rohtak	1972	1,971	15,359	180	0.35	42.03
Sonepat	1980	507	7,364	40	0.15	40.64
Karnal	1984	96	2,798	60	0.02	36.42
Sirsa	1984	108	2,233	50	0.05	29.97
Faridabad	1986	n.d.	n.d.	n.d.	n.d.	39.11
Kurukshetra	1986	214	2,717	95	0.06	32.70

Source: Ratta.
Note: 1—year of establishment; 2—membership; 3—total book collection; 4—average issue/return of books; 5—membership as percentage to literate population; 6—literacy percentage.

From the Table 6.67, it is evident that the growth of district libraries has been gradual and so also the collection development in these libraries. What is glaring in these is that the literacy percentage has no much of relationship with the district public library growth. Whether there is a district library or not, the literacy rate is not much different. Compare the first few district with the last few district libraries in the Table 6.67. There is hardly any difference in general.

Library Finance

Most of the library developments have taken place in the Seventh Plan period: including, the establishing of three more district libraries (already existing were five); opening of five sub-divisional libraries, etc. During the years 1988-89, 6 more sub-divisional libraries were started. These are run by different agencies and departments. For instance, the Directorate of Higher Education runs all the sub-divisional and district libraries. There are libraries run by local government, Public Relations Department, etc.

TABLE 6.68: Grants to Sub-Divisional Libraries

Year	*Grant (in Rs. lakhs)*
1985-86	1.91
1986-87	2.07
1987-88	1.81
1988-89	3.02

While this is the pattern of grant a few libraries in the State, the trend is not very happy. One has no reason to understand the fluctuations in the budget that is sanctioned for libraries, in the Table 6.68!

Library Expenditure

TABLE 6.69: Expenditure on Public Libraries in States (1986-87)

Expenditure (in lakhs)	*Population (in lakhs)*	*Per Capita (in Rs.)*	*Literacy % 1980s*
35.0	129.2	0.27	35.84

These figures, Table 6.69, are representative of what is the priority in the State for expenditure related to libraries. The State has grown in its socio-economic status and its industrial output is well advanced. And despite these developments the State is 19th in literacy rate, and in terms of per capita of the State in the last decade it stands at 25th place among all the States in the country.

Efforts for Enactment

1972 Haryana Public Libraries Bill—prepared by M.L. Bhagi

1982 Haryana Public Libraries Bill—prepared by Dr. Janak Raj

1988 Haryana Public Libraries Bill—prepared by N.K. Sharma.

It is hoped that the recently, passed, Haryana Public Libraries Act, 1989, will improve the working condition of the library system of the State.

Academic Libraries

Of all the experiments to make the library more accessible, Haryana Agricultural University, has a different experience. The library running a Book Shop for the benefit of students. The book shop provides the advantage of the required discount and ease in supply for the library as well. This in-house facility saves the botheration of ordering books/ serial through other book dealers and agencies. And since the book shop gets trade discount, the savings in this regard boosts the acquisition budget also.

The book shop is managed by the library staff, under the guidance of Library Advisory Committee. A glance at the sales and savings is given in the Table 6.70.

TABLE 6.70: Performance of the Book Shop

(Rupees in thousand)

Year	*Sales*	*Savings*
1975-76	40.20	25.01
1976-77	529.53	6.20
1977-78	471.27	8.04
1978-79	548.24	12.08
1979-80	796.45	19.78
1980-81	820.10	19.25
1981-82	834.68	22.45
1982-83	n.d.	n.d.
1983-84	710.00	19.00
1984-85	1,124.21	19.68

Source: Goyal & Singh.

The figures given in Table 6.70 reveal the positive image the book shop has created in this experimentation. Given the non-profit making status the book shop has it is an example for others to get into this venture. The ICAR Review Committee, infact, in its recommendations stated. "The Library is operating a book shop for the benefit of the students and is able to pass on the benefit of wholesale discount to the students, except a small margin for handling charges. This is a useful scheme, and should be adopted as a model by all other universities" (quoted by Goyal and Singh: 52).

Library Profession

Haryana Library Association (*f.* 1967) publishes its own newsletter. As a part of its professional activities, it offers a certificate course in library science. The duration is one year. A diploma course for women is offered which is a two-year programme. University of Kurukshetra commenced its professional training programme in 1969, by offering a degree course in library science.

STATE: HIMACHAL PRADESH

Being in the lap of the Himalayas, it gets its name, from the Hima, and was formed in 1971, though its formation started with the Punjab Reorganization Act, 1966. Its the land of Kangra and Kullu valleys, Manali and the Rohtang Pass, and most importantly the summer capital of Britishers, Simla.

Its area is 55,673 sq. kms. The population density is 92 persons per sq. km. The sex ratio of the State is 996 females per 1000 males. The literacy rate of this State is 63.54 per cent in 1991—males is 74.5 per cent and females is 52.4 per cent. The main language groups as per 1981 Census are: Hindi (88.4%); Punjabi (5.7%); Kinnauri (1.2%); Gorkha/ Nepali (0.9%); Kashmiri (0.7%); Lahauli (0.4%). The religious groups as per the 1981 Census are: Hindus (95.7%); Muslims (1.6%); Buddhists (1.2%); Sikhs (1.2%); etc.

Public Libraries

Starting afresh in the post-independent India, this State's public library system, had its first steps in library development in 1960, with the establishment of 6 District Libraries and a Central State Library at Solan. With the re-organization of the boundaries of the State in 1966, it received from Punjab 3 District Libraries. By 1985, the State had apart from one State Central Library, 11 District Public Libraries, and 13 Tehsil/Community Centre Public Libraries. Interestingly, during the Seventh Plan Period much development took place. A State Central Library at Shimla was also established, among other libraries. This library is being developed as a multilingual library in a phased manner.

According to a news report in *Granthana*, January 1991, an organ of the RRLF, the State is experimenting the practice of setting up school-cum-public libraries in the premises of secondary schools. This according to Justa (1993), was a process that started in the Seventh Plan Period. It was the opening of 101 Senior Secondary School Libraries were declared as public libraries. These libraries are open for the local public daily in the evening hours, and these libraries have trained assistant librarians.

Library Finance

Administratively, the State public library system in under the control of Director of Education. The whole system is run by the State Government, as there is hardly any privately managed library system.

Annual budget allocation is by the grants which the State government gives and the matching grant received from RRLF. There is no cess or any other source of income.

Library Expenditure

The figures, Table 6.72, are representative of what is the priority in the State for expenditure related to libraries. The State has grown in its socio-economic status and its industrial output is well advanced. And despite these developments the per capita of the State in the last decade stands at 18th place among all the States in the country.

TABLE 6.71: Budget Allocation

Income:	
Plan budget Non-plan budget	Combined Rs. 50 lakhs*
RRLF	Rs. 4 lakhs
Expenditure:	
Books	2,00,000

* Non-plan budget allocation does not exceed Rs. 28 lakhs.

TABLE 6.72: Expenditure on Public Libraries in States (1986-87)

Expenditure (in lakhs)	*Population (in lakhs)*	*Per Capita (in Rs.)*	*Literacy % 1980s*
25.0	42.8	0.58	42.48

Efforts for Enactment

1982 Himachal Pradesh Public Libraries Bill—prepared by Dr. A.S. Chandel

STATE: JAMMU & KASHMIR

This State combines the barren lands of Laddakh, the verdant valley of Kashmir, and the sandstone slopes of the Shivalik range of Jammu. It is the land of chinars and shikaras, Vaishnodevi and Hazratbal, Waswan, apples and saffron. It was acceded to India in October 1947.

Its total area (including the occupied territories by Pakistan and China) is 2,22,236 sq. kms. The population density is 76 persons per sq. km. The sex ratio of the State is 923 females per 1000 males. Its literacy rate has grown from 11 per cent in 1961; 18.6 per cent in 1971; 27 per cent in 1981 to 32.68 per cent in 1991. This is the lowest literate State in the country. The literacy rate of males is 44.1 per cent and females is 19.5 per cent. The main language groups as per 1981 Census are: Kashmiri (52.3%); Dogri (24.2%); Hindi (16.9%); Punjabi (2.7%); Ladhaki (1.2%); Shina (0.2%) and Lahnda (0.2%). The religious groups according to 1981 Census are: Muslims (64.2%); Hindus (32.2%); Sikhs (2.2%); Buddhists (1.1%); Christians (0.1%); and others.

Public Libraries

There are two Central Libraries at Srinagar and Jammu. The State Central Libraries, District and Tehsil Libraries are all managed by the Government. The State receives regular support from the RRLF, for working and improvement of rural libraries.

Library Expenditure

TABLE 6.73: Expenditure on Public Libraries in States (1986-87)

Expenditure (in lakhs)	*Population (in lakhs)*	*Per Capita (in Rs.)*	*Literacy % 1980s*
17.3	59.8	0.29	27.00

These figures, Table 6.73, are representative of what is the priority in the State for expenditure related do libraries. The State has grown in its socio-economic status and its industrial output is well advanced. And despite these developments the per capita of the State in the last decade stands at 24th place among all the States in the country.

Efforts for Enactment

1951 Library Bill for Jammu & Kashmir—prepared by Kaula. This bill was not passed in the Assembly. Such attempts by professionals, however, did result in preparing the authorities for the groundwork relating to library development. In 1963 the Government framed rules and regulations for managing public libraries, and named this document as J & K Library and Reading Room Rules.

1975 Jammu & Kashmir Public Library Bill—by M.S. Randhawa

While efforts from different quarters did not make much progress in terms of getting a public library enactment, these did however, resulted in the appointment of a Committee with Dr. M.S. Randhawa, as Chairman, to look into the working of the Department of libraries, and to make further recommendations in improving the same. The Committee report, submitted soon after, still awaits Government's approval and implementation.

Academic Libraries

A survey of 19 college libraries in the State, conducted by Baba gives interesting results. The observations are as follows: "The major function of all these college libraries is the circulation. . . . Most follow the ledger

TABLE 6.74: College Library Status

College	*Books*	*Subscribed Periodicals*	*Separate Library Building*	*Daily Users*	*Charging System/ Staff*	*Professionals*	*Others*
SPCS	32,000	30	yes	50	Ledger	3	3
ASCS	25,000	32	no	65	Ledger	2	4
CWMARS	20,000	35	no	70	Ledger	1	3
CWNS	27,000	22	no	95	Ledger	3	7
VBWCS	9,000	10	no	75	Ledger	2	1
ACSCS	30,000	62	yes	200	Newark	3	6
DCS	15,000	60	no	250	Ledger	2	1
ICWS	10,000	20	no	125	Ledger	—	—
DCB	21,019	56	yes	100	Ledger	1	5
DCA	6,000	40	no	85	Ledger	3	3
DCBS	15,000	35	no	250	Ledger	1	3
DCWA	18,000	10	no	300	Newark	2	2
MCS	28,000	75	no	225	Ledger	1	5
RECS	32,000	135	yes	150	Newark	6	23
CES	19,000	20	no	75	Ledger	1	4
ACS	12,321	166	no	100	Ledger	2	3
CMCS	17,500	23	no	65	Ledger	2	3
METTCS	5,040	32	no	50	Ledger	1	1
CPES	3,000	20	no	10	Ledger	1	—

Source: Baba.

system (for this purpose). Only three libraries have Newark charging system. Average daily issues and returns range between 20 to 500, with a provision of maximum 2 or 3 books per student, with no such limit for faculty. . . . The librarians check the circulation records to assess the interests of the users".

The Table 6.74 shows that of the 19 surveyed college libraries only 4 have separate libraries; 3 have modernized library charging system, from the antiquated ledger (record) system to the Newark system; 9 have comparatively higher visitor rates, and so on. But these higher figures are not comparable with larger collections. For instance, a library with the highest number of books (SPCS) does not have high number of periodicals, nor its daily visitors are high as in the case of other comparable collections. Further, the size of the collection is not a criteria to match its application of modernized charging system, for instance, more libraries with higher collections have ledger charging system.

One glaring difference for a viewer will be the figures of RECS (Regional Engineering College, Srinagar). It has no comparison with other libraries in the sense that these professional colleges receive higher funds and are expected to perform better than others. An indepth survey of the performance of such professional colleges will reveal the actual situation and this is not attempted here.

These are faced with many problems, and the list includes:

- The expectation of the management to pay for the loss of books, from the salary of the librarian;
- One person has to manage all services, a few have more than two professionals;
- No separate building exists for library in most cases, and wherever it exists, it is not according to the standards;
- librarians are not well paid, nor have proper status, they have no sufficient financial powers;
- close access is the fashion of most libraries;
- lack of user orientation, and user motivation programmes;
- lending rules for the faculty are not stated clearly;
- reader's suggestion regarding various library activities are neglected.

Library Profession

Due to various circumstances, the development of library profession in the State has been considerably slow. It was not until 1964, that the first professional body emerged in the State. Library training and education was all being dealt at Delhi and other neighbouring States, until the State had its own establishment, which was only in 1971, at Srinagar, in Kashmir University. Today both Jammu and Kashmir universities offer training programmes.

STATE: KARNATAKA

It is the land of the Tiger of Mysore—the dead Tiger was also fearful for the British Generals—land of Shravanabelagola and Gold mines, coffee of Bababudangiri Hills, Coorg of Manekshaw and Kariappa's and sandalwood and ivory products. The State, originally called, Mysore, emerged in 1956. Its area is 1, 91,791 sq. kms. The population density is 234 persons per sq. km. The sex ratio of the State is 960 females per 1000 males. It has a literacy growth rate of 3.0 per cent in 1951; 25.4 per cent in 1961; 31.5 per cent in 1971; 38.4 per cent in 1981; and 55.9 per cent in 1991—male literacy is 67.2 per cent and female is 44.3 per cent. The main language groups are as per 1981 Census: Kannada (65.1%); Urdu (9.4%); Telugu (8.0%); Marathi (3.7%); Tamil (3.7%); Tulu (3.2%); Hindi (1.7%); Konkani (1.7%); Malayalam (0.6%); Coorgi/Kodugu (0.2%). The religious groups according to the 1981 Census reports are: Hindus (85.7%); Muslims (11.2%); Christians (2.1%); Jains (1.7%); Buddhists (0.1%). etc.

Public Libraries

The State has enacted the Public Libraries Act in 1965, and the Act has 52 sections. The Act benefited and incorporated large number of improvements in the enactment, as compared to the provisions of the preceding public library acts of Tamil Nadu and Andhra Pradesh.

Library Expenditure

TABLE 6.75: Expenditure on Public Libraries in States (1986-87)

Expenditure (in lakhs)	*Population (in lakhs)*	*Per Capita (in Rs.)*	*Literacy % 1980s*
232.1	371.4	0.63	38.41

These figures, Table 6.75, are representative of what is the priority in the State for expenditure related to libraries. The State has grown in its socio-economic status and its industrial output is well advanced. And despite these developments the per capita of the State in the last decade stands at 17th place among all the States in the country. The State made a provision in the budget, 1987-88, for opening of libraries down to the mandal level. The State funds 3 per cent of revenue collection of the District. In Sixth plan Rs. 16.5 lakhs, was meant for library development.

TABLE 6.76: Seventh Plan Outlay for Library Development

(Rupees in lakhs)

Library	*Grant*
Voluntary Organizations	5
Mobile Libraries	26
Book Delivery Stations	21.5
Branch Libraries	14
City Libraries	2
Library Buildings	43

Public Library System

A glance at the figures of the existing number of libraries in the State is pertinent here, to provide an overview of the total system.

TABLE 6.77: Karnataka Public Library System at a Glance

	1988	*1995*
State Central Library	1	1
City Central Libraries	11	14
District Central Libraries	20	20
Branch Libraries	346	334
Panchayat Libraries (Mandal or Rural)	120	1,051
Book Delivery Stations	285	300
Raja Rammohun Roy Library Foundation Centres	1,905	1,922
Service Stations	—	150
Mobile Libraries	8	11
Hospital and Prison Libraries	—	40
Public Technical Library	1	1
Children's Library	—	1
Aided Libraries	—	83
Others	2	24
Total		4,410

Rural Library System

In accordance with the Zilla Parishad Act, 1987, the Karnataka State Government, directed the Directorate of Public Libraries, to establish Panchayat Libraries. The Directorate could establish 1,151 libraries, by the year 1995-96. The Directorate provides about 300 books to these libraries, along with one Kannada Newspaper, three Kannada weekly magazines, and Rs. 200 for miscellaneous expenditures. The respective panchayat was expected to appoint staff and provide free building for the library. The problems that these libraries face include lack of trained staff; meagre salaries and lack of incentives, and lack of good collections.

With the establishment, in 1972, of the Raja Rammohun Roy Library Foundation (RRLF), by the Central Government, the development of libraries in general, and of rural libraries, in particular, received a boost all over. This was reflected in Karnataka as well. The following is a map of the RRLF information centres, as of the 1970s, when the Foundation initiated the programme.

TABLE 6.78: RRLF Information Centres in Each District

	Number	*Percentage*
Bangalore (Rural)	42	2.1
Bangalore (Urban)	30	1.5
Belgaum	291	15.1
Bellary	114	5.9
Bidar	76	3.9
Bijapur	174	9.0
Chikmagalur	31	1.5
Chitradurga	78	4.0
Dakshina Kannada (Mangalore)	167	8.6
Dharwad	187	9.7
Gulbarga	166	8.6
Hassan	13	0.1
Kolar	30	1.5
Mandya	80	4.0
Mercara (Coorg)	24	1.2
Mysore	162	8.4
Raichur	80	4.2
Shimoga	63	3.3
Tumkur	74	3.8
Uttar Kannada (Karwar)	40	2.0
Total	1,922	100.0

While the original spirit was to provide seed money and develop rural libraries, everywhere, the development soon came to standstill. Some of these information centres have been converted as panchayat libraries, and most of these are not existing at present (Ijari, 1996: 96).

In fact the State Government had the responsibility to sustain and support the development of these libraries. The reasons for the decay of the programme of public library development, despite the continued support of the RRLF, has been highlighted by Prof. Ijari, as follows:

(a) Beginning in 1972, the Directorate of Public Libraries, Bangalore, bought books from its own funds as well as from the RRLF funds, and sent the books to the District Central Library (DCL), for distribution to respective centres in their jurisdiction, without any guidelines about the *modus operandi*;
(b) Some DCL's distributed books to panchayats and primary schools; and
(c) The recipients of these load of books, accepted the bundles, but did not receive any funds and the paraphernalia to manage and serve the users, resultingly the bundles were kept unopened—if opened the suspicion was about loss of books and the persisting threat that any loss of books leads to salary deduction of the teachers who were assigned this task.

State Central Library, Bangalore

This library, which was called as Bangalore Public Library, was established in 1914, as a result of the recommendations of the Education Committee, which was constituted under the Chairmanship of Dr. M. Vishveshwarayya, the then Diwan of Mysore State. Ranganathan remarks, that the Bangalore Public Library is, I am told, a brain child of Mokshagundam Vishveshwarayya. He conceived it in accordance with the ideas about a Public Library prevailing 50 years ago. It was in effect to provide reading materials to scholastic minded, fairly rich, and leisured class of people. It began as subscription library. It was a public library in the sense that it was open to any member of the public to become a paying member. The message sent on its formal opening on 1st May 1915, by Vishveshwarayya had, however, the pregnant words, 'Cherish the hope that it will be a lasting benefit to the citizens of Bangalore'. "The management of Bangalore Public Library continuously liberalized its services. From the very beginning it maintained a 'Free Reading Room' for the use of newspapers and periodicals by any person without payment. It also allowed non-subscribers to read the books of the library within the library premises. But the privilege of taking books home was denied to non-members" (quoted in Ijari, 1997: 180).

District Central Library, Dharwad

It was established in 1969, as per the provision of the Public Library Act.

Collection: It had 2,31,965 books in 1990, 2,33,614 in 1991 and 2,61,737 in 1992. It subscribes to 138 Kannada and 32 English newspapers and 382 Kannada and 68 English magazines, which is probably only next to the State Library subscriptions.

Service: This District Library does not provide any public service. It however provides all technical service to its 35 branch libraries, 23 mandal libraries, service stations, 14 book depository centres, and aided libraries. The total population in the area is 28,51,405 (55% male and 45% female), and literates are 45 per cent male and 29 per cent female.

The District Library is responsible for centralized acquisition of books, magazines and newspapers, processing, and delivery of these to the respective libraries, for decentralized storage and dissemination.

District Central Library, Tumkur

The services rendered in this district in particular, and in the State in general, received an appreciative note in the Tumkur District Gazetteer, 1969, "A feature of the library movement in the State was the starting of an integrated library service in compact areas under a Government of India Scheme of Educational Development. Each such area was supplied with periodicals, and books of interest, which were circulated in the villages of that area" (quoted in Ijari, 1997: 181).

Efforts for Enactment

1963 Mysore Public Libraries Bill—prepared by SRR for the Mysore Public Libraries Bill Committee, 1961.

1965 Mysore Public Libraries Act.

The support received by B.V. Baliga, the Speaker of the Legislature, and S.R. Kanthi, the Education Minister, was tremendous in passing the bill, in the Legislative Assembly. Based on this Bill, and the efforts of professionals and friends of the library, the Bill was passed and in 1965 the State had the enactment. Later when the State was re-named it became essential to re-name the Act, and hence in 1973, it came to be known as Karnataka Public Libraries Act.

Academic Libraries

There are few old universities, like Mysore University, Mysore, (*f.* 1916); Karnataka University, Dharwad, (*f.* 1950); Bangalore University, Bangalore (*f.* 1965); University of Agricultural Sciences, Bangalore (*f.* 1965); The Indian Institute of Sciences, Bangalore (*f.* 1911), etc.

A host of new ones, like Kuvempu University, Shimoga; Mangalore University, Mangalore, (*f.* 1980); Gulbarga University, Gulbarga, (*f.* 1980); etc. According to Prof. Deshpande "The credit of establishing the first University in an Indian Princely State goes to Mysore" (1983: 28).

A glance at the acquisition of one of these is pertinent, to understand the trends. Mysore University Library (*f.* 1916) is the oldest and biggest in Karnataka. The library was started with 2, 311 books—320 by purchase, 1961 that were transferred from Government Oriental Library, Mysore, and 30 by gift.

TABLE 6.79: Mysore University Library Development

	1981-82	*1982-83*
Books added	4,671	8,569
Total collection	n.d	3,70,000
Periodicals subscribed	2,133	2,145
Members enrolled	2,773	2,297
Reader's attendance	1,26,998	1,40,792
Books issued	56,519	49,187
Books consulted	87,832	96,834
Inter-library loan		
Lent	154	189
Borrowed	41	32

These are the figures, Table 6.79, of collection development and use pattern for two years. A sample of this size, of an established library, speaks much about the reader's information seeking behaviour, as well as collection development and maintenance patterns. For instance, in a city like Mysore, with nearly ten educational academies and research institutions, the level of interaction, in terms of inter-library borrowing from a university library, rightly has a higher lending rate, and lesser borrowing rate. The primary borrowers are the Central Food Technological Research Institute, Regional College of Engineering, and so on.

Further, by the figures of membership and book consultations, it can be implied that each member has on an average higher number of consultations, and the text books and reference resources must be quite adequate.

In sixty years of its existence; it has improved from 2,311 books to 3,70,000 total collection, with an average annual addition of 6,000 volumes. The average addition is also indicated, by the book collections added, in the Table 6.79.

Mysore University Library has all the traditional services and facilities, and hence the above discussion does not speak of any innovative experiences or innovations that are carried out in this library. It is a good library, may not be very user-friendly, but does have a few librarians who are sought after by every user. User friendliness does exists, but it is that variety of user-friendliness which suits the librarians, and not as the user's desire—and this defect in planning of libraries based on user needs is visible everywhere.

State Government's Role

To bring uniformity in the administration and academic programmes in the universities of Karnataka, the Government enacted the State Universities Act, 1976. As a provision of the Act, the first review committee was set up in 1980, under the Chairmanship of Dr. K.N. Raj. The Committee included in its scope a detailed assessment of the finances of university and college libraries. It recommended that 20 per cent of the total university budget must be marked for development of libraries. Based on this some universities, like Karnataka University, raised their budget to 10 per cent instead of a meagre allotted amount.

The Raj Commission also recommended a network for the libraries in the State, provision of liberal photocopying facility, sponsoring cooperative acquisition programmes, etc. Commenting on the dire need for cooperative acquisition, a seasoned professional the librarian of Mysore University (1965-67), Karnataka University, Bangalore University, etc. Prof. Deshpande states. "If at all a ceiling is to be put on the number of documents that a library should have, I would put it at above 10 lakhs of life books, and about 2,000 current periodicals for each library" (1983: 34).

Karnataka has another ruling for the University libraries. According to this rule, no person is eligible to hold simultaneously two offices—University Librarian and Head of the department of library science. This has resulted in bifurcation of the professional activity, theory away from laboratory. There are advantages in the dictum one person one office, but there are also disadvantages that abound. Karnataka has been experiencing this rule for decades.

Special Libraries

Special libraries, traditional and modernized, are abundant in this State, with most concentration of such libraries in its capital city, Bangalore. One finds here a mix of both traditional and ultra-modern libraries in ample. A list of these can be found in any directory, such as Holmes. H.W., Research facilities series, booklet dealing with Bangalore. Indian Library Association's Directory of ILA Members, IASLIC Directory of Libraries, Directory of Special and Research Libraries in India, etc.

Two libraries are of special importance here, one is the National Aeronautical Laboratory Library, and the other is Mythic Society of India Library, both located in Bangalore, The first is the most modern—super speciality library—serving with all the online technologies, and is up-to-date; the other is a traditional library, collecting books at a slow speed, and keeping it open to the research and public needs in the field of mythology, culture, and society. The scientific research that the former promotes, has been given all the essentials of a modern library, whereas the latter deals with abstract knowledge and hence this library does not find itself in the priority list of the management. If the library, promoting in a descent fashion, cultural understanding of one's own country, does not find a priority for modernization and improvement of its age-old image, then it is the society, which should take up the matter and demand for a change.

Another special library, neither too traditional, nor too advanced, is the example of a newspaper library. *Deccan Herald* and *Prajavani* (started in 1948) are two newspapers, which are published in English and Kannada, respectively, from Bangalore, and they have maintained a good library (Ramamurthy; 1982). The publishers also have two other papers in the network, that is, *Sudha* and *Mayura*, both in Kannada (Ramamurthy; 1983).

Since the newspaper library has a different information need and information demand pattern, this Newspaper Library reflects this dimension. As the newspaper constantly needs background information for every news story, the collection then not only includes books, journals, etc., it also has newspaper clippings from its own publications, and papers published in the region, in the country and so on. To manage the clippings, the Library uses, Kolatkar's Scheme of Classification. Its collection has the following categories of resources. Books, magazines and periodicals; Backfiles in hard copy; Backfiles in microform; Photographs, Backgrounders, and Current clippings.

The library receives 600 books for the purpose of review in the magazine. Most books are marked to the reviewers, but if not worth a review, some are directly accessioned, and some are given away to other institutions.

Given the age of information explosion, and shortage of information sources in the library, inter-library lending is the only resort, and the libraries, in the neighbourhood and in the region are requested for material. The inter-library requests are sent within Bangalore to Bangalore University Library, Indian Institute of Management Library, British Library, etc. and sometimes to Chennai, which includes British Council Library, United States Information Service, etc.

Thus to cater to nearly hundreds of potential journalists working in this newspaper system, the library has a well trained staff, and it keeps updating its professional skills in information searching and handling. The newspaper has entered the world of INTERNET, and the staff are therefore into surfing and browsing the Web and the kind to provide more direct access to the world of information.

Library Profession

Library Association

Professional affiliation in the State is demonstrated through the bodies, such as Mysore Library Association (*f.* 1929), later its name was changed as Karnataka Library Association, as soon as the name of the State was changed. It has led a good example by initiating various professional works, such a journal, and conducting professional meetings regularly. The post-independent India saw the growth of library science literature at a very fast level, and there is now significant material in Kannada. Karnataka Granthalaya is a serial in this language. A doctoral research has also surveyed the reference sources that are available in this language—such studies have been done in Telugu and probably in one or two more languages. But such studies will show how strong is the reference resource in the respective language, and what else is required to provide efficient and effective reference service to the majority who are aware of only the regional language.

Library Education

Providing a catalogue of the universities that offer the courses is not intended here. What is aimed at is a review of the situation, gains and fruits that have enabled the library development in the State.

All the universities offering general education have a full-fledged department of library science (now re-named as Library and Information Science, or as Post-Graduate Department of Library and Information Science). All these have a programme of research too, given the UGC stipulation that the academic librarians, to get faculty status, have a research degree.

DRTC, Bangalore

A little detailed review of one of the significant training institution, Documentation Research Training Centre, Bangalore, will give a glimpse of the state-of-the-art. DRTC, as it is popularly known, (*f.* 1962), had the benevolent advice and support of two stalwarts, Prof. P.C. Mahalanobis, a member of the National Planning Commission, and Director of Indian Statistical Institute, and Dr. S.R. Ranganathan.

Unlike the library science departments in the Indian universities, and all other training programmes for library science, DRTC, from its day one, had the objective of training documentalists that is, those who can perform the advanced reference service as a holistic mission, and not as an isolated activity.

Towards the fulfilment of this mission, a team of faculty supports the training and research programme of DRTC. A few selected participants each year enroll and get into this mission oriented area, and in the last three decades of its existence DRTC has produced hundreds of documentalists.

Appreciating its approach and methodology, Prof Kumbhar and Karisiddappa state: "Though all the universities in the State have changed the nomenclature of the course curriculum . . . there remains much more to be changed in order to prepare the professionals to suit the changing needs of the modern libraries and information centres. These academic institutions should adopt best possible course contents and methodologies as provided in the courses of DRTC and INSDOC, to produce future professionals to work in the special libraries—industrial, R&D, and Business Information Centres" (1983: 59).

The quality of these documentalists, and the quantum of the work they produce, requires a thorough analysis, which is not attempted here. Such an analysis must compare the input, thru' put, and output of the university trained and DRTC trained professionals. Also such a comparison may include a similar institution, INSDOC, New Delhi, to find out the similarities and dissimilarities. Such a comparison calls for a team work and must be considered as an evaluative process, rather than finding faults with the courses and training offered by respective institutions.

Continuing Education

To provide continuing education facility, DRTC, like all other professional institutions, conducts courses, seminars and workshops. Its annual seminars and annual refresher courses are two regular features, which allow not only its alumni to upgrade their skills and knowledge, but also for non-DRTC alumni to participate in such continuing education programmes.

A sister organisation, Sharda Ranganathan Endowment, organises annual lecture series, and has sponsored the visits of world renowned professionals like Lancaster, Fosket, and others, to address its audience in Bangalore.

There are other agencies in the State who are providing facility for continuing education programmes. Mysore University is recognised centre for the UGC Refresher Courses, and the Academic Staff College, coordinates one-month long continuing education programmes as in-service training for librarians in the region.

In one such refresher course, this writer, was invited. The audience, totally forty participants, a lively group, expected more current and realistic approach to information access, rather than utopian or antique elements. Most were college librarians, and had never used, until 1996, a computer for the library work, yet were inclined to actively learn the know-how of the emerging information technology. Back at home, these participants, would again have the same chorus of all the traditional tasks—performed single-handedly, and probably acting in a slightly changed manner. They needed at the best, motivation and inspiration, and the course gave some opportunity for the introspection.

STATE: KERALA

The name of the State probably originate from the coconut palm, in Malayalam, Keram. It is the land of cashew and coconuts, snakeboats, and Kathakali, spices and rubber, Adi Sankara and Communism and Onam.

The State emerged in 1956, incorporating the Malabar district, earlier under the Madras Province, Tavancore and Cochin. This State takes the lead in re-naming anglicised names, beginning with the year 1990, of many districts and other places, such as, Kozhikode (for Calicut): Thiruvananthapuram (for Trivandrum); etc.

The State has 14 districts. The literacy rate, interestingly, grew from mere 6.0 per cent, in 1951; to 46.8 per cent in 1961 (this hike emerged due to the inclusion of the complete district of Malabar—earlier under Madras Province), 60 per cent in 1971; 69.71 per cent in 1981, and 90.59 per cent in 1991—the literacy rate of males is 94.4 per cent and females is 86.9 per cent.

The literacy in Kerala is the highest in the country, and this record achievement is due to a number of factors. The primary reason could be in its high standards of education, literacy campaigns, urge among the people to know and be informed, and so on.

The State was declared as fully literate on 18 April 1991 at the end of a year long literacy drive named Aksharakeralam. The programme was implemented by the Kerala Saksharatha Samiti, a Government organization, in which about 2,50, 000 (or 2.5 lakh) people participated, most were high school dropouts (or failed in the State Board examination). The Samiti aimed at helping 12.5 lakh illiterates to become literates. Of the 28.5 illiterates, in the age group of 6-60, as identified in a one-day survey on 8 April 1990, 12.5 lakh attended the literacy classes held all over the State, and passed the evaluation test (Silvera, 1991: 72).

This project took the State's literacy level to 93.6 per cent, higher than the norm set by National Literacy Mission (NLM). The stated norm of NLM for this is 90 per cent literacy in the State. Interestingly, literacy, a fashion and common talk of the day, is a census based figure, which defines a literate as 'if he or she can read and write any language with understanding'.

Also pertinent is the fact, that its political consciousness of the public, is probably the highest in the country. It is the first State in the world where communism was accepted as a political ideology, through the medium of the ballot box as early as 1957 (Silvera, 1991: 73).

Its area is 38,863 sq. kms. The population density is 747 persons per sq. km. The sex ratio of the State is 1040 females per 1000 males. The main language groups as per 1981 Census are: Malayalam (95.2%); Tamil (2.3%); Tulu (0.4%) Konkani (0.4%); Kannada (0.2%) Telugu (0.2%). The religious groups as per the 1981 Census are: Hindus (58.1%); Muslims (21.2%); Christians (20.5%); etc.

Public Libraries

The history of public libraries in Kerala dates back to the opening of the Trivandrum Public Library, later named as State Central Library, (*f.* 1829). Its original intention was to open it to the British aristocracy, and at the most to those who were permitted by the Maharaja. A change in fact took place, in 1898, with the Trivandrum Public Library Society's initiative. The Society agreed to hand over the library to the Government and H.H. The Sreemoolam Thirunal declared that the library would be opened to the public.

Library Finance

The library movement has been better in this State, as is evident, otherwise, from the following norms that have been devised for granting financial support to libraries in the State. The Table 6.80 shows the required standards as they are prescribed if one expects help from the Kerala Grandhalaya Sangham or Kerala Library Association (*f.* 1956) later re-named as Kerala Granthsala Sanghom (1957).

TABLE 6.80: Financial Assistance

	Norms for Grading (figures in '000s)				*Annual Grant*	*Librarians (Pay) (Rs.)*	*Librarian's Allowance (Rs.)*
Grade	*Collection Size*	*Annual Lending*	*Dailies*	*Periodicals*			
A	Above 8	12,000	5	15	175	2,200	900
B	5—8	8,000	5	12	398	1,250	900
C	4—5	6,000	5	10	503	1,000	900
D	3—4	5,000	4	8	1,147	700	600
E	2—3	4,000	4	8	731	600	360
F	1—2	2,000	3	6	70	450	300

Source: Bavakutty, 1988: 79.

The Granthsala Sangham distributes the Government grants, both, recurring and non-recurring to grant-in-aid to libraries. During 1980-85, on an average Rs. 1,80,000 were spent on non-recurring items, and Rs. 26,76,000 was spent on recurring items.

In addition to this grant distributing pattern, the Malabar District Library Authority, which functioned until recently under the Tamil Nadu Public Libraries Act, establishes and maintains large number of libraries.

TABLE 6.81: Public Library Budget

(Rs. in lakhs)

Year	*Plan*	*Non-Plan*	*Total*
1985-86	7.00	60.68	67.68
1986-87	7.00	75.52	82.52
1987-88	8.00	84.87	92.87
1988-89	6.00	85.29	91.29

Incidentally, the non-plan budget is considerably higher than the plan budget head. This must be then proportional each year to the State's plan budget.

Library Expenditure

TABLE 6.82: Expenditure on Public Libraries in States (1986-87)

Expenditure (in lakhs)	*Population (in lakhs)*	*Per Capita (in Rs.)*	*Literacy % 1980s*
113.0	254.5	0.44	69.17

These figures, Table 6.82, are representative of what is the priority in the State for expenditure related to libraries. The State has grown in its socio-economic status and its industrial output is well advanced. And despite these developments the per capita of the State in the last decade stands at 20th place among all the States in the country.

TABLE 6.83: Amount Spent by State Central Library

Budget Category	*Expenditure (in rupees)*
Library Services	9,22,276
Reading Material	2,59,930
Total	11,82,206

The figures, Table 6.83, relates to the amount spent by the SCL, at Trivandrum, in fulfilling its objective. The amount of money spend on the reading material is not commensurate with the requirement of the users, and this is evident in the proportionate of per capita that it spends on the libraries, as low as 20th place. Even the operational charges of 2 per cent suggested by the RRLF is not implemented by the State, and this enhancement, according to Sukumaran Nair (1993), is necessary for increasing efficiency.

Efforts for Enactment

1947 Cochin State Public Libraries Bill—prepared by SRR

1947 Travancore State Public Libraries Bill—by SRR

1959 Kerala Public Libraries Bill—by SRR, on the request of the Chief Minister of Kerala, E.M.S. Namboodripad

1969 Kerala Public Libraries Bill—by SRR

1971 Kerala Public Libraries Bill—presented in the Assembly by the Chief Minister, C.H. Mohamed Koya, but the assembly did not consider it.

1974 Draft Bill—reintroduced in the Assembly by Chakkari Ahammed Kutty, Minister of Education, and the Assembly referred it to the Select Committee, but before the report could be submitted the term of the Assembly was over.

1977 Draft Bill—presented before the Assembly, and again referred to the Select Committee, and the Select Committee could not submit its report because of the dissolution of the Legislature.

1977 Library Bill was drafted by combined effort of Kerala Library Association, ILA, and Central Libraries Association of Kerala.

1985 Draft Bill—prepared by T. M. Jacob

Another draft bill—prepared by K.G. Kunjukrishna Pillai, MLA, presented a non-official bill.

A Draft Bill—by Justice V.R. Krishna Iyer, and sent it to the Chief.

The passing of the Kerala State Public Libraries (Kerala Granthasala Sangham) Act, 1989, has sought to regularise the working of the otherwise adhoc library network in the State. The enactment of the Public Libraries Act, has many advantages and limitations. The Act has an added advantage, as compared to all other Library Acts in India, in the fact that "In all the bills prepared in Kerala and in the acts in other States the President/Chairman of State Council/Board/Authority is either the education minister or minister in-charge of the libraries. In this Act it is the elected President. Even in the bye-laws of former Kerala Granthasala

Sangham, voting rights and rights to compete in elections were provided to nominated member. There were many nominated members in the Sangham. But in this Act, nominated member has no voting right and no right to compete" (Chandran, 1990; 57).

The limitations of the Act include, "An amount not exceeding one per cent of the education budget is allotted for the library movement. The Chattopadhyaya Commission report had suggested to set apart ten per cent amount of the education budget. It is natural that the financial support from the public will diminish when it is felt that more money is derived from the Government. This will effect the functioning of libraries. This deficiency is to be rectified" (Chandran, 1990: 59).

What has been the response from the library professionals, on the enactment of the long awaited, enactment?

"It is possible that library professionals are generally disappointed as the Act does not provide much scope for any radical change in the library set up in the State. Professional involvement in the policy making and decision making activities will be almost insignificant. Out of the three bodies, *viz*, State Library Council (SLC), District Library Council (DLC), and Taluk Library Council (TLC), only in SLC there is provision for nomination of a librarian as its member DLC's and TLC's can very well be without librarians as per the Act. Similarly there is no representation from the Panchayats, Municipalities and Municipal Corporations. After experiencing the defects and shortcomings of cess based public library service for more than a century, United Kingdom has enacted legislation making it obligatory on the part of local governments to provide adequate library and information service to the people of their area. Unfortunately we have to go a long way to realize this and make necessary compulsory legislation for adequate library service" (Ramakrishnan, 1990: 60).

Academic Libraries

TABLE 6.84: Types of Academic Libraries in State

Type of Library		*Number*
School Libraries:	Secondary	2,429
	Upper Primary	2,870
	Primary	6,845
College Libraries:	General Education	250
	Medical Colleges	2
	Engineering Colleges	4
	Ayurveda Colleges	2
	University Libraries	3

School Libraries

Though all secondary and upper primary schools have a library for namesake, but as a rule the majority are not in a functional situation. The reasons for this include

(a) lack of qualified full-time professional staff: a teacher is assigned the task of managing the library. The teacher has to see her/his convenience of teaching hours, and the library work is a real burden with no extra monetary benefit. The library if at all functions each day, it is hardly for an hour or two.
(b) lack of variety in the collection. Malayalam fiction is predominant—for the use of school children.
(c) no separate room for the school library is designed, it is part of the teachers room or some other multi-purpose location.
(d) lack of sense of deprivation among teachers, administrators, etc., none recognises that there is no proper reading room facility.

College Libraries

A detailed analysis of the growth, development and prospects of academic library situation, including college and academic libraries has been done by Bavakutty (1988) and others.

The survey of the college libraries shows that the situation in the State is the same as elsewhere in the country:

(a) no professional staff to manage the libraries, most college librarians at the best have a matriculation with Certificate in Library Science, the staff do not get UGC pay scales;
(b) most colleges have departmental libraries, as well, in addition to the main library, compounding the problems of bad management which are even otherwise prevailing in these libraries.
(c) many college libraries do not have good arrangement system—the books are kept on shelves according to accession numbers or alphabetically by writers, thereby the 'shelf arrangement' saves the time of the staff, and none cares if this wastes the staff time;
(d) working hours of most college libraries are from 10 a.m. to 5 p.m. This is suitable for the library staff to go home early, but not for the students, who attend the classes during these hours;

(e) lending of books is the only service performed. Even this service is offered based on close access. Open access is not the rule in the college libraries;

(f) almost all these libraries lack proper furniture and human care for the users—lack of proper ventilation, lighting, functional building, etc.

Financial resources of a college library include:

Library fees	Rs. 3,150.00
Government grant	Rs. 5,500.00
UGC Library grant	Rs. 40.000.00
Average library expenditure (in total of the college)	0.6 to 0.9
Average No. of seats in college libraries	25
Average No. of students per college	1,500

Library fees of Rs. 2 per student in a year is collected. The entire fund is insufficient for any planned collection development, let alone acquire standard reference sources.

TABLE 6.85: Functioning with Limited Facilities of Library

University Libraries	*Collection Books*	*Central Library Periodicals Sub.*	*Dept. Library Books*
Calicut (*f.* 1968)	1,00,000	650	n.d.
Kerala (*f.* 1937)	2,25,000	822	n.d.
Cochin (*f.* 1971)	50,000	740	1,00,000
Kerala Agri.	n.d.	n.d.	n.d.
Mahatma Gandhi	n.d.	n.d.	n.d.

These figures, Table 6.85, though inadequate in many respects, yet give an inclination of the pattern that prevails in three of the five universities that have libraries which are functioning with limited facilities and not so congenial atmospheres. For instance, the departmental libraries, function as immediate resources for the faculty and students. Hence most of these users do not turn upto the Central Library.

A visit to some of these departmental libraries, such as those in Calicut University library system, demonstrates the utility of having such small libraries. Each of these departmental libraries is supervised by a professional librarian—trained in art and craft of the trade. The departmental libraries are equipped, if not with all reading material, at least with minimum reference and study material, periodicals, and so on. The lending here decentralised. All technical processing and public services are centralised. Newspapers and textbook collections do not find a place in these departmental libraries.

Special Libraries

There are many technical, research and other types of special libraries in the State. There are six libraries attached to respective specializations, working under the umbrella of the Indian Council of Agricultural Research (ICAR); two libraries under the CSIR, namely, ISRO, Trivanthapuram, and Kerala Forest Research Institute, Trichur, and in addition to these there are specialised research institutes attached to the universities in the State.

Library Profession

The leading professional body is Kerala Grandhalaya Sangham or Kerala Library Association (*f.* 1956) later re-named as Kerala Granthsala Sanghom (1957). The efforts of the Association are all oriented towards making the library facility available for the users. The State had unique experience with literacy reaching the high mark, even before the newly enacted Library Act could show its impact. The question that can be asked to the professionals in the State is simple; what was their role in promoting literacy, and if they had any opportunity of playing a role? The answer calls for an in-depth interview and survey of the length and breadth of the State, which is not in the scope of this work. The study of this literacy growth pattern has to find out from the literacy workers about the level of support they received from libraries in this mission, and so on.

Grandhalokam and Vijnana Kairali are two prominent serials that are published in Malayalam for the continuing education of the professionals in the State. There is a lot of literature in Malayalam for the same purpose.

Library Education

There have been library training programmes in the State, ranging from training programmes offered by the Association, the State Library, Trivanthapuram, and the departments of library science at the Universities of Calicut and Kerala. The Certificate courses offered by the Association and the State Library, are of four months duration, and provide a base for the novice and unskilled to get initiated.

There are a few library science books and periodicals in Malayalam, the State language. A survey conducted by Dr. Bavakutty, in 1988, showed that there are 34 books, in the field. These are mostly single author contributions, and not much effort has been seriously made to bring team work in this regard. There is no periodical contributing exclusively to library science, however, Grandhalokam, and Vijnana Kairali, over many articles relating to library and information science.

The two universities, Kerala University and Calicut University offer, training programmes regularly. Both have bachelor's, master's and doctoral programmes. Like other States in the country, degree colleges, such as Farook College, Calicut, offers library science as a part of the degree programme.

Library Networks

Networking: A traditional sense of networking does exist in the departmental libraries, for instance, in the Calicut University Library System. Humanities collection is placed in one location, though managed independently by discipline and area of study. The Arabic Departmental Library, as a case on hand, is managed and serves its users independent of the neighbouring section dealing with Sanskrit, or other subjects.

In terms of automated networks there is some attempt made in the scientific libraries, for instance, in the CSIR laboratories, and their associates. Similarly, ISRO Centre, Trivanthapuram, is appropriately hooked up to its sister organizations in the country.

UNION TERRITORY: LAKSHADWEEP

This archipelago of 36 coral islands, inhabited by only 10 of these islands, emerged as Union Territory in 1956, with the name Laccadive, Minicoy and Amindivi Islands and it was re-named in 1983 as Lakshadweep (lit. thousand lamps).

Its area is 32 sq. kms. The population density is 1,615 persons per sq. km. The sex ratio of the State is 944 females per 1000 males. The literacy rate of males is 87.06 per cent and females is 70.8 per cent. The main language groups as per 1981 Census are: Malayalam (83.8%); and others (16.2%). The religious groups as per the 1981 Census are: Muslims (94.8%); Hindus (4.4%); Christians (0.6%).

Public Libraries

Library Expenditure

TABLE 6.86: Expenditure on Public Libraries in States (1986-87)

Expenditure (in lakhs)	*Population (in lakhs)*	*Per Capita (in Rs.)*	*Literacy % 1980s*
0.5	0.4	1.24	44.65

These figures, Table 6.86, are representative of what is the priority in the State for expenditure related to libraries. The State has grown in its socio-economic status and its industrial output is well advanced. And despite these developments the per capita of the State in the last decade stands at 11th place among all the States in the country.

STATE: MADHYA PRADESH

This is the land of Khajuraho and Sanchi, tribal Gonds and 'Barasingha' deer, and covering the area which Fahien called as Madhya-desa, and Scindias. More pertinently, it is the State whose capital city, Bhopal, is now universally famous, for the gas leak disaster of 1984.

Madhya Pradesh (lit. middle of the country, and Pradesh=State), was formed in 1956, with the parts of the territories that were earlier under Marathas, Rajputs, Muslims and other rulers, and presently its adjacent States are Maharashtra, Bihar, Uttar Pradesh, Orissa, and Rajasthan. With all these influences it has a multi-cultural background. Its literacy has grown from 6 per cent in 1951; 17 per cent in 1961; 22 per cent in 1971; 27.8 per cent in 1981; to 43.4 per cent in 1991—The literacy rate of males is 57.4 per cent and females is 28.3 per cent.

Its area is 4,43,446 sq. kms. The population density is 149 persons per sq. km. The sex ratio of the State is 932 females per 1000 males. The main language groups are as per 1981 Census: Hindi (84.0%); Gondi (2.5%); Marathi (2.2%); Urdu (2.2%); Kurukh/Oran (0.6%); Sindhi (0.5%); Korku (0.5%). The religious groups as per the 1981 Census are: Hindus (92.9%); Muslims (4.7%); Jains (0.8%); Christians (0.6%); Sikhs (0.2%); Buddhists (0.1%); etc.

Public Libraries

The State library system has three administrators of public libraries, *viz.*, a part-time officer in the Department of Education for urban libraries, that is, State Central Library, Regional Libraries, District Libraries, and Aided-Libraries. A part-time officer in the Department of Panchayat and Social Welfare for rural libraries, that is, Block Libraries, and Panchayat Libraries, and a part-time officer in the Department of Tribal Welfare, Harijan and Backward Classes for libraries in tribal areas. In this the State has a good example of three State departments providing library services. This is reflected in the library scenario which is as follows.

TABLE 6.87: Library Scenario in the State

Type of Library	*Number*
State Central Library	1
Regional Libraries	5
District Libraries	42
Information Centres	6
Private Public Libraries	80
Gram Panchayat Libraries	15,800
Total	15,934

Library Expenditure

TABLE 6.88: Expenditure on Public Libraries in States (1986-87)

Expenditure (in lakhs)	*Population (in lakhs)*	*Per Capita (in Rs.)*	*Literacy % 1980s*
120.0	521.7	0.23	27.82

These figures, Table 6.88, are representative of what is the priority in the State for expenditure related to libraries. The State has grown in its socio-economic status and its industrial output is well advanced. And despite these developments the per capita of the State in the last decade stands at 26th place among all the States in the country.

Efforts for Enactment

1946 Central Provinces and Benaras Public Libraries Bill—prepared by SRR.

1950 Madhya Pradesh Public Libraries Bill

1958 Madhya Pradesh Public Libraries Bill—by Maulana Azad Central Library Committee

1959 Madhya Pradesh Public Libraries Bill—by Madhya Pradesh Library Association

1968 Madhya Pradesh Public Libraries Bill—by G.D. Bhargava and V.S. Moghe

1970 Madhya Pradesh Public Libraries Bill—by Indore Library Association. This was the result of the 17th All-India Library Conference, held at Indore. The Association authorised MP Library Association to push the matter further. The bill was presented to the Education Minister, Jadgishnarayan Avasthi, who could not get the bill cleared.

1978 Madhya Pradesh Public Libraries Bill—presented by MP Public Libraries Association, to the Education Minister, Omprakash Rawal, but before anything could happen, the minister was ousted.

1990 Madhya Pradesh Public Libraries Bill—by K.M. Ujlambkar.

Each time the draft is forwarded and put up for the discussion in the Assembly, but the matter of passing the library act get postponed.

As a stop gap arrangement, the Government has taken different steps, one such is reported in Granthana, "The Madhya Pradesh Government is developing school-cum-public libraries in primary schools located in tribal areas, and they have been named as 'Saraswathi Sanghams'. According to available reports these are mostly functioning as school libraries rather than dual libraries" (Granthana, 1991: 86).

Academic Libraries

There are many institutions of higher learning in the State, and there are more than 8 universities in this large State. An attempt is made to see how the financial management of the academic libraries is being viewed by the authorities.

TABLE 6.89: University's Allocation for Libraries

(Rupees in lakhs)

University	*I*	*II*	*III*	*Yearly*	*IV*	*V*	*Total*
Bhopal	—	—	—	—	1.06	1.19	2.26
Gwalior	—	—	1.68	3.07	3.51	9.36	17.63
Indore	—	—	0.04	0.85	0.33	9.28	10.52
Jabalpur	3.45	2.65	6.22	7.79	9.08	—	29.20
Raipur	—	—	0.14	0.70	5.69	3.89	10.44
Rewa	—	—	—	—	1.50	0.61	2.12
Saugar	1.91	7.18	0.43	5.02	8.51	11.13	34.19
Vikram	—	5.58	4.41	4.64	5.05	13.31	33.01

TABLE 6.90: Recurring UGC Grants to Universities

(Rupees in lakhs)

University	*I*	*II*	*III*	*Yearly*	*IV*	*V*	*Total*
Bhopal	—	—	—	—	1.10	6.60	7.70
Gwalior	—	—	0.75	1.35	6.46	14.00	22.56
Indore	—	—	0.35	1.20	8.30	14.01	23.87
Jabalpur	1.00	6.59	—	4.39	10.00	—	21.98
Raipur	—	—	0.40	1.71	0.57	8.79	17.60
Rewa	—	—	—	—	1.12	5.02	6.14
Saugar	1.30	4.12	3.81	—	12.50	15.00	36.73
Vikram	—	1.12	4.45	—	6.76	3.00	15.41
Total	1.30	6.32	16.35	4.26	46.44	77.33	152.02

TABLE 6.91: Non-recurring UGC Grants to Universities

(Rupees in lakhs)

University	*III*	*Yearly*	*IV*	*V*	*Total*
Bhopal	—	—	—	10.00	10.00
Gwalior	—	—	6.20	1.00	7.20
Indore	—	0.25	10.00	6.30	16.55
Jabalpur	6.65	—	—	—	6.65
Raipur	—	10.00	5.10	—	15.10
Rewa	—	n.d.	—	—	—
Saugar	5.53	—	—	—	5.53
Vikram	4.21	—	1.11	0.80	6.12
Total	16.40	10.25	22.42	18.10	67.18

Source: Tejomurthy, 1991.

The Tables 6.89, 6.90 and 6.91 reflect the State of financial income for the universities in the State. University's allocation for libraries is on the lowest priority, as elsewhere in the country, and this not anything new about this State. Further, the recurring grants given by UGC, to supplement the State funds, for library management, are also inadequate. These recurring grants are for the purchase of books and periodicals.

What is glaring is the fact that each university follows its own pattern of funding for the libraries, some are as high as ten lakhs, and some are as low as meagre sum of eighty thousand!

Library Profession

Library Association

The formation of Madhya Pradesh Library Association, in 1957, has had important contribution which history has conveniently ignored.

Ranganathan was invited to Ujjain, as a Visiting Professor. During this visit, he helped formation of Madhya Pradesh Library Association. To find some suitable head for the new body, in line with the professional demands, Ranganathan set out in search of some personality who could be appropriate. In the person of the then Governor of MP, H.V. Patsaker, he did find a good leader. Patsaker accepted the offer and led the Association towards progress.

S.R. Ranganathan and his contemporaries felt important, that they must involve public, and leaders from the society. The reason for this involvement was to put the library movement on a firm footing. This has been the basis of many associations which our library leaders initiated in this country. An association by the profession, for the profession and of the profession, has no charm, no support from the public, and no outside influences to lead it towards progress. Such a historic lesson does not charm any more!

Apart from the MP Library Association, there is another important body, Madhya Pradesh College Librarians Association. Keeping in line with regional needs, Indore Library Association emerged. It did promote the publication of regional language material, including the quarterly serial, *Pustakalaya Sandesh*, started in 1967.

The scene today is really disturbing, according to the words of Late Prof. A. Tejomurthy, "Though the Madhya Pradesh Library Association exists in name, for all practical purposes, it is a defunct body. Though certain attempts at library legislation have been made in the State, no progress has been made . . . it is deplorable that there is no library association, worth the name, representing the whole State. Professional problems remain unsolved" (p. 125).

Coming to library education, there are eleven universities in the State, and the first to impact library science degree programme was Vikram University, in 1957. In addition to the attempts to train professionals at the university level, the public libraries at Bhopal and Gwalior, also offer certificate courses.

STATE: MAHARASHTRA

This is the land of Shivaji, Shirdi Sai Baba, Gateway of India, and Bollywood. Its capital, Bombay (now Mumbai), came to the British as dowry from the Portuguese in 1662. This tradition of goodwill still retains its colour in the huge goodwill the business dons extract—each time a site is rented out—at a unparalleled rate.

It is the third largest State in India, (lit. maha=big, rashtra=State). It was formed, in 1960, based on the territories of the then state, differently called, Greater Bombay, Bombay State and Bombay Presidency. Its literacy growth rate is visible from the figures, that it was better off comparatively, in 1951 at 13 per cent, 29.8 per cent in 1961; 39.2 per cent in 1971; 47.3 per cent in 1981; and 63 per cent in 1991—The literacy rate of males is 74.8 per cent and females is 50.5 per cent.

Its area is 3,07,690 sq. kms. The population density is 256 persons per sq. km. The sex ratio of the State is 936 females per 1000 males. The main language groups are as per 1981 Census: Marathi (72.9%); Urdu (6.8%); Hindi (6.6%); Gujarati (2.6%); Khandeshi (1.7%); Telugu (1.4%); Kannada (1.4%); Sindhi (0.8%). The religious groups according to 1981 Census are: Hindus (81.4%); Muslims (9.2%); Buddhists (6.2%); Jains (1.5%); Christians (1.2%); Sikhs (0.1%), etc.

Public Libraries

While the Directorate of public libraries is at the head of the State library system, however, it has a decentralized public library system—1 State central library, 6 regional libraries, and 8 district libraries. The State library is designated as a national depository under the Delivery of Books Act. The State Public Libraries Act, 1967 also, designated, two regional libraries (Pune and Nagpur) to act as depositories of all the publications of the State. Further the Act identified two other regional libraries (Nasik and Ratnagiri) as reference libraries.

Collection Development

The collection in the public libraries, has grown considerably, primarily because of the support the State provides, and also because of the RRLF funds, that have continuously supported the library development plans in the State, as they are doing all over the country. The Table 6.92 gives an idea of the level and patterns of growth of the collection in the public library system.

The figures in the Table 6.92 represent the collection in different public libraries in the State, as well as, the number of books that are received under the respective Acts.

Library Finance

The funding for these public libraries is primarily by the State, and additional support is from Raja Rammohun Library Foundation and

TABLE 6.92: Book Collection, as of March 1988

Libraries	*Number*	*Collection*
Govt. Divisional Library	5	5,53,744
Govt. District Library	8	2,32,648
Aided District Library	28	11,05,545
Aided Taluka Library	236	23,81,143
Other Aided Library	3,963	48,58,337
Central Library	1	
Press & Regn. of Books Act		2,07,024
Delivery of Books Act		3,33,749

Source: Chahande, 1991.

other sources. There are at the local level, registered societies, which raise funds, and appoint staff to acquire and maintain the reading materials. The State library system does get library cess, as other State eligible to get from the respective State acts.

Library Budget

The State budget for the libraries, plan and the non-plan are given below:

TABLE 6.93: Budget Estimates (Rs. in thousands) (1988-89)

Head	*Non-plan*	*Plan*	*Total*
(i)	30.59	1.00	31.59
(ii)	40.84	—	40.84
(iii)	142.34	7.06	149.40
Total	213.77	8.06	221.83

The (i), (ii), and (iii) heads or categories of the budget are the estimates for the three separate categories of the public library system, *viz*, (i) Directorate of Libraries, (ii) Government Divisional and District Libraries, and (iii) Assistance to Central, District and Taluka Libraries.

The source of income of the aided public libraries are Government grants, grants from local self-government, donation from charitable institutions and individual, and subscription from members. The income and expenditure, in terms of balance sheet, of the three types of libraries in the Table 6.94, clarifies the actual funds scenario.

TABLE 6.94: Statement of Accounts, 1987-88

(Rs. in lakhs)

Libraries	*Income*	*Expenditure*
District	53.88	42.05
Taluka	95.74	79.52
Village	165.36	156.40
Total	315.00	277.98

Library Expenditure

TABLE 6.95: Expenditure on Public Libraries in State (1986-87)

Expenditure (in lakhs)	*Population (in lakhs)*	*Per Capita (in Rs.)*	*Literacy % 1980s*
123.7	627.8	0.20	47.37

These figures, Table 6.95, are representative of what is the priority in the State for expenditure related to libraries. The State has grown in its socio-economic status and its industrial output is well advanced. And despite these developments the per capita of the State in the last decade stands at 28th place among all the States in the country.

Trends in Library development: To encourage the library development, the State has the following awards Dr. Babasaheb Ambedkar Award for the best public library; Dr. S.R. Ranganathan Grantha Mitra Award for best librarian, and Dr. B.R. Ambedkar Award for the best user. The last mentioned is instituted by a Public Trust, which manages the Garde Vachanalya, Buldana (Anil, 1996: 62).

To list more details, about the description of how and what of each public library, may be undesirable, but a glance at the set up would be relevant to give a feel of what is it.

Regional Library

Government Divisional Library, Mumbai Division, Nasik: Collection: 44,380 books,in languages, such as, Marathi, Hindi, and English, subscribes to 38 magazines, and 15 newspapers.

Services: Since it is designated as reference library, it does not lend books directly. It has however institutional membership, and to these it lends 50 books at a time. In addition to providing reference service, at no cost, it arranges book exhibitions, and cooperates in professional matters at the district level.

District Library

Sarvajanik Vachnalaya, Nasik, Nasik District: Founded in 1840, it is one of the oldest libraries in Nasik. It has 4,000 members (comprising life members, ordinary members, and children). This is recognised as 'A' type library at district level.

Collection: 1,35,000 books, including 6,000 rare titles (published between 1800 and 1930), 9,000 Mss, it also has a Museum attached.

Service: Reading facility, reference service; separate section for women and children; arranges exhibitions on topics, events, conducts seminars, debates, etc.

Taluk Library

Sinnar Sahakari Vachanalaya, Sinnar: Sinnar is 20 miles away from Nasik. This library is recognised as 'A' type library at taluk level. It has 500 members.

Collection: 20,000 books, subscribes to 58 magazines, and 14 newspapers.

Service: Reading room facility, provides separate section for women and children, organises weekly story-telling for children, organises library week celebrations, arranges a parade through the Taluk on its foundation day (which falls on the Ugadi Day), and to perform this, it collects donations, called as MUSHTI DAN (lit. handful gift).

Village Library

Gram Panchayat Sarvajanik Vachnalaya, Pimpalgaon (Basvant): This is a 'B' type library at the village (rural) level. It is 30 miles away from Nasik. Managed by Gram Panchayat (local government), the Library receives grant from the State. It also manages two branch libraries, and has a total membership of 650 members.

Collection: 15,380 books, subscribes to 80 magazines and 15 newspapers, all primarily in Marathi language Additionally, it has a special collection of Gazettes, published during 1800-1940.

Service: Offers a special section for women and children; maintains newspaper clippings on topics such as, gram panchayat, local agricultural practice, etc.

District Library

Buldana District Library, Buldana: It is identified as 'A' grade District Library, and is managed by the State Government. It has 1,289 members.

The Library offers training programme for Certificate course in library science, and provides consultancy and guidance for establishment of new libraries at the District level.

Collection: 25,000 books, subscribes to 45 magazines, and 22 newspapers.

Service: Reading room facility, book lending, reference service on demand and in anticipation; organises seminars, book exhibitions, and cultural programmes.

Taluk Library

Bharatiya Rashtrabhasha Pustakalaya: This is situated in Khamgaon Taluk, which is 80 miles away from Buldana. It is designated as 'B' grade library. It has 381 members.

Collection: 18,000 books, subscribes to 20 magazines, and 25 newspapers, all in Marathi language.

Service: Reading room facility, reference service on demand; separate sections for women and children.

Village Library

Saraswati Library, Paturda, Buldana District: Paturda is a village in the Sangrampur Taluk and is 100 miles away from Buldana. This library (*f.* 1967), has 350 members.

Collection: 17,000 books, subscribes to 25 magazines and 16 newspapers all in Marathi.

Service: Book lending reference service on demand; inter-library lending, maintains a separate sections for women and children.

Efforts for Enactment

1936 Bombay Presidency Public Libraries Bill—by S.K. Bole.

1945 Kolhapur State Public Libraries Act

1947 Public Libraries Bill for Bombay Province—by SRR

1959 Bombay State Public Libraries Bill—by M.V. Donde

1965 Maharashtra Public Libraries Bill—by Maharashtra Library Association

1967 Maharashtra State Public Libraries Act.

Academic Libraries

The development of academic libraries is comparatively better and systematic, in the urban areas, and less so in the rural area. For instance in the Vidarbha region, which includes the Nagpur district also, has major concentration of the developmental activities in the urban area of Nagpur. Nagpur has a well established university system, and Nagpur University (*f.* 1923) has led to considerable library development in the region. In the Vidarbha only in 1983, for all the nine districts, yet another university was established at Amravati. The slow progress for the development of academic activity is also reflected in the libraries attached to these academic institutions.

A glance at the state-of-the-art in terms of the college libraries is worth, to understand these further. A survey conducted by Dr. Baheti (1994), of the affiliated colleges of the two universities, namely, Amravati University and Nagpur University, reveal the results, which are discussed herein.

The college library must have adequate facilities, resources, and an environment congenial to permit the reading of library materials by the college user community. Bearing this ideal in mind, it is worth assessing the existing conditions of the college libraries in the Vidarbha region.

The collection that is acquired in the college libraries in this region, is depicted in the Table 6.96.

TABLE 6.96: Collection in the Libraries, 1991-1992

Books	*Libraries*
Upto 10,000	20
Upto 20,000	35
Upto 30,000	27
Upto 40,000	11
More than 40,000	7

The average size of these libraries then is, around 30,000. The normal collection is a college library is primarily of textbook type, and reference books hardly get a priority status, given the funding position in these libraries. Table 6.97 is given the fund status, which itself speaks of the collection development pattern that is possible in the given circumstances.

TABLE 6.97: Acquisition's Budget

Funds (in rupees)	*Libraries*
Upto 10,000	37
Upto 20,000	31
Upto 30,000	19
Upto 40,000	8
More than 40,000	5

On an average the annual budget, then for the acquisition of books, periodicals, etc., is only around 20,000. Given the high rate of inflation, increasing prices and increasing needs the question is how many reading materials can be acquired in this meagre amount?

The significant findings of the study are:

1. Relating to needs there is a great paucity of funds. This has led to inadequate collections;
2. The library staff, including the clerical and custodial, is inadequate, which is obvious in the inefficient management of the system, of the resources, and services to the clients;
3. The working hours of most are also inadequate, because of the reason that there is no money for employing more staff. Facilities for night study are lacking completely;
4. There is inadequate reading facility, and the arrangement of the reading rooms is very poor;
5. Provision of toilet, drinking water, canteen, etc., is simply non-existent in most of the cases; and
6. Virtually there is no provision for inservice training for the librarians.

TABLE 6.98: College Library Buildings

Type of Accommodation	*Libraries*
Separate building	26
Separate building, but performs multiple functions	30
No separate building, functions as part of college building	62
Without even proper reading rooms	50

The Table 6.98 indicates the trends, let alone the existence of functionally planned and designed library buildings, there are no separate library buildings, and not to mention of independent reading rooms that are lacking in these college libraries.

Special Libraries

The State has been lucky in having Bombay (now called Mumbai), as its State capital, which has many libraries, representing the different tastes and interests of the fields of sciences, social sciences and humanities.

The networking of a few special libraries, such as the IIT and the scientific libraries in Mumbai, has led to a separate network, which is working successfully.

Library Profession

Library associations are trying their best to promote the cause of professional advancement. A number of bodies have emerged in the State, and to name a few, these are: Maharashtra Library Association (*f.* 1921), Maharashtra Rajya Granthalaya Sangha (*f.* 1962), Marathwada Library Association (*f.* 1959), etc. The education for librarianship in the State started in 1943, at Bombay University, Poona took a lead in starting a course sponsored by the library association. There are as many as 17 centres offering certificate courses and seven universities offering higher degrees in the field of library and information science.

STATE: MANIPUR

It is the land of Loktak lake, and the Land lily, dancing deer on a floating sanctuary. Its capital is Imphal.

Manipur came under Japanese attack during the war, from 1942 to 1944. In 1949 the ruler, signed an agreement with the Government of India and thence the State was integrated with the Indian union. It was given a Part C status, as the Union Government was not in favour of accepting the recommendation of the States Reorganization Commission. It, however, became a Union Territory, as per the States Reorganization Act, 1956. Georgraphically, the State has three districts on the plains and five districts on the hills.

Among the newly formed States, Manipur, emerged in 1972, as an independent State, has 8 districts in its boundary. Its literacy stands at: 30 per cent in 1961; 32.9 per cent in 1971; 41.9 per cent in 1981; and 60.96 per cent in 1991—male literacy is 72.9 per cent and female is 48.6 per cent.

Its area is 22,327 sq. kms. The population density is 82 persons per sq. km. The sex ratio of the State is 961 females per 1000 males. The main language groups as per 1981 Census are: Manipur/Meithei (61.8%); Tangkhul (5.5%); Thado (4.0%); Mao (3.7%); Kabui (3.5%); Kuki (2.6%); Gorkha/Nepali (2.6%); Hmar (2.0%); Bengali (1.3%); Vaiphei (1.1%); Paita (1.0%); etc. The religious groups as per the 1981 Census are: Hindus (60.0%); Christians (29.6%); Muslims (7%); etc.

Public Libraries

The library development starts with the growth of the public library as an institution. The founding of the subscription based Imphal Public Library in 1938 (*Circa* 1940), and its being recognized by the State Darbar, laid to a beginning of the spirit of the public library.

In post-independent India, the establishment in the year 1958, of Manipur District Library (later named as State Central Library), led to a true beginning in this developmental process. Till 1980 all public library activity was under the administrative control of Directorate of School Education. But in 1980, with further advancement of the public libraries, the opening of many districts and local libraries, it was felt appropriate by the State Government to attach these public libraries under the Directorate of Arts and Culture.

Library Finance

The financial income of the public libraries is based on the plan and non-plan budget allocated by the State Government. The Table 6.99 gives an idea of the type of funding that the public libraries receive each year.

TABLE 6.99: Library Budget at a Glance

(Rs. in lakhs)

Year	*Plan*	*Non-plan*	*Total*
1984-85	200	238	438
1985-86	200	250	450
1986-87	300	352	652
1987-88	383	683	743
1988-89	475	300	775
1989-90	580	480	1,060

Source: Singh, 1993.

In the Table 6.99, there is no pattern, sometimes the plan amount exceeds the non-plan and *vice-versa.* The budget however is progressive, and this is an advantage. The figures, Table 6.99, also include the matching grants received from RRLF. The State's contribution has been increased from Rs. 15,000 in 1984-85, to Rs. 2 lakhs, in 1988-89. As per the RRLF guidelines, the amount is for distribution of books to libraries attached to clubs, voluntary organization, etc.

How much is being spent under the State grants and from the RRLF Book Assistance Scheme? This is shown in the Table 6.100.

TABLE 6.100: Development of Book Collection

Year	*Purchase of Books*		*RRLF Book Assistance*		*Gift*	
	Adult	*Child*	*Adult*	*Child*	*Adult*	*Child*
1984-85	367	146	89	27	—	—
1985-86	748	485	435	—	—	—
1986-87	1,385	640	403	—	108	—
1987-88	1,494	357	335	63	13	—
1988-89	941	488	50	—	5	—

Source: Singh, 1993.

From the Table 6.100 pattern of acquisition, it is obvious that, there is a regular inflow of books for the public use. It is also obvious that these funds are, by and large, being used very appropriately for users of all ages, the young and the old, alike. But what is not obvious is given the very little material available for the children in Indian regional languages, how much of the material that is bought for the child, is really useful for the child—the child who is brought up in the mother tongue alone, and for the child who is literate, but has no culture to read any books. May be more useful for this category of users are the non-book materials, which can entertain and provide information for a growing mind through different media. Are the policy makers aware of these alternatives? In the context of diversifying the acquisition of reading materials, it is pertinent to note that while RRLF funds the schemes for development of children's section and purchase of equipment, can be advised to consider these suggestions. It is more than 25 years that RRLF has been funding for books in these areas, and now it is probably appropriate to change the priorities. Even in the case of rural libraries where the print material is supposed to be acquired, under the RRLF assistance, it is worth considering these strategies, to satisfy the long awaited information needs to neo-literates as well as totally neglected user community non-literates.

Library Expenditure

The figures given in the Table 6.101 representative of what is the priority in the State for expenditure related to libraries. The State has grown in its socio-economic status and its industrial output is well advanced. And despite these developments the per capita of the State in the last decade stands at 13th place among all the States in the country.

A detailed analysis of the State's performance in wake of the enactment will be pertinent, but due to lack of data this is not attempted here.

TABLE 6.101: Expenditure on Public Libraries in States (1986-87)

Expenditure (in lakhs)	*Population (in lakhs)*	*Per Capita (in Rs.)*	*Literacy % 1980s*
15.0	14.2	1.05	41.91

Efforts for Enactment

1988 Manipur Public Libraries Bill

The public library development received some impetus, by the enactment of the Manipur Public Libraries Act, 1988.

Academic Libraries

As per the survey conducted in the Capital, Imphal, the situation of the schools is as follows.

The survey was aimed at finding out if there are libraries attached to schools in the urban area of the capital, and if there are how far are they developed and how well are they organized.

* There was hardly anything in most of the schools, which could be worth noting. The concept of library was missing.
* Most of the libraries have some collection but without room, furniture, clearly stated consultation hours, and budget.
* The annual budget of a fortunate higher secondary school, received from the Government, is totally Rs. 300.
* Some of the 'A' grade schools had the minimum facilities, which include, Central School, Sainik School, Public School, Navodaya School, and some missionary schools.

Such is the sad state of affairs. To help schools have their own libraries, the Manipur Library Association, has been recommending to all the concerned authorities that school libraries must be set up and maintained well in all schools.

Another body which is promoting the cause of school libraries is the Manipur Language Development Society (MALADES). It has recognised the impact of the school libraries for 'the rapid growth of Manipuri Language', which 'depends on its active use by the people of different places'. It has, therefore, been working with missionary zeal in opening

Manipuri medium schools and libraries wherever Manipuri speaking people are permanently settled.

Library Profession

The State had its first professional body, Manipur Library Association (*f.* 1987). The training programme for the State was started within the State at the university level in 1986. The training programme is also offered by the State Library—beginning in 1982—like many State libraries in the country.

STATE: MEGHALAYA

This is the land of the Khasis (a tribe of Austro-Asiatic stock). Jaintias and Garos (having Tibetan origins), music and festive dances, orchids, waterfalls and Cherrapunji (the wettest place in the world, with very heavy rainfall), and the land whose capital, Shillong, is called, 'Scotland of the East. Meghalaya (lit. megha=clouds; and alaya=home, home of clouds).

This is yet another State, like Manipur and other North-Eastern States, was also formed in 1972. The growth of literacy was 18.5 per cent in 1961; 29.5 per cent in 1971; 33.22 per cent in 1981; and in 1991 it is 48.62 per cent literacy rate of males is 51.5 per cent and females is 44.7 per cent.

Its area is 22,429 sq. kms. The population density is 78 persons per sq. km. The sex ratio of the State is 947 females per 1000 males. The main language groups are as per 1981 Census: Khasi (37.2%); Garo (23.5%); Bengali (7.0%); Gorkha/Nepali (3.6%); Hindi (1.7%); Assamese (1.3%). The religious groups as per 1981 Census are: Christians (52.6%); Hindus (18.0); Muslims (3.1.%); Buddhists (0.2%); Sikhs (0.1%); other tribals (25.8%).

Public Libraries

Library Expenditure

TABLE 6.102: Expenditure on Public Libraries in States (1986-87)

Expenditure (in lakhs)	*Population (in lakhs)*	*Per Capita (in Rs.)*	*Literacy % 1980s*
30.0	13.35	2.24	33.22

These figures, Table 6.102, are representative of what is the priority in the State for expenditure related to libraries. The State has grown in its socio-economic status and its industrial output is well advanced. And despite these developments the per capita of the State in the last decade stands at 2nd place among all the States in the country.

Like many of the recently emerged States, this State has to develop its professional body and programmes for training its librarians.

UNION TERRITORY: MIZORAM

This is the land of blue mountains, and deep valleys, cheraw (bamboo) dance and chheihlam. Mizo is a generic term meaning hillmen or highlanders.

Mizoram is the former Lushai Hills District of Assam State, which was formed in 1898 by the British Government. As per the North-Eastern Reorganization Act, 1972, it received status of a Union Territory in 1972, to be centrally administered, and after the Union Government signed a Memorandum of Settlement with Mizo National Front (MNF) in 1986; it got its independent statehood only in 1987. The literacy rate of the State is 81.23 per cent, just next to Kerala.

The male literacy in this State is 84.0 per cent and female literacy is 78.09 per cent. The primary reason for its high literacy is the missionary activity, which brought in its wake education. Mizo language has no script of its own. The missionaries introduced the Roman script for Mizo language and thereby promoted formal education. The Inner Line System introduced by the Crown, only missionaries through, resulting in a predominant Christian and highly illiterate population.

Its area is 21.081 sq. kms. The population density is 33 persons per sq. km. The sex ratio of the State is 924 females per 1000 males. The main language groups are as per 1981 Census: Lushai/Mizo (83.8%); Bengali (8%); Tripuri (4.0%); Laker (3.1%). The religious groups as shown in the1981 Census are: Christians (83.8%); Buddhists (8.1%); Hindus (7.1%); Muslims (0.4%), etc.

Public Libraries

Its public library history starts from 1969, with the starting of the first public library, at Aizwal, it was named as Sub-Divisional Library. A series of libraries were opened by the Government. The State recognised 83 village libraries managed by Young Mizo Association. This recognition led to receiving regular Government grants, as well as, the RRLF assistance.

The public libraries are presently under the control of the Education Department. The State Library is headed by a professional, whereas the other library heads are under the Education Department.

Library Finance

The total budget for public libraries in the State is Rs. 22 lakhs, as of 1987-88, and the matching fund received from RRLF was Rs. 1.45 lakhs.

Library Expenditure

TABLE 6.103: Expenditure on Public Libraries in States (1986-87)

Expenditure (in lakhs)	*Population (in lakhs)*	*Per Capita (in Rs.)*	*Literacy % 1980s*
10.0	4.93	2.02	54.91

These figures, Table 6.103, are representative of what is the priority in the State for expenditure related to libraries. The State has grown in its socio-economic status and its industrial output is well advanced. And despite these developments the per capita of the State in the last decade stands at 5th place among all the States in the country.

Efforts for Enactment

1980 Mizoram Public Libraries Bill—by State Library

1988 Mizoram Public Libraries Bill

The State library development finally got into the stage of an enactment of library bill, and in 1989, the Mizoram State Public Libraries Act, was passed by the State legislative assembly.

STATE: NAGALAND

This is the famous land of Angamis and the martial Semas, Kohimas (where Japanese, and the INA forces, during World War II, were stopped from what would have been otherwise leading to the conquest of India), Mount Tiyi, the mythical abode of departed souls.

It has a special history of secessionists, who resisted the move to join the Union Government, but were finally forced to surrender and this led to the formation of Union Territory status in 1957, followed by independent statehood in 1963.

It has in 1991 a literacy rate of 61.3 per cent—male literacy is 66.0 per cent and female literacy is 55.7 per cent. The official language of the State is English and the main language groups are based on the 16-odd tribes and sub-tribes each with their own dialect. Majority of the population, as per the 1981 Census, is Christians (80.2%); the other minorities are Hindus (14.3%); Muslims (1.5%); others (3.7%). Its area is 16,579 sq. kms. The population density is 73 persons per sq. km. The sex ratio of the State is 890 females per 1000 males.

Public Libraries

Library Expenditure

TABLE 6.104: Expenditure on Public Libraries in States (1986-87)

Expenditure (in lakhs)	*Population (in lakhs)*	*Per Capita (in Rs.)*	*Literacy % 1980s*
15.0	7.74	1.94	42.57

These figures, Table 6.104, as representative of what is the priority in the State for expenditure related to libraries. The State has grown in its socio-economic status and its industrial output is well advanced. And despite these developments the per capita of the State in the last decade stands at 7th place among all the States in the country.

STATE: ORISSA

This is land of Lord Jagannath, Konark and Chilika, Odissi and Keertan; the land of revival of Hinduism, spread of Buddhism under the Ashoka's conquest of Kalinga. It was given independent status of State in 1936, by the Crown, which was re-organised in 1949 after independence as retained its name as it is. The origin of the name is lost in the legends, but it was also called as Kalinga, Utkal, and Udra.

The first language of the State is Oriya, used by of 81.5 per cent and the other languages used are Telugu (2.3%); Hindi (2.3%); Santali (2%); Kuli (1.9%); Bengali (1.4%); Urdu (1.4%). Its literacy growth rate is 3 per cent in 1951; 21.7 per cent in 1961; 26 per cent in 1971; 34.1 per cent in 1981; and 58.5 per cent in 1991—literacy rate of males is 62.3 per cent and females is 34.4 per cent. Its area is 1,55,07 sq. kms. The population density is 202 persons per sq. km. The sex ratio of the State is 972 females per 1000 males. The religious groups as shown in the

1981 Census are: Hindus (95.4%); Christians (1.8%); Muslims (1.6%); Sikhs (0.05%); etc.

Public Libraries

The public libraries in the State are administered and maintained by the Department of Culture. In this Orissa has a different pattern, as against the general trend in the country's library system. It is appropriate to list the organizational structure of the State, which is as given below:

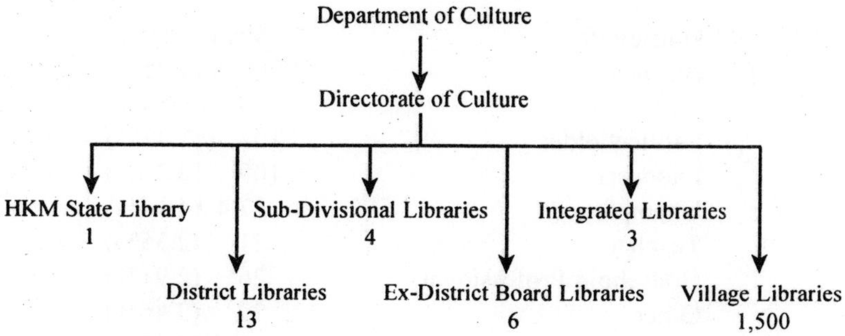

Under the Directorate of Culture, the HKM State Library is headed by a professional Director, and all the others are headed by an Assistant Director of Library.

The State Library (*f.* 1967), is the apex library in the State. It houses 86,000 volumes, and has 6,000 members. The State Library is headed by a professional librarian.

Interestingly, there are agencies which are providing library service in the State. The Department of Housing and Urban Development also renders public library service, through its 39 Municipalities which maintain library-cum-reading room facilities. The collection ranges between 500 to 10,000 volumes, and each subscribes to a good number of newspapers and magazines.

The Department of Information and Public Relations maintain Information Centre-cum-Reading Rooms. The aim is to acquaint the local residents about plans, policies, programmes of the Government and the schemes undertaken during the respective plan periods. A variety of books, journals, reports, etc., are made available for this dissemination of information. There are in all 69 such libraries, located in the 58 sub-divisions and other cities/towns of the State.

Community Information Service

A survey of 1,500 electorates, living in four zones of the Puri District, was undertaken to identify the willingness of the public to accept community advisory services through the libraries of the respective areas. The community services are aimed at providing information on day-to-day affairs.

Of the 1,500, 892 were interviewed on the subject. The respondents of the interview belonged to the categories as follows:

Housewife	389 (43.60%)
Business	100 (11.21%)
Cultivator	86 (9.64%)
Serviceholder	102 (11.43%)
Labourer	109 (12.21%)
Unemployed	37 (4.14%)
Teacher	21 (2.35%)
Household Professional	26 (2.91%)
Other	22 (2.46%)
Literate	487 (54.60%)
Illiterate	405 (45.40%)

The results of the survey are:

TABLE 6.105: Acceptance of the Service

Respondents	*Percentage*
Literates	89.93
Illiterates	64.69
Housewives	55.26
Fee based service	90.00

The interest in community related services, both by the literate and illiterate public is interesting outcome of the survey. Supposing if the public receives information about their daily survival needs, and that too at a price 90 per cent, of the public, as shown above are willing to pay the cost and receive the same. Are there any policy makers and decision makers aware of this high level of public interest?

Furthermore, except housewives, more than 90 per cent respondents indicated their desire to have such community services in their locality, Of those who were willing to pay for the service, were ready to even travel a distance upto three miles for such a service.

Thus there is a high potential for any innovative exercise on the part of public libraries! Are there any takers of this idea?

Library Finance

The Table 6.106 lists the budget allocation for three successive years.

TABLE 6.106: Budget Allocation for Public Libraries

Year	*Non-plan*	*Plan*	*RRLF Assistance*	*Total (Rs. in lakhs)*
1990-91	17.58	48.95	10.00	76.53
1991-92	20.59	39.21	10.00	69.80
1992-93	15.62	45.24	13.00	73.86

Source: Srichandan.

In addition to this allocation, the State has allocated Rs. 45 lakhs and 20 lakhs for the expenditures under the two respective departments, *viz.*, Information & Public Relations, and Department of Housing and Urban Development.

Library Expenditure

TABLE 6.107: Expenditure on Public Libraries in States

Year	*Expenditure (Rs. in lakhs)*	*Population (in lakhs)*	*Per Capita (in Rs.)*	*Literacy %*
1986-87	60.00	263.7	0.22	34.10
1992-93	138.86	315.0	0.44	58.50

These figures, Table 6.107, are representative of what is the priority in the State for expenditure related to libraries. The State has grown in its socio-economic status and its industrial output is well advanced. And despite these developments the per capita of the State in the last decade stands at 27th place among all the States in the country.

Presently the total expenditure on public library system in the State is higher, even the per capita expenditure of Re. 0.44 indicates the progress. This is appreciable improvement in a short period of time.

Efforts for Enactment

1974 Orissa Public Libraries Bill—by Prof. B.B. Shukla

The Utkal Library Association submitted a draft bill called 'Public Library Act for Orissa', in March.

1974 The Government showed no interest in its implementation.

1983 Orissa Public Libraries Bill (Revised)—Shukla. A group of professionals, after lapse of nine years from the date of the proposed bill, held discussions on the idea of updating the public library bill. The bill was revised and submitted to the State Government.

1983 Orissa Public Libraries Bill—Utkal Library Association

1982 Orissa Public Libraries Bill (Revised)—Shukla and Dr. P.K. Rath

1991 A State level conference was held on "Library legislation for Orissa and UGC pay scales for college and university librarians", on 2nd October, 1991. The aim was to recommend to the Government of Orissa for implementation of Public Library Act/Law in Orissa and enable maximization of the use of graphic records.

1992 The Government has formed a High Power Committee to analyse the details of the Draft Public Library Bill. The report of the Committee still awaits acceptance and none of these attempts have succeeded in getting the end result—library legislation in the State. The attempts by several library related agencies, societies, as well individual efforts by scholars, librarians, and leaders, have received no appreciation from the powers that be.

Academic Libraries

In the State, the academic libraries, are as deplorable as any other State. This is true here of all types of libraries. For instance, the school libraries are in a very neglected condition. A survey of 183 school libraries from four educational districts in Ganjam District, in 1990-91, reveals that the facts are all the same, *i.e.*, meagre funds, non-recognition of the value of library, rigid book selection pattern, etc. There are some exceptions, in the case of public schools.

The picture looks better in terms of collections these have. The collection in these surveyed libraries, ranges between 148 volumes to 35,983 volumes. Compared to "other developing countries (the total volumes in schools were) impressive. . . . Even the books per student was also very satisfactory. In smaller schools their ratio ranged from 1 : 5 to 1 : 9, whereas in larger schools their ratio increased to even from 1 : 11 to 1 : 18. But in comparison to the standards set in other countries, they were, however, found to be less" (Das and Mahapatra, 1994: 251).

Physical facilities are lacking in most of the school libraries. Most lacked separate reading rooms, the collection being stored in offices, meant for administrators, teachers, etc., or even in class rooms. Minority of the schools have a fixed library period of 35 minutes duration each week. There are some exceptions which have professionally trained staff, some have the facility of checking out books beyond school's working hours.

The survey highlights the following findings:

* the slenderness of the financial resources which are only for establishment and development of the school libraries;
* poor conception and imagination of the school administration about the value of libraries; and
* library consciousness in these education institutions is insufficient, improper, and uneven.

Library Profession

Library Association

Several library associations sprang up in the State. The Utkal Library Association (*f.* 1944), has been less active, as compared to the Orissa Association of Academic and Public Libraries (*f.* 1970).

Library Education

The education of the professionals in the State is offered in the following manner.

TABLE 6.108: Education for Librarianship

Name of the Course	*Institutions*
(1)	(2)
Certificate (duration 6 to 12 months)	(a) Institute of Lib. Sc. (since 1974-75) (b) Utkal Library Association (since 1978) (c) Affiliated College: SMIT Berhampur University (since 1984)
Diploma (2 years)	S.K.D.A.V. Women Polytechnic, Rourkela (since 1967-68)
Undergraduate level included in +2 level	NCERT's Institutes.
IA and BA stage	S.B. Women's College, Cuttack
Bachelor's Degree (1 year)	(a) Sambalpur University (since 1976-77)

(*Contd.*)

TABLE 6.108 (*Contd.*)

(1)	(2)
	(b) Pandit Nilkantha College (1981-82)
	(c) Affiliated College: SMIT (since 1984-85)
Bachelor's Degree (Correspondence)	IGNOU Centre
Master's Degree (1 year)	(a) Utkal University (since 1983-84)
	(b) Affiliated Colleges: SMIT
Master's Degree (Correspondence)	IGNOU Centre
Ph.D.	Utkal University
D.Litt	Utkal University
Inservice training/short term courses	(a) Libraries
	(b) Documentation Centres
	(c) Library Associations

Note: Since Orissa is one of the few States, which has started library science at the undergraduate level, it is appropriate to view some of the course details. the post-metric, or plus two level, two years diploma course deals with general subjects, like English, MIL, and general knowledge, in addition to theory and practice about library and information science. The National Council of Educational Research and Training, New Delhi, has prepared a vocational course in library science at the plus 2 level. The course prescribes 1500 marks, and a teaching programme of 2400 hours for the entire period. The Department of Education, Orissa, introduced this course in eight Higher Secondary Schools, but in 1992, it discontinued the same. Presently, the SCERT, Orissa, has constituted a Text Book Development Committee, for preparing course material in Oriya. The course thus prepared, has ten papers, each paper of 100 marks. By its external outlook, though it must be far better, it looks like the contents of a certificate course. The papers prescribed include: (1) organization and administration (theory and assignment); (2) classification theory; (3) classification practice; (4) cataloguing theory; (5) cataloguing practice; (6) reference service theory; (7) reference practice; (8) English; (9) MIL; and (10) Basic Foundation Course.

Utkal University started a course at the degree (or +3 level), in library science, as a pass and also as Honours subjects. The pass course contains 4 papers of 100 marks each, which includes (1) fundamentals of libarianship; (2) cataloguing theory; (3) classification; and (4) cataloguing practice, etc.

The Honours course, has in addition to the above four papers, the following: (5) reference service; (6) documentation and information science; (7) bibliography and book selection; (8) documentation and reference practical.

The above scenario of educational programmes at different levels speaks amply about the provision for education for librarianship in the State. What is not ascertained here is the intensity and extensity of the training programmes, how far the programmes make the workmanship more effective and efficient. These questions require extensive research which is not attempted here.

UNION TERRITORY: PONDICHERRY

This State joined the Indian Union in 1954, and in 1962 it received the status of Union Territory. Its official language is Tamil. Also used as official languages are Telugu, Malayalam, English and French. This multiplicity is because the four districts which it has, had been formerly under Kerala, Tamil Nadu, and Andhra Pradesh. Its literacy rate in 1991 is 74.91 per cent—male literates are 83.9 per cent and female are 65.7 per cent.

Its area is 429 sq. kms. The population density is 1,605 persons per sq. km. The sex ratio of the State is 982 females per 1000 males. The main language groups are as per 1981 Census: Tamil (88.4%); Malayalam (5.1%); Telugu (3.9%). The religious groups are: Hindus (85.5%); Christians (8.2%); Muslims (6.0%); etc.

Public Libraries

Library Expenditure

TABLE 6.109: Expenditure on Public Libraries in States (1986-87)

Expenditure (in lakhs)	*Population (in lakhs)*	*Per Capita (in Rs.)*	*Literacy % 1980s*
15.0	6.04	2.48	45.71

These figures, Table 6.109, are representative of what is the priority in the State for expenditure related to libraries. The State has grown in its socio-economic status and its industrial output is well advanced. And despite these developments the per capita of the State in the last decade stands at 1st place among all the States in the country.

Academic Libraries

The recently established Pondicherry University has many faculties and the library is on a rapid growth. Like Goa, Delhi and other places, this City-State is dependent on its neighbouring States, rather than having its own independent institutions of higher learning.

STATE: PUNJAB

Its distinction lies in being the land of the Golden Temple, Bhakra and Baisakhi, Bhangra and sarsonv da saag (curry of mustard oil). Golden Temple appeared in news when the Government under Prime Minister Indira Gandhi, forcibly entered its precincts, and thereby attempted to quell the terrorist movement.

The name Punjab is derived on the five rivers (punj=five, ab=water) that flow in this region. The official language of the State is Punjabi. The main language groups in the State are Punjabi (84.5%); Hindi (14.5%); Urdu (0.1%); Dogri (0.1%). The religious groups are (1981 Census): Sikhs (60.7%); Hindus (36.9%); Christians (1.1%); Muslims (1%); and others.

Its area is 50,362 sq. kms., its capital is Chandigarh, its population density is 401 persons per sq. km. Its literacy growth was 3 per cent in 1951; 24 per cent in 1961; (till then this figure included Haryana—now an independent State); 33.7 per cent in 1971; 40.7 per cent in 1981; and 57.1 per cent in 1991—male literates are 63.6 per cent and female are 49.7 per cent.

Political axe fallen on this State many a times. In 1947 it was divided into East Punjab and West Punjab, the former remained in India, and the latter became a part of Pakistan. The East Punjab was divided into three provinces, *viz.*, Himachal Pradesh, PEPSU and Punjab. While PEPSU and Punjab together were declared in 1956 as Punjab State, the province of Himachal Pradesh and Punjab were again reorganized in 1966, resultingly, there emerged, *viz.*, the State of Haryana and the Union Territory of Chandigarh. The States of Himachal Pradesh and Punjab were reduced in size, by this reorganization. And this whole mix-up resulted in Chandigarh being declared as the capital of Punjab as well as Haryana,

The State is divided into 14 districts, 110 towns, 10 cities, 118 blocks, and 12,342 villages. Nearly 70 per cent of the population is engaged in agriculture, and yet the State is advanced in industrialization, more so in terms of the development of small scale industries.

Public Libraries

Punjab library movement, has the Punjab Carnegie, in the person of Dayal Singh Majithia, who set the Dayal Singh Library in Lahore, in 1908 for the benefit of the common people. Such individuals, though not many, include Sir Ganga Ram who made history by establishing Sir Ganga Ram Commercial Library (*f.* 1921), in Lahore, which aimed at providing library services to commercial institutions, like banks, industry, as so on. Lala Lajpat Rai was instrumental in the founding of Dwarka Das Library, (*f.* 1921), in Lahore, which was meant for the public. The more deserving name of Dr. M.S. Randhawa, cannot be omitted here, who promoted the cause of establishment of panchayat and rural libraries in the State. Except for the last person, most of these were part of the pre-independence library movement.

Punjab public library system has its origins in the Punjab Public Library (*f.* 1884), in Lahore. The library was managed by a committee of 23 members, appointed by the Punjab Government. The users were of three types; life members, annual subscribers, and the visitors who used the reading room, free of charge. Incidentally, it was in this State, probably only next to Bengal, the Government invested in establishing and maintaining village libraries, in the early decades of the present century.

Due to the pressures from the public, the State Government in 1950, set up a Central Library Committee and some District Library Committees. Apart from the growth of a few libraries in number, not much has been achieved in terms of library legislation, library development, and so on.

TABLE 6.110: Number of Libraries in Each District

District	*Municipal Libraries*	*Districts Libraries*
Ambala	11	1
Amritsar	6	—
Bhatinda	7	—
Dharamshala	—	1
Ferozepur	10	—
Gurdaspur	10	1
Hoshiarpur	7	—
Hissar	5	1
Jalandhar	5	1
Kangra	2	—
Kapurthala	2	—
Kamal	9	—
Kulu	1	—
Ludhiana	5	—
Mahendergarh	2	—
Naranul	—	1
Patiala	8	1
Sangrur	6	1
Shimla	1	—
Total	97	8

A glance at the number of libraries in each district is appropriate here. The Table 6.110 lists the number of libraries in each of the 17 districts, as of 1966, before Shimla was made the capital of the State of Himachal Pradesh.

At the helm of the State affairs relating to the library system of the public services, the State established the Central State Library, in 1956, at Chandigarh. The library has a vast resource of books, manuscripts, etc. A break up of the manuscript collection indicates the variety:

TABLE 6.111: Collection of Manuscript in Central State Library

Language	*Collection*
Hindi & Sanskrit	687
Persian	1,122
Panjabi	907
Others	243

Its rare collection is the real resource, having some rarities like, Jain Vipak Sutra, which is 800 years old, dating back to 1216 Brahmi; Siasat Nama; etc.; for which even foreign scholars reach this library—one scholar from Oxford University came to use Siasat Nama (Singh & Satija, 1994: 237).

Library Expenditure

TABLE 6.112: Expenditure on Public Libraries in State (1986-87)

Expenditure (in lakhs)	*Population (in lakhs)*	*Per Capita (in Rs.)*	*Literacy % 1980s*
30.0	167.8	0.18	40.71

These figures, Table 6.112, are representative of what is the priority in the State for expenditure related to libraries. The State has grown in its socio-economic status and its industrial output is well advanced. And despite these developments the per capita of the State in the last decade stands at 29th place among all the States in the country.

Efforts for Enactment

1962 Punjab Public Libraries Bill—by R.L. Mittal

1962 Punjab Public Libraries Bill—by Punjab Library Association

1992 Public Libraries Bill—prepared on the basis of the Model Act of Dr. Venkatappaiah

Academic Libraries

The repeated reorganization of the State had its effects on the academic libraries too. The first university library in the State was established in 1882 (Punjab University, Lahore) and its library was set up in 1915. The growth of the university libraries in the States is as shown in the Table 6.113.

TABLE 6.113: Collection *versus* Use

University Library	*Collection (in lakhs)*	*Periodicals*	*Members*	*Books Borrowed (in lakhs)*
(a)	6.0	1,500	13,500	3.0
(b)	2.5	—	—	—
(c)	2.0	1,500	3,800	0.9
(d)	2.0	—	—	—

Source: Bansal and Tikku.

TABLE 6.114: Services at a Glance

University Library	*Compilation/Editing Service*					*User Education*
	Biblio-graphy	*New Addi. List*	*Indexing*	*Abstrac-ting*	*CAS*	
(a)	no	yes	no	no	no	no
(b)	no	yes	no	no	no	no
(c)	yes	yes	yes	yes	no	yes
(d)	no	yes	yes	yes	no	no

Source: Bansal and Tikku.
Note: (a) Punjab University, Chandigarh (*f.* 1983) (includes Punjab University Extension Library, Ludhiana); (b) Punjab University, Patiala (*f.* 1983); (c) Punjab Agricultural University, Ludhiana (*f.* 1981); (d) Guru Nanak Dev University, Amritsar (*f.* 1983).

As the Table 6.114 figures, based on a survey of the statewide network of university libraries, in 1991, by Bansal and Tikku, the university libraries have a low profile, in terms of their collection, use and services. An exception in providing services, the lead taken by Agricultural University, is not surprising, rather it is the scientific and technological institutions in the country that have taken the lead to provide all services and be modernized in their overall outlook and performance as well. The Agricultural library has a lead in providing user education, or as some call it bibliographical instruction. In fact all academic libraries, and more so university libraries were expected to provido this service, but as seen in Table 6.114, only one library offers it! The teaching function of the university library is more so in teaching the users how to use, and in fulfilling this objective of the academic enterprise, the university libraries have by and large failed, and this is not the sole representation in this State, it is a national failure.

College Libraries

According to a survey of college libraries in the State of Punjab carried by Arora (1994), 145 colleges were respondents, and the data reveals the following. The collection in these colleges varies from 500 to 50,000. The ranges is seen in the Table 6.115, where the average collection of the responding 122 colleges, is around 30,000.

TABLE 6.115: Collection Size in College Libraries

Libraries	*Collection*
33	upto 10,000
61	upto 30,000
22	upto 50,000
6	more than 50,000

As per the survey the colleges have their subscriptions equally divided into two, general magazines and research and scholarly periodicals. The figures in the Table 6.116 describe the trends, in terms of the subscription patterns of these college libraries:

TABLE 6.116: Periodical Subscription

Type of Periodicals	*Libraries*
Popular magazines	131
Research journals:	
Indian	108
Foreign	40

The present century made reading and assimilation of information easier and simpler, by the introduction of non-book reading sources, including audio-visual materials. The college libraries in the State have also stepped into the world of non-book aids, and the Table 6.117 shows the patterns that exists in acquiring such non-book materials.

TABLE 6.117: Non-book Materials

Availability	*Collection*
Available	27
Not available	52
No response	66

Providing reading materials is a part of the library service, but more important is making the resources available and keeping the doors open to the community of users. The college libraries have different working hours, ranging from mere four hours in a day to more than 8 hours of working schedule. Mere four hours is a distinct status of all such institutions which have less awareness of the need as well the potential value of the library. The Table 6.118 shows that most of these libraries work for 6 or less hours each day. Whereas the working hours of all colleges are normally more than 8 hours a day—for instance the college office, laboratory and other departments are expected to put in a work hour of no less than 8 hours each day.

TABLE 6.118: Working Hours of Libraries

Libraries	*Hours*
53	4
40	6
27	8
2	more than 8

The working hours are a part of the user services, and so also are the other public service activities. Table 6.119 shows the trends in providing the respective service, and the type of methods adopted in saving the time of the readers. The table indicates that the reference service is existing in a few colleges, so also is the user education. Xeroxing is more common service, and this facility is more important given the advantage it has in document delivery process. In terms of methods adopted in fulfilling the service objectives, providing user education is as important as is the adopting of issue methods, in terms of saving the time of the users. Register method is most common method of recording the issues of books to all methods, which has its own advantages and disadvantages in the operational procedures.

The size of the staff that work in each library speak of the attitude of the management in terms of priority towards maintenance and upkeep

TABLE 6.119: User Services

Reference		*User Education*		*Xerox*		*Issue System*		
Yes	*No*	*Yes*	*No*	*Yes*	*No*	*Browne*	*Register*	*Passbook*
25	85	20	95	90	55	38	87	20

of the library as an institution. Table 6.120 shows that most libraries have only two or three librarians, and more have not more than 4 or 5 librarians. The range of staff in these libraries varies between 1 and 18, and this variety of numbers in college libraries shows how much could the input from the staff could be if there are fewer staff, and how much it could be if there are enough staff. If 46 libraries are maintained by 3 staff, then it is easy to infer the kind of services that can be offered, and the nature of duties these three will be expected to perform. In short, the three staff will be spending more time in technical routines and will be left with no time for public services, or for that matter, to render any sort of personalized reference service.

TABLE 6.120: Staff Size

Total Staff	*Libraries*
1	4
2	24
3	46
4	16
5	16
6	5
7	6
8	1
9	1
10—15	4
More than 15	2

"The investigations reflect that the college libraries in Punjab are low on performance scale specially in regard to non-book material, subscription of journals, reprographic services, reference services, stock verification, user education, maintenance and documentation. The librarians are also professionally inert as per modern library standards. They lack motivation for participation in research oriented professional activities" (p. 272).

The reasons for this slackness are listed as follows:

1. Absence of library committee for all purposes;
2. Lack of funds;
3. The management is not interested in library development;
4. Faculty has not library oriented;
5. Librarians have no professionalism;
6. Inservice training is missing;
7. Required working hour schedule is not followed;
8. Absence of proper infrastructure;
9. Librarians are made to perform non-library tasks; and
10. Syllabi and teaching in the college is not library oriented.

Special Libraries

Apart from traditional references to special libraries, that this State has in many varieties, a most significant library does exist here. It is unique in its aim and collection. This is the Sikh Reference Library, attached to the Sikh History Society (both founded in 1945), aimed at collecting all relevant material under one roof, for the easy and convenience of the concerned scholar and lay alike. Its aim was to be a, non-lending, reference collection. It is located in the Golden Temple, and intends to make available to any one desiring to study the subject, all types of resources in the field—books, records, deeds, paintings, arms, etc. Unfortunately, the library was destroyed in the Operation Bluestar, in 1984. There are attempts to resurrect it.

Library Profession

Library Association

The Punjab Library Association, originally founded in 1916, retained its spirit, in one form or the other, even after the partition of the State in the post-independent era. This spirit has been manifested in different times, with degrees varying from regular activities to irregular initiative. For instance, it soon got rehabilitated in 1984, with its headquarters at Simla and it organised book fairs, library seminars, and so on. With the emergence of the new capital, Chandigarh, the headquarters of the Association was also shifted to Chandigarh. Its revival in 1957 led to the publication of Punjab State Library Service Year Book, during the years 1957 to 1962. In another spirit of activism the Association led a series of activities, and among other activities it instituted meritorious Library Service Awards for outstanding librarians. This example was later taken up by Indian Library Association—which confers the Best Librarian Award—and so also by other professional bodies.

Library Education

Library movement received a great impetus from the formal and informal training programmes that are offered in the universities and other institutions. The leading institution, since the beginning of the century, has been Punjab University, which has again the distinction of having the first library school in the post-independent Punjab, commencing from 1960. The other two school of library and information studies, are at Guru Nanak Dev University at Amritsar, and Punjabi University at Patiala. These annually train 80 librarians with Bachelor's, about 35 with Master's, and a few doctoral degrees.

STATE: RAJASTHAN

It is the land of pink city, lake cities, Pushkar and Teej, camels and desert festivals, also the land of Ajmer's Saint palaces, and Mount Abu. This State has its name derived from the former State Rajputana, (lit abode of rajas). The Government of India has continued to have, the former capital city Jaipur, as its capital.

Its area is 3,42,239 sq. kms. Its population density is 128 persons per sq. km. Its official language is Hindi. The main language groups as per 1981 Census are as follows: Hindi (89.6%); Urdu (2.1%); Punjabi (2.1%); Sindhi (0.8%); Gujarati (0.1%). Its main religious groups according to 1981 Census are: Hindus (89.3%); Muslims (7.2%); Jains (1.8%); Sikhs (1.4%); Christians (0.2%); Buddhists (0.01%), etc. Its literacy rate has grown from 3 per cent in 1951; 15 per cent in 1961, 19 per cent in 1971; 25 per cent in 1981; and 38.8 per cent in 1991—male literacy is 55.07 per cent and female 20.84 per cent.

Public Libraries

The reorganization of the State, in 1949, necessitated the streamlining of library development programmes. In 1953-54, that is the First Five Year Plan period, there was a reorganization of the public library set-up under the direct responsibility of the Department of Education. During the Second Five Year, 1955-56, thirty new libraries were established, including, a State Central Library, five regional libraries (with travelling libraries), and 24 district libraries. In the Third Five Year period the public libraries were redesignated as divisional, district and tahsil libraries. There was no development worth mentioning in the Fourth and Fifth Plan periods.

A survey by Nandwana reveals that "major part (more than 75%) of the collections in public libraries are fictions" (1996: 158).

According to a survey done by Vyas (1994), the public library system in the State has "undergone superfluous and marginal changes" in the last four decades. Further, "there has been no perceptible change in the public library system except that their names have been changed from Regional Libraries to Divisional Libraries and headquarters from Bikaner to Jaipur. This has rather created more confusion" (p. 257).

Even in the 7th Plan period there is not much of library development in the State, though this Plan period is supposed to be more involved in the development of libraries.

Library Finance

If libraries are important, the question is how important are these in the society. If formal education is a must for the development of society, how much in informal education centres like libraries, are important. A glance at the comparison of the grants for education and libraries in the State is pertinent in this context (Table 6.121).

TABLE 6.121: Comparison of Budgets

(Rs. in lakhs)

Year	*Education*		*Public Libraries*		*% of Education for Public Libraries*
	% State Budget	*Amount*	*% State Budget*	*Amount*	
1984-85	1.29	0.29	22.42	37.58	0.1292
1985-86	1.51	0.32	21.56	41.52	0.1274
1986-87	1.91	0.40	20.96	45.79	0.1138
1987-88	2.49	0.45	18.06	49.08	0.1089
1988-89	2.36	0.51	21.76	52.82	0.1027

Source: Sharma & Sharma.

The gradual progress in the annual outlay for education is not even matching with what is meant for public libraries—rather the educational budget is going up, and contrarily the public library budget is constantly declining! Is the policy making body unaware that informal education is the fashion of the day, and any decrease or even stagnation in the spending in this direction is harmful to the healthy development of the society.

Library Expenditure

Interestingly, the State had no clear budget for libraries. The picture became evident only later, with the increasing pressures for library legislation. The budget that was made available for library development, however, has been as follows, as per the survey by Mohan Rao.

TABLE 6.122: Budget for Library

Year	*Expenditure (in Rs.)*	
1950-51	18,00,000	(government and non-government libraries)
1956-57	3,00,000	(only government libraries)
1970-71	10,00,000	(only government libraries)
1985-86	41,52,000	(government and non-government libraries)
1986-87	1,20,00,000	(government and non-government libraries)

The figures given in Table 6.122 have, despite their non-systematic coverage, a growth pattern in funding for libraries. This is interesting given the irony that the State does not have a library legislation to support the development of libraries. This may be yet a meagre sum given the un-systematic development of libraries, lack of a clear policy on spending for different areas in developing a useable library system, and more than all this the lack of material that is available in a low literacy State such as Rajasthan. Indian public libraries are yet to come to terms with fulfilling the needs of neo-literates and non-literates. All the orientation as of this day in the country is towards providing reading material that is suitable only for the literates.

The Table 6.123 displays the comparative picture of library expenditure—making it obvious that this State is no exception in the per capita expenditure as well:

TABLE 6.123: Expenditure on Public Libraries in States (1986-87)

Expenditure (in lakhs)	*Population (in lakhs)*	*Per Capita (in Rs.)*	*Literacy % 1980s*
120.0	342.6	0.35	25.00

The sanctioned amount was increased in the year, 1986-87, to meet the regular expenditures, as well as, for the establishment of three district libraries in the State. The figures in the Table 6.123 are representative of priority in the State for expenditure related to libraries. The State has grown in its socio-economic status and its industrial output is well advanced. And despite these developments the per capita of the State in the last decade stands at 21st place among all the States in the country.

A further glance at the growth details in the Table 6.124, demonstrate the trends that the State, like all other States, in the country needs to make the growth and development a planned affair, rather than leaving it to winds.

TABLE 6.124: Growth and Development a Planned Affair

Year	*Expenditure on books (Rs.)*	*Staff*	*Registered Members*	*Visiting Readers*
1956-57	1,60,000	200	5,600	4,49,000
1969-70	3,88,000	240	11,000	12,50,000

In a period of 12 years that the table provides the figures, the growth of the book expenditure, members and visitors have all doubled. What has remained least important is the size of the staff. If staff, books and users are the three cornerstones of the library, how can two progress and one remain of least interest?

Efforts for Enactment

1965 Rajasthan Public Libraries Bill—by Rajasthan Library Association.

1969 The government accepted the memorandum submitted by the Association, containing the proposal of the Public Libraries Bill. The Administrative Department was asked to prepare the Draft Bill. The assistance in this regard was provided by N.N. Gidwani and Mohan Rao. The draft bill was sent to Legal department for further assessment. But the result of this was the usual game of postponement.

1972 Public Library Act—Draft Bill.

1990 Rajasthan Public Libraries Bill—by K.M. Ujlambkar

1991 Rajasthan Public Library—Revised draft bill submitted by the Committee constituted under the Chairmanship of Prof. S.N. Srivastava.

Despite these series of attempts and assurances by the State, there has been no Library Act, that can regulate the working of the public library system. There is also a proposal, kept in pending by the government for creating a separate directorate of libraries in the State. All these efforts are hindered by the political imbalance the State has been facing, with more recent changes in the governmental machinery.

Academic Libraries

This State has one of the old universities—Rajasthan University (*f.* 1947) but it has no catalogue! In this it ranks first in the country for having a full-fledged university library system without any proper access and control mechanism.

Library Profession

Library Association

The establishment of the Rajasthan Library Association (1962), resulted in the series of attempts at raising the issue of library legislation at appropriate levels, but led to no results. The State had a constant financial limitations as a reason for lack of any movement in this regard. Professionally, this State has been a very active State, and has taken a lead in preparing a sense of professionalism. It has had many leaders who directed the course of action of professionals who spread all over, not only in India, but also abroad.

The training programme for librarians however took some time to get started, and this is an interesting fact, given the kind of leaders and stalwarts, the State has produced. The first training programme was offered by the State Government in 1956. It was only in 1961 that the Rajasthan University started a degree course.

STATE: SIKKIM

This is the land of Kanchenjunga, snowleopards, and red pandas. Its name, Sikkim, owes its origin to some legend.

Its area is 7,096 sq. kms. The population density is 57 persons per sq. km. The sex ratio of the State is 880 females per 1000 males. The literacy rate of males is 64.34 per cent and females is 47.23 per cent. The main language groups as per 1981 Census are: Gorkha/Nepali (60.9%); Lepcha (7.0%); Bhotia (6.8%); Lumbu (5.6%); Hindi (4.7%); and Sherpa (3.3%). The religious groups are (as per 1981 Census): Hindus (67.2%); Buddhists (28.7%); Christians (2.2%); Muslims (1.0%).

Public Libraries

Library Expenditure

TABLE 6.125: Expenditure on Public Libraries in States (1986-87)

Expenditure (in lakhs)	*Population (in lakhs)*	*Per Capita (in Rs.)*	*Literacy % 1980s*
5.0	3.16	1.58	34.05

These figures, Table 6.125, are representative of what is the priority in the State for expenditure related to libraries. The State has grown in its socio-economic status and its industrial output is well advanced. And despite these developments the per capita of the State in the last decade stands at 9th place among all the States in the country.

STATE: TAMIL NADU

This is the land of Bharata Natyam and Carnatic Music, Kanyakumari and Rameswaram, Pongal, sambar and dosa.

This State was named as Madras State. The new State then, Madras State, was based on the areas that came under the Madras Province and Madras Presidency, but lost much to the neighbouring States in the re-organization of the States.

Its area 1,30,058 sq. kms. The population density is 428 persons per sq. km. The sex ratio of the State is 972 females per 1000 males. The main language groups as per 1981 Census are: Tamil (84.7%); Telugu (8.2%); Kannada (2.3%); Urdu (1.7%) and Malayalam (1.2%). The religious groups are (1981 Census): Hindus (88.8%); Christians (5.7%); Muslims (5.2%); Jains (0.1%); etc. The literacy has grown from 18 per cent in 1951 (included in this is Malabar District, later the district was transferred under Kerala State); 31 per cent in 1961; 39.5 per cent in 1971; 45.78 per cent in 1981; and 63.7 per cent in 1991—rate of male literacy is 74.8 per cent and females is 52.2 per cent.

Public Libraries

The public library development in the State has been historic in one single sense, that it received all the required attention and efforts of Ranganathan. The Madras Public Libraries Act, 1948, was the first public library act in free India. The Act, though had many shortcomings, nevertheless has led to remarkable progress of the public libraries in a number of ways.

TABLE 6.126: Growth of Libraries

Type of Library	*1980s*	*1990s*
State Central Library	1	1
District Central Libraries	14	22
Branch Libraries	1,440	1,531
Mobile Libraries	n.d.	9
Part-time Libraries	n.d.	999

Hierarchically under the District libraries are Branch Libraries, Circle Libraries, Mobile Libraries, and Part-time Libraries.

According to Ramesh Babu the figures of Branch Libraries includes the number of Circle libraries, that the Government established in the City of Chennai. These are working administratively under the District Library. The idea of Circle libraries is a decade old, and the State has been successful in running 6 such circle libraries in the city, to meet the needs of the 150 divisions of the corporations, proportionately. These circles libraries collect their own deposits and check out books.

A word of what is part-time libraries is not out of place. Since bulk of the material in the public libraries is unused, it was decided by the Directorate of Public Libraries to open part-time libraries, in villages having no public library system around. Hence the part-time libraries were initiated as outreach services.

Since such a service without local support would be less effective, it was decided that to ensure local participation each intending part-time library of the village has to fulfil the following four conditions:

(a) five to ten cents of land to be registered with the concerned Local Library Authority;
(b) to provide rent-free building;
(c) to provide Rs. 2,000 cash or furniture worth Rs. 2,000; and
(d) enroll at least 100 members.

The success of the scheme is visible in the nearly1,000 libraries flourishing in the State. Some such libraries are more popular than the regular public libraries. One instance of this popularity is seen in the part-time library at Athipatti village, in the Kamarjar District, established in 1990, it has 1,050 members, the public contributed 5 cents of land, built a structure worth 1.75 lakhs, to house this part-time library. Not only this, they contribute by subscribing to magazines, donate books, etc. A weekly magazine which is purchased for domestic use, is read at home, on the first day of its publication, and the next day it reaches the library shelf. Under this type of generosity, this village library has books worth Rs. 7 lakhs and journals worth Rs. 3.20 lakhs.

Another attempt to promote library interests in the public in the State, has been in terms of the Government introducing the programme of enrolling friends or patrons for each and every library. Under this scheme one who pays Rs. 1,000 to any public library is enrolled as a 'Patron' of that library. The amount so collected is deposited as a long term deposit, and the interest that accrues is used for subscription to journals of the Patron's choice and supplied to library under his seal. This scheme has benefited the entire public library system in the State. In 1992-93, the public library system had more than 4,500 patrons in all. One patron donated Rs. 1,00,000 to the Connemara Public Library under this scheme.

TABLE 6.127: Population and Literacy

Year	*Population (in lakhs)*	*Literacy*	*Total Books (in lakhs)*	*Literate Users*	*Registered Borrowers (in lakhs)*
1980	483	45.78%	85	0.51	294
1990	556	63.72%	162	n.d.	397

Source: G. Ranganathan.
n.d. = No data available.

The Table 6.127 displays the rate of increase in literacy in the State *vis-a-vis* the growth of the library system in the State. How far the literates are using the library is visible from the above, but how far the neo-literates and non-literates are able to get from these public resource centres is worth assessing, which is not attempted here.

What has been the trends in providing service to the users and what has been the proportion of the growth of the system in terms of increase in collection, users, staff, etc. The Table 6.128 indicates these at length for a decade.

Pattern of Table 6.128 reflects on the stagnant *versus* active growth in the State library system. The stagnant areas are service units, and number of staff who are expected to be at the helm of the affairs—which have remained constantly the same for all the years, the active areas are visible in the regular increase in the collection, use and users size. The

TABLE 6.128: Growth of the Library System

1	*2*	*3*	*4*	*5*	*6*	*7*	*8*	*9*	*10*
1972-73	n.d.	n.d.	45	n.d.	n.d.	n.d.	n.d.	n.d.	n.d.
1973-74	n.d.	n.d.	58	n.d.	n.d.	n.d.	n.d.	n.d.	n.d.
1974-75	1,456	3,671	53	150	60	5	67	270	106
1975-76	1,456	3,809	59	152	58	6	71	290	159
1976-77	1,456	3,742	102	195	61	6	64	296	133
1977-78	1,456	3,751	127	190	65	7	70	286	136
1978-79	1,448	3,284	96	328	72	7	70	297	138
1979-80	1,456	3,432	145	203	79	8	71	297	135
1980-81	1,456	3,432	n.d.	212	85	9	72	294	134
1981-82	1,477	2,937	n.d.	161	89	9	75	308	152*
1990-91	1,588	3,193	n.d.	n.d.	160	18	126	409	111**

Source: * Thillainayagam; 1994. ** Ramesh Babu, 1994.

Note: 1—year, 2—service units, 3—staff, 4—cost collected in lakhs, 5—expenditure Rupees in lakhs, 6—book stock in lakhs, 7—members in lakhs, 8—books borrowed in lakhs, 9—visitors in lakhs, 10—books referred.

entire library system is a living organism according to Ranganathan. If staff size and the service centres are not taken care to be on par with other parts of the body as growing organisms, then the disease infects the body and the resultant is the lack of first aid mechanisms to diagnose and provide necessary help for the system.

Another glance from a different perspective gives the picture of the public libraries in the State. The Table 6.128 shows the figures for one year growth of different main and branch libraries.

Library Finances

The income and expenditure pattern of the public library system is displayed in the Table 6.129, and is a sample of the resource, such as

TABLE 6.129: Library Finances at a Glance

(in lakh rupees)

Category	*1985-86*	*1986-87*	*1987-88*	*1988-89*
Income				
Cess	204.2	222.6	233.4	292.8
Expenditure:				
Staff	338.4	414.5	413.5	487.2
Books	81.2	55.6	84.1	98.9
Periodicals	11.1	14.3	12.8	23.9
Furniture	16.0	15.4	11.1	14.6
Miscellaneous	49.5	117.0	111.1	141.1
Total	496.2	616.2	632.6	767.7

Source: Thillainayagam, 1994.

cess, and the amount spent on different categories. Library cess and the matching grant received from the Government are the basis of the library finances.

The growth of library expenditure by the State Government has increased considerably. A glance at the pattern of growth of the expenditure is pertinent.

Library Expenditure

It should not surprise that the expenditure is more than the Grant received from the Government, because as per the provision of the Madras Public Libraries Act, the library also receives funds from the cess collected from the public. From another point of view the expenditure of the State in terms of per capita is shown in the Table 6.131 to demonstrate the place in the national scenario.

TABLE 6.130: Expenditure on Library Service

(in rupees)

Years	*Expenditure*	*Government Grant*
1951-52	n.d.	2,71,703
1952-53	n.d.	6,34,210
1953-54	n.d.	6,72,608
1954-55	n.d.	n.d.
1955-56	12,95,951	4,94,463
1956-57	14,18,655	7,82,764
1957-58	18,12,393	5,34,876
1958-59	n.d.	9,99,376
1959-60	21,86,892	6,93,237
1950-61	n.d.	n.d.
1961-62	46,02,966	11,15,420
1962-63	n.d.	10,51,690

Source: Cited in Thillainayagam, 1994, from the Annual Reports of the Madras Library Association.

TABLE 6.131: Expenditure on Public Libraries in States (1986-87)

Expenditure (in lakhs)	*Population (in lakhs)*	*Per Capita (in Rs.)*	*Literacy % 1980s*
451.5	484.0	0.93	45.78

These figures, Table 6.131, are representative of what is the priority in the State for expenditure related to libraries. The State has grown in its socio-economic status and its industrial output is well advanced. And despite these developments the per capita of the State in the last decade stands at 14th place among all the States in the country.

Efforts for Enactment

1931 Public Libraries Bill for the Presidency of Madras—by Madras Library Association

1937 Public Libraries Bill for the Presidency of Madras—by Madras Library Association

1946 Madras Public Libraries Bill—by SRR

1948 Madras State Public Libraries Act

1993 Madras Public Libraries Comprehensive Bill—by Venkatappaiah

A Case of Madurai District Library Network

There is a comparatively well-knit example in the State of Tamil Nadu, which is a result of the Public Library Act. This district has 113 full-time library units, 70 part-time village community libraries, one mobile library, one hospital library and one prison library.

Working Hours: These work between 9.00 am and 11.00 am, and 4.00 p.m. and 6.00 p.m. The part-time libraries work beyond this schedule; the village assembly finds leisure time only in the evenings, in turn becoming a cause for late working hours for these libraries.

Collection: Since the community needs information primarily in two areas, namely, government development programme information for the rural community and people's personal information need fulfilment, these centres try to collect information on these. Every District Central Library, and main library of the taluk, receives and makes it available to its users, a copy of the State Gazette. Since these village libraries work as community information centres, these collect information resource files, about local issues, local problems, local leaders or experts, etc.

Service: Reference and referral service are provided sometimes in anticipation and mostly on demand. The Gazette is not lent, whereas other books do circulate. To enable outside the library reading possible, the Gazette is photocopied for larger use.

The branch libraries perform the role of community information centres, by promoting an understanding and awareness of Government programmes among the rural community. As against the normal public library service, in a community context, the human resources are more frequently consulted, and a document in the traditional library collection only supplements the information need.

To keep the professionals up-to-date with the information services and information needs, the District Central Library at Madurai, provides the opportunity of continuing education for its professionals. It also collaborates programmes with other professional institutions in the neighbourhood, including the Department of Library Science at Madurai Kamaraj University, for this purpose.

Connemara Public Library: The one significant aspect of this library is that it had the privilege to become one of the four national depositories in the country, in 1956, under the Delivery of Books Act.

TABLE 6.132: Growth of the Library

	*1970**	*1990***
Total Books	2,14,359	4,69,000
Periodicals received	6,818	—
Newspaper	266	—
Book consultations (per month)	36,590	2,01,000
Books issued (per month)	10,270	4,000
Visitors (annual)	1,44,000	7,45,000

* Thillainayagam, 173.
** Ranganathan, G., 91.

Academic Libraries

The lead taken by Ranganathan in developing the Madras University Library made it a place of envy for all, as it had open access to all seekers of knowledge.

Special Libraries

The City has made considerable progress in its special libraries. The field of sciences are its hotbed. Its IIT and CSIR libraries supporting the national network of science libraries have a well-knitted network and are efficiently serving their users. Madras (now called Chennai) has a city based library network in budding, and is yet to demonstrate its ability to be fully active system.

Library Profession

Library Association

Madras Library Association, Tamil Nadu Library Association, etc., are the leading bodies. The spirit of professionalism is very high in this State, given the effective background which was left by Ranganathan.

Professional education, which was first commenced at Madras University, in 1931, and in a gradual progression, it was called in 1937 as post-graduate diploma, and in 1961 it was called Bachelor's degree. Today Madras University has also a correspondence course and so has Annamalai, both offering bachelor and master programmes, in the accepted informal methods. Additionally there are other institutions offering training and education in librarianship.

STATE: TRIPURA

It emerged as a Union Territory in 1956; and received the status of a State in 1972. It owes its origins to an ancient Hindu Kingdom, and is a land of 'Khrachi' and Ganga pujas.

Its area 10,486 sq. kms. The population density is 262 persons per sq. km. The sex ratio of the State is 946 females per 1000 males. The main language groups as per 1981 Census are: Bengali (68.9%); Tripuri (22.8%); Hindi (1.3%); etc. The religious groups (1981 Census) are: Hindus (89.3%); Muslims (6.7%); Buddhists (2.6%); Christians (1.2%); and others. Its literacy (combined ratio of male and female) has grown from 42.1 per cent in 1981 to 60.4 per cent in 1991—male literacy is 70.8 per cent and female rate is 50.0 per cent.

Public Libraries

The history of the public library movement lies in the scattered history of the Eastern India. A leading palace library was established in the latter half of the nineteenth century, by Maharaja Bir Chandra Manikya Bahadur. This was later named as Bir Chandra Public Library, and in 1953, it was taken over by the State Government and named it as State Central Library. Agartala, the State capital, is the location of the State Central Library.

Public library service in the State is under the control of Directorate of Higher Education, Government of Tripura. There is no separate directorate for public libraries in the State. In fact the Head Librarian of the State Central Library supervises all activities including the management of financial and administrative matters of the library system. There is a centralized acquisition of all reading materials and equipment. While most of the libraries are now functioning under the direct supervision of the State, there are, however, some private libraries, run by clubs, sanghas, and samitis.

The staffing pattern of the public libraries is seemingly well taken care in the case of the State and district libraries, but in the case of lower level libraries, a few have two professionals, and more are one man libraries. for instance, the State Central Library, has 15 professionals, and 28 non-professionals. The North District Library has 3 professionals and 7 non-professionals; the South District Library has 2 professionals, and 5 non-professionals; etc.

Collection Development: The collection in different public libraries in the State as of 1988 November is shown in the Table 6.133. The collection represents different languages.

TABLE 6.133: Book Collection in Public Libraries

Library	*Regional Languages*	*Other Languages*	*Total*
State Central Lib. (and West Dist. Lib)	86,529	27,072	1,13,061
South Dist. Lib, Udaipur	22,414	5,998	28,402
North Dist. Lib, Kailashahar	22,103	3,884	25,987
Dharmanagar Pub. Lib.	19,447	3,660	23,107
Kamalpur Pub. Lib.	16,996	3,334	20,330
Ambasa Pub. Lib.	4,704	243	2,947
Khowai Pub. Lib.	16,267	3,557	19,824
Teliamura Pub. Lib.	5,595	375	5,970
Mohanpur Pub. Lib.	4,020	48	4,068
Bishalgarh Pub. Lib.	11,479	2,254	13,733
Melaghar Pub. Lib.	10,673	2,870	13,543
Sonamura Pub. Lib.	13,530	3,592	17,122
Kakraban Pub. Lib.	4,165	62	4,227
Amarpur Pub. Lib.	13,926	1,992	15,918
Santirbazar Pub. Lib.	4,421	38	4,459
Belonia Pub. Lib.	17,676	2,639	20,315
Rajnagar Pub. Lib.	3,770	32	3,802
Sabroom Pub. Lib.	15,505	3,241	18,746
Gandhighat Pub. Lib.	5,779	0	5,779

Source: Gupta, 1993.

The figures, Table 6.133, of respective libraries do indicate the strengths and weaknesses of these in regional language and other language collection. Any public library has to provide, in a country like India, with a multi-lingual environment. And, interestingly, most are very good in collecting languages which belong to non-regional type of reading materials.

What are the rules for using and borrowing in these libraries? The answer is that to use the reference books, there is no open access, rather it requires seeking permission. To borrow, like all other public libraries in India, a security deposit is required. While non-book material is acquired in the State Central Library, these are non-useable as the operator is not available.

Financial Resources

The public library system receives funds both from the plan and non-plan heads in its annual budget. A break up of the budget is shown in the Table 6.134, to see the expenditure and budget in a comparative perspective.

TABLE 6.134: Annual Outlay and Expenditure at a Glance

(Rs. in lakhs)

Year	*Plan Budget*	*Plan Expenditure*	*Non-plan Budget*	*Non-plan Expenditure*
1985-86	2.00	1.30	17.43	17.43
1986-87	2.20	1.50	19.75	19.75
1987-88	4.05	2.50	24.50	24.50
1988-89*	4.30	0.31	22.20	22.22

Source: Gupta.
* Upto November, 1988.

The expenditure and the budget at a glance speak about the income and expenditure patterns in the State library system. The above figures do not include other income and expenditures. Hence the figures given in the Table 6.135 should not seem contradictory. Below is yet another comparative perspective for further analysis.

Library Expenditure

The figures, Table 6.135, are representative of what is the priority in the State for expenditure related to libraries. The State has grown in its socio-economic status and its industrial output is well advanced. And despite these developments the per capita of the State in the last decade stands at 10th place among all the States in the country.

TABLE 6.135: Expenditure on Public Libraries in States (1986-87)

Expenditure (in lakhs)	*Population (in lakhs)*	*Per Capita (in Rs.)*	*Literacy % 1980s*
30.0	20.0	1.46	42.12

One significant development that has taken place in this State is the various types of libraries, that are under different bodies and Government departments. One such department is the Social Education Directorate, which has 1,900 adult education schools, and 262 rural libraries—containing 5,000 volumes. Similarly, 704 elected village panchayats are also trying to create a library for each of the panchayats. The government spent Rs. 5.46 lakhs for the collection development. Of these 200 have set up reading rooms in space owned under this developmental fund.

A word about the support of RRLF is also appropriate. The RRLF support has been in the following order (Table 6.136).

TABLE 6.136: RRLF Assistance

	1985-86		*1986-87*
Income:			
State funds	2,62,000	Same amount	
RRLF funds	2,62,000		
Total	5,24,000		
Expenditure:			
Bi-cycles	2,256	Mobile Van	1,38,000
Book carriers	2,930	Books	2,68,000
Book for 19 libs.	5,18,814	Books (non-matching funds)	1,58,000
Total	5,24,000	Total	5,64,000

Library Legislation

The State is yet to have a Library Act for regularization and systematization of the public library services. Attempts are being made to prepare a draft public library bill for the State.

Library Profession

Library Association

The tiny State has as many as three professional bodies, *viz.*, Nikhil Tripura Granthagahar Parishad, Library Employee's Local Committee, and Tripura Library Association. One of their popular demand is the establishment of library directorate in the State. This would enable in bringing under one umbrella all the 19 public libraries, 704 Panchayat Libraries, and about 200 libraries which are under the Social Education Department.

Library Education

Apart from the regular library science courses that are offered in the university level, in the region, the Government under the aegis of the Higher Education Directorate, organizes annual programme of library related seminar, All the Government and non-Government library personnel are allowed to attend in these seminars. The topics of the seminars have been of practical value, and have included the following:

* Orientation in rural libraries (first seminar, 1972);
* Sharpening of reference service in the libraries of Tripura (fifth seminar, 1985); and
* Libraries and readers of Tripura (seventh seminar, 1987).

STATE: UTTAR PRADESH

This is the land of the Taj Mahal, and the Ganga, Kumbh Mela, Vrindavan and Benaras, the Oudh of Wajid Shahs and Imambaras of Lucknow. It is here that the language Urdu or Hindustani developed and prospered—through the literature of Kabir and Lucknow—and it is still the hub of this language. A land important for Buddhists (in its place of first sermon at Sarnath), for Jains and for the Hindu revival under the Jagadguru Sankaracharya.

A mix of Bengal province, Agra province, and others, this State was called United Province, and in 1950 it was called Uttar Pradesh (lit Uttar=north, Pradesh=State). By its size, population it is the largest State of India. Its area 2,94,411 sq. kms. The population density is 471 persons per sq. km. The sex ratio of the State is 882 females per 1000 males. The main language groups as per 1981 Census are: Hindi (89.4%); Urdu (9.7%); Punjabi (0.4%); Bengali (0.08%). The religious groups (1981 Census) are: Hindus (83.3%); Muslims (15.9%); Sikhs (0.4%); Christians (0.2%); Jains (0.1%); Buddhists (0.05%); etc. Its literacy has grown from 12 per cent in 1951; 17.6 per cent in 1961; 21.8 per cent in 1971; 27.38 per cent in 1981; and 41.71 per cent in 1991. The literacy rate of males is 55.3 per cent and females is 26.0 per cent.

Public Libraries

The State has not made much progress in the development of public libraries. Only after the inclusion of the State under the 5th Five Year Plan period, there has been some concern and concerted effort in this regard. This is evident from the progress made since independence, which is as follows:

The opening of the State Central Library, in 1949, at Allahabad, gave a hope of progress, but not much was achieved.

Under the First Five Year Plan (1951-56), some recurring and non-recurring grants were given to a few voluntary public libraries. The one development that took place during this period was the establishment of nine districts libraries. In the Second Plan (1956-61), the support to voluntary agencies continued, along with grants to State Central Library and the district libraries. But all this funding and support enabled providing some sort of lending and reading room facility. Not much improvements were made during the Third Plan period (1961-66). In the Fourth Plan (1969-74), was the establishment of the RRLF, and the willingness of the State Government to actively participate in the public library developmental programmes. During the Fifth Plan (1974-78), the Allahabad Public Library (*f.* 1893) was provincialized in 1975, a scheme to develop district libraries was introduced in the Plan budget. The 'Development of library policy and system', incorporated in the Plan budget, led to creation of Library Cell, in the State Secretariat, under the charge of Officer on Special Duty, who would be a library professional. During the Sixth Plan (1980-85) the State established 14 more district libraries, in addition to already existing 14 district libraries, and the State Library. In the Seventh Plan (1985-90) seven schemes

TABLE 6.137: **Budget for Public Library Development**

Years	*Rs. in lakhs*
1980-81	20.00
1981-82	22.00
1982-83	31.50
1983-84	35.39
1984-85	79.64
1985-86	118.32
1986-87	137.56
1987-88	183.57
1988-89	184.15
1989-90	227.80

were introduced to develop the libraries in hill regions. The level of support that came up in the Sixth and Seventh Plan periods can be seen in the budget provisions in these for public library development, which is given in Table 6.137.

While the growth in the budget is at times considerable, it is on the whole progressive.

Library Expenditure

TABLE 6.138: Expenditure on Public Libraries in States (1986-87)

Expenditure (in lakhs)	*Population (in lakhs)*	*Per Capita (in Rs.)*	*Literacy % 1980s*
137.5	1,108.6	0.12	27.38

These figures, Table 6.138, are representative of what is the priority in the State for expenditure related to libraries. The State has grown in its socio-economic status and its industrial output is well advanced. And despite these developments the per capita of the State in the last decade stands at 30th place among all the States in the country.

Efforts for Enactment

1948 Library Bill for the United Provinces—by SRR. The draft bill and the plan for the library development in the State was published, with a foreword by Ranganathan: "The Draft Library Act can form the basis of legislation on the subject not only of Uttar Pradesh, but in any other Province as well".

1958 Uttar Pradesh Public Libraries Bill—revised by SRR. In 1960 as a follow up of this bill the Uttar Pradesh Library Association, made all pleas to the State for this enactment.

1964 The Model Public Library drafted by the Union Government, was sent to the State Government for preparing a Library Act in the State, but no action was taken on it, by the State.

1969 Uttar Pradesh Public Libraries Bill—by U.P. Library Association. This draft borrows much from the immediate predecessor, Maharashtra Public Libraries Act, with modifications suiting conditions in the State. According to B.N. Tiwari (1972), "the Maharashtra Act is an unusual one. In the long run it may fail to be helpful. The latest Act to be used as model is the Mysore Public Libraries Act, 1965" (p. 203).

1973 Uttar Pradesh Public Libraries Bill—by Goswami Committee.

Shri Radhakrishna Goswami was made the Chairman of the Library Committee, during the Fourth Five Year Plan, to consider the possibilities of developing library system in the State. The Committee submitted its report along with a draft bill for Public Libraries.

1983 Uttar Pradesh Public Libraries Bill—by Venkatappaiah

1983 Uttar Pradesh Public Libraries Bill—by Vishwanathan Committee

1992 Uttar Pradesh Public Libraries Bill—by Venkatappaiah

Academic Libraries

The university libraries in the State began much earlier in this century, with Allahabad, Aligarh and Banaras, in the lead. The book stock, as of March 1991, follows in the Table 6.139 (and for this the survey of Dr. Sonal Singh has been handy).

TABLE 6.139: Book Collection in the University Libraries in the State

University Library	*1947*	*1957*	*1967*	*1977*	*1987*	*1991*	*Annual Acquisition 1990-91*
(1)	(2)	(3)	(4)	(5)	(6)	(7)	(8)
Agra							
Books*	0.17	0.48	0.86	1.12	1.43	1.60	<10,000
Journals	—	—	—	—	52	172	300
Allahabad							
Books	1.19	1.71	2.56	3.09	4.70	4.98	<10,000
Journals	—	—	—	173	300	402	—
Avadh							
Books	—	—	—	—	0.04	0.05	<1,000
Journals	—	—	—	—	129	160	
Bundelkhand							
Books	—	—	—	—	0.07	0.09	<1,000
Journals	—	—	—	—	—	122	125
Garhwal							
Books	—	—	0.43	—	0.30	0.55	<10,000
Journals	—	—	—	150	240	400	—
Gorakhpur							
Books	0.65	0.90	1.75	2.50	3.00	—	<20,000
Journals	—	—	—	—	300	650	750
Kanpur							
Books	—	—	—	0.10	0.36	0.40	<5,000
Journals	—	—	—	—	30	100	250

(*Contd.*)

TABLE 6.139 (*Contd.*)

(1)	(2)	(3)	(4)	(5)	(6)	(7)	(8)
Kashi Vidyapith							
Books	0.27	0.50	0.97	1.40	—	1.60	<10,000
Journals	—	—	—	—	103	119	140
Kumaun							
Books	—	—	—	—	—	0.01	<1,000
Journals	—	—	—	—	—	—	—
Lucknow							
Books	—	—	—	4.30	5.00	—	<20,000
Journals	—	—	—	—	300	700	1,200
Meerut							
Books	—	—	0.43	0.80	0.80	—	<1,000
Journals	—	—	—	—	123	392	500
Rohilkhand							
Books	—	—	—	—	0.12	—	<5,000
Journals	—	—	—	—	—	—	52

* All book figures are in lakhs <= less than.

The Table 6.139 displays the growth pattern in a comparative perspective, of all the university libraries in the State. What is clear from the above is the point that three of the twelve university libraries, have more than 3 lakh books, and more than four of these libraries subscribe to more than 400 periodical titles. The glaring distinction in the matter of periodical subscription is that of Lucknow University Library which receives 1,200 periodicals, and all others are less than 750 titles.

What is not clear from the above, is that, what is the proportion of the acquisition that matches the annual new users, new research areas, and new subjects that are added in the curriculum. Further, what is not clear, and more intense studies need to be done is to assess the use pattern of these collections. Use of books, by language is pertinent, because Uttar Pradesh is in the heartland of the Hindi belt, and the assessment must include the language influence in acquisition and use patterns.

What are the other types of reading materials these universities have in their libraries? The answer to this is seen in the Table 6.140, which lists the variety of resources that are housed in these libraries.

The Table 6.140 shows that the most common source of information, after books and journals, is thesis (includes Ph.D and M.Phil). The next important resource available in most libraries is the Government reports. What is the need of all libraries becoming depositories of all governmental publications, and documents, is a question, which is not discussed here.

What is missing and therefore striking, in the survey of resources that are in these libraries, is the microforms—major part of the library world in 1970s and 1980s was flooded with these resources. But these university libraries do not have this supposedly advantageous technological information storage and preservation tool.

TABLE 6.140: Reading Materials (Other than Books and Journals)

University Library	*Rare Books*	*Govt. Reports*	*Thesis*	*Mss*	*Microforms*
Agra	y	y	y		
Allahabad		y			
Avadh	y				
Bundelkhand	y	y			
Garhwal	y	y	y		
Gorakhpur		y			
Kanpur		y			
Kashi Vidyapith	y	y	y		
Kumaun	y		y		
Lucknow		y	y	y	
Meerut	y	y	y	y	
Rohilkhand	y	y			

The survey of Sonal Singh concludes with a critical, but appropriate remark, "majority of the books selected are not in consonance with the requirements of students and research scholars. The collection development will come out only when its librarian and the library staff are in know-how of new trends, new publications, newer editions, and understand the various dimensions of subjects in the growing universe of knowledge. But, in Uttar Pradesh university libraries, there is an unhealthy practice of appointing a professor incharge as head of the library under the cadre of Honorary Librarian.

A professor's approach would be to cater to individual and immediate needs rather than to long range needs of future ones. Moreover, he spends much of his time for teaching and visits library only for one or two hours. Hence, he is not familiar with reader's needs. Many times he is away on an assignment or on vocation. Thus, he is unable to devote attention to the job of selection (of books). As a result the collection is incomplete (pp. 343-44).

Goswami has given the findings of his survey on the state of academic libraries in the State. According to this "Only 55 per cent intermediate colleges have libraries in one form or the other. Those colleges which have libraries, are managed by a single person designated as librarian-cum-clerk, who has to look after the office work of the college as well as the library". He has cited another survey done by the Department of Education U.P. in 1987, which revealed that among the colleges where libraries exist, only 2 per cent are spending more than Rs. 5,000 for the purchase of reading materials, 34 per cent college spent about Rs. 1,000, 20 per cent spent Rs. 2,000 and only 7 per cent spent more than Rs. 2,000, during the year 1986-87. In the preceding years 37 per cent intermediate colleges did not spend any amount on acquiring reading material, despite the fact that library fees is regularly collected from the students! (Goswami, 1996: 69).

Special Libraries

U.P. and more so, its State capital, Lucknow, has a variety of special libraries. The leading sectoral information centre for Drugs, under the NISSAT, is at Lucknow. Similarly there are many other scientific and industrial libraries in the city and the State. There are other special libraries in the city, such as the world famous, Nadwat-ul-Ulama, which is a university status academy in Oriental studies and research.

Library Profession

Library Association

The leading and one of the most pro-active body in the State is the Uttar Pradesh Library Association, was founded in 1935, and has been actively involved in professional advancement more so since, 1965. Its official organ, published in English is Lucknow Librarian, and the Hindi news quarterly is called Pustakalaya Samvad Patrika.

Library Education

Of the 16 universities offering education in general, only seven are offering degree courses in library science. The Uttar Pradesh Library Association offers four-month course, and a two-year programme is being offered since a few years.

STATE: WEST BENGAL

Here are the Sunderbans and the Bengal Tiger, Durga and Kali, rossogullas and Darjeeling tea. The name Bengal or Bangla has its origin in the ancient Kingdom of Vangor Ranga (or Venga), and this is corroborated in the Sanskrit literature of 3rd century. The division of Bengal into East and West, led to what Majumdar calls "the destruction of the bond that united the Bengalis, under colour of providing for administrative efficiency, considerably weakened the politically advanced Bengali intelligentsia. It split them into two separate Provinces, in both of which they would be outnumbered by other elements of the population, and kindled religious animosities, thus interfering with the growth of a true national spirit transcending creed and community" (1967: 976).

Its area 88,752 sq. kms. The population density is 766 persons per sq. km. The sex ratio of the State is 917 females per 1000 males. The main language groups as per 1981 Census are: Bengali (85.7%); Hindi (5.9%); Santali (2.8%); Urdu (2.2%); Gorkha/Nepali (1.3%); The religious groups (1981 Census) are: Hindus (76.9%); Muslims (21.5%); Christians (0.6%); Sikhs (0.09%); Jains (0.07%) and others. The growth of literacy has been not very remarkable, despite the literary waves that the State has since a hundred years. The literacy growth is seen in 9 per cent in 1951; 29.3 per cent in 1961; 33 per cent in 1971; 40.8 per cent in 1981; and 57.7 per cent in 1991—The literacy rate of males now is 67.2 per cent and female is 47.1 per cent.

Public Libraries

The history of public libraries in Calcutta, more specifically, and in the State in general, is associated with the growth of British power as well as the rise of Bengali intellectualism. The growth of nationalism provided an added support for the library development. In the post-independence era, however, libraries in West Bengal, are not the centre of political activism, nor it has a library enactment until 1979.

Of the nearly 5,000 libraries that were managed by the public, until the independence, some were taken over to be directly managed by the Government.

It was in the election manifesto of the Left Front Government, issued in 1977 which stated that if they win the election they would develop the public library system through library legislation. In fact, for the first time in the sub-continent, library legislation as an issue was explicitly stated in an election manifesto. The Left Front demonstrated this by improving the library system in terms of increasing the number of libraries, increasing the funds, and so on.

The changed outlook of the Government thus manifested in a number of ways with libraries and librarianship, which was already one of the better systems, in terms of historic origins, and in terms of the level of professionalism that it had imbibed, now renewed its activism.

A word in passing is worth mentioning about the historic roles the profession in West Bengal played in the days before independence. It was here that the public interest in library movement was witnessed, in the development of various libraries and library related associations, including, ILA, IASLIC, BLA, etc. It was here that the roots of national library were laid, and the roots of modern public library system took birth, in the Calcutta Public Library. Let alone the professional inspiration that came in this process, the writings and speeches of scholars and elite, including Rabindranath Tagore, regarding the role of the library, the type of collection that would be useful, the kind of service expected from libraries, and so on.

The State Central Library (*f.* 1962), was established to meet the requirement of the West Bengal Public Library Act, 1979. It is located on the Emerald Bower Campus of the Rabindra Bharathi University, Calcutta. Hence the primary users are 6,150, of which 5,500 are students, 250 faculty, and among others 450 administrative staff of the university. When it moves to the new location at V.I.P. Road, then it will have the general public as its main users.

Collection: 86,100 volumes, and 369 periodicals. A language breakup of these shows the pattern in the Table 6.141.

TABLE 6.141: Language-wise Collection of Book and Periodicals

Language	*Book*		*Periodicals*	
	Collection	*Percentage*	*Collection*	*Percentage*
English	38,620	44.8	295	80.0
Indian			(163)	
Non-Indian			(132)	
Fiction	(250)			
Non-fiction	(38,370)			
Bengali	46,756	57.2	74	20.0
Fiction	(14,523)			
Non-fiction	(32,233)			
Hindi	400	0.5		
Sanskrit	120	0.2		
Assamese	101	0.1		
Bi-lingual	40	0.1		
Urdu	25	0.1		
Total	81,600		369	

As a State level depository of the printed books, it received 19,000 books under the Delivery of Books Act; it purchased 56,100 books; 11,000 were received as gift—including those from late Prof. M.M. Ghosh collection it received 1,100 books, and from late P. Sen Collection 3,000 books.

Services: Reading room and reference service only. No arrangement is made for lending books. It is opened between 11 a.m. and 6 p.m., with almost five-day week pattern, and State holidays are applicable. It offers bibliographical services, reference and referral services—a printed bibliography compiled in 1980, and an annual list of books are to its credit.

A recent survey of its users indicates, 50 per cent users are in the age group of 20-29 years, 30-39 years are about 20 per cent, and so on. Indicating that the student population is crowding the reference and textbook sections. This is supported by the user categories that frequent the library: Students are 40 per cent; Faculty 20 per cent; Researchers 28 per cent; etc.

An attempt had also been made to train librarians, during 1988 and 1991 by offering Certificate Course in Library Science, but has not been continued.

But, like all State libraries, it is not befitting the type of State library, which the Act has described. It has many problems, probably due to various reasons, including odd location, imbalanced collection so far as the public library context is concerned, etc. (Ohdedar, 1996: 338).

A glance at the State library system is also pertinent here to see how the system works (Table 6.142).

TABLE 6.142: A Glance at the State Library System

District	*Central Library*	*District Library*	*Area Library*	*Rural Library*
(1)	(2)	(3)	(4)	(5)
Bankura	—	1	1	24
Birbhum	—	1	1	22
Burdwan	—	2	1	29
Calcutta	1	—	—	—
Cooch Behar	—	1	1	18
Darjeeling	1	1	6	10
Hooghly	1	2	29	—
Howrah	—	1	—	29
Jalpaiguri	—	1	—	12
Malda	—	1	—	10

(*Contd.*)

TABLE 6.142 (*Contd.*)

(1)	(2)	(3)	(4)	(5)
Midnapore	—	2	2	39
Murshidabad	—	1	—	24
Nadia	—	1	1	14
Purulia	—	1	—	21
24 Parganas	—	3	8	38
West Dinajpur	—	1	—	23

Source: Mookerjee, 1969: 513.

The growth pattern of public libraries has been interesting in the State. The Table 6.143 depicts this pattern.

TABLE 6.143: Comparison of Library Growth by Periods

	1947-1977	*1977-1986*
State Library	1	—
District Library	20	1
Central Library	3	—
Town Library	37	83
Rural Library	701	1,575

The growth pattern is tremendous of town libraries and rural libraries. Given the RRLF funding that started from 1972 onwards, rural library development received a boost, which was unprecedented. Formation of reading circles with the rural population, in collaboration with local clubs is made under the scope of the patha-sibiras, along with group sessions of reading, poetry recitation, and enacting plays.

The travelling library, or mobile reading camp (Bharmyaman Patha Sibira) has developed much of interest in libraries and reading. The mobile van service is highly appreciated. "It has been found that a considerable number of farmers, tillers of land and school children read books and use this library for a maximum period of 4 hours at a stretch". The library employees attending this service read out the books and explain with the help of posters, and such other materials, the various facets of life and its necessities, like, how to grow more food, how to have more yields, etc. (Mookerjee, 1969: 507).

The Directorate of Social Education under the office of District Social Education Officer supervises the working of the district library system. The other two offices to whom the District Librarian is responsible are Block Development Officer, and the Circle Assistant. But this creates problems for the independent functioning of the librarian. The District Librarian, who is subordinate of District Social Education Officer, is frustrated and quits the position. To fill this vacancy, some deputy inspector of schools is given short training of a make-believe course in library science and is appointed District Librarian. This is the sad state of affairs, and this haphazard practice is not only in this State, it is practiced everywhere in the country (Mookerjee, 1969: 390).

Library Finance

TABLE 6.144: Budget Allocation for Libraries

(Rupees in lakhs)

Year	*Amount*
1979-80	2.26
1980-81	4.01
1981-82	4.28
1982-83	4.66
1983-84	5.00
1984-85	5.50
1985-86	7.50
1986-87	9.28

TABLE 6.145: Annual Grant Allocation to Libraries

(Rupees in thousands)

Books & Pdls.	*SCL*	*U*	*DL*	*S/T*	*R/O*
1975-76	50	25	3	1.8	—
1985-86	105	37	32	9	3
Furniture					
1975-76	—	—	—	—	—
1985-86	1	3	2	1	0.5
Bind. & Preser.					
1975-76	—	—	—	—	—
1985-86	15	10	3	1	0.5
Contingency					
1975-76	31	11	2	1.2	0.6
1985-86	35	11	8	2.5	1
Mobile Van					
1975-76	42	—	—	—	—
1985-86	42	—	15	—	—
Total					
1975-76	123	36	5	3	0.6
1985-86	207	61	60	13.5	5

Note: SCL=State Central Library; U=Uttapara J.K. Library; DL=District Libraries; S/T=Sub-divisional/Town Libraries; R/O=Rural/Area/Primary Unit Libraries.

The Table 6.145 shows the glaring jump on the whole library allocations received before 1977 and after 1977. The reason for the higher allocation, according to one school of thought, which sounds reasonable, is that the Left Front Government took over the State in 1977, and liberalized funding for libraries.

Interestingly, the increase has been considerable for some libraries. While the State Library is yet to receive an appropriate funding and allocation, the role played by rural and town libraries is significant.

Library Expenditure

The expenditure on libraries has grown at a considerable rate, and the State ranks as the highest spending State in the country. The Table 6.146 demonstrates the pattern of expenditure on libraries.

TABLE 6.146: Comparison of Expenditure on Public Libraries

(Rs. in lakhs)

Year	*Non-plan*	*Plan*	*Total*
1985-86	2.06	6.00	8.06
1986-87	4.30	6.14	10.91
1987-88	3.22	6.05	9.28

Source: Kaula, 1991: 27.

TABLE 6.147: Expenditure *vis-a-vis* Per Capita (1986-87)

Expenditure (in lakhs)	*Population (in lakhs)*	*Per Capita (in Rs.)*	*Literacy % 1980s*
928.2	545.8	1.70	40.88

These figures, Table 6.147, are representative of what is the priority in the State for expenditure related to libraries. The State has grown in its socio-economic status and its industrial output is well advanced. And despite these developments the per capita of the State in the last decade stands at 8th place among all the States in the country.

Efforts for Enactment

1931 Bengal Public Libraries Bill—drafted by Kumar Munindra Deb Raj Mahasay, MLA. This bill was introduced in Bengal Legislature by him, but it was rejected.

1958 West Bengal Public Libraries Bill—by SRR. During the

Conference of the Bengal Library Association (BLA), in 1958, Ranganathan, presented a draft bill on public library service. This was probably most congenial period for an enactment to succeed, as the then Chief Minister and the Finance Minister (the latter being the President of BLA), were sympathetic to the cause of library development. But no library related act was passed and not an inch progress made in terms of library legislation then. In 1967 the United Front Government made an unsuccessful attempt at enacting the library law, but its short term did not give any time to proceed in this regard.

1978 West Bengal Public Libraries Bill—by State Government. The Left Front Government on assuming power, in 1977, constituted an Expert Committee to draft a Public Library Bill. The Committee constituted thus, had professionals and bureaucrats, among others. A draft bill was made, based on the past drafts prepared by Kumar Munindra, Ranganathan, etc., as well taking into consideration the contemporary needs of public libraries in the State.

1979 West Bengal State Public Libraries Act—The draft bill, prepared by the Expert Committee was submitted to the State Legislature with certain modifications. After debates and series of discussions the bill was passed and the Public Libraries Act came into force. The Act brought a relief to much degraded status that the public libraries in the State were in. The Act also resulted in improvement of status and working conditions of the staff in the public library system in the State. The Act had two Amendments in 1982 and 1985 to the Public Libraries Act. The improved Act has given a distinct status to the State of having massive investment in the form of Government grants to implement the developmental schemes, providing organisational structures, to maintain library services, establishment of new libraries, organizing book fairs, and so on and so forth.

Academic Libraries

West Bengal has an outstanding contribution in the number of academic libraries that it had in the pre-independence era. Some have made remarkable progress in the annals of library history. Shantiniketan has been one major illustration of the kind of books which Tagore wanted it to have and how it has served as a basis of professional growth in the State.

Special Libraries

Special libraries here have set new standards working, and they made serious attempts to coordinate and cooperate their activities.

Library Profession

Library Association

The library associations in the State have always led to progress and been exemplary in their performance. It was this land which led to the formation of many associations, including the Indian Library Association, Bengal Library Association, Government of India Library Association, etc. It was here that the first All-India library meeting was held, to start a series of All-India Library Conferences under the aegis of ILA. It was the first to produce professional literature in regional language at a very large scale, and in a variety of forms. It made history, when it used radio to create a mass movement for library development—25 radio lectures were relayed on topics relating to libraries and library movement.

Library Education

It was here that the first professional in-service training programme was started in the National Library. The first diploma course was started by Khan Bahadur Asadullah at the Imperial Library (now National Library of India), in 1935. The Bengal Library Association started the certificate course in 1937. Calcutta University was the first agency at the higher level to start a course in 1945.

Library Networks

It made another history when it first launched a local library network, CALIBNET, using established procedures and practices to integrate the library systems in the metropolitan city—Calcutta. Though it is a sad story, that CALIBNET did not even get a take of stage, it went into cold storage immediately after its birth.

SUMMING UP

According to the survey by Thakur and Gopinath, the library development in India has not made much progress. "Only in a few States of India some attempts have been made by State Governments to develop public libraries, though there are many limitations in those programmes. In most of the States of India, the inadequate, unorganized and scattered public libraries have been left to the care of some voluntary workers. Recommendation of the Advisory Committee on Libraries and the

Planning Commission Working Group on Libraries, both appointed by the Union Government and different proposals of Dr. S.R. Ranganathan for development of public library system in India have been ignored" (1994: 153).

These statements are very true, and there can be no dispute about the whole matter. The added stand that the Constitution of India has placed in the case of library development is not one which can facilitate the unified and holistic approach to the entire subject of setting up a library system in the country—The Constitution has placed library development as a subject which is the concern of the State, and not of the Centre. This Federalism has though advantages of allowing free hand in State matters and in implementation of schemes, has nevertheless dampened the process of a systematic library development programme for the entire country.

REFERENCES

Andhra Pradesh

Andhra Pradesh, Public Libraries (Department of). Report (Chairman: Justice Ekbote). Hyderabad, 1978.

Andhra Pradesh, Report of the Committee on Private Libraries (Chairman: Vavilala Gopalkrishnayya), Hyderabad, 1978.

Burhanuddin, Mohammed and Taher, Mohamed, "State Central Library, Andhra Pradesh: A Centennial Review (1891-1990)", in *Humanities Information Systems and Services* (Handbook of Libraries, Archives and Information Centres, Series, Vol. 9, Part 1), New Delhi, Aditya, 1991.

Chandran, D. and Ramesh Babu, B., "Non-Users of the Regional Library: A Survey", in *Public Library Systems: Services and Networking*, A festschrift presented to Prof. K. Sarada, ed. by L.S. Ramaiah and others, New Delhi, Ess Ess Publications, 1997, Vol. 1, 280-86.

Chandraiah, I "Circulation Libraries: A Study", *Granthana*, 4:1&2 (Jan. and July, 1993), 37-40.

Haravu, L.J., "Hyderabad Libraries Network (HYLIBNET): Approaches to Planning and a Conceptual Architecture", in *Souvenir, CALIBER-95*, Second National Convention on Information Access Through Networks, Feb. 1995, Hyderabad. Hyderabad, University of Hyderabad, 1995.

Inamdar, N.B., "Institute of Library Science, Hyderabad", in *Souvenir*, National Workshop on Library Science Education at the Certificate Level and Library Service in Rural Areas, Dec. 15-17, 1991, Hyderabad, 1991.

————, and Shakira, A.W., "Management of Libraries in the State of Hyderabad: An Overview", in *Library Development in India* (Handbook of Libraries, Archives, and Information Centres in India, Series, Vol. 16), Ed. by B.M. Gupta, New Delhi, Segment Books, 1996, pp. 84-100.

Isenberg, Artur, *Profile of Andhra Book Readers*, Masulipatam, Hindu Press, 1960 (A report of the survey of reading habits of the subscribers of the Andhra Pradesh Book Distributors's Home Library Plan).

Jagga Rao, N.V. and Prafulla Chandra, T.V., "Need for Andhra Pradesh State Bibliography", in *Public Library Systems: Services and Networking*; A festschrift presented to Prof. K. Sarada, Ed. by L.S. Ramaiah and others, New Delhi, Ess Ess Publications, 1997, Vol. 1, pp. 176-90.

Janardhana Rao, S.S. "Autonomous Colleges and the Challenges of the Librarian", in *College Libraries in India*, Proceedings of National Seminar on College Libraries in India, Delhi, 31 Oct.-1 Nov., 1988. Ed., Krishan Kumar, and J.K. Anand, Delhi, ILA, 1988, pp. 92-95.

Kamaiah, P., and Paul, G. Sarojini, "Library Movement in Rayalseema in Andhra Pradesh: A New Look", in Vashishth, C.P., *Library Movement and Library Development in India*, Seminar Papers, 39th All-India Library Conference, Bangalore, 7-10 January 1994, pp. 32-43.

Mohanvo, "Book Industry in Andhra Pradesh (1800-1995)", in *Souvenir*, 41st All-India Library Conference, Vijayawada, 1996.

Rajeswari, D., "Growth and Development of Sri Padmavathi Mahila University Library, Tirupati", in Vashishth, C.P., *Library Movement and Library Development in India*, Seminar Papers, 39th All-India Library Conference, Bangalore, 7-10 January 1994, pp. 298-308.

Raju, A.A.N., *History of Library Movement in Andhra Pradesh*, 1900-1956, Delhi, Ajanta, 1988.

————, "What Ails Library Service in Andhra Pradesh", *The Hindu*, 114:89 (1991), 19.

Ramaiah, L.S., "Public Libraries and Access to Information in India", in *Public Library Systems: Services and Networking*; A festschrift presented to Prof. K. Sarada, Ed. by L.S. Ramaiah and others, New Delhi, Ess Ess Publications, 1997, Vol. 1, pp. 111-24.

Rao, C. Gopinatha, Library Movement in Andhra Pradesh, Hyderabad, Department of Public Libraries, Govt. of Andhra Pradesh, 1981. Reddy, P. Janardhan, "Network of Public Library Services in Twin Cities", in *Souvenir*, National Workshop on Library Science Education at the Certificate Level and Library Service in Rural Areas, 15-17 December 1991, Hyderabad, 1991.

Riswadkar, M.R., "Six Years with Institute of Library Science", in *Souvenir*, National Workshop on Library Science Education at the Certificate Level and Library Service in Rural Areas, 15-17 December 1991, Hyderabad, 1991.

Satish, N.G., "Bare Foot and Far to Go: Stray Impressions on Role of Library in Our Rural Setting", National Seminar on Community Information Centres Under Panchayat Raj, 19-21 February 1997. K.A. Raju, Seminar Director; Reading material, Hyderabad, NIRD, pp. 79-83.

Satyanarayana, M., "Use of Public Libraries", *Annals of Library Science and Documentation*, 43(1996), pp. 108-115.

Taher, Mohamed, "Functions of the State Libraries: A Case Study of A.P. State Central Library, Hyderabad", in *Public Library Systems: Services and Networking*, A festschrift presented to Prof. K. Sarada, Ed. by L.S. Ramaiah and others, New Delhi, Ess Ess Publications, 1997, Vol. 1, pp. 15-25.

————, and Fatimy, M.A.K., "Mosque Library: A Case Study", *ILA Bulletin*, 22 (April-September 1984), pp. 38-42.

————, and Gupta, B.M., "American Studies Research Centre: Library & Information Services (Developmental history)", in *Social Sciences: Information Systems and Centres* (Handbook of Libraries, Archives and Information Centres, Series, Vol. 8), New Delhi, Aditya, 1990.

Takalkar, Anil and others, "Case Studies of Rural Libraries in Andhra Pradesh and Maharashtra", National Seminar on Community Information Centres Under Panchayat Raj, 19-21 February 1997. K.A. Raju, Seminar Director; Reading material, Hyderabad, NIRD, pp. 55-65.

Venkatappaiah, Velga, "Developing Rural Libraries as Rural Information Centres", National Seminar on Community Information Centres Under Panchayat Raj, 19-21 February 1997. K.A. Raju, Seminar Director; Reading material, Hyderabad, NIRD, pp. 35-46.

————, "Developing Rural Libraries as Rural Information Centres", National Seminar on Community Information Centres Under Panchayat Raj, 19-21 February 1997. K.A. Raju, Seminar Director; Reading material, Hyderabad, NIRD, pp. 35-46.

————, "Need for Library Legislation in South Asian Countries", in *Public Library Systems: Services and Networking*; A festschrift presented to Prof. K. Sarada, Ed. by L.S. Ramaiah and others, New Delhi, Ess Ess Publications, 1997, Vol. 1, pp. 76-110.

————, "Andhra Pradesh Governmental Oriental Manuscripts Library and Research Institute, Hyderabad" in Gupta B.M. (Ed.), *Humanities Information Systems and Centres* (Handbook of Libraries, Archives, and Information Centres in India, Series, Vol. 9, Part 2), New Delhi, Aditya Prakashan, 1991, pp. 261-65.

————, "Sri Venkateshwara Oriental Research Institute, Tirupati", in Gupta, B.M. (Ed.) *Humanities Information Systems and Centres* (Handbook of Libraries, Archives, and Information Centres in India, Series, Vol. 9, Part 2), New Delhi, Aditya Prakashan, 1991, pp. 289-92.

————, *Granthalaya Darshani*, Eluru, Sanchalana Samiti, 1968. March of Library Science, Kaula Festchrift, New Delhi, Vikas, 1979.

Andaman & Nicobar

Adak, Tapan, "Development of Public Libraries in Andaman & Nicobar Islands", *Granthana*, 4: 1&2 (Jan. & July 1993), pp. 117-19.

Dutta, Ajit Kumar, "Andaman and Nicobar Islands: Marching Towards Modernized Public Library System", in *Souvenir*, 34th All-India Library Conference, and 13th National Seminar of the IASLIC, Calcutta, Bengal Library Association, 1988, pp. 29-32.

Assam

Barman, Rajani Kanta, "University Library Development in Assam: A Study in the Context of Fifth Law of Library Science", in Vashishth, C.P., *Library Movement and Library Development in India*, Seminar Papers, 39th All-India Library Conference, Bangalore, January 7-10, 1994, pp. 284-97.

Hazarika, B. "Status Report on the Public Library Development in Assam", *Granthana*, 4: 1&2 (Jan. & July, 1993), pp. 41-44.

Lahkar, Narendra, "College Libraries of Assam: Problems and Prospects", in *College Libraries in India*, Proceedings of National Seminar on College Libraries in India, Delhi, 31 Oct.-1 Nov., 1988. Ed. Krishan Kumar, and J.K. Anand, Delhi, ILA, 1988, pp. 142-49.

Phukan, Alka Burgohain, "Library Situation in the State of Assam: A Status Report", in *Souvenir*, 34th All-India Library Conference, and 13th National Seminar of the IASLIC, Calcutta, Bengal Library Association, 1988, pp. 39-43.

Bihar

Esperanza, M., "College Libraries in Bihar", in *College Libraries in India*, proceedings of National Seminar on College Libraries in India, Delhi, 31 Oct.-1 Nov., 1988. Ed. Krishan Kumar, and J.K. Anand, Delhi, ILA, 1988, pp. 49-58.

————, "Library Development in Bihar (1900-1990)", in *Library Development in India* (Handbook of Libraries, Archives, and Information Centres in India, Series, Vol. 16). Ed. by B.M. Gupta, New Delhi, Segment Books, 1996, pp. 146-74.

Mishra, B.N., "Veterinary College Libraries in Bihar—A Study", in *College Libraries in India*, proceedings of National Seminar on College Libraries in India, Delhi, 31 Oct.-1Nov. 1988. Ed. Krishan Kumar, and J.K. Anand, Delhi, ILA, 1988, pp. 59-63.

Mishra, Jogesh, *et al.*, "Library Movement in Bihar, Maharashtra, Madhya Pradesh and Punjab", *Herald of Library Science*, 3: 2-3 (1964), 185-206.

Singh, R.S.P., "Public Library Development in Bihar", *Granthana*, 2: 2 (July 1991), 193-203.

Chandigarh

Anand, Virender K., "Library and Librarianship in the 'City Beautiful': An Overview", in *Souvenir*, 34th All-India Library Conference, and 13th National Seminar of the IASLIC, Calcutta, Bengal Library Association, 1988, pp. 44-47.

Arora, Madhuri, "College Libraries in Punjab and UT Chandigarh", in Vashishth, C.P., *Library Movement and Library Development in India*, Seminar Papers, 39th All-India Library Conference, Bangalore, January 7-10, 1994, pp. 261-74.

Bansal, G.C., assisted by Preeti Goel, "The Public Library System in the 'City Beautiful' (Chandigarh)", in Gupta, B.M., Ed., *Library Development in India* (Handbook of Libraries, Archives, and Information Centres in India, Series, Vol. 16), New Delhi, Segment Books, 1996, 350-55.

Ramola, K.C. "Chandigarh Public Library System", *Granthana*, 4: 1&2 (Jan. & July, 1993), pp. 121-26.

————, and Arora, Sanjay, "Computerization of Central State Library, Chandigarh", in Vashishth, C.P., *Library Movement and Library Development in India*, Seminar Papers, 39th All-India Library Conference, Bangalore, January 7-10, 1994, pp. 420-25.

Delhi

Anand, J.K., "College Libraries in Delhi: Problems and Prospects", in *College Libraries in India*, proceedings of National Seminar on College Libraries in India, Delhi, 31 Oct.-1 Nov. 1988, Ed. Krishan Kumar, and J.K. Anand, Delhi; ILA 1988, pp. 1-15.

Kumar, Krishan, and Datta, N. "Delhi University College Libraries: An Overview", in *Current Problems and Trends in Library and Information Services*, Prof. K.S. Deshpande commemoration volume, Ed. by H.A. Khan and S.R. Ijari, Varanasi, Indian Bibliographic Centre, 1990, pp. 72-81.

Kumar, Sunil, "School Libraries in Delhi: A Study", in Kumar, R.P. *et al.* (ed), *Role of Libraries in National Development*, 42nd All-India Library Conference, Calicut, 21-24 Dec. 1966, pp. 222-25.

Madan Lal, and Jyothirmayi, S., "Library Finance in Delhi University Colleges", in *College Libraries in India*, Proceedings of National Seminar on College Libraries in India, Delhi, 31 Oct.-1 Nov. 1988, Ed. Krishan Kumar, and J.K. Anand, Delhi, ILA, 1988, pp. 21-31.

Vashishth, C.P. Ed. and Singh, Dev. Raj. "Libraries in Delhi: A Scenario", in *Souvenir*, 34th All-India Library Conference, and 13th National Seminar of the IASLIC, Calcutta, Bengal Library Association, 1988, pp. 48-56.

Walia, P.K. and Gautam, Shalini, "Library Services in Colleges of Delhi: A Survey", in *College Libraries in India*, Proceedings of National Seminar on College Libraries in India, Delhi, 31 Oct.-1 Nov. 1988, Ed. Krishan Kumar and J.K. Anand, Delhi ILA, 1988, pp. 16-20.

Goa

Rodrigues, Pia de Menezes, "Library Movement in Goa", in *Souvenir*, 34th All-India Library Conference, and 13th National Seminar of the IASLIC, Calcutta, Bengal Library Association, 1988, pp. 57-61.

————, "Development of Public Library Service in Goa", *Granthana*, 4: 1&2 (Jan & July 1993), pp. 45-48.

————, "Goa State Central Library: Past, Present, and Future", in Gupta, B.M. Ed. *Library Development in India* (Handbook of Libraries, Archives, and Information Centres in India, Series, Vol. 16), New Delhi, Segment Books, 1996, pp. 271-85.

Gujarat

Borden, W.A. "Baroda, India and Its Libraries", *Library Journal*, 38 (1913), pp. 659-63.

Gopinath, M.A., "History of Library Legislation in India", in *Public Library System*, S.R. Ranganathan, and A. Neelameghan, (Ed.), Bangalore, Sarada Ranganathan Endowment for Library Service, 1972, pp. 12-38.

Kesavan, R. Venkata, and Sharma, R.S., "Promoting Local Library Networks Towards Self-sufficiency: Strategies and Techniques with Special Reference to ADINET", in *Meeting the Information Challenge for Development and Self-sufficiency*, Papers: XVII National Seminar of IASLIC, Dec. 10-13, Calcutta, pp. 99-104.

Majumdar, K.J., and Shukla, K.H., "Public Library Finance in Gujarat: An Analysis", in Vashishth, C.P., *Library Movement and Library Development in India*, Seminar Papers, 39th All-India Library Conference, Bangalore, January 7-10, 1994, pp. 320-27.

Shah, P.C., "Libraries in Gujarat--A Bird's Eye View", in *Souvenir*, 34th All-India Library Conference, and 13th National Seminar of the IASLIC, Calcutta, Bengal Library Association, 1988, pp. 62-65.

Shukla, K.H. and Soni, N.N., "Public Library Development in Gujarat: An Appraisal", in Vashishth, C.P., *Library Movement and Library Development in India*, Seminar Papers, 39th All-India Library Conference, Bangalore, January 7-10, 1994, pp. 309-19.

Shukla, K.H. and Thaker, Kiran, "Women Library in Gujarat: Some Observations and Suggestions", in Vashishth, C.P., *Library Movement and Library Development in India*, Seminar Papers, 39th All-India Library Conference, Bangalore, January 7-10-1994, pp. 220-30.

Thaker, Urmila A., "Library Movement in Gujarat", in Vashishth, C.P., *Library Movement and Library Development in India*, Seminar Papers, 39th All-India Library Conference, Bangalore, Jan.7-10, 1994, pp. 44-51.

Thaker, Urmila, A. and Mehta, P.V., "Public Libraries in Gujarat: Appraisal and Performance", in Mangla, C.P., *et al.*, Ed., *Fifty Years of Librarianship in India: Past, Present and Future,* 29th All-India Library Conference, Mysore, Dec. 5-9, 1983, pp. 310-17.

Upadhaya, H.J. "Gujarat and Its Libraries", *Granthana*, 2: 2 (July 1991), pp. 123-33.

Haryana

Goyal, S.P. and Singh, Balbir, "University Book Depot: Theory and Practice", in Prasher, R.G. Ed. *University Libraries in India: 1980s and Beyond,* New Delhi, Medallion Press, 1991, pp. 41-52.

Janak Raj, "Library Movement in Haryana", in *Souvenir*, 34th All-India Library Conference, and 13th National Seminar of the IASLIC Calcutta, Bengal Library Association, 1988, pp. 66-70.

————, "State Central Library, Haryana", in Gupta B.M., Ed., *Library Development in India* (Handbook of Libraries, Archives, and Information Centres in India, Series, Vol. 16), New Delhi, Segment Books, 1996, pp. 286-92.

————, and Sachdeva, B.R., "Guidelines for Norms of Collection and Organization of Material in College Libraries in Haryana", *ILA Bulletin*, 19: 4 (Jan.-March 1984).

Ratta, W.D., "Status Report on Development of Public Libraries in Haryana", *Granthana*, 4: 1&2 (Jan & July 1993), pp. 49-55.

Himachal Pradesh

Chandel, A.S., "Library Movement in Himachal Pradesh: Past and Present", in *Library Development in India*, (Handbook of Libraries, Archives, and Information Centres in India, Series, Vol. 16), Ed. by B.M. Gupta, New Delhi, Segment Books, 1996, pp. 188-99.

Justa, H.R., "Development of Public Libraries in Himachal Pradesh", *Granthana*, 4: 1&2 (Jan. & July 1993). pp. 57-60.

Jammu & Kashmir

Baba, Abdul Majid, "College Libraries in Kashmir Valley: A Survey", in Mangla, C.P., *et al.*, Ed, *Fifty Years of Librarianship in India: Past, Present and Future,* 29th All-India Library Conference, Mysore, Dec. 5-9, 1983, pp. 26-39.

Lattoo, R., "Role of Public Libraries in Adult Education with Special Reference to Jammu & Kashmir", in Vashishth, C.P., *Library Movement and Library Development in India*, Seminar papers, 39th All-India Library Conference, Bangalore, January 7-10, 1994, pp. 165-70.

Shafi, S.M. and Rufai, Reyaz, "Public Libraries in Jammu & Kashmir: An Appraisal", *Granthana*, 2: 2 (July 1991) pp. 169-77.

Karnataka

Deshpande, K.S., "University Libraries in Karnataka", in *Souvenir*, 29 All-India Conference, Mysore, Dec. 5-9, 1983, pp. 27-35.

————, "Library Movement in Mysore State", *Indian Librarian*, 17 (1962-63).

Ijari, S.R., "Survey of Public Library Development in Karnataka", in *Public Library Systems: Services & Networking;* A festschrift, presented to Prof. K. Sarada, Ed. by L.S. Ramaiah and others, New Delhi, Ess Ess Publications, 1997, Vol. 1, 176-190.

————, "March of Libraries in Karnataka", in *Souvenir*, 34th All-India Library Conference, and 13th National Seminar of the IASLIC, Calcutta, Bengal Library Association, 1988, pp. 71-77.

————, "Panchayat Libraries Under Public Library System in Karnataka: A Micro-analysis", National Seminar on Community Information Centres Under Panchayat

Raj, February 19-21, 1997, K.A. Raju, Seminar Director, Reading material, Hyderabad, NIRD, 95-105.

————, *Development Plan for Public Library System in Karnataka State*, Dharwad, 1983, Ph. D. Thesis.

————, and Khan, H.A, "State Central Reference Library", in *Library Development in India* (Handbook of Libraries, Archives, and Information Centres in India, Series, Vol. 16), Ed. by B.M. Gupta, New Delhi, Segment Books, 1996, pp. 293-301.

Karisiddappa, C.R. and Kumbhar, B.D., "Public Library Services in Rural Area: A Case Study of Dharwad District", in *Public Library Systems: Services & Networking*; A festschrift presented to Prof K. Sarada; Ed. by L.S. Ramaiah and others, New Delhi, Ess Ess Publications, 1997. Vol. 1, pp. 193-202.

Khan, H.A., "Public Library's Response to Rural Information Needs", in *Public Library Systems: Services & Networking*; A festschrift presented to Prof. K. Sarada, Ed. by L.S. Ramaiah and others, New Delhi, Ess Ess Publications, 1997, Vol. 1, pp. 216-27.

Khan, H.A., "Issues in Public Library Development in Karnataka", in *Souvenir*, 29 All-India Library Conference, Mysore, Dec. 5-9, 1983, pp. 36-44.

————, "Public Library's Response to Rural Information Needs", in *Public Library Systems: Services & Networking*; A festschrift presented to Prof. K. Sarada, Ed. by L.S. Ramaiah and others, New Delhi, Ess Ess Publications, 1997, Vol. 1, pp. 216-27.

————, *Problems and Prospects of Public Libraries in Four Library Law States in India*, Karnataka University, Dharwad, 1985 Ph.D. Thesis.

————, "Public Libraries and the Contemporary Indian Society", in *Current Problems and Trends in Library and Information Services*, Prof. K.S. Deshpande commemoration volume, Ed. by H.A. Khan and S.R. Ijari, Varanasi, Indian Bibliographic Centre, 1990, pp. 166-72.

————, "Role of Rural Libraries in the Promotion of Literacy and Adult Education", *Granthana*, 2: 2 (July 1991), pp. 135-45.

Kumbhar, M.R., and Karisiddappa, C.R., "Library and Information Science Education in Karnataka", in *Souvenir*, 29 All-India Conference, Mysore, Dec. 5-9, 1983, pp. 54-59.

Rammurthy, J.R., "Media Information System in Karnataka: A Case Study of Deccan Herald and Prajavani", in *Souvenir*, 29 All-India Conference, Mysore, Dec. 5-9, 1983, pp. 45-48.

Sainath, J.S., "Mysore University Library", in *Souvenir*, 29 All-India Conference, Mysore, Dec. 5-9, 1983, pp. 12-15.

Kerala

Augustine C.A. and Devarajan, G. Ed., *Public Library System in India*, New Delhi, Ess Ess Publications, 1990. (contains a number of Essays of the Library Act and Legislation in Kerala).

Bavakutty, M., "Book Collection in College Libraries", in *Current Problems and Trends in Library and Information Science*, (1990);.

————, *Libraries in Higher Education*, Delhi, Ess Ess Publications, 1991.

————, "College Libraries in India", *Int. Lib. Rev.*, 14 (1982) 391-7.

————, "Development of Book Collection in College Libraries in Kerala", 30th All-India Library Conference, 1985.

Bavakutty, M., "College Libraries in Kerala: A Survey Report", *Int. Lib. Rev.* 16 (1984), 437-446.

————, "Libraries and Library Science Education in Kerala", in *Souvenir*, Calcutta, Bengal Library Association, 1988, pp. 78-83.

————, "Organisation of College Libraries", *ALIS Bulletin*, (1981).

————, "Organisation of College Libraries: Centralization *vs* Decentralization", ILA South Zone Conference, 1979;

————, "College Libraries in India: Some Observations", in 29th All-India Library Seminar, 1983.

————, "Staff Pattern in College Libraries in Kerala", 31st All-India Library Conference, 1985.

————, "Quality of Book Collection", 32nd All-India Library Conference, 1989.

————, "Standards for College Libraries", 35th All-India Library Seminar, 1989.

————, "Towards Better Education", in *Hundred Years of Library Education and Its Future*, Ed., P.S.G. Kumar, paper CC. 1987.

————, "Academic Status for University Library Staff", in *University Libraries in India*; 1980s and beyond, Delhi, Medallion Press, 1991.

————, "School Libraries in Kerala", *Int. Lib. Rev.*, 13 (1981), pp. 447-51.

————. "College Libraries in Kerala: The State-of-the-art", in *College Libraries in India*, proceedings of National Seminar on College Libraries in India, Delhi, 31 Oct-1 Nov. 1988, Ed., Krishan Kumar, and J.K. Anand, Delhi, ILA, 1988, pp. 105-12.

————, "Development of Public Libraries in Kerala: A Review", 28th All-India Library Seminar, 1982.

————, "Kerala Public Libraries Bill, 1972: An Evaluation", *Library Herald*, 15 (284), 1973-74, pp. 146-50.

Chandran, Manayath, "Kerala Granthasala Sangham Act: Background and Special Features", in *Public Library System in India*, Ed. by C.S. Augustine and G. Devarajan, New Delhi, Ess Ess Publications, 1990, pp. 52-59.

Devarajan, G., "Changing Concept of Public Library Development in Kerala", *in Public Library System in India*, Ed. by C.A. Augustine and G. Devarajan, New Delhi, Ess Ess Publications, 1990, pp. 34-42.

————, "Library Science Literature in Malayalam", *Herald of Library Science*, 26: 1&2, (1987), 95-99.

Isaac, K.A., "Library Movement in Kerala", *Timeless Fellowship*, 8(1973), pp. 45-56.

Kerala Granthasala Sanghom, Annual Reports.

Nair, K. Sukumaran, "Public Libraries in Kerala-origin and Development", *Granthana*, 4: 1&2 (Jan. & July 1993), pp. 61-67.

Nair, R. Raman, "Origins of People's Library Movement in Kerala", *Granthana*, 4: 1&2 (Jan. & July 1993), pp. 29-36.

Rajashekaran, K., "College Libraries Under Kerala Agricultural University: Present Situation and Future Directions", in *College Libraries in India*, Proceedings of National Seminar on College Libraries in India, Delhi, 31 Oct. 1 Nov. 1988, Ed. Krishan Kumar, and J.K. Anand, Delhi, ILA, 1988, pp. 113-19.

Ramakrishnan, M.N., "Kerala Public Libraries (Kerala Granthalaya Sangham) Act, 1989: An Overview", in *Public Library System in India*, Ed. by C.A. Augustine and G. Devarajan, New Delhi, Ess Ess Publications, 1990, pp. 60-63.

Lakshadweep

Hamsath, K., "Public Libraries in Union Territory of Lakshadweep", in 25th All-India Library Conference, Trivandrum, 14-18 May, 1979, *Souvenir*, pp. 141-42.

Madhya Pradesh

Bhargava, G.D., and Nigam, B.S., "Madhya Pradesh Needs Library Legislation", in Vashishth, C.P., *Library Movement and Library Development in India*, Seminar Papers, 39th All-India Library Conference, Bangalore, January 7-10, 1994, pp. 52-60.

Kumar, S., and Kumar, Abha, "Promotion Avenues for College Librarians in Madhya Pradesh: Prospects and Challenges", in *College Libraries in India*, Proceedings of National Seminar on College Libraries in India, Delhi, 31 Oct.-1 Nov. 1988, Ed. Krishan Kumar, and J.K. Anand, Delhi, ILA, 1988, pp. 64-72.

Moghe, V.S., "Madhya Pradesh", in *Public Library System*, Ed. by S.R. Ranganathan, and A. Neelameghan, Bangalore, Sarada Ranganathan Endowment for Library Service, 1972, pp. 195-98.

Tejomurthy, A., "Madhya Pradesh Library Association", in Vashishth, C.P., *Library Movement and Library Development in India*, Seminar Papers, 39th All-India Library Conference, Bangalore, January 7-10, 1994, pp. 120-25.

————, "University Library Finance Management: Theory and Practice", in Prasher R.G. Ed., *University Libraries in India: 1980s and Beyond*, New Delhi, Medallion Press, 1991, pp. 140-61.

Wadikar, A.L., "Library Scene in Madhya Pradesh", in *Souvenir*, 34th All-India Library Conference, and 13th National Seminar of the IASLIC, Calcutta, Bengal Library Association, 1988, pp. 84-88.

Maharashtra

Baheti, S.R., "Status: Pay Scales and Service Conditions of College Librarians in Vidharbha Region (Maharashtra)", in *College Libraries in India*, Proceedings of National Seminar on College Libraries in India, Delhi, 31 Oct.-1 Nov. 1988, Ed.,Krishan Kumar, and J.K Anand, Delhi, ILA, 1988, pp. 154-66.

————, "Development of College Libraries in Maharashtra with Special Reference to Vidharbha Region", in Vashishth, C.P., *Library Movement and Library Development in India*, Seminar Papers, 39th All-India Library Conference, Bangalore, January 7-10, 1994, pp. 275-83.

Borkar, V.M. "Problems of College Libraries in Ahmednagar City", in *College Libraries in India*, Proceedings of National Seminar on College Libraries in India, Delhi, 31 Oct.-1 Nov. 1988, Ed., Krishan Kumar, and J.K. Anand, Delhi, ILA, 1988, pp. 150-53.

Chahande, M.S. "Development of Public Libraries in Maharashtra", *Granthana*, 2: 2 (July 1991), pp. 183-92.

Mahajan, S.G., "Library Development in Maharashtra", in *Souvenir*, 34th All-India Library Conference, and 13th National Seminar of the IASLIC, Calcutta, Bengal Library Association, 1988, pp. 89-94.

Mahajan, S.G., "Legal Aspects in University Library Management", in *Academic Libraries Role in the National Development*, Ed., Dorothy Isaac and Others, Madras, T.R. Publications, 1993, pp. 133-51.

Manipur

Lahiri, Ramansu, "Library Development and the School Phenomenon: A Highlight on Manipur", in Vashishth, C.P., *Library Movement and Library Development in India*, Seminar Papers, 39th All-India Library Conference, Bangalore, January 7-10, 1994, pp. 240-48.

Singh, N. Giridhari, "Development of Libraries in Manipur", in *Souvenir*, 34th All-India Library Conference, and 13th National Seminar of the IASLIC, Calcutta, Bengal Library Association, 1988, pp. 95-99.

Singh, P. Achouba, "Public Library Development in Manipur", *Granthana*, 4: 1&2 (Jan. & July 1993), pp. 69-74.

Meghalaya

Chandel, A.S., "Library Services in Meghalaya", in *Souvenir*, 34th All-India Library Conference, and 13th National Seminar of the IASLIC, Calcutta, Bengal Library Association, 1988, pp. 100-04.

———, "College Libraries in Bihar", In *College Libraries in India*, Proceedings of National Seminar on College Libraries in India, Delhi, 31 Oct.-1 Nov. 1988, Ed., Krishan Kumar, and J.K. Anand, Delhi ILA, 1988, pp. 49-58.

Mizoram

Lianzama, C., "History and Development of Library Movement of Mizoram State", in *Souvenir*, 34th All-India Library Conference, and 13th National Seminar of the IASLIC, Calcutta, Bengal Library Association, 1988, pp. 105-06.

———, "Status Report of Public Library Development in Mizoram", *Granthana*, 4: 1&2 (Jan & July 1993), pp. 75-78.

Orissa

Das, Kailash Chandra, and Mohapatra, M., "Development of Secondary School Libraries in Orissa", in Vashishth, C.P., *Library Movement and Library Development in India*, Seminar Papers, 39th All-India Library Conference, Bangalore, January 7-10, 1994, pp. 249-55.

Jena, Puspanjali, "A Study of Book Selection and Acquisition Policy in College Libraries of Orissa", in *College Libraries in India*, Proceedings of National Seminar on College Libraries in India, Delhi, 31 Oct.-1 Nov. 1988, Ed., Krishan Kumar and J.K. Anand, Delhi, ILA, 1988, pp. 78-80.

Joshi, S.C., "Library Legislation in Orissa: What, Why and When?" in Vashishth, C.P., *Library Movement and Library Development in India*, Seminar Papers, 39th All-India Library Conference, Bangalore, January 7-10 1994, pp. 61-67.

Mahapatra, M. "Libraries and Library Movement in Orissa—An Overview", in *Souvenir*, 34th All-India Library Conference, and 13th National Seminar of the IASLIC, Calcutta, Bengal Library Association, 1988, pp. 107-11.

Panda, B.D., *History of Library Development*, New Delhi, Anmol, 1992 (Major focus is the history of developments in Orissa).

Padhi, P., and Panda, K.C., "Harekrishna Mahtab State Library, Orissa", in *Library Development in India* (Handbook of Libraries Archives, and Information Centres in India, Series, Vol. 16) Ed., B.M. Gupta, New Delhi, Segment Books, 1996, pp. 307-20.

Parida, Baman, "Status and Pay Scales of College Library Staff of Orissa: An Evaluation", in *College Libraries in India*, Proceedings of National Seminar on College Libraries in India, Delhi, 31 Oct.-1 Nov. 1988, Ed., Krishan Kumar, and J.K. Anand, Delhi, ILA, 1988, pp. 81-87.

Samantaray, M. and Rath, P.K., "Public Library System and Service in Orissa", in Vashishth, C.P., *Library Movement and Library Development in India*, Seminar

Papers, 39th All-India Library Conference, Bangalore, January 7-10, 1994, pp. 74-79.

Shukla, B.B., "Role of Public Libraries and Impediments on Their Development in Orissa with Reference to Library Legislation", in Vashishth, C.P., *Library Movement and Library Development in India*, Seminar Papers, 39th All-India Library Conference, Bangalore, January 7-10, 1994, pp. 80-84.

Srichandan, G.K., "Public Library Service in Orissa—A Status Report", *Granthana*, 4: 1&2 (Jan & July 1993), pp. 79-82.

Pondicherry

Rajan, K. Sounder, "Romain Rolland Library, Pondicherry", in Gupta B.M. Ed., *Library Development in India* (Handbook of Libraries, Archives, and Information Centres in India, Series, Vol. 16), New Delhi, Segment Books, 1996, pp. 302-06.

Punjab

Arora, Madhuri, "College Libraries in Punjab and UT Chandigarh", in Vashishth, C.P., *Library Movement and Library Development in India*, Seminar Papers, 39th All-India Library Conference, Bangalore, January 7-10, 1994, pp. 261-74.

Bansal, G.C., and Tikku U.K., "University Library Services in Punjab", in Prasher, R.G., Ed., *University Libraries in India: 1980s and Beyond*, New Delhi, Medallion Press, 1991, pp. 31-40.

Sharma, M.L., *A Critical Study of the Role and Contribution of the Private Enterprise in Education in Punjab, 1954-1966*, Punjab University, Chandigarh, 1981, Ph.D. Thesis.

Singh Sewa, "History of Library Movement in Punjab", in Gupta, B.M., Ed., *Library Development in India* (Handbook of Libraries, Archives, and Information Centres in India, Series, Vol. 16), New Delhi, Segment Books, 1996, pp. 208-24.

————, "Public Library Development in Punjab", *Granthana*, 2 : 2 (July 1991), pp. 147-54.

————, "Library Movement in Punjab: Roles and Outlook", in Vashishth, C.P., *Library Movement and Library Development in India*, Seminar Papers, 39th All-India Library Conference, Bangalore, January 7-10, 1994, pp. 85-94.

Singh, Sukhdev, and Satija, M., "Development of Academic and Public Libraries in Punjab: A Historical Perspective", in Vashishth, C.P., *Library Movement and Library Development in India*, Seminar Papers, 39th All-India Library Conference, Bangalore, January 7-10, 1994, pp. 231-39.

Trehan, G.L. "Library Development in Punjab—An Overview", in *Souvenir*, 34th All-India Library Conference, and 13th National Seminar of the IASLIC, Calcutta, Bengal Library Association, 1988, pp. 112-14.

Rajasthan

Bhardwaj, C.B. "Public Library System in Rajasthan—A Bird's Eye View", *Granthana*, 4: 1&2 (Jan. & July 1993), pp. 83-87.

Boonlia, Naresh, "Deplorable and Discouraging Pay Scales of College Assistant Librarians in Rajasthan", in *College Libraries in India*, Proceedings of National Seminar on College Libraries in India, Delhi, 31 Oct.-1 Nov. 1988, Ed., Krishan Kumar, and J.K. Anand, Delhi, ILA 1988, pp. 43-48.

Nandwana, H.B. "Role of Public Libraries in Distance Education with Special Reference to Rajasthan", in R.P. Kumar, *et al.*, (Ed.), *Role of Libraries in National Development*, 42nd All-India Library Conference, Calicut, Dec. 21-24, 1996, pp. 154-59.

Sharma, C.D. and Sharma, Narendra, "Library Movement in Rajasthan", in *Souvenir*, 34th All-India Library Conference, and 13th National Seminar of the IASLIC, Calcutta, Bengal Library Association, 1988, pp. 115-24.

Sharma, Narendra, "Library Development in Rajasthan", in Gupta, B.M., Ed., *Library Development in India* (Handbook of Libraries, Archives, and Information Centres in India, Series, Vol. 16), New Delhi, Segment Books, 1996, pp. 225-35.

Vyas S.D. "School and Public Library System with Special Reference to Rajasthan", in Vashishth, C.P., *Library Movement and Library Development in India*, Seminar Paper, 39th All-India Library Conference, Bangalore, January 7-10, 1994, pp. 256-60.

Tamil Nadu

Amudavalli, A., "Library Services of Foreign Cultural Centres at Madras", in *Current Problems and Trends in Library and Information Services*, Prof. K.S. Deshpande Commemoration Volume, Ed. by H.A. Khan and S.R. Ijari, Varanasi, Indian Bibliographic Centre, 1990, pp. 104-13.

Dilli, K.T., and Srinath, Manorama, "Role of Public Libraries in Promoting Literacy Programmes in Tamil Nadu: A Comparative Study with JSN", in R.P. Kumar, *et al.*, Ed., *Role of Libraries in National Development*, 42nd All-India Library Conference, Calicut, Dec. 21-24, 1996, pp. 77-85.

Manoharan, A., "Perspectives of College Library Services and Management in Tiruchirapalli", in *College Libraries in India*, Proceedings of National Seminar on College Libraries in India, Delhi, 31 Oct.-1 Nov., 1988, Ed. Krishan Kumar, and J.K. Anand, Delhi, ILA, 1988, pp. 96-100.

Palanivelu, C., and Raghavan, K.S. Eds., *Education Through Public Libraries—A Practical Approach*, National Seminar on Public Library Movement. Proceedings, Madras, Directorate of Public Libraries 1991.

Pandithurai, C., "Concept of Community Information System for Integrated Rural Development: Madurai District Experience—Considerations for a Model", National Seminar on Community Information Centres Under Panchayat Raj, February 19-21, 1997, K.A. Raju, Seminar Director; Reading material, Hyderabad, NIRD, pp. 55-65.

Ponamian, R., "The Services of the Connemara Public Library", in *Public Library Systems: Services & Networking*, A festschrift presented to Prof. K. Sarada, Ed. by L.S. Ramaiah and Others, New Delhi, Ess Ess Publications, 1997, Vol. 2, pp. 8-14.

Ramesh Babu, B., "Public Library Systems in Tamil Nadu: Emergence of Circle Libraries", *Vashishth*, C. P. and Others, Ed. New Horizons in Library and Information Science. Dr. Velaga Venkatappaiah Festschrift, Madras, T.R. Publications, 1994, pp. 225-33.

Ranganathan, G. "Public Libraries: Tamil Nadu", *Granthana*, 4: 1&2 (Jan. & July 1993), pp. 89-98.

Rani, B.S. Swaroop, "Access System in Trichy College Libraries", in *College Libraries in India*, Proceedings of National Seminar on College Libraries in India, Delhi, 31 Oct.-1 Nov., 1988, Ed. Krishan Kumar, and J. K. Anand, Delhi, ILA 1988, pp. 101-04.

Sarma, K.V. "Manuscript Collections in Tamil Nadu: A Survey", *Granthana*, 2: 2 (July 1991), pp. 155-62.

Thillainayagam, V.E., "Library Act Based Library Service in Tamil Nadu: A Critical Review", in Vashishth, C.P., *Library Movement and Library Development in India*, Seminar Papers, 39th All-India Library Conference, Bangalore, January 7-10, 1994, pp. 100-19.

Thillainayagam, V.E., "Tamil Nadu", in *Public Library System*, edited by S.R. Ranganathan, and A. Neelameghan, Bangalore, Sarada Ranganathan, Endowment for Library Service, 1972, pp. 169-73.

Venkatappaiah, Velaga, "Connemara (State Central) Public Library, Madras", in Gupta, B.M., Ed., *Library Development in India* (Handbook of Libraries Archives, and Information Centres in India, Series, Vol. 16) New Delhi, Segment Books, 1996, pp. 321-26.

Tripura

Chakraborty, G.P., "College and Academic Institutional Libraries in Tripura: A Survey", in *College Libraries in India,* Proceedings of National Seminar on College Libraries in India, Delhi, 31 Oct.-1 Nov., 1988 Ed., Krishan Kumar, and J.K. Anand, Delhi, ILA, 1988, pp. 120-41.

Chakraborty, Debabrata, "The Development of Library Service in Tripura", in *Souvenir*, 34th All-India Library Conference, and 13th National Seminar of the IASLIC, Calcutta, Bengal Library Association, 1988, pp. 125-28.

Gupta B.B. "Status Report on Development of Public Libraries in Tripura", *Granthana*, 4: 1&2 (Jan. & July 1993) pp. 99-106.

Uttar Pradesh

Chaturvedi, C.C. "College Libraries in Uttar Pradesh: Working Conditions and Major Problems", in *College Libraries in India*, Proceedings of National Seminar on College Libraries in India, Delhi, 31 Oct. 1-Nov., 1988, Ed., Krishan Kumar, and J.K. Anand, Delhi, ILA, 1988, pp. 32-42.

Goswami, Dinesh Chandra, "Libraries and Librarianship in Uttarkhand: A Perspective", in Kumar, R.P. *et. al.*, *Role of Libraries in National Development*, Papers of the 42nd All-India Library Conference, Calicut, Dec. 21-24, 1996, pp. 66-72.

Mehrotra, R.K. "Public Library Development in Uttar Pradesh", *Granthana*, 4: 1&2 (Jan. & July 1993), pp. 107-11.

Sahu, K.C., and Azad, G.C., "U.P. Library Association—A Brief History", *Lucknow Librarian* (Special Souvenir issue) 14:2-3 (1982), xli-xliv.

Singh, Sonal, "Collection Development in Libraries of Uttar Pradesh", in Vashishth, C.P., *Library Movement and Library Development in India*, Seminar Papers, 39th All-India Library Conference, Bangalore, January 7-10, 1994, pp. 328-44.

Srivastava Rachna, "Library Movement in Uttar Pradesh: A State of the Art", in *Souvenir*, 34th All-India Library Conference, and 13th National Seminar of the IASLIC, Calcutta, Bengal Library Association, 1988, pp. 129-34.

Taher, Mohamed, "Madarsa Libraries in India: A Case Study of Nadwat-al-Ulama, Lucknow", in *Humanities Information Systems and Services*, (Handbook of Libraries, Archives and Information Centres, Series, Vol. 9. Part I), New Delhi, Aditya, 1991.

Tiwari, B.N. "Uttar Pradesh" in *Public Library System*, edited by S.R. Ranganathan, and A. Neelameghan, Bangalore, Sarada Ranganathan Endowment for Library Service, 1972, pp. 202-03.

West Bengal

Kabir, Abulfazal M. Fazle, *The Libraries of Bengal, 1700-1947: The Story of Bengali Renaissance*, New Delhi 1988.

Mukherjee, Nirmal, "Development of Library Services in the State of West Bengal", *Granthana*, 4: 1&2 (Jan. & July 1993), pp. 113-16.

Ohdedar, A.K., "State Central Library, West Bengal", Gupta, B.M. Ed., *Library Development in India* (Handbook of Libraries, Archives, and Information Centres in India, Series, Vol. 16), New Delhi Segment Books, 1996, pp. 327-39.

Roychoudhury, Prabir, "Public Library Development in West Bengal: A Review", In *Souvenir*, 34th All-India Library Conference, and 13th National Seminar of the IASLIC, Calcutta, Bengal Library Association, 1988, pp. 135-48.

Saha, Ramkrishna, "Library Movement in West Bengal", in *Souvenir*, 34th All-India Library Conference and 13th National Seminar of the IASLIC, Calcutta, Bengal Library Association, 1988, pp. 153-59.

7

TECHNIQUE OF MAINTENANCE AND PRESERVATION OF LIBRARIES

"It is estimated that the average scientist spends between 20 and 25 per cent of his working time searching for information. Because of this it is obvious desirable that information needs should be studied with a view to improving the libraries' role as information transfer agent . . . the anomalous dilemma of rising costs and decreasing service suggests that libraries are straying from their essential business of gathering, putting in order and giving".

"Current emphasis on the mechanical aspects of acquisitions and cataloguing not only overlooks the prime importance of collection usage but also fails to realize that the giving function must be expanded to include self service use (*i.e.*, a user orientation). Unless libraries are successful in the area of uniting book and reader, their very existence, as we currently know them, is threatened" Dano L. Roth, Library Advisor, IIT Kanpur, (1972).

Maintenance and Preservation: Trends and Practices

Maintenance here concerns keeping the collection in a way that it is useable, and that the collection is kept in a temperature that is most suitable to the specific type of reading materials that the library has, and to keep library safe from hazards of different types—human, insects, natural calamities, climatic influences, etc.

History

Libraries always collected information and also did take steps to maintain the library and preserve their contents in a shape useful for posterity. In the age of advances in recording and storing all types of information, libraries did adopt methods most suitable to each type of reading material, be it a printed book, or audio record, or a manuscript. Maintenance includes processing of books, dusting, keeping the place useable, as well repair of damaged reading materials. The main idea of maintaining a library is to classify and catalogue books, and this was done since long in India. For instance, in the ancient period, the Indian libraries had arranged the books according to some classification scheme. There were variations of languages, of literature's from Buddhists to Brahmins, and so on. Buddhists literature had, for instance, three main divisions, Jains had six groups, and Brahminical Classification had four divisions.

Black ink was commonly used for writing. In Sanskrit, it is called *Mashi* or *Mas*, meaning *Kajal*. Most of the presently available manuscripts, using *Kajal*, date back to Seventh century AD. There are also evidences of the use of iron powder, being used for writing in Ancient India. In terms of ink that has longer life, the Mss. belonging to Punjab are still in readable condition.

In preservation of books Jains took the lead. The library was, usually, in the basement to save the manuscripts (Mss.) from the rays of sun and dust. Leather and wooden boxes were in use to store these books. A knot of cotton thread was used for the Mss. to protect from the changing atmospheric conditions as well as dust. Further, Birch Bark and palm leave Mss. were held together by a cord drawn together by a single hole in the middle, and this was how they bound the books. The outer cover of this book would sometimes be of cloth. But normally outer covers were of thin sliced wood pieces, rarely of skin and hide covers. Birch Bark often breaks, when folded, and hence large number of these ancient Mss. on bark have been found in roll form, not bound at all.

In the ancient India, while hides of tiger and deer, were used, all other skins were considered as impure. In Subandhu's Vasavadatta, there is an explicit reference to the use of hide for writing Palm leaf Mss. belonging to the period of Eleventh or Twelfth centuries, are still available in various libraries and manuscript depositories of India. In areas of very high temperatures, in Rajasthan and other areas, many manuscripts were lost due to such unhealthy climatic conditions.

Paper was a rare commodity, though already invented, even in Seventh century India. The oldest Indian Mss. traced by the famous paleologist, G. Buhler, dates 1223 AD. Interestingly, India has even today handwritten manuscripts, and these both for official and non-official reasons, will continue for ages. Official transactions are made on handwritten or typewritten, manuscripts, and will serve as valuable documents for all purposes.

Medieval period witnessed advances in maintenance and preservation in libraries. There are elaborate references to scholars being responsible for this task. The Imperial Library of the Mughals, for example, classified the collection in thirteen subjects, and arranged the books on shelf according to different languages.

The period saw another development in the form of illuminated manuscripts, in quantity unheard before. This did have a direct impact on need to improve preservation of such artistic and aesthetic books. Calligraphy and the art of binding were the other advances made in this period of Indian library history. The Mughuls produced leather for binding, and this period saw the development of book-binding as an art. They initiated yet another trend, that is of, decorative book binding.

By the end of Seventeenth century Western interests in India necessitated the building of printing and mass production of books. This had a direct effect on means of maintenance and preservation in the libraries. The Westerners also therefore imported various techniques. One of these was the idea itself of modern librarianship. By the end of Nineteenth century India received much impetus in this regard and the country witnessed many improvements in libraries. It transformed the idea of library from storehouse to information resource centres, declaring that the library has its collection only for use. Ranganathan imported many ideas of library management, and much more were innovated in the process by himself and by those all who received the Western inspiration. He initiated the system of management, storage, preservation and retrieval based on standards for libraries, as an all-round concept. A list of standards evolved by the Indian Standards is given in the appendix of the present work.

Shelves for keeping books in libraries have been in use for ages. The difference that appeared in the present century was in opening the closed shelves. Open access to information, that was otherwise locked for ever, revolutionized the idea of providing direct access to information. Based on these modern tenets, Ranganathan gave his first law, that books are not for storing, rather these are for use, and that these are not to be locked up, rather these are to be kept open for browsing by one and all; thereby re-stated the purpose of libraries as resource centres, and public libraries as free for all, and open for all.

Libraries did preserve the material using indigenous methods of safeguarding, from hazards such as, insects, environment, etc. Not that Indians left all their libraries to winds, and to the floods. India had its own ways of maintaining its books and libraries. For instance, binding of books, using locally developed pest control systems, all were available. Indians have carefully preserved their ancient heritage of manuscripts, in different forms, even to this day.

Open shelf was not the method adopted for manuscripts in Indian libraries. These are generally kept under closed access, and in steel almirahs, with no provision for air to pass through. While air-conditioning is a costly affair, the Indian libraries have not developed alternative means for safety of these sources. Naphthalene balls are generally used to avoid insects destroying the manuscripts. Fewer institutions have adopted fumigation technique for preservation. A few libraries have initiated the process of laminating the manuscripts, to save the decaying condition. Some have instituted microfilming projects for the manuscripts, for which they have microfilming equipment too.

Nevertheless, what was lacking was (a) supply of these for mass consumption—like population explosion and information explosion, libraries also grew leaps and bounds; (b) knowledge of using various medicinal techniques for preserving books; and (c) the techniques of protecting the newer devices of information storage, such as, non-book materials.

Record Management

How have libraries preserved their own records of growth and development? This is a question which is sometimes, answered in affirmative, by stating that each library has its annual report. Each university, for instance, has its report approved by its board of management, and records its annual additions, its annual progress, and so on. What one expects from these annual reports, drafted as a ritual, and submitted to fulfil an obligation, is rather different. For a historian, the statistics which some of these annual reports provide act as mere pathfinders. But there is no further guidance on a number of questions, which are raised to indicate the patterns of growth, level of growth, type of growth, year by year and period by period.

For instance, Thillainayagam, has identified the significant ingredients which makes an annual report really useful, in his paper "Annual Report of the public library system in Tamil Nadu: Suggestions for rapprochement" published in *Public Library System: Services and Networking*, edited by L.S. Ramaiah, and others (1997).

The author, makes a thorough analysis of the type of response the public libraries have initiated in preparing annual reports. He finds that the idea of annual report is by and large a missing feature, and hence suggests a detailed plan for what are the essential features which a public library annual report must have. Such a report will be largely a survey of the quantitative aspects, and to some extent it gives hint on qualitative aspects. In fact, an annual report, to be useful for current and historic survey, must focus on providing equal emphasis on qualitative and quantitative matters.

What otherwise is expected of libraries is that they maintain systematic records of their past performance, and past growth patterns. For a historian, while it is important to have such records, it is worth re-stating that, libraries maintain no serious records and leave the researcher in the field in utter state of chaos and confusion. What was expected from others—by the very librarians—to maintain all documentary evidences of societal affairs, is ironically set aside, when it comes to their own unwillingness to document the library development.

The hypothesis of the present study, in this context, referred to the lack of records in libraries. The hypotheses, is as follows: "Libraries are underdeveloped in maintaining records of their own development; indicating a lack of attitude in record maintenance and a lack of scope for retrospection".

Recent Advances in Maintenance and Preservation

With the changing times and user needs, there emerged different sources of information in a variety of physical forms. For instance, microforms appeared as an alternative storage system to save space, cost and with many more advantages. So also, audio and video cassettes revolutionized the idea of storage mechanisms. These inventions of different types of information sources, necessitated the development of means and methods of storing these in the libraries, in areas other than the book shelf. Moreover, to use these audio-visual it became imperative that libraries must have necessary infrastructure and capabilities to make use of these, and provide ready service to users.

The Indian libraries with only manuscripts, later also added books, but, were soon crowded with these multiple forms of storage and retrieval. Soon multi-media became the fashion of the day, and each library started envying each other in adding up these non-print forms.

If information is stored easily in these non-book materials, it is also true that it is easy to retrieve information from these sources. The additional advantage of these appeared with media sources entrain the field, for instance, newspaper in microforms, enabled storing very old issues of the paper, without any problem which old and worn out paper or manuscript would pose. Similarly, children's libraries needed audio tapes and video cassettes containing educative and informative material, and for such libraries these soon became indispensable sources.

These advantages made it necessary for libraries to venture into this area of adding material that was not their making. It was the technological innovations which were facilitated by the industrial advances in storing information in multiple formats. Hence when these non-book forms were acquired in the libraries, these led to a series of connected issues. The issues were all around acquiring the right type of source, at a minimum price, and most importantly, getting suitable people to maintain these. Librarians in India were aware of book stock maintenance, but maintaining machines, with each having an altogether different mechanism, called for appointing or training staff, for operating as well as maintaining machines.

With the development of photocopying technology, document delivery and document preservation achieved another high mark all over, but more specifically in India. While the country still imports the equipment for photocopying, the procedure being simple and the cost effectiveness of the process, has led to user satisfaction which is very remarkable. Another revolution in the field of automation, that is, computers brought a flood of problems of storage and retrieval for libraries. Libraries, as usual shied away from these automatic information storage mechanisms. They presumed that these are not for bibliographic data storage. This misunderstanding led to a cleavage, which has resulted in late entry of libraries in the competitive world of automating their collections, and automatic retrieval of information contained in these documents.

The libraries in India gradually got acquainted, in the post-independence era, with the preservative and pesticides, to safeguard the resources. With the advances in these techniques it is easy for libraries today to preserve the documents for posterity in a far better way, as compared to the facilities available for the same in the pre-independence era.

With the advent of computers there began a serious consideration for standardization of data entry formats for uniformity in processing of library documents, all over the country. The developments in ISBN, CCF, MARC, CDS/ISIS, and so on, are only some of the representative ones. To create and preserve the bibliographic databases of each and every library, a few leading private entrepreneurs have evolved library friendly software packages. And this has opened up a new era of linking national resources to the world at large. DELNET, the Delhi based library network of libraries in Delhi, has been hooked to Internet, thereby providing access to the world all resources in the libraries of the city. The discussion on maintenance and preservation, is therefore, related to the procedures adopted for input of information, throughput, and output of information. These are a part of the cycle that reflects the routine tasks in the library. Traditionally, input in library was the acquisition of different sources of information. Today, the input is also from the on-line catalogue, which are connected throughout the world. Similarly, the throughput and the output have also undergone change in their basic and overall performance.

One of the main hypothesis of the present study is that libraries do not carefully maintain records of their own growth. Keeping themselves busy with daily routines, and involving themselves in trivial matters, they forget their own origin and the processes that have made them whatever they are!!! Most libraries have no records of all the transactions that they make, whether in terms of annual evaluations, or annual performance appraisal records. The only exception is that all libraries religiously maintain an accession register, which is hardly sufficient for writing the growth of the entire library. A survey of major libraries in the country shows that there is an unconscious disregard for maintaining records of past. If one were to measure the performance of today with that of the recent past, even that in most of the cases is impossible, as there is no track of any sort to link the past with the present, to measure the present, based on the set policies of the institutions, it is not any way easy. The first reason for this is, there are no stated policies. Each administrator in the library manages the show according to his own whims and fancy, and each successor overturns the decisions and ideas of the predecessor for good or for bad. The second reason for this measurement being difficult, is the fact that apart from the acquisition statistics, there are hardly any facts or figures documented, let alone for the past years, even for the same year. There is no such thing called decision making record or documentation of what decisions were made in, let alone small time affairs, in major policies and practices—such as why a particular software was selected and why others were all ignored, or why did the library decide to order CD-ROM rather than hard copies of serials, breaking the back volumes and creating a maze for the users—to run from pillar to post. There are many such mysterious reasons, and matters which necessitate record keeping in libraries, but there is no such practice. It is hoped that Internet will bring some relief in recording the transactions, that would otherwise go unrecorded. All this is, however, the concern of a historian, which the practitioners care not!

In terms of preserving the cultural and literary heritage of India, the Government has already initiated steps in this regard. The establishment of Indira Gandhi Centre for Fine Arts, is a leading resource trying to collect Indian literary resources and preserve them for posterity. So also, the news comes that Khuda Bakhsh Oriental Public Library, is building up cassette collection. The aim is to collect a comprehensive collection of audio and video cassettes of distinguished writers, poets and eminent people of India. According to its Annual Report, 1995-96, placed before the Parliament, the library has so far brought out 36 volumes dealing with manuscripts of Persian poetry, Hadith literature and Sufism. It has, as a part of resource sharing programme, acquired microfilms of selected Mss. from other libraries in the country, including, Aligarh Muslim University Library, Aligarh; Asafiya Library, Hyderabad, Bhagalpur; and Asiatic Society, Calcutta.

One instance at hand is the idea of preserving the decaying collection of late Raja Muttiah Chettiar Collection, at Chennai. Tha Raja, a lover of books, who died in 1992, left an impressive collection of a variety of literary masterpieces in Tamil—the collection having 100 rare books, 1,500 journals and newspapers, and half a million clippings.

The project of microfilming all these documents, was initiated by the University of Chicago recently. James Nye, was assigned the task of being the chief coordinator of this project. The programme is to prepare microfilm, preserve the precious resource and catalogue the same, and make it accessible to the concerned scholars all over the world. As per the plans, the entire collection is being catalogued using library software, under the guidance of a local library expert. Once the project is completed, its access to local as well as international scholars would be freely available. In the US the microfilm collection will be available through inter-library loan. There will also be facilities where individuals can buy copies at very low prices.

Such an ambitious project, with the help of University of Chicago, and by the efforts of James Nye, is also being undertaken to similarly process another rare and valuable resource in Hyderabad, all in Urdu, Scholars all over the world are interested in this one man collection—Subhan's collection. Subhan, an ordinary car mechanic, spent his life earnings to acquire unique prints and complete runs of many Urdu periodicals, and primary documents. The collection running to 25,000 volumes is presently under process. With the advancement in technology, it is rather easier to find and correlate, the past performance. This is possible at the best in certain conditions. For example, if the historian desires to find the patterns of growth of users, collection, size of population, increase in prices and level of incomes and expenditure, all in one go, can make it possible because all these figures are available in the computerized system. What is still difficult, despite the advancement, is the areas of qualitative and behavioural issues pertaining to the same topics and same growth patterns. Rather, it is simple to state that with automated procedures that libraries follow, a few areas of records of library development are easily identifiable. Whereas a large number of areas of historical research interest are still in a disarray.

Conclusion

The art and craft of maintaining and preserving library materials has been progressing in the country. By and large, during the last fifty years there has been many attempts in this regard, and the aim of satisfying the maximum user needs with minimum resources is getting possible support from the libraries.

8

LIBRARIES FOR A BETTER TOMORROW

Futuristic Perspectives: Need for Useable Libraries

To begin with it is relevant to quote a senior professional, Prof. Vashishth, reiterates, in 1993—exactly seven years before the millennium—a seven point programme of library development. This programme, he hoped, would help achieving the objective of 'library service for all' by 2000 AD. The seven points are (Vashishth, 1994: xxi-xxviii):

(i) Make 'library' an essential component in all schemes of literacy, education and development;
(ii) Community library status to school library after-school hours;
(iii) Network of rural libraries;
(iv) Modernization of libraries;
(v) Library service under mandate of law;
(vi) Regular supply of funds to libraries of higher-education; and
(vii) Moratorium on opening of new library science schools.

The point is based on the fact that the level of literacy at the national level is just 50 per cent, with a 'dubious distinction of having the largest number of illiterates in the world'. He opines that the schemes launched by the Government, such as, " 'Total literacy campaign', the 'District Primary Education Programme', and 'Operation Black Board', have all been done with good intention. But even after 50 years of our independence, we are still lagging behind 33 years so far as the target of universal primary education is concerned. . . . There are massive resource requirements for meeting the goal of 'Education for all by 2000'. Our policy planners need to realize the importance of 'Libraries' in the scheme of things. The component of 'Library' must be included with all seriousness in all the schemes of literacy, education and development. . . . Libraries are very potent instruments for creating general awareness, building mass movements, effecting social changes and speeding the process of development. No more now we can ignore the role of library in the development of nation as a whole" (p. xxii).

On the basis of a very high level of dropouts—50 per cent dropout before reaching class V, and this combined with lack of public library resource for the neo-literate, Prof. Vashishth recommends that for these "the doors of school libraries should be thrown open after the regular school hours. The concerned ministries and departments should work out a scheme for the linkage of school library . . . and the services of its librarian commissioned. As an incentive, the librarian and his support staff may be paid honorarium for extra load of work" (p. xxiii).

Considering the lack of rural libraries, for the rural masses, and considering the failure of even the States where library legislation could have improved the situation, he is hopeful that the proposed plan of the Union Ministry of Rural Development of establishing 1,00,000 community centres in every Panchayat in the Eighth Five Year Plan, he feels a strong need for a people's movement to make the plan and proposal a success. Hence he states "The peoples movement such as Chipko Movement, Narmada Bachao, Arak, and other movements which enjoy the support of the masses at large are mostly due to increasing awareness of the people. The library movement will have to be made a people's movement. The Non-Governmental Organizations can play a significant role in mass education programmes and in spread of library culture. They may be invited to play their role effectively and necessary incentives given" (p. xxiv).

On the need to get modernized he strongly suggests that libraries, which are all in the race for getting automated, must follow standard formats for uniformity and easy exchange of data, within the country and at international level. "Our National Bibliography can make the ball rolling in this respect" (p. xxv).

Regarding the lack of legislation in several States of India, and despite the attempts of ILA and other State level associations to get the State Government enact the laws, he feels "it is certainly the lack of political will on the part of our State Governments which delaying the enactment of library legislation . . . Library service must find a place in the agenda of all such States which have remained without library law all these years. The Governments which are afraid of imposing any cess may adopt the 'West Bengal Model' and pass the Library bill. Cess or no cess, the citizens of the land must not be denied the pleasure of reading" (pp. xxv-xxvi).

Given the provision of the New Education Policy, proclaimed by the Rajiv Gandhi Government in 1985, it was expected by all that it would get reflected at least in the national planning, strangely, in these plan allocations. India ranks 115th among the countries of the world in terms of investing in education as percentage of GNP. Similarly, the place of India, is visible in the per capita expenditure on education—the developed countries spend Rs. 10,000 to Rs. 25,000 whereas in India it is Rs. 600. In addition to this, the picture has further worsened, due to the share that goes to the distance education, from the already meagre budget for higher education. Hence one direct effect has been in the fall in the library acquisition programmes, and the budget cut is more obvious in sharp fall in the subscription to periodicals in universities and research centres. "Often education gets relegated to backstage and libraries are subjected to huge cuts. Let it not happen any more" (p. xxvi).

From five universities, imparting education for librarians, to 90 such institutions, offering certificate, diploma, degree and doctoral programmes, there is a level of production which has not been in accordance with the principle of supply and demand. Further, these courses have been added, despite the lack of infrastructure to offer programmes. Lack of adequate funds with these institutions, and departments in the universities, is evident from the fact that these are not in a position to buy even current editions of reference books, as well as, basic tools for conducting practical classes. "Sometime back, the members of the Association of Unemployed Librarians of Rajasthan sat on *dharna* in Jaipur demanding suitable jobs for them" (p. xxviii). Lack of employment opportunities for fresh graduates, and lack of promotional chances for the existing employees, is creating a serious problem and needs to be arrested before it takes a serious turn.

The overall question still remains behind the head: How to survive the present while preparing for the future? The answer lies in using a systems' approach in libraries, that is, talking the matters in a holistic sense.

The trend today is to find alternative means of access to information, given the fact that information technology is making the access simpler and easier, day by day. If we presume that soon the majority will have access to INTERNET type of resource, then the major problem—need to acquire and maintain enormous information sources—will be considerably diminished. While this is more so true of research libraries, it does not however disqualify the other libraries also coming under this changed scenario. While today a library is measured by its size and funds, it must be easier to begin the measurement of libraries, based on a single criterion: current user satisfaction. This is based on the premise that once users are able to get a document, irrespective of its presence in the library, ownership becomes irrelevant.

Future of Library History and Historiography

As stated in the previous chapter, library history and historiography in India is gaining momentum, and a variety of agencies are feeling the need to work in this direction. The scenario of uninterestedness is vanishing. Further, those who were remaining aloof from this field, of library history, are also, finding interest in this activity, and this is a sign of life for the historians all over. Further, the interest in library history can be more also because of the fact that the scope of the field is wide enough to include a variety of people in the name of writing a fresh library history.

A fresh approach to the history of libraries, here refers, to writing the history in a holistic sense, encompassing all library related matter, library related issues, and library related fields, in its definition. That is, a history of library, has to take care of all forces and factors that are responsible, and there cannot be any history, for that matter, in isolation.

The historians of libraries need to re-consider their conceptual framework to facilitate the study, teaching and research of the field. The conceptual framework includes dimensions such as, psychological, sociological, philosophical, etc. Psychological, here connotes, a study of the behaviour of the institutions in their respective environment. Sociological, connotes, study of group behaviour in an environment. Both the group and the environment receive emphasis and need a coherent approach. Philosophical point of view relates to the value systems held by the group as well by the institutions. This framework helps in clarifying the implicit and explicit matters related to the field.

A history in this sense, aims at inviting different specialists, different agencies, and different resources to combine under one umbrella the purpose of writing a new outlook on libraries in India. This is necessary, more so, in a country, which has a rampant oral culture, and a level of literacy matched by no other developed country. Given this special background, it is expected that library historians in the country will use this as a base to guide others in the country, for writing a holistic history. In short, a history of library here intends to cover all agencies; libraries, archives, museums, and so on; and receive a support for subject content from historians of education, politics, economics, sociology, public administration, law, etc.; and take the help of all available, tapped and hitherto untapped sources; primary, secondary and tertiary sources, in all languages, land in all States.

India can present in this vision of a broad based library history, a sample and a framework for library historians all over the world.

Areas of Research for the 21st Century

A review of the fifty years development of libraries, has to highlight what areas are over worked, what areas are left untouched, and what areas, in a comparative perspective, can be still taken for research and study.

Any quantitative or qualitative study of historical investigation, must employ a method of investigation, such as cliometrics, or, celebration charting. The present study has greatly focused on the first, and a future researcher in the area can concentrate on other methods, including the second method. As stated earlier, cliometrics is concerned with counting and reporting of events or behaviours, and celebration charting, is the method of reporting frequency counts on semi-logarithmic charts.

A study of the society can be quantitatively measured by sociometrics, including indicators such as quality of life; economic progress can be measured by econometrics; information generation can be measured by infometrics; library growth can be measured by librametrics; and so on. But there is a need to measure the library development in the context of quality of life which libraries try to promote. There are various sources which provide basic data regarding the quality of life, and the list of such sources includes, UN's Statistical Year Book, World Education Report, Human Development Report, Asian Development Report, etc. But there is a need to develop a measure for the library development in relation to the level of national development. Also important is the analysis of the issues that revolve around the question: How access to or no access to information helps in the development of the society. These are very significant issues for research and study.

There is, again, a need for an Indian work, similar to what is Frederick William's Measuring the information society (Sage, 1988). In terms of emerging information society there must be systematic attempts to measure and analyze the level and type of society that is emerging with improved means of access to information. The book deals with conceptual and methodological issues; the information economy, promoting change; attitudes toward change; media, information technology, and change; etc.

Another foreign attempt, has been made in a similar way. This is a dissertation by Jesus G. Law, entitled, "A study of selected social factors influencing information development in low, middle, and highly developed countries. An assessment for the period 1960-1977. University of Sheffield, Ph.D thesis, 1988 (DAI 52/04, p. 1117, Oct. 1991). The interest and relevancy of this work for a developmental perspective is obvious from the framework it has adopted. Information was narrowed to three components: (1) centres storing information for public use, (2) stocks of information accumulated by countries, and (3) recording of information. The first two components were characterized by ten library indicators, the third information component was represented by five publishing indicators. Socio-economic development was limited to five social components: health, education, food, water supply, and sanitation. These factors were represented by five indicators of human basic needs.

A review of the doctoral work completed in the field of library science, as surveyed by Prof. A.A.N. Raju, the number of dissertations in India between 1980 and 1991, are in the descending order as follows: University libraries 12; Personnel 7; Information systems and networks 7; Information, reference and bibliographic sources and services 6; Public libraries 6; Classification 5; User needs and studies 4. Other topics receiving lesser attention are library cooperation; Organization; Information storage and retrieval; development of periodical literature; LIS education; special libraries; etc. Interestingly, from our topical interest, there is one dissertation each in history of conditions and library movement and legislation. This is to re-state that there is yet a serious gap in writing Indian library history.

Speaking in terms of quantitative historical studies, there are a number of references in the bibliography of the present work, on Cliometrics, Bibliometrics, and Librametrics.

Furthermore, there are clear statistics, accessible easily to the needy, dealing with food calories, health status, education, transport, communication, literacy, population, energy consumption, ecology, trade and so on. But there is nothing available, on per capita figures relating to growth of libraries, production, distribution and consumption of book and other reading materials. Similarly, figures relating to use of libraries and use of other media in a comparative perspective, book and other print media-reading rates, book purchasing and subscribing patterns, and so on, are non-existent. A source like Bowker's Annual provides some such statistics for the different areas of activity, mostly in the USA, and sometimes for other countries. But there is no other ready source for this information. A researcher must be prepared to search many such sources to gather some bits here and there.

A study of the possible areas of measuring scientific progress in the country, *vis-à-vis*, national development is discussed by Sikka, in a recent issue of University News. This gives a framework for a researcher to develop the idea of library progress *vis-à-vis* national development. Its relevance here, is both, as an indigenous model and as a related citation. To quote:

"The Government's concern for S&T and its involvement in management, promotion and evaluation are now universally recognized in countries with market economies. The concern has primarily been due to some of the key questions related to scientific and technological developments, such as:

(i) how to develop mechanisms for the effective application of science and technology to national development?
(ii) what products and/or product groups constitute the proper vehicle for technological development of the country?
(iii) how to determine the optimum size of investment for R&D related with imported and indigenous technologies and involve private organizations and industries for funding R&D?
(iv) how to increase the absorptive capacity for the imported technology?
(v) how to improve the effectiveness of R&D units?
(vi) how to ensure a gradual growth of basic research?
(vii) how to create a favourable technology climate? (1996: 2).

The author admits, that, 'The main constraint in the construction and application of technology indicators to developing countries is the lack of an integrated information system on technology relevant information in these (*i.e.*, developing) countries. Secondly, the experience of industrialization and the usefulness of established technology indicators in developing countries vary according to their level of development and industrialization policies" (p. 3).

While the present work is a solo research, it is necessary that team research in this area must be initiated to replicate the findings presented here. In this context, there is a need to conduct detailed and systematic research in finding out the influences that have contributed or failed to contribute for the library development in the country. The factors must revolve around environment, infrastructure, input, throughput, output, quality control devices, marketing strategies, feedback and R&D.

Again in terms of the sources which the management, policy-makers, government, and the decision makers, use to arrive at conclusive decisions, there is a need to make an in-depth survey of the following:

(a) types of sources which are relied upon, example, National survey results, Census reports, MARG studies, media, reports of committees, Government documents, etc.;
(b) information base that is easily accessible, for instance, departmental libraries, Internet/intranet resources, personal collection, etc.;
(c) resources other than documentary that help in the process friends, lobby's, intuition, political pressures, etc.

A series of research must be initiated to identify the level of involvement, if any—of people, Government, and the professionals—in library development. One has to assess the internal and external parameters in each role that these play. The presumptions that are underlying such role need to be thoroughly analyzed, and the list of presumptions includes:

(a) lack of social consciousness of information needs;
(b) lack of professional responsiveness to information needs for image building;
(c) lack of Government's attitude in providing information its proper place in the society;
(d) lack of any library movement worth its name in the country today;
(e) lack of desire to work among the professionals in India;
(f) lack of motivation for the professionals to work;
(g) availability of alternative information resources which the public have access to; and so on.

The agenda for the research can be listed in following lines:

Funds

Inadequate funds hamper smooth and effective running of libraries.

What are the ways of raising alternative funds and fund raising sources that can make libraries less shaky.

Accommodation

Mainly because of the low priority which libraries receive, many of the library services suffer due to lack of suitable land sufficient accommodation. What are the ways in which libraries can tackle this problem and have the cake and eat it too?

Staffing

Libraries are expected to operate with a mediocre of staff, *i.e.*, both in qualitative and quantitative sense. How can the libraries motivate the staff, to be service minded and/or can libraries remove the tag of service institution, and become commercial information centres, which in turn may bring in the staff a spirit of business like—in business what matters is how you can earn more.

Stocks

Many libraries face the problem of being inadequately stocked, due to shortage of funds, foreign exchange restraints, and other reasons. Can all libraries develop some specialization to avoid the duplication of collections in all areas in all languages, and in all ways. It is possible that public libraries, like super-speciality hospitals, agree to concentrate in only specified and agreed areas, than be super markets of all, which infact means nothing in library stocks—still aimlessly duplicating all resources and wasting precious little money. Changing characteristics of sources used by the end-users, and its implications on the need fulfilment in libraries.

Information infrastructure: The country lacks a national information system for the development of libraries and for the systematic planning of information services. While there is a need for a well coordinated and directed national plan within the total framework of the nation's development plan. This is not coming up. Without such an infrastructure, the contribution of libraries and other related services can only be marginal in the national scene. And despite the failure of the nation to elevate its literacy an educational levels, the national planners are still unable to think of the possible avenues which could make things better. The question requiring in-depth study and analysis, from grass-roots to the level of policy-makers in the country is: Why does the national development plan ignore/marginalize, most segments of the society, including libraries and information related agencies.

Consider the scope of information infrastructure, which appeared in print (*Economic Times*, Hyderabad edition, 15 January 1996, p. 6). The proposed 'national information infrastructure' has the following elements: "communications infrastructure basic and value added; the computers and appliances that process information and allow people to physically interface with it; the software and applications that enable people to use information; content or information (whether audio, video, text or images) the people land companies who develop, manufacture, sell and service the networks".

To get a clear idea let us also list the agenda that is given in the same article: "enable private organizations to set up and run datacom networks, enable universal access to data networks for both domestic and international traffic; reform legislation to accord a legal basis to electronic financial transactions; establish national standards for cryptography to enable electronic transactions; establish norms for privacy and confidentiality of information to protect citizen rights, encourage investments in infrastructure by permitting depreciation of assets over their actual productive life".

If a plan for information handling agencies—is the sole prerogative of telecommunications—than such an infrastructure should be named only as telecommunication infrastructure and network, and not information network, as there are many agencies—handling information—that are missing from the focus, including libraries, archives, etc. The simple question one can pose is has the society removed the information content from the libraries, if yes, has it been replaced with food stuff, or what else???

To quote Gessesse,

> "Libraries are tools of economic and socio-cultural development. No planner or public administrator can perform his role effectively without the support of a good library. Thus, by virtue of their being an infrastructure to the whole development process of a nation and also by virtue of their importance for manpower development, library services must belong to the first order priorities in the planning of a national development. . . . People in the developing world today require information and materials systematically organized to develop their country's resources and direct such

resources to economic, social and cultural growth. Thus, to fulfil its purpose a library, must be readily accessible and its door open for free and equal use by all types of users regardless of race, colour, nationality, age, sex, religion, status or educational attainment" (1986: 207-08).

The findings of the present study has been to work differently, and to present a picture of the library development in an altogether a new fashion. This was necessitated based on the survey of the Indian library history as well as the American library history. The trends in Indian library history are analyzed and interpreted in a previous chapter. The American attempts to write library history are also not very different. A quantitative analysis of one recent bibliography on library history, reveals that there are hardly any studies that a historian considers as developmental study. Most are descriptive and are least analytical. Most studies have made general surveys of regions, and of literature. Few have concentrated to write specific case histories. There are 53 articles, 11 books, 3 master's dissertations, and 5 reports, that are listed in the bibliography, compiled by Donald Davis. This counting deals with the data on private libraries alone, and represents the trends in library history abroad.

What is missing in detailed study and analysis of growth and development of individual institutions, and detailed study of individual factors that effect or influence the growth of libraries, or otherwise. A future research of Indian library system, must therefore concentrate on writing case histories, narrating all the possible influences that have promoted or hindered the developmental activities. Such a study must be least descriptive—avoid stating all through the objectives and goals of the library with no space left for critical evaluation, analytical commentary, and so on.

9

SUMMARY

"The function of the library historian is not to celebrate libraries, either as arsenals of democracy, the people's university, or the heart of the university. Lamentation for a form of library that is passing is also not the aim of a history of libraries. Understanding their function within the book world and within the larger society must be our goal". —*Kenneth E. Carpenter*, Harvard University Library.

"Readers and Libraries: Toward a History of Libraries and Culture in America", in *News from the Center for the Book*, LC Information Bull., Oct. 16, 1995.

While it is customary to write a conclusion, I however admit that much still remains to be accomplished, and in lieu of conclusion, it would be preferable, to call this last chapter as summary of the research that is undertaken. The idea of summing up, also, is to re-state that this book is not directed itself so much to answering all questions, and clarifying the stand libraries/society has taken, rather its purpose is to stimulate discussion on the problems of useable libraries in the post-independent India.

To sum up, this study aimed at finding out how far there is a development of user-friendly libraries in the framework of the fifty years of Indian national development. The study has presented developmental perspective, both in its theoretical and practical dimensions. In terms of a framework for the libraries this study has used the critical view to assess the place which libraries have in national development, and *vice-versa*, that is, the place which nation has in library development.

The stated hypotheses have been tested all through. The discussions that have followed have made it explicit and obvious that all the stated hypotheses were correct. These presuppositions, stated again are as follows:

(a) That there is no proper record maintaining practice in libraries—which a historian must find—regarding their own growth and development patterns;

(b) That libraries are isolated in all respects in national planning, and the society has also not played its role in library development;

(c) That society is by and large unaware of its democratic right to information, and the profession has failed to do its best in removing this ignorance; and

(d) That libraries have not made their presence felt in the society and hence planners and policy-makers have left libraries to be marginalized.

The study has given a bird's eyeview of the landmarks, and the significant posts that appear in the length and breadth of the fifty year old, independent nation. The library development though not a part and parcel of the overall national development, has nevertheless been significant. Two full chapters review the progress made in a variety of areas and the study has highlighted the main currents.

There is a unanimity among the intellectuals that there must be an integrated approach in planning and implementation of the national development programmes. This integrated approach must include libraries as an essential segment of the entire process of social growth, and society must in turn get involved in the library development, which in turn will lead to emergence of useable libraries. But who should bell the cat, and put this in practice? No one knows the answer!

A significant style adopted in the chapterisation is that of case studies, quoting cases from all corners, relevant and related, but creating a sense of involvement in the whole context. Including cases was worth since a lot of such instances are scattered in the literature and it makes good history, and reading this stimulates the reader. Writing history is different from making history readable, and enjoyable. The present work has tried to infuse something of this sort.

Exhaustive surveys throughout the length and breadth of the country have made this study, unique, valuable, and worth, the attempt. It has used all methods in direct and mixed combination to achieve maximum results and effective correlation of the matter that is interpreted. A travel across the country was combined with interviews with all types of library users, non-users, and rare users, to find the pulse of the people at large. Meeting experts and specialists was also on the agenda and the study maximised these opportunities. Questionnaires were served to all major libraries and users from different walks of life in the country. The results are all summarised and interpreted in the chapter on libraries and national development.

Treating the issue of library movement in its holistic sense and as is understood both in India and abroad, the study has drawn its interpretations to identify that library movement did start here and there, but it did not last long to lead the country. So also the role of the profession, on the whole, has neither been very positive, nor does it shows that they have done their best, in the wake of the crisis the libraries in the country have been undergoing. The question still remains unanswered, since, neither the librarians, nor the users in their responses, made it clear as to who is to be blamed for the 'lack of recognition and status for libraries in the society'. If libraries are not involved in planning of the country, and if nation is not participating in library development, the primary responsibility must either be with the profession or with the society? But none is willing to be blamed, nor any one is apologetic about the whole tragic situation. The losers are the libraries in this drama of sorts!

The goal of 'libraries for all' and information for all, are still on paper. If Ranganathan has laid down guidelines in 1930s—that Books are for use, books must find readers, every reader must get the required information, save the time of the reader, and library is a growing organism—the problem still remains the same: who should bell the cat? That is, to whom Ranganathan is addressing these 'laws', as he calls it. If he is addressing these to the profession, then the profession has not fulfilled its responsibility.

If these are guidelines for the society to show that in a free society they have 'right to information' and hence, they can get whatever and wherever information they need, then they have also equally well failed to do their democratic duty, and the survey highlights more and more people need to be made information literates, that is, they are unaware of their own information related rights.

This speaks on its own about the social attitudes towards information, professional attitudes towards the society, and in general it also goes to indicate that oral cultures, as against the written and book cultures, will always behave differently. It is, therefore, probably incorrect to expect too much from a developing book culture, such traits and such moves which are not in their veins! There are other countries who are already in the information society and have useable libraries, and theirs is an information culture, not ours!!!

There is a need to immediately initiate the establishment, of a long awaited, body for continuously working on the intellectual role book has been playing in the country. An organisation, such as, the SHARP, (Society for the History of Authorship, Reading and Publishing), will help fostering study and research of the history and the development of book related institutions. This can be a voluntary body, or a chapter of the existing historical or social research institutes.

In short the study unravels the inroads towards a saga of information culture in India. It should help all people know: Where is India standing in its fiftieth year; Where India must recoup to do better in the coming century; and Where India can do better if it involves libraries in its national planning, not as mere advisors, and dignatories, but as essential components in the process of nation building.

APPENDICES

APPENDIX-I

QUESTIONS FOR SELF-ASSESSMENT OF ACADEMIC LIBRARIES

[*Note:* The following are taken from the *Self-Study Manual for Indian Universities and Colleges*, prepared by Malcolm M. Willey and J. Arthur Branch, Ford Foundation consultants, and submitted to the UGC, 1968] (Part IV, Section 5, deals with libraries).

Library Resources

1. Do the holding reflect the needs of the institution in relation to its educational programme?
2. Is the collection 'culled' from time to time and useless or antiquated materials eliminated?
3. Has a systematic check been made, using standard check lists, to compare the library's holdings in general areas of scholarship with what is regarded as a desirable minimum?
4. What is the opinion of the teachers concerning the adequacy of the library collection?
5. Are teachers satisfied that the library does enable them to keep abreast of their fields?
6. Has the library committee formulated any acquisition policy of priorities?

Library Use

7. Are the figures to show library use? What do they indicate concerning the role that the library plays?
8. Does the library provide reference assistance, bibliographical service, abstracting. duplicating service, etc.?
9. Does the library regularly and systematically inform teachers of new acquisitions?

10. What days and hours is the library open?
11. Are materials readily accessible?
12. How long, on an average, would a user have to wait for a book?
13. Is the seating capacity for reading adequate?
14. Is the library physically conducive to the effective, easy and stimulating use of the resources?
15. Does the library arrange an orientation programme? Is there a guide for library users?
16. How long does it take to acquire and place on the shelves any book that it is decided to purchase?

Management

17. Is there a clear recognition (on the part of the library staff) of the diverse functions which the library performs?
18. Are there staff members sufficiently trained and motivated to convert the library into an intellectual workshop?
19. Does the budget allow any flexibility in the use of funds?
20. What do teachers think about the efficiency of the purchasing procedure, cataloguing, and circulation desk?

APPENDIX-II

GLOSSARY

Information Revolution: First revolution: speech; second revolution: writing; third revolution: printing; fourth revolution: computers and networking.

Literacy: Learned, ability to read and write; Scientific, literacy refers to ability to read, comprehend and communicate on scientific matters, in particular, and any subject in general; Technical literacy refers to ability to operate, understand the mechanism, and ability to practice; Computer literacy refers to ability to use the computers and its related technology, in terms of technique and problem solving.

User Interface: Links which make it convenient for the user to handle a library system, or any machine.

UNION/STATE LIBRARY BILLS

1930 Model Library Act—prepared by Dr. S.R. Ranganathan (hence SRR)
1931 Draft Model Public Libraries Bill—prepared by SRR
1950 Union Library Bill—prepared by SRR
1957 Model Library Act—prepared by SRR
1963 Model Public Libraries Bill—prepared by Dr. M. D. Sen, on the basis of Sinha Committee Report
1965 Model Public Library Bill—prepared by the Planning Commission, of the Government of India
1972 Model Union Libraries Act—prepared by SRR
1972 Model Public Libraries Act (Revised)—prepared by SRR
1972 Model State Libraries Act—prepared by SRR
1989 Model Public Libraries Act—prepared by Dr. V. Venkatappaiah
1991 Model Public Libraries Act (Revised)—prepared by Dr. Venkatappaiah and Indian Library Association

Statewise Library Bills/Acts

Andhra Pradesh

1953 Hyderabad Public Libraries Bill—drafted by Dr. S.R. Ranganathan (hence SRR)
1957 Andhra Pradesh Public Libraries Bill—drafted by SRR
1959 Andhra Pradesh Public Libraries Bill
1969 Andhra Pradesh Public Libraries Amendment Bill
1979 Andhra Pradesh Public Libraries (Comprehensive) Bill—drafted by Dr. Venkatappaiah
1986 Andhra Pradesh Public Libraries Amendment Bill
1989 Andhra Pradesh Public Libraries Amendment Bill to amend the name: Andhra Pradesh Granthalaya Parishad
1990 Andhra Pradesh Public Libraries Amendment Bill

Assam

1964 Public Libraries Bill for Assam—prepared by SRR

1972 Assam Public Libraries Bill—prepared by Dr. R.L. Mittal
1986 Assam Public Libraries Bill

Bihar

1973 Bihar Public Libraries Bill—prepared by Bihar Library Association
1981 Bihar Public Libraries Bill—prepared by R.S.P. Singh

Delhi

1955 Delhi Public Libraries Bill—prepared by Prof. P.N. Kaula

Goa

1983 Goa Public Libraries Bill—prepared by State Library Advisory Board
1990 Goa Public Libraries Bill—prepared by K.M. Ujlambkar

Gujarat

1965 Gujarat Public Libraries Bill—prepared by Library Committee, Gujarat Government
1969 Gujarat Public Libraries Bill—tabled in the Assembly by Manohar Sinhji P. Jadeja, MLA
1973 Gujarat Public Libraries Bill—prepared by Maneklal Gandhi
1978 Gujarat Public Libraries Bill—prepared by Manohar Sinhji Jadeja
1981 Gujarat Public Library Bill—by Lakkani
1990 Gujarat Library Bill—H.J. Upadhyaya

Haryana

1972 Haryana Public Libraries Bill—prepared by M.L. Bhagi
1982 Haryana Public Libraries Bill—prepared by Dr. Janak Raj
1988 Haryana Public Libraries Bill—prepared by N.K. Sharma

Himachal Pradesh

1982 Himachal Pradesh Public Libraries Bill—prepared by Dr. A.S. Chandel

Karnataka

1963 Mysore Public Libraries Bill—prepared by SRR for the Mysore Public Libraries Bill Committee, 1961

Kerala

1947 Cochin State Public Libraries Bill—prepared by SRR
1947 Travancore State Public Libraries Bill—by SRR
1959 Kerala Public Libraries Bill—by SRR
1969 Kerala Public Libraries Bill—by SRR

Jammu & Kashmir

1951 Library Bill for Jammu & Kashmir—prepared by Kaula
1975 Jammu & Kashmir Public Library Bill—by M.S. Randhawa

Madhya Pradesh

1946 Central Provinces and Benaras Public Libraries Bill—prepared by SRR
1950 Madhya Pradesh Public Libraries Bill
1958 Madhya Pradesh Public Libraries Bill—by Maulana Azad Central Library Committee
1959 Madhya Pradesh Public Libraries Bill—by Madhya Pradesh Library Association
1968 Madhya Pradesh Public Libraries Bill—by G.D. Bhargava and V.S. Moghe
1970 Madhya Pradesh Public Libraries Bill—by Indore Library Association
1978 Madhya Pradesh Public Libraries Bill
1990 Madhya Pradesh Public Libraries Bill—by K.M. Ujlambkar

Maharashtra

1936 Bombay Presidency Public Libraries Bill—by S.K. Bole
1947 Public Libraries Bill for Bombay Province—by SRR
1959 Bombay State Public Libraries Bill—by M.V. Donde
1965 Maharashtra Public Libraries Bill—by Maharashtra Library Association

Manipur

1988 Manipur Public Libraries Bill

Mizoram

1980 Mizoram Public Libraries Bill—by State Library
1988 Mizoram Public Libraries Bill

Orissa

1974 Orissa Public Libraries Bill—by Prof. B.B. Sukla.
1983 Orissa Public Libraries Bill (Revised)—Sukla
1983 Orissa Public Libraries Bill—Utkal Library Association
1982 Orissa Public Libraries Bill (Revised)—Sukla and Dr. P.K. Rath

Punjab

1962 Punjab Public Libraries Bill—by R.L.Mittal
1962 Punjab Public Libraries Bill—by Punjab Library Association
1992 Punjab Public Libraries Bill—prepared on the basis of the Model Act of Dr. Venkatappaiah

Rajasthan

1965 Rajasthan Public Libraries Bill—by Rajasthan Library Association
1990 Rajasthan Public Libraries Bill—by K. M. Ujlambkar

Tamil Nadu

1931 Public Libraries Bill for the Presidency of Madras—by Madras Library Association
1937 Public Libraries Bill for the Presidency of Madras—by Madras Library Association
1946 Madras Public Libraries Bill—by SRR
1993 Madras Public Libraries Comprehensive Bill—by Venkatappaiah

Uttar Pradesh

1948 Library Bill for the United Provinces—by SRR
1958 Uttar Pradesh Public Libraries Bill—by SRR
1969 Uttar Pradesh Public Libraries Bill—U.P. Library Association
1973 Uttar Pradesh Public Libraries Bill—by Gowswami Committee
1983 Uttar Pradesh Public Libraries Bill—by Venkatappaiah
1983 Uttar Pradesh Public Libraries Bill—by Vishwanathan Committee
1992 Uttar Pradesh Public Libraries Bill—by Venkatappaiah

West Bengal

1931 Bengal Public Libraries Bill—by Kumar Munindra Deb Raj Mahasay

1958 West Bengal Public Libraries Bill—by SRR
1978 West Bengal Public Libraries BIll—by State Government
1982 Amendment to the West Bengal Public Libraries Act
1985 Amendment to the West Bengal Public Libraries Act

APPENDIX-IVA

INDIVIDUAL USER'S QUESTIONNAIRE

Dear friend

This questionnaire is for you with a request to respond, if not so badly occupied, and as you may be a regular visitor of a library, we have in you a good choice to help us in this enquiry. The purpose of this exercise is to know what you feel about libraries, and what kind of satisfaction the library provides. Your response may help us to understand role of library in society and to plan a strategy for better libraries.

About Yourself

1. Present qualification: Masters/M.Phil/Ph.D/D.Litt (tick any)
2. Present academic status: teacher/researcher/student/other (mention)
3. What libraries have you used in past: (tick any) private collection/public library/school library/college library/university library/research library/other collections (mention)
4. Have you used libraries abroad: (name the countries)
5. Have you sought the help of librarians there: yes/no
6. Have you faced any difficulties in finding information: yes/no
7. What other source of information you find useful (please rank) news from friends/newspaper/Doordarshan/cable TV/radio/ electronic mail/internet/others (please name)
8. Do you know that the Government of India has a national network (called NICNET), to provide the rural and urban public, some essential information for survival: yes/no
   - 8.1 If yes, where do you use this: (tick any) university library/ public library/research library/others.
   - 8.2 Are you aware that there are private and public access points of electronic mail/letter/information anywhere in the world: yes/no.
9. Are you aware that there are many institutions and foundations who can help in funding your research/travel, etc.: yes/no
   - 9.1 If yes, have you availed such a facility from: (tick any) Indian institution/American/British/others (name it)

About the Library You Use Most

10. Please name it:
11. Do you visit your library: (tick any) frequently/rarely/not at all
12. Your evaluation of library collection: (tick any) adequate/inadequate/fairly well
    12.1 If inadequate, in what ways: (tick any) books/journals/reports/services/staff.
    12.2 Is the library catalogue: (tick any) computerised/card catalogue/no proper catalogue
13. Are you familiar with catalogue: yes/no
    13.1 If yes, do you think it is: easy/difficult to use
    13.2 If easy, how often you consult the same: regularly/sometimes
    13.3 If difficult: do you normally ignore the catalogue: yes/no
    13.4 If no, ask library staff/go directly to the shelf/struggle with catalogue
    13.5 If difficult to use, it is because of: (tick any) its arrangement/its inconvenient location/unimaginable order
    13.6 Is your searching of the catalogue by subject helpful: yes/no
14. Arrangement (or classification) of books on the shelf is understandable: yes/no
    14.1 If yes, is it helpful: yes/no
    14.2 If no, do you ask for help: yes/no
    14.3 If yes, are the staff available: yes/no
15. Do you find the library staff: (tick any) helping/sincere/concerned
    15.1 Are they: professionally trained/up to date in their skills/motivated (tick any)
    15.2 Or are they: careless/negligent/misbehaving
16. Do you know that the library has many indexes and bibliographies on your subject matter in articles/books/dissertations: yes/no
    16.1 If yes, how often do you use: (tick any) regularly/occasionally/ never
    16.2 Can you name two or three indexes (please list)
    16.3 If you do not use indexes, how do you find articles/essays/chapters: (tick any) through friends/through citations/others

16.4 How often do you scan through periodicals: (tick any) regularly/occasionally/never

17. If you do not find the required materials, do you still try: yes/no

    17.1 If yes, through whom: (tick any) friends/library staff/ colleagues/other libraries

18. Do you know that the library can borrow materials from other libraries for you: yes/no

    18.1 If yes, how often do you use this privilege: (tick any) regularly/occasionally/never

19. Do you pay for any service in the library: yes/no

    19.1 How happy are you with the charges: (tick any) very much/not much/O.K.

20. Do you use your library for other than research: yes/no

    20.1 If yes, is it for: (tick any) recreation/information/ knowledge/meeting friends

    20.2 Do you have friendly relations with library staff: yes/no

    20.3 If yes, how friendly they are: (tick any) very much/not so much/only for finding information

21. Do you think the library must train the users: yes/no

    21.1 If yes, to what level (tick any) use catalogue/use all areas/ use indexes/new technologies

    21.2 Have you ever undergone this training: yes/no

    21.3 How do you feel its impact: useful/not necessary (tick any)

    21.4 If you are positive, does this training help you understand the staff and resources: yes/no

    21.5 Do you think the library must be user-friendly: yes/no

    21.6 If yes, is it lacking in its: (tick any) services/products/ staff/resources/performance

22. Is the library always useful in development of your career/ status: yes/no

    22.1 If no, what you think are the sources of information for keeping yourself abreast: (tick any) personal library/ friends/teachers/others (mention)

23. *Right to Information*

    23.1 Did you know that you have a democratic right to demand library services or facilities in the library: yes/no

    23.2 If yes, how to communicate this right to people: (tick any) publicity/propaganda/movement by masses

23.3 Do you think library is a societal need, as important as education, health, sanitation, market, social welfare: yes/no

23.4 Do you think that libraries are unable to attract users for serious readings: yes/no

23.5 What remedial measures you suggest to improve the library performance for social change: (state it in a few lines please; like ways of improvement in searching literature; providing quick access to literature; providing more help and save time; increase user training methods; mail recent acquisition lists; etc.)

23.6 Do you think library is an indispensable institution for your information needs: yes/no

23.6.1 If yes, how will you help its survival (*e.g.*, if the library is declared as closed what will you do): (tick any) react/protest/remain neutral

23.6.2. How will you react: (tick any) take up the matter/raise funds/go to other library

23.7 Does right to information means no censorship: yes/no

23.7.1 If yes, do you recommend freedom of access to reading materials on: (tick any) antireligion/obscene/pornographic/unhealthy books/politically sensitive information/others (any comments).

APPENDIX-IVB

INSTITUTIONAL QUESTIONNAIRE

Dear colleague

The purpose of this enquiry is to see how far Indian academic and research libraries are developed, and to interpret the results in assessing or measuring this development *vis-a-vis* the national development. The assessment may reveal as to where and how far is the link or participation of the library development process with national development. Hope you will help in my understanding of what your library does (service/ products) and how to change for the better.

Organisation

[Questions here relate to staff development, collection development, storage, services and the by-products (called as library products), how do we promote/market and get a feedback about the services]

Personnel

1. How many professionals work in library: 1-10/10-20/20-30/ more (tick any)
    - 1.1 How may other staff are in library: 1-10/10-20/20-30/ more (tick any)
    - 1.2 Is there a job description for the staff: yes/no
    - 1.3 Is there a performance evaluation for staff: yes/no
2. Do the staff have continuing education: yes/no
    - 2.1 Is it: internal/external (tick any)
    - 2.2 Duration: one week/more/not fixed (tick any)
    - 2.3 Nature: planned/adhoc (tick any)
    - 2.4 Faculty: librarians/outsiders (tick any)
3. Are there any promotional chances: merit/seniority/open (tick any)
4. Do the staff have internal meetings and discussions: yes/no
    - 4.1 If yes, how often: weekly/monthly/rarely/none (tick any)
5. How often new staff are appointed: (tick any) yearly/rarely/ only if position vacant

6. Are the staff generally: (tick any) committed/motivated/ dedicated
7. Do staff agree for transfer with the system: yes/no
   7.1 If yes, how frequently are transfers: (tick any) daily rotation/once in a year/once in five years/longer
8. Desire for a: change/new ideas must come from below (tick any)
9. As a librarian rank three major areas in which you spend at least 20 per cent of your time as part of the routine: (rank your priorities) finding user needs/processing/acquisition/ administration/developing new products/staff interaction/ management

Acquisition .

10. Is there is policy for collection development: yes/no
    10.1 If yes, is it written: yes/no
    10.2 Who decides finally: library professional/others
    10.3 How is the demarcation done: (tick any) subjectwise/ randomly/budgetwise/on demand/none
11. What is yearly budget: (tick any) below 10 lakh/above 20/ unstated
    11.1 How much is the yearly increase: (tick any) 10%/15%/ limited/no limit
    11.2 It is proportional to other departments: yes/no
    11.3 It is taking care of inflation: yes/no
    11.4 It is taking care of changing needs: yes/no
12. Is there a planning to increase collection: yes/no
    12.1 If yes, how much was last year's annual increase (tick any)

Books	1—5%	5—10%	10—15%
Journals	1—5	5—10	10—15
Reports	1—5	5—10	10—15
a/v/	1—5	5—10	10—15
CD-ROM	1—5	5—10	10—15

13. How long the user must wait for a suggested title: (tick any) six months/around two years/more than two years
14. What is the total collection now (total volumes)
15. What was the last year's collection (total volumes)

Storage

16. What major equipment is added since last four years: (tick any) xerox machine/computer PCs/terminals/fax machine/microfilm equipment
17. Is the planning adequate to place equipment/furniture: yes/no
    17.1 If yes, is it enough for computers/audio-visuals: yes/no
    17.2 Does its maintenance call for training staff: yes/no
    17.3 If yes, are the computers managed by a library staff: yes/no
    17.4 How frequently machines break down: usually/rarely (tick any)
18. Is the budget sufficient for adding new equipment: yes/no
    18.1 If yes, does the maintenance take away large chunk: yes/no
19. How often users complain about missing items from shelf: (tick any) few users/most users
20. Do you have shelf rectification/shelf reading by staff: yes/no
21. How many books are processed per day: (tick any) 5—10/10—20/20—40/more
22. Technical processing is: manual/automated (tick any)
23. How many pcs/computer terminals are in library (figures)
24. How many other audio/visual equipment are available: (figures)

Service

25. Does the library have the following services: (tick any) circulation/xerox/translation/inter library loan/online/library products+abstracts/indexes/CAS/SDI
26. Is there any survey done on the need of library products: yes/no
    26.1 What type of users were surveyed: regular/rare users/non-users (tick any)
    26.2 Survey by: (tick any) questionnaire/interview/observation
    26.3 Did the respondents knew the library: yes/no
    26.4 Did the respondents understood the library services: yes/no
    26.5 If yes, were they: happy/insensible (tick any)
    26.6 Did the respondents desired free services: yes/no
    26.7 If yes, what type of services are expected free: (tick any) circulation/xerox/indexes/CD-ROM/etc.
    26.8 If no, what was acceptable price to receive library products: (tick any) subsidised/actual/nominal/no charges at all

27. If no survey done, any other means for feedback on services (circulation/xeroxing/online/CD-ROM searching): yes/no
    27.1 Are the services having full use: yes/no
    27.2 Are the services actual need based: yes/no
    27.3 If yes, how are the needs ascertained: (tick any) observation/past behaviour/circulation pattern/shelf use behaviour/other methods
    27.4 Are there any user satisfaction records: yes/no
    27.5 If yes, how are these used as feedback to improve the work (please comment)
28. What do users think about the library: (tick any) very good/all right/requires improvement/below average
    28.1 If requires improvement what measures are planned: (tick any)
29. Any study done to assess cost-benefit to services: yes/no
30. What is the daily number of visitors: (tick any) 5—50/50—100/100/200/more
31. What is the daily number of issues: (tick any) 5—50/50—100/100/200/more
32. Is xeroxing service: free/priced (tick any)
33. Is online computer searching: free/priced (tick any)
34. Is CD-ROM searching free/priced (tick any)
    34.1 Any count of daily CD-ROM users: 5—25/25—50/more/no record
    34.2 Any count of daily reference queries: (tick any) 5—25/25—50/50—75/more/no limit

Technology and Changing User Needs

35. What are the technological implications on the library: (rank these) manpower/collection/storage/acquisition/processing
36. Is there any priority in implementation of technology: yes/no
    36.1 If yes, what is to be done first: (tick any) acquisition/cataloguing/serials/online searching/CD-ROM
37. What are the implications of changing needs of the users (rank these) on manpower/collection/storage/acquisition/processing/funds
38. Is there any priority in meeting the needs: yes/no
39. If yes, priorities the programme of action: (rank these) acquisition/cataloguing/serials/online searching/others

User Education

(Questions here concern what are the ways adopted to make the users develop self-help, as an essential attitude for managing the library)

40. Any courses of educating users are introduced? yes/no
    - 40.1 If yes, (tick the following name of the programme: user education, bibliographic instruction)
    - 40.2 Duration: an hour/a week/two weeks/others (mention)
    - 40.3 Level at which it is offered: (tick any) freshmen/regular/advanced/others
    - 40.4 Curriculum detail: yes/no (please enclose, if any already prepared)
    - 40.5 What does it improve: retrieval/note taking/evaluation/communication (tick any)
    - 40.6 Who teaches: library staff/others (tick any)
    - 40.7 Teaching methods: lectures, tours, audio/visuals, practicals (tick any)
    - 40.8 What learning packages are included: self-instruction manual/computer aided instruction, etc.
    - 40.9 Promotional guides: (tick any) how to use manual/product details/etc.
41. Since how many years is the programme offered: (tick any) less than one year, less than five years, more than five years
42. If user education programme exists (give reasons):
    - 42.1 Lack of resources: yes/no
    - 42.2 Lack of interest in the staff: yes/no
    - 42.3 Users are acquainted and prefer timely assistance: yes/no

Future

(Questions are on the strategies being adopted to face an era of changing technology, changing user needs, literature explosion, inflation and shrinking budgets, with other information providers competing in the society)

43. What are future plans to keep pace with changing needs, check the following: (considering technological advances/user needs/financial cuts)
    - 43.1 By improving processes and implementation: yes/no
    - 43.2 By making staff changes: yes/no
    - 43.3 By asking for more resources from the management: yes/no

43.4 By sending staff for continuing education: yes/no
43.5 By other methods of strategic planning: yes/no

44. What are the implications of the future on the following:
    44.1 Collection development: alter interests/withdraw/adhoc (tick any)
    44.2 Processing: changes in record entry format: yes/no
    44.3 Changes in output format: yes/no
    44.4 Plans to download cataloguing records: yes/no
    44.5 Storage increase in capacity: yes/no
    44.6 Change medium/methods: yes/no
    44.7 Change systems of storage: yes/no
    44.8 Services: increase new services: yes/no
    44.9.1 Price the products: yes/no
    44.9.2 Produce/increase in phases library products: yes/no
    44.9.3 Marketing: survey the needs: yes/no
    44.9.4 Feasibility studies of products/services: yes/no
    44.9.5 Get regular feedback: yes/no
    44.9.6 Evaluate the products regularly: yes/no
45. As a librarian what knowledge/skills/training you think are critical for your future (state in few lines) (critical issues like automation, continuing education, networks, staff motivation, fund raising, etc.)

Professional Issues

46. Can you divide library work into administrative and specialists tasks (two/more divisions): yes/no
47. If yes, two/more librarians will have equal status, and the headship will rotate (as per UGC faculty pattern): (tick any) agree/do not agree/not possible/no comment
48. Can library get involved in national development? yes/no
    48.1 If yes, can the Government involve library in the planning and implementation?: yes/no
49. How you think library can get that level of priority: (any comment on how to go about doing this, who should come forward: the society, Government, professional, etc.: do you see any parallels, in this idea of linkages, that are found in health, education, literacy, science, technology, etc. Can the library also find a place of priority among the developmental areas).
50. Will this involvement improve social image of library?: yes/no

51. Any views on building a useable library to the society you serve (please comment)
52. Do you agree that right to information means no censorship: yes/no
    52.1 If yes, do you recommend freedom of access for all: (tick any) irreligious/obscene/pornographic/unhealthy books/ politically sensitive information (any comments)
53. Did you ever think that users have a democratic right to demand library services or facilities in the library?: yes/no
    53.1 If yes, what are the ways of communicating this right to people?: (tick any) publicity/propaganda/mass movement.

BIBLIOGRAPHY

HISTORIOGRAPHICAL WORKS

India

Bhatt, R.K., and Bhatt, S.C., "Applications of Historical Method of Research in the Study of Library and Information Science: An Overview", *Annals of Library Science and Documentation*, 41(4), 1994, 155-60

Chatterjee, Partha, *The Nation and Its Fragments: Colonial and Postcolonial Histories*, New Delhi, Oxford University Press, 1995.

Davis, Donald Gordon, "Status of Library History in India: A Report of an Informal Survey and a Selective Bibliographic Essay", *Journal of Library and Information Science*, 14:2 (Dec. 1989), 98-114; also in Libraries and Culture, 25:4 (1990), 575-89.

———, and Taher, Mohamed, "Library History in India: Historiographical Assessment and Current Trends", *Third World Libraries*, 3 (1993), 40-44.

Dutt, Newton Mohan, "History of Indian Libraries from Earliest Times to the Present Day", *Modern Libraries*, 2 (1932), 69-76.

Murthy, M.K., "Examination of Primary Sources in Indian Library Historiography", *Library History Review*, 1 (1974), 77-96.

Negers, Daniel, "The Bura Haal of Burrakatha in State", *Deccan Chronicle*, Hyderabad, March 10, 1997.

Nair, Raman, "Nature and Use of Library History", in *Library Movement and Library Development in India*, Seminar Papers of All-India Library Conference, 1994, held at Bangalore, pp. 1-13.

Sharma, O.P., "Literature of the History of the Library Movement", *Herald of Library Science*, 7: 1968, 8-16.

Sheikh Ali, B., *History: Its Theory and Method*, New Delhi, MacMillan, 1978.

Taher, Mohammed, "Library Historiography: Methodological Issues", a note prepared for the ILA's Central Sectional Committee, 1995.

Others and General

Alston, R.C. "Library History: A Place in the Education of Librarians?" *Library History*, 9 (1991), 37-51.

Baum, Willa K., "The Expanding Role of the Librarian in Oral History", in *Oral History: An Interdisciplinary Anthology*, (Ed.), by David K. Dunaway and Willa K. Baum, 2nd Ed., New Delhi, Sage, 1996.

Bedarida, Francois, "Historical Practice and Responsibility", *Diogenes*, Number 168, Vol. 42: 2, 1994, 1-6.

Davis, Donald Gordon and Tucker, John M., *American Library History: A Comprehensive Guide to the Literature*, Santa Barbara, ABC-CLIO, 1989.

Ditzion, Sidney, "The Research and Writing of Library History", in *Toward a Theory of Librarianship*, Papers in honour of Jesse Hauk Shera, Ed. Conrad Rawski, Metuchen, Screcrow, 1973, pp. 55-59.

Gallerano, Nicola, "History and the Public Use of History", *Diogenes*, Number 168, Vol. 42: 2, 1994, 85-102.

Harris, Michael H., *Fugitive Literature in Library Science: American Library History as a Test Case*, Albany State University of New York, 1968.

———, *A Guide to Research in American Library History*, Methushen, Scarecrow, 1974.

———, and Hannah, Stanley, "Why Do We Study the History of Libraries?: A Meditation on the Perils of a Historicism in the Information Era", *LISR*, 14, 1992, 123-30.

Haselden, R.B., *Scientific Aids for the Study of the Manuscripts*, London, Oxford University Press, 1935.

Jackson, Holbrook, *The Anatomy of Bibliomania*, London, The Soncino Press, 1932.

Kaegbein, P. and Sturges, P., "Introduction: Library History Research in the International Context", *Libraries & Culture*, 25 (1990), 1-3.

Krzys, Richard, "Library Historiography", in *Encyclopedia of Library and Information Science*, Ed., Allen Kent, Vol. 15, New York, Dekker, 1975, pp. 294-330.

Manley, K.A. with the assistance of Denis F. Keeling, "Sunshine in the Gloom: The Study of British Library History", *Libraries & Culture*, 25 (1990), 80-85.

Passet, Joanne M., "Historiography of Library History", in *Encyclopedia of Library History*, Ed., by Wayne E. Wiegand and Donald G. Davis, Jr., New York, Garland, 1994, pp. 260-62.

Pum, Gabriele, *Library Catalogues as Historical Sources: A Contribution to Library History and Sociology of Literature*, showing with the private library of Emperor Ferdinand II, D. Phil Thesis, University of Wien (Austria), 1992. (DAI, 57/01, p. 7, Spring 1996).

Reiff, Janice L., *Structuring the Past: The Use of Computers in History*, American Historical Association, 1991.

Schneiders, Paul, "Library History in the Netherlands: Problems and Suggestions", *Libraries and Culture*, 25 (1990), 4-10.

Shera, Jesse H. "The Literature of American Library History", in *Knowing Books and Men: Knowing Computers Too*, Colarado, Libraries Unlimited, 1973, pp. 126-27.

———, *Foundations of the American Public Libraries*, 1949.

———, "Without Reserve: What the Historian has been Missing", *Wilson Library Bulletin*, 40 (1966).

Welsch, Erwin K., "Historical Literature", in *Encyclopedia of Library and Information Science*, Ed., Allen Kent, Vol. 10, New York, Dekker, 1973, pp. 423-35.

Wiegand, Wayne, A., "Library History Research in the United States", *Libraries & Culture*, 25 (1990), 103-14.

———, and Davis, Donald G. Jr., Ed., *Encyclopedia of Library History*, New York, Garland, 1994.

Willison, I.R., *On the History of Libraries and Scholarship*, Washington, Library of Congress, 1980.

CLIOMETRICS/BIBLIOMETRICS/LIBRAMETRICS

Ali, M. Farooq, *The Concept of a Balanced Collection: An Analysis of the Collection Development Literature*, 1970-1900, Ph.D. thesis, Texas Women's University, 1992 (DAI: 53/05, p. 1307, Nov. 1992).

Attia, Abdel-Hameed Mohammed, *Application of Information Theory Concepts in the Investigation of the Growth Pattern of Production, Distribution, and Velocity of Information*, Ph.D. thesis, University of North Texas, 1987 (DAI: 48/08, p. 1918, Feb. 1988).

Burhanuddin, Muhammad and Taher, Mohamed, *Indian Contribution to American Studies: An Assessment*, New Delhi, Anmol, 1997.

Burns, Robert W., "A Generalized Methodology for Library Systems Analysis", *College and Research Libraries*, July 1971, 295-303.

Cunningham, Melvin Charles, *Johnson Community College Library: A Quantitative History of the First Years with Projections to the Year 2000*, Ph.D. thesis, University of Kansas, 1989 (DAI: 50/11, p. 3398, May 1990).

Du Mont, Rosemary, and Du Mont, Paul F., *Measuring Library Effectiveness: A Review and an Assessment* (Advances in Librarianship, Vol. 9), New York, Academic Press, 1979.

Jones, Norgah, and Jordan, Peter, "Checklist on Library Measurement", in *Case Studies in Library Management*, London, Bingley, 1988, pp. 179-80.

Kunz, Arthur H., "The Use of Data Gathering Instruments in Library Planning", *Library Trends*, 24:3, Jan. 1976, 459-72.

Marchant, Maurice P., *University Libraries as Economic Systems*, College and Research Libraries, Nov. 1975, 449-56.

McGrath, William E., "A Pragmatic Book Allocation Formula for Academic and Public Libraries with a Test for Its Effectiveness", *Library Resources & Technical Services*, 19:4, Fall 1975, 356-90.

Monat, William R., "The Role of the Social and Behavioural Sciences in Determining Library Operation and Impact", *Library Trends*, 24:3, Jan. 1976, 583-96.

Nancy, A. *et al.*, *Measuring Academic Library Performance: A Practical Approach*, Chicago, ALA, 1990.

Pizer, Irwin H., and Cain, Alexander M., "Objective Tests of Library Performance", *Special Libraries*, Nov. 1968, 704-08.

Sikka, Pawan, "The Measurement of Science and Technology", *University News*, 34:51, Dec. 16, 1996, 1-4.

Taher, Mohamed, *Studies in Librarianship*, Vol. 2; Quantitative Studies in Library Science, New Delhi, Anmol, 1997.

Waldhart, Thomas J., and Marcum, Thomas P., "Productivity in Academic Libraries", in *Productivity Measurement in Libraries*.

Williams, Robert V., "The Making of Statistics of National Scope on American Libraries, 1836-1986: Purposes, Problems, and Issues", in *Reading & Libraries: Proceedings of Library History Seminar VIII*, Ed. by Donald G. Davis, Jr. Austin, University of Texas, 1991.

Library Development: Case Studies

India

Allauddin, Sheikh and Rout, R.K., *Libraries and Librarianship During the Muslim Rule in India*, New Delhi, Reliance, 1996.

Amudavalli, A., "Library Services of Foreign Cultural Centres at Madras", in *Current Problems and Trends in Library and Information Services*, Prof. K.S. Deshpande Commemoration Volume, Ed. by H.A. Khan and S.R. Ijari, Varanasi, Indian Bibliographic Centre, 1990, pp. 104-13.

Bensal, G.C., assisted by Preeti Goel, "The Public Library System in the 'City Beautiful' (Chandigarh)", in Gupta, B.M., Ed. *Library Development in India* (Handbook of Libraries, Archives, and Information Centres in India, Series, Vol. 16), New Delhi, Segment Books, 1996, 350-55.

Bhardwaja, B.L., "Presidential Address" (on the role of the professional associations, with special reference to IASLIC), *IASLIC Bull*, 20:4, Dec. 1975, 81-88.

Bordon, W.A., "Baroda, India and Its Libraries", *Library Journal*, 38 (1913), 659-663.

Burhanuddin, Mohammed and Taher, Mohamed, "State Centre Library, Andhra Pradesh: A Centennial Review (1891-1990)", in *Humanities Information Systems and Services* (Handbook of Libraries, Archives and Information Centres, Series, Vol. 9, Part 1), New Delhi, Aditya, 1991.

Chandran, D. and Ramesh Babu, B., "Non-users of the Regional Library: A Survey", in *Public Library Systems: Services & Networking*, A festschrift presented to Prof. K. Sarada, Ed. by L.S. Ramaiah and others, New Delhi, Ess Ess Publications, 1997, Vol. 1, 280-86.

Chatterjee, Ashis, "Need for Information Support for Company Shareholders", *ILA Bulletin*, 24:3, Oct.-Dec., 1988, 164-67.

Das, K.C., and Mahapatra, M., "Development of Secondary School Libraries in Orissa: A Proposal", in *Library Movement and Library Development in India*, Seminar papers of All-India Library Conference, 1994, held at Bangalore, pp. 249-55.

Esperanza, Sister M., "The State Central Library, Patna", in Gupta, B.M., Ed. *Library Development in India* (Handbook of Libraries, Archives, and Information Centres in India, Series, Vol. 16), New Delhi, Segment Books, 1996, pp. 258-70.

Gangu, B.T., "Reaching Out Beyond the Walls: A Case for Extra-Mural Services in University Libraries," *ILA Bull.*, 25:2, July-Sept., 1989, 89-94.

Ghosh, S.B., "Problems for Development: An Integrated Library and Information Network for India, Some Issues", in *Problems of Information Science*, Ed. by N.R. Satyanarayana, and R. Satyanarayana, New Delhi, New Age International Ltd. Publishers, 1996, pp. 80-88.

Gupta, B.M., Ed. *Library Development in India* (Handbook of Libraries, Archives, and Information Centres in India, Series, Vol. 16), New Delhi, Segment Books, 1996 (The series specializes in covering case studies and survey of Indian library history and the related developments).

Ijari, S.R., and Khan, H.A., "State Central Reference Library", in *Library Development in India* (Handbook of Libraries, Archives, and Information Centres in India, Series, Vol. 16), Ed. by B.M. Gupta, New Delhi, Segment Books, 1996, pp. 293-301.

Karisiddappa, C.R., and Kumbar, B.D., "Public Library Services in Rural Areas: A Case Study of Dharwad District", in *Public Library Systems: Services & Networking*, A festschrift presented to Prof. K. Sarada, Ed. by L.S. Ramaiah and others, New Delhi, Ess Ess Publications, 1997, Vol. 1, pp. 193-202.

Kesavan, B.S., *India's National Library*, Calcutta, 1961.

Khan, H.A., "Public Library's Response to Rural Information Needs", in *Public Library Systems: Services & Networking*, A festschrift presented to Prof. K. Sarada, Ed. by L.S. Ramaiah and others, New Delhi, Ess Ess Publications, 1997, Vol. 1, pp. 216-27.

Kumar, P.S.G., "Some Lessons from the Sixty Years History of ILA", in Vashishth, C.P., *Library Movement and Library Development in India*, Seminar papers, 39th All-India Library Conference, Bangalore, January 7-10, 1994.

Nagaraj, M.N., "The Asiatic Society of Calcutta—Early Years", in *Public Library Systems: Services & Networking*, A festschrift presented to Prof. K. Sarada, Ed. by L.S. Ramaiah and others, New Delhi, Ess Ess Publications, 1997, Vol. 2, pp. 3-7.

Ohdedar, A.K. "Calcutta Public Library: A Historical Profile", in *Library Development in India* (Handbook of Libraries, Archives, and Information Centres in India, Series, Vol. 16), Ed. by B.M. Gupta, New Delhi, Segment Books, 1996, pp. 30-51.

———, "Imperial Library, Calcutta", in *Library Development in India* (Handbook of Libraries, Archives, and Information Centres in India, Series, Vol. 16), Ed. by B.M. Gupta, New Delhi, Segment Books, 1996, pp. 52-83.

———, "State Central Library, West Bengal", in *Library Development in India* (Handbook of Libraries, Archives, and Information Centres in India, Series, Vol. 16), Ed. by B.M. Gupta, New Delhi, Segment Books, 1996, pp. 327-39.

Padhi, P., and Panda, K.C., "Harekrishna Mahtab State Library, Orissa", in *Library Development in India* (Handbook of Libraries, Archives, and Information Centres in India, Series, Vol. 16), Ed. by B.M. Gupta, New Delhi, Segment Books, 1996, pp. 307-20.

Raj, Janak, "State Central Library, Haryana", in *Library Development in India* (Handbook of Libraries, Archives, and Information Centres in India, Series, Vol. 16), Ed. by B.M. Gupta, New Delhi, Segment Books, 1996, pp. 286-92.

Rajan, K. Sounder, "Romain Rolland Library, Pondicherry", in *Library Development in India* (Handbook of Libraries, Archives, and Information Centres in India, Series, Vol. 16), Ed. by B.M. Gupta, New Delhi, Segment Books, 1996, pp. 302-06.

Rammurthy, J.R. Media Information System in Karnataka: A Case Study of Deccan Herald and Prajavani", in *Souvenir*, 29 All-India Conference, Mysore, Dec. 5-9, 1983, p. 45-48.

Rani, B.S. Swaroop, "Access System in Trichy College Libraries", in *College Libraries in India*, Proceedings of National Seminar on College Libraries in India, Delhi, 31 Oct.-1 Nov., 1988, Ed. Krishan Kumar, J.K. Anand, Delhi, ILA, 1988, pp. 101-04.

Reddy, V. Pulla, "Job Satisfaction of Librarians: A Study", in *Public Library Systems: Services & Networking*, A festschrift presented to Prof. K. Sarada, Ed. by L.S. Ramaiah and others, New Delhi, Ess Ess Publications, 1997, Vol. 2, pp. 29-40.

Rodrigues, Pia De Menezes, "Goa State Central Library: Past, Present and Future", in *Library Development in India* (Handbook of Libraries, Archives, and Information Centres in India, Series, Vol. 16), Ed. by B.M. Gupta, New Delhi, Segment Books, 1996, pp. 271-85.

Sahu, K.C., and Azad, G.C., "U.P. Library Association—A Brief History", *Lucknow Librarian* (Special Souvenir issue), 14: 2-3 (1982), xli-xliv.

Sainath, J.S., "Mysore University Library", in *Souvenir*, 29 All-India Conference, Mysore, Dec. 5-9, 1983, pp. 12-15.

Sarda, M., "Extracts from the Writings of Prof. Sarada", in *Public Library Systems: Services & Networking*, A festschrift presented to Prof. K. Sarada, Ed. by L.S. Ramaiah and others, New Delhi, Ess Ess Publications, 1997, Vol. 2, pp. 220-31.

Suseela Kumar, *Changing Concepts of Reference Service*, Delhi, Vikas, 1974.

Taher, Mohamed, "Madrasa Libraries in India: A Case Study of Nadwat al Ulama, Lucknow", in *Humanities Information Systems and Services* (Handbook of Libraries, Archives and Information Centres, Series, Vol. 9, Part 1), New Delhi, Aditya, 1991.

———, "Collection in University Libraries: A Case for Balanced Development of Books", in Isaac, Dorothy, and others, Ed. *Academic*

Libraries: Role in the National Development, Madras, T.R. Publications, 1993, pp. 105-11.

Taher, Mohamed, "Dargah Libraries in India: A Comparative Study", *International Library Review*, 18 (1986), 337-46.

———, "Functions of the State Libraries: A Case Study of A.P. State Central Library, Hyderabad", in *Public Library Systems: Services & Networking*, A festschrift presented to Prof. K. Sarada, Ed. by L.S. Ramaiah and others, New Delhi, Ess Ess Publications, 1997, Vol. 1, pp. 15-25.

———, "Madrasa Libraries in India", *International Library Review*, 21 (1989), 83-98.

———, *Studies in Librarianship*, Vol. 3; Qualitative Studies in Library Science, New Delhi, Anmol, 1997.

———, and Fatimy, M.A.K., "Mosque Library: A Case Study", *ILA Bulletin*, 22 (April-Sept. 1984), 38-42.

———, and Gupta, B.M., "American Studies Research Centre: Library & Information Services (developmental history)", in *Social Sciences: Information Systems and Centres* (Handbook of Libraries, Archives and Information Centres, Series, Vol. 8), New Delhi, Aditya, 1990.

"US Varsity Helps Preserve Indian Library" (A Case Study of late Raja Muttiah Chettiar Library, Chennai)—PTI, *Indian Express*, July 12, 1993, p. 6.

Venkatappaiah, Velaga, "Connemara (State Central) Public Library, Madras", in *Library Development in India* (Handbook of Libraries, Archives, and Information Centres in India, Series, Vol. 16), Ed. by B.M. Gupta, New Delhi, Segment Books, 1996, pp. 321-26.

Venkateshwara Rao, L., "Library Service with Library Cess or Without Library Cess", in *Library Movement and Library Development in India*, Seminar papers of All-India Library Conference, 1994, held at Bangalore, pp. 181-83.

Others and General

Reed, Mary Marth, *History of the Lakewood Public Library*, Master's thesis, Western Reserve University, 1958.

Weaver, B., "What on Earth is a State Library?: Issues in State Library Management", *Wilson Library Bulletin*, 65 (1990), 28-30.

White, Carl, *A Survey of the University of Delhi Library*, Delhi, University of Delhi, 1965, p. 184 [see also: Mehta, R.C., "White Report and University Libraries in India", *Indian Librarian* 21:4 (March 1967), 195-98].

Library Development: Surveys

India

Anand, J.K., "College Libraries in Delhi: Problems and Prospects", in *College Libraries in India*, Proceedings of National Seminar on College Libraries in India, Delhi, 31 Oct.-1 Nov., 1988, Ed. Krishan Kumar and J.K. Anand, Delhi, ILA, 1988, pp. 1-15.

Anand, Virendra K., "Library and Librarianship in the 'City Beautiful': An Overview", in *Souvenir*, 34th All-India Library Conference, and 13th National Seminar of the IASLIC, Calcutta, Bengal Library Association, 1988, pp. 44-47.

Asundi, A.Y., "Library Developments in Karnataka: Nineteenth Century and Earlier", in *Library Development in India* (Handbook of Libraries, Archives, and Information Centres in India, Series, Vol. 16), Ed. by B.M. Gupta, New Delhi, Segment Books, 1996, pp. 119-28.

Baheti, S.R., "Status, Pay Scales and Service Conditions of College Librarians in Vidharbah Region (Maharashtra)", in *College Libraries in India*, Proceedings of National Seminar on College Libraries in India, Delhi, 31 Oct.-1 Nov., 1988, Ed. Krishan Kumar and J.K. Anand, Delhi, ILA, 1988, pp. 154-66.

Bavakutty, M., "Book Collection in College Libraries", in *Current Problems and Trends in Library and Information Services*, Prof. K.S. Deshpande commemoration volume, Ed. by H.A. Khan and S.R. Ijari, Varanasi, Indian Bibliographic Centre, 1990, pp. 60-71.

———, "Libraries and Library Science Education in Kerala", in *Souvenir*, 34th All-India Library Conference, and 13th National Seminar of the IASLIC, Calcutta, Bengal Library Association, 1988, pp. 78-83.

Bharadwaja, B.L., "The All-India Library Conference in Retrospect and Prospect", *Lucknow Librarian* (Special Souvenir issue), 14: 2-3 (1982), xlv-xlxi.

Bhatt, R.K., *History and Development of Libraries in India*, New Delhi, Mittal, 1995 (Special focus on the library development of Delhi in post-Independent India).

Chakraborty, Debabrata, "The Development of Library Service in Tripura", in *Souvenir*, 34th All-India Library Conference, and 13th National Seminar of the IASLIC, Calcutta, Bengal Library Association, 1988, pp. 125-28.

Chakraborty, G.P., "College and Academic Libraries in Tripura: A Survey", in *College Libraries in India*, Proceedings of National Seminar on College Libraries in India, Delhi, 31 Oct.-1 Nov., 1988, Ed. Krishan Kumar and J.K. Anand, Delhi, ILA, 1988, pp. 120-41.

Chandel, A.S. "Library Movement in Himachal Pradesh: Past and Present", in *Library Development in India* (Handbook of Libraries, Archives, and Information Centres in India, Series, Vol. 16), Ed. by B.M. Gupta, New Delhi, Segment Books, 1996, pp. 188-99.

———, "Library Services in Meghalaya", in *Souvenir*, 34th All-India Library Conference, and 13th National Seminar of the IASLIC, Calcutta, Bengal Library Association, 1988, pp. 100-04.

Chandler, G., *Libraries in the East: An International and Comparative Study,* New York, Seminar Press, 1971 (deals with developmental perspectives in Calcutta and Delhi).

Datta, N., *Academic Status for University and College Librarians in India*, 3rd ed., Delhi, Indian Bibliographies Bureau, 1989.

Deshpande, K.S., "University Libraries in Karnataka", in *Souvenir*, 29th All-India Conference, Mysore, Dec. 5-9, 1983, pp. 27-35.

Dutta, Ajit Kumar, "Andaman and Nicobar Islands: Marching Towards Modernised Public Library System", in *Souvenir*, 34th All-India Library Conference, and 13th National Seminar of the IASLIC, Calcutta, Bengal Library Association, 1988, pp. 29-32.

Dutta, B.K., *Libraries and Librarianship in Ancient and Medieval India*, Delhi, Atma Rama & Sons, 1970.

Dutta, Dwijendranath, *Libraries and Their Uses: A Guide for the Users*, Calcutta, World Press, 1975.

Esperanza, M., "Library Developments in Bihar (1900-1990)", in *Library Development in India* (Handbook of Libraries, Archives, and Information Centres in India, Series, Vol. 16), Ed. by B.M. Gupta, New Delhi, Segment Books, 1996, pp. 146-74.

———, "College Libraries in Bihar", in *College Libraries in India*, Proceedings of National Seminar on College Libraries in India, Delhi, 31 Oct.-1 Nov., 1988, Ed. Krishan Kumar and J.K. Anand, Delhi, ILA, 1988, pp. 49-58.

Gaddagimath, R.B., *Information Management Programmes for Users in Indian Agricultural Libraries: An Indepth Study of Resources, Curriculum Design and Development of Learners Packages*, Dharwad, Karnataka University Ph.D. thesis, 1995.

Gidwani, N.N. (Ed.), *Comparative Librarianship: Essays in Honour of Professor D.N. Marshall*, New Delhi, Vikas, 1973.

Gopinath, M.A., "History of Library Legislation in India", in *Public Library System: India, Sri Lanka, U.K., U.S.A*, Comparative legislation—based on the Papers and Proceedings of the All-India Seminar on Public Library System, Bangalore, 28 to 30 April, 1972. Ed. by S.R. Ranganathan and A. Neelameghan, Bangalore, Sarada Ranganathan Endowment for Library Service, 1972, pp. 12-38.

Gour, P.N., "Bihar", in *Public Library System: India, Sri Lanka, U.K., U.S.A.*, Comparative legislation—based on the Papers and Proceedings of the All-India Seminar on Public Library System, Bangalore, 28 to 30 April, 1972. Edited by S.R. Ranganathan and A. Neelameghan, Bangalore, Sarada Ranganathan Endowment for Library Service, 1972, pp. 185-89.

Government of India Librarians' Association (GILA), 50 Years of Government of India Librarian's Association, 1933-83, New Delhi, The Association, 1983.

Goyal, Sat Pal (Ed), *Indian Librarianship: Essays in Honour of S.R. Bhatia*, Delhi, Scientific Book Store, 1972.

Gupta, Anuradha, *Government of India Libraries: Their Growth, Development and Services*, Delhi, B.R. Publishing Corp., 1994.

Gupta, O.P., *Development of University Libraries in India after Independence*, New Delhi, Concept, 1992.

Haravu, L.J., "Hyderabad Libraries Network (HYLIBNET): Approaches to Planning and a Conceptual Architecture", in *Souvenir*, CALIBER-95, Second National Convention on Information Access Through Networks, Feb. 1995, Hyderabad, University of Hyderabad, 1995.

Ijari, S.R., "Survey of Public Library Development in Karnataka", in *Public Library Systems: Services & Networking*, A festschrift presented to Prof. K. Sarada, Ed. by L.S. Ramaiah and others, New Delhi, Ess Ess Publications, 1997, Vol. 1, pp. 176-90.

———, "March of Libraries in Karnataka", in *Souvenir*, 34th All-India Library Conference, and 13th National Seminar of the IASLIC, Calcutta, Bengal Library Association, 1988, pp. 71-77.

———, and Khan, H.A., "State Central Reference Library Karnataka", in *Library Development in India* (Handbook of Libraries, Archives, and Information Centres in India, Series, Vol. 16), Ed. by B.M. Gupta, New Delhi, Segment Books, 1996, pp. 293-301.

Inamdar, N.B., and Shakira, A.W. "Management of Libraries in the State of Hyderabad: An Overview", in *Library Development in India* (Handbook of Libraries, Archives, and Information Centres in

India, Series, Vol. 16), Ed. by B.M. Gupta, New Delhi, Segment Books, 1996, pp. 84-100.

Isaac, Dorothy, and others, (Ed.), *Academic Libraries: Role in the National Development*, Madras, T.R. Publications, 1993.

Issac, K.A., "Kerala", in *Public Library System: India, Sri Lanka, U.K., U.S.A.*, Comparative legislation—based on the Papers and Proceedings of the All-India Seminar on Public Library System, Bangalore, 28 to 30 April, 1972. Edited by S.R. Ranganathan and A. Neelameghan, Bangalore, Sarada Ranganathan Endowment for Library Service, 1972, pp. 190-94.

Jagga Rao, N.V. and Prafulla Chandra, T.V., "Need for Andhra Pradesh State Bibliography", in *Public Library Systems: Services & Networking*, A festschrift presented to Prof. K. Sarada, Ed. by L.S. Ramaiah and others, New Delhi, Ess Ess Publications, 1997, Vol. 1, pp. 176-90.

Janak Raj, "Library Movement in Haryana", in *Souvenir*, 34th All-India Library Conference, and 13th National Seminar of the IASLIC, Calcutta, Bengal Library Association, 1988, pp. 66-70.

Kabir, Abulfazal M. Fazle, *The Libraries of Bengal, 1700-1947: The Story of Bengali Renaissance*, New Delhi, 1988.

Kaula, P.N. (Ed.), *Library Science Today: Ranganathan Festschrift*, Bombay, Asia Publishing House, 1965.

———, "Observation on School and Public Library Development in India", *Granthana*, 2:1 (Jan. 1991), 21-30.

Kesavan, B.S., *Book in India: A Compilation*, Delhi, National Book Trust, 1992.

———, "History of Printing and Publishing in India: A Story of Cultural Re-awakening", Volume 1, South Indian Origins of Printing (National Book Trust, 1984).

Khan, H.A., *Problems and Prospects of Public Libraries in Four Library Law States in India*, Karnataka University, Dharwad, 1985, Ph.D. thesis.

———, Public Libraries and the Contemporary Indian Society", in *Current Problems and Trends in Library and Information Services*, Prof. K.S. Deshpande commemoration volume, Ed. by H.A. Khan and S.R. Ijari, Varanasi, Indian Bibliographic Centre, 1990, pp. 166-72.

Konnur, M.B., *Transnational Library Relations: The Indo-American Experience*, New Delhi, Concept, 1988.

Kumar, Girija, *Library Development in India*, New Delhi, Vikas, 1986.

Kumar, Krishan, "University Libraries: Problems and Solutions", in Isaac, Dorothy, and others, Ed. *Academic Libraries: Role in the National Development*, Madras, T.R. Publications, 1993, pp. 4-12.

———, and Datta, N., "Delhi University College Libraries: An Overview," in *Current Problems and Trends in Library and Information Services*, Prof. K.S. Deshpande commemoration volume, Ed. by H.A. Khan and S.R. Ijari, Varanasi, Indian Bibliographic Centre, 1990, pp. 72-81.

Kumbhar, M.R., and Karisiddappa, C.R., "Library and Information Science Education in Karnataka", in *Souvenir*, 29 All-India Conference, Mysore, Dec. 5-9, 1983, pp. 54-59.

Lahkar, Narendra, "College Libraries of Assam: Problems and Prospects", in *College Libraries in India*, Proceedings of National Seminar on College Libraries in India, Delhi, 31 Oct.-1 Nov., 1988, Ed. Krishan Kumar and J.K. Anand, Delhi, ILA, 1988, pp. 142-49.

Lal, Madan, and Jyothirmayi, S., "Library Finance in Delhi University Colleges", in *College Libraries in India*, Proceedings of National Seminar on College Libraries in India, Delhi, 31 Oct.-1 Nov., 1988, Ed. Krishan Kumar and J.K. Anand, Delhi, ILA, 1988, pp. 21-31.

Lianzama, C., "History and Development of Library Movement of Mizoram State", in *Souvenir*, 34th All-India Library Conference, and 13th National Seminar of the IASLIC, Calcutta, Bengal Library Association, 1988, pp. 105-06.

Mahajan, S.G., "Legal Aspects in University Library Management", in *Academic Libraries: Role in the National Development*, Ed. Dorothy Isaac and others, Madras, T.R. Publications, 1993, pp. 133-51.

———, Library Development in Maharashtra", in *Souvenir*, 34th All-India Library Conference, and 13th National Seminar of the IASLIC, Calcutta, Bengal Library Association, 1988, pp. 89-94.

Mahapatra, M., "Libraries and Library Movement in Orissa—An Overview", in *Souvenir*, 34th All-India Library Conference, and 13th National Seminar of the IASLIC, Calcutta, Bengal Library Association, 1988, pp. 107-11.

Mangla, P.B. and others, *Fifty Years of Librarianship in India: Past, Present and Future*, seminar Papers, 29 All-India Library Conference, Bangalore, 1983, Delhi, Indian Library Association, 1983.

Manoharan, A., "Perspectives of College Library Services and Management in Tiruchirapalli", in *College Libraries in India*, Proceedings of National Seminar on College Libraries in India, Delhi, 31 Oct.-1 Nov., 1988, Ed. Krishan Kumar and J.K. Anand, Delhi, ILA, 1988, pp. 96-100.

Mishra, B.N., "Veterinary College Libraries in Bihar—A Study", in *College Libraries in India*, Proceedings of National Seminar on College Libraries in India, Delhi, 31 Oct.-1 Nov., 1988, Ed. Krishan Kumar and J.K. Anand, Delhi, ILA, 1988, pp. 59-63.

Mishra, Jogesh, *History of Libraries and Librarianship in Modern India since 1850*, Delhi, Atma Ram & Sons, 1979.

Mitra, D.P., "A Census of Library and Information Science Periodicals", *ILA Bull.*, 24:2 (July-Sept. 1988), 76-86.

Moghe, V.S., "Madhya Pradesh", in *Public Library System: India, Sri Lanka, U.K., U.S.A.*, Comparative legislation—based on the Papers and Proceedings of the All-India Seminar on Public Library System, Bangalore, 28 to 30 April, 1972. Edited by S.R. Ranganathan and A. Neelameghan, Bangalore, Sarada Ranganathan Endowment for Library Service, 1972, pp. 195-98.

Mookerjee, Subodh Kumar, *Development of Libraries and Library Science in India*, Calcutta, World Press, 1969 (Special focus on public library and national development).

Nagar, Murari Lal, *Foundation of Library Movement in India*, Ludhiana, Indian Library Institute and Bibliographic Centre, 1983.

Nagaraj, M.N., "National Committees and Commissions on Libraries", in *New Horizons in Library and Information Science*, Dr. Velaga Venkatappaiah Festschrift, Ed., C.P. Vashishth, and others, Madras, T.R. Publications, 1994, 309-18.

Naik, M.K., "The Decline and Fall of the Well-Read Man", in *Current Problems and Trends in Library and Information Services*, Prof. K.S. Deshpande commemoration volume, Ed. by H.A. Khan and S.R. Ijari, Varanasi, Indian Bibliographic Centre, 1990, pp. 6-8.

Nair, R. Raman, "Public Library Systems in Ancient South India", in *Library Development in India* (Handbook of Libraries, Archives, and Information Centres in India, Series, Vol. 16), Ed by B.M. Gupta, New Delhi, Segment Books, 1996, pp. 129-37.

Navlani, K., "Promotion: The Least Satisfying Aspect of Library Profession", in *Current Problems and Trends in Library and Information Services*, Prof. K.S. Deshpande commemoration volume, Ed. by H.A. Khan and S.R. Ijari, Varanasi, Indian Bibliographic Centre, 1990, pp. 128-37.

Ohdedar, A.K., *The Growth of the Library in Modern India*, 1498-1836, Calcutta, 1966.

Palanivelu, C., and Raghavan, K.S. Eds. *Education Through Public Libraries—A Practical Approach*, National Seminar on Public

Library Movement: Proceedings, Madras, Directorate of Public Libraries, 1991.

Panda, B.D., *History of Library Development*, New Delhi, Anmol, 1992 (Major focus is the history of developments in Orissa).

Pandithurai, C., "Concept of Community Information System for Integrated Rural Development: Madurai District Experience—Considerations for a Model", National Seminar on Community Information Centres under Panchayat Raj, February 19-21, 1997. K.A. Raju, Seminar Director, Reading material, Hyderabad, NIRD, pp. 55-65.

Phukan, Alka Burgohain, "Library Situation in the State of Assam: A Status Report", in *Souvenir*, 34th All-India Library Conference, and 13th National Seminar of the IASLIC, Calcutta, Bengal Library Association, 1988, pp. 39-43.

Ponamian, R. "The Services of the Connemara Public Library", in *Public Library Systems: Services & Networking*, A festschrift presented to Prof. K. Sarada, Ed. by L.S. Ramaiah and others, New Delhi, Ess Ess Publications, 1997, Vol. 2, pp. 8-14.

Rajagopalan, T.S., *Year's Work in Indian Librarianship*, Delhi, ILA, 1988.

———, "An Integrated Information System for Socio-economic Development of India", (Presidential Address), *IASLIC Bull.*, 28:4, 1983, 143-50.

Rajasekharan, K., "College Libraries under Kerala Agricultural University: Present Situation and Future Directions", in *College Libraries in India*, Proceedings of National Seminar on College Libraries in India, Delhi, 31 Oct.-1 Nov., 1988, Ed. Krishan Kumar and J.K. Anand, Delhi, ILA, 1988, pp. 113-19.

Raju, A.A.N., *History of Library Movement in Andhra Pradesh, 1900-1956*, Delhi, Ajanta, 1988.

———, "What Ails Library Service in Andhra Pradesh", *The Hindu*, 114:89 (1991), 19.

Ramaiah, L.S. "Public Libraries and Access to Information in India", in *Public Library Systems: Services & Networking*, A festschrift presented to Prof. K. Sarada, Ed. by L.S. Ramaiah and others, New Delhi, Ess Ess Publications, 1997, Vol. 1, pp. 111-24.

Ranganathan, S.R., *Library Movement by Diverse Hands*, Madras, Madras Library Association, 1929.

———, *Library Developmental Plan*, Bangalore, Sarada Ranganathan Endowment for Library Service.

Ranganathan, S.R., "Library Organization and the Constitution in India", in *Public Library Provision and Documentation Problems*, Papers for discussion at the Ninth All-India Library Conference, Indore, 11-14 May 1951, G. Blunt & Sons, London, and Delhi, Indian Library Association, 1951.

———, "Library Way for India", in *Library Movement in India*, Papers for discussion at the First Delhi Library Conference, 30-31 March 1957, and the proceedings of the Conference, Edited by P.N. Kaula, Delhi, Delhi Library Association, 1958.

———, and Jayarajan, P., *New Education and School Library: Experience of Half a Century*, Bangalore, Sarada Ranganathan Endowment for Library Service, 1973.

Rao, C. Gopinatha, *Library Movement in Andhra Pradesh*, Hyderabad, Dept. of Public Libraries, Govt. of Andhra Pradesh, 1981.

Rao, Mohan, "Library Service in Rajasthan", in *Public Library System: India, Sri Lanka, U.K., U.S.A.*, Comparative legislation—based on the Papers and Proceedings of the All-India Seminar on Public Library System, Bangalore, 28 to 30 April, 1972. Edited by S.R. Ranganathan and A. Neelameghan, Bangalore, Sarada Ranganathan Endowment for Library Service, 1972, pp. 330-32.

Rao, Ramakrishna, K., "Library Development in India", *Library Quarterly*, 31 (1961), 135-53.

Rao, S. Sudarshan, "University Libraries in India: Their Role in Academic Research", in Isaac, Dorothy, and others, Ed. *Academic Libraries: Role in the National Development*, Madras, T.R. Publications, 1993, pp. 35-46.

Rath, P.N., and Mohanta, R.N., "Free or Fee Based Public Library Service: An Observation in Indian Context", in *Library Movement and Library Development in India*, Seminar papers of All-India Library Conference, 1994, held at Bangalore, pp. 184-91.

Rawal, M.M., "Library Service in Gujarat", in *Public Library System: India, Sri Lanka, U.K., U.S.A.*, Comparative legislation—based on the Papers and Proceedings of the All-India Seminar on Public Library System, Bangalore, 28 to 30 April, 1972. Edited by S.R. Ranganathan and A. Neelameghan, Bangalore, Sarada Ranganathan Endowment for Library Service, 1972, pp. 324-29.

Reddy, P. Janardhan, "Network of Public Library Services in Twin Cities", in *Souvenir*, National Workshop on Library Science Education at the Certificate Level and Library Service in Rural Areas, Dec. 15-17, 1991, Hyderabad, 1991.

Riswadkar, M.R., "Evaluation of Academic Library Services", in Isaac, Dorothy, and others, Ed. *Academic Libraries: Role in the National Development*, Madras, T.R. Publications, 1993.

Rodrigues, Pia de Menezes, "Library Movement in Goa", in *Souvenir*, 34th All-India Library Conference, and 13th National Seminar of the IASLIC, Calcutta, Bengal Library Association, 1988, pp. 57-61.

Rout, R.K., Ed. *Library Legislation in India*, New Delhi, Reliance Publishing Co., 1986.

Roychoudhury, Prabir, "Public Library Development in West Bengal: A Review", in *Souvenir*, 34th All-India Library Conference, and 13th National Seminar of the IASLIC, Calcutta, Bengal Library Association, 1988, pp. 135-48.

Rupail, Nirmal, "India", in Organization of Social Science Information and Documentation; Reports on 11 Asian countries. Presented at the First Asian Seminar on Information Sources, Systems, and Services in the Social Sciences, organized by UNESCO, 11 to 22 July, 1983, Bangkok, UNESCO Regional Office, 1983.

Saha Ramakrishna, "Library Movement in West Bengal", in *Souvenir*, 34th All-India Library Conference, and 13th National Seminar of the IASLIC, Calcutta, Bengal Library Association, 1988, pp. 153-59.

———, (Ed.), *Library Movement in India*, Calcutta, Bengal Library Association, 1988.

Sarin, Ashok Kumar, and Sharma, Janak Raj, "Bibliographical Services in India, 1958-67", in *IX IASLIC Conference Papers*, Ed. by Abdul Rahman and others, Calcutta, IASLIC, 1972, pp. 309-28.

Satyanarayana, M., "Government Policies Towards Public Libraries", in *Public Library Systems: Services & Networking*, A festschrift presented to Prof. K. Sarada, Ed. by L.S. Ramaiah and others, New Delhi, Ess Ess Publications, 1997, Vol. 1, pp. 125-35.

Sen, N.B., *Development of Libraries in New India*, New Delhi, New Book Society, 1965, p. 353.

———, *Progress of Libraries in Free India*, New Delhi, New Book Society of India, 1967, p. 247.

Shah, P.C., "Libraries in Gujarat—A Bird's Eye View", in *Souvenir*, 34th All-India Library Conference, and 13th National Seminar of the IASLIC, Calcutta, Bengal Library Association, 1988, pp. 62-65.

Sharma, C.D., and Sharma, Narendra, "Library Movement in Rajasthan", in *Souvenir*, 34th All-India Library Conference, and 13th National Seminar of the IASLIC, Calcutta, Bengal Library Association, 1988, pp. 115-24.

Sharma, J.N., "ICAR: Its Role in the Development of Libraries", *Lucknow Librarian* (*Special Souvenir issue*), 14:2-3 (1982), 53-59

Sharma, Jagdish S., "India's Contribution in the Field of Bibliography", *Library Herald*, 16:3&4 (Oct. 1974-March 1975), 87-139.

Sharma, Narendra, "Library Development in Rajasthan", in *Library Development in India* (Handbook of Libraries, Archives, and Information Centres in India, Series, Vol. 16), Ed. by B.M. Gupta, New Delhi, Segment Books, 1996, pp. 225-35.

Singh, Hukam, "Punjab", in *Public Library System: India, Sri Lanka, U.K., U.S.A.*, Comparative Legislation—based on the Papers and Proceedings of the All-India Seminar on Public Library System, Bangalore, 28 to 30 April, 1972. Edited by S.R. Ranganathan and A. Neelameghan, Bangalore, Sarada Ranganathan Endowment for Library Service, 1972, pp. 199-201.

Singh, N. Giridhari, "Development of Libraries in Manipur", in *Souvenir*, 34th All-India Library Conference, and 13th National Seminar of the IASLIC, Calcutta, Bengal Library Association, 1988, pp. 95-99.

Singh, Sewa, "History of Library Movement in Punjab", in *Library Development in India* (Handbook of Libraries, Archives, and Information Centres in India, Series, Vol. 16), Ed. by B.M. Gupta, New Delhi, Segment Books, 1996, pp. 208-224.

Srivastava, Rachna, "Library Movement in Uttar Pradesh: A State of the Art", in *Souvenir*, 34th All-India Library Conference, and 13th National Seminar of the IASLIC, Calcutta, Bengal Library Association, 1988, pp. 129-34.

Taher, Mohamed, "India", in *Encyclopedia of Library History,* New York, Garland, 1994.

———, "Libraries as Instruments of Socio-economic Development", *Hindu* (March 20, 1990), 19.

———, "Mosque Libraries: Bibliographical Essay", *Libraries & Culture*, 27 (1992), 43-48.

———, and Davis, Donald Gordon, *Librarianship and Library Science in India: An Outline of Historical Perspectives*, New Delhi, Concept, 1994 [book review, Girja Kumar, "Intellectual History and Librarianship in India", in *The Book Review*, 19:5, (1995?), 22-23].

Takalkar, Anil and others, "Case Studies of Rural Libraries", in *Andhra Pradesh and Maharashtra,* National Seminar on Community Information Centres Under Panchayat Raj, February 19-21, 1997, K.A. Raju, Seminar Director, Reading material, Hyderabad, NIRD, pp. 55-65.

Thakur, Ranjan Sinha, and Gopinath, M.A., "Role of State and Central Governments in Public Library Development in India", in Vashishth, C.P. Ed., *Library Movement and Library Development in India,* Seminar papers, 39th All-India Library Conference, Bangalore, January 7-10, 1994, pp. 139-55.

Thillainayagam, V., "Tamil Nadu", in *Public Library System: India, Sri Lanka, U.K., U.S.A.*, Comparative legislation—based on the Papers and Proceedings of the All-India Seminar on Public Library System, Bangalore, 28 to 30 April, 1972. Edited by S.R. Ranganathan and A. Neelameghan, Bangalore, Sarada Ranganathan Endowment for Library Service, 1972, pp. 169-73.

Thomas, M.O., "Literature, Learning and Libraries in Ancient India", J. Annamalai University, 3 (1934).

Tiwari, B.N., "Uttar Pradesh", in *Public Library System: India, Sri Lanka, U.K., U.S.A.*, Comparative legislation—based on the Papers and Proceedings of the All-India Seminar on Public Library System, Bangalore, 28 to 30 April, 1972. Edited by S.R. Ranganathan and A. Neelameghan, Bangalore, Sarada Ranganathan Endowment for Library Service, 1972, pp. 202-03.

Trehan, G.L., *Modern Public Library Movement and Services in India*, Chandigarh, Library Literature House, 1982.

———, "Library Development in Punjab—An Overview", in *Souvenir*, 34th All-India Library Conference, and 13th National Seminar of the IASLIC, Calcutta, Bengal Library Association, 1988, pp. 112-14.

Vashishth, C.P. (Ed), *Quality Life Through Libraries*, Presidential address, delivered at 38th All-India Library Conference, Nov. 21, 1992 Bhubaneswar.

———, *Library Movement and Library Development in India,* Seminar papers, 39th All-India Library Conference, Bangalore, January 7-10, 1994.

———, and others, Ed., *New Horizons in Library and Information Science*, Dr. Velaga Venkatappaiah Festschrift, Madras, T.R. Publications, 1994.

———, and Singh, Dev Raj, "Libraries in Delhi: A Scenario", in *Souvenir*, 34th All-India Library Conference, and 13th National Seminar of the IASLIC, Calcutta, Bengal Library Association, 1988, pp. 48-56.

Wadikar, A.L., "Library Scene in Madhya Pradesh", in *Souvenir*, 34th All-India Library Conference, and 13th National Seminar of the IASLIC, Calcutta, Bengal Library Association, 1988, pp. 84-88.

Walia, P.K., and Gautam, Shalini, "Library Services in Colleges of Delhi: A Survey", in *College Libraries in India*, Proceedings of National Seminar on College Libraries in India, Delhi, 31 Oct.-1 Nov., 1988, Ed. Krishan Kumar and J.K. Anand, Delhi, ILA, 1988, pp. 16-20.

Yash Pal, "Beyond Information, Beyond Technology", *IASLIC Bull.*, 40:1 (1995), 9-16.

Others and General

Black, Alistair Matthew, *The English Public Library as an Agency for Social Stability, C. 1850-1919*, Ph.D. Thesis, Council for National Academic Awards (UK), 1989 (DAI: 50/10, p. 3095, April 1990).

Bordon, Arnold K., "The Sociological Beginnings of the Library Movement", *Library Quarterly*, 1 (1931), 278-83.

Bundy, Mary Lee and Stielow, Frederick J., *Activism in American Librarianship, 1962-1973*, New York, Greenwood, 1987.

Butler, Pierce, *Introduction to Library Science*, Chicago, Chicago University Press, 1933, (reprinted 1961).

Lorence, John G., "The Role of Libraries in Economic and Social Development", *UNESCO Bull. for Libraries*, 15:5, Sept.-Oct., 1962, 226-33.

Manning, Leslie A., "The Public Library in the American West: A Bibliographic Essay", *Journal of the West*, 30:3, July 1991, 90-91.

Marquant, R., "Archives and Economic and Social Development", *UNESCO Bull. for Libraries*, 15:5, Sept.-Oct., 1962, 234-38.

———, "Place of Libraries in National Economic Development", *UNESCO Bull. for Libraries*, 15:5, Sept.-Oct., 1962, 248-52.

———, "Reading for Self-Improvement in Eastern Nigeria", *UNESCO Bull. for Libraries*, 15:5, Sept.-Oct., 1962, 244-46.

Van Niekerk, Rona Vernon, *Information in South African Agriculture: The Role of the Library*, D.Phil Thesis, University of Pretoria, 1991 (DAI 52/06, p. 1927, Dec. 1991).

History (In General)

Majumdar, R.C. and others, *An Advanced History of India*, Macmillan, 1967.

Nehru, Jawaharlal, *An Autobiography*, with musings on recent events in India, London, John Lane the Bodley Head, 1936.

Nehru, Jawaharlal, *The Discovery of India*, New Delhi, Oxford University Press, 1989.

Ritter, Harry, *Dictionary of Concepts in History*, New York, Greenwood, 1986.

Thapar, Romila, *Cultural Transaction and Early India: Tradition and Patronage*, New Delhi, Oxford University Press, 1994.

———, *Interpreting Early India*, New Delhi, Oxford University Press, 1993.

Other Areas in Librarianship

India

Aslam, M., "Towards Designing a Strategy for Establishing Community Information Centres in Rural India", in *National Seminar on Community Information Centres Under Panchayat Raj*, February 19-21, 1997, K.A. Raju, Seminar Director, Reading material, Hyderabad, NIRD, pp. 7-13.

Elahi, Fazal, *Reference Assistance to Indian Readers: A Text Book for Librarians*, Lucknow, Maxwell Press, 1940.

Gaur, P.N., "Public Library Services in India and National Adult Education Programme: A Plea for their Integration", in 24 All-India Library Conference, New Delhi, 1980, Ed. Krishan Kumar and C.P. Vashishth, New Delhi, ILA, 1980, pp. 3-9.

Ijari, S.R. "Panchayat Libraries under Public Library System in Karnataka: A Micro-Analysis", in *National Seminar on Community Information Centres Under Panchayat Raj*, February 19-21, 1997, K.A. Raju, Seminar Director, Reading material, Hyderabad, NIRD, pp. 95-105.

Inamdar, N.B., "Institute of Library Science, Hyderabad", in *Souvenir*, National Workshop on Library Science Education at the Certificate Level and Library Service in Rural Areas, Dec. 15-17, 1991, Hyderabad, 1991.

Jagga Rao, N.V., and Prafulla Chandra, T.V., "Role of Public Relations in University Libraries", in Isaac, Dorothy, and others, Ed. *Academic Libraries: Role in the National Development*, Madras, T.R. Publications, 1993, pp. 183-95.

Janardhana Rao, S.S., "Autonomous College and the Challenges of the Librarian", in *College Libraries in India*, Proceedings of National Seminar on College Libraries in India, Delhi, 31 Oct.-1 Nov., 1988, Ed. Krishan Kumar and J.K. Anand, Delhi, ILA, 1988, pp. 92-95.

Kapoor, S.K. and Ghosh, S.B., Ed. *Planning of National Information Network*, Papers of the 11th IASLIC Conference, November 2-5, 1977, Dharwar, Calcutta, IASLIC, 1977.

Khan, H.A., "Role of Rural Libraries in the Promotion of Literacy and Adult Education", *Granthana*, 2:2 (July 1991), 135-45.

Kumar, Girja, "Librarians and Publishers in Dialectical Relationship", Isaac, Dorothy, and others, Ed. *Academic Libraries: Role in the National Development*, Madras, T.R. Publications, 1993, pp. 57-70.

Kumar, Krishan and Vashishth, C.P. Ed., *Seminar on 'Library Services for a Developing Society'*, 24 All-India Library Conference, New Delhi, 1980, New Delhi, ILA, 1980.

Kumar, P.S.G., "Panchayat Libraries as Community Resource Centres: Some Suggestions", in *National Seminar on Community Information Centres Under Panchayat Raj*, February 19-21, 1997, K.A. Raju, Seminar Director, Reading material, Hyderabad, NIRD, pp. 15-18.

———, and Tejomurthy, A., "Printing and Publishing: Technologies and Trends—Impact on Library and Information Science", in *Current Problems and Trends in Library and Information Services*, Prof. K.S. Deshpande commemoration volume, Ed. by H.A. Khan and S.R. Ijari, Varanasi, Indian Bibliographic Centre, 1990, pp. 173-78.

Murthy, C.N.N., "Reaching the Message to Rural Areas"," in *National Seminar on Community Information Centres Under Panchayat Raj*, February 19-21, 1997, K.A. Raju, Seminar Director, Reading material, Hyderabad, NIRD, pp. 47-53.

Neelameghan, A., "Social Change, Communication of Ideas and Library Service with Special Reference to Developing Societies", *Library Science with a Slant to Documentation*, 10:1, 1973, 1-23.

———, and Gopinath, M.A., "An Annual Review for Library Science in India: Its Need, Scope and Publications", *IX IASLIC Conference Papers*, Ed. by Abdul Rahman and others, Calcutta, IASLIC, 1972, pp. 41-50.

Raja Rammohun Roy Library Foundation and Indian Library Association, Documents on National Policy on Library and Information System, 1985.

Ranganathan, S.R., *Library Manual: For Library Authorities, Librarians and Library Workers*, Bangalore, Sarada Ranganathan Endowment for Library Service, 1988.

———, "A Century's Journey to Documentation Service: Responsiveness to User's Needs", in *IX IASLIC Conference Papers*, Ed., by Abdul Rahman and others, Calcutta, IASLIC, 1972, Part II, Paper A, pp. 1-12.

Ranganathan, S.R., "Integrated Public Library System: Five Tiers", in *Public Library System: India, Sri Lanka, U.K., U.S.A.*, Comparative legislation—based on the Papers and Proceedings of the All-India Seminar on Public Library System, Bangalore, 28 to 30 April, 1972. Edited by S.R. Ranganathan and A. Neelameghan, Bangalore, Sarada Ranganathan Endowment for Library Service, 1972, pp. 208-12.

———, *Reference Service*, Bangalore, Sarada Ranganathan Endowment for Library Service, 1961.

———, and others (Ed.), *Free Book Service for All: An International Survey*, Bombay, Asia Publishing House, 1968.

Riswadkar, M.R., "Six Years with Institute of Library Science", in *Souvenir*, National Workshop on Library Science Education at the Certificate Level and Library Service in Rural Areas, Dec. 15-17, 1991, Hyderabad, 1991.

Roth, Dano L., "The Needs of Library Users", in *IX IASLIC Conference Papers*, Ed., by Abdul Rahman and others, Calcutta, IASLIC, 1972, Part II, Paper C1, pp. 31-34.

Sahay, P.N., *Historical and Indological Institutions in India*, Delhi, S.S. Publishers, 1987.

Sarada, K., "Public Libraries in India: Status and Resources", in *National Seminar on Community Information Centres Under Panchayat Raj*, February 19-21, 1997, K.A. Raju, Seminar Director, Reading material, Hyderabad, NIRD, pp. 29-30.

Satish, N.G., "Bare Foot and Far to Go: Stray Impressions on Role of Library in Our Rural Setting", in *National Seminar on Community Information Centres Under Panchayat Raj*, February 19-21, 1997, K.A. Raju, Seminar Director, Reading Material, Hyderabad, NIRD, pp. 79-83.

Sundaram, K.V., "Information Needs and Systems for Decentralized Development Planning with Special Reference to India", Regional Seminar on Development Information, (n.d.), 57-77.

Venkatappaiah, Velga, "Developing Rural Libraries as Rural Information Centres", in *National Seminar on Community Information Centres Under Panchayat Raj*, February 19-21, 1997, K.A. Raju, Seminar Director, Reading material, Hyderabad, NIRD, pp. 35-46.

———, Need for Library Legislation in South Asian Countries", in *Public Library Systems: Services & Networking*, A festschrift presented to Prof. K. Sarada, Ed. by L.S. Ramaiah and others, New Delhi, Ess Ess Publications, 1997, Vol. 1, pp. 76-110.

Venkateshwara Rao, L., "Opening of School and College Libraries to the Public", in *New Horizons in Library and Information Science*, Dr. Velaga Venkatappaiah Festschrift, Ed., C.P. Vashishth, and others, Madras, T.R. Publications, 1994, 363-73.

Others & Miscellaneous

Gessesse, Kebede, "Libraries and Their Contribution to National Development", *Herald of Library Science*, 25: 3-4, 1986, 205-08.

Library Friends, University of Illinois at Urbana-Campaign, Annual Report 1990-91, Urbana, IL Library Office of Development and Public Affairs, UIUC, 1991.

Lorence, John G., "The Role of Libraries in Economic and Social Development",*UNESCO Bull. for Libraries*, 15:5, Sept.-Oct., 1962, 226-33.

Marquant, R., "Archives and Economic and Social Development", *UNESCO Bull. for Libraries*, 15:5, Sept.-Oct., 1962, 234-38.

Penniman, W. David, and Jacob, Mary Ellen, "Libraries as Communicators of Information", in *The New Media: Communication, Research and Technology*, Ed. by Ronald E. Rice, and Associates, New Delhi, Sage, 1984, pp. 251-68.

"Place of Libraries in National Economic Development", *UNESCO Bull. for Libraries*, 15:5, Sept.-Oct., 1962, 248-52.

"Reading for Self-Improvement in Eastern Nigeria", *UNESCO Bull. for Libraries*, 15:5, Sept.-Oct., 1962, 244-46.

Related Works

Dubey, Y.P., Menon, V.V. and Prasad, H.N., *Information Technology and National Development*, Agra, Y.K. Publishers, 1994.

Fransman, Martin, "Conceptualising Technical Change in the Third World in the 1980s", in *Technology and Economic Development*, Boulder, CO., Westview Press, 1986.

India, 1992: A Reference Annual, Compiled and edited by Research and Reference Division, Ministry of Information and Broadcasting, Government of India, New Delhi, 1993.

Mohanvo, "Book Industry in Andhra Pradesh (1800-1995)", in *Souvenir*, 41st All-India Library Conference, Vijayawada, 1996.

"Production of Books: National Trust to be Set Up—Azad Reveals Decision", *The Hindu* (New Delhi), 7 Oct. 1955, reprinted in *The*

Hindu Speaks on Libraries, Compiled by Editor, Madras, Kasturi & Sons, 1992, pp. 138-40.

Raghvachari, C., "The Role of Mass Media", in *Souvenir*, 41st All-India Library Conference, Vijayawada, 1996.

Sharma, M.L., *A Critical Study of the Role and Contribution of the Private Enterprise in Education in Punjab, 1954-1966*, Punjab University, Chandigarh, 1981, Ph.D. Thesis.

Silvera, D.M., *The India Book, 1991*, New Delhi, News India Publications, 1991.

Committee, Commissions, Reports and Documents

Andhra Pradesh, Public Libraries (Department of) Report (Chairman: Justice Ekbote), Hyderabad, 1978.

———, Report of the Committee on Private Libraries (Chairman: Vavilala Gopalkrishnayya), Hyderabad, 1978.

Calcutta University Commission, 1917-18 Report (Chairman: Michael Sadler).

India, Culture, Dept. of Committee on National Policy on Library and Information Systems, A Presentation (Chairman: D.L. Chattopadhyaya), New Delhi,1986.

India, Education, Ministry of Advisory Committee for Libraries, Report (Chairman: K.P. Sinha), New Delhi, 1959.

India, Government of The Constitution of India, New Delhi, Manager of Publications, 1949.

India, Finance, Ministry of Standard of Work for Jobs in Departmental Libraries, Report submitted by The Staff Inspection Unit, Delhi, 1965. See also: Sen, Ashis, "Plea for Performance Budgets and National Standards for Libraries in India", *IASLIC Bull.*, 12: 4 (December 1967), 280-90.

India, Planning Commission, First Five Year Plan, New Delhi, 1952.

———, Second Five Year Plan, New Delhi, 1956.

———, Third Five Year Plan, New Delhi, 1961.

———, Fourth Five Year Plan, New Delhi, 1966. See also (1) *Libraries in Fourth Five Year Plan*, A paper prepared for the Planning Commissions' Working Group on Libraries, by N.C. Chakravarty, Delhi, 1964, 14p. (2) Kalia, D.R., "Libraries in Fourth Five-Year Plan", *Bull. Ind. Lib. Assn.*, 1:1 (Jan.-Mar. 1965), 1-76. (3) Mittal, R.L., "Education for Librarianship during Fourth Five Year Plan Period in India", *Libri*, 17:1 (1967), 21-28. (4) Ranganathan, S.R.,

"Academic Library System: Fourth Plan Period", *Lib. Sc.* with Slant to Documentation, 2:4 (1965), 335.

———, Fifth Five Year Plan, New Delhi.

———, Sixth Five Year Plan, New Delhi.

———, Seventh Five Year Plan, New Delhi.

———, Eighth Five Year Plan, New Delhi.

———, Ninth Five Year Plan, New Delhi.

———, "Working Group on Modernization of Library Services and Informatics", Report for the Seventh Five Year Plan, 1985-90, New Delhi, July 1984.

———, "Working Group on Libraries: A Survey of Public Library Services in India", conducted by Planning Commission. Tabulated and analysed by D.R. Kalia, Delhi, ILA, 1965, 66p.

India, "University Education Commission", 1948-49, Report (Chairman: S. Radhakrishnan), Delhi, 1949.

India, "Education Commission, 1964-66", Report: Education and National Development (Chairman: D.S. Kothari), New Delhi, NCERT, 1971.

India, Ministry of Human Resource Development, Department of Education, *Programme of Action*, New Delhi, 1986.

India, Registrar General & Census Commissioner, Census of India, 1991.

India, Universities Commission, 1902, Report, Calcutta.

India, UGC Library Committee: College and University Libraries (Chairman: S.R. Ranganathan), New Delhi, 1966. See also (1) Agarwal, D.S., "Recommendations of the Review Committee on Library Science: An Evaluation", *Herald of Library Science*, 6:2-3 (April-July 1967), 167-74. (2) Srivastava, A.P., "Recommendations of the U.G.C., Review Committee's report on Library Science in Indian Universities, "A Critical Evaluation", *IASLIC Bulletin*, 11:3 (Sept. 1966), 17-182.

India, UGC Development of Library Facilities in Universities and Colleges, New Delhi, 1968, 52p.

———, Development of an Information and Library Network, Report of the Inter-agency Working Group/UGC, New Delhi, 1988.

Right to Information

Baxi, Upendra, "Democratic Dimensions of the Right to Information", in *New Horizons in Library and Information Science*, Ed., C.P. Vashishth, *et al.*, Madras, T.R. Publications, 1994, pp. 85-93.

Bidwai, Praful, "The Right to Information: Legal Codification An Imperative", *Frontline*, September 6, 1996, 103-04.

Calvert, P.J., "A Literate Profession", *Assistant Librarian*, 86:11, Nov. 1993, 168-72.

Castelli, Jim, "National Issues Forums: Promoting Democracy in Libraries—National Issues Forums (NIFS) (USA)", *American Libraries*, 23:6 June 1992, 510-12.

Dervin, B., "Information-Democracy: An Examination of Underlying Assumptions", *JASIS*, 45:6, July 1994, 369-85.

Durrance, J.C., "The White House Conference and Democracy: A Missed Opportunity", *Government Information Quarterly*, 9:3, 1992, 341-46.

Leivrouw, L.A., "Information Resources and Democracy: Understanding the Paradox", *JASIS*, 45:6, July 1994, 350-57.

Marston, Betsy, "Libraries and Democracy: Information for All", *Wilson Lib. Bull.*, 65:7, March 1991, 47-50.

Noorani, A.G., "The Press Council's Bill on Right to Information", *Economic and Political Weekly*, Dec. 21, 1996, p. 3283.

Pande, S.K., "Right to Information: Committee to Prepare Draft Bill", *Frontline*, September 6, 1996, p. 110.

Roode, J.D., and Plooy, N.F. du., "A Bill of Rights for the Information Age which Recognizes the Third World", *IFIP WG9*. 4 Conference Proceedings, (1995?), 227-39.

Webb, Sylvia P., "Censorship", (Article 19 World Report) (Index on censorship), *Outlook on Research Libraries*, Oct. 1990, 1-3.

Standards for Libraries

Indian Standards (issued by Bureau of Indian Standards):

IS: 382-1952. Practice for alphabetical arrangement.

IS: 382-1952. Guidelines for presentation of information in technical manuals.

IS: 793-1956. Specification for the author statements in the title page of a book.

IS: 790-1956. General structure of preliminary pages of book.

IS: 1553-1960. Code of practice relating to primary elements in the design of library buildings.

IS: 2550-1963. Glossary for classification terms.

IS: 2960-1964. Specification for book binding leather.

IS: 3050-1965. Reinforced binding for library books and periodicals, code of practice.
IS: 3083-1966. Code of practice for processing of microfilms (Silver halide).
IS: 796-1966. Glossary of cataloguing terms.
IS: 2672-1966. Code of practice for library lighting.
IS: 1358-1967. Practice for layout of library catalogue code.
IS: 18-1970. Guide to abbreviations of words in titles of periodicals using alphabet (first revision), 41p.
IS: 3130-1972. Code of practice for handling and storage of transparencies (microfilms and microfische).
IS: 1829. Specifications for library furniture and fittings, Part I (1978) Timber, Part II (1993) Steel.
IS: 7400-1974. Guide for preparation and production of textbooks.
IS: 1883-1975. Metal shelving racks (adjustable types).
IS: 3312-1984. Steel shelving cabinets (adjustable type) (second revision).
IS: 4116-1976. Wooden shelving cabinets (adjustable type) (first revision).
IS: 1553-1976. Recommendations relating to primary elements in the design of library buildings.
IS: 1275-1976. Rules for making alphabetical indexes.
IS: 8310-1977. Guide for print area margins and type sizes for textbooks, Part I, Textbooks in English.
IS: 2663-1977. Recommendations relating to the primary elements in the design of building archives.
IS: 2381-1978. Recommendations for bibliographical references: essential and supplementary elements (first revision), 16p.
IS: 9400-1980. Guide for preparation of bibliographic description sheet technical reports.
IS: 9430-1980. Guide for placement of images in roll microfilms.
IS: 10455-1983. Guidelines for presentation of abstract sheets in serial publications, 8p.

Bibliography

Bavakutty, M., "Standards for College Libraries", 35th All-India Library Conference, Poona, 1989.
Deshpande, K.S., and Byadge, T.L., "Staff Pattern in the University and College Libraries in India", *Timeless Fellowship*, 10 (1975-76), 45-6.
Gopinath, M.A., "Standards for Use in the Planning of Library and

Documentation Systems: Comparative Data from India, UK, USA, and Canada", *Library Science Slant Doc.*, 11 (1974), Paper N.

———, "Standardization in Documentation and Book Science", *Library Science Slant Doc.*, 9:3 (1972), 657-76.

India, Education, Ministry of Advisory Committee for Libraries, Report, Rev. Ed. Delhi, Manager of Publications, 1961.

India Finance, Ministry of Standard of Work for Jobs in Departmental Libraries, Report submitted by The Staff Inspection Unit, Delhi, 1965.

See also: Sen, Ashis, "Plea for Performance Budgets and National Standards for Libraries in India", *IASLIC Bull.*, 12:4 (December 1967), 280-90.

Janak Raj and Sachdeva, B.R., "Guidelines for Norms of Collection and Organization of Material in College Libraries in Haryana", *ILA Bulletin*, 19:4 (Jan.-Mar. 1984).

Kasiviswanadham, S., "Role of Standardization in Computerized SDI", Sixteenth Indian Standards Conventions, Bhopal 1975, Doc: S-4/D-1.

Malwad, N.M., "Standardization of Bibliographic Record Format", in *Standardization of Computerized Information Systems,* Sixteenth ISE Convention, Bhopal, 19-25 October, 1975, New Delhi, The Author, 1975, Section B.

"NISSAT", Status Report on Bibliographical Information Processing in India, New Delhi, 1966.

Qureshi, Naimuddin, "Standards for Libraries", in *Encyclopedia for Library and Information Science*, Ed. Allen Kent, Vol. 28, New York, Marcel Dekker, 1980, 470-99.

Rajan, T.N., and Ramaswami, K. "International Standard Book Number", *Ann. Lib. Sci. Doc.*, 19:1 (1972), 25-29.

Ranganathan, S.R., "Document, Documentation and Standardization", *ISI Bulletin*, 10:1 (Jan. 1958), 10-14.

Sangameswaran, S.V., and Gopinath, M.V., "Standards and Guidelines Applicable to Contents Description of Current Awareness Services", Sixteenth Indian Standards Convention, Bhopal, 1975, Doc: S-4/0-2.

Sardana, J.L., "Indian Standards in Library and Information Science: A Review", *ILA Bulletin*, 19: 1-3 (April 1983), 53-60.

Seetharama, S. "Staffing of Libraries and Information Centres", in *Current Problems and Trends in Library and Information Services*, Prof. K.S. Deshpande Commemoration volume, Ed. by H.A. Khan and S.R. Ijari, Varanasi, Indian Bibliographic Centre, 1990, pp. 138-46.

Sharma, M.S., *International Standard Book Numbering in India*, New Delhi, Saraswati Book Co., 1987.

Tayal, A.S., "Standards and Specifications in Libraries", *UNESCO Bull.*, 15 (1961), 203-05.

———, "Acquisition and Updating of Standards and Specifications in Technical Libraries", *UNESCO Bull. of Libraries*, 25 (1971), 199.

Umapathy, K. Setty, "Standards for Libraries", *Indian Librarian*, 32:1 (1977), 15-18.

Vashishth, C.P., Ed. "Standardization in Library and Information Work and Services", Seminar papers, 35th All-India Library Conference, Pune, 1989 (It has exhaustively dealt with the topic and the 49 papers in it have extensively discussed. The report of the proceedings, which is published after the seminar in the *ILA Bulletin* will be useful).

"What Standardization Can Do?" *ISI Bulletin*, 36 (Sept. 1984), 319.

Use and User Studies

Isaac, K.A., *Literature Search*, New Delhi, Concept, 1990.

Kumar, Girja, "Information Needs of Social Scientists in India: A User Education Perspective", in Kumar, Girija, *Library Development in India*, New Delhi, Vikas,1986, pp. 471-87.

———, and Kumar, Krishan, *Philosophy of User Education*, New Delhi, Vikas, 1983.

"Libraian's Role: Mr. Nehru's Analysis—Need to Promote Reading Habit", *The Hindu* (New Delhi), 21 Oct. 1955. Reprinted in *The Hindu Speaks on Libraries*, Compiled by Editor, Madras, Kasturi & Sons, 1992, pp. 141-42.

Maheswarappa, B.S., and Nagappa, B., "Information Needs of Indian Social Scientists", in *Current Problems and Trends in Library and Information Services*, Prof. K.S. Deshpande commemoration volume, Ed. by H.A. Khan and S.R. Ijari, Varanasi, Indian Bibliographic Centre, 1990, pp. 357-65.

Maheshwarappa, B.S., and others, "The Foreign Language Barrier Among the Indian Statisticians", in Isaac, Dorothy, and others, Ed. *Academic Libraries: Role in the National Development*, Madras, T.R. Publications, 1993, pp. 223-35.

Narayan, R.K., "A Library Without Books", *The Hindu*, 5 April, 1953. Reprinted in *The Hindu Speaks on Libraries*, Compiled by Editor, Madras, Kasturi & Sons, 1992, pp. 125-26.

"Problems of Publishers", editorial, *The Hindu*, 14 Feb. 1960, Reprinted in *The Hindu Speaks on Libraries*, Compiled by Editor, Madras, Kasturi & Sons, 1992, p. 177.

Sahai, Shrinath, *Bibliographic Methods and Reading Behaviour*, Delhi, Oriental Publishers, 1976.

Satish, N.G., *Attitude Towards Information: A Study of Social Scientists*, New Delhi, Concept, 1994.

"Students and extra Reading", editorial, *The Hindu*, June 10, 1973. Reprinted in *The Hindu Speaks on Libraries*, Complied by Editor, Madras, Kasturi & Sons, 1992, p. 230-31.

Taher, Mohamed, "User Education", in *Encyclopedic Dictionary of Library and Information Science*, London, Routledge, 1997.

INDEX